AMERICAN ORIENTALISM

American

Orientalism

*The United States
and the Middle East
since 1945*

DOUGLAS LITTLE

The University of North Carolina Press

Chapel Hill and London

© 2002 The University of North Carolina Press
All rights reserved
Manufactured in the United States of America

Designed by April Leidig-Higgins
Set in Aldus by Copperline Book Services, Inc.

"Arabian Nights," music by Alan Menken, lyrics by
Howard Ashman, © 1992 Walt Disney Music Company, Wonderland Music Company, Inc., all rights
reserved, used by permission.

The paper in this book meets the guidelines for per-
manence and durability of the Committee on Production Guidelines for Book Longevity of the Council on
Library Resources.

Library of Congress Cataloging-in-Publication Data
Little, Douglas. American orientalism: the United
States and the Middle East since 1945 / Douglas Little.
p. cm. Includes bibliographical references and index.
ISBN 0-8078-2737-1 (cloth: alk. paper)
1. Middle East—Relations—United States. 2. United
States—Relations—Middle East. 3. Orientalism—
United States. 4. Nationalism—Middle East.
5. Arab-Israeli conflict. I. Title.
DS63.2.U5 L58 2002
327.73056'09'045—dc21   2002003989

06 05 04 03 02   5 4 3 2 1

For Colin and Alison

CONTENTS

Acknowledgments ix

Abbreviations xiii

INTRODUCTION Gideon's Band in the Holy Land:
We're Not in Kansas Anymore 1

CHAPTER ONE Orientalism, American Style:
The Middle East in the Mind of America 9

CHAPTER TWO Opening the Door: Business, Diplomacy,
and America's Stake in Middle East Oil 43

CHAPTER THREE The Making of a Special Relationship:
America and Israel 77

CHAPTER FOUR A Tale of Four Doctrines:
U.S. National Security, the Soviet Threat,
and the Middle East 117

CHAPTER FIVE   Sympathy for the Devil?:
                America, Nasser, and Arab Revolutionary
                Nationalism 157

CHAPTER SIX   Modernizing the Middle East:
                From Reform to Revolution in
                Iraq, Libya, and Iran 193

CHAPTER SEVEN   Kicking the Vietnam Syndrome:
                Waging Limited War from the
                Mediterranean to the Persian Gulf 229

CHAPTER EIGHT   Opportunities Lost and Found:
                The United States and the Arab-Israeli
                Peace Process 267

CONCLUSION   Fool's Errand or Kodak Moment?:
                America and the Middle East at the
                Dawn of the Twenty-first Century 307

                Notes 319

                Bibliography 365

                Index 389

ACKNOWLEDGMENTS

Although I am not fond of self-indulgent acknowledgments where the author thanks everyone but his pet ferret for help along the way, I have been at work on this project for so long that I have incurred an amazing array of intellectual and personal debts.

I truly believe that I could have completed this project only at Clark University. First things first. It was a Clarkie (he must remain anonymous) who inspired me to switch my focus from Africa to the Middle East eighteen years ago when he wrote a mediocre research paper on JFK and Israel that convinced me that there had to be more to the story than met the eye. Four other undergraduates, Pamela Phillips, Marisara Melendez, Emily Douglas, and Lai Jin Wong, provided wonderful research assistance. A fifth, Nichole Dupont, not only checked notes and tracked down obscure references but also read the entire manuscript and reminded me to keep my audience in mind. A sixth, Heather Sensibaugh, handled last-minute fact checking with remarkable aplomb and good humor. Three Ph.D. students, Margaret Manchester, Teresa Thomas, and John Murnane, read some of what I wrote, listened patiently to my ideas, and occasionally let me borrow theirs. My colleague George Lane shared his ambassadorial yarns about Libya, Lebanon, and Yemen and helped connect me with his friends in the U.S. Foreign Service. The magnificent staff at Goddard Library, especially Mary Hartman, Irene Walch, Ed McDermott, and Rachael Shea, always went the extra mile to obtain whatever materials I needed. Anne Gibson, one of Clark's geographic information science wizards, made the map. The Clark University Faculty Development Fund and the Higgins School for the Humanities helped defray the cost of travel to archives on both sides of the Atlantic. My administrative assistant, Ellen Staples, reminded me that meetings and writing do not mix, saved me from countless interruptions, and laughed at my jokes. Three old friends, Paul Ropp, Drew McCoy, and particularly George Billias, boosted my spirits and prodded me when the book dragged into its second decade. Four new comrades, Fred Greenaway, David Angel, Debbie Merrill, and Andrea Michaels, tolerated my crankiness and made me look good as an administrator while I completed the eleventh-hour revisions on the manuscript.

I have been lucky to have many friends whose comments have helped make this a better book than it would otherwise have been. Andy Rotter and Clea Bunch sharpened the chapter on orientalism, and Ann Heiss did the same for the chapter on oil. David Langbart lent a critical eye to the chapter on Israel and, even more important, constantly provided me with recently declassified documents on a broad range of topics. Jim Goode and Bob Vitalis, my Middle East hands, critiqued the chapters on nationalism and modernization and saved me from several embarrassing errors. Rich Immerman, Gerry Haines, and Mark Gasiorowski carefully read a chapter on covert action, sections of which are now sprinkled throughout the text. Bob Buzzanco gave the chapter on military intervention the once-over and, with Bill Walker, helped me appreciate not only Lyndon Johnson's worst decisions in the Third World but also the best barbecue in Austin. Salim Yaqub and Matt Jacobs graciously shared their research findings while making me envious of their mastery of Arabic. Steve Rabe helped me distinguish between modernization in Latin America and the Middle East during late-night bull sessions in some of the most memorable dorm rooms on the North American continent.

Peter Hahn and Bob McMahon read the entire manuscript and offered excellent advice regarding where to trim the fluff without losing the substance. Diane Kunz encouraged me to write the topical book that I wanted rather than a dreary monograph detailing what one clerk said to another. Bob Divine pushed me to expand my research into the late 1960s and beyond. As always, Walt LaFeber quietly encouraged me to think big and then persuaded me that I could stitch the book back together after surgically removing 200 pages.

Working with the staff of the University of North Carolina Press has been a truly splendid experience. Paula Wald, Amanda McMillan, and Stephanie Wenzel oversaw the prepublication details with amazing good cheer. Furthermore,

I had the good fortune to work with not one but two excellent editors who remain committed to publishing diplomatic history. Lew Bateman let me bend his ear about this project for years before he saw a single word and then, after reading 300,000, reminded me that less is often more. Chuck Grench ensured that the project never became an orphan and guided the manuscript through two sets of revisions and several missed deadlines before putting it on a fast track for publication. Chuck, Lew, and the others mentioned above are responsible for most of what is good about this book. The errors, by contrast, belong to me and me alone.

This book is dedicated to Colin and Alison, who grew up to be fine young adults despite having a father whose perpetual obliviousness to the world around him was a source of endless amusement. They have agreed not to reveal any state secrets, and I have agreed to forgive them for being more interested in science than in history. Finally, there is Pat. For thirty years she has brightened my life with grace and wit and awesome patience. Although she still finds diplomatic history terribly dry and draws the line at proofreading, the introduction and the conclusion did meet with her approval. And that has made all the difference.

ABBREVIATIONS

AIOC	Anglo-Iranian Oil Company
AIPAC	American Israel Public Affairs Committee
ARAMCO	Arabian-American Oil Company
CASOC	California Arabian Standard Oil Company
CENTCOM	Central Command
CFP	Compagnie Française des Petroles
CIA	Central Intelligence Agency
IPC	Iraq Petroleum Company
IRS	Internal Revenue Service
ISI	Inter-Services Intelligence Agency
JCS	Joint Chiefs of Staff
MEC	Middle East Command
MEDO	Middle East Defense Organization
NATO	North Atlantic Treaty Organization
NPT	nonproliferation treaty

NSC	National Security Council
OPEC	Organization of Petroleum Exporting Countries
PLO	Palestine Liberation Organization
PRC	Petroleum Reserves Corporation
RCC	Revolutionary Command Council
TAPLINE	Trans-Arabian Pipeline
TPC	Turkish Petroleum Company
TVA	Tennessee Valley Authority
UAE	United Arab Emirates
UAR	United Arab Republic
UNRWA	United Nations Relief and Works Agency
UNSCOP	United Nations Special Committee on Palestine
USIA	U.S. Information Agency
YAR	Yemen Arab Republic

AMERICAN ORIENTALISM

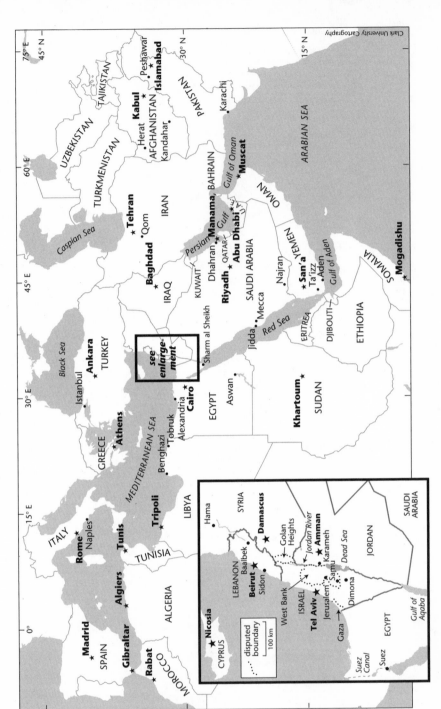

The Middle East 2001

The people stared at us every where, and we stared at them. We generally made them feel rather small, too, before we got done with them, because we bore down on them with America's greatness until we crushed them. . . .

If ever those children of Israel in Palestine forget when Gideon's Band went through there from America, they ought to be cursed once more and finished. It was the rarest spectacle that ever astounded mortal eyes, perhaps. —Mark Twain, *The Innocents Abroad* (1869)

Crush USA—Graffiti in Karachi, Pakistan, *New York Times*, 30 September 2001

Gideon's Band in the Holy Land

We're Not in Kansas Anymore

On a crisp and cloudless Tuesday morning in September 2001, two Boeing 767 jetliners commandeered by Arab terrorists streaked across the New York skyline and slammed into the World Trade Center. Ninety minutes later the twin glass and steel towers imploded, killing nearly 3,000 office workers, firemen, and passersby and crushing whatever collective illusions of innocence or omnipotence Americans may have had. In ways that few could ever have imagined, Osama bin Laden and his Afghan-based terrorist network al-Qaeda had brought the Middle East to America. As rescue workers probed the smoldering rubble in lower Manhattan and policymakers in Washington hammered out plans for military retaliation against bin Laden and his Taliban allies, President George W. Bush[1] posed a question that most Americans were already asking themselves: "Why do they hate us?"

The president's answer came during a nationally televised address nine days after the tragedy. "They hate our freedoms—our freedom of religion, our freedom of speech, our freedom to vote and assemble and disagree with each other," Bush asserted on 20 September. "These terrorists kill not merely to end lives, but to disrupt and end a way of life," he insisted. "They stand against us, because we stand in their way."[2] Although Bush's remarks seemed to capture a contemporary truth, the full answer to his question was deeply rooted in the past. Some initial clues had surfaced 130 years earlier, when Mark Twain and a band of self-styled pilgrims hailing from Boston, St. Louis, and points west first brought America to the Middle East. In June 1867 Twain hurried down Wall Street and clambered aboard the first-class steamer *Quaker City* bound for the Holy Land, where he and his fellow travelers stumbled into terra incognita. Although his voyage took place more than a century before the Middle East became a national obsession, Twain provided Americans with an enduring portrait of an unpredictable and unforgettable region at the moment when the United States was beginning to emerge as a world power.

U.S. interests in the Middle East have deepened since Twain first steamed east across the Atlantic, but in some respects American attitudes have changed little since the nineteenth century. The public at large, of course, is now far more likely to get its information from CNN or the *New York Times* than from an epic travelogue like *Innocents Abroad*. The hundreds of students who have attended Hebrew University in Jerusalem or American University in Beirut, the thousands of emigrants who have made new lives for themselves in Israel, and the tens of thousands of tourists who have touched the Wailing Wall or surveyed the ruins at Luxor have helped create a more nuanced picture of the Middle East in the United States. And the oil executives, national security managers, and academic experts who shape U.S. policy today have a far better grasp of the cultural, ideological, and commercial forces at work in the Middle East than did the passengers aboard the *Quaker City*.

Yet early in the new millennium many Americans remain frustrated by the slow pace of social change, disturbed by the persistence of political autocracy, and appalled by the violent xenophobia of groups such as al-Qaeda emanating from a part of the world whose strategic and economic importance remains unsurpassed. From the dawn of the Cold War through the twilight of the twentieth century, U.S. policymakers insisted time and again that Islamic radicals, Israeli prime ministers, and Iraqi dictators had merely misunderstood America's good intentions and that better understanding would produce better relations. Over the years, however, critics from Tel Aviv to Tehran have retorted that they understood those intentions all too well and that the peculiar blend of ignorance and arrogance that characterized U.S. policy would effectively prevent Americans from ever truly understanding the region and its peoples.

The terrorist attacks of 11 September 2001 constituted both a brutal reminder of how very different the Middle East is from the Middle West and a stunning confirmation that, as Dorothy told Toto in *The Wizard of Oz*, "We're not in Kansas anymore." Having spent his boyhood on the other side of the river in Missouri, Mark Twain would have known this intuitively. Indeed, Twain was among the first to interpret the U.S. relationship with the Middle East as the byproduct of two contradictory ingredients: an irresistible impulse to remake the world in America's image and a profound ambivalence about the peoples to be remade. I explore that irony in the pages that follow.

The definition of the Middle East employed here is expansive and encompasses not merely Israel, the Arab states, and Iran but also the Muslim lands stretching from the Sahara Desert to the Khyber Pass and from Algeria to Afghanistan. Although it is intended to be of interest to specialists in diplomatic history and area studies, this book is also designed to provide the general reader with a broad understanding of the political, cultural, and economic considerations that have influenced U.S. policy since 1945. In recent years some outstanding monographs have appeared on topics such as multinational oil, the special relationship with Israel, and the Iranian revolution.[3] Some fine case studies have been written on the Suez crisis, the Six Day War, and the conflict in the Persian Gulf.[4] Most overviews of U.S. policy, however, have been long on chronology and short on analysis and have usually sacrificed depth for breadth.[5]

American Orientalism combines the best of both approaches through a series of eight thematic chapters that, read in sequence, tell the story of America's relationship with a very complicated region. Each chapter is devoted to a single topic and is designed to stand alone, with a beginning, a middle, and an end. But each chapter also touches on a broader aspect of diplomatic history with relevance beyond the Middle East (for example, the persistence of racial and cultural stereotypes, the rise of the national security state, and the challenges of modernization in the Third World). Taken as a whole, then, this book helps make sense of the complex and sometimes inconsistent attitudes and interests that determined U.S. policy in the region.

The central premise of Chapter 1 is that if one wishes to understand America's encounter with the Middle East after 1945, one must appreciate the cultural baggage and the racial stereotypes that most Americans carried with them. A quick look at eighteenth- and nineteenth-century popular culture shows that Muslims, Jews, and most other peoples of the Middle East were "orientalized" and depicted as backward, decadent, and untrustworthy. By

1900 anti-Semitic and anti-Islamic sentiments were as American as apple pie. During the early twentieth century, businessmen, missionaries, and archaeologists reinforced this orientalist outlook, with help from popular magazines like *National Geographic*. With the coming of the Second World War, the Holocaust, and the founding of Israel, however, anti-Semitism abated somewhat, and Jews were "westernized" while Arabs and Muslims were "demonized" as anti-Western terrorists. By the late 1990s these more complicated orientalist messages were being projected not only onto America's movie screens through Hollywood blockbusters such as *Schindler's List* and *True Lies* but also into America's living rooms through nightly news footage that contrasted telegenic Israeli moderates with ruthless, rich, or radical Arabs.

Notwithstanding such orientalist imagery, the most recognizable symbol of the Middle East for most Americans has probably been the oil well. After briefly tracing the emergence of the international oil industry, Chapter 2 zeroes in on the question of whose interests have been served by multinational corporations. During the quarter-century after 1945, policymakers and oil executives developed a symbiotic relationship that allowed the United States to provide aid and exert influence in the Arab world while keeping shareholders and friends of Israel relatively happy. What was best for Exxon and Texaco seemed also what was best for America, and vice versa. With the emergence of the Organization of Petroleum Exporting Countries (OPEC) after 1970, however, corporate and national interests diverged sharply. Many on Main Street and Capitol Hill attributed the ensuing energy crunch to collusion between greedy Arab sheiks and profit-hungry multinational corporations, who conspired to cut back output, jack up prices, and fleece American consumers while U.S. policymakers were preoccupied with Cold War crises. Outraged at having their loyalty called into question, oil executives screamed foul, pushed patriotic themes in their public relations, and blamed America's energy woes principally on the special relationship between the United States and Israel.

America, of course, *has* had a special relationship with Israel, and that relationship *has* created problems with the Arab oil states. A common faith in democratic values and an uncommon reliance on interest group politics have been the glue binding Americans and Israelis together since the late 1940s. Chapter 3 shows that what made that relationship truly special, however, was Israel's development of nuclear weapons and its potential to serve as America's strategic asset in the Middle East. Once the United States became convinced that the Israelis possessed both the will and the way to build an atomic bomb, conventional arms sales became part of a concerted but ultimately unsuccessful U.S. effort to convert Israel into a regional partner and prevent it from going nuclear. Although the Israelis never really accepted the notion that what was good for the United States was necessarily good for the Jewish state, down through the 1991 Gulf War both sides acknowledged that geopolitics was at least as important as interest group politics in shaping the special relationship.

Cultivating Israel as America's geopolitical asset seemed more and more essential for U.S. policymakers as they struggled to prevent the Soviet Union from filling the vacuum created by Britain's slow-motion withdrawal from its empire east of Suez after 1945. Chapter 4 traces U.S. efforts to contain the Soviet Union by utilizing the newly created Cold War "national security state" to enforce what amounted to a Monroe Doctrine for the Middle East. The Truman Doctrine envisaged the United Kingdom providing the military muscle and the United States bankrolling a regional security system that stretched from Turkey to Pakistan. The Suez crisis, however, showed that U.S. and U.K. interests were not identical, and America moved to convert Britain into its junior partner under the Eisenhower Doctrine during the late 1950s. Following the Labour Party's decision to liquidate the remnants of British imperialism during the 1960s, Presidents John F. Kennedy and Lyndon B. Johnson laid the groundwork for what would become the Nixon Doctrine, a "twin pillars" policy in which Iran and Saudi Arabia would serve as anti-Soviet regional proxies. But after the Iranian revolution and the Soviet invasion of Afghanistan in 1979 revealed the limitations of such an arrangement, U.S. officials decided to stand alone with the Carter Doctrine, a policy reminiscent of President Harry Truman's approach, with America cast in Britain's role.

Although such doctrinal thinking may have helped keep the Soviets out of the Middle East, it could not hold back the rising tide of revolutionary nationalism that surged out of Egypt and swept through the Arab world after 1945. Chapter 5 suggests that America's ambivalent reaction to Gamal Abdel Nasser's nationalist revolution was rooted in deep misgivings about radical political change that dated from the nineteenth century. After Nasser seized power in July 1952, U.S. officials hoped he would become a Middle Eastern Thomas Jefferson. But his nasty divorce from Whitehall over Suez and his noisy flirtation with the Kremlin thereafter led the administration of Dwight D. Eisenhower to dismiss him as at best the Egyptian equivalent of Alexander Kerensky and at worst the Egyptian equivalent of Vladimir Ilyich Lenin. Despite a brief display of sympathy for the devil during the Kennedy years, LBJ and his advisers regarded Nasser and like-minded revolutionary nationalists as Arab equivalents of the Viet Cong and welcomed Israel's attempt to cut them down to size in June 1967.

Chapter 6 argues that the United States hoped to avoid a replay of revolution in Egypt by modernizing and reforming traditional Muslim societies from North Africa to the Persian Gulf. Relying on modernization theories similar to those at the heart of JFK's Alliance for Progress in Latin America, U.S. policymakers deluded themselves into thinking that by initiating evolutionary change in Iraq, Libya, and Iran, they could make revolutionary change unnecessary. In Baghdad the Eisenhower administration worked with Britain to reform the Hashemite monarchy, only to touch off a revolution of rising expectations punctuated by a series of ever more bloody coups that eventually brought Saddam Hussein to power. In Tripoli U.S. officials encouraged King Idris to modernize his regime, only to trigger an anti-Western revolt led by Muammar al-Qaddafi. And in Iran Kennedy, Johnson, and President Richard M. Nixon invested heavily in the shah's "White Revolution," only to be repaid with an Islamic backlash led by Ayatollah Ruhollah Khomeini. In short, America's attempt to modernize the Middle East backfired, igniting the very revolutions it was supposed to squelch and inadvertently sparking a bloody war in the Persian Gulf between Iran's thoroughly traditional Ayatollah Khomeini and Iraq's brutally modern Saddam Hussein.

The Iran-Iraq War ended in stalemate in 1988 without significant U.S. military involvement. Two years later, however, President George Bush would send a half-million GIs to Saudi Arabia after "the butcher of Baghdad" invaded Kuwait. Chapter 7 shows that the 1990–91 Gulf War must be understood not merely as a response to Saddam Hussein's smash-and-grab tactics but also as a reaction to the "Vietnam Syndrome" that had curtailed armed U.S. intervention in regional conflicts for nearly two decades. The Middle East had actually served as the testing ground for an early application of the doctrine of "limited war" in 1958, when Eisenhower sent the Marines to Beirut and back in just 100 days. But the model of controlled escalation so central to Ike's success in the Middle East eventually produced disaster in Southeast Asia, where LBJ's no-win war left both the public and policymakers in the United States wary of military intervention anywhere. The Ronald Reagan years were marked by abortive efforts to reverse that mentality from the Shouf Mountains of Lebanon to the sea lanes of the Persian Gulf. With the overwhelming victory in Operation Desert Storm, the White House claimed that America had finally kicked the Vietnam Syndrome. But George Bush's reluctance to march on Baghdad in 1991 and President Bill Clinton's equivocal policies in the Balkans eight years later suggested that antiinterventionism remained alive and well in Washington.

If the U.S. victory in the Gulf War did not quite cure the Vietnam Syndrome, it certainly helped pave the way for Israeli and Palestinian peace negotiations during the 1990s. Chapter 8 argues that for more than fifty years the U.S. prescription for an Arab-Israeli settlement has been based on one simple truth: If there is to be an end to bloodshed, both Arab and Jew must accept the principle of "peace for land." From 1947 to 1967 the Arabs rejected this principle and, as Abba Eban said, never missed an opportunity to miss an opportunity. Truman, Eisenhower, and Kennedy all floated some variant of the peace-for-land formula only to be greeted with Arab intransigence. After the Israelis conquered the Sinai, the West Bank, and the Golan Heights during the 1967 war, however, they seemed to lose interest in the American formula. After fifteen years of unabashed expansionist policies from Menachem Begin and Yitzhak Shamir, the other Yitzhak—Rabin—finally put the Jewish state back on the path to compromise with the 1993 Oslo Accords.

Despite high hopes that the breakthrough in the land of the midnight sun would mark the dawn of a new era of peace and reconciliation between Arab and Jew, the final years of the old millennium brought a season of rising frustrations for all parties. To be sure, the swift establishment of a Palestinian Authority led by a "new" and seemingly more pragmatic Yasser Arafat raised hopes that Israel had at last found a reliable negotiating partner. The assassination of Rabin in November 1995, however, rapidly polarized the Jewish state between Benjamin Netanyahu, a right-wing opportunist who irritated Washington by backing away from the peace-for-land formula at the heart of the Oslo process, and Ehud Barak, who rallied Israeli voters to the banner of peace in May 1999 with help from Rabin's widow and the man in the Oval Office. But when Bill Clinton convened a "minisummit" at Camp David fourteen months later, Barak's maximum offer fell short of Arafat's minimum demands, the peace talks deadlocked, and the Israelis and Palestinians blamed each other. When violence rocked the West Bank and Gaza with Arafat's tacit blessing in September 2000, Israeli support for Barak's conciliatory policies plummeted, and the electorate swung toward hard-liners such as Ariel Sharon, whose victory at the polls in February 2001 signaled that the Jewish state was shifting its strategy from "peace for land" to "peace through strength."

Dismissing Clinton's eleventh-hour bid to broker an Israeli-Palestinian settlement as little more than diplomatic grandstanding, George W. Bush saw no hope for resolving the Middle East conflict in the near future and distanced himself from the peace process during his first months in office. The inability of Clinton or Bush to break the Arab-Israeli stalemate would have come as no surprise to Mark Twain, who had toured the Middle East eighty years before America's forty-second and forty-third presidents were born. Unlike most of the other passengers aboard the *Quaker City*, Twain was a shrewd judge of character and a lifelong student of irony who observed that wherever they went, from Damascus to Jerusalem to Cairo, Americans tended to underestimate the resourcefulness of Arabs and Jews while overestimating their own Yankee ingenuity. This seemed to him a prescription for frustration that, under the wrong circumstances, might tempt Uncle Sam to bear down on the peoples of the Middle East with America's greatness until it crushed them. To a very great degree the United States succumbed to that temptation after 1945, unleashing a dynamic whose most significant unintended consequence was Osama bin Laden's monstrous bid to crush the United States on 11 September 2001. This book explores the impact of that dynamic on five decades of U.S. policy toward the Middle East.

To see a camel train laden with the spices of Arabia and the rare fabrics of Persia come marching through the narrow alleys of the bazaar . . . is a genuine revelation of the Orient. The picture lacks nothing. It casts you back at once into your forgotten boyhood, and again you dream over the wonders of the Arabian Nights; again your companions are princes, your lord is the Caliph Haroun Al Raschid, and your servants are terrific giants and genii that come with smoke and lightning and thunder, and go as a storm goes when they depart!
—Mark Twain, *The Innocents Abroad* (1869)

Most Americans now know better than to use nasty generalizations about ethnic or religious groups. Disparaging stereotypes—the avaricious Jew, the sneaky Chinese, the dumb Irishman, the lazy black person—are now so unacceptable that it's a shock to hear them mentioned.

Thanks to current international politics, however, one form of ethnic bigotry retains an aura of respectability in the United States: prejudice against Arabs. Anyone who doubts this has only to listen to the lyrics in a song [titled "Arabian Nights"] from the animated Disney extravaganza "Aladdin."—*New York Times* editorial, 14 July 1993

1

Orientalism, American Style

The Middle East in the Mind of America

Few parts of the world have become as deeply embedded in the U.S. popular imagination as the Middle East. The Puritans who founded "God's American Israel" on Massachusetts Bay nearly four centuries ago brought with them a passionate fascination with the Holy Land and a profound ambivalence about the "infidels"—mostly Muslims but some Jews—who lived there. Raised on Bible stories and religious parables laced liberally with a fervently Christian sense of mission and a fiercely American Spirit of '76, the citizens of one of the New World's newest nations have long embraced a romanticized and stereotypic vision of some of the Old World's oldest civilizations. The missionaries, tourists, and merchants who sailed from America into the Eastern Mediterranean during the nineteenth century were amazed by the Christian relics and biblical landscapes but appalled by the despotic governments and decadent societies that they encountered from Constantinople to Cairo. The diplomats, oil men, and soldiers who promoted and protected U.S. interests in the Middle East during the twentieth century converted these earlier cultural assumptions and racial stereotypes into an irresistible intellectual shorthand for handling the "backward" Muslims and the "headstrong" Jews whose objectives frequently clashed with America's.

That intellectual shorthand, reflected in everything from feature films and best-selling novels to political cartoons and popular magazines, has had a profound impact on Main Street and in the nation's capital. Over the years the public and policymakers in the United States have frequently employed what historian Michael Hunt has termed a "hierarchy of race" in dealing with what used to be called the Third World. As early as 1900, Hunt argues, Anglo-Saxon racism and Social Darwinism had fused in the collective mind of America to generate a powerful mental map in which, predictably, the "civilized" powers—the United States and Western Europe—controlled a descending array of underdeveloped, even "primitive" Asians, Latinos, American Indians, and Africans. Although Hunt discusses the Middle East only in passing, his brief references suggest that U.S. policymakers tended to place Arabs and Jews nearer the bottom than the top of the hierarchy of race.[1]

More than a decade ago Columbia University's Edward Said suggested *why* this should have been so. Borrowing from intellectual history, literary criticism, and classical philology, Said showed how eighteenth-century British officials embraced "orientalism," a self-serving view of Asians, Africans, and Arabs as decadent, alien, and inferior, a view that Whitehall later used to rationalize its own imperial ambitions from the Indian subcontinent to the banks of the Nile. For British orientalists, Ottoman despotism, Islamic obscurantism, and Arab racial inferiority had combined to produce a backward culture that was badly in need of Anglo-Saxon tutelage. With the waning of Britain's power and the waxing of America's after 1945, something very like Said's orientalism seems subconsciously to have shaped U.S. popular attitudes and foreign policies toward the Middle East.[2]

More recently anthropologists Catherine Lutz and Jane Collins have suggested *how* orientalism made its way into U.S. popular culture. Utilizing insights from postmodern social theory, photojournalism, and cultural anthropology, Lutz and Collins trace the process through which orientalist images of the Middle East and other parts of the Third World were generated and disseminated by one of the most widely circulated magazines in the United States, *National Geographic*. The subliminal messages encoded in the magazine's eye-catching photos and intriguing human interest stories seem clear. The Arabs, Africans, and Asians who grace the pages of *National Geographic* are backward, exotic, and occasionally dangerous folk who have needed and will continue to need U.S. help and guidance if they are successfully to undergo political and cultural modernization.[3]

Once the orientalist mindset of imperial Britain insinuated its way into the White House, the Pentagon, and Foggy Bottom during the late 1940s, and once the orientalist worldview epitomized by *National Geographic* found its way onto America's coffee tables and movie screens during the early 1950s, U.S. policies and attitudes toward the Middle East were shaped in predictable ways. Influenced by potent racial and cultural stereotypes, some imported and some homegrown, that depicted the Muslim world as decadent and inferior, U.S. policymakers from Harry Truman through George Bush tended to dismiss Arab aspirations for self-determination as politically primitive, economically suspect, and ideologically absurd. Meanwhile, Zionist pioneers were ineluctably transforming the dream of a Jewish state into Middle Eastern reality through blood, sweat, and tears. Both the dream and the reality soon prompted most Americans to shed their residual anti-Semitism and to regard the children of Isaac, now safely more Western than oriental, as a strategic asset in America's increasingly nasty confrontation with the children of Ishmael.

As the twentieth century drew to a close, Hollywood confirmed that orientalism American style had sunk deep roots into U.S. popular culture. In 1992 Disney Studios released *Aladdin*, the latest in a long line of animated classics, which opens with a Saddam Hussein look-alike crooning "Arabian Nights." The lyrics evoke long-standing sinister images of the Muslim world punctuated by an orientalist punch line: "It's barbaric, but hey it's home." Two hundred years earlier, Americans familiar with the Middle East would not have disagreed.

Of Pirates, Prophets, and Innocents Abroad

In 1776 what little the average American knew about the Middle East and its peoples likely came from two sources: the King James Bible and Scheherazade's *Thousand and One Arabian Nights*. Few Americans could have found Baghdad or Beirut on a map, and fewer still had climbed the great stone pyramids at Giza or waded the holy waters of the River Jordan. But most Americans remembered the Gospel according to St. Matthew and the tale of Ali Baba and his forty thieves, most recalled the crucifixion and the crusades, and most regretted that the Holy Land was peopled by infidels and unbelievers, Muslims and Jews beyond the pale of Christendom.[4]

Because it wedded the religious teachings of the Koran with the secular power of sultans and sheiks from Turkey to Morocco, the specter of Islam loomed larger in late-eighteenth-century U.S. popular culture than did Judaism. Alongside *Arabian Nights* on library shelves from Boston to Charleston were biographies of the Prophet Mohammed depicting the Islamic messenger of God as the founder of a wicked and barbarous creed that had spread from Arabia to North Africa by offering conquered peoples a choice between conversion and death. The revolutionary statesmen who invented America in the quarter-century after 1776 regarded the Muslim world, beset by oriental despotism, economic squalor, and intellectual stultification, as the antithesis of the republicanism to which they had pledged their sacred honor.[5] Three decades of sporadic maritime warfare with the Barbary pirates helped spread these orientalist images to the public at large through captivity narratives such as Caleb Bingham's *Slaves in Barbary* and plays like Susanna Rowson's *Slaves in Algiers*.[6]

Greater American familiarity with the Muslim world during the nineteenth century seems merely to have bred greater contempt. When Greek patriots rebelled against Turkish domination of their homeland in 1821, the widely read *North American Review* labeled the ensuing struggle "a war of the crescent against the cross" and claimed that "wherever the arms of the Sultan prevail, the village churches are levelled with the dust or polluted with the abominations of mahometanism."[7] American missionaries such as Harrison Gray Otis Dwight, who hoped to spread the gospel throughout the Ottoman Empire during the late 1820s, certainly shared these sentiments.[8] Indeed, when Dwight visited Washington and called on John Quincy Adams in early 1839, he painted "a melancholy picture" of the peoples of the Middle East for the aging statesman. "They consist of Turks, Greeks, Armenians, and Jews," Adams confided in his diary, of whom "the Jews [were] the worst" because, according to Dwight, "their hatred of all Christians is rancorous beyond conception."[9]

Dwight's anti-Semitism was not unusual among America's nineteenth-century Anglo-Saxon elite, most of whom regarded Jews as one part Judas and one part Shylock, a suspect people wedded to a set of cultural and economic values that seemed vaguely un-American. Although most of the 150,000 Jews who arrived in the United States before the Civil War had fled persecution in Germany and were eager to Americanize themselves by shedding many of their Old World customs, Jewish Americans were nevertheless the targets of ugly racial stereotypes depicting them as greedy, greasy, and grasping.[10]

Yet despite such anti-Semitic caricatures, many Christian citizens of God's American Israel felt a peculiar sense of kinship with Jews. Evangelical Protestant revivalists interpreted the Book of Revelation to mean that the millennium would arrive once the Jews returned to the Holy Land, and hundreds of American pilgrims trekked east to worship at sacred sites in Jerusalem and

Nazareth.[11] "We know far more about the land of the Jews," *Harper's Magazine* announced smugly in January 1855, "than the degraded Arabs who hold it."[12]

The orientalist assumptions explicit in *Harper's Magazine* were implicit in much of nineteenth-century U.S. popular culture. Illustrated editions of *The Arabian Nights* and trusty McGuffey readers brought a frequently exotic and often evil Middle East to life for a new generation of schoolchildren. Popular authors like Washington Irving published books such as *Mahomet and His Successors* that presented stereotypic portraits of a Muslim world whose benighted inhabitants were far better suited for theocratic or autocratic rule than for American-style democracy.[13] Landscape artists such as Minor Kellogg and Edward Troye painted Middle Eastern vistas littered with biblical ruins and peopled with Bedouins and other orientals who had clearly fallen from grace.[14] Portrait painter Frederick Arthur Bridgman produced dozens of sexually charged canvases modeled on those of his mentor Jean-Léon Gérôme, a leading French orientalist famous for works like *The Snake Charmer* and *The Slave*. It is not surprising that one of the most popular attractions at the 1893 Columbian World Exposition in Chicago was the Ottoman Pavilion, complete with mosque, bazaar, harem, and belly dancers to titillate Victorian Americans.[15]

No one probably did more to shape nineteenth-century U.S. views of the Middle East, however, than Mark Twain, whose darkly humorous account of his calamitous tour of the Holy Land sold nearly 100,000 copies in the two years after it was published in 1869. A master of irony, Twain titled his saga of this eastward odyssey *The Innocents Abroad* and provided scathing sketches of his fellow travelers, most of whom he found guilty of tactlessness, excessive pride, and what twentieth-century critics would call cultural imperialism.[16]

What may well have stood out in the minds of Twain's readers, however, were the venomous vignettes he offered of the local population. Terming Muslims "a people by nature and training filthy, brutish, ignorant, unprogressive, [and] superstitious" and calling the Ottoman Empire "a government whose Three Graces are Tyranny, Rapacity, [and] Blood," Twain found little correlation between the "grand oriental picture which I had worshipped a thousand times" in *Arabian Nights* and the gritty reality he encountered during his Arabian days. The Arabs of Palestine were mired in dirt, rags, and vermin, he observed, and "do not mind barbarous ignorance and savagery." Nor was Twain fond of Egyptians, whose constant cries of "bucksheesh" echoed down Cairo's back alleys. "The Arabs are too high-priced in Egypt," he remarked acidly at the end of his voyage. "They put on airs unbecoming to such savages."[17] To be sure, some readers of Twain's account must have marveled at the author's sarcastic wit, but many more probably put down *Innocents Abroad* with their orientalist images of a Middle East peopled by pirates, prophets, and paupers more sharply focused than ever.[18]

Americanizing the Middle East

The Middle East began to loom larger on America's diplomatic and cultural horizon during what Mark Twain called "the Gilded Age," not only because U.S. missionaries sought to save more souls but also because U.S. merchants sought to expand trade. By the 1870s American entrepreneurs were buying nearly one-half of Turkey's opium crop for resale in China while providing the Ottoman Empire with everything from warships to kerosene. "Even the sacred lamps over the Prophet's tomb at Mecca," one U.S. diplomat gloated in 1879, "are fed with oil from Pennsylvania."[19]

Meanwhile a new generation of American missionaries made their way to Armenia, Syria, and other corners of the Ottoman realm, spreading not only the gospel but also subversive New World ideas. Indeed, by the 1890s two institutions of higher learning established by U.S. missionaries three decades earlier—Robert College just outside Constantinople and the Syrian Protestant College in Beirut—had become notorious anti-Turkish hotbeds, where Arabs, Kurds, and Armenians began to dream of and scheme for national independence.[20] "Quite without intention," British orientalist and adventurer T. E. Lawrence observed a generation later, these two colleges had actually "taught revolution" to subject peoples throughout the Turkish empire.[21]

While most U.S. observers seem to have agreed that the Christians of Armenia and Syria might profit enormously from these lessons, few churchmen or diplomats expected such revolutionary teachings to spell anything but disaster in the Muslim world. When angry mobs of Iranian students and peasants toppled the royal government and forced the shah to proclaim a constitutional monarchy in August 1906, for example, Ambassador Richmond Pearson offered a bleak forecast laced with orientalism: "History does not record a single instance of successful constitutional government in a country where the Mussulman religion is the state religion."[22] Ambassador John Leishman, Pearson's counterpart in Constantinople, was no more sanguine about the prospects for constitutional rule in Turkey, where reformist military officers—"the Young Turks"—staged a coup and curbed the sultan's powers in July 1908. "The fanatical element" among Muslim students, soldiers, and mullahs, Leishman reported nine months later, had triggered antigovernment riots, an army mutiny, and "a reign of terror and a succession of murders."[23]

President Theodore Roosevelt, who had appointed both Pearson and Leishman, was even more skeptical about the possibility of reform and progress in the Middle East. A firm believer in a hierarchy of race in which "civilized nations" like the United States must shoulder "the White Man's Burden" and attempt to westernize the "benighted" peoples of Asia, Africa, and Latin America, Roosevelt confessed privately in 1907 that "it is impossible to expect moral, intellectual and material well-being where Mohammedanism is supreme." The Egyptians, for example, were "a people of Moslem fellahin who have never in all time exercised any self-government whatever." Britain's Lord Cromer, Roosevelt added, "is one of the greatest modern colonial administrators, and he has handled Egypt just according to Egypt's needs"—military occupation, foreign tutelage, and Christian patience.[24]

If Roosevelt ranked Muslims near the bottom of his hierarchy of race, he placed Jews closer to the top. To be sure, like many other members of the patrician elite that still ruled America at the turn of the century, Roosevelt harbored some patronizingly offensive stereotypes of Jewish Americans.[25] But he was also highly critical of the wave of anti-Semitism that swept Turkey and Russia during the First World War, and he was an early supporter of the idea of establishing a Jewish state in the Holy Land. The United States and its allies, Roosevelt observed in July 1918, should "pledge themselves never to make peace until the Turk is driven from Europe, and . . . the Jews [are] given control of Palestine." It seemed, he added two months later, "entirely proper to start a Zionist State around Jerusalem."[26]

As the war to end all wars drew to a close, the establishment of a Jewish homeland in Palestine had become a goal widely shared on both sides of the Atlantic. Famous mainly for its biblical ruins and its fruit exports, Palestine had until very recently remained little more than a sleepy backwater controlled by the dying Ottoman Empire. Overwhelmingly Muslim, Palestine had counted just 25,000 Jews among a total population of 300,000 as late as 1880.[27] Fifteen years later, however, Theodore Herzl, a thirty-five-year-old Jewish lawyer-turned-journalist born in Budapest, published what might be called the first Zionist manifesto. Outraged by the pogroms in Russia and Poland and appalled by the resurgence of anti-Semitism farther west in France, Herzl warned his brethren in the pages of The Jewish State that only by establishing a national home in Palestine could they be safe from persecution. Working tirelessly, Herzl brought together Jews from seventeen countries, including the United States, in Basel, Switzerland, where in August 1897 they founded the World Zionist Organization committed to accelerating Jewish immigration to Palestine by purchasing land from the Arabs. Zionist efforts bore fruit in short order and helped swell the Jewish community in Palestine to 85,000, 12 percent of the total population, on the eve of the First World War.[28]

Although very few of these immigrants had come from the United States, American Zionists hoped that President Woodrow Wilson's wartime pledge to make the world safe for democracy would apply to Jewish aspirations in the

Holy Land. Well before the United States entered the war in April 1917, Louis Brandeis, a Harvard-educated reformer whom Wilson had named America's first Jewish Supreme Court justice, apprised the White House of Zionist objectives in Palestine. Across the Atlantic in London Chaim Weizmann, a brilliant chemist and Britain's leading Zionist, was likewise pressing Foreign Secretary Arthur Balfour to endorse the idea of a Jewish state as U.K. forces prepared during the autumn of 1917 to wrest control of Palestine from the Ottoman Turks. Fearful that the German government might soon embrace Zionism in a cynical bid to undermine support for the Allied war effort among British, Russian, and American Jews, Whitehall drafted what came to be known as the Balfour Declaration, one of the most controversial, compound-complex sentences ever written: "His Majesty's Government view with favor the establishment in Palestine of a national home for the Jewish people, and will use their best endeavours to facilitate the achievement of this object, it being clearly understood that nothing shall be done which may prejudice the civil and religious rights of existing non-Jewish communities in Palestine, or the rights and political status enjoyed by Jews in any other country."[29]

Before releasing the Balfour Declaration, however, the British government sought the blessing of the Americans. The United States was not formally at war with the Ottoman Empire, and Wilson was not willing to see U.S. troops become embroiled in what seemed certain to be a nasty, three-cornered quarrel among Turks, Arabs, and Jews. But once he realized that the British intended the Balfour Declaration to be merely a statement of principles rather than a prescription for specific policies, Wilson quietly sent word across the Atlantic that he "concurred in the formula suggested from the other side."[30] Relieved to have U.S. approval, Foreign Secretary Balfour unveiled Britain's new approach toward Palestine on 2 November 1917 in a letter to Lord Lionel Walter Rothschild, a recent convert to Zionism who was working closely with Weizmann and Brandeis.[31]

When Woodrow Wilson and British prime minister David Lloyd George journeyed to Versailles fourteen months later to negotiate what one historian has called "a peace to end all peace," they found it extremely difficult to translate the Balfour Declaration from diplomatic principle into political practice. To be sure, Wilson publicly reaffirmed his commitment to a Jewish homeland in an August 1918 open letter to Rabbi Stephen Wise, a Hungarian-born Zionist with close ties to Brandeis and other White House insiders, and Lloyd George briefly lent a sympathetic ear to Chaim Weizmann during the spring of 1919. But conflicting Jewish and Arab claims to Palestine and mounting pressure from Armenians, Kurds, and other peoples formerly subject to Turkish rule for full and complete independence led the peacemakers to proceed with extreme caution.[32]

Before the summer was over, Wilson would send a fact-finding mission to the Middle East headed by General James Harbord, who uncovered both good and bad news among the ruins of the Ottoman Empire. "Without visiting the Near East," he reported in October 1919, "it is not possible for an American to realize even faintly the respect, faith and affection with which our country is regarded throughout that region." Thanks to "the world-wide reputation which we enjoy for fair dealing" and to "unselfish and impartial missionary and educational influence exerted for a century," he added, "it is the one faith which is held alike by Christian and Moslem, by Jew and Gentile, by prince and peasant in the Near East." Unfortunately, Harbord warned Washington, the peoples of the Middle East exhibited much less faith in each other. In short, should America decide to become more involved in the Middle East, U.S. policymakers would face not only familiar quarrels among peoples who shared their own Judeo-Christian heritage but also the "bloodthirsty, unregenerate and revengeful" attitude of "the indolent and pleasure-loving Turk" and the "traditional lawlessness of migrating Kurds and Arabs," among whom "the temptation to reprisals for past wrongs will be strong for at least a generation."[33]

Of Sheiks, Sphinxes, and Final Solutions

Grounded in a Social Darwinistic belief in the racial inferiority of Arabs, Kurds, and Turks and sustained by an abiding faith in the superiority of the United States, orientalism American style became a staple of popular culture during the 1920s through such media as B movies, best-selling books, and mass circulation magazines. Hollywood blockbusters such as *The Sheik* (1921), *The Thief of Baghdad* (1924), and *Beau Geste* (1926) propelled Rudolph Valentino, Douglas Fairbanks, and Ronald Colman to stardom while reinforcing popular stereotypes of the Arabs as a culturally backward, sexually depraved, and congenitally violent people.[34] In 1927 T. E. Lawrence's *Revolt in the Desert*, an abridged version of his massive *Seven Pillars of Wisdom*, became an overnight best-seller in U.S. bookstores, providing American readers with a predictable portrait of the Arabs as brave and brutal primitives, noble savages badly in need of Western guidance and tutelage.[35]

Many of the orientalist stereotypes of the Arabs evoked by films and books were reinforced by popular magazines such as *National Geographic*, which by the late 1920s had become a window on the world for millions of middle-class Americans. *National Geographic's* entire May 1923 issue, for example, was devoted to the recently discovered tomb of King Tutankhamen and other wonders of the Muslim world. Articles like "Egypt, Past and Present" and "East of Constantinople" contrasted the imperial grandeur of ancient Egyptian and medieval Islamic civilizations with the hardscrabble realities of the twentieth century. In "A Visit to Three Arab Kingdoms" *National Geographic* took its subscribers on a tour of three newly independent states—Transjordan, Iraq, and the Hejaz (later incorporated by King Abdul Aziz Ibn Saud into modern-day Saudi Arabia)—ruled by the Hashemite clan, who had spearheaded the revolt in the desert chronicled by T. E. Lawrence. Despite the political fragmentation of the region, the article emphasized that the Arabs had long been united by race, language, and religion. "To all this has been added, largely since the war, a new and broader bond, a sympathy between the Orient and Mid-East, a resentment of world domination by the white races of the Occident." In short, the magazine warned its readers, "the tinder is ready whenever the spark may strike."[36]

Over the next decade *National Geographic* published nearly a dozen articles highlighting the widening political and cultural gap between Occident and Orient in the Middle East. A December 1927 article titled "East of Suez to the Mount of the Decalogue," for example, focused on "the fatalistic and irresponsible Arabs" who wandered the Sinai Desert as childlike camel jockeys, shunning Western technology and embracing Mohammedan superstition.[37] Three years later a photoessay on Libya, where Benito Mussolini was waging one of the most brutal colonial wars of the twentieth century, downplayed the imperial carnage and emphasized instead westernization and modernization. "To-day the will of New Italy dominates this long derelict land and Italian agriculturalists are teaching new ways to Berber, Arab, and black Sudanese."[38] An October 1932 piece called "Into Burning Hadhramaut" detailed a trek into the interior of Southwest Arabia straight out of the tales of Scheherazade. "That Arabia has been able to guard its mysteries so long against the inquisitive Westerner," the author informed his readers, "is due partly to the physical features of the country and partly to the religious fanaticism of its sparse population."[39]

Nowhere did Muslim religious fanaticism and anti-Western radicalism come through more clearly, however, than in Palestine, where in a series of five articles published between 1926 and 1938 *National Geographic* tracked the descent of the Holy Land into sectarian strife between Arab and Jew. Three early pieces focusing on Bethlehem and Jerusalem presented a portrait as familiar to most Americans as the nearest Bible of a land where "three great faiths" managed to live in relative harmony.[40] But by the mid-1930s the magazine's readers learned that the rapid modernization of the Holy Land was generating considerable religious and cultural tension. "Changing Palestine," a photoessay that appeared in April 1934, described how hundreds of British bureaucrats and thousands of Jewish settlers were transforming "the land of milk and honey" into a Western outpost in the Eastern Mediterranean. "In Palestine, possibly more dramatically than anywhere else in the world, modern inventions [and] modern methods" disseminated among the Arabs were "developing pastoral people to a higher plane of life."[41]

Not until *National Geographic* published "Change Comes to Bible Lands" in December 1938, however, did middle America gain a full appreciation for the Old Testament ferocity fueling the clash between Arab and Jew. "The Balfour Declaration and Europe's anti-Semitic waves brought thousands of new settlers, especially from Germany," the magazine noted, and these Zionist pilgrims had converted a vast expanse of scrub brush and sand dunes into "the world's first new-made, 100-per-cent-Jewish city," Tel Aviv. "The influx of Jews from all over the world aroused the hostility of the Arabs," whom *National Geographic* depicted as colorful primitives capable of extraordinary acts of violence. Yet although "Arab terrorism paralyzed all Palestine in the summer of 1938," many readers doubtless put down the magazine confident that the swelling tide of Jewish immigration was likely to sustain a wave of economic growth and social progress that would soon give the Holy Land "the look of Southern California."[42]

Before 1938 was over, however, developments 1,700 miles to the northwest in Berlin would unleash a vicious outburst of anti-Semitism whose genocidal outcome would dramatize for Zionists on both sides of the Atlantic that establishing a Jewish homeland in Palestine had truly become a matter of life or death. During the preceding two decades fewer and fewer Americans remembered Woodrow Wilson's wartime promises to Louis Brandeis and Stephen Wise. Instead, more and more isolationists from coast to coast applauded Warren Harding, Calvin Coolidge, and Herbert Hoover for minimizing U.S. political entanglements abroad, whether in Western Europe or the Middle East. Meanwhile U.K. officials, such as Colonial Secretary Winston Churchill, who were responsible for administering the Palestine mandate Britain had received from the newly created League of Nations, edged away from the Balfour Declaration in the face of violent resistance from Arabs opposed to the establishment of a Jewish homeland in their midst.[43]

As enthusiasm for a Jewish state in Palestine faded at the White House and at Whitehall during the 1920s, an upsurge of nativism eroded support on Main Street for the Zionist dream. From Atlanta to Anaheim the Ku Klux Klan burned crosses and staged rallies to intimidate African Americans, Catholics, and Jews, while on the banks of the Potomac Congress was erecting restrictive quotas to stem the flow of Jews and other "undesirable" groups from Eastern Europe. Fearful that a Zionist success in Palestine might inadvertently call into question the loyalty of the entire Jewish community in the United States, influential American Jews such as *New York Times* publisher Arthur Hays Sulzberger distanced themselves from lobbying efforts on Capitol Hill. By the early 1930s membership in the Zionist Organization of America, an umbrella agency founded by Brandeis and Wise a generation earlier, had plummeted from a postwar high of 175,000 to just 25,000, convincing the State Department's elitist and sometimes anti-Semitic Middle Eastern experts that they could safely ignore this first Jewish foray into interest group politics.[44] By late 1936 the State Department's Wallace Murray had convinced his superiors to do nothing that might "entangle us in any other way in the most delicate problem of Palestine."[45]

Murray's brief for U.S. noninvolvement could not have come at a worse time for American Zionists or their comrades in Europe. Claiming that the influx of 250,000 European Jews during the decade and a half since the First World War was more than the overloaded Palestinian economic and political system could bear, in 1936 the Arabs launched a violent revolt to resist Zionism. While Palestinian militias battled the Haganah, the Jewish underground army, in the streets of Jerusalem and the foothills of Nablus, even more ominous events were unfolding in Germany, where Adolf Hitler's anti-Semitic policies were growing ever more blatant. Since coming to power in early 1933 the Nazi dictator had tarred German Jews with the brush of communism, stripped them of their civil rights, and branded them scapegoats for the Third Reich's economic woes. After Nazi tanks rolled into Vienna in March 1938 and after Hitler's storm troopers went on an anti-Semitic rampage in Berlin eight months later, thousands of German and Austrian Jews sought refuge abroad, some in Britain and America, but most in Palestine.[46]

At the time when European Jewry was most desperate for a safe haven in a national homeland, however, the British government moved to reduce Jewish immigration to Palestine sharply. Having just completed a costly two-year campaign to suppress the Arab revolt, Whitehall issued a White Paper on 17 May 1939 limiting the total number of Jewish refugees permitted to enter the Holy Land to just 75,000 during the next five years; after that, all further immigration would be subject to Palestinian approval. Among the most outspoken critics of the 1939 White Paper was fifty-three-year-old David Ben Gurion, the charismatic unofficial leader of the Yishuv, as the 350,000-member Jewish community in Palestine was now known. Convinced that persuading Whitehall to rescind the White Paper would prove an exercise in futility, Ben Gurion and his comrades hoped American Zionists might be more successful at the White House, where Franklin D. Roosevelt was preparing to seek an unprecedented third term with support from Jewish liberals.[47]

Long sympathetic to the aims of the Balfour Declaration, FDR was clearly troubled during the late 1930s by signs that Britain intended to repudiate its commitment to a Jewish homeland. "I was at Versailles," he recalled in 1938, "and I know that the British made no secret of the fact that they promised Palestine to the Jews. Why are they now reneging on their promise?"[48] Britain's actions during the spring of 1939 only raised more questions. "I have read with interest and a good deal of dismay the decisions of the British Government regarding its Palestine policy," he told Secretary of State Cordell Hull in mid-May. "This White Paper," Roosevelt hastened to add, "is something that we cannot give approval to."[49] During the following eighteen months well-connected Zionists such as Stephen Wise and Felix Frankfurter, whom FDR had recently tapped to fill Brandeis's seat on the Supreme Court, quietly encouraged the president to press Whitehall to honor its commitments regarding Palestine. At the State Department, however, Hull and his advisers insisted that U.S. meddling would only serve to undermine the U.K. position in the Middle East at a time when Britain, in the wake of the fall of France in June 1940, was the sole remaining barrier to complete Nazi domination of Europe. Judging geopolitical considerations to be more important than domestic politics, Roosevelt kept his doubts about the White Paper to himself and still managed to win a third term by a healthy margin.[50]

Thousands of European Jews unable to find refuge abroad would soon be among the earliest victims of the Holocaust. During 1939 and 1940 the Nazis had targeted the Jewish population of occupied Europe for relocation to concentration camps in Poland. After the German invasion of the Soviet Union in June 1941, agents of the Gestapo, Hitler's secret police, began systematically to murder all Russian Jews who fell into their hands. By the time that Germany's Japanese allies attacked Pearl Harbor on 7 December 1941, rumors of the Gestapo's anti-Semitic butchery were already filtering into the United States. In January 1942 Hitler formally approved a "final solution for the Jewish problem" and authorized the Schutzstaffel, or SS, an elite corps of the German army whose commanders spoke with the voice of Cain, to begin the wholesale extermination of hundreds of thousands of Jews then imprisoned at Auschwitz, Buchenwald, and other concentration camps. During the next three years nearly 6 million Jewish men, women, and children would die.[51]

The unspeakable slaughter unfolding in Nazi-occupied Europe removed any remaining doubts among most American Jews about the importance of a Jewish homeland in Palestine. In May 1942, 600 American Zionists gathered at the Biltmore Hotel in New York City and passed a unanimous resolution demanding "that Palestine be established as a Jewish Commonwealth integrated in the structure of the new democratic world." While insiders such as Stephen Wise sought to win White House support for the Biltmore declaration, outsiders like Abba Hillel Silver, a fiery Cleveland rabbi born in Lithuania and educated at Hebrew Union College, founded the American Zionist Emergency Council, whose 200 local chapters funneled a half-million dollars into national headquarters to finance a lobbying effort in Washington.[52]

Nineteen forty-four was an election year, and U.S. advocates of a Jewish homeland in Palestine worked tirelessly to gain bipartisan endorsements for their plans. Relying on his close ties with Senator Robert Taft, an Ohio Republican with a perennial case of Potomac fever, Abba Hillel Silver managed to persuade the Grand Old Party to insert a plank in its platform calling for the immediate implementation of the Balfour Declaration. Not to be outdone, Zionist Democrats saw to it that when their party gathered in Chicago for its national convention, it endorsed the creation of "a free and democratic Jewish commonwealth" in Palestine.[53] As his campaign for a fourth term drew to a close, Franklin Roosevelt publicly reiterated his support for the Balfour Declaration and vowed that "if re-elected, I shall help to bring about its realization."[54]

A few days after the voters had handed Roosevelt yet another triumph at the polls on 7 November, however, American Zionists began to detect signs that, like the exhausted chief executive's health, his commitment to their objectives was quite fragile. Just one week after election day the Roosevelt administration cautioned Rabbi Stephen Wise "that it would be a mistake to stir things up at this time" by seeking a congressional resolution calling for a Jewish state in Palestine. When Senator Robert Wagner, an Empire State Democrat, pressed the White House to honor its campaign promises to the Zionists in late November, FDR replied that it would be most unwise to "add fuel to the flames" in Palestine. "There are about half a million Jews there. Perhaps another million want to go," Roosevelt informed Wagner on 3 December. "On the other side of the picture there are approximately seventy million Mohammedans who want to cut their throats the day they land."[55]

Roosevelt learned just how ferocious Arab opposition to Zionism had become when, on the return leg of his trip to the great power summit at Yalta in early 1945, he sat down with Saudi Arabia's King Abdul Aziz Ibn Saud. During a three-hour Valentine's Day meeting with FDR the Saudi ruler demanded that the United States and Britain halt Jewish immigration and vowed that "the Arabs would choose to die rather than yield their lands to the Jews." Somewhat taken aback, Roosevelt assured Ibn Saud that the United States "would do nothing to assist the Jews against the Arabs and would make no move hostile to the Arab people."[56] After his return to Washington, the aging and ailing president could not shake the image of the hawklike Saudi monarch, ensconced in a gold chair and surrounded by six slaves, thundering against Zionist plans to carve out an enclave in Palestine. "Ibn Saud made the point that he had no trouble with native Palestine Jews," Roosevelt told an aide on 14 March 1945, "but the immigration from Europe was more than he could cope with and if things went wrong the millions of surrounding Arabs might easily proclaim a Holy War and then there would be no end of trouble."[57]

When Rabbi Stephen Wise called at the White House the next day, however, FDR was far more sanguine. Despite "a momentary sense of failure" after his encounter with Ibn Saud, the president remained committed to "the establishment of a free and democratic Jewish Commonwealth."[58] After Wise relayed this news to the Jewish community at Roosevelt's request, State Department officials forecast stormy weather for U.S. interests in the Middle East. "The statement which [the White House] authorized Rabbi Wise to make is certain to cause consternation and dismay in the Arab world . . . and damage to our position," Wallace Murray warned his superiors on 20 March. "The President's continued support of Zionism may thus lead to actual bloodshed in the Near East and even endanger the security of our immensely valuable oil concession in Saudi Arabia."[59] Seeking to limit the damage, Roosevelt reminded Ibn Saud several weeks later that the United States still intended to consult the Arabs before acting on Palestine. But FDR's cardiovascular system gave out before he could see whether his soothing message would prevent the Saudi monarch from launching his jihad.

During the first weeks of his administration, Harry Truman was more concerned with ending the hot war in Europe than with avoiding a holy war in the Middle East. The day before Truman had taken the oath of office, tanks and half-tracks from General George Patton's U.S. Third Army had rolled into Buchenwald, a Nazi death camp just outside Weimar in central Germany, where American GIs discovered gruesome proof of Hitler's unspeakable brutality. Photographs from Buchenwald, Auschwitz, and other concentration camps imprinted indelibly in the world's collective memory ghastly images of corpses stacked like cordwood and emaciated bands of "displaced persons," as the survivors of the Holocaust were known, too weak to walk or talk. In the weeks and months after the guns fell silent on 9 May 1945, the number of displaced persons in the custody of U.S. and U.K. forces would swell to nearly 1 million, 250,000 of whom were stateless Jews who desperately sought to immigrate to Palestine.[60]

As they frequently had done when confronted with the horrors of war and revolution, the editors of *National Geographic* downplayed the carnage of Hitler's final solution, choosing instead to publish upbeat stories hinting that the best solution for those who had survived the Nazi death camps was the creation of a Jewish state in the Holy Land. Readers thumbing through a June 1945 pictorial titled "Americans Help Liberated Europe Live Again," for example, found not the grisly photos of the victims of Buchenwald taken six weeks earlier but, rather, inspirational portraits of clean-cut GIs helping the people of France, Belgium, and Germany begin to put their shattered societies back together. The article mentioned neither Hitler's anti-Semitism nor his concentration camps, nor did it include Jews on its list of nationalities victimized by the Nazis. Indeed, few *National Geographic* subscribers would have realized that at least one-quarter of the "refugees and displaced persons" targeted by Allied relief and relocation efforts were Jewish.[61]

When *National Geographic* finally got around to acknowledging the Holocaust sixteen months later, it did so in "Palestine Today," a matter-of-fact account of relatively westernized Jews reclaiming their rightful place in the Holy Land from orientalized Arabs. One photo, for example, showed "Singing, Shouting Fugitives from Concentration Camps" marching beneath the Star of David into a promised land that, according to the magazine, "is, in a broad sense, the United States of the middle 1800s at the same time that it is, paradoxically enough, California of today." Another photo captured "Westernized Haifa's Streamlined Balconies Stretch[ing] for Oriental Breezes" along the Mediterranean, where "the Jews have lived since Biblical times." The photos of Arabs, on the other hand, showed smiling but simple people dressed in native garb carrying fruit, picking vegetables, and performing other menial tasks.[62]

Most Americans reading this article must surely have come away with the impression that the Zionist dream was not very different from their own. After all, the Jewish refugees arriving in Palestine, like the Puritans who had settled New England three centuries earlier, were victims of religious persecution determined to make new lives for themselves in an unforgiving landscape. "On a miniature—almost a laboratory scale," the magazine assured its subscribers, "a visit to Palestine today is much like a visit to America of yesterday." A pair of snapshots juxtaposed near the end of the article left little doubt regarding who was cast as Prospero and who as Caliban. The first photo shows a pretty teenager, whose "parents may have been among the six million Jews massacred in Europe," planting tomato seedlings in Palestine. "Buchenwald and Belsen behind her," the caption reads, "a survivor of Horror Camps tills the land of her dreams." The second photo shows a grungy Arab farmer clad in a kaffiyeh and armed with an ornamental sword overseeing three Palestinians doing stoop labor. "A semifeudal economy," *National Geographic* explained, "prevails in isolated Arab farm communities."[63] Projected into America's living rooms by mass circulation magazines, these powerful images of brave Jews who had survived Hitler's final solution in order to make new lives on an old frontier, and of exotic Arabs, one part sheik and one part sharecropper, would do much to shape the U.S. approach to the Middle East after 1945.

David, Goliath, and the Arab-Israeli
Conflict, 1948–1967

During the nineteen years between the founding of Israel in May 1948 and the stunning Israeli victory in the June 1967 Six Day War, the U.S. public and policymakers gradually came to see the tiny Jewish state's confrontation with its much larger Arab rivals as a reenactment of the biblical story of David and Goliath. Cast by much of the American media as a geopolitical underdog whose occidental values were anathema to its oriental neighbors, Israel relied on courage, ingenuity, and increasingly, Western weapons to defeat people whose Muslim faith and tribal culture seemed to magazines such as *National Geographic* more and more out of step with twentieth-century realities. The November 1948 issue of *National Geographic*, for example, included "Sailing with Sindbad's Sons," an account of the voyage of the *Bayan*, a square-rigged "Winged Galleon of Araby" that retraced the route of the old slave and spice trade from Aden at the mouth of the Red Sea to Zanzibar off the East African coast. The description of the *Bayan's* crew reaffirmed the classic orientalist myth of the primitive but happy native. "Like Monkeys in Treetops, Arabs Climb a 130-Foot Yard," reads one caption. "Their pay is a pittance and their food poor, yet they are cheerful."[64]

The sharp contrast that *National Geographic* drew for its readers between westernized Israelis and backward Arabs came through most clearly, however, in a pair of articles that appeared in the autumn of 1947. In "An Archaeologist Looks at Palestine," photographs of Bronze Age skeletons and biblical ruins alternate with snapshots of Zionist irrigation projects that "Make the Desert Bloom" and sun-drenched Tel Aviv beachgoers clad in Bermuda shorts.[65] The color photos at the end of the article, on the other hand, highlight the exotic and dangerous Arab lands to the east. "Sheiks of the Wealthy Majali Bedouins Relax on Rugs and Soft Cushions before Their Tent," reads one caption. A few pages later a Jordanian desert warrior, sporting a rifle, a pistol, two bandoliers, and a silver dagger, stares menacingly at the camera from beneath his red-checkered kaffiyeh.[66]

National Geographic's subscribers got their longest look at the primitivism of the Arab world in October 1947 with the publication of "Yemen: Southern Arabia's Mountain Wonderland," a forty-one-page photoessay written by Harlan B. Clark, a U.S. Foreign Service officer based next door in Britain's Aden protectorate. One aerial shot showed Imam Yahya watching his "Parading Troops Perform the Dagger Dance" amidst racing camels and black stallions, a moment Clark likened to "a scene out of *Arabian Nights*." The article closed with a photo of Harry Truman, clad in a double-breasted suit, chatting in the

Oval Office with Yahya's youngest son, Prince Saif, who had arrived at the White House carrying worry beads and wearing a fez and a prayer shawl.[67]

Saif's July 1947 visit doubtless helped persuade Truman that Arabs were exotic figures straight out of *Innocents Abroad*. After meeting with Abdullah Suleiman, King Ibn Saud's minister of finance, in August 1946, Truman had likened the second most powerful man in Saudi Arabia to "a real old Biblical Arab with chin whiskers, a white gown, gold braid, and everything." When Suleiman asked for U.S. help on a Saudi irrigation project, Truman replied that "he should send for a Moses to strike rocks in various places with his staff and he'd have plenty of water."[68]

Other top U.S. officials held the Arabs in even lower esteem. When Saudi Arabia and its Arab allies nearly sidetracked U.S. plans for the early recognition of Israel in the spring of 1948, for example, White House counsel Clark Clifford urged decisive action. "The United States appears in the ridiculous role of trembling before threats of a few nomadic desert tribes," he wrote Truman in early March. "Why should Russia or Yugoslavia, or any other nation treat us with anything but contempt in light of our shilly-shallying appeasement of the Arabs."[69] Even across town at Foggy Bottom, where State Department Middle East experts had a reputation for being much more sympathetic to Arabs than to Jews, key officials regarded Israel's neighbors as irrational and unrealistic. "As for the emotion of the Arabs, I do not care a dried camel's hump," acid-tongued Palestine desk officer Robert McClintock growled on 1 July. "It is, however, important to the interests of this country that these fanatical and overwrought people do not injure our strategic interests through reprisals against our oil investments."[70] Like McClintock, George Kennan, the State Department's reigning Soviet specialist and newly appointed chief of its Policy Planning Staff, questioned the wisdom of U.S. support for Israel. But he was no friend of the Arabs, who had left a lasting impression on him during a wartime visit to Iraq as a people prone to "selfishness and stupidity" and "inclined to all manner of religious bigotry and fanaticism."[71]

Few U.S. policymakers saw any reason to challenge Clifford's or Kennan's orientalist interpretation of Muslim behavior during Truman's second term. After all, according to a 1949 Central Intelligence Agency (CIA) psychological profile of the Middle East, the Arabs were not only "non-inventive and slow to put theories into practice" and "skillful mainly at avoiding hard work" but also capable of "astonishing acts of treachery and dishonesty."[72] Carleton Coon, a State Department whiz kid whose first assignment abroad had come in Damascus during the early 1950s, recalled long afterward that "the Syrians had a well deserved inferiority complex" that predated the creation of Israel.[73] Adolf Berle, a Democratic Party insider who served in Truman's kitchen cabinet, remarked privately during the summer of 1952 that this well-documented psychological profile of instability extended to non-Arab Muslims such as the Iranians as well. "Fanatic Mohammedan nationalism" seemed about to sweep away the shah of Iran, opening the door to a "Communist takeover" in Tehran, Berle confided in his diary on 13 August. There was a very real danger, he concluded gloomily, "that the Russians would be on the Persian Gulf by Christmas."[74]

In short, as the Truman administration drew to a close, officials from the bottom to the top of the policymaking pyramid were convinced that the peoples of the Muslim world were an unpredictable lot whose penchant for political and religious extremism constituted a grave threat to U.S. interests in the region. Indeed, most U.S. policymakers would likely have seconded the orientalist assessment that Britain's ambassador to Iraq forwarded to London in late 1952. The Iraqi, like most Arabs, "is embittered, frustrated and fanatical," Sir John Troutbeck cabled Whitehall on 31 October. "Seeing little but squalor and stagnation around him, he will not admit even to himself the obvious answer, that he belongs to a peculiarly irresponsible and feckless race."[75]

The man who replaced Harry Truman in the Oval Office in January 1953 was equally comfortable with such orientalist stereotypes of the Middle East. Dwight Eisenhower's view of the Muslim world was colored by his wartime experiences in North Africa, where a decade earlier he had tried unsuccessfully to bridge the gap between French colonialists and Algerian nationalists. "Arabs are a very uncertain quantity, explosive and full of prejudices," he remarked privately in November 1942. "Many things done here that look queer are just to keep the Arabs from blazing up into revolt."[76] Eisenhower's close encounter with the Arabs during the 1950s did nothing to soften his earlier assessment. Despite Britain's "modern program of independence for countries once part of the Empire," Ike complained in his memoirs, Egyptian president Gamal Abdel Nasser had unleashed a crusade of "virulent nationalism and unreasoning prejudice" in which there was "evidence of Communist meddling."[77]

Nasser's seizure of the Suez Canal during the summer of 1956 reinforced Eisenhower's belief that the Arabs were irrational, resentful, and dangerous to Western interests. "Nasser," Ike observed on 31 July, "embodies the emotional demands of the people of the area for independence and for 'slapping the White Man down.'"[78] When Eisenhower sent U.S. marines to Lebanon two years later to shore up a pro-American regime besieged by pro-Nasser dissidents, he reminded the National Security Council (NSC) that "the underlying Arab thinking" remained deeply rooted in "violence, emotion and ignorance."[79] As his term drew to a close, Ike complained that Nasser and like-minded nationalists were little more than oriental despots. "If you go and live with these Arabs, you will find that they simply cannot understand our ideas of freedom or human dignity," he told the NSC in June 1959. "They have lived so long under dictatorships of one form or another, how can we expect them to run successfully a free government?"[80]

Eisenhower's top advisers echoed the president's growing frustration with the Arabs. Shortly after taking over at Foggy Bottom, for example, John Foster Dulles took a two-week fact-finding trip to the Middle East that confirmed all of his Presbyterian fears of the Muslim infidel. Following visits to Cairo and other Arab capitals in May 1953, Eisenhower's secretary of state pronounced Nasser and like-minded Arab nationalists "pathological" in their suspicion of the Western powers and "naive" in their trust of the Kremlin.[81] It is no surprise that in private conversations with U.K. officials in early July, Dulles described Iran's anti-Western prime minister, Mohammed Mossadegh, as "a wily oriental."[82] When anti-Western violence rocked Baghdad, Beirut, and Amman five summers later, White House troubleshooter Robert Murphy undertook a "twenty-nine-day Magic Carpet tour of the fabled East" at the behest of Eisenhower, with whom he had worked to curb "the restiveness of the indigenes" in Muslim North Africa during the Second World War. After visiting "Godforsaken stretches of Iraq," where "mobs whose violence surpassed all expectations" held sway, he informed his boss in August 1958 that little had changed since the early 1940s.[83]

U.S. diplomats stationed in the Middle East helped reinforce the orientalist views of Eisenhower, Dulles, and Murphy. When Ambassador Henry Villard found himself mired down in endless negotiations over a U.S. air base in June 1954, he cabled Washington that the tactics of Libyan officials were "tantamount to blackmail and show[ed] little change from [the] barbary pirate tradition."[84] Two years later Henry Byroade, the U.S. ambassador to Egypt, confirmed that Nasser and his followers were volatile, unpredictable, and quixotic. "Arabs are quite capable of getting completely beside themselves" on matters related to Israel, Byroade warned Dulles on 14 March 1956, "because by nature they [are] inclined to fight windmills."[85] A White House study completed four years later reiterated the importance of "psychological" factors in U.S. relations with the Middle East. American officials, the drafters of NSC-6011 pointed out in July 1960, must understand that "the Arabs' experience with and fear of Western domination" had generated hostility and suspicion that were in turn exacerbated by "their belief that the United States is the special friend and protector of Israel."[86]

Indeed, by the time that Eisenhower retired to his farm just outside Gettysburg, Pennsylvania, in January 1961, the Arabs could see that Israel had won not only a special spot in the hearts of everyday Americans, who identified with the underdog status of the new nation, but also the grudging respect of U.S. policymakers, who were impressed by its military prowess.[87] As they had during the mid-1940s, so too during the Eisenhower era many Americans seemed to regard sympathy for a Jewish homeland in the Middle East as a form of symbolic atonement for having done too little too late to prevent the Holocaust in Europe. For the United States during the 1950s perhaps the most powerful reminder of Hitler's genocide was a grainy, black-and-white snapshot of a teenage Jewish schoolgirl that graced the cover of her heartbreaking, posthumous account of life and death in Nazi-occupied Holland. When first published in 1952, *Anne Frank: Diary of a Young Girl* became an instant bestseller. By the end of the decade the haunting visage of Anne Frank had been imprinted even more deeply onto U.S. popular culture, first by a Pulitzer Prize–winning play that drew standing-room-only crowds on Broadway in 1956 and then by a Hollywood box-office smash that received two Academy Awards three years later.[88]

The literary and cinematic connections between the nightmare of the Holocaust and the dream of Israel were drawn most clearly for readers and moviegoers in Eisenhower's America, however, in the work of novelist and screenwriter Leon Uris. Few novels have sold 4 million copies faster while winning wide critical acclaim than *Exodus,* a thinly fictionalized account of the tireless Zionist crusade to run food, guns, and Jewish refugees into Palestine after the Second World War. Published in 1958, the book contained a plot that pitted survivors of the Nazi death camps against callous British colonial bureaucrats and ruthless Arab demagogues as well as a message that trumpeted the eventual triumph of good over evil. Hollywood wasted little time producing its version of the heroic founding of Israel. In December 1960 United Artists released *Exodus,* a four-hour epic starring rising young screen idol Paul Newman as an indomitable Jewish freedom fighter and featuring a stirring soundtrack that would win an Oscar for best musical score. Appearing seven months after a well-publicized, stranger-than-fiction operation whereby Israeli intelligence had snatched Adolf Eichmann, one of the chief architects of the final solution, off the streets of Buenos Aires and spirited him to Jerusalem to stand trial as a Nazi war criminal, *Exodus* reminded American audiences that with the creation of a Jewish state in the Holy Land, Anne Frank had not died in vain.[89]

Eighteen months after Paul Newman enthralled friends of Israel with his gallantry and good looks in *Exodus,* a white-robed Peter O'Toole stormed out of the heart of Arabia and into movie theaters from coast to coast as the reincarnation of T. E. Lawrence. Directed by British filmmaker David Lean and shot on location in the desert just outside Seville, where the Spaniards had finally driven the Muslims out of Europe in 1492, *Lawrence of Arabia* recaptured the romance, the adventure, and the orientalism of Britain's errand among the Arabs during the First World War. Despite the bravery and skill of the Bedouin warriors, millions of filmgoers went home convinced that without Lawrence's help, the Arabs could never have thrown off the Ottoman yoke. Unlike the Zionists in *Exodus*, whose singleness of purpose ensured the establishment of a strong and independent Jewish state, the Arabs in *Lawrence of Arabia* saw their dreams of self-determination dashed by their self-destructive penchant for tribal infighting and political scheming. *Lawrence of Arabia*'s orientalist message, its breathtaking camera work, and its talented cast combined to win six Oscars, including those for best actor, best director, and best picture.

The images of noble Israelis surrounded by unruly Arabs projected by Hollywood were reinforced by mass market monthlies such as *National Geographic*, whose circulation soared during the early 1960s. The magazine's December 1963 issue, for example, included "Holy Land Today," a brief photoessay that described Israeli pioneers, "a trowel in one hand and a Bible in the other," methodically "reversing the ordinary course of history" through "the transformation of ancient ruins into living communities."[90] By way of contrast, a March 1964 *National Geographic* piece on Yemen began with this lead-in: "Wracked by civil war, an ancient Arabian land struggles to find its place in the world of the twentieth century." Even a brief look at the wild-eyed mountain tribesmen brandishing daggers and submachine guns or the bearded worshipers "pour[ing] out of Yemen's Arabian Nights capital" must have persuaded many American readers that the Yemenis were unlikely to win that struggle without the second coming of T. E. Lawrence.[91] Subscribers thumbing through a March 1965 pictorial on Israel, on the other hand, discovered a "Land of Promise" where "smooth new highways hum with traffic" and where "fields of soft green gleam amid the old desert wastes."[92]

Like the editors of *National Geographic*, the insiders who advised John F. Kennedy and Lyndon B. Johnson on the Middle East seem subconsciously to have embraced a hierarchy of race and culture in which the Arabs ranked far below the Israelis. A June 1961 CIA national intelligence estimate on U.S. relations with Nasser, for example, predicted that his brand of nationalism was likely to grow stronger "because it provides an excuse—the wickedness of the great powers—for a host of deficiencies and inadequacies in Arab society."[93] Nasser was not above employing "an oriental bargaining tactic," White House Middle East expert Robert Komer complained to Kennedy in November 1962, whenever he needed to extract himself from a military or diplomatic tight spot.[94] It was always important, Komer mused a year later, to "tak[e] adequate account of the inferiority of the Arab soldier as compared to the Israeli."[95] Perhaps the most pronounced orientalist views, however, were expressed by U.S. diplomats serving overseas, like Harold Glidden, who was stationed in Iraq. "If Arabs ever took over [the] world, they would start instantly to tear it down," Glidden told a reporter shortly after a bloody military coup rocked Baghdad in early 1963. "Arab values of vengeance, prestige and obsession with feuding are not acclimated to urban society."[96]

The hulking Texan who succeeded Kennedy in the Oval Office later that year did not disagree with this harsh assessment. An ardent friend of the Jewish state and an outspoken foe of radical Arab nationalism since his days as Senate majority leader during the late 1950s, President Lyndon Johnson regarded the Middle East as a backward and exotic corner of the world straight out of *Arabian Nights* and badly in need of westernization. At a White House dinner in April 1964, for example, Johnson toasted King Hussein of Jordan for having "brought that ancient land of the camel, the date, and the palm to the threshold of a bright and a hopeful future."[97] On the other hand, LBJ neither liked nor trusted militant Arab leaders such as Nasser, who seemed to be a cross between Ho Chi Minh and Geronimo. Johnson's sentiments became very clear after Egyptian students staged violent anti-American demonstrations and burned down the U.S. Information Agency (USIA) library in Cairo in December 1964. "One way to react," LBJ told a group of congressmen shortly afterward, was to tell Nasser "to go to hell."[98]

According to Mohamed Heikal, a leading Egyptian journalist and one of Nasser's closest advisers, the feeling was mutual. After Johnson threatened to suspend U.S. economic aid to Egypt in retaliation for the destruction of the USIA facility, Nasser delivered a blistering reply. "Those who do not accept our behavior can go and drink from the sea," he thundered on 23 December. "We will cut the tongues of anybody who talks badly about us." Lest LBJ miss the point, Nasser added, "We are not going to accept gangsterism by cowboys."[99] This outburst helped place America's confrontation with the Arabs into a context any self-respecting Texan could appreciate: cowboys and Indians. While neither Johnson's memoirs nor his private papers make it clear whether he ever cast the problem explicitly in terms of Western civilization versus oriental barbarism, the newly created Palestine Liberation Organization (PLO) did remind him of the Viet Cong.[100] When PLO raids against Israeli villages along the Syrian frontier lit the fuse for the Six Day War during the spring of 1967, the Johnson administration knew who wore white hats and who wore black. White House aide John Roche probably put it best in late May when he told LBJ in the vernacular of the Lone Star State, "I confess that I look on the Israelis as Texans and Nasser as Santa Ana."[101]

Israel's stunning victory over the combined forces of Egypt, Jordan, and Syria in June 1967 seemed to confirm a verdict British orientalists had handed down about the Arab East a century earlier. Nasser might invoke the memory of Saladin and appeal to "the 'Holy War' psychology of the Arab world," Secretary of State Dean Rusk prophesied as the clock ticked down toward H-hour in early June, but in the face of superior Western firepower, the Egyptians would cut and run.[102] Israel's swift seizure of the Sinai, the West Bank, and the Golan Heights with the blessing of Lyndon Johnson touched off "a riotous wave of anti-Americanism" from Cairo to Kuwait City that John Badeau, Kennedy's ambassador to Egypt, likened to "the Boxer Rebellion in China" seven decades earlier.[103] The implications of the Six Day War for U.S. policy-makers were spelled out several years later in a CIA study of the Arab-Israeli conflict. "The June [1967] war was frequently invoked by analysts as proof," the agency's experts concluded in late 1973, that "many Arabs, as Arabs, simply weren't up to the demands of modern warfare and that they lacked understanding, motivation, and probably in some cases courage as well."[104]

For the U.S. public, however, the lessons of the Six Day War grew out of popular culture rather than foreign policy and probably ran more in the direction of David and Goliath tempered by knowledge of the Holocaust. Opinion polls taken shortly after the shooting stopped showed that Americans sympathizing with Israel outnumbered those sympathizing with the Arabs by a whopping 19-to-1 ratio.[105] Predisposed to siding with the underdog, most Americans seemed to regard Israel's smashing victory as the fulfillment of a biblical prophecy. Indeed, one of the hottest-selling paperbacks in June 1967 was James Michener's *The Source*, a 1,000-page epic recounting 2,000 years of Jewish exile, torment, and eventual redemption symbolized by the creation of Israel. Dismissing the notion that his country should remain "a little enclave that thrills the world because its fighters defend themselves against the Arab circle," Michener's Israeli protagonist insisted that the Jewish state could "become a beacon of pure, burning light, illuminating this entire area, forming an alliance with a prospering Arab world."[106] Readers thumbing through the *National Geographic*'s fifteen-page photoessay on the Six Day War six months later were reminded of just how close that light had come to burning out. "I am the only member of my family who survived Buchenwald," reads the caption alongside a snapshot of an Israeli commando who had helped defeat three Arab armies. "This time I have a gun to fight with, a country and a cause to serve."[107]

In short, for Americans Israel's military triumph in June 1967 completed the transformation of Jews from victims to victors while branding the Arabs as feckless, reckless, and weak. For a generation that remembered appeasement as a dirty word and regarded Nasser as a Hitler on the Nile, the Six Day War closed the book on Anne Frank and fulfilled the dream of *Exodus*. The burned-out tanks that littered Egypt's Sinai Desert and Syria's Golan Heights and the angry mobs who burned Uncle Sam in effigy from the Gulf of Sidra to the banks of the Euphrates confirmed for many Americans that the Arabs did not have an inferiority complex; they were simply inferior. As Lyndon Johnson settled into a Vietnam-induced early retirement at the LBJ Ranch in January

1969, his disappointment that the Indians held the upper hand in Southeast Asia was tempered by his realization that, in the Middle East, the cowboys were winning.

True Lies?: From Black September to Desert Storm

For many Americans the darkest and most chilling image to emerge from the Middle East before 11 September 2001 may well date from September 1972. As Richard Nixon moved inexorably toward a landslide victory in his bid for a second term inside the Beltway, a small band of Palestinian commandos shot their way into the Israeli compound at the Olympic Village just outside Munich, the city that thirty-four years earlier had become synonymous with totalitarianism and appeasement. While the whole world watched in horror, seven Black September terrorists mowed down eleven defenseless Israeli athletes during an airport shootout with German police. For the next twenty years both U.S. popular attitudes and foreign policy toward the Middle East would be preoccupied with combating Palestinian terrorists and their patrons such as Iraqi dictator Saddam Hussein.

Like most Americans, Richard Nixon was appalled by the awful news from Munich. After watching the Olympic tragedy unfold live via satellite, he denounced Black September as "international outlaws of the worst sort who will stoop to anything in order to accomplish their goals" and pledged to help the Israelis rid themselves of the Palestinian terrorists whose cruelty knew no bounds.[108] Indeed, although he occasionally lambasted Jews critical of his administration in language that shocked insiders like national security adviser Henry Kissinger, Nixon was a staunch friend of the Jewish state. "In every crisis Nixon stood by Israel more firmly than almost any other President save Harry Truman," Kissinger recalled in his memoirs. "He admired Israeli guts. He respected Israeli leaders' tenacious defense of their national interest. [And] he considered their military prowess an asset for the democracies." Speaking for himself, Kissinger confessed that Israel was also an intensely personal issue. "I could never forget that thirteen members of my family had died in Nazi concentration camps," he noted grimly. "I had no stomach for encouraging another holocaust by well-intentioned policies that might get out of control."[109]

For both Kissinger and Nixon this meant working quietly behind the scenes to broker an Arab-Israeli truce with moderates such as Egypt's Anwar Sadat while isolating extremists like the Black September guerrillas. Despite his role in masterminding the Syro-Egyptian attack on Israel in October 1973, by the end of the decade Sadat was regarded by most Americans and by many Israelis as the quintessential "good Arab." In Egyptian-Israeli disengagement parleys extending through three U.S. administrations, Sadat struck American policy-makers as shrewd, pragmatic, and willing to take enormous risks for peace. Nixon praised Sadat's "great subtlety and sophistication" and called him "a constructive and essential influence for any future Middle East negotiations."[110] Gerald Ford, who had once inadvertently toasted Sadat as the leader of "the great people of the Government of Israel," appreciated the Egyptian president's sense of humor, his straightforward manner, and his diplomatic flexibility.[111] Jimmy Carter, who without Sadat's help could never have launched the Camp David peace process in September 1978, came to admire his Egyptian friend "more than any other leader" and called him "a man who would change history."[112]

Carter, Ford, Nixon, and most other Americans were shocked and saddened on 6 October 1981 when Anwar Sadat was gunned down in Cairo by "bad Arabs," Muslim militants linked to the shadowy Islamic Group. The funeral three days later produced a media frenzy reminiscent of Valentino's death fifty-four years earlier, with a sad-eyed Barbara Walters beaming an informal eulogy of her friend Anwar into millions of American living rooms. The *National Geographic* crew that witnessed Sadat's assassination never forgot the "exceptional beauty about his dark, complex face, noble as a pharaoh's," as he rose to confront his killers, and they never forgave the Bedouin tribesmen who shortly thereafter celebrated the Islamic Group's awful deed.[113] "Sadat was a great and good man," Jimmy Carter remarked upon hearing the sad news, a victim of "his most bitter and dangerous enemies," anti-Western extremists "obsessed with hatred for his peaceful goals."[114] A latter-day pharaoh, Carter added four years later, Anwar Sadat had died "at the hands of misguided religious fanatics."[115]

Although few Americans realized that "assassin" was an Arabic word, many probably believed that the brutal act of terrorism in the streets of Cairo, like Black September's bloody raid outside Munich nine years earlier, was very much in keeping with the Arab character. Seven months before the Olympic massacre, a retired State Department Middle East expert had published a psychological profile warning that the repeated humiliations inflicted by Israel would unleash a "collective need for vengeance" deeply rooted in Arab culture. "It is difficult to describe the depth of the Arabs' emotional need for revenge, but suffice it to say that Islam itself found it necessary to sanction revenge," Harold Glidden observed in February 1972. "The felt need for revenge is as strong today as it was in pre-Islamic times."[116]

Other orientalist broadsides followed in quick succession. Raphael Patai, an Israeli-educated anthropologist who had taught Middle Eastern studies at Princeton, Columbia, and other American universities, offered his readers a bleak view of the "backwardness, cultural decline, indeed, fossilization" of the Arab world in 1973. The troubled relationship with the West, Patai explained, was the result of everything from prolonged breast-feeding to faulty toilet training, all of which "produced a disturbing inferiority complex in the Arab mind which in itself made it more difficult to shake off the shackles of stagnation."[117] Two years later British orientalist John Laffin informed the American public that "violence exists at every level of Arab life," thanks mainly to "poverty and frustration—sexual, economic, [and] political." Long ago, Laffin added, "history 'turned wrong' for the Arabs," leaving them subordinate to the Western powers. The "consequent trauma," he concluded, was "a principal reason for the great psychological sickness which fell like a plague upon the Arab race."[118] William Brown, a U.S. diplomat posted to Cairo and Beirut during the 1960s, confirmed Patai's and Laffin's orientalist diagnoses in a 1980 retrospective aptly titled *The Last Crusade*. Arab nationalism was "beyond the control apparatus of any state" and had "a reactive quality arising from the Arabs' experience with the West," Brown observed. "A relative and tolerant perspective is not possible within the Arabs' world of absolute and God-given truth."[119]

Critics such as Edward Said were quick to challenge these orientalist assumptions. As early as 1978 Said insisted that such pathological stereotypes of the Arabs constituted little more than self-serving rationalizations for Western cultural and economic imperialism. "Lurking behind all of these images is the menace of *jihad*," he observed bluntly. "Consequence: a fear that the Muslims (or Arabs) will take over the world." The net effect of this fear was ignorance, Said concluded in the final chapter of *Orientalism*, ignorance that seemed destined "to keep the region and its people conceptually emasculated, reduced to 'attitudes,' 'trends,' statistics: in short, dehumanized."[120] Throughout the 1980s and into the early 1990s Said broadened his critique, stressing that America's habit of viewing "Arabs as basically, irrecusably, and congenitally 'Other'" clearly reflected "racist overtones in its elaboration of an 'Arab' anti-democratic, violent, and regressive attitude to the world." This, Said pointed out in *Culture and Imperialism* in 1993, "contributed to the polarity that was set up between democratic Israel and a homogeneously non-democratic Arab world, in which the Palestinians, dispossessed and exiled by Israel, came to represent 'terrorism' and little beyond it."[121]

Said's trenchant criticism notwithstanding, the reading public was treated to a steady diet of orientalism American style during the Reagan and George Bush years. In a revised edition of *The Arab Mind* that appeared in 1983, Raphael Patai saw little hope for peace or progress in the Middle East unless the children of Ishmael could "devote their best talents not to fighting windmills, but to constructing the new Arab man."[122] Six years later David Pryce-

Jones, a crusty veteran of Britain's Suez War and a self-styled orientalist, published *The Closed Circle*, a scathing anti-Arab diatribe that recycled many of the stereotypes popularized by Glidden, Patai, and Laffin. Because the Arabs remained trapped in a brutal, patriarchal, and tribal society whose members "really believe in their inalienable right to be exploited by people of their own nationality," Pryce-Jones concluded that autocracy, not democracy, would always carry the day: "Instead of construction, destruction; instead of creativity, wastefulness; instead of body politic, atrocities."[123]

The most widely disseminated orientalist screed of the decade, however, was probably Bernard Lewis's "The Roots of Muslim Rage," *Atlantic Monthly*'s cover story for September 1990. A British-born, Princeton-based founding father of the modern academic discipline of Middle Eastern studies, Lewis attributed the wave of anti-Americanism sweeping the Muslim world to an irrational hatred of Judeo-Christian civilization exacerbated by "the revival of ancient prejudices" among Islamic extremists. Reminding the *Atlantic*'s readers that "America had become the archenemy, the incarnation of evil," for theocratic zealots from Lebanon to Iran, Lewis prophesied that Islam's "war against modernity" would eventually escalate into "a clash of civilizations."[124]

Anyone studying the magazine's cover, which showed a bearded and turbaned Muslim whose scowling eyes were riveted on the stars and stripes, might reasonably have concluded that the clash was already under way. Anyone reading the blurb in the *Atlantic*'s table of contents, which insisted that the "intense—and violent—resentment of the West" was merely the latest in "a long series of attacks and counterattacks, jihads and crusades, conquests and reconquests," might well have wondered whether Lewis had uttered a self-fulfilling prophecy. Indeed, critics such as Georgetown University's John Esposito have suggested that academic orientalists, U.S. policymakers, and the American media had, like twentieth-century Scheherazades, conjured up the genie of rampaging "Islamic fundamentalism" to fill a "threat vacuum" created by the collapse of the Soviet Union and the end of the Cold War.[125]

A quick look at how Arabs have been depicted in everything from pulp fiction to television during the past twenty years confirms that orientalism American style remained alive and well in both popular culture and the mass media. A "Saturday Night Live" spoof during the 1979 oil shortage, for example, featured "The Bel Airabs," poor Bedouins transplanted to California like latter-day Beverly Hillbillies thanks to the dumb luck of Abdul, the leader of the clan: "And then one day he was shootin' at some Jews, and up through the sand came a bubblin' crude."[126] Nor was such imagery uncommon in prime time, where during the late 1970s Arabs were the frequent butt of jokes delivered by everyone from Sonny and Cher to Archie Bunker on "All in the Family." Angered by the shoddy treatment he received from an Arab dry cleaner, Archie orders Edith, "Don't go near that Ay-rab again unless you got a dirty camel to wash." When son-in-law Michael objects to the nasty stereotype, Archie retorts, "They're born pirates, all of 'em."[127]

Arabs have fared little better in American cartoons. When Tarzan inadvertently insulted a thin-skinned sheik during the 1980s, a sword-wielding comic-book Arab shrieked, "Only this blade will satisfy me . . . letting flow your coward's blood!" Later that decade *Marvel Comics'* GI Joe and a band of U.S. commandos rescued two Americans held hostage by a stereotypical Arab potentate who "has been known to behead jaywalkers." In 1985 one political cartoonist provided a nasty portrait of "the Arab mind" that included "vengeance," "fanaticism," and "blackmail" among its many lobes. "What is the difference between a rat and [Yasser] Arafat?" another asked after sketching two vermin, only one of whom was a rodent, crawling out of the garbage. "Answer: The rat has more friends." Still another humorist drew a captionless panel showing a white-robed Arab executioner holding a bleeding globe in one hand and a bloody scimitar in the other.[128]

This orientalist imagery was no less pronounced among newspaper reporters and television journalists. "It became very clear to me," Jim Hoaglund of the *Washington Post* recalled in early 1982, "that in Western writing in general—not just newspapers but in books and certainly in cartoons—there was quite a distorted image" of a Middle East peopled by "Arabs sneaking about with knives in their teeth."[129] A year later John Cooley of the *Christian Science Monitor* agreed that "certainly Arabs have been unfairly portrayed" in both print and electronic media. Indeed, Cooley added, "Arabs are probably still the only group in the U.S. that anyone dares to portray in pejorative terms."[130] As early as 1975 ABC television anchorman Peter Jennings acknowledged that "there is definitely an anti-Arab bias in America," a bias that had led "unfortunately, [to] stereotyping in the media."[131] In the early 1980s Jim Lehrer, cohost of the PBS evening news hour, agreed that network television's fascination with terrorism and sectarian strife in the Middle East "feeds the stereotype that many Americans have of Arabs as bloody people who just go out killing each other all the time."[132]

When pressed by an interviewer to suggest what Arabs and, more generally, Muslims might do to counteract this stereotype, Lehrer did not mince words. "This is not a public relations image problem," he observed archly, his mind's eye doubtless riveted on the fifty-two Americans recently released from 444 days of captivity in Iran and on the never-ending civil war in Lebanon; "it's a reality problem."[133] Anthony Lewis of the *New York Times* agreed. "When Mr. Arafat goes on an American television program," Lewis told Arab American media consultant Edmund Ghareeb, "he comes through as a mixture of that romantic desert Arab you spoke of, but without the romance."

When Ghareeb retorted that many Americans mistakenly seemed to regard Arafat as "a bloodthirsty terrorist," Lewis shot back, "But you know, he does look a bit bloodthirsty."[134]

What Lehrer termed "a reality problem" was clearly exacerbated, however, by how Arabs were portrayed in pulp fiction. Beginning in 1975 with the publication of Thomas Harris's *Black Sunday*, which revolved around a Palestinian plot to commandeer the Goodyear blimp and terrorize the Super Bowl, a slew of paperback potboilers with titles such as *Jihad*, *Phoenix*, and *On the Brink* routinely depicted Arabs as either ruthless and brutal thugs or greedy sheiks eager to bankroll their bloodthirsty brethren. But the most widely read mass market novel extolling orientalist stereotypes of the Arabs was probably *The Haj*, a prequel written by Leon Uris in 1984, a quarter-century after the publication of *Exodus*. Set in the Holy Land during the 1930s, *The Haj* describes Palestinians in language that would have made even right-wing Israeli leaders like Menachem Begin blush. "Every last Arab is a total prisoner of his society," a British officer tells Uris's proto-Israeli protagonist. "The Arabs will never love you for what good you've brought them. They don't know how to really love. But hate! Oh God, can they hate!"

Lest readers miss the point, Uris hammered home this orientalist verdict in terms that prefigured those employed by Bernard Lewis six years later. The Arabs "have a deep, deep, deep resentment because you have jolted them from their delusions of grandeur and shown them for what they are—a decadent, savage people controlled by a religion that has stripped them of all human ambition . . . except for the few cruel enough and arrogant enough to command them as one commands a mob of sheep." This anti-Arab soliloquy ends with a message intended not only for Zionists during the 1930s but also for Americans during the 1980s: "You are dealing with a mad society and you'd better learn how to control it." With nearly 2 million copies of *The Haj* in print by 1985, that message seems to have been well received by the reading public.[135]

As it had for more than a generation, the film industry projected orientalist images from the printed page onto the silver screen throughout the 1980s and into the 1990s. As early as 1977, when the big-budget *Black Sunday* became the summer's hottest hit, Hollywood's Arabs were consistently depicted as homicidal fanatics who were, more often than not, too clever by half. Occasionally Arabs came across as comical, as in *Back to the Future*, a 1985 blockbuster in which bungling Libyan hitmen out to steal enough plutonium to build an atomic bomb shoot Christopher Lloyd and inadvertently send Michael J. Fox and his nuclear-powered DeLorean back to 1955.

U.S. audiences, however, were more likely to cringe than chuckle when an Arab appeared on the screen. In *Delta Force*, a 1986 action film loosely based on the brutal murder of a U.S. sailor aboard a hijacked TWA jetliner a year earlier in Beirut, Chuck Norris and a team of commandos rescued a planeload of Americans held hostage by psychopathic Palestinian terrorists. Eight summers later in *True Lies*, a CIA superman played by Arnold Schwartzenegger single-handedly thwarted "Crimson Jihad," a gun-toting band of Arab wildmen planning to launch a nuclear attack on Miami from their base in the Florida Keys.[136] Despite protests from Arab Americans, at the end of the twentieth century the film industry continued to offer orientalist fare like *Executive Decision* (1996) or *The Mummy* (1999), with Arabs depicted as airborne fanatics or feckless and foul-smelling opportunists. "To Hollywood, the Arab is the wife-abuser who wants to buy Steve Martin's house in *Father of the Bride II*," Ray Hanania complained in *Newsweek* in late 1998. "We Arabs murder innocent airline passengers in *Executive Decision* simply because it makes us feel good."[137]

The Israelis, by contrast, tended to fare somewhat better than the Arabs at the hands of Hollywood and the mass media. To be sure, the *New York Times* and the major television networks were highly critical of both Israel's invasion of Lebanon in June 1982 and its repression of the Palestinian "Intifada" uprising that erupted on the West Bank in December 1987. Ze'ev Chafets and Stephen Karetzky responded by publishing stinging exposés in which they charged that the media were employing a double standard. Why was there so much coverage of the massacre of nearly 1,000 Palestinian refugees just outside Beirut in September 1982 by Lebanese Christians allied with Israel, Chafets and Karetzky wondered, and so little outcry over the far greater slaughter seven months earlier at Hama, a city 100 miles north of Damascus, where Syria's president Hafez al-Assad ordered his troops to kill more than 10,000 Syrians whose only crime was to oppose his dictatorship?[138] Israeli foreign minister Moshe Arens reacted in a similar fashion to U.S. criticism of Israel's crackdown on the West Bank. "The media coverage of the Intifada," Arens told U.S. Jewish leaders in early 1989, "had successfully switched the focus from the Arab-Israeli conflict—in which Israel appeared as little David—to the Israeli-Palestinian conflict, in which Israel was being made to appear as Goliath."[139]

Yet despite a tendency among militantly pro-Israeli pundits such as *Commentary*'s Norman Podhoretz to imply that media figures critical of the Jewish state were closet anti-Semites, journalists at NBC, *Newsweek*, and the *Los Angeles Times* found fault with Israel because of what its government was doing in Lebanon and on the West Bank, not because most of its citizens were Jews. In any case, Moshe Arens's complaint notwithstanding, most Americans still seemed to identify Israel as more like David than Goliath. Much of the reason probably lies in Hollywood. The 1981 made-for-television movie *Masada*, for example, retold the legendary story of a besieged Jewish fortress on the shores of the Dead Sea whose heroic defenders, like Davy Crockett at the Alamo, had chosen death rather than submission to Roman imperialism almost 2,000 years earlier.

It was the Holocaust, however, painfully and painstakingly relived with the help of Hollywood, that probably did the most to reaffirm subconsciously Israel's status as an underdog in the hearts and minds of most Americans. The eight-hour miniseries *The Holocaust*, which starred Meryl Streep as a beautiful but doomed twenty-something version of Anne Frank, won the network ratings war during sweeps week in 1978 and later captured eight Emmys. Four years later Streep won an Oscar for her moving performance in *Sophie's Choice*, where she played a concentration camp survivor haunted by having had to choose which of her two children would die at Auschwitz. Once television and film viewers turned their attention from these emotionally charged histories of the Holocaust to the here and now of the modern Middle East, more than a few must have taken comfort from the knowledge that, whatever Israel's faults, it remained the best insurance available against a replay of Hitler's final solution.

An even more riveting cinematic treatment of the Holocaust appeared a decade later with the premiere of *Schindler's List* in December 1993. Shot on location just outside Auschwitz in grainy black and white and directed by Hollywood wunderkind Steven Spielberg, the film told the story of Oskar Schindler, a German businessman whose growing doubts about Nazism and whose simple humanity led him to risk everything to save several hundred Jewish slave-laborers imprisoned at the death camp. Although *Schindler's List* won seven Oscars, including those for best director and best picture, the film was banned in April 1994 by many Islamic countries, less because its brief nude scenes and graphic violence offended Muslim sensibilities than because its subliminal message ran counter to the abiding anti-Israel and anti-Semitic sentiments of some Arab audiences.[140]

A year earlier a very different movie, Disney's *Aladdin*, had won two Oscars while offending the sensibilities of many Arab Americans. Ostensibly an animated love story about two rather westernized Arabs, Aladdin and Princess Jasmine, whose English was flawless, Disney's animators and lyricists depicted most of the other inhabitants of their imaginary oriental sheikdom as frightful thugs sporting turbans, daggers, and thick accents. The Academy Award–winning soundtrack written by Alan Menken and Howard Ashman summed up *Aladdin*'s subconscious orientalism most succinctly. The first song, "Arabian Nights," contains an opening lyric straight out of *Innocents Abroad*. "Oh I come from a land, from a faraway place, where the caravan camels roam," a swarthy merchant croons, "where they cut off your ear if they don't like your face, it's barbaric, but hey, it's home." The second tune, "A Whole New World," won a Grammy in March 1993 as "song of the year." Evoking images of a patriarchal oriental past and an egalitarian Western future, Aladdin serenades Jasmine with the promise of "a new fantastic point of view," if only she will let her heart decide. Although repeated protests from the Arab-American Anti-Discrimination Committee persuaded Disney Studios to remove the most offensive lyrics from the home video distributed later that year, *Aladdin* revised still reflected the orientalism deeply embedded in U.S. popular culture during the preceding two centuries.[141]

As it did for many people living next door to hostile neighbors, xenophobia came naturally to most citizens of the fledgling United States, surrounded as they were by Spanish imperialists, British provocateurs, and Indian infidels who seemed determined to destroy God's American Israel. Because Jews and Muslims were neither Christian nor Anglo-Saxon, both groups were suspect in the eyes of most Americans, who throughout the nineteenth century and into the twentieth relied on a well-defined hierarchy of race and culture in dealing with foreigners who looked and prayed differently. The missionaries, merchants, and archaeologists who shaped America's understanding of the Middle East from the Barbary Wars through the discovery of King Tut's tomb reaffirmed orientalist stereotypes as old as the Crusades depicting Arabs as exotic, fanatical, and congenitally predisposed toward autocracy. Likewise, America's blue-blooded elite and its blue-collar workforce usually greeted the millions of Jewish immigrants who arrived in the United States between the Civil War and the Balfour Declaration with anti-Semitic epithets and ethnic slurs.

Beginning in the 1920s, however, the images of Muslims and Jews as represented in U.S. popular culture began to diverge sharply. Well into the last quarter of the twentieth century, films, books, and magazines continued to depict Arabs as primitive, untrustworthy, and malevolent figures who bore close watching. By contrast, the eagerness of Jewish newcomers to assimilate themselves into Main Street's mainstream and the awfulness of the Holocaust combined to reduce American anti-Semitism and to stimulate U.S. support for the creation and preservation of Israel, despite Arab objections.

Down through the 1990s, media giants as diverse as *National Geographic* and Disney Studios presented a Middle East in which Israel was cast as an occidental David while Arabs, and Muslims in general, were depicted as oriental Goliaths. Predictably, the Oscar for best documentary in March 2000 went to *One Day in September*, the heartbreaking story of the Israeli Olympians massacred at Munich twenty-eight years earlier. Meanwhile the season's first box-office smash, *Rules of Engagement*, saw Samuel L. Jackson mow down a wild-eyed mob of Islamic zealots in Yemen, and Nelson DeMille's *The Lion's*

Game, a potboiler recounting the fictional exploits of a ruthless Libyan terrorist, topped the *New York Times* best-seller list.

Nevertheless, in the wake of the airborne terrorist attacks on Washington and New York City on 11 September 2001 there were some reassuring signs that life need not always imitate art. Three summers earlier Twentieth Century Fox had released *The Siege,* an eerily prescient film about an ever escalating Muslim reign of terror in the streets of Manhattan that culminates with a group resembling al-Qaeda attacking a skyscraper with a truck bomb and killing 600 New Yorkers. "You have to learn the consequences of telling the world how to live," the terrorist ringleader informs the FBI's Denzel Washington in words that must have made Osama bin Laden smile. Shortly thereafter the Pentagon's Bruce Willis rounds up Arab Americans and briefly places them in detention centers.

Despite causing many more deaths, however, bin Laden's real-life assault on the World Trade Center generated a relatively mild orientalist backlash against America's Muslims. Sadly, there was some racial profiling at airports, a few hate crimes, and even one or two murders. But there was no wholesale violation of the civil liberties of Arab Americans. Indeed, during a visit to Washington's Islamic Center on 17 September, George W. Bush took pains to emphasize that "Islam is peace" and reminded all Americans that they "must treat each other with respect," regardless of race or religion. "The terrorists are traitors to their own faith," Bush told a joint session of Congress three days later, "trying to hijack Islam itself."[142]

Yet lurking just beneath Bush's rhetoric of toleration was a subliminal impulse to demonize Islamic terrorists that echoed earlier orientalist diatribes. "By sacrificing human life to serve their radical visions—by abandoning every value except the will to power—they follow in the path of fascism, and Nazism, and totalitarianism," America's forty-third president concluded. "And they will follow that path all the way, to where it ends: in history's unmarked grave of discarded lies."[143] As the grim task of recovering the remains of thousands of Americans entombed beneath the ruins of the World Trade Center entered its sixth month, a truck bomb here or an oil embargo there seemed very likely to resurrect ugly anti-Arab prejudices from the not so distant past. With popular culture saturated by an American-style orientalism dating from the nineteenth century, it should come as no surprise that since 1945 the U.S. public and policymakers have ostracized Arab radicals who threaten Israeli security or challenge Western control over Middle East oil.

The fact cannot be ignored that the reported resources of Mesopotamia have interested public opinion of the United States, Great Britain, and other countries as a potential subject of economic strife. . . . The Government of the United States assumes that there is a general recognition of the fact that the requirements for petroleum are in excess of production and it believes that opportunity to explore and develop the petroleum resources of the world wherever found should without discrimination be freely extended, as only by the unhampered development of such resources can the needs of the world be met.
—Bainbridge Colby, 20 November 1920

Vital issues of principle are at stake. Saddam Hussein is trying to wipe a country off the face of the Earth. . . . Vital economic interests are at stake as well. Iraq itself controls some 10 percent of the world's proven oil reserves. Iraq plus Kuwait controls twice that. An Iraq permitted to swallow Kuwait would have the economic and military power, as well as the arrogance, to intimidate and coerce its neighbors—neighbors who control the lion's share of the world's remaining oil reserves. We cannot permit a resource so vital to be dominated by one so ruthless. And we won't.
—George Bush, 11 September 1990

2

Opening the Door

Business, Diplomacy, and America's
Stake in Middle East Oil

While the earliest images of the Middle East in the mind of America were products of traditional Bible stories refracted through nineteenth-century orientalist literature and twentieth-century popular culture, the region's most recognizable symbol has probably been the oil well. By 1900 some business leaders and government officials were predicting that the black gold oozing to the surface from western Pennsylvania to east Texas would eventually propel the United States to industrial and military supremacy. The discovery of huge pools of crude oil in Iran, Iraq, and Saudi Arabia during the first half of the twentieth century prompted America's largest petroleum firms to obtain concessions in the Middle East and, in the process, to transform themselves into giant multinational corporations.

Founded and managed by entrepreneurs who favored maximizing profits by minimizing taxes and regulations, these multinational oil companies usually remained aloof from U.S. foreign policy and practiced their own brand of corporate diplomacy down through the eve of the Second World War. Eager to avoid being drawn into imperial rivalries and political squabbles in the Persian Gulf, Woodrow Wilson and his successors were content with prying open the door to Middle East petroleum for firms such as Standard Oil of New Jersey and Texaco and then watching it swing closed behind them. As late as 1939 U.S. oil executives wielded more influence in Baghdad and Riyadh than did U.S. diplomats.

Two wars, one hot and one cold, highlighted the importance of Middle East oil for U.S. national security and altered the relationship between businessmen and policymakers dramatically. Persian Gulf petroleum would power the Allied armies and navies that defeated the Axis, it would fuel the Marshall Plan that helped stimulate the economic recovery of Western Europe, and it would eventually flow into the automobiles of millions of commuters from Long Island to Los Angeles whose demand for gasoline was gradually outstripping America's supply. Because both stability abroad and prosperity at home seemed to hinge on secure access to Middle East crude, in short order the U.S. government cleared the way for new pipelines, subsidized the construction of a fleet of supertankers, and exempted U.S. multinationals from the antitrust laws. During the Suez crisis and the Six Day War, Washington worked closely with Wall Street to shield U.S. petroleum concessions from attacks by Arab radicals and to prevent producing countries from disrupting the flow of oil to consumers in Europe and Asia.

Mounting competition inside the international petroleum industry and the growing sophistication of the Muslim oil states, however, rapidly eroded this informal partnership between U.S. multinationals and policymakers after 1970. Long dominated by the "Seven Sisters," a cartel of powerful American- and British-controlled giants that included Jersey Standard and Royal Dutch Shell, Middle East crude was targeted during the late 1950s by smaller and more aggressive competitors. By offering terms far more generous than their larger rivals, independent companies such as Occidental Petroleum won the right to exploit rich new oil fields like those in Libya. As supplies rose, prices and profits fell, sharply reducing the revenues to which the producing states had become accustomed and prompting them to form OPEC in 1960. After a decade of financial wrangling among themselves, OPEC's Middle Eastern members managed to wrest control of production, pricing, and distribution from the big multinationals during the 1970s. By 1980 almost all of the region's petroleum operations had been nationalized thanks to the efforts of OPEC.

As they lost their ability to control both price and supply, the oil companies distanced themselves from the U.S. government. When some of the petroleum giants struck lucrative refining and distribution agreements with the producing countries during the early 1980s, critics charged that big oil was putting corporate profits ahead of U.S. national security. Yet if what was best for Standard Oil was not always what was best for America during the Reagan years, corporate and national interests once again converged in late 1990, when U.S. multinationals worked closely with policymakers to boycott Iraqi crude after Saddam Hussein invaded Kuwait in a reckless bid to monopolize Persian Gulf petroleum. Seventy years earlier in the aftermath of the century's first great war, the Wilson administration had opened the door for U.S. oil companies in the Middle East. In 1991 George Bush would wage the century's last great war to prevent that door from slamming shut.

Of Open Doors and Oil Wells, 1900–1941

Sweltering through the heat and the humidity of yet another Washington summer, President William McKinley and his secretary of state, John Hay, watched with growing concern in July 1899 as America's commercial rivals proceeded with their plans to carve up East Asia into exclusive spheres of influence. Urged by State Department officials determined "to maintain the open door for ordinary commerce in China," Hay, with McKinley's blessing, sent diplomatic notes to Britain, Russia, and the other great powers announcing that the United States would tolerate no discrimination against U.S. trade or investment in the Celestial Kingdom. Enshrined after the turn of the century as "the open door policy," Hay's initiative became a lodestar for successive generations of U.S. businessmen and diplomats who linked economic opportunity abroad with prosperity at home.[1]

Among the U.S. firms doing business in China when John Hay proclaimed the open door was the Standard Oil Company, which supplied much of the kerosene that lighted the lamps of Shanghai and Beijing. Founded in 1870 by John D. Rockefeller, a shrewd entrepreneur who employed cutthroat tactics against his competitors, Standard Oil quickly became a virtual monopoly, controlling every aspect of the petroleum industry from securing concessions and drilling wells to building refineries and developing marketing networks. Convinced that Standard Oil was too rich and too powerful, the U.S. Supreme Court issued a landmark ruling in 1911 dissolving Rockefeller's giant trust and replacing it with several separate corporations, the largest of which, Standard Oil of New Jersey, was stripped of most of its domestic crude reserves and forced to seek new supplies overseas.[2]

Prospects for replenishing Jersey Standard's petroleum reserves initially seemed most promising in Latin America, but the firm's top executives soon learned that the richest oil fields were halfway around the world in the Persian

Gulf. The first major gusher had been struck in May 1908 by the Anglo-Persian Oil Company at Masjid-i-Suleiman in southwestern Iran. Once the Royal Navy decided to convert its warships from coal-fired boilers to diesel motors, the British government acquired a 51 percent interest in Anglo-Persian, which would give Whitehall a monopoly over Iranian oil for the next forty years. Even larger petroleum deposits were rumored to lie next door in Mosul, a remote corner of the Ottoman Empire that would eventually be incorporated into northern Iraq. Eager to secure oil for their country's expanding military machine, German entrepreneurs took the lead in establishing the Turkish Petroleum Company (TPC), whose early explorations in Mosul were short-circuited by the guns of August 1914. Following Germany's defeat four years later, Anglo-Persian and Royal Dutch Shell gained a controlling interest in the TPC, turned the German stake over to the French, and moved to bring Iraqi petroleum squarely into Britain's sphere of economic influence.[3]

Although Jersey Standard and other major U.S. oil firms believed that their reserves in the Western Hemisphere were probably sufficient to meet America's petroleum needs for the foreseeable future, the Wilson administration anticipated a postwar shortage of crude and pressed Britain to open the door to U.S. participation in the TPC consortium. Ignoring Uncle Sam's grumbling, British and French leaders met at San Remo on the Italian Riviera, where in April 1920 they signed an accord formally excluding the United States from Iraqi oil. Outraged by the San Remo agreement, Secretary of State Bainbridge Colby reminded British officials seven months later that America remained committed to the principle "that opportunity to explore and develop the petroleum resources of the world wherever found should without discrimination be freely extended."[4] Fearful that its U.K. rivals would use their monopoly position in Iran and Iraq to start a price war by dumping low-cost Middle East crude onto world markets, Jersey Standard echoed Colby's call for the open door and began seeking oil concessions in the Persian Gulf.[5]

The U.S. firm that pressed hardest for the open door in the Middle East, however, was the Standard Oil Company of New York (Socony), another crude-short stepchild of the Supreme Court's breakup of Rockefeller's petroleum trust. Its prospects for securing oil in the Middle East dashed by the San Remo agreement, Socony persuaded the State Department to step up its pressure on the British to permit U.S. multinationals to buy into the TPC consortium.[6] Worried that discrimination against U.S. oil interests might provoke retaliation against British commerce, Whitehall offered American firms a substantial stake in Iraqi petroleum in late 1922. By the time that a British drilling team brought in the first gusher 200 miles north of Baghdad five years later, the TPC consortium had been rechristened the Iraq Petroleum Company (IPC), and its ownership had been reconfigured. Socony and Jersey Standard combined to control 23.75 percent of IPC's stock; Anglo-Persian, 23.75 percent; Royal Dutch Shell, 23.75; and the state-owned Compagnie Française des Petroles (CFP) 23.75 percent. The remaining 5 percent went to Calouste Gulbenkian, a smooth Armenian deal-maker who had helped win the original concession from the Turks.[7]

Having slipped through the open door into Middle East petroleum with the State Department's help, Socony and Jersey Standard moved quickly to close it behind them. By the late 1920s the world was awash in oil, and the firms inside the IPC consortium feared that once Iraqi crude began to pour onto the market, prices and profits would fall sharply. In July 1928 representatives of the two U.S. firms and their IPC partners secretly crafted a self-denying ordinance designed to restrict production and retard exploration throughout most of the Middle East. Working with a large outline map of the region dating from 1914, Calouste Gulbenkian drew a thick red line around the prewar Ottoman Empire, an area that included Iraq and Saudi Arabia but not Iran or Kuwait, and proposed that all IPC members refrain from seeking new concessions inside that territory without the approval of the consortium as a whole. Jersey Standard and Socony jumped at Gulbenkian's proposal, as did Anglo-Persian, Royal Dutch Shell, and CFP. Preoccupied with negotiations over European war debts, the Coolidge administration seemed content to leave the making of U.S. foreign oil policy in private hands. By restraining competition with Washington's tacit blessing, the Red Line Agreement guaranteed the U.S. and U.K. multinationals what they wanted most: secure sources of supply in the Middle East and stable prices.[8]

Smaller crude-hungry companies like Standard Oil of California (Socal), yet another stepchild of the dissolution of Rockefeller's empire, were far less content, however, with Gulbenkian's scheme. Insisting that those firms outside the IPC consortium should be free to seek new oil fields inside the red line, Socal executives contacted Saudi Arabia's King Abdul Aziz Ibn Saud in late 1931. After months of wrangling, in May 1933 Socal agreed to pay Ibn Saud £35,000 in gold in exchange for a sixty-year concession stretching from the Persian Gulf to the Red Sea. To help defray its exploration costs and ensure future markets, three years later Socal sold a 50 percent interest in its Saudi subsidiary, the California Arabian Standard Oil Company (CASOC), to Texaco, a Houston-based multinational eager to obtain Middle Eastern crude. In March 1938 CASOC engineers drilling just outside Dhahran struck oil a mile beneath the Saudi desert. By 1940 Socal and Texaco's subsidiary was pumping 5 million barrels per year out of Ibn Saud's realm, where reserves were estimated to surpass those of Iraq or Iran.[9]

While Socal and Texaco were tapping a huge pool of petroleum inside the red line in Saudi Arabia, Pittsburgh-based Gulf Oil was securing an equally lucrative concession next door in Kuwait. Although the tiny sheikdom at the head of the Persian Gulf lay outside Gulbenkian's red line, the British had exercised a protectorate over Kuwait since 1899 and were not eager to open the door to U.S. multinationals. Gulf Oil, however, was extremely well connected on both sides of the Atlantic. Andrew Mellon, the firm's principal shareholder, served as ambassador to Great Britain during the Hoover years and had little trouble securing State Department support for Gulf's initiative during the early 1930s. Shortly after Mellon returned home, Whitehall permitted Gulf Oil to undertake a fifty-fifty joint venture with Anglo-Persian in Kuwait. Gulf's persistence paid off in 1938 when its engineers discovered an enormous pool of oil in southeastern Kuwait. Although its British partners insisted on keeping Kuwaiti crude off the market indefinitely, Gulf Oil had gained what Andrew Mellon had wanted all along: access to an almost limitless supply of Middle Eastern petroleum.[10]

By 1941 five U.S. multinationals—Jersey Standard, Socony, Socal, Texaco, and Gulf—had moved through the open door to drill oil wells in the Middle East. With occasional assistance from the State Department, they had sunk nearly a billion dollars into petroleum concessions in Iraq, Saudi Arabia, and Kuwait. The United States, with its immense domestic reserves in Texas, Oklahoma, and California, imported little oil on the eve of the Second World War, but U.S. multinationals expected eventually to see hefty earnings from the sale of Middle Eastern crude to consumers in Europe and Asia. Even as the war clouds loomed, the Roosevelt administration preferred to leave both the problems and the profits of Persian Gulf oil in private hands. Indeed, when CASOC executives pleaded for U.S. financial help to shore up their Saudi Arabian concession, FDR suggested that Whitehall might be better suited to this task than the White House. "Will you tell the British I hope they can take care of the King of Saudi Arabia," Roosevelt instructed one of his advisers on 18 July 1941. "This is a little far afield for us!"[11] The White House would feel very differently during the years to come.

Oil, War, and National Security, 1941–1947

America's rapidly expanding energy needs during the Second World War highlighted the crucial link between oil and national security and persuaded the Roosevelt administration that decisions about the petroleum of the Persian Gulf were too important to be left entirely in the hands of private enterprise. Well before the sneak attack on Pearl Harbor, top U.S. officials had realized that Japan's imperial ambitions in the South Pacific and the Indian Ocean were fueled largely by its determination to control the oil-rich Dutch East Indies and by its desire to win access to Middle Eastern crude. Nor could FDR and his advisers fail to notice that Adolf Hitler's drive to the east stemmed to a very great degree from a Nazi obsession with solving Germany's energy woes by conquering the oil fields of Romania and Russia and, perhaps, of Iraq and Iran as well.[12]

In order to clarify America's strategic oil policy in the Persian Gulf and elsewhere, Roosevelt asked Secretary of the Interior Harold Ickes to head the newly created Petroleum Administration for War in late 1942. A world-class curmudgeon and legendary New Deal bureaucratic infighter, Ickes believed that only by gaining the upper hand over Wall Street and Whitehall in the Middle East could the U.S. government secure access to the oil it needed to win the war and ensure the peace that would follow. At first U.S. businessmen and U.K. diplomats welcomed Ickes's activist approach to foreign oil problems. Convinced that unless Washington helped Ibn Saud solve his war-related financial woes, his "independent kingdom, and perhaps the entire Arab world, will be thrown into chaos," CASOC lobbyists had repeatedly urged the Roosevelt administration to provide Saudi Arabia with substantial economic assistance since early 1941.[13] U.K. policymakers likewise worried that financial chaos inside the House of Saud, which controlled the Muslim holy places at Mecca, might reverberate through Britain's imperial outposts from Palestine to India. Shortly after taking over at the Petroleum Administration for War, Ickes took the lead in winning FDR's approval on 18 February 1943 for a controversial ruling that made Saudi Arabia, a nonbelligerent state, eligible for a multimillion-dollar U.S. aid package under the auspices of the wartime Lend Lease Act.[14]

Long before the war was over, however, Ickes had worn out his welcome on Wall Street and at Whitehall. The trouble started in June 1943, when he persuaded Roosevelt to establish the Petroleum Reserves Corporation (PRC), a government agency empowered to expand U.S. oil supplies by seeking concessions overseas. Determined that the United States should acquire a formal stake in Middle Eastern petroleum analogous to the British government's controlling interest in Anglo-Persian, Ickes approached Socal and Texaco executives two months later about selling their Saudi Arabian subsidiary to the PRC. Rebuffed by both firms, neither of which had any interest in encouraging the creation of a state-owned oil company, Ickes unveiled an even more ambitious scheme in February 1944. Would Britain, he wondered, be willing to turn over its 50 percent interest in the Kuwait oil fields as partial repayment for U.S. Lend Lease assistance?[15]

The short answer was clearly no. The British government and Gulf Oil, which owned the other half of the concession in Kuwait, rejected the proposal out of hand and warned that Ickes's bureaucratic maneuvering risked disrupting the war effort. Undaunted, the unreconstructed New Dealer bounced back later that spring with yet another innovative plan for a 1,000-mile pipeline to carry Saudi and Kuwaiti crude to the Eastern Mediterranean, where the PRC would establish a huge storage facility. Although U.S. multinationals and U.K. officials found Ickes's latest scheme more attractive than his earlier projects, smaller domestic oil firms feared that the government-owned pipeline would flood U.S. markets with cheap Persian Gulf crude and put them out of business. So did senators and congressmen from Texas and Oklahoma, who forced Ickes to withdraw the pipeline proposal in June 1944.[16]

Ickes's failed quest to secure a government stake in Persian Gulf oil evoked mixed emotions among his bureaucratic rivals at the State Department. Secretary of State Cordell Hull, an aging Tennessee Democrat who had spent a lifetime preaching the gospel of free enterprise and the open door, questioned most PRC projects on the grounds that they were likely to stimulate the growth of exclusive spheres of economic influence inimical to the expansion of international trade and investment. Like Ickes, however, Hull and his top advisers agreed that foreign oil reserves in general, and the 26 billion barrels of crude estimated to lie beneath the Middle East in particular, were critically important not only to the successful prosecution of the war but also to postwar national security. Without secure access to those reserves, State Department economic adviser Herbert Feis warned Hull in March 1943, "the United States will be in hazard (a) of having to pay an economic or political toll to secure the oil, or (b) [of] actually fail[ing] to secure it."[17] After all, PRC geologist E. L. De Golyer pointed out in early 1944, "the center of gravity of world oil production is shifting from the Caribbean area to the Middle East—to the Persian Gulf."[18]

Yet while Hull and Feis may have shared Ickes's diagnosis of America's looming oil woes, they rejected his prescription. Convinced that deeper government involvement in Middle Eastern petroleum would inevitably evoke fierce criticism from small business at home and nationalist leaders abroad, the State Department pressed instead for an Anglo-American oil agreement designed to hold the door open for U.S. private enterprise. In pursuing a petroleum pact with Whitehall, Hull and his advisers had strong support from the man in the White House, who was "disturbed by the rumor that the British wish to horn in on Saudi Arabian oil reserves," and from U.S. multinationals, whose concessions were vulnerable to U.K. poaching.[19]

To this end Hull and Roosevelt arranged a series of meetings in Washington, where U.K. and U.S. petroleum experts, assisted by oil executives, hammered out a compromise. Signed with much fanfare on 8 August 1944, the Anglo-American Oil Agreement affirmed the sanctity of existing concessions and acknowledged Whitehall's preeminence in the Middle East while, at Hull and Roosevelt's insistence, applying the "principle of equal opportunity" to any U.S. petroleum firm seeking to enter the region. State Department officials and multinational oilmen tried to sell the Anglo-American pact as a relatively cheap way to protect and promote U.S. interests in the Middle East, but domestic petroleum producers and their friends on Capitol Hill charged that the Roosevelt administration was proposing to create, in the words of Sun Oil's Joseph Pew, a "super-state cartel" whose costs would be borne primarily by small business and middle-class consumers.[20] In the face of stiff congressional opposition, Hull's successor, Edward R. Stettinius, reluctantly scuttled the Anglo-American Oil Agreement in January 1945.[21]

Critics on Capitol Hill may have killed Roosevelt's plan for a formal petroleum agreement between Washington and London during the final months of the Second World War, but the domestic oil lobby could not prevent the Truman administration from seeking to integrate Persian Gulf crude into America's Cold War strategy. Although few Americans during early 1945 expected a serious postwar petroleum shortage, top State Department and Pentagon officials felt that the United States, which had provided 85 percent of the 7 billion barrels of crude consumed by the Allied armed forces since 1941, must have secure access to foreign oil supplies to offset its depleted domestic reserves. John Loftus, the chief of the State Department's Petroleum Division, spelled out the implications of this line of reasoning later that spring. U.S. national security, he pointed out on 31 May 1945, required "a relative increase in the rate of exploitation in the Eastern Hemisphere (particularly Middle Eastern) petroleum reserves, and a relative decrease in the rate of exploitation in the Western Hemisphere." To this end Loftus recommended that the Truman administration seek "a cessation of British political interventionism in the process of obtaining petroleum concessions" in the Persian Gulf so that U.S. multinationals could operate more freely in the region.[22]

American efforts to utilize Middle Eastern oil reserves more effectively were complicated by the rapid disintegration of the wartime Grand Alliance, whose demise rekindled simmering commercial rivalries with Britain and ignited explosive political and economic clashes with Russia. U.K. officials, for example, proved quite willing to rely more on the Persian Gulf and less on the Western Hemisphere to meet the energy needs of European consumers, but Whitehall was reluctant to open the door any wider for U.S. oil firms seeking to enter the Middle East. To make matters worse, evidence was also mounting that the Soviet Union, which had exercised enormous influence in Tehran during the Second World War, might soon attempt to wrest control of Iranian oil from Britain. This, U.S. ambassador to Iran Wallace Murray warned Washington on 25 September 1945, "would mean extension of Soviet influence to the shores of the Persian Gulf creating a potential threat to our immensely rich oil holdings in Saudi Arabia, Bahrain, and Kuwait."[23]

The deepening great power rivalry in the Persian Gulf highlighted the strategic importance of the region's petroleum in the eyes of top U.S. policy-makers. "If we ever got into another world war it is quite possible that we would not have access to reserves held in the Middle East," Secretary of the Navy James Forrestal pointed out on 5 April 1946, "but in the meantime the use of those reserves would prevent the depletion of our own, a depletion which may be serious within the next fifteen years."[24] With postwar U.S. oil consumption up 20 percent from prewar levels and with America's proven reserves up only 7 percent, national security did seem increasingly to hinge on the expansion of Middle Eastern petroleum output. Although the United States still produced more oil than it consumed, the State Department's John Loftus prophesied that "within a few years we shall of necessity be as a nation a significant net importer of petroleum." To minimize its vulnerability, the United States had to tap "the oil rich areas of the Middle East" and reduce the "drain upon Western Hemisphere reserves which has characterized the pattern of world oil trade in the past." This would mean "diplomatic assistance to and support of American oil companies in their various dealings with foreign governments" in the Persian Gulf.[25]

Washington, Wall Street, and Middle Eastern Oil, 1947–1954

By the spring of 1947 the Truman administration and the largest U.S. multinational oil firms had established what amounted to an informal partnership based on a mutual conviction that national security and corporate profitability required expanded American access to the petroleum reserves of the Middle East. Among the first steps toward securing such access was the abrogation of the IPC consortium's Red Line Agreement, which for nearly twenty years had prevented a pair of U.S. petroleum giants—Jersey Standard and Mobil, as Socony was now known—from expanding their operations inside the former Ottoman Empire. When the two multinationals proposed erasing the red line in late 1946, their British-controlled partners inside the Iraqi concession— Anglo-Persian and Royal Dutch Shell—acquiesced. But the French-owned CFP balked, as did "Mr. Five Percent," Calouste Gulbenkian. When French officials charged that they were being unceremoniously crowded out of Middle Eastern oil, the State Department unfurled the tattered banner of the open door and retorted that the Red Line Agreement or any other petroleum pact based on "restraint of competition" would henceforth be regarded as "incompatible with the economic foreign policy" of the United States.[26] Frustrated by Washington's position, CFP and Gulbenkian initiated a lengthy legal battle with their IPC partners before settling out of court in November 1948.[27]

Having escaped the red line in Iraq with help from Foggy Bottom, Jersey Standard and Mobil were free to pursue plans to join forces with Socal and Texaco, which were seeking an infusion of capital to expand their operations next door in Saudi Arabia. Eager to increase both the revenues and the royalties generated by their recently rechristened subsidiary, the Arabian-American Oil Company (ARAMCO), Socal and Texaco unveiled plans in mid-1945 for a pipeline to carry Saudi crude from Dhahran to the Mediterranean coast. To help finance the $200 million Trans-Arabian Pipeline (TAPLINE), ARAMCO's parents offered Jersey Standard and Mobil a minority interest in the Saudi concession in early 1946. Neither firm was willing to join the ARAMCO cartel, however, unless the Truman administration waived prosecution under the antitrust laws. The Justice Department obliged in March 1947 by announcing that it had "no legal objections to the deal." Eighteen months later Jersey Standard and Mobil accepted the offer from Socal and Texaco and became full partners in ARAMCO.[28]

Truman and his advisers waived the antitrust laws and acquiesced in the cartelization of Saudi Arabian oil because they regarded both ARAMCO and TAPLINE as critically important to U.S. national security during the first years of the Cold War. While Socal, Texaco, Jersey Standard, and Mobil were preparing to pool their resources at Dhahran, U.S. policymakers were putting the finishing touches on what would become the Marshall Plan, a multibillion-dollar program to help reconstruct war-torn Western Europe. To fuel the European Recovery Program that Secretary of State George Marshall unveiled in June 1947, the Truman administration intended to rely not on the oil fields of east Texas or Venezuela but, rather, on the 300,000 barrels of Saudi crude that ARAMCO would soon be pumping through TAPLINE each day. When the domestic oil lobby and its friends on Capitol Hill renewed their refrain that cheap Middle Eastern petroleum would put U.S. producers out of business, James Forrestal, who had just taken over the newly created Department of Defense, reiterated the strategic and economic importance of the pipeline project. TAPLINE would carry oil "mostly to Europe and the Far East," he told a Senate committee in January 1948. "To the extent to which the Middle East oil is made available to Europe, it lifts the burden from us."[29] If this burden were not lifted, the secretary of defense confided in his diary, "within ten years" U.S. automakers would "be faced with the conversion to 4 cylinder cars."[30]

To ensure that Rovers, Citroens, and Volkswagens continued to roll along the highways of Western Europe and that V-8s continued to roll off the assembly lines in Detroit, the Truman administration was already clearing the path for TAPLINE. Political and topographical feasibility studies suggested that the pipeline should run west-northwest from Dhahran across the Saudi desert through Jordan's panhandle and Syria's Golan Heights to the Lebanese coast.[31]

U.S. officials and ARAMCO executives worked closely together to secure the necessary rights-of-way. Their task was easiest in Lebanon, where the pro-Western regime signed off on a deal calling for ARAMCO to pay an annual fee of £150,000 for the right to build a pipeline terminus and refinery complex at Sidon, forty miles south of Beirut. A hundred miles to the east in Amman, the Emir Abdullah likewise proved amenable to routing TAPLINE through his realm once ARAMCO offered to pay him a transit fee of £60,000 per year. Next door in Damascus, however, neither U.S. diplomats nor businessmen could make any headway with President Shukri Quwatly, a militant Arab nationalist who believed that TAPLINE needed Syria much more than Syria needed TAPLINE. Frustrated by two years of wrangling over the pipeline, the Truman administration secretly encouraged Syrian army chief of staff Husni Zaim to overthrow the Quwatly regime on 31 March 1949. Six weeks later Zaim granted ARAMCO its elusive right of way, removing "the last major barrier to the building of the long-pending Trans-Arabian pipeline."[32]

Once the path through Syria, Jordan, and Lebanon was cleared with help from Washington, ARAMCO completed the pipeline on schedule in December 1950. Almost immediately TAPLINE paid huge dividends for European consumers, the Truman administration, and the House of Saud. Each day 320,000 barrels of Saudi crude coursed through the 1,100-mile steel tube from Dhahran to Sidon, where a fleet of tankers stood by to ferry it to refineries in France and Italy. This in turn reduced European reliance on oil from the Western Hemisphere and enabled U.S. strategic planners to build up petroleum reserves from Texas to Venezuela for eventual domestic consumption. By linking the Dhahran oil fields more directly to Western markets, TAPLINE helped trigger a 60 percent increase in Saudi production from 477,000 to 770,000 barrels per day and a whopping 135 percent jump in royalties flowing to King Ibn Saud. By 1954 ARAMCO payments to the House of Saud totaled more than a quarter-billion dollars, four times what the firm had paid just five years earlier.[33]

The sharp rise in oil revenues received by the Saudi government, however, stemmed not merely from TAPLINE but also from changes in ARAMCO's financial relationships with Riyadh and Washington. Under the terms of the original concession, ARAMCO was obligated to pay Ibn Saud royalties amounting to 12 percent of its net profits. Although the cash-hungry king frequently pressed the firm to sweeten the deal, he did not insist on renegotiating financial arrangements with ARAMCO until November 1948, when Venezuelan oil minister Juan Pablo Perez Alfonso announced that his country had forced subsidiaries of Jersey Standard and Royal Dutch Shell to split their profits fifty-fifty with the government in Caracas. Few in Washington expected Ibn Saud to overlook the implications of Perez Alfonso's action. "The Saudis knew the Venezuelans were getting 50/50," Assistant Secretary of State for Near Eastern Affairs George McGhee recalled long afterward. "Why wouldn't they want it too?"[34]

The king and his oil experts soon made it clear that they did want a larger percentage and pressed ARAMCO to accept a profit-sharing formula modeled on Venezuela's. The firm's executives were willing to accommodate the House of Saud, provided that Uncle Sam approved a tax break. According to Internal Revenue Service (IRS) regulations, U.S. corporations operating overseas could not claim a foreign tax credit for royalties paid to local governments. If ARAMCO received a credit offsetting increased royalty payments, however, it would split its profits fifty-fifty, Venezuelan style, with the Saudis. Although a few policymakers "expressed some concern over what in effect would amount to a subsidy of Aramco's position in Saudi Arabia by U.S. taxpayers," in November 1950 State and Treasury Department officials agreed that the foreign tax credit made sense in terms of U.S. national security.[35] Having secured the Truman administration's blessing for an arrangement that critics dubbed "the golden gimmick," ARAMCO signed an agreement guaranteeing Ibn Saud one-half of its profits in late December. Five years later the IRS formally confirmed that the scheme was legitimate, a ruling that eventually saved the firm over a billion dollars in U.S. taxes.[36]

The same concerns about U.S. national security that had prompted the Treasury and State Departments to support ARAMCO's golden gimmick in Saudi Arabia would soon lead the White House to bend the antitrust laws to accommodate U.S. multinationals operating throughout the Middle East. Following a three-year investigation of U.S. corporations producing oil in the Persian Gulf, the Federal Trade Commission issued a scathing report in mid-1952 recommending criminal antitrust proceedings against five firms—Jersey Standard, Mobil, Socal, Texaco, and Gulf—for price gouging and other unfair business practices. The multinationals, led by Jersey Standard, countered by claiming that such litigation would undermine America's national security. "Jersey believes that the current attack against the oil companies has in fact already prejudiced American petroleum interests in the Middle East," a corporate spokesman warned U.S. Attorney General James P. McGranery in late 1952. "Deserted and repudiated by their own Government, as they appear to be in the Middle East mind, the American companies are marked as fair game for attacks and hostile action by different nationalist, Communist, or religious factions, which would not occur if the companies were thought to have the full backing and confidence of their Government."[37] The Justice Department was unmoved, however, and pressed ahead with its antitrust case against Jersey Standard and the four other multinationals.[38]

With a grand jury on the verge of handing down indictments, on 6 January

1953 State, Defense, and Interior Department officials urged President Harry Truman to shield the oil companies from criminal prosecution. The three departments reminded the man in the Oval Office that by "giving strength to the claim that the American system is one of privilege, monopoly, private oppression, and imperialism," the Justice Department's antitrust suit would disrupt plans for the economic recovery of Western Europe, dash hopes for the economic development of the Middle East, and play into the hands of the Soviet Union.[39] The Justice Department responded with a report of its own urging Truman to allow the antitrust suit to go forward as scheduled.[40] The president settled the matter at an NSC meeting three days later. The State, Defense, and Interior Departments "emphasized the damaging effects to our national security," while "Justice on the whole presented a rather weak case." After hearing both sides Truman agreed "that considerations of national security were overriding" and instructed the attorney general to "terminate the criminal suit" against the multinationals and prepare instead for "a civil action."[41]

Truman's eleventh-hour decision to halt criminal antitrust proceedings came as welcome news to U.S. oil companies, which could now turn their attention from battling the Federal Trade Commission and the Justice Department at home to facing down a nationalist regime halfway around the world in Iran, where an assault on British petroleum operations boded ill for Americans doing business in the region. For nearly a half-century Britain's recently rechristened Anglo-Iranian Oil Company (AIOC) had held an exclusive concession in Iran, pumping a billion barrels of Persian Gulf crude into the Royal Navy's strategic petroleum stockpile and huge profits into Whitehall's sterling reserves while paying royalties amounting to just $35 million per year. After smoldering for decades, Iranian resentment against the British oil monopoly flared into full-scale confrontation during the early 1950s when Mohammed Mossadegh, a fiery nationalist, called for legislation forcing AIOC to split its profits with Iran fifty-fifty, as ARAMCO had recently done across the Persian Gulf in Saudi Arabia. Terming Mossadegh's proposal outrageous, the British firm refused to budge, confident that the shah of Iran, whose pro-Western proclivities were well known, could arrest the drift toward nationalization. Following a series of anti-British riots and assassinations in early 1951, however, the Iranian parliament passed a tough new national petroleum law in mid-March and forced the shah to appoint Mossadegh prime minister a month later.[42]

Before the end of 1951 the new prime minister stunned Whitehall by issuing a decree expropriating AIOC without compensation and requiring all British business and military personnel to leave the country as soon as possible. Having tried for months to persuade the British that a profit-sharing arrangement modeled on those in Venezuela and Saudi Arabia was inevitable in Iran, top U.S. officials were frustrated by the AIOC's head-in-the-sand approach to Middle Eastern oil. "Never had so few," Secretary of State Dean Acheson growled long afterward, "lost so much so stupidly and so fast."[43] Any remaining hope for a negotiated settlement evaporated once Mossadegh moved forward with his plans to establish a state-owned National Iranian Oil Company in late 1951. Well aware that Mossadegh's strong-arm tactics would set a dangerous precedent jeopardizing U.S. petroleum concessions throughout the Middle East, State Department officials quietly encouraged Jersey Standard and other U.S. multinationals to assist AIOC in organizing a worldwide boycott of Iranian crude. By the time Harry Truman turned the White House over to Dwight Eisenhower in January 1953, Iranian oil exports had plummeted from 666,000 to 20,000 barrels per day.[44]

Hard pressed for revenue, Mossadegh pleaded for U.S. financial help during the spring of 1953 and hinted that the boycott might eventually force him to seek markets inside the Soviet bloc for Iran's oil. Troubled by signs that left-wing political influence was mounting in Tehran, the Eisenhower administration rejected Mossadegh's plea and worked instead behind the scenes to arrange his overthrow in August 1953 by right-wing Iranian officers loyal to the shah. Convinced that Iranian oil must rapidly find its way back into the international marketplace if the shah and other pro-Western elements were to retain the upper hand over the long haul, Washington moved swiftly to secure a compromise between AIOC and the government of Iran. The key figure in these negotiations was Herbert Hoover Jr., an international petroleum expert whose father had sat in the Oval Office a quarter-century earlier. After shuttling between Tehran and London, Hoover managed to broker a settlement before the year was out whereby AIOC would receive $90 million for relinquishing three-fifths of its exclusive concession to its U.S. rivals and for agreeing to allow the National Iranian Oil Company to oversee day-to-day operations in the Iranian oil fields.[45]

Because Hoover's proposal to transform AIOC's Iranian monopoly into a multinational consortium called for the participation of several big U.S. oil firms, the Eisenhower administration, like its predecessor, had to weigh national security considerations abroad against antitrust regulations at home. The State Department favored bending the rules, but the Justice Department did not. After a brief discussion at an NSC meeting on 14 January 1954, Ike sided with Foggy Bottom and "agreed to advise the Attorney General that the security interests of the United States require that United States petroleum companies participate in an international consortium to contract with the Government of Iran, within the area of the former A.I.O.C. concession."[46] Nine months later the shah formally approved an oil consortium in which AIOC retained a 40 percent interest, five U.S. firms—Jersey Standard, Mobil,

Socal, Texaco, and Gulf—shared another 40 percent, and Royal Dutch Shell received 14 percent, with the remaining 6 percent going to the French CFP.[47]

Thanks to close cooperation between Washington and Wall Street, by late 1954 Iran had joined the growing list of Middle Eastern nations whose oil fields were integrated into America's national security empire. By clearing the path for TAPLINE and facing down intransigent nationalists from Damascus to Tehran, public policymakers helped private enterprise shift the burden of fueling the economic recovery of Western Europe during the decade after 1945 from the Western Hemisphere to the Persian Gulf. By stretching the IRS tax code and waiving the antitrust laws, the Truman and Eisenhower administrations believed they had converted U.S. multinational oil companies into informal instruments of American foreign policy in the Middle East.

OPEC and Creeping Nationalization, 1955–1967

The partnership between businessmen and diplomats that had helped consolidate U.S. control over Middle Eastern crude after the Second World War would be sorely tested during the decade after 1955 thanks to profound changes in the international petroleum industry and in the policies of the oil-producing states. The movement of smaller and more aggressive U.S. firms overseas and the discovery of rich new reserves in North Africa meant rising competition, falling prices, and declining revenues for the House of Saud and other oil-rich regimes that rimmed the Persian Gulf, who banded together in September 1960 to establish OPEC. The rapid expansion of Middle Eastern oil production during the early 1960s to meet rising demand not only in Western Europe and Japan but also in America raised the possibility that OPEC and the largest oil companies might eventually establish an informal partnership of their own, to the detriment of U.S. national security interests in the Persian Gulf.

Perhaps the last time that corporate interests and national security converged fully in the Middle East was late 1956, when Washington and Wall Street managed to prevent the Suez crisis from wreaking havoc on international oil markets. After a series of bitter diplomatic exchanges with Britain and the United States, on 26 July 1956 Egypt's president Gamal Abdel Nasser had nationalized the Suez Canal, through which passed three-quarters of the oil consumed in Western Europe. When Britain and France, with Israel's help, resorted to armed intervention in early November to retake the canal, Nasser scuttled a dozen ships in the narrow waterway while his allies in Syria dynamited the pipelines carrying Iraqi crude to Lebanon for transshipment to European refineries. "If we really get the Arabs sore at us," Dwight Eisenhower grumbled as the showdown at Suez reached its climax, "they could embargo all oil" and touch off an energy crisis.[48]

Averting such a grim scenario was likely to require close collaboration among the U.S. petroleum giants in violation of Justice Department guidelines. More convinced than ever that national security must trump antitrust considerations, in early November Eisenhower authorized the creation of the Middle East Emergency Committee, a standing group composed of U.S. policymakers and multinational executives who juggled oil contracts and prepared to divert Western Hemisphere petroleum across the Atlantic. Should participation in the Emergency Committee mean that "the heads of these oil companies landed up in jail or had to pay a big fine," Eisenhower told his advisers with a smile on 8 November, "he would pardon them (laughter)." Once Britain had pulled its troops out of Egypt in early December, Jersey Standard and other U.S. firms launched a massive "oil lift" under Emergency Committee auspices that averted a full-scale energy crisis in Western Europe.[49]

By dramatizing how easily anti-Western leaders could disrupt the flow of Persian Gulf crude to European consumers, the Suez crisis prompted U.S. policymakers to seek more secure means of supply. One alternative under active consideration was the construction of a new pipeline from Iraq and Iran through Turkey to the Mediterranean coast, bypassing the pro-Nasser regime in Syria.[50] Because such a pipeline would do little to reduce Western dependence on petroleum shipments passing through the Suez Canal, however, top U.S. officials had recommended as early as November 1956 that "a super tanker program should be carried out in American shipyards" to build giant vessels capable of carrying Middle Eastern oil safely around the Cape of Good Hope to Western Europe.[51] By late 1957 the State Department was confident that with "the completion of the tanker fleet presently in the shipyards or on the drawing boards, the West should be in a much stronger position" regarding Persian Gulf oil.[52]

The discovery of rich new oil fields in Libya and Algeria during the late 1950s promised to reduce Western dependence on canals, pipelines, and supertankers still further. Lower in sulfur and a thousand miles closer than Persian Gulf oil, Libyan and Algerian crude seemed tailor-made to meet Europe's expanding energy needs in the coming decade. In times of crisis, U.S. officials were quick to point out in August 1959, Libya in particular, with the pro-American King Idris in control, "affords a more readily accessible emergency oil reserve than do the areas east of the Suez canal." Once Libyan oil began to reach European consumers in commercial quantities in the mid-1960s, Western Hemisphere reserves could be devoted exclusively to supplying the rapidly growing U.S. domestic market.[53]

King Idris hoped to prevent the big multinationals from gaining monopoly control by inviting smaller U.S. firms to invest in his realm. The crude-short Continental Oil Company (Conoco) obliged by working nonstop during 1959 and 1960 to pump as much oil as possible from beneath the Libyan desert.

What was good for Conoco and Libya, however, was not necessarily good for the U.S. and U.K. petroleum giants operating in the Persian Gulf or for the governments to which those firms paid royalties. Faced with a growing world-wide surplus of crude, the Seven Sisters—Jersey Standard, Mobil, Socal, Texaco, Gulf, Royal Dutch Shell, and British Petroleum, as AIOC was now known—cut their prices in August 1960 and abruptly reduced their payments to the oil states by 7 percent. Outraged by such high-handedness, oil ministers from Saudi Arabia, Iran, Iraq, and Venezuela gathered hastily in Baghdad, where on 14 September 1960 they founded OPEC.[54]

American policymakers had been worrying about just such an eventuality for nearly two years. "Arab unity," John Foster Dulles had remarked privately as early as 2 January 1958, "may make it more difficult for the oil companies to maintain a decent position" in the Middle East.[55] Six months later in the wake of the sudden overthrow of the pro-Western regime that had sat atop Iraq's enormous petroleum reserves, anxious U.S. officials warned that unless the Seven Sisters "give more tangible recognition to the need of the populations of the host countries for a greater share of the oil reserves and a better distribution of those resources towards social and economic ends, Western access to the oil in the area may be in the future threatened."[56] Fearful that Persian Gulf leaders would "get together on a unified petroleum policy" during the inaugural meeting of the new Arab Petroleum Congress to be held in Cairo, Jersey Standard's Eugene Holman reminded Secretary of State Christian Herter on 18 March 1959 that it was "extremely important that American officials should emphasize their support for the 'sanctity' of contracts."[57] ARAMCO executives, by contrast, believed that Holman was overreacting and assured U.S. diplomats in late April that the Cairo affair was "not seriously damaging [to the] interests [of the] western producing companies."[58]

What ARAMCO did not realize, however, was that Venezuela's legendary oil minister, Juan Pablo Perez Alfonso, had held a series of long talks in Cairo with Sheik Abdullah Tariki, Saudi Arabia's director of petroleum affairs, who was determined to gain even greater leverage over the Seven Sisters. A petroleum engineer trained at the University of Texas and briefly employed by Texaco, Tariki impressed the Venezuelan as a passionate nationalist. Convinced that by banding together, the oil-producing states could force the multinational giants to pay higher royalties, Tariki and Perez Alfonso persuaded their Kuwaiti and Iranian colleagues to initial a "Gentlemen's Agreement" calling for the creation of a joint Oil Consultative Commission designed to present the Seven Sisters with a common front.[59] "The oil companies screamed they were being ruined, but they're still in business in Venezuela," Tariki pointed out after returning to Riyadh. "The industry didn't collapse. It won't collapse in the Middle East when the Arabs get more."[60]

As the balance of power in the Persian Gulf tilted inexorably away from the multinationals and toward the host countries, U.S. policymakers did what they could to minimize the damage to their own interests. In the short run there were few good options. "As long as Middle Eastern oil continues to be as cheap as it is," Eisenhower told NSC members on 13 May 1959, "there is probably little we can do to reduce the dependence of Western Europe on the Middle East."[61] What U.S. officials could do, however, was to reaffirm their desire that the U.S. oil firms remain unified in the face of mounting pressure exerted by the producing states. This meant blocking Justice Department plans to resume criminal antitrust proceedings against the five largest U.S. multinationals in early 1960. The mere hint that the attorney general might reopen the case, Assistant Secretary of State Lewis Jones warned on 20 April, would tempt Saudi Arabia to undertake the "Arabization" of its oil industry, something that might trigger "a chain effect bringing into question the equity of petroleum concession terms generally" and reduce "availability to the West of ME oil on reasonable terms."[62]

It did not take Eisenhower very long to agree that the risks associated with the Justice Department proposal outweighed any possible gains. State Department petroleum experts made a compelling case during an NSC meeting on 9 May 1960 that the proposed litigation would mean "a reduction in the U.S. control over the supply of oil for U.S. and Free World needs" and would also "provide propaganda ammunition to leftists, nationalists and the Soviet Union," all of whom sought to discredit U.S. firms operating overseas. Four days later Eisenhower informed his attorney general not to proceed with the antitrust suit without the approval of the State and Defense Departments.[63] Taking their cues from the White House, Foggy Bottom and the Pentagon quietly bottled up the Justice Department's proposed litigation in short order. It was Secretary of the Treasury Robert Anderson, a wealthy Texas oilman, however, who summed up most succinctly just how high the stakes were in the Persian Gulf. "Middle East oil," Anderson told the NSC on 15 July 1960, "was as essential to mutual security as atomic warheads."[64]

The news that the five most important oil producing states—Saudi Arabia, Iran, Iraq, Kuwait, and Venezuela—had banded together two months later to establish OPEC did not bode well for long-term Western security interests in the Middle East. To be sure, Eisenhower pooh-poohed the threat posed by the new OPEC cartel, insisting in late September that "anyone could break up the Organization by offering five cents more per barrel for the oil of one of the countries."[65] Jersey Standard executives likewise expected little trouble from the producers' cartel in the short run, provided the Eisenhower administration was willing "to use its influence in urging the OPEC countries to go slowly in completing the OPEC organization and implementing its program."[66]

Over the long haul, however, most U.S. officials expected rising demand among Western consumers and a rising tide of nationalism among Arab leaders eventually to give OPEC the upper hand over the multinational oil firms. In a national intelligence estimate completed just a month before Eisenhower left office, CIA experts predicted that "the producing states will probably work more effectively through OPEC to bring pressure upon the companies than they have in the past." Although wholesale expropriation of the multinational giants operating in the Middle East seemed unlikely, the CIA cautioned that "there may develop a kind of 'creeping' nationalization under which the companies gradually retreat to a position where they are little more than managing agents of the local governments."[67]

Although the CIA did not expect a serious challenge to the Seven Sisters to materialize in the Middle East for a decade or more, the pace of nationalization in at least one Arab state—Iraq—threatened to accelerate from a creep to a sprint during the early 1960s. After seizing power in July 1958 during a bloody military coup that toppled a pro-Western regime in Baghdad, Colonel Abdel Karim Qassim had moved his country steadily leftward. An ardent nationalist, Qassim soon took aim at the Iraqi Petroleum Company, whose British and U.S. parents had reaped more than a billion dollars in profits during the three decades since the Mosul oil fields had come on line. Qassim signaled his intention to confront IPC as early as September 1960 when, after hosting OPEC's organizational conference in Baghdad, he vowed that Iraq would become "a thorn in the eyes of those who deviate from the right path."[68] Determined to force IPC back onto that path, Qassim demanded that the firm relinquish the unutilized portions of its concession and grant the Iraqi government 20 percent ownership and 55 percent of the profits. When the Anglo-American consortium balked, Qassim issued Public Law 80 on 11 December 1961, a decree that would, if implemented on schedule in February 1963, strip IPC of 99.5 percent of its concession, impose taxes that the Seven Sisters regarded as confiscatory, and establish a state-owned Iraq National Oil Company to oversee the Iraqi petroleum industry.[69]

Welcomed enthusiastically by Iraqi nationalists and applauded by the Kremlin, the assault on IPC outraged British and U.S. officials, who interpreted Public Law 80 as proof that Qassim was drifting rapidly into the Soviet orbit. Terming the proposed expropriation of IPC a "unilateral violation of a major Western arrangement with Iraq," Assistant Secretary of State Phillips Talbot expected Jersey Standard and other U.S. multinationals to urge the Kennedy administration "to retaliate against and place other pressures on" the Qassim regime.[70] The U.S. government, ambassador to Iraq John Jernegan recalled several years later, was understandably reluctant "to call out the battleships every time somebody changes the terms of a concession or even in the case of an expropriation, as long as there's some effort made to pay compensation."[71] But once it became clear Qassim seemed "determined to push IPC to the wall," the Kennedy administration began quietly to encourage dissident army officers to seize power.[72] On 8 February 1963, just a few days before Public Law 80 was to go into effect, Qassim was deposed and executed by ruthless military rivals who quickly distanced themselves from the Soviet Union, "put out feelers for Western aid," and agreed to reopen negotiations with IPC. In early 1965 the new regime privately reaffirmed IPC control over Iraq's richest oil fields, Mosul in the north and Rumaila in the south. Working together, U.S. businessmen and policymakers had prevented Baghdad from expropriating IPC, an action that would have set a dangerous precedent for Iraq's oil-rich neighbors.[73]

Blunting the Iraqi assault on IPC was part of a broader U.S. effort during the Kennedy and Johnson years to prevent OPEC from becoming too powerful. During the early 1960s the cartel added Libya, Indonesia, and Qatar, a small, thumb-shaped sheikdom that jutted into the Persian Gulf, to its ranks, so that fully one-half of the oil produced in the Free World came from OPEC's eight members.[74] Well aware that petroleum output was expanding most rapidly in the Arab world, State Department experts and multinational executives got together in January 1965 to discuss "a program aimed at attacking the notion that the Near Eastern oil producing countries can dominate and thereby control the international energy market both now and in the future." Although U.S. officials felt that "this task is and should remain the main responsibility of the oil companies," they acknowledged that it might be necessary for Washington to "play an expanded role to supplement company efforts" to persuade Saudi Arabia and other OPEC producers to back away from their more extreme demands. "There was," ARAMCO president Thomas Barger confessed, "an appropriate US Government role aimed at preventing unthinking use of oil as a political weapon by radical Arabs."[75]

Just how important that role might be was dramatized two years later when the Arabs unsheathed their oil weapon on the eve of the Six Day War. "If the US directly supports Israel, Aramco can anticipate being nationalized 'if not today, then tomorrow,'" the House of Saud warned Barger's firm on 24 May 1967. "If the US does not stay out of this conflict, the US is finished in the Middle East."[76] Furious about Israel's surprise attack against Egypt twelve days later, Saudi Arabia ordered ARAMCO to halt oil exports to the United States and the United Kingdom at once. "You should see that this is strictly implemented," Saudi officials informed ARAMCO on 7 June, "and your company shall be gravely responsible if any drop of our oil reaches the land of the said two states."[77] Within days Iraq and OPEC's other Arab members followed suit. Meanwhile, striking oil workers forced all U.S. and U.K. multinationals operating in Kuwait and Libya to suspend their operations. By mid-June Arab petroleum exports to the West had plummeted 60 percent from their prewar levels.[78]

U.S. policymakers and petroleum executives were hardly surprised by the Arab oil embargo. ARAMCO officials were well aware that the Egyptians had been pressing the House of Saud for months to place its petroleum resources in the service of the wider Arab cause, and just one week before the Six Day War erupted, White House national security adviser Walt W. Rostow prophesied that the United States might "have to face issues like the cancelling of oil contracts."[79] To prevent just such an eventuality and to counteract the effects of the June embargo, the Johnson administration established the Foreign Petroleum Supply Committee and invited two dozen oil executives to Washington, where they managed quietly to expand crude exports from the Western Hemisphere to Western Europe to offset cutbacks by the Arab producers. U.S. officials also worked closely with the Paris-based Organization for Economic Cooperation and Development to meet the energy needs of European consumers.[80]

While U.S. policymakers, the multinational oil companies, and European officials collaborated to reconfigure Western petroleum distribution patterns, the Arabs began to bicker among themselves. As early as 18 June U.S. intelligence detected a serious rift between Egyptian and Syrian radicals, who insisted that a prolonged embargo would force Britain and the United States to abandon Israel, and Saudi and Kuwaiti moderates, who feared that such tactics would merely reduce markets for and revenues from Persian Gulf oil. By early July Kuwait was ready to resume petroleum shipments to the United States and Western Europe, and the House of Saud was complaining that "restrictions on oil exports are harming the Arab producers more than the boycotted nations." By the end of the summer the embargo had fizzled, and in September 1967 Arab oil exports were actually 8 percent higher than they had been on the eve of the Six Day War.[81]

The Arab oil weapon had been neutralized during the decade after the Suez crisis by a complex set of circumstances. Despite occasional disagreements, Washington and Wall Street were usually able to coordinate their actions to promote U.S. national security in the Middle East through 1967. Despite increasingly shrill calls from Cairo and Damascus for the destruction of Israel, neither the Saudis nor their oil-rich neighbors were eager to subordinate their economic resources to the political agenda of the Arab radicals. Despite growing indications that worldwide demand for oil would soon outstrip supply, a global petroleum surplus throughout the 1960s enabled Western governments and multinationals to play Middle Eastern producers against competitors from West Africa to Latin America. During the decade ahead dramatic economic and political changes would alter the balance of power among the Western governments, the multinational petroleum giants, and the host countries in ways few could have imagined in June 1967.

The Making of an Energy Crisis, 1967–1973

The average U.S. citizen hardly noticed the abortive Arab oil embargo during the 1967 Six Day War. Within five years, however, Americans would become painfully aware of an energy crisis that was rooted in their growing dependence on Middle Eastern petroleum. With domestic oil reserves estimated to exceed 250 billion barrels, the United States had remained largely self-sufficient during the decade after 1945. But by the late 1950s America was importing 350 million barrels of oil each year, mostly from Canada and Venezuela, to fuel the ever growing number of automobiles that cruised the urban expressways and interstate highways built during the Eisenhower years. Hoping to prevent Americans from becoming overly dependent on foreign oil, in 1959 Ike limited imports, except for those from Canada, to 10 percent of total U.S. consumption. This formula would cap the flow of petroleum into the United States from outside North America at roughly 450 million barrels per year during the 1960s.[82]

Through 1969 less than one-quarter of those imports originated in the Middle East. Because America's demand for oil was rapidly outstripping its domestic output, however, the Nixon administration decided to phase out petroleum import quotas. By 1972 annual U.S. consumption of foreign oil had skyrocketed to 811 million barrels, nearly one-third of which came from the Middle East. During the first nine months of 1973 the United States imported 413 million barrels, almost 10 percent of its total oil consumption, from the Persian Gulf and North Africa.[83]

While America's soaring demand for foreign crude was helping to transform a modest surplus into a global shortage, OPEC's Middle Eastern members were preparing to wrest control of the pricing and production of oil from the Seven Sisters. When OPEC representatives gathered in Vienna in June 1968, the Iraqis and Saudis secured passage of Resolution XVI 90, a "Declaration of Oil Policy" that specified that within five years the producing countries, not the U.S. and U.K. multinationals, would set prices and regulate output of Middle Eastern petroleum.[84] Three months later in Beirut, oil ministers from the Persian Gulf and North Africa founded the Organization of Arab Petroleum Exporting Countries, whose first director was Ahmed Zaki Yamani, a Harvard-educated Saudi technocrat determined to maximize the revenues accruing to the House of Saud and other member states. With his neatly trimmed goatee and his tenacious negotiating style, Yamani, who had succeeded Abdullah Tariki as the Saudi petroleum minister in 1962, would in short order become instantly recognizable to Western consumers.[85]

Turmoil in Libya during the summer of 1969 soon placed even greater leverage in the hands of Yamani and OPEC's Arab oil producers. After overthrowing the pro-Western regime of King Idris in Tripoli on 1 September, Colonel Muammar al-Qaddafi adopted an aggressive approach toward the multinational oil companies operating in his country and insisted that the price of Libyan crude be raised sharply to fund his ambitious development projects. Although giant firms such as Exxon, as Jersey Standard was now called, could afford to ignore Qaddafi's demands, Occidental Petroleum, a mid-sized, crude-short, California-based independent controlled by seventy-one-year-old Armand Hammer, could not stay in business without its Libyan reserves.[86]

Qaddafi was well aware of Occidental's vulnerability. In early 1970 he warned Hammer that unless the firm hiked prices by 15 percent and increased Libya's share of profits to 55 percent, its concession would be revoked. When Occidental balked, Qaddafi ordered sharp cutbacks in the production of Libyan crude, creating spot shortages in Western European markets in May and June. Hoping to prevent the Qaddafi regime from setting a precedent that might be emulated by other OPEC members, Hammer sought to identify alternate sources of supply should his firm be forced to shut down its Libyan operation entirely. After Exxon declined to guarantee Occidental enough crude to offset its potential losses, however, Hammer reversed course, flew to Tripoli in late July, and accepted all of Qaddafi's demands.[87]

Troubled by Exxon's shortsightedness and stunned by Occidental's capitulation, top State Department officials asked John J. McCloy, a corporate lawyer widely regarded as the founding father of the "American Establishment," to bring a group of multinational oil executives to Foggy Bottom in late September to discuss how best to limit the damage. McCloy's group and U.S. Middle East experts had little trouble diagnosing the nature of the problem. "It seemed clear that the Libyan Government was attempting to apply pressure piecemeal against the companies," McCloy recalled several years later, "thus forcing acceptances which could be leap-frogged against the other operators." Unless Washington and Wall Street moved quickly, other OPEC members were certain to follow Qaddafi's lead.[88]

Identifying a prescription acceptable to both policymakers and businessmen, however, proved much more difficult. Everyone agreed that, as in the past, the Justice Department would have to waive the antitrust laws in order to enable the multinational petroleum firms to cooperate against Libya and the other producing countries. But by early 1971 tactical differences began to emerge. Convinced that "they would be leap-frogged to death if they did not join together" to "conduct negotiations with OPEC as a whole," the oil companies favored seeking a single short-term agreement with the producers' cartel covering the entire Middle East. The State Department, on the other hand, worried that such an all-embracing approach would actually strengthen OPEC by driving Persian Gulf moderates closer to North African radicals and preferred to see the multinationals negotiate separate long-term deals with each of the producing countries.[89]

Groping for compromise, the Nixon administration and the oil companies settled on a two-track approach in January 1971 calling for two sets of talks, one in Tehran and the other in Tripoli. With OPEC members already insisting on higher prices and profits, this was a prescription for disaster. On 14 February the multinationals initialed an agreement in Tehran raising prices for Persian Gulf crude by 40 cents per barrel and increasing the host country's share of profits to 55 percent. Six weeks later in Tripoli Qaddafi forced the oil companies to hike the price of Libyan crude by 90 cents per barrel and to hand over 60 percent of their profits. Almost at once pressure built in Tehran to raise Persian Gulf prices again to match those in Tripoli. Even worse, before the year was out Libya and Algeria announced plans to nationalize state-owned foreign oil firms such as British Petroleum and the French CFP operating in North Africa.[90]

By early 1972 the State Department favored establishing a National Advisory Committee of Foreign Petroleum in order to increase U.S. government influence over American multinationals doing business in the Middle East. "We were in a new day and age," Foggy Bottom oil expert James Akins told John McCloy on 21 January. "There was a growing urge for nationalization or participation and one had to recognize the realities in the world in which we live." Because "the position of the oil companies in relation to O.P.E.C. was not strong," the Nixon administration "was anxious to work out a national policy to protect legitimate United States interests" in Middle Eastern petroleum. Although McCloy welcomed the State Department's help in the region, he worried that too close an association between Washington and Wall Street might make his clients "more vulnerable to political action by oil producing countries who did not approve of certain United States Government policies." Without even mentioning Israel, McCloy had in effect offered a prophecy whose fulfillment eighteen months later would highlight how far U.S. national security and American corporate interests now diverged.[91]

Throughout 1972 the U.S. multinationals distanced themselves from what they regarded as America's pro-Israel foreign policy and edged toward an accommodation with the Arab oil-producing states. On 12 March, for example, ARAMCO indicated that it was prepared to offer the House of Saud 20 percent ownership in order to retain long-term access to the Dhahran oil fields. Within days Gulf and Texaco's subsidiaries in Kuwait and the other oil sheikdoms announced similar arrangements with the host governments. Later that spring the military regime in Baghdad stunned Exxon and Mobil by nationalizing their Iraqi subsidiary, IPC, without compensation, a development that tempted Saudi Arabia's Yamani and other OPEC moderates to press for the "Arabianization"—51 percent ownership by the producing states—of all multinationals operating in the Middle East.[92] "There is a worldwide trend toward nationalization and Saudis cannot stand against it alone," Yamani warned U.S. oil executives. "The industry should realize this and come to terms," he added, "so that they can save as much as possible under the circumstances." Heeding his advice the U.S. multinationals signed a "participation agreement" with Saudi Arabia and its Persian Gulf neighbors in October 1972 that immediately increased host country ownership to 25 percent, with an understanding that within a decade that figure would rise to 51 percent.[93]

By early 1973 some State Department officials worried that America's deepening dependence on Middle Eastern crude, OPEC's mounting leverage over the multinationals, and growing Arab frustration with Washington's special relationship with Israel could easily trigger an oil crisis. In a controversial article subtitled "This Time the Wolf Is Here" that appeared in the April 1973 issue of *Foreign Affairs*, Foggy Bottom's James Akins predicted that accelerating energy consumption in the Western world and continuing diplomatic stalemate in the Middle East would inevitably lead to a doubling of oil prices and to serious fuel shortages. During the previous year, Akins pointed out, "Arabs in responsible or influential positions made no less than 15 different threats to use oil as a weapon against their 'enemies,'" and "almost all of them singled out the United States as the prime enemy." Even the House of Saud, long the most pro-American regime in the Arab world, had begun to distance itself from Washington. "King Faisal of Saudi Arabia, who has said repeatedly that he wishes to be a friend of the United States and who believes that communism is a mortal danger to the Arabs," Akins reminded his readers, "insists to every visitor that U.S. policy in the Middle East, which he characterizes as pro-Israeli, will ultimately drive all Arabs into the Communist camp."[94]

Akins's grim forecast, however, seemed to go largely unnoticed in the Oval Office, where Richard Nixon was increasingly preoccupied with the Watergate scandal at home and with détente abroad. When Exxon relayed word to the White House in May 1973 that Arab radicals might soon force King Faisal once again to unsheath the oil weapon, the firm was told that "His Majesty is calling wolf where no wolf exists except in his imagination."[95] But before the summer was over, the Saudi monarch would demonstrate vividly that what top U.S. policymakers had dismissed as an imaginary threat was in fact all too real. On 2 September Faisal was asked by a U.S. journalist whether Saudi Arabia might use its petroleum as a weapon against America. "We have no wish to restrict our oil exports to the United States in any way," the king replied, "but, as I have just pointed out, America's complete support for Zionism and against the Arabs makes it extremely difficult for us to supply the United States with oil."[96]

Faisal's remarks sent shock waves through Washington. Three days later a reporter posed a blunt question during a White House news conference: "What exactly are you doing to meet these threats from the Arab countries to use oil as a club to force a change in our Middle East policy?" Hinting that he would handle fresh threats the same way that Eisenhower had dealt with the Iranian radicals who had challenged Western control of their nation's petroleum two decades earlier, Nixon did not mince words. "Oil without a market, as Mr. Mossadeg learned many, many years ago, does not do a country much good," Nixon growled. "We and Europe are the market, and I think that the responsible Arab leaders will see . . . that if they continue to up the price, if they continue to expropriate, if they do expropriate without fair compensation, the inevitable result is that they will lose their markets and other sources will be developed."[97] What Nixon seems not to have realized, however, was that the Middle East was a far different place in 1973 than it had been in 1953, that U.S. consumers were much more dependent on Persian Gulf crude than ever before, and that U.S. multinationals were much less willing than in the past to serve as instruments of American foreign policy. The man in the White House and the U.S. public were about to receive a painful lesson in the politics of oil.

Private Profits, Public Policy, and OPEC Oil since 1973

In the early hours of 6 October 1973, while executives from Exxon and several other U.S. multinationals were high above the Atlantic en route to a critically important meeting with OPEC oil ministers in Vienna, Egyptian and Syrian troops fired the opening shots in what came to be known as the October War. By the time the American oilmen sat down with the OPEC delegates in the Austrian capital four days later, the U.S. government was airlifting badly needed military hardware to Israel to repel the two-pronged Arab assault. Saudi Arabia's Yamani, who now led the producers' cartel, had indicated weeks earlier that he intended to drive a hard bargain in Vienna—a 15 percent price increase to offset the recent devaluation of the U.S. dollar and a larger share of the resulting profits for the OPEC countries. Worried by Yamani's hints of "unilateral action," representatives of the Seven Sisters huddled in New York City with John McCloy, who knew that the Nixon administration's "overt moves to support" Israel might mean that "oil supplies [were] jeopardized as well as [the] whole U.S. oil position in [the] Middle East." Eager to prevent matters from spiraling out of control, the multinationals tried to strike a quick deal by accepting the 15 percent price hike without debate. Yamani laughed. With one eye on the Arab-Israeli conflict and the other on skyrocketing Western demand for Middle Eastern oil, he indicated that OPEC now thought that perhaps an increase of 100 percent was in order.[98]

Stunned by OPEC's latest proposal, the oilmen held the line at 15 percent, packed their bags, and flew home on 12 October. "They made a terrible, terrible mistake," Iranian oil minister Jamshid Amouzegar told reporters, "by refusing to improve their offer." A few hours later Yamani announced that the cartel was unilaterally increasing the average price of Persian Gulf crude by 70 percent, from $3.00 to $5.10 per barrel. Worse was to come four days later in Kuwait, where OPEC's Arab members agreed to cut back their output progressively by 5 percent each month and imposed an embargo on all oil exports to the United States until Israel made major territorial concessions. Having lost control over both pricing and production, the multinationals feared that they might soon be stripped of their oil concessions as well unless they came to terms with OPEC. Convinced that they could pass the increased prices along to Western consumers and minimize shortages in the United States by expanding production in Africa and Latin America, the petroleum giants acquiesced in Yamani's power play. After another round of discussions between OPEC and the oil companies in mid-December, the average price of Persian Gulf crude climbed to $11.65 per barrel, nearly four times higher than it had been on 6 October.[99]

While U.S. consumers turned down their thermostats and waited in long lines for gasoline, policymakers pondered their options. The 1973 energy crisis, Secretary of State Henry Kissinger confessed years later, had caught Washington unprepared. Lulled into a false sense of security by a quarter-century of prosperity fueled by cheap and plentiful petroleum and "reluctant to interfere with the operation of a market that seemed both efficient and consonant with our long-term interests," the Nixon administration, like its predecessors, had been content to leave Middle Eastern oil policy largely in the hands of the big multinationals. Too late, Kissinger admitted, did U.S. officials realize that a worldwide petroleum shortage and OPEC's plans for "creeping nationalization" could easily "reduce the major oil companies to marketing and management organizations" serving as "instruments of nations whose interests did not necessarily parallel our own."[100] Relying on his legendary diplomatic wizardry, Kissinger persuaded OPEC to lift its embargo in early 1974. But the price of Middle Eastern crude continued to spiral upward during the mid-1970s, as did American consumption. Indeed, between 1974 and 1977 U.S. imports from the Persian Gulf and North Africa tripled to an all-time high of 1.3 billion barrels per year. By the time Kissinger departed from Foggy Bottom, one-quarter of all the petroleum consumed in the United States originated in the Middle East, a constant reminder for policymakers that oil might once again be employed "as a weapon of economic blackmail."[101]

Because rising prices for Middle Eastern crude during the mid-1970s coincided with rising profits for U.S. multinational oil companies, many Americans suspected that the OPEC producers were not the only ones engaging in economic blackmail. Average earnings for America's largest petroleum firms rose by 70 percent in 1973 and climbed another 40 percent in 1974, prompting angry calls from Capitol Hill for an investigation. Frank Church, an Idaho Democrat who chaired the Senate's recently established Subcommittee on Multinational Corporations, agreed and announced that his panel would explore much broader issues growing out of the complex relationship between private enterprise and U.S. national security in the Middle East. Having represented Exxon, Gulf, Mobil, Socal, and Texaco in the courts and before Congress for many years, John J. McCloy charged that Church was downplaying the importance of the Arab-Israeli conflict in order to "concentrate the chief blame on the oil companies" for OPEC's recent price hikes and America's energy woes.[102]

Frank Church, on the other hand, insisted that the energy crisis was the "inexorable" result of a quarter-century of decision making based on the myth that corporate interests were usually compatible with national security in the realm of oil. In 1947, he reminded McCloy, the Truman administration had permitted "four American companies to control exclusively the greatest oil pools in the world in Saudi Arabia." Over the next two decades the NSC, the State Department, and the IRS had run interference for the multinationals with the courts and the bureaucracy at home while the White House, the Pentagon, and the CIA had helped shield the petroleum giants from nationalist regimes abroad. By the late 1960s, Church noted, the production of Persian Gulf oil was dominated by a handful of McCloy's most influential clients, whose complacency in the face of rising demand, stagnating supplies, and emerging nationalism had eventually forced them to capitulate to OPEC in October 1973. "Quite frankly," Church concluded, "the roots of our present energy problems go to the core assumption of postwar U.S. oil policy: that what was good for the established international majors was best for the nation."[103]

Neither John McCloy nor his clients were willing to accept Church's contention that only greater government oversight could cure what ailed U.S. oil policy in the Middle East. Almost all the petroleum industry representatives who testified before Church's subcommittee insisted that the Arab-Israeli imbroglio, not collusion between OPEC and the multinationals, had touched off the energy crisis. "The fact is that up until 1970–71, there was little need for the government's active involvement or intervention," George Piercy, director of Exxon's Middle Eastern operations, told Church and his colleagues. "Oil was flowing in ever-growing quantities at low prices."[104] Echoing Piercy, McCloy challenged Church's assertion that corporate objectives were incompatible with national security in the Persian Gulf. "The interests of American industry and the country's welfare do coincide, and in this instance judged by the continuity of the flow of oil at reasonable, if not low, prices over a substantial period," he informed the Idaho Democrat on 30 May 1974, "these interests did coincide."[105] Unmoved by this line of reasoning, the Church subcommittee reached a far different verdict after the hearings drew to a close in the spring of 1975: "In a democracy, important questions of policy with respect to a vital commodity like oil, the lifeblood of an industrial society, cannot be left to private companies acting in accord with private interests and a closed circle of government officials."[106]

Ironically, a concerted OPEC drive to nationalize the holdings of all foreign oil firms operating in the Middle East would soon make the debate between McCloy and Church academic. Following the lead of the Iraqis, who had taken control of the IPC in 1972, a year later Qaddafi expropriated a dozen U.S., British, and Italian firms that had been pumping Libyan oil for more than a decade. In 1974 the shah of Iran announced that the state-owned National Iranian Oil Company was assuming full control over all aspects of petroleum production in his realm, a move that effectively reduced the multinational consortium established during the Eisenhower years to an elaborate marketing agency. Within twelve months Kuwait had persuaded British Petroleum and Gulf Oil to relinquish their joint concession, for which they received just $50 million in compensation. After a year of tortuous negotiations with Yamani, Exxon, Mobil, Socal, and Texaco agreed to turn ARAMCO over to the Saudi government in exchange for the right to market 80 percent of the output from the Dhahran oil fields. By the end of the decade even tiny Persian Gulf sheikdoms like Qatar and Dubai had followed suit.[107]

With the Middle Eastern host countries having wrested complete control from the multinationals and with Western demand for imported petroleum still rising steadily, the stage was set for a second "oil shock." Between 1974 and 1978 the average price of Persian Gulf crude had climbed steadily from just under $12.00 to slightly more than $15.00 per barrel. Then a revolution rocked Iran in early 1979, toppling the shah, disrupting oil production, and sending prices soaring to $28.00 per barrel. The eruption of the Iran-Iraq war ratcheted that figure upward to $34.00 in January 1981. During the following twelve months, despite spot prices for Saudi and Kuwaiti crude that exceeded $40.00 per barrel in some Western markets, the United States still imported 18 percent of its oil from the Middle East.[108]

Although some officials inside the newly inaugurated Reagan administration hinted darkly at military intervention to prevent further "economic blackmail," U.S. policymakers and petroleum executives preferred to rely on "the magic of the marketplace" to address America's energy woes during the 1980s. Convinced that Persian Gulf prices could not remain artificially high in the face of worldwide competition, Exxon and other giant oil companies shifted their gaze closer to home and began relying heavily on cheaper and relatively more secure sources of supply in Canada, Mexico, and Venezuela. Between 1980 and 1990 annual U.S. oil imports from the Middle East fell by 25 percent to 681 million barrels, while the influx of Western Hemisphere crude swelled by 240 percent to 729 million barrels. Faced with a shrinking share of the market, OPEC cut average posted prices for Persian Gulf oil by 15 percent to $29.00 per barrel in March 1983, then slashed them again by almost 40 percent three years later.[109]

As government oil revenues plummeted during the late 1980s, bitter recriminations erupted between Iraq, whose economic development projects and military ambitions required an ever growing flow of petrodollars generated by higher prices, and the sparsely populated oil-producing states of the Arabian Peninsula, whose more modest needs could be met by lower prices. By early 1990 U.S. multinationals were paying just $18.00 per barrel for Middle Eastern crude, a figure that, when discounted for inflation, translated into a price 25 percent lower than the $11.65 that OPEC had imposed during the first oil shock seventeen years earlier. Bowing to relentless pressure from Iraq's Saddam Hussein, OPEC's Arab members hiked prices for their oil to $21.00 per barrel in July. Less than a month later Iraqi armored columns rolled into Kuwait, rumors circulated that Baghdad's next target would be Saudi Arabia, and the price for a barrel of Persian Gulf crude soared to nearly $30.00 on the spot market.[110]

Halfway around the world in the White House, George Bush pondered America's options. A transplanted Connecticut Yankee who had made a small fortune in west Texas oil before assuming a series of high-level posts in Washington, Bush did not intend to stand idly by while Saddam Hussein slammed shut the door to Middle Eastern petroleum that U.S. businessmen and diplomats had pried open seventy years earlier. "An Iraq permitted to swallow Kuwait would have the economic and military power, as well as the arrogance, to intimidate and coerce its neighbors—neighbors who control the lion's share of the world's remaining oil reserves," he told the American people on 11 September 1990. "We cannot permit a resource so vital to be dominated by one so ruthless. And we won't."[111] Before the year was over, Bush dispatched more than a half-million U.S. troops to the Persian Gulf, secured United Nations approval for economic sanctions against Baghdad, and, with help from America's largest petroleum companies, organized a very effective boycott of Iraqi oil exports. When Saddam Hussein refused to reverse course, a coalition led by the United States drove his troops back across the Iraqi border in February 1991 and marched into Kuwait City, whose skyline was shrouded by suffocating clouds of thick black smoke from hundreds of burning oil wells.

Although Bush claimed that the triumphant military crusade against Iraq in 1991 reflected America's emerging faith in a "New World Order" based on democratic values, the Gulf War actually reaffirmed an abiding commitment to an open door for Middle Eastern oil that had shaped the foreign policy of the United States for nearly a century. Having helped win the First World War, U.S. policymakers fought hard to prevent their British and French allies from excluding American multinationals from the oil-rich Arab states that replaced the defeated Ottoman Empire. Having worked closely together to prevent Persian Gulf petroleum from falling under Nazi control during the Second World War, U.S. diplomats and oilmen forged an informal partnership during the quarter-century after 1945 to ensure the flow of ever increasing amounts of low-cost Middle Eastern crude to Western consumers on both sides of the Atlantic.

During the 1970s, however, America's seemingly insatiable demand for oil and OPEC's relentless quest for higher prices spawned an energy crisis that strained relations between Washington and Wall Street. Many on Capitol Hill and Main Street blamed corporate greed, which allegedly had led the multinationals to place a higher premium on their own profitability than on U.S. national security. Petroleum executives, on the other hand, blamed diplomatic myopia, which had allegedly led the American public and its leaders to advocate increasingly close ties with Israel that alienated the Arab oil producers. Oil company cooperation in the 1990 boycott of Iraq crude exports, however, showed that under the right circumstances, corporate interests could still coincide with those of the nation as a whole. Washington's ability to secure active Saudi support for the 1991 Gulf War despite America's obvious commitment to Israel likewise showed that, at least for some Arabs, oil was thicker than blood.

The early 1990s would bring falling prices for Middle East oil, rising hopes for Arab-Israeli peace, and growing confidence that public policy and private enterprise had finally resolved the nation's energy woes. As the decade drew to a close, however, America's love affair with gas-guzzling sport utility vehicles was pumping up demand while a reinvigorated OPEC was ratcheting down supply. By the summer of 2000 oil cost more than $30.00 a barrel, gasoline prices in the United States were approaching $2.00 a gallon, and Israeli-Palestinian peace talks were running on empty.[112] After George W. Bush took over on 20 January 2001 with an administration top-heavy with executives from Halliburton, Enron, and other Texas energy conglomerates, few Americans expected oil prices to drop any time soon.

The terrorist attacks on the World Trade Center and the Pentagon eight months later raised the specter of the most serious energy crisis in three decades. Although some observers feared that U.S. military intervention in Afghanistan might trigger a regional conflict that would disrupt the flow of crude from the Caucasus and Central Asia, the Bush administration's biggest worries centered on the Arabian Peninsula. The next target of Osama bin Laden and al-Qaeda was rumored to be the House of Saud, which remained the largest supplier of oil to the United States. "If they do a similar operation in Saudi Arabia," one Persian Gulf petroleum executive prophesied as the year drew to a close, "the price of oil will go up to one hundred dollars a barrel."[113] Even if the royal government was not toppled by the Saudi-born bin Laden, the escalating Israeli-Palestinian conflict would almost certainly force Riyadh to consider using its oil as a diplomatic weapon, much as it had a generation earlier. In short, at the dawn of the new millennium, U.S. policymakers and oil executives had to wonder whether, under the wrong circumstances, America's special relationship with Israel might once again complicate the exceedingly complex political and economic challenges confronting the United States in the Middle East.

We Americans are the peculiar, chosen people, the Israel of our time. We bear the ark of the liberties of the world. —Herman Melville, 1849

The United States, the President said, has a special relationship with Israel in the Middle East really comparable only to that which it has with Britain over a wide range of world affairs. —John F. Kennedy, 27 December 1962

3

The Making of a Special Relationship

America and Israel

While the lure of oil always loomed large in the eyes of the business leaders and diplomats who shaped U.S. policy toward the Middle East during the decades after the Second World War, the vision of a stable and secure Jewish state in the Holy Land loomed even larger in the eyes of other Americans. During the mid-1940s non-Jews appalled by Washington's do-nothing response to the Holocaust joined forces with Jewish Americans all too familiar with anti-Semitism in a campaign to win U.S. support for Zionist aspirations in Palestine. Despite some ferocious bureaucratic infighting among his top advisers, President Harry Truman gave Israel America's blessing by recognizing the new nation just a few minutes after its birth on 15 May 1948.

During the following half-century Israel and the United States became ever more deeply involved in a complicated "special relationship" that some observers have compared to a durable but informal alliance and that others have likened to an unstable common-law marriage. Although Washington formalized relations by opening an embassy in Tel Aviv, Israel's administrative capital, in early 1949, the honeymoon between the two governments was short lived. The Truman administration tangled repeatedly with Prime Minister David Ben Gurion over Israeli territorial ambitions, and Dwight Eisenhower very nearly imposed sanctions on the Jewish state in the aftermath of the Suez crisis. By the late 1950s, however, a mutual desire to contain radical Arab nationalism led Israel and the United States to edge closer together, a process that accelerated after John F. Kennedy moved into the White House in 1961. U.S. military and diplomatic support for the Jewish state during the Johnson and Nixon years convinced many on Main Street and Capitol Hill that Israel would serve as America's strategic asset during the 1970s. After running cold under Ford and Carter, hot under Reagan, and then cold again during the early 1990s, the special relationship between Israel and the United States seemed by the Clinton years to have become a permanent fixture of U.S. foreign policy.

For more than a generation scholars have sought to identify the mainspring of Israeli-American relations. Critics of the special relationship have attributed its persistence to election-year arithmetic and domestic politics. Although their numbers have always been relatively small in absolute terms and although their views on many issues have been relatively diverse, Jewish voters have been quite sympathetic to Israel, and their ballots have been important in key states such as New York, Illinois, and California. Moreover, the rise of powerful lobbying groups such as the American Israel Public Affairs Committee (AIPAC) since the 1960s has enhanced the influence of both Jewish voters and the Jewish state on Capitol Hill and at the White House.

Supporters of the Israeli-American special relationship, on the other hand, have insisted that the calculus of Cold War and geopolitics has always been more important than ballot counting on the first Tuesday after the first Monday in November. Indeed, U.S. officials determined to contain the Soviets without blundering into another Vietnam frequently regarded Israel, with its democratic tradition and its military prowess, as an attractive partner in the Middle East. Moreover, many analysts in Washington hoped that diplomatic support and conventional military hardware would make Israel more likely to accept territorial compromise with its Arab neighbors and less likely to develop a nuclear arsenal. A careful examination of the ambivalent and informal alliance that emerged between the United States and Israel during the fifty years after 1945 reveals that, more often than not, both simple arithmetic and differential calculus were at work.

Israel has always held a special place in the U.S. imagination. From the moment that the *Arabella* dropped anchor in Massachusetts Bay in 1630, the Puritans identified themselves as citizens of God's American Israel, destined for greatness "as a City upon a Hill."[1] Herman Melville updated those words two centuries later in one of his first novels. "We Americans are the peculiar, chosen people, the Israel of our time," he wrote in 1849, echoing his Puritan ancestors. "We bear the ark of the liberties of the world."[2] Although twentieth-century isolationists and anti-Semites dismissed Zionism as "messianic globaloney," many Americans saw religious significance in the Jews reclaiming their ancient home in Palestine, and most would confess at some time that Israel was one of their favorite nations.

Yet Uncle Sam's special relationship with the Jewish state could not claim pride of place, nor was Israel the first foreign nation ever to win favor in American eyes. Those honors fell to France, which had helped Britain's American colonies win their independence after 1776. Once Paris was rocked by revolution, however, George Washington feared that the French connection would draw America into the widening wars that plagued Europe, polarizing politics and weakening the foundations of stable government.[3] As he prepared to leave office, America's first president discreetly outlined his concerns regarding overly close ties with France. In a valedictory message that has come to be known as his "Farewell Address," Washington warned the American public in May 1796 that "a passionate attachment of one nation for another produces a variety of evils" and cautioned against forming "an habitual fondness" for any foreign country. Washington's successors heeded his warning, dismantled the alliance, and concluded that the French were really not very special at all.[4]

Indeed, 150 years later the United States maintained a special relationship with only one nation: Great Britain. Because they spoke the same language and shared many cultural and political values, Franklin Roosevelt and Winston Churchill managed to bury the hatchet during the Second World War, raising hopes on both sides of the Atlantic that the mutual trust and affection spawned by the Grand Alliance would be long lasting. But as the war wound down, many of the prewar problems that had worked against a special relationship resurfaced.[5]

Among the most controversial matters confronting U.S. and U.K. policymakers was how to handle Palestine, which had been a British mandate for a quarter-century. Although Chaim Weizmann was pressing Whitehall in early 1945 to rescind the ban on Jewish immigration imposed by the White Paper six years earlier, Churchill seemed more determined than ever to keep the door to the Holy Land closed. Across the Atlantic, on the other hand, FDR seemed more receptive to Zionist aspirations, notwithstanding bitter recriminations from Arab leaders such as Saudi Arabia's King Ibn Saud.[6] On 12 April, four weeks after he issued a carefully worded statement endorsing a Jewish state in the Holy Land, Roosevelt died of a massive stroke, leaving Harry Truman to decide whether his predecessor's ambiguous commitments regarding Palestine should be transformed into a special relationship with Israel despite Arab objections and British reservations.

Midwife from Missouri: Harry Truman and the Birth of Israel

Harry Truman was a shrewd politician and a lifelong friend of the underdog who instinctively placed greater weight on the promises that Roosevelt had given to the Zionists than on those given to the Arabs. During the Missouri Democrat's first weeks in office U.S. troops swept across Germany, liberating Buchenwald and the other death camps, whose Jewish inmates dreamed of starting new lives in Palestine. In late June Truman sent Earl G. Harrison, the former U.S. commissioner of immigration, to Europe to assess the needs of the Holocaust survivors.[7] Appalled to discover that many of Europe's quarter-million stateless Jews were being housed in abandoned Nazi facilities, Harrison recommended in August that the White House help them find refuge in the Holy Land. As long as the British White Paper of 1939 remained in force, however, Palestine would be off limits for all but a handful of Jewish refugees. "To anyone who has visited the concentration camps and who has talked with the despairing survivors," Harrison emphasized, "it is nothing short of calamitous to contemplate that the gates of Palestine should soon be closed."[8] Convinced that "America could not stand by while the victims of Hitler's racial madness were denied the opportunities to build new lives," Truman urged the British to rescind their prewar White Paper and permit 100,000 Jewish refugees to immigrate to Palestine at once.[9]

Truman's proposal found favor at neither the Foreign Office nor the State Department. Tough-talking Ernest Bevin, foreign secretary in Britain's new Labour government, believed that increased Jewish immigration into the Palestine mandate would undercut U.K. influence among the Arabs, and he frankly resented White House meddling in what he regarded as Whitehall's business. On the other side of the Atlantic, high-ranking State Department officials had been urging Truman to go slow in the Holy Land almost from the moment he set foot in the Oval Office. "The question of Palestine," Secretary of State Edward Stettinius warned the new president on 18 April, was "a highly complex one and involves questions which go far beyond the plight of the Jews of Europe."[10] Five months later State Department Middle East experts were still telling Truman that "we should stay out of any activity that might offend the Arabs."[11]

In the face of stiff opposition from Whitehall and widespread second-guessing at the State Department, Truman tabled the immigration scheme and accepted a British proposal to establish a joint Anglo-American Committee of Inquiry on Palestine later that autumn. During the first three months of 1946 the twelve members of the committee (six British and six American) held hearings in Washington and London, visited refugee camps in Germany, and traveled to Palestine, where they marveled at the achievements of the Zionist pioneers and heard the mufti of Jerusalem vow that the Arabs would drive the Jews into the sea. Upon returning to London the committee recommended that 100,000 Jewish refugees be permitted to enter Palestine at once, with the scope of future immigration to be linked to the economic absorptive capacity of the land. But the Anglo-American Committee stopped short of endorsing the creation of an independent homeland for the Jews and proposed a binational state composed of two provinces, one Jewish and one Arab, to be administered by Britain under the auspices of a United Nations trusteeship.[12]

Few Zionists were satisfied with the binational scheme. To be sure, Chaim Weizmann tried to persuade his comrades to accept the Anglo-American Committee's recommendation as a first step toward an independent Jewish commonwealth. But David Ben Gurion and most other Zionist leaders inside Palestine insisted that only by partitioning the land between the Mediterranean Sea and the Jordan River into two separate states could the Jews ever hope to defend themselves against their Arab enemies. On the other hand, a few zealots such as Menachem Begin, the Polish-born founder of the Irgun Zvai Leumi (National Military Organization), rejected partition and advocated terrorist methods to drive both the British and the Arabs out of Palestine to clear the way for an expansive Jewish state.[13]

Convinced that Begin's violent tactics went too far but that Weizmann's conciliatory approach did not go far enough, most American Zionists sided with Ben Gurion. Jewish leaders publicly endorsed partition and privately hoped that Harry Truman would reject the binational formula favored by the Anglo-American Committee of Inquiry. When Truman obliged by issuing a statement on 30 April 1946 endorsing the committee's recommendation that 100,000 Jewish refugees be permitted to enter Palestine but ignoring its controversial proposal for a binational trusteeship, British officials fumed and anti-American protests rocked Arab capitals. Truman's response was characteristically blunt. "I have to answer to hundreds of thousands who are anxious for the success of Zionism," he told a State Department critic. "I do not have hundreds of thousands of Arabs in my constituents."[14]

With tensions rising between Washington and Moscow during the spring and summer of 1946, however, the president and his advisers had to think twice about a policy in Palestine that promised to alienate America's Cold War allies in Britain and that threatened to propel the Arabs, with all their oil, into the Soviet orbit. In mid-June Henry F. Grady, Truman's diplomatic trouble-shooter on Palestine, and Herbert Morrison, one of Foreign Secretary Bevin's closest advisers, crafted an ambiguous scheme proposing two self-governing but loosely federated provinces in Palestine, one Arab and the other Jewish, over which Britain would exercise a United Nations trusteeship for an indefinite period.[15]

While State Department officials saw the Grady-Morrison plan as a step in the right direction, American Zionists and their supporters on Capitol Hill regarded it as a betrayal of a long-standing U.S. commitment to a Jewish homeland. Sorting through his options during a cabinet meeting on 30 July, Truman grew testy. Commerce Secretary Henry Wallace, an Iowa liberal openly sympathetic to partition, warned that the Grady-Morrison plan "was loaded with political dynamite" and reminded him that "the Jews had expected more than 1500 square miles." Truman shot back that he was "very much 'put out' with the Jews," adding that "Jesus Christ couldn't please them when he was here on earth, so how could anyone expect that I would have any luck?" Playing on Truman's mounting frustration, Secretary of the Navy James Forrestal warned that support for a Jewish state in Palestine might jeopardize U.S. access to the oil of Saudi Arabia, where King Ibn Saud's anti-Zionism was reaching explosive levels. But the president was not interested in petro-politics. "Truman said he wanted to handle this problem not from the standpoint of bringing in oil," Henry Wallace noted in his diary, "but from the standpoint of what was right."[16]

By the autumn of 1946 Truman was convinced that partitioning the Holy Land was the right thing to do. With off-year elections looming in November and with Democrats widely regarded as soft on communism and wrong on the economy, Jewish ballots counted for more than Arab oil. "You let me have the Jewish vote of New York and I will bring you the head of Ibn Saud on a platter," Democratic party high-roller and White House insider Bernard Baruch told a fellow Zionist as the campaign got under way. "The Administration will sell all seven Arab states," Baruch added, "if it is a question of retaining the support . . . of the Jews of New York alone; never mind the rest of the country."[17]

Yet the decisive consideration in the Truman administration's tilt toward partition seems to have been peace in the Holy Land, not victory on election day. On 7 August 1946 Nahum Goldmann, a director of the Jewish Agency, a group founded in 1929 by Chaim Weizmann to assist destitute European Jews seeking refuge in Palestine, advised the State Department that the Zionists would never permit the Arabs to finish the job that the Nazis had started. Many Jews in Palestine were already taking up arms against the Grady-Morrison proposal, Goldmann explained, and without partition, "the extremists will win." Just two weeks earlier Begin's Irgun had detonated a bomb inside Jerusalem's King David Hotel, the headquarters for British military operations in Palestine, killing ninety-one people and wounding forty-five. "There will be terror. Weizmann and I will resign," Goldmann noted sadly. "You will be in a hell of a fix. You will have to help the English fight the Jews after Auschwitz, or what else would you do?" Goldmann would get his answer on the eve of Yom Kippur, when Truman issued a statement endorsing an independent Jewish commonwealth in Palestine.[18]

Outraged by what they interpreted as stark evidence that the White House accorded a higher priority to placating its Jewish constituents than to accommodating its British allies, in February 1947 Whitehall announced that it was turning the Palestine imbroglio over to the United Nations. Hardly surprised by Britain's decision but eager to avoid being drawn into the dispute, the Truman administration worked behind the scenes with United Nations secretary general Trygve Lie, who persuaded the General Assembly on 13 May to set up the United Nations Special Committee on Palestine (UNSCOP), composed of diplomats from "eleven relatively neutral states," who were to make their recommendations no later than 1 September 1947.[19]

When the eleven UNSCOP representatives arrived in Jerusalem on 16 June to commence their work, Palestine was on the verge of civil war. Throughout the spring Begin and the Irgun had slowly escalated their hit-and-run campaign against the British, who responded by imposing martial law. Meanwhile, Palestinian Arabs, with the blessing of the mufti of Jerusalem, were mobilizing forcibly to prevent further Jewish immigration and to block Zionist efforts to purchase more land. After five weeks in Palestine few UNSCOP members believed that the binational state proposal favored by many in London and some in Washington was workable. Reconvening in Geneva, Switzerland, the committee approved a plan calling for the partition of Palestine into two fully independent states, with the understanding that Jerusalem was to remain an international city controlled by neither Arabs nor Jews but, rather, by United Nations peacekeepers.[20]

The UNSCOP's recommendations ignited a ferocious parliamentary battle at Lake Success, the Long Island suburb twenty miles east of New York City that served as the temporary headquarters of the United Nations while architects prepared blueprints for a skyscraper in Manhattan. Needing a two-thirds majority to implement partition, Zionist lobbyists pulled out all stops to win the votes of wavering states such as the Philippines and Liberia. Requiring a minority of just one-third-plus-one to reject the UNSCOP report, the five Arab members of the United Nations sought support from their Muslim neighbors in Turkey and Iran and from newly independent neutrals like India. By early November the General Assembly echoed with Arab charges that their Jewish rivals were buying votes and Jewish countercharges that the Arab oil states were blackmailing undecided countries dependent on petroleum imports from the Middle East.

Arab and Zionist politicking among the rank and file at Lake Success notwithstanding, both sides realized that the outcome hinged on the attitudes of the Big Three: Britain, Russia, and the United States. Although British officials remained convinced that partition would undermine the U.K. position in the Arab world, Whitehall abstained to avoid crippling the United Nations by opposing the UNSCOP report. Ever eager to fish in troubled waters, the Kremlin supported partition precisely because it seemed certain to erode British influence in the Middle East. As it had for most of the preceding eighteen months, U.S. policy toward Palestine remained murky as the crucial vote drew near. State Department officials still saw a hands-off approach as the best way to avert civil strife and Soviet subversion in the region. White House aides such as David Niles, however, outflanked Foggy Bottom by seeing to it that staunch proponents of partition ranging from Eddie Jacobsen, the president's old Kansas City business partner, to Chaim Weizmann, the world's most prominent Zionist, were able to make their case personally to Harry Truman. Thanks to such well organized lobbying in the Oval Office, the United States was among the thirty-three nations at Lake Success that supported partition on 29 November, not among the eleven that abstained or the thirteen that stood in opposition. By just two votes the Zionists had achieved their two-thirds majority.[21]

Implementing the United Nations partition resolution proved extraordinarily difficult. The day after the vote Palestinian Arabs machine-gunned a Jewish bus just outside Tel Aviv, marking the start of an increasingly bloody civil war. With violence escalating rapidly, the British government announced on 11 December that it would pull out of Palestine no later than 15 May 1948. Anarchy and terror, U.S. consul general Robert Macatee warned his superiors from Jerusalem on New Year's Eve, seemed inevitable. With Britain determined to relinquish its mandate and with Russia eager to meddle in the Palestinian imbroglio, many at Foggy Bottom worried that the United Nations would turn to the United States if troops were needed to restore peace in the Holy Land.[22]

By early 1948 at least one high-ranking Pentagon official was complaining privately that the U.S. approach to Palestine was being dictated by election-year political considerations, not by national security interests. Terming the deepening crisis in Palestine "too deeply charged with grave danger to this country to allow it to remain in the realm of domestic politics," James Forrestal, recently promoted to secretary of defense, feared that partition would do "permanent injury to our relations with the Moslem world" or, even worse, lead the United States to "stumble into a war."[23] War, whether in the Middle

East or Central Europe, did not strike U.S. officials as far-fetched. On 25 February communist hard-liners with close ties to the Kremlin seized power in Czechoslovakia, heightening fears that a Soviet military offensive against American forces next door in Germany might come with dramatic suddenness. Preoccupied with the war scare in Europe and eager to avoid stumbling into military quicksand in the Middle East, Harry Truman authorized the State Department to resurrect its earlier plans for a binational trusteeship in Palestine later that spring should the United Nations decide that partition was no longer feasible. Not wishing to rule out an independent Jewish state, however, Truman assured Chaim Weizmann during an "off the record" Oval Office meeting on 18 March 1948 that "I knew what it was he wanted."[24]

So did State Department officials, but they made it clear the next day that they were far less inclined than Truman to accommodate Zionist aspirations. On 19 March Warren Austin, U.S. ambassador to the United Nations, informed the Security Council that the United States now believed that partition was unworkable and would support a "temporary trusteeship" instead. "The State Dept. has reversed my Palestine policy" despite recent assurances to Weizmann, Truman fumed, and "I'm now in the position of a liar and a double-crosser." Noting that "there are people on the 3rd and 4th levels of the State Dept. who have always wanted to cut my throat," the man from Missouri confessed that "they are succeeding in doing it."[25]

A few hours later the president summoned Clark Clifford, a shrewd young St. Louis lawyer who was completing his second year as White House special counsel, to the Oval Office to discuss how best to stop the bleeding. Truman instructed Clifford to "read the riot act" to the State Department, and Clifford was only too happy to oblige.[26] Although he always contended that domestic political considerations played no role in shaping White House attitudes on Palestine, Clifford was very well aware that his boss badly trailed the Republican front-runner, Governor Thomas E. Dewey of New York, in most polls and faced an uphill battle in his bid for a second term in November. The president, Clifford admitted privately, was going to need every vote he could get, and in the wake of the recent flip-flop on Palestine, "every Jew thought that Truman was a no good son-of-a-bitch."[27]

Just as the presidential campaign was beginning to heat up, Ben Gurion and his Zionist comrades formally rejected a United Nations trusteeship and announced plans to set up a provisional government in Tel Aviv once the last British troops departed on 15 May. Convinced that Ben Gurion meant business, Truman's aides believed that only by promptly recognizing the as yet unnamed Jewish state could the president win back the support of unhappy American Zionists by election day. "Frankly, the President could not carry the state of New York in the present circumstances," one well-placed Empire State

Democrat warned the White House on 5 May. "The Jewish vote against him would be overwhelming."[28]

In less than a fortnight Truman's prospects would take a dramatic turn for the better. On 12 May the president refereed a debate between Secretary of State George C. Marshall and Clark Clifford over Palestine. "A separate Jewish state is inevitable," Clifford insisted, and since the Kremlin was likely to establish relations with the new regime sooner rather than later, "it is better to recognize now—[and] steal a march on [the] U.S.S.R." Terming this a "transparent dodge to win a few votes," Marshall retorted that "the counsel offered by Mr. Clifford was based on domestic political considerations, while the problem which confronted us was international." Moreover, "if the President were to follow Mr. Clifford's advice and if in the elections I were to vote," the normally even-tempered secretary of state added bluntly, "I would vote against the President."[29] As the meeting broke up, Clifford recalled shortly afterward, Marshall's "righteous God-damned Baptist" fulminations seemed to have carried the day against recognition.[30]

"Well that was rough as a cob," Truman winced a few moments after Marshall and his aides had departed; "I never saw the General so furious." The president, however, remained deadly serious about recognizing the Jewish state. "Suppose we let the dust settle a little," Truman told Clifford, "and see if we can get this thing turned around."[31] Later that same evening Clifford called on Undersecretary of State Robert Lovett, who hoped to avert a messy public parting of the ways between Truman and Marshall. Like his boss, Lovett believed that "to recognize the Jewish state prematurely would be buying a pig in a poke."[32] Clifford begged to differ. "Bob, there is no chance whatsoever that the President will change his mind on the basic issue," Clifford explained. "He wants to recognize the new state." Sipping a bourbon and branch water, the White House special counsel urged the State Department to back off. "All I can say," Clifford concluded, "is that if anyone is going to give, it is going to have to be General Marshall, because—I can tell you now—the President is not going to give an inch."[33]

During the following thirty-six hours Lovett managed to persuade the secretary of state to give a mile. Gradually Marshall's loyalty to the chief executive overcame his fury with the Missouri Democrat. Just before 4:00 P.M. on Friday, 14 May 1948, the White House got what it wanted. "I have talked to the General," Lovett informed Clifford. "He cannot support the President's position, but he has agreed that he will not oppose it."[34] Clifford in turn relayed the good news to Truman, who replied, "That is all we need." Two hours later the White House issued a statement recognizing the new state of Israel just eleven minutes after it came into being. Rankled by what he regarded as the triumph of short-term political expediency over long-term national interests, Lovett conducted a Monday-morning postmortem on the decision to recognize Israel. "My protests against the precipitate action and warnings as to consequences with the Arab world appear to have been outweighed by considerations unknown to me," Lovett observed on 17 May, "but I can only conclude that the President's political advisers having failed last Wednesday afternoon to make the President a father of the new state, have determined at least to make him the midwife."[35]

Lovett, of course, knew very well, as did White House advisers, that domestic political considerations had figured prominently in Truman's decision to recognize Israel. During the final hours before the historic announcement on 14 May, Clifford told Lovett that "the President was under unbearable pressure to recognize the Jewish state promptly" and that the issue was "of the greatest possible importance to the President from a domestic point of view."[36] Years later Foggy Bottom's Loy Henderson, who had warned the White House repeatedly that recognizing Israel would harm U.S. interests, could still remember David Niles replying sharply, "Look here, Loy, the most important thing for the United States is for the President to be reelected."[37]

Election-year politics, however, was not the only factor in the decision. Emphasizing that "my soul [sic] objective in the Palestine procedure has been to prevent bloodshed," Truman seems genuinely to have believed that recognizing Israel would remove the endless speculation that had helped keep Arabs and Jews at each other's throats for a generation. Deeply concerned about possible Soviet inroads into the Middle East, he seems also to have regarded a Jewish state as a stronger bulwark against communism than anything the Arabs could muster.[38] Added to all of this were moral considerations stemming from U.S. inaction during the Holocaust. In the eyes of the president the horrors of Auschwitz and Buchenwald made the case for U.S. support for Zionist objectives in the Holy Land all the more compelling. Yet Truman was far too shrewd a politician not to realize that his recognition of Israel in the spring would reap handsome dividends from American Jews before the year was out. On 2 November 1948 Truman accomplished one of the most stunning political upsets in U.S. history when he defeated Dewey and secured a second term. As always, no single issue determined the outcome. It is safe to assume, however, that Jewish and Christian friends of Israel cast their ballots for Truman in overwhelming numbers.

Years of Estrangement, 1948–1957

Although the Truman administration had served as midwife at the birth of the Jewish state, by the mid-1950s the relationship between the United States and Israel resembled a power struggle between a domineering stepparent and a rebellious stepchild. Signs of estrangement between Washington and Tel Aviv had surfaced as early as the summer of 1948, when Ben Gurion tangled with U.S. policymakers over the appropriate boundaries for the Jewish state. Convinced that Israel controlled too much territory in the wake of its smashing victory, State Department officials quietly encouraged the United Nations to draw boundaries more favorable to the Arabs. By late August, Count Folke Bernadotte, a Swedish aristocrat who served as United Nations mediator for Palestine, was pressing Israel to return the Negev Desert to the Arabs, something that Ben Gurion and Israeli foreign minister Moshe Sharett rejected out of hand. Determined to thwart the proposal by killing its chief proponent, extremists far to the right of the Israeli government assassinated Count Bernadotte on 17 September 1948 as he drove through Jerusalem.[39]

Stunned by the assassination, the Truman administration realized that the Bernadotte plan was dead on arrival. In a series of election-eve statements, the man in the Oval Office publicly affirmed his support for a Jewish state "large enough, free enough and strong enough to make its people self-supporting and secure." Privately, however, Truman regarded further expansion as out of the question, something he made very clear after Israel attempted to gain unimpeded access to the Red Sea by seizing part of the Sinai peninsula from Egypt in late December. Noting that this was "not an accidental maneuver but a deliberately planned military operation," Truman warned Ben Gurion on 30 December that unless Israeli forces withdrew at once, the United States "would have no other course than to undertake a substantial review of its attitude toward Israel."[40] Insisting that the Sinai operation had been motivated by self-defense but unwilling to risk an open breach with the United States, Ben Gurion assured the White House on New Year's Day that "orders for the withdrawal of the Israel units have already been given."[41]

Although Truman was preoccupied during his second term with far more acute crises in China and Korea, Israel's territorial ambitions remained a nagging concern. When violence erupted along the Syrian frontier in 1951, for example, the Truman administration held the Israelis responsible and condemned them for attempting to occupy the demilitarized zone that the United Nations had set up to keep the peace between Arab and Jew. While 1952 was an election year, a war-weary and scandal-plagued Truman had decided not to seek another term, and thus he was less sensitive to pressure from pro-Israel groups such as the American Zionist Council, a lobbying organization founded in 1951 that would eventually give rise to AIPAC. In short, as the Missouri Democrat prepared to turn the White House over to Dwight Eisenhower, relations between Israel and the United States were far cooler than they had been four years earlier.[42]

The new administration that took office on 20 January 1953 quickly proved more attentive to the complaints of Israel's Arab foes and less sensitive to the concerns of the new nation's American friends. Although Eisenhower acknowledged America's moral obligation to support Israel, he insisted that the United States must also address Arab concerns. Friction between the Eisenhower administration and Israel surfaced in mid-May, when Secretary of State John Foster Dulles arrived in Tel Aviv as part of a two-week fact-finding trip to the Middle East. A cagey corporate lawyer whose vision of the United States as God's American Israel rivaled that of the Puritans, Dulles admired the Israelis for their pioneering spunk and their anticommunist zeal but resented their uncompromising approach toward the Arabs and their unabashed involvement in interest group politics on Capitol Hill. This ambivalence flared into outright hostility after Ben Gurion refused even to consider making boundary concessions. Frustrated by what he regarded as Israeli intransigence, Dulles insisted that peace and stability in the Middle East hinged on redressing the grievances of the Arabs, who "feel Roosevelt and Truman administration[s] so subject to Jewish influence that Arab viewpoint ignored." The Eisenhower administration, Dulles added with characteristic bluntness, would not make decisions regarding the Arab-Israeli dispute "under pressure [from] United States Jewish groups."[43]

Neither Dulles nor the president he served sought to conceal the new administration's desire to revamp America's approach to the Middle East. "United States policies should be impartial," Dulles told the American public in a nationally televised address on 1 June, "so as to win not only the respect and regard of the Israeli but also of the Arab peoples." U.S. policymakers must constantly ask themselves, Eisenhower told his NSC five weeks later, "whether we were being as tough with the Israelis as with any other nation." On 14 July 1953, Eisenhower approved NSC-155/1, a directive on Middle East policy calling for the "reversal of the anti-American trends of Arab opinion" by making it clear that "Israel will not, merely because of its Jewish population, receive preferential treatment."[44]

Before the end of the year the Eisenhower administration would demonstrate that it meant business. When the Jewish state refused to honor a United Nations request to halt work on an irrigation project at Banat Ya'acov in the no-man's-land separating Israel from Syria in early September, Washington quietly froze $40 million in U.S. economic aid that Truman had earmarked for Tel Aviv before he left office. U.S. officials publicly confirmed the freeze five weeks later after a bloody Israeli retaliatory raid on the Jordanian village of Qibya in mid-October that left sixty-six West Bank Palestinians dead.[45] After meeting with unhappy representatives of the American Jewish Committee, the American Zionist Council, and B'nai B'rith on 26 October, John Foster Dulles icily suggested that "the group might spend some time working with representatives of the Israeli Government to try to change their policy of presenting the world with *faits accompli*." Although the Eisenhower administration did agree to release a $26 million technical aid package a few days later, relations between the United States and Israel remained quite chilly as 1953 drew to a close.[46]

Despite periodic hints of a thaw, by the end of Eisenhower's first term the temperature of the American-Israeli relationship was rapidly approaching the diplomatic equivalent of absolute zero. After Moshe Sharett succeeded the exhausted Ben Gurion as prime minister in December 1953, some U.S. officials expected the Israeli negotiating position to become more flexible. Born in Russia but raised in an Arab village after his parents immigrated to Palestine in 1906, the fifty-seven-year-old Sharett was an outspoken critic of the Irgun and preferred to see Israel achieve its objectives through diplomacy rather than through force of arms. With this in mind Sharett initiated back-channel negotiations with Egypt's Gamal Abdel Nasser during early 1954 and sought U.S. help in reducing Arab-Israeli tensions. Determined to disrupt these peaceful initiatives, hard-liners inside the government of Israel led by Defense Minister Pinhas Lavon, one of Ben Gurion's protégés, secretly arranged for Israeli intelligence to firebomb several U.S. facilities in Cairo, hoping thereby to poison relations between the United States and Egypt and between Nasser and Sharett. Nasser's police uncovered the conspiracy in July 1954 and arrested thirteen Egyptian Jews, two of whom were executed early in the new year. Meanwhile a stunned Sharett demanded Lavon's resignation, opening the door to Ben Gurion's return to the cabinet as defense minister on 17 February 1955.[47]

Just eleven days later Israeli commandos acting on orders from Ben Gurion attacked Egyptian military installations in the Gaza Strip, killing thirty-seven of Nasser's troops and two civilians. U.S. policymakers suspected that the retaliatory raid signaled "the beginning of a less moderate policy" that would eventually enable Ben Gurion to gain the upper hand over Sharett.[48] Nasser's decision to strengthen his arsenal by swapping Egyptian cotton for Soviet arms in September 1955 further undermined the position of Israeli doves such as Sharett, who stepped down as prime minister on 2 November in favor of the more hawkish Ben Gurion. Although Sharett remained in the cabinet as foreign minister, hard-liners like Israeli chief of staff Moshe Dayan, a vocal advocate of preventive war against Egypt, had Ben Gurion's ear. To be sure, Sharett did manage to rally the cabinet in late 1955 against Operation Omer, Dayan's plan to attack Nasser before he could integrate Soviet weapons into the Egyptian arsenal. In the long run, however, he saw a preemptive strike against Egypt as inevitable. "Israel will act," Sharett lamented privately on 5 December 1955, "at a time and place which it deems appropriate."[49]

The Eisenhower administration was deeply disappointed but hardly surprised when Ben Gurion decided that the appropriate time had arrived eleven months later. Nasser himself lit the fuse in July 1956 by seizing control of the Suez Canal from Britain and France, who secretly approached Israel about joint operations against Egypt. In mid-October Ben Gurion and Moshe Dayan flew to Paris, where they secured French and British approval for a surprise attack on Nasser. Worried that an Arab-Israeli conflagration might spiral into a superpower showdown, Eisenhower warned Ben Gurion on 27 October that a "forcible initiative" at this critical juncture "would endanger the peace and the growing friendship between our two countries."[50] The next day, with "new evidence of heavy Israeli mobilization" and with no sign of a reply from Ben Gurion, Eisenhower visited Walter Reed Hospital for gastrointestinal x-rays. "Israel and barium," Ike growled, "make quite a combination."[51] In a last-minute bid to restrain the Israelis, the president urged Ben Gurion "to do nothing which would endanger the peace." Eisenhower got his reply just before dinner on 29 October, when word arrived that Israeli troops had invaded the Gaza Strip and the Sinai.[52]

Upon hearing the news, Eisenhower lost both his appetite and his temper. Noting that the Israelis had launched their attack just as the 1956 presidential campaign was reaching its crescendo, Ike nevertheless moved swiftly to seek United Nations condemnation of the Jewish state and declared that he "did not care in the slightest whether he is re-elected or not."[53] On 7 November 1956, just twenty-four hours after sweeping to a second term in a landslide over Adlai Stevenson and the Democrats, Eisenhower sent Ben Gurion a blistering note demanding that Israel comply with a series of United Nations resolutions calling for speedy withdrawal from all Egyptian territory.[54] Eager to avoid an open breach with the United States, Ben Gurion sent word the next day that "upon conclusion of satisfactory arrangements with the United Nations," he and his government would "willingly withdraw our forces."[55]

Over the next four months both Eisenhower and United Nations secretary general Dag Hammarskjöld would discover that satisfying Ben Gurion was no easy task. Although the Israelis did honor a U.N. request to begin a phased withdrawal from the Sinai in mid-December, the pace was so slow that few U.S. officials believed that the Jewish state would ever accept a return to the pre-1956 territorial status quo. Convinced that Israel's unwillingness to pull out of Gaza and the Sinai would exacerbate existing U.S. problems with pro-Nasser Arab radicals and generate new tensions with oil-rich Arab conservatives, Eisenhower warned the Israeli prime minister on 3 February that continued occupation of Egyptian territory "would almost surely lead to the invoking of further UN procedures," including sanctions.[56]

Eisenhower's words had an electric effect in both Tel Aviv and Washington. "Tell him to bomb us with guided missiles," Ben Gurion thundered after receiving the president's message. "He has atomic missiles; why shouldn't he fire them at us? Let them carry out their sanctions!" Threats or no threats, he told Eisenhower on 8 February, the Jewish state would withdraw from the territory in question only after the United Nations took steps to prevent further Palestinian raids emanating from Gaza and to guarantee Israeli vessels the right of free passage through the Straits of Tiran at the mouth of the Gulf of Aqaba.[57] As word of the Israeli-American rift spread, the Eisenhower administration was bombarded with letters and phone calls opposing sanctions. Meanwhile I. L. "Si" Kenen, the director of the American Zionist Council, mobilized Israel's friends in the U.S. Senate. By early February both majority leader Lyndon B. Johnson, a Texas Democrat, and minority leader William Knowland, a California Republican, were warning that sanctions against Israel would undermine support for Eisenhower's foreign policy on Capitol Hill.[58]

The crisis deepened four days later when Ben Gurion rejected an American aide-mémoire offering oblique support for the Israeli position on Gaza and the Gulf of Aqaba in exchange for Tel Aviv heeding the United Nations call for withdrawal from all the occupied territories. Dulles flew to Thomasville, Georgia, where Eisenhower was vacationing, to deliver the bad news on 16 February. "We had gone just as far as was possible to try to make it easy and acceptable to the Israelis to withdraw," Dulles said. "To go further would almost surely jeopardize the entire Western influence in the Middle East." Sanctions, possibly including an embargo on all private U.S. assistance to Israel (which had totaled nearly $100 million in 1956), seemed the only way to get the Israelis to pull out of Egyptian territory.[59]

Eisenhower agreed and hurried back to Washington, where he sought bipartisan support from Congress for a tough new policy regarding Israel. "Nobody liked the idea of sanctions," Ike told House and Senate leaders on 20 February, but there were few other options. "Much of the world, including the Israeli government, believed Israel could in crucial moments control US policy," Dulles added. "Should the Arab nations see any confirmation of this belief, they would . . . turn to Russia." But both Lyndon Johnson, who wore what one observer called "an expression which seemed to say that he was not going to give an inch," and William Knowland, who sported "his classical toga of lofty defiance," were unmoved. "There were times," the Texas Democrat explained, "when Congress must of course express its viewpoint."[60]

Undaunted by congressional second-guessing, Eisenhower appeared on national television a few hours later to express his viewpoint. To accept the Israeli argument that "armed attack can properly achieve the purposes of the assailant," he explained, "would be a blow to the authority and influence of the United Nations." Therefore the United States had no choice but to support U.N. sanctions against Israel.[61] Shocked by Eisenhower's speech, Ben Gurion instructed Israeli ambassador Abba Eban to strike the best possible bargain in Washington. The Israelis were prepared "to make an unconditional statement that they would withdraw," Eban told Dulles on 24 February, provided that Hammarskjöld gave "reasonable assurances" that a United Nations Emergency Force would prevent Palestinian guerrillas from returning to Gaza.[62]

Deeply mistrustful of the Israelis, Hammarskjöld balked at assuming such open-ended peacekeeping responsibilities and seemed determined to impose sanctions on Israel. Hoping to break the deadlock, Dulles met with Eban and Foreign Minister Golda Meir, Moshe Sharett's American-born successor, on 28 February. If Israel agreed to "complete and prompt withdrawal" from the occupied territories, Dulles promised to support both its "right of innocent passage" through the Straits of Tiran and "its freedom to act to defend its rights" should conditions in Gaza deteriorate. Convinced that this eleventh-hour U.S. initiative would make the risks more manageable, Hammarskjöld agreed to station United Nations peacekeepers in Gaza and the Sinai as soon as the Israelis completed their withdrawal. Meir confirmed the Israeli-American understanding before the U.N. General Assembly the next day, narrowly averting a vote on sanctions.[63] Although the United States and Israel had avoided an open breach, their bitter clash during early 1957 revealed a level of reciprocal mistrust and diplomatic estrangement that would once have seemed unthinkable but that now seemed unavoidable.

The Israeli-American Reconciliation, 1958–1968

Estranged though they might be during the mid-1950s, however, neither the United States nor Israel was willing to demand a divorce, because each side realized that the only winners in an American-Israeli breakup would be anti-Western radicals like Egypt's Nasser. Indeed, as early as 1958 Eisenhower and Ben Gurion began to edge toward a diplomatic reconciliation in order to help shore up moderate regimes in Lebanon and Jordan, long the most pro-Western and the least anti-Israel of the Arab states. When Muslim radicals seemed poised to seize power in Beirut, the Israelis welcomed Washington's decision to send U.S. marines to Lebanon on 15 July 1958. When King Hussein appealed for U.K. help against pro-Nasser subversives in Amman two days later, Ben Gurion honored Eisenhower's request that Britain be permitted to airlift its troops from Cyprus through Israeli airspace into Jordan.[64]

The Israeli prime minister, however, regarded these operations as at best stopgap measures. Before the month was over, Ben Gurion proposed to transform Israel from a strategic liability to a strategic asset by linking it to a "peripheral pact" of pro-Western, non-Arab regimes such as Iran, Ethiopia, and

Turkey.[65] Delighted by this offer to help "erect effective sandbags" against the rising tide of radical Arab nationalism, John Foster Dulles assured Ben Gurion on 1 August that the United States was "happy to encourage Israel in its efforts to stand on its own feet."[66] Three weeks later the Eisenhower administration agreed to sell Israel arms—100 recoilless rifles and "reasonable quantities" of half-tracks—for the first time.[67] By the end of the year, Ambassador Abba Eban recalled long afterward, "a sense of common purpose" had finally begun to emerge between Israel and the United States after nearly a decade of estrangement.[68]

Israel's friends on Capitol Hill added their voices to the chorus heralding more harmonious relations during 1959. In February Si Kenen's newly rechristened AIPAC began to press hard in Congress for more U.S. aid for the Jewish state.[69] Later that spring Senate majority leader Lyndon Johnson proposed making Israel eligible for a multimillion-dollar military assistance credit under the Mutual Security Program.[70] Reluctant to conclude a major arms deal with the Israelis, the Eisenhower administration did agree later that summer to provide $100 million in technical and financial assistance over the next two years, a sum larger than all previous U.S. aid to Israel since 1948.[71]

Further evidence that the thaw in Israeli-American relations was real came in March 1960, when Ben Gurion arrived in Washington seeking military hardware, including Hawk antiaircraft missiles. Although Eisenhower "questioned the desirability of the U.S. becoming the arsenal for Israel" and refused to provide any Hawks, before the end of the year he agreed to sell the Israelis $10 million worth of sophisticated radar equipment.[72] While Eisenhower had not given Ben Gurion all he wanted, it did seem that, as Abba Eban put it many years later, the two men had finally emerged from their post-Suez squabbling "with the basic elements of the American-Israeli partnership unimpaired."[73]

That partnership, however, soon faced new strains, because by late 1960 many observers in Washington feared that Israel might utilize the nuclear reactor it was secretly constructing with French help at Dimona in the Negev Desert to develop atomic weapons. The CIA believed that when it was completed, the reactor could produce eight to ten kilograms of weapons-grade plutonium a year, enough for one atomic bomb.[74] Despite informal Israeli assurances that the Dimona facility would be used only for peaceful purposes, when Eisenhower demanded in mid-January 1961 that Israel "declare unreservedly that she had no plans to manufacture atomic weapons," Ben Gurion balked. Insisting that the reactor was necessary to meet Israel's growing energy needs, he indignantly told U.S. ambassador Ogden Reid that "you must talk to us as equals, or not talk to us at all."[75]

Eisenhower, of course, left office at the end of the month, leaving John F. Kennedy to do all the talking. A Massachusetts Democrat and longtime admirer of the Zionist dream who had called Israel "the bright light now shining in the Middle East" following a 1951 visit to Tel Aviv, JFK would win the hearts and votes of many American Jews nine years later on election day. During a transition briefing on 6 December 1960, however, the president-elect told Eisenhower "that an atomic development in Israel is highly distressing."[76] Kennedy's distress mounted during the spring of 1961 after he learned that Israel intended to buy medium-range French bombers capable of carrying atomic weapons. "While the reactor is clean as a whistle today," national security adviser McGeorge Bundy informed JFK on 29 May, "it could be turned in a dirty direction at any time."[77]

As one might have predicted, the Dimona reactor was the first issue Kennedy raised when he met with Ben Gurion the next day at New York City's Waldorf Astoria. Israel, Ben Gurion maintained, was not developing a nuclear deterrent and intended to use atomic power to desalinize seawater. Greatly relieved, Kennedy persuaded the Israeli prime minister to permit U.S. physicists to visit Dimona periodically and to share their findings with nervous Arab leaders. In return Ben Gurion hoped that Kennedy would be more receptive to Israel's request for "defensive weapons" such as Hawk missiles. JFK, however, worried that if the United States said yes, the regional arms race "will escalate fast," with the Arabs seeking more sophisticated weaponry from the Kremlin. "We are reluctant to give Israel missiles and you understand," Kennedy concluded, "but we would be disturbed if Israel should get into a situation that would invite attack." In any event, he assured Ben Gurion that "we will keep the matter under continuing review."[78]

Having won assurances regarding Dimona and having placed the Hawks on hold, Kennedy began to move steadily toward a rapprochement with Egypt, which he felt held the key to a comprehensive regional settlement that would do far more to bolster Israel's security than would atomic bombs or surface-to-air missiles. Relying on personal diplomacy and economic aid, Kennedy charmed Nasser and generated so much goodwill that even the announcement that Washington would sell eight batteries of Hawks to Israel did not provoke anti-American demonstrations in Cairo. On 18 August 1962 White House counsel Myer Feldman, JFK's informal liaison to the American Jewish community, flew to Tel Aviv to offer the Israelis the antiaircraft missiles they coveted in exchange for fresh assurances regarding nuclear nonproliferation.[79] According to McGeorge Bundy, Ben Gurion agreed that "Israel would permit regular visits by Americans to Dimona, where they could judge for themselves whether or not the installation was part of a weapons program."[80] Several weeks after Feldman returned to Washington, a team of U.S. physicists inspected the reactor and confirmed that "there [was] no evidence of preparation for nuclear weapons production."[81]

By selling the Israelis defensive weapons while working to restrain Nasser, the Kennedy administration hoped to make them more willing to make concessions to the Arabs and less likely to go nuclear. To this end JFK invited Foreign Minister Golda Meir to the winter White House at Palm Beach, Florida, just after Christmas. "The United States," Kennedy told Meir, "has a special relationship with Israel in the Middle East really comparable only to that which it has with Britain," and it was "quite clear that in case of an invasion the United States would come to the support of Israel." In return, however, Kennedy hoped "that Israel would give consideration to our problems on this atomic reactor," not merely because "we are opposed to nuclear proliferation" in principle, but also because a regional arms race would prevent progress on other Middle East issues. "Our relationship," Kennedy reminded Meir, must be "a two-way street." Before she left, Meir assured JFK that "there would not be any difficulty between us on the Israeli nuclear reactor" or on the Palestinian problem.[82]

The Kennedy administration, however, made little headway on either front during the new year. In early 1963 mobs of angry West Bank Palestinians protesting King Hussein's relatively benign policies toward Israel nearly toppled the Hashemite monarchy. To make matters worse, pro-Nasser and anti-Israel officers seized power first in Iraq and then in Syria, heightening Israeli fears of encirclement by Arab radicals. Predictably, Israel began to press for still more explicit security guarantees, in the absence of which the CIA fully expected the Jewish state to develop atomic weapons "to intimidate the Arabs." Deeply disturbed by the implications of Israel's nuclear option, Kennedy created an interagency task force in late March "to develop proposals for forestalling the development of advanced weapons in the Near East."[83]

Meanwhile, Kennedy and his advisers reaffirmed their commitment to the security of the Jewish state. In early May the president personally assured Ben Gurion that "we have Israel's defense problems very much in mind," while Myer Feldman promised AIPAC officials that Washington would assist Tel Aviv at once in the event of an "unprovoked attack on its territory."[84] But Israel's supporters in the U.S. Senate wanted more. On 6 May Kennedy learned that New York's Jacob Javits and Minnesota's Hubert Humphrey intended to propose "collective defense arrangements with Israel." When Israeli chargé d'affaires Mordechai Gazit arrived at the White House a week later, he informed Robert Komer, Kennedy's Middle East expert, that the "hullabaloo" on Capitol Hill "was likely to get worse unless we did 'something' to meet Israeli security requirements." Like many inside the Kennedy administration, Komer believed that Gazit and his superiors were exaggerating the Arab threat as "part of a campaign to justify Israeli development of nuclear weapons."[85]

Fortunately the interagency task force Kennedy had created in March was putting the finishing touches on a plan "to stop nuclear/missile escalation" in the Middle East. To achieve this objective the task force recommended on 14 May that Kennedy send John J. McCloy, his special coordinator for disarmament, on "a highly secret probe" to obtain promises of "no nuclear weapons," first from Egypt and then from Israel. If all went according to plan, by midsummer the White House would be well on the way toward an Egyptian-Israeli "arms limitation arrangement and security guarantee."[86] State Department officials believed that Nasser would welcome the U.S. nonproliferation proposal as the best way to avoid choosing between a nuclear Israel and a shotgun marriage with the Kremlin. When McCloy arrived in Cairo at the end of the month, however, the Egyptian leader proved far less accommodating than Foggy Bottom had expected, and Kennedy's emissary returned to Washington empty-handed without even having bothered to stop in Tel Aviv.[87]

Nasser's rebuff of McCloy increased the danger of a nuclear arms race in the Middle East and made Israel's insistence on a security guarantee in exchange for its own promise to forgo nuclear weapons seem less unreasonable. Levi Eshkol, the soft-spoken moderate who succeeded the combative Ben Gurion as prime minister on 16 June 1963, capitalized on the growing rift between Washington and Cairo by reiterating that Israel was not building an atomic bomb at Dimona.[88] Eshkol's newfound cooperativeness and Nasser's born-again rejectionism soon evoked fresh assurances that the United States would "come to Israel's assistance if Israel were the victim of aggression."[89]

Kennedy himself spelled this out in a recently declassified letter to Eshkol dated 2 October 1963. Reiterating America's "determination to see a prosperous Israel securely established in the Near East and accepted by her immediate neighbors," the president pointed to the U.S. Sixth Fleet—"our quick reaction forces in the Mediterranean"—as proof that "we can back up our assurances." This informal security guarantee, however, was linked to Israel's promise to refrain from developing nuclear weapons, a pledge that Kennedy and his advisers regarded as suspect. "It was strange to me that Israel was so consistently coy about describing its own defense plans and programs to its guarantor, banker, and strongest friend in the world," NSC Middle East expert Robert Komer told Mordechai Gazit on 21 November. Did such evasiveness, he wondered, "mask an intent to acquire nuclear capability?"[90] Although JFK never received an unambiguous answer to this question, he went to his grave firmly committed to America's emerging special relationship with Israel.

Lyndon B. Johnson would consummate the Israeli-American reconciliation initiated by Eisenhower and accelerated by Kennedy. The Israel lobby had regarded Senator Johnson as one of its leading friends on Capitol Hill during the late 1950s and counted Vice-President Johnson among its most loyal allies inside the Kennedy administration. The new president did not disappoint. "The

United States will continue its warm friendship with Israel," LBJ assured Golda Meir at the reception following Kennedy's funeral on 25 November 1963. "Israel can count on this."[91] During the months that followed, Johnson placed other friends of Israel in key posts. He selected Hubert Humphrey, a longtime advocate of closer U.S. ties with the Jewish state, as his running mate in 1964, named Supreme Court Justice Arthur Goldberg, an enthusiastic Zionist, as America's new ambassador to the United Nations, and assigned the avowedly pro-Israel Rostow brothers to influential policymaking positions. MIT economist Walt W. Rostow was named national security adviser, and Yale-educated lawyer Eugene Rostow became undersecretary of state for political affairs.[92]

Despite the pro-Israel complexion of his administration, the new president was not eager to expand U.S. military assistance. When Israel requested 200 American M-48 tanks in early 1964, for example, Johnson hesitated. Secretary of State Dean Rusk cautioned that selling Israel such advanced offensive weapons was certain to spark a regional arms race.[93] Two White House holdovers from Kennedy's staff tried to persuade Johnson to supply the tanks. Myer Feldman cited America's moral commitment to Israel, and Robert Komer pointed toward the upcoming presidential campaign. In May 1964, however, LBJ decided that, at least for the time being, geopolitical considerations must take precedence over domestic politics. Rather than providing U.S. tanks, he opted instead for indirect aid via the West Germans, who were quietly encouraged to sell M-48s to Israel.[94]

After soundly thrashing Barry Goldwater at the polls on 3 November, Johnson took another hard look at the military balance in the Middle East. For months the Arabs had been stockpiling Soviet weapons while calling for an anti-Israel variant of the Kremlin-backed "war of national liberation" wracking Vietnam, trends that seemed certain to accelerate the Jewish state's quest for an atomic bomb. Like his predecessor, Johnson placed a high priority on preventing nuclear proliferation. To this end LBJ had informed Prime Minister Eshkol during an Oval Office meeting on 1 June 1964 that "he was foursquare behind Israel on all matters that affected their vital security interests" but that he was also "violently against nuclear proliferation." In return for U.S. help in securing tanks from West Germany, Johnson asked Israel to reaffirm its pledge not to build atomic weapons. Eshkol obliged, but West German foot-dragging and Egyptian saber-rattling led to new requests for U.S. military hardware when Averell Harriman, LBJ's ambassador-at-large, visited Israel in February 1965. Harriman returned home with a shopping list that included not only 210 M-48 tanks but also 75 B-66 medium bombers, which led to suspicions that the Jewish state might be "looking down the road toward an aircraft capable of carrying an Israeli developed nuclear weapon."[95]

Determined to avert a nuclear arms race in the Middle East, the White

House moved in late March to make Israel eligible for almost any conventional weapon in the American arsenal. U.S. officials quickly agreed to provide 210 M-48 tanks but postponed a decision on Eshkol's request for a squadron of A-4 Skyhawk jets until Israel determined whether the French might make similar aircraft available.[96] After being rebuffed in Paris, the Israelis returned to Washington in October 1965 seeking either A-4 Skyhawks or, preferably, F-4 Phantom jets capable of carrying nuclear weapons. Following months of wrangling with White House officials, in March 1966 the Israelis finally agreed to accept forty-eight of the slower Skyhawks instead of the supersonic Phantoms.[97] To no one's surprise the sale drew "heavy criticism from the Arabs." But as the State Department reminded LBJ four months later on the eve of his meeting with Israeli president Zalman Shazar, "if Israel is unable to obtain its valid conventional arms requirements, those in Israel who advocate acquisition of nuclear weapons will find a much more fertile environment for their views."[98]

Convinced that Israel intended to acquire atomic bombs whether it received U.S. tanks and planes or not, during late 1966 the Arabs began to prepare for a military confrontation. In November Palestinian commandos staged a series of bloody raids against Israel from base camps on the West Bank, while Syrian radicals urged the Kremlin to speed up deliveries of sophisticated Soviet weaponry, including MIG-21s. Outraged by these Arab provocations, Israel filled the skies with its warplanes during the spring of 1967, downing six Syrian MIGs on 7 April in a dogfight over the Golan Heights. Nasser, who had until then done little to assist either the Palestinians or the Syrians, warned the Israelis later that month not to attack Damascus and began to mobilize Egyptian troops for a showdown.[99]

Hoping to avert a full-scale war, White House troubleshooter Harold Saunders undertook a fact-finding mission to the Middle East. The stakes had never been higher, nor had the prospects for peace ever been bleaker. Well aware that President Johnson had "a political need as well as a personal desire to maintain a warm relationship with Israel," Saunders reported that the Israelis now saw "Arab terrorism as the greatest threat to their security today" and were doing everything possible to combat it. "The 'war of national liberation' as a technique," he concluded, "has come to the Middle East." Having seen Johnson invest so much blood and treasure "in demonstrating that he will not tolerate this brand of aggression" in Southeast Asia, America's friends would soon be asking, "How can he stand against terrorist attackers in Vietnam and not in Israel?"[100]

Moreover, unless the United States stood firm against the Arab radicals, how could Johnson expect Israel to endorse the nuclear nonproliferation treaty he was peddling in Tel Aviv and elsewhere? "Before signing an NPT," Saunders predicted, the Israelis would "want assurances from the US and USSR that major arms suppliers will keep the lid on the Arab arms inventory while the conventional balance is still in Israel's favor." Few in Israel or the United States, however, expected Moscow to exercise that level of statesmanship. "What this adds up to," Saunders noted gloomily on 16 May, "is great pressure on us to join in a confrontation with Nasser and prediction that US will lose its stature in the area if we refuse and fail to stop him, the USSR and the liberation armies."[101]

That pressure mounted sharply the next day after Nasser sent troops into the Sinai to replace the United Nations Emergency Force that had patrolled the Egyptian-Israeli frontier since February 1957. When Israel mobilized to parry Egypt's thrust, Johnson cautioned Eshkol not to overreact. Heeding this warning, the Israelis held back. Then, on 22 May, Nasser closed the Straits of Tiran to Israeli shipping, a move that Tel Aviv interpreted as an act of war. Johnson urged the Israelis to be patient while he organized a multinational flotilla to challenge Nasser's blockade.[102]

Patience, however, was in increasingly short supply inside Levi Eshkol's cabinet. "The last thing Israel wanted would be a war," Israeli diplomat and longtime LBJ crony Ephraim "Eppie" Evron assured State Department officials as news of Nasser's blockade spread. But because "the Arabs felt that the United States would not act," war might soon be Eshkol's only option.[103] The Gulf of Aqaba "was where all the oil from Iran came in," Democratic bigwig and outspoken friend of Israel Abraham Feinberg remembered telling LBJ as the crisis deepened. Should Eshkol permit Nasser to sever that petroleum lifeline, Feinberg concluded in words that must have made Johnson wince, "Israel would be economically castrated."[104] Nevertheless, Johnson and his advisers did what they could to discourage Eshkol from striking the first blow against Nasser. Should the Jewish state launch a preemptive attack, CIA director Richard Helms warned the NSC on 24 May, the United States would be "fully blackballed in the Arab world as Israel's supporter."[105]

The longer the Middle East crisis dragged on, however, the less interest there was in preventing an Israeli first strike. When Foreign Minister Abba Eban visited the White House on 26 May to review plans for a "Red Sea regatta" to break the Egyptian blockade, for example, LBJ did not say categorically that the United States would part company with Israel if it launched a preemptive war against Egypt. Instead Johnson cryptically remarked three times, "Israel will not be alone unless it decides to go it alone."[106] LBJ held out little hope that his words would restrain Israel for very long. Indeed, during a late-night debriefing session attended by White House speechwriter John Roche, the president sipped "some of that poisonous low-cal Dr. Pepper," waxed comical, and even "did a takeoff on Eban" agonizing over Israel's options. But when the conversation turned to "what we thought the Israelis were going to do," LBJ suddenly turned very serious. "They're going to hit [Nasser]," he said. "There's nothing we can do about it."[107]

During the following ten days the Johnson administration did next to nothing to discourage the Israelis and may actually have encouraged them through the back channel to hit Nasser hard. To be sure, Dean Rusk did counsel patience when he met with Israeli ambassador Avraham Harman on 2 June, emphasizing that "the question of who fired first would be significant."[108] But when Harman arrived at National Airport a few hours later for a flight bound for Tel Aviv, he received a phone call from Abe Fortas, Supreme Court justice, presidential confidant, and staunch friend of Israel. According to a law clerk Fortas said, "Rusk will fiddle while Israel burns. If you're going to save yourself, do it yourself."[109]

These "Delphic" comments, Abba Eban recalled long afterward, had an electric effect inside Eshkol's cabinet. Fortas had "praised our restraint in the past without any hint that it should continue in the future," leaving little doubt in Tel Aviv that Israeli military action "would now be received with unspoken relief even in Washington."[110] Eppie Evron likewise remembers thinking that finally, at the eleventh hour, the White House was tilting toward Israel. "From a red light, opposing war, we understood that the light had changed to yellow," Evron recently told an interviewer. "The Americans didn't give us a green light to go to war, but they signaled to us that they would not repeat what the Eisenhower administration had done in 1957."[111]

Just after dawn on Monday, 5 June, jets marked with the Star of David swooped low over the Nile Delta and knocked out the Egyptian air force before it could get off the ground. Dean Rusk claimed to have been "astonished and dismayed" by this surprise attack and flashed word to his Soviet counterpart, Andrei Gromyko, that "we had assurances from the Israelis that they would not initiate hostilities pending further diplomatic efforts."[112] Nevertheless, U.S. support for the Jewish state never wavered throughout the Six Day War. Clearly, Lyndon Johnson's handling of the crisis was influenced in part by pressure from friends of Israel in Congress, on the White House staff, and among the American Jewish community. He also probably hoped that his staunch support for Israel would be popular enough to help quell mounting criticism of his increasingly unpopular policies in Southeast Asia. But domestic politics was only part of the story. Johnson seems to have taken vicarious pleasure from Israel's ability to thwart an Arab war of national liberation not unlike the one the United States faced in Vietnam.[113]

Johnson and his top aides also hoped that a strong Israel convinced of its own invincibility would be more likely to compromise with Arab moderates and less likely to go nuclear. Shortly after the shooting stopped on 10 June

Dean Rusk discussed peace terms with Abba Eban. Distressed to learn that Israel intended to keep much of the land seized during the Six Day War, Rusk reminded Eban that his country had always denied having territorial ambitions. "We have changed our minds," Eban retorted. Worried that Israel might also change its mind about the atomic bomb, Rusk shot back, "Don't you be the first power to introduce nuclear weapons into the Middle East." "No," Eban replied with a smile, "but we won't be the second."[114]

This exchange symbolized the uneasy partnership that had emerged between Israel and the United States by 1967. The Israeli triumph over Soviet-backed Arab radicals seemed to vindicate Eisenhower and Ben Gurion, both of whom had envisioned their nations as allies in the struggle to curb Kremlin influence as early as 1958. Israeli troops armed with U.S. weapons had shown friend and foe alike that Third World wars of national liberation need not always be successful. Yet the danger that the Israelis might develop atomic weapons continued to keep U.S. officials on edge. "We'll make sure Israel has our political support and the equipment it needs to defend itself," Harold Saunders wrote Walt Rostow on 29 December. "But we can't tie ourselves to a 'fortress Israel,'" especially if "Israel gets SSMs [surface-to-surface missiles] or decides to build nuclear weapons."[115]

Levi Eshkol arrived at the LBJ Ranch in January 1968 seeking fifty supersonic F-4 Phantom jets. Although Johnson faced an uphill battle for a second term in just ten months, he seemed less concerned with election-year politics than with the dimming prospects for peace in the Middle East. "We can't support an Israel that sits tight," he told Eshkol on 7 January. Unless Israel showed its good faith by "avoiding permanent moves in [the] occupied lands" and forswearing "Nuclear Weapons and Missiles," there would be no Phantoms.[116] And so there were not, despite one of the most hotly contested presidential elections in the twentieth century. To be sure, deepening problems in Southeast Asia forced Johnson out of the race in March and left him little time for what must have seemed to be far less pressing troubles in the Middle East. The Israelis and their friends in Washington, of course, hinted that by providing the Phantoms before election day, a lame-duck Johnson might secure just enough extra votes to ensure a Democratic victory.[117] Nevertheless, LBJ would not release the Phantoms, Dean Rusk informed Ambassador Yitzhak Rabin in mid-September, until Israel "dispelled the ambiguity" surrounding its nuclear program and clarified the fate of Arab territory seized during the Six Day War.[118]

Johnson's position softened somewhat later that autumn after AIPAC persuaded seventy U.S. senators to sign a letter supporting the sale of F-4s to Israel. But "the irrationality of trying to make peace by force alone" continued to rub the president the wrong way. "Our own experience," LBJ reminded

Eshkol on 23 October, "has proved that real peace is not found alone on the walls of a fortress—or under the umbrella of air power—or behind a nuclear shield."[119] The Phantom deal remained stalled until 25 November, three weeks after Richard Nixon had eked out a razor-thin victory over the ardently pro-Israel Hubert Humphrey. The sticking point remained what it had been for nearly a year. "We are . . . concerned with Israel's missile and nuclear plans," Assistant Secretary of Defense Paul Warnke told Ambassador Rabin during the last stages of the Phantom negotiations. "This is why we need to 'up-date' your assurances to us on these matters."[120]

The best assurance, of course, would have been Israeli ratification of the nonproliferation treaty. In the end, however, Washington settled for Tel Aviv's renewed pledge not to be the first nation in the Middle East to acquire an atomic bomb. This was a hollow victory for policymakers such as Warnke, who noted long afterward that "at the time I believed, and subsequent information has tended to confirm, that Israel had in fact developed a small arsenal of nuclear weapons."[121] Ironically, the quest for nuclear nonproliferation had been at least as important as the quest for votes in cementing closer ties and completing the reconciliation between the United States and Israel during the 1960s.

Strategic Asset or Liability?: Israel and the United States since 1969

When Lyndon Johnson turned the White House over to Richard Nixon, he left behind a special relationship with Israel that, over the next thirty years, would become the subject of intense debate among U.S. policymakers who could not agree whether the Jewish state constituted a strategic asset or a diplomatic liability. A Republican street fighter who had helped orchestrate America's post-Suez showdown with Israel from his post as Eisenhower's vice-president, Nixon took office in January 1969 knowing that 85 percent of Jewish voters had cast their ballots for Hubert Humphrey.[122] Less receptive to Israel's friends than his Democratic predecessor had been, the new president quickly signed off on National Security Study Memorandum 2, which called for a thorough review of the U.S. position in the Middle East. "Is it eroding drastically?" Nixon wondered. "Is an early Arab-Israeli settlement essential to preserving the U.S. position?"[123] While it was unclear where the review was headed, Nixon tipped his hand during a news conference on 27 January 1969. "I believe we need new initiatives and new leadership on the part of the United States in order to cool off the situation in the Mideast," he told a packed house in the East Room. "I consider it a powderkeg, very explosive. It needs to be defused."[124]

Defusing the Mideast powderkeg frequently put Richard Nixon on a collision course with Israel during his first eighteen months in office. Troubled in early 1969 by fresh signs that the Israelis were developing an atomic bomb at Dimona and frustrated that they showed so little interest in United Nations efforts to restart the deadlocked peace process, Nixon postponed indefinitely the delivery of the F-4 Phantoms that Johnson had promised Israel just before he left office. "I am beginning to think," Nixon complained privately as the year drew to a close, that "we have to consider taking strong steps unilaterally to save Israel from her own destruction."[125]

Strong steps were just what Secretary of State William P. Rogers recommended. A Wall Street attorney who had watched Washington tangle with Tel Aviv a decade earlier from his perch atop Eisenhower's Department of Justice, Rogers approached the Israelis as though they were targets in a hostile corporate takeover. By the autumn of 1969 the Israelis had learned that before the year was over the State Department intended to propose a comprehensive settlement that would require the return of all Egyptian territory conquered during the Six Day War in exchange for peace talks with Nasser. "You are in for a hard time," one White House insider informed Yitzhak Rabin in early October. "The administration has decided to give in on a total Israeli withdrawal, at least in the Sinai."[126] Two months later Nixon's secretary of state confirmed that the future of Israel's relationship with the United States hinged on its willingness to accept the territorial concessions outlined by the State Department.[127]

The Israelis were outraged. Golda Meir, who had succeeded Eshkol as prime minister ten months earlier, termed the U.S. proposal "a disaster for Israel" and thundered that "any Israeli government that would adopt and implement such a plan would be betraying its country." Yitzhak Rabin relayed Meir's message to the White House. "Let me tell you in complete frankness, you are making a bad mistake," he told the NSC's Harold Saunders in late December, by "fostering an imposed solution that Israel will resist with all her might." As he got up to leave, Rabin vowed to "do everything within the bounds of American law to arouse public opinion against the administration's moves!"[128]

True to his word Rabin applauded when Israel's friends came out against the Rogers initiative early in the new year. "Some 1,400 leading American Jews from 31 states descended on Washington on January 25 and 26," AIPAC's Si Kenen recalled long afterward, "to voice their protest."[129] In the weeks that followed, Kenen's allies on Capitol Hill joined the rising chorus calling for the White House to scuttle the peace plan and to deliver the long-awaited F-4 jets to Israel's air force. Bridling at what he regarded as "the unyielding and shortsighted pro-Israeli attitude prevalent in large and influential segments of the American Jewish community, Congress, the media, and in intellectual and cultural circles," in early March Nixon once again postponed the release of the supersonic Phantoms.[130]

Nixon's decision grew out of his conviction that America's relationship with Israel must reflect the national interest, not merely interest group politics. "Our interests are basically pro-freedom and not just pro-Israel because of the Jewish vote," he remarked privately as the dust began to settle later that spring. "We are *for* Israel because Israel in our view is the only state in the Mideast which is *pro*-freedom and an effective opponent to Soviet expansion." Eager to dispel any doubts about U.S. staying power in Southeast Asia, Nixon vowed to "oppose a cut-and-run policy" in the Middle East. "This is the kind of friend that Israel needs and will continue to need particularly when the going gets very tough in the next five years."[131]

When the going got tough sooner than Nixon had anticipated, Israel proved to be just the kind of friend the United States needed as well. During the spring and summer of 1970 the Kremlin shipped eighty batteries of surface-to-air missiles and a squadron of MIG-21 jet fighters to Egypt, then dispatched several thousand Russian military advisers and several hundred Soviet pilots to ensure that the Egyptians made their new hardware operational as soon as possible. Moscow's decision to escalate the arms race in the Middle East while Washington was working to scale back its own military involvement in Southeast Asia did not sit well with Nixon or with Henry Kissinger, his national security adviser. "Once the Soviets established themselves with a combat role in the Middle East and we accepted that role," Kissinger recalled in his memoirs, "the political balance would be drastically changed, and the military balance could be overthrown at any moment of Soviet choosing."[132] Disturbed by the steady growth of Russian influence and angered by Nasser's decision to move his new military hardware within striking distance of Israeli positions in the Sinai Desert, the Nixon administration finally agreed on 1 September 1970 to deliver the squadron of F-4 Phantom jets that Tel Aviv had been seeking for a year and a half.[133]

Israel would repay the favor when civil war erupted next door in Jordan later that same month. During the week after Nixon released the Phantoms, Palestinian commandos hijacked three jetliners—one American, one British, and one Swiss—and flew them to an abandoned airfield thirty miles outside Amman, where several hundred passengers, many of whom were U.S. citizens, were held hostage. Hoping to spark an uprising against Jordan's King Hussein, the terrorists released their hostages unharmed on 12 September and then blew up the aircraft while television cameras whirred. With Washington's blessing Hussein struck back hard, imposing martial law and sending the Jordanian army into the refugee camps that ringed Amman to disarm the commandos and capture their leaders. With the king poised to liquidate his Palestinian foes, the pro-Soviet regime in Damascus moved to help its Palestinian friends. As Syrian tanks rolled into northern Jordan on 20 September, Henry Kissinger huddled with Israeli ambassador Yitzhak Rabin, who confirmed that his government was willing to launch air and ground strikes if Washington thought this would save Hussein's throne. Kissinger relayed the news to his boss in the Oval Office, who swiftly agreed to support Israel. "I have decided it," Nixon remarked just after breakfast on 21 September. "Tell him [Rabin] 'go.'"[134]

Now that the Middle East was on the verge of a Syro-Israeli war that might easily have escalated into a superpower conflict, Moscow evidently told Damascus to stop. With Israel's warplanes poised for attack, Syria's tanks reversed course and clanked back out of Jordan on 22 September. Buoyed by this Israeli-American show of support, King Hussein drove thousands of Palestinian guerrillas and their families out of Jordan in an operation that the PLO labeled "Black September." For top U.S. policymakers the outcome of the Jordanian crisis confirmed what Ben Gurion, Eshkol, and Meir had been saying for more than a decade: Israel could serve the United States as a strategic asset. "The President will never forget Israel's role in preventing the deterioration in Jordan," Kissinger informed Rabin on 25 September 1970. "He said that the United States is fortunate in having an ally like Israel in the Middle East."[135]

Over the next three years Nixon and Kissinger would demonstrate time and again that they meant what they said. During 1971, for example, the White House repeatedly undercut State Department efforts to force the Israelis to return Egyptian territory seized during the Six Day War. In February 1972 the United States agreed to sell Israel another forty-two F-4 Phantoms and eighty-two A-4 Skyhawks. By the summer of 1973 the CIA and the Mossad, the chief Israeli intelligence agency, were comparing notes on Palestinian terrorists and Arab radicals.[136]

The acid test of the Nixon administration's strategic relationship with Israel, however, would come in the autumn of 1973, when Egypt and Syria launched a surprise attack on the Jewish state during Yom Kippur. With the Syrian army threatening to retake the Golan Heights and with Egyptian forces inflicting heavy losses on Israeli troops in the Sinai, Prime Minister Meir urgently requested that Washington airlift everything from small arms to tanks to replace the war matériel destroyed by the Arabs. Following a series of round-the-clock meetings with Kissinger and other NSC officials, Nixon approved Meir's request on 14 October and instructed the Pentagon to "send everything that will fly."[137] By the time the airlift ended on 15 November 1973, U.S. Air Force C-5As and C-130s had flown nearly 700 sorties and had ferried 11,000 tons of military hardware to Israel.[138]

Interest group politics seems to have been less important than geopolitical considerations in Nixon's decision to rearm Israel during the October War. To be sure, a bipartisan delegation of pro-Israel senators and representatives did visit the White House on 10 October. AIPAC did mobilize American Jewish organizations to support the emergency airlift in the days that followed. And Nixon did assure friends of the Jewish state on Capitol Hill that "we will not let Israel go down the tubes."[139] Larger issues, however, influenced deliberations inside the Nixon administration. According to Secretary of Defense James Schlesinger, some U.S. policymakers feared that if Washington did not replenish Tel Aviv's conventional arsenal, the Israelis might resort to nuclear weapons to avoid defeat. "From where we sat," Schlesinger recalled long afterward, "there was an assumption that Israel had a few nukes and that if there was a collapse, there was a possibility that Israel would use them."[140] Moreover, with the Watergate scandal slowly sapping Nixon's authority at home and eroding his credibility abroad, Schlesinger and other high-ranking U.S. officials regarded the highly visible airlift to Israel as the best way to signal the world that the United States had no intention of abandoning its friends in the Middle East.[141]

On 16 June 1974 Air Force One touched down just outside Tel Aviv, and Richard Nixon became the first U.S. president to visit Israel. Greeted cordially by Yitzhak Rabin, who had recently succeeded Golda Meir as prime minister, both Nixon and Henry Kissinger assured their host that they regarded the Jewish state as a strategic asset. "Israel was our friend and ally; we stood together through grave crises," Kissinger recalled telling Rabin. Before returning to Washington, Nixon likewise "stressed his willingness to continue long-term economic and military aid." But he was also quick to add "that in return he expected Israeli flexibility at the conference table."[142] As he prepared to step down, Nixon reflected on his many achievements in the Middle East and realized that he was bequeathing a paradoxical legacy in that troubled region. "We would make Israel strong enough that they would not fear to negotiate," he confided in his diary, "but not so strong that they felt they had no need to negotiate."[143]

Navigating between Israel's fears and needs was something that would preoccupy Gerald Ford as he completed the final twenty-nine months of Nixon's second term. A Michigan Republican who had developed a reputation as a quiet but firm friend of Israel during his eight years as House minority leader and his eight months at Blair House, President Ford worried in early 1975 that Prime Minister Rabin's "nitpicking" and "shortsighted" attitude toward negotiations with Egypt and Syria might jeopardize broader U.S. efforts to reduce tensions in the Middle East.[144] Upon learning that Henry Kissinger's latest round of Arab-Israeli shuttle diplomacy had reached a dead end in Tel

Aviv, Ford wrote Rabin on 21 March to express "profound disappointment over Israel's attitude in the course of the negotiations" and to announce "a reassessment of United States policy in the region, including our relations with Israel." Hinting strongly that the Jewish state was fast becoming a diplomatic liability, Ford also pointedly postponed any decision on Israel's latest request to purchase a squadron of F-15 jets until the reassessment was completed.[145]

Ford laid out the rationale for his painful decision a week later. "Since I have been in office, we have worked with Israel to try and get a settlement," he reminded the NSC on 28 March. "But when the chips were down they showed a lack of flexibility which was needed for an agreement." Insisting that he had "always liked and respected the Israeli people," Ford confessed that he had "never been so disappointed" as he was now by Israeli leaders, who seemed "unable to see that we are trying to do something for their interest as well as for our own." Waxing categorical about "more Israeli flexibility being in the best interests of peace," he concluded that "the time has come for a good hard look" at the special relationship. "I will catch flak for my position," Ford admitted, "but in the final analysis our commitment is to the United States."[146]

The flak generated by Gerald Ford's reassessment of U.S. relations with Israel caught up with him very quickly. The Israelis and their American supporters were not happy, but neither were they surprised. Ford's action, Rabin recalled in his memoirs, "heralded one of the worst periods in American-Israeli relations." Morris Amitay, the hard-driving former congressional staffer who had succeeded Si Kenen as director of AIPAC a few months earlier, mounted an aggressive pro-Israel campaign on Capitol Hill. On 21 May 1975 Gerald Ford received a letter signed by seventy-six U.S. senators from both sides of the aisle advising him to "be responsive to Israel's urgent military and economic needs" and to be wary of Arab promises of peace. "We urge you to make it clear, as we do," the senators concluded, "that the United States acting in its own national interests stands firmly with Israel in the search for peace." Bristling at what he regarded as a heavy-handed Israeli attempt to exert "home-front political pressure," Ford engaged in "a test of wills" with Rabin throughout the summer of 1975. "The Israelis," Ford complained in his memoirs, "were always insisting that we supply them more military equipment than our own experts thought they needed."[147] The Americans, Rabin retorted in his memoirs, seemed intent on "singling out Israel as the principal culprit" for the diplomatic stalemate in the Middle East.[148]

After wrangling all summer, Ford and Rabin struck a deal on 1 September 1975 that enabled them to paper over their differences. In exchange for $1.5 billion in U.S. military assistance and a commitment to station 200 American civilian observers in the Sinai Desert, the Israelis promised to evacuate oil fields and other strategically important positions seized from Egypt. Relieved that

U.S. relations with the Jewish state had finally taken a turn for the better, Ford assured congressional leaders three days later that "Israel is in very good shape" and pledged that "we will continue to provide Israel [with] the defensive weapons it needs."[149] But despite greater cooperation in the struggle for peace and closer coordination in the battle against terrorism, Ford and Rabin never succeeded in rekindling the diplomatic magic ignited by Johnson and Eshkol during the late 1960s and perfected by Nixon and Meir during the early 1970s.

Election results in both the United States and Israel dampened the special relationship still further. On 3 November 1976 Gerald Ford was narrowly defeated by Jimmy Carter, a Georgia Democrat and born-again Christian who shocked the Israelis and their U.S. supporters shortly after his inauguration by publicly endorsing the concept of a Palestinian homeland.[150] Yitzhak Rabin, whose Labor Party already faced an uphill battle against Menachem Begin's right-wing Likud coalition in Israeli elections scheduled for the spring of 1977, concluded that "Israel would probably have to pay heavily until the new American government acquired expertise and political maturity." But this price proved too high for many Israeli voters, who chose Begin as their new prime minister by a narrow margin on 17 May. Rabin interpreted the outcome as a signal that nasty diplomatic weather lay ahead. "If Israel was unable to rely upon the United States as a friend and ally," he explained in a postelection postmortem, "then she would have to entrust her fate to a 'tough' and 'uncompromising' leadership to protect her vital interests."[151]

Menachem Begin was as tough and uncompromising in May 1977 as he had been three decades earlier when he had led the Irgun into battle during Israel's war for independence. A staunch expansionist, Begin made no secret of his intention to incorporate the West Bank—what he liked to call Judea and Samaria—into Israel, sooner rather than later. "It was frightening," Jimmy Carter confided in his diary on 23 May, "to watch his adamant position on issues that must be resolved if a Middle Eastern peace settlement is going to be realized." Throughout the last half of 1977 and well into 1978 Carter tangled repeatedly with Begin over everything from Israeli territorial concessions in the Sinai to U.S. arms for Saudi Arabia. Carter's task was not made any easier by complaints from Capitol Hill and Main Street that the new administration seemed to be tilting toward the Arabs. The Georgia Democrat tried to shore up his "damaged political base among Israel's American friends" by assuring key members of Congress and Jewish leaders that the United States remained firmly committed to Israeli security.[152] But when Carter proposed selling F-15 jets to Saudi Arabia and Egypt in February 1978, a political firestorm exploded inside the Beltway, where AIPAC's Morris Amitay charged that the White House was betraying Israel. Although the president secured congressional approval for the arms sales in May, many friends of Israel voted Republican in the off-year elections six months later to protest what they regarded as Carter's pro-Arab and anti-Israel policies.[153]

Nothing cast the strains in America's special relationship with Israel into sharper relief during the Carter years than the Camp David Accords of September 1978. After months of prodding and cajoling, Israel's Menachem Begin and Egypt's Anwar Sadat accepted Jimmy Carter's invitation to commence peace talks at the presidential retreat in Maryland's Catoctin Mountains. Following two weeks of grueling negotiations, Carter was able to broker an eleventh-hour compromise, with Israel agreeing to withdraw from the Sinai and to commence Palestinian autonomy talks within three years in exchange for a formal peace treaty with Egypt. Although Carter was all smiles as he watched Sadat and Begin initial the accords on 17 September 1978, he worried privately that Israel was far more interested in a separate peace with Egypt than in a lasting peace with the Palestinians. After a series of nasty diplomatic exchanges with Israel, the Carter administration opted in March 1980 to support a United Nations resolution affirming Arab rights on the West Bank and in East Jerusalem. Influenced by AIPAC's claims that Carter was selling out the Jewish state, many of Israel's American friends declined to vote for the Georgia Democrat eight months later and helped widen Ronald Reagan's margin of victory on election day.[154]

The Reagan administration briefly breathed new life into America's tattered special relationship with Israel. A California Republican who had long admired the Israelis for their pluck and perseverance, Ronald Reagan confessed in his memoirs that "no conviction I've ever held has been stronger than my belief that the United States must ensure the survival of Israel." It is not surprising that candidate Reagan labeled the Jewish state a "strategic asset," nor was anyone shocked when President Reagan embraced Prime Minister Begin as an ally in America's battle against international terrorism.[155] Secretary of State Alexander Haig, an unreconstructed Cold Warrior who had earlier served as Nixon's chief of staff, likewise sought Israeli support during early 1981 for an anti-Communist "strategic consensus" designed to combat the Kremlin and its Arab clients. On 30 November 1981 Reagan and Begin unveiled a new Israeli-American memorandum of understanding heralding a "mutual security relationship" designed "to enhance strategic cooperation to deter all threats from the Soviet Union" in the Middle East.[156]

Notwithstanding their common anti-Soviet rhetoric, however, U.S. and Israeli policymakers diverged sharply regarding how best to approach the Arab world. Convinced that the House of Saud required sophisticated AWACS (airborne warning and control system) surveillance aircraft to protect itself from its radical neighbors in Iraq and Iran, the Reagan administration fought and won a bitter battle on Capitol Hill, where AIPAC, with Begin's blessing, tried unsuccessfully during the autumn of 1981 to prevent congressional approval of an $8.5 billion Saudi-American arms deal. As the year drew to a close, the White House was equally unsuccessful in preventing the Jewish state from formally annexing the Golan Heights, territory the Israelis regarded as essential in protecting themselves against the radical regime next door in Syria. Hoping to force Begin to rethink his unilateral policies, the White House rescinded the recent memorandum of understanding just before Christmas and froze $300 million in military aid. But Begin held his ground. "What kind of talk is this—'penalizing' Israel?" he snapped at U.S. ambassador Samuel Lewis on 20 December. "Are we a banana republic?" Begin was quick to provide his own answer. "The people of Israel lived without the memorandum of understanding for 3700 years," he reminded Lewis, "and will continue to live without it for another 3700 years."[157]

Begin's decision to invade Lebanon six months later threatened to drive Israel and the United States still farther apart. As early as December 1981 Israeli defense minister Ariel Sharon had warned Philip Habib, a State Department troubleshooter in the Middle East, that unless the Palestinians halted their guerrilla forays into northern Israel from base camps just across the Lebanese border, "we will have no choice but to wipe them out completely in Lebanon [and] destroy the PLO's infrastructure there." Stunned by Sharon's vow "to eradicate the PLO in Lebanon," Habib tried to flash him a red light. "General Sharon, this is the 20th century and times have changed," Habib explained. "You can't go around invading countries just like that, spreading destruction and killing civilians."[158]

Unfazed by this history lesson, in May 1982 Sharon flew to Washington, where he bluntly informed Habib's boss that Israel was about to "deliver a knockout blow to the PLO." Secretary of State Haig recalls telling his Israeli visitor "privately, in the plainest possible language," that "unless there was an internationally recognized provocation, and unless Israeli retaliation was proportionate to any such provocation, an attack by Israel into Lebanon would have a devastating effect in the United States."[159] The diplomatic signal that Haig claims was unmistakably red, however, struck some of his colleagues as being a different color. "There was a clear, strong amber light," Ambassador Samuel Lewis recalled a decade later, an amber light that tempted Israeli leaders to seek a pretext to invade Lebanon. Raymond Tanter, a Middle East expert in the Reagan White House, agreed. "Washington officials charged with the conduct of U.S.-Israeli relations must play by explicit rules of the road," Tanter recently told an interviewer, "lest they leave an opening through which Israeli tanks might rumble."[160]

In June 1982 Israeli tanks would rumble all the way to Beirut after Palestinian terrorists attempted to kill an Israeli diplomat in London. Billed as a surgical strike to root out the PLO infrastructure, Operation Peace for Galilee quickly became a bloody military stalemate. It sparked murderous sectarian violence between Lebanese Christians and Palestinian refugees and prompted the Reagan administration to dispatch a battalion of U.S. Marine peacekeepers to Lebanon, where before the end of the year they would become targets for Muslim extremists. Relations between the United States and Israel sank to a new low in January 1983, when U.S. and Israeli troops engaged in a series of highly publicized military shoving matches just outside Beirut.[161]

After Yitzhak Shamir replaced the exhausted Begin in the autumn of 1983, the Reagan administration briefly hoped that the situation might take a turn for the better. On 29 October Reagan approved National Security Decision Directive 111, which proposed resurrecting the earlier strategic consensus between Israel and the United States, and sent Undersecretary of State Lawrence Eagleburger to Jerusalem with one overriding message. "The President and everyone in the Administration want to sit down with you and really talk about strategic cooperation in the future—in Lebanon, in the Middle East generally, and everywhere," Eagleburger assured Shamir. "You and we have a long-standing special relationship. This is the time for defining it."[162] Israel's new prime minister, however, was a firm believer in unilateralism and self-reliance and rejected Reagan's overture. Instead, he insisted on a security zone in southern Lebanon, expanded Jewish settlements on the West Bank and in Gaza, and permitted Israeli intelligence to buy U.S. military secrets from Jonathan Pollard, a low-level Pentagon employee whose arrest in 1985 embarrassed Israel's American friends. Israel's role as middleman in the Iran-Contra arms-for-hostages fiasco a year later proved even more embarrassing.[163]

Bitter disagreements between Shamir and Reagan's successor, George Bush, over the expansion of Jewish settlements in the occupied territories created the impression that relations between the United States and Israel were not really very special at all. Indeed, after Secretary of State James Baker publicly labeled Shamir's handling of those settlements "unrealistic" in May 1989, Israel's friends and foes alike wondered whether the Bush administration might be headed for a collision with the Jewish state unprecedented since the Eisenhower era. Despite barbed comments from Bush and Baker, however, at key moments during the early 1990s Israel and the United States managed to warm up to each other. Because both sides realized that Israel's involvement in the Gulf War would undermine Arab support for the broad coalition the United States was mobilizing against Saddam Hussein, Israeli and U.S. officials agreed that the Pentagon should deploy Patriot surface-to-air missiles to protect Tel Aviv from Iraqi Scud missiles. After the shooting stopped in the Persian Gulf, Shamir sent an Israeli delegation to Madrid to resume the process of making peace with the Palestinians.[164]

Only with the election of Yitzhak Rabin as prime minister in June 1992, however, did the old special relationship show signs of resurfacing between Israel and the United States. Within weeks Rabin was privately assuring Secretary of State Baker that he would reduce the Israeli presence in the occupied territories.[165] A year later, with help and encouragement from President Bill Clinton, a longtime supporter of the Jewish state, the Israelis agreed to freeze settlements on the West Bank, setting the stage for Yitzhak Rabin's Rose Garden rendezvous with Yasser Arafat in September 1993. A few moments after the historic handshake, Clinton reminded everyone that "the United States is committed to the security of Israel," insisted that "we want to do some more joint strategic thinking," and hinted that "we may wind up doing more in terms of shared technology."[166]

Rabin's assassination in November 1995 and the defeat of his successor, Shimon Peres, at the polls six months later, however, led many inside the Clinton administration to suspect that the special relationship might once again be in jeopardy. Prime Minister Benjamin Netanyahu, a U.S.-educated hawk and longtime supporter of Begin and Shamir's plans for a Greater Israel, did nothing to dispel those suspicions when he distanced himself from Rabin's peace initiatives during his first visit to the White House in July 1996. "Clinton came out of the meeting saying that Netanyahu behaved and spoke in a tone that didn't seem to let on that he knew that Clinton was President of a friendly superpower, and that Netanyahu was the leader of a small nation who needs the superpower's support," Israeli ambassador Itamar Rabinovich remarked afterward. Nor did the prime minister endear himself to the Arkansas Democrat with a mocking reference to the United States as Israel's strategic asset a year later.[167]

But Netanyahu had maintained that the special relationship must be reshaped to reflect diverging Israeli and U.S. interests long before he became prime minister. "The task of Israel's leaders is to try to *convince* the American government that it is in the interest of the United States to follow policies that cohere with Israeli interests, not vice versa," Netanyahu observed in May 1993. In the United States "the administration, the Congress, and especially popular opinion" were "very much open to persuasion," he added, and "Israel has every fair opportunity to try to convince each of them of the justice of its case."[168]

Unpersuaded by Netanyahu's bluntness, U.S. policymakers hoped that Ehud Barak would be elected prime minister in May 1999. Two months after a landslide victory orchestrated by Clinton confidant James Carville, Barak made a triumphant visit to Washington, where he affirmed his commitment to the peace process and signed a $2.5 billion dollar arms deal for fifty F-16E fighter-bombers. But he also chided Clinton for his "patronizing" attitude and insisted that the United States must never become the "policeman, judge and arbitrator" of Israel's relations with the Arabs.[169] Barak's decision to pull Israeli forces out of southern Lebanon in May 2000 demonstrated that he was willing to take risks for peace, as did his eagerness for summit talks with Yasser Arafat later that summer. When Israeli, Palestinian, and U.S. officials sat down at Camp David in mid-July, however, sparks flew, not only because Arafat proved intransigent from the start but also because at the last moment Barak retracted an offer to transfer three villages on the outskirts of Jerusalem to Arab control. Having assured the Palestinians that the Israeli offer was a done deal, Clinton was humiliated by the eleventh-hour reversal and angrily informed Barak that he was tired of being treated "like a wooden Indian doing your bidding."[170]

Despite Clinton's best efforts, the summit collapsed, Barak and Arafat returned home amidst bitter recriminations, and violence flared in the occupied territories. By the end of the year the Palestinian body count was approaching 200, Israel was plagued by suicide bombings and drive-by shootings, and Ariel Sharon, who had succeeded Netanyahu as the leader of the Likud, was denouncing the U.S.-backed peace process as little more than appeasement. Coming just three weeks after George W. Bush moved into the Oval Office, Sharon's victory over Barak in February 2001 prompted the new administration to reassess America's special relationship with Israel. Seven months later, as Washington scrambled to secure Arab support for an antiterrorist coalition following the attacks on the World Trade Center, the Bush administration shocked Sharon by announcing that the United States stood ready to endorse a Palestinian state. In an emotional speech that evoked memories of the Holocaust, the Israeli prime minister likened George W. Bush to Neville Chamberlain. "Do not repeat the dreadful mistake of 1938, when enlightened European democracies decided to sacrifice Czechoslovakia for a convenient temporary solution," Sharon thundered on 4 October. "Do not try to appease the Arabs at our expense." Although Sharon was quick to apologize for his "unfortunate metaphor" after the White House termed his remarks "unacceptable," many Israeli and U.S. observers wondered whether their two nations were headed for another showdown like the one between Eisenhower and Ben Gurion forty-five years earlier.[171]

In short, a half-century after Harry Truman helped put the Jewish state on the map, the Israeli-American special relationship was being restructured, largely because neither side could agree whether Israel should be America's partner or merely its proxy. Every administration from Truman's to Bush's believed that it possessed the economic and military leverage to force Israel to fall into line on everything from Palestinian refugees to nuclear weapons. AIPAC's political potency and Israel's military prowess, on the other hand, convinced David Ben Gurion and his successors that their country need not always do America's bidding. Viewed from Washington, Israel sometimes proved a strategic asset and other times constituted a diplomatic liability. Viewed from Moscow, the complex relationship between the United States and Israel seemed to offer an unequaled opportunity to expand Soviet influence and undermine U.S. interests in the Middle East. During the five decades after the Second World War, U.S. leaders would fashion a succession of strategic doctrines designed to prove the Kremlin wrong.

If you want a war, nourish a doctrine. Doctrines are the most fearful tyrants to which men ever are subject, because doctrines get inside of a man's own reason and betray him against himself. Civilized men have done their fiercest fighting for doctrines.
—William Graham Sumner, *War* (1903)

The region which is now threatened by Soviet troops in Afghanistan is of great strategic importance: It contains more than two-thirds of the world's exportable oil. . . .

Let our position be absolutely clear: An attempt by any outside force to gain control of the Persian Gulf region will be regarded as an assault on the vital interests of the United States of America, and such an assault will be repelled by any means necessary, including military force.
—Jimmy Carter lays out the Carter Doctrine, 1980

A Tale of Four Doctrines

*U.S. National Security, the Soviet Threat,
and the Middle East*

Although the promise of Israel as America's strategic asset was never quite fulfilled, Washington's pursuit of such a relationship was part of a more ambitious quest to promote regional defense and prevent communist inroads in the Middle East after 1945. Wedded to an evolving doctrine of national security that defined the Soviet Union as a mortal threat to the United States and that dictated global vigilance against Russian-backed communist subversion, U.S. policymakers from Harry Truman to Jimmy Carter waged a Cold War against the Kremlin from the sun-drenched shores of the Eastern Mediterranean to the snow-capped mountains of Afghanistan. Some historians point to the Red Army's belated departure from Iran in early 1946 and to its sudden arrival in Kabul in late 1979 as proof of Moscow's unwavering drive to dominate the Middle East. Other scholars, however, argue that U.S. leaders overreacted to Russian diplomatic pressure during the late 1940s and overestimated Soviet responsibility for the anti-Western upheavals that rocked the Muslim world during the decades that followed. While definitive answers regarding Soviet motivation must await further revelations from the Russian archives, a careful examination of the U.S. documentary record confirms that Uncle Sam's reliance on doctrinal prescriptions to cure diplomatic insecurity has deep roots in the American past.

A fragile republic in a world dominated by imperial powers such as Great Britain, the newly independent United States relied more on geographic remoteness than military preparedness to defend itself well into the nineteenth century. But in December 1823 the specter of European aggrandizement from the Pacific Northwest to Cape Horn prompted President James Monroe to stake America's claim to a sphere of influence in the Western Hemisphere in a doctrine that bears his name. Proclaiming that the independent nations of the New World were "henceforth not to be considered as subjects for future colonization by any European powers," Monroe declared that the United States would regard "any attempt on their part to extend their system to any portion of this hemisphere as dangerous to our peace and security."[1] The most formidable challenge to the Monroe Doctrine came from the British, whose designs on Texas, Cuba, and Venezuela triggered periodic clashes with the United States through the 1890s. By the turn of the century, however, Britain had lost interest in the Western Hemisphere and turned its attention to matters both more pressing and more profitable, such as the acquisition of oil concessions in the Persian Gulf and imperial lines of communication in the Eastern Mediterranean.[2]

Among the first Americans to appreciate the strategic importance of the Middle East for the British was Captain Alfred Thayer Mahan, a naval historian whose books on sea power had become Gilded Age best-sellers. Indeed, Mahan inadvertently provided the region with its modern name. "The middle East, if I may adopt a term which I have not seen, will some day need its Malta as well as its Gibraltar," Mahan prophesied in a 1902 essay detailing Britain's ceaseless efforts to keep Russia out of the Eastern Mediterranean and the Indian Ocean. He expected the British to expand their naval base in Aden at the mouth of the Red Sea and to establish new outposts in the tiny sheikdoms that rimmed the Persian Gulf. Whitehall's most important regional stronghold, however, was certain to be the isthmus of Suez, bisected by a British-controlled canal whose commercial and military significance was, in Mahan's eyes, unsurpassed in the entire Eastern Hemisphere.[3] Although Whitehall managed to fulfill most of Mahan's prophecy during the first two decades of the twentieth century, the Second World War badly damaged the British Empire and fundamentally altered the balance of power in the Middle East.

Having served as the cornerstone for U.S. diplomacy in the Western Hemisphere for more than 100 years, the Monroe Doctrine seems subconsciously to have become an intellectual lodestone for U.S. policymakers seeking to stabilize the Middle East after 1945. Hoping to avoid a vacuum in a region whose strategic importance was fast becoming unparalleled, the White House agreed in March 1947 to assume Britain's long-standing commitments in Greece and Turkey under the auspices of the Truman Doctrine, with the understanding that Whitehall would retain primary responsibility for the defense of the Arab world. Following a decade of ugly Anglo-Arab confrontations that undermined regional security and invited Soviet meddling, in 1957 U.S. policymakers unveiled the Eisenhower Doctrine, which made Washington the senior member of the Anglo-American partnership in the Middle East. When Britain's deepening financial woes eventually forced Whitehall to liquidate its last imperial outposts in the Arabian Peninsula and the Persian Gulf in the late 1960s, U.S. officials edged toward what came to be known as the Nixon Doctrine, which envisioned regional proxies such as Iran and Saudi Arabia serving as junior partners against the Kremlin. When events in Iran and Afghanistan showed that America's proxies simply could not do the job, Jimmy Carter promulgated his own doctrine and, with a bow to Harry Truman, informed the world in January 1980 that the United States had vital security interests in the Middle East for which it was willing to fight, whether it had dependable partners or not.

To the Truman Doctrine and Beyond, 1941–1952

When Harry Truman took the oath of office thirty-five years earlier, he hoped that the British would remain reliable partners in the Middle East. Throughout the early 1940s the Roosevelt administration had assumed that postwar Britain would continue to play its historic role as the chief guarantor of security in the region. "The Indian Ocean, Persian Gulf, Red Sea, Libya and the Mediterranean," FDR had cabled Prime Minister Winston Churchill in a March 1942 recap of the Anglo-American plan of battle against the Axis, "would fall directly under British responsibility."[4] But Hitler made Churchill's task as difficult as possible, and U.S. officials soon questioned whether Whitehall was capable of fulfilling its regional duties. "Great Britain," Patrick Hurley, one of FDR's roving ambassadors, remarked after visiting Egypt in May 1943, "no longer possesses within herself the essentials of power needed to maintain her traditional role as the dominant influence in the Middle East area."[5]

Hurley's diagnosis was confirmed by the steady erosion of Whitehall's position and by subtle indications that the Kremlin was quietly preparing to fill the resulting vacuum. As early as the spring of 1944 U.S. observers were reporting that "Soviet policy in the Arab world appears to be aimed at the reduction of British influence in that area and the acquisition of the balance of power."[6] By V-E Day, State Department experts had concluded that if Britain could no longer prevent the Soviet Union from fishing in troubled waters, the United States might have to assume responsibility for "fostering the economic advancement of the Middle East peoples" and "facilitating freedom from external interference and exploitation."[7]

That the Kremlin sought to expand its influence along Russia's southern flank after the Second World War is beyond doubt. After all, Josef Stalin, the brutal and ruthless dictator who had held sway in Moscow for nearly two decades, had sent thousands of Soviet troops into northern Iran in 1941 and had recently stepped up diplomatic pressure on Turkey, which had long refused to allow the Red Navy to pass through the Dardanelles, the narrow straits that connected the Black Sea with the Mediterranean. Although the nature of Stalin's ultimate objectives remained far from clear, by the autumn of 1945 U.S. policymakers tended to expect the worst. "The British publicly admit that they are no longer able to keep the Middle East in order without our help," State Department officials warned the White House in mid-October, and "Soviet Russia is showing marked interest in the area." Unless the United States responded "firmly and adequately," Foggy Bottom's experts concluded, "a situation might well develop in the Near East which would result in another World War."[8]

Loy Henderson, one of the State Department's leading authorities on Soviet foreign policy, outlined the implications of the impending crisis in the Middle East in a graphic memorandum that found its way to the Oval Office early in the new year. "The national objectives of two Great Powers, namely the Soviet Union and Great Britain," he pointed out on 28 December 1945, "collide head-on in this region." Whitehall was still "endeavoring to use the Near Eastern area as a great dam . . . to hold back the flow of Russia towards the south." The Kremlin, on the other hand, "seems to be determined to break down the structure which Great Britain has maintained so that Russian power and influence can sweep unimpeded across Turkey and through the Dardanelles into the Mediterranean, across Iran and through the Persian Gulf to the Indian Ocean." Henderson believed that Washington could ill afford to allow Moscow to succeed. "During the last five years, two great barriers to Russian expansion have disappeared, namely Germany in the West and Japan in the East," he concluded. "Judging from recent events in the Near East, Russia now appears to be concentrating upon the removal of a third barrier in the South."[9] For Truman's administration as for Monroe's 120 years earlier, an autocratic Old World power seemed to pose a threat to vital U.S. security interests in a region whose people were in the process of winning their independence from imperial rule.

It did not take long for a consensus to emerge in Washington that the United States must establish a national security state capable of preventing Soviet encroachments in the Middle East and other parts of the world. The Truman administration's most pressing concern was the situation in Iran, where despite the Kremlin's assurances to the contrary, the Red Army was tightening its grip on Azerbaijan province, 200 miles northwest of Tehran. When Stalin failed to fulfill his wartime pledge to withdraw his troops from Iran no later than 2 March, the State Department fired off a blistering protest condemning the prolonged Soviet occupation as a "gross violation" of Iranian sovereignty and territorial integrity that held "many dangerous implications."[10]

Washington's point man during the Iranian crisis was James F. Byrnes, a feisty South Carolina Democrat who had headed Roosevelt's Office of War Mobilization until Truman named him secretary of state shortly after V-E Day. Once it was clear that the Soviets had ignored the U.S. protest and were reinforcing the Red Army and encouraging a left-wing separatist movement in Azerbaijan, Byrnes beat one fist into his other hand on 6 March and growled, "Now we'll give it to them with both barrels."[11] Barrel number one was a U.S.-sponsored United Nations resolution branding the Kremlin's presence in northern Iran a threat to world peace. Barrel number two consisted of vague hints that the United States stood ready to use armed force to expel the Soviets from Azerbaijan, a scenario that generated a flurry of headlines forecasting a third world war. In the event, Byrnes's double-barreled shotgun proved less effective than the single-minded diplomatic horse-trading of Iranian prime minister Ahmad Qavam, who flew to Moscow in mid-March and persuaded the Kremlin to withdraw all of its troops from Azerbaijan in return for assurances of Soviet access to Iranian oil reserves.

Although many scholars have recently interpreted the Soviet withdrawal on 6 May 1946 as evidence that the Kremlin's objectives were relatively limited, Truman and his senior advisers regarded the Red Army's prolonged presence in northern Iran as a probing action that presaged a more general Russian offensive in the Middle East. As the Soviet-American confrontation in Iran had moved toward its climax, George Kennan, the insightful U.S. chargé d'affaires in Moscow, had warned Washington on 22 February in his famous "Long Telegram" that the "Kremlin's neurotic view of world affairs" and its "traditional and instinctive Russian sense of insecurity" were likely to spell serious trouble for other neighboring states such as Turkey. Six months later Stalin unveiled a proposal calling for joint Soviet and Turkish control of the Dardanelles. Fearing that Moscow was ready to resort to armed force if the straits remained closed, the Turks sought help from Britain and the United States.[12]

The traditional and instinctive American sense of insecurity helped ensure that U.S. policymakers adopted a worst-case scenario in dealing with the Turkish request. During an Oval Office meeting on 15 August, Truman and his top advisers concluded that "the primary objective of the Soviet Union is to obtain control of Turkey." Dismissing the possibility that the Kremlin would limit itself to securing safe and unimpeded passage through the Dardanelles, U.S. officials worried that a Russian triumph in Turkey would make it "extremely difficult, if not impossible, to prevent the Soviet Union from obtaining control over Greece and over the whole Near and Middle East."[13] U.K. policymakers were as determined as their U.S. counterparts to prevent Soviet inroads into Turkey and elsewhere in the region. Coordinating their actions, Whitehall and the White House privately advised the Turks to reject the Kremlin's unilateral power play and publicly suggested that the fate of the Turkish straits be resolved by an international conference to be attended by all maritime powers, including Britain and the United States.[14]

Notwithstanding the apocalyptic scenarios popular on both sides of the Atlantic, the Turco-Soviet crisis ended with a whimper rather than a bang. Although Moscow continued to harass Ankara diplomatically, Stalin never tried to force his way through the Dardanelles, nor did the Red Army occupy eastern Turkey. Moreover, Stalin expressed no interest in attending an international conference on the Turkish straits, where he was certain to be outvoted by the United States and Great Britain. As the year drew to a close, a combination of U.S. diplomatic and economic support and British military aid seemed to have assuaged Turkish anxieties. Yet the Truman administration was well aware that its policy in Turkey, and in the region as a whole, hinged on help from Washington's faltering partner in London. "If a case should arise where Britain is not in a position to furnish the necessary arms and military equipment" to the Turks or their neighbors, the State Department observed on 21 October 1946, the United States would have to "consider furnishing certain supplies direct."[15]

Just such a case arose a few months later across the Aegean Sea in Athens, where a deepening political crisis forced Washington to assume most of London's responsibilities under the auspices of the Truman Doctrine. By the autumn of 1946 Greece was embroiled in a bloody civil war that pitted communist-led guerrillas against a right-wing government armed and financed by Britain. In early 1947 U.K. officials informed the Truman administration that acute economic problems required a drastic reduction in London's role in Athens and urged Washington "to afford financial assistance to Greece on scale sufficient to meet her minimum needs, both civil and military."[16] Having monitored the deteriorating situation for more than two years, U.S. policymakers privately acknowledged that most of Greece's woes were homegrown, not imported from Moscow. But American officials were also well aware that a left-wing victory in the Greek civil war would be widely interpreted as a triumph for the Kremlin. "Soviets feel that Greece is a ripe plum ready to fall into their hands in a few weeks," Mark Ethridge, the U.S. representative on the U.N. observation team stationed in Athens, cabled Foggy Bottom on 17 February.[17] Undersecretary of State Dean Acheson could not have agreed more. "The capitulation of Greece to Soviet domination through lack of adequate support from the U.S. and Great Britain," he observed grimly on 21 February, "might eventually result in the loss of the whole Near and Middle East and northern Africa."[18]

Acheson's boss was equally pessimistic. Whitehall's withdrawal from Greece, Secretary of State George Marshall sighed on 24 February, was "tantamount to British abdication from the Middle East with obvious implications as to their successor."[19] Three days later Harry Truman invited congressional leaders to the White House, where Marshall and Acheson briefed them on the bleak situation in the Eastern Mediterranean. "Soviet pressure on the Straits, on Iran, and on northern Greece had brought the Balkans to the point where a highly possible Soviet breakthrough might open three continents to Soviet penetration," Acheson told the stunned lawmakers. "Like apples in a barrel infected by one rotten one, the corruption of Greece would infect Iran and all to the east."[20] With so much at stake, the president informed his visitors that he had "decided to extend aid to Greece and Turkey" and expressed his hope that "Congress would provide the means to make this aid timely and sufficient."[21]

On the afternoon of 12 March Truman delivered a momentous eighteen-minute address to a joint session of Congress declaring that U.S. national security required the containment of the Soviet Union. Promulgating what soon became known as the Truman Doctrine, the president vowed that "it must be the policy of the United States to support free peoples who are resisting attempted subjugation by armed minorities or by outside pressures" and won swift congressional approval for a $400 million military and economic aid package to shore up anticommunist forces in Greece and Turkey.[22] The Truman administration broadened the agenda in early June by proposing a multibillion-dollar European Recovery Program that eventually became the Marshall Plan. On 25 July Congress passed the National Security Act, landmark legislation that established both the NSC and the CIA and that laid the groundwork for the creation of a single unified Department of Defense. By the autumn of 1947 the Truman Doctrine and other key components of America's Cold War national security state were in place.[23]

In mid-October Truman's top advisers invited British policymakers to the Pentagon for a series of skull sessions to determine how best to utilize these new components in the Middle East. As the Pentagon talks progressed, a rough consensus began to emerge. "Greece and Turkey are, politically and strategically, the North Western bastions of the Middle East," Foreign Office briefing papers pointed out, and "primary responsibility for aid to those countries now lies with the United States." For their part U.K. strategic planners would be free "to concentrate on those Middle East points which are our primary interest," such as the Persian Gulf oil fields and the Suez Canal.[24] This sort of arrangement was quite attractive to the Americans, who were preoccupied with combating the Kremlin in Europe and Asia. Noting that vital Western interests in the Middle East made it "essential that Soviet expansion in that area be contained," State Department officials hoped to cast "Britain in the role of a benevolent and welcome senior partner," with "primary responsibility for military security" throughout the Muslim world.[25] After hammering out position papers on everything from Afghanistan to Yemen, the two delegations affirmed their mutual desire "to follow parallel policies" and "to cooperate with and support the other in the area."[26]

The informal Anglo-American partnership in the Middle East foreshadowed by the Truman Doctrine and fleshed out during the Pentagon talks would be sorely tested in the months ahead. Assuming the role of the aggrieved senior partner, Whitehall complained throughout 1948 and well into 1949 that U.S. support for the creation of Israel was undermining Western security in the region by tempting the Arabs to seek Soviet help. Playing the part of the frustrated junior partner, Foggy Bottom retorted that British inflexibility in dealing with Muslim aspirations for self-government was equally important in driving pro-Western leaders in Egypt and Iran toward the Kremlin. When U.S. and U.K. experts gathered in Washington in November 1949, Assistant Secretary of State George McGhee wondered whether it might be time for a thorough reevaluation of the explosive situation in the Middle East. "Should the United States Government choose to assume greater responsibility in the area," Sir Michael Wright, McGhee's British counterpart, replied, "such a decision would be welcomed by the United Kingdom as being to the common advantage."[27]

McGhee's call for a review of America's approach to the Middle East was just one part of a much broader reassessment of U.S. national security policy that was taking shape as the year drew to a close. Distressed by a series of unexpected setbacks during the last half of 1949—the Kremlin's acquisition of nuclear weapons in August, the U.S. economy's sudden slide into a sharp recession in September, and the triumph of communism in China in October—many in Washington feared that the tide in the Cold War was turning decisively against the United States. Among those most troubled was Harry Truman, who on 31 January 1950 instructed the Departments of State and

Defense "to undertake a reexamination of our objectives in peace and war and of the effect of these objectives on our strategic plans."[28]

After ten weeks of nonstop brainstorming, on 7 April the Pentagon and Foggy Bottom sent President Truman NSC-68, an eye-opening sixty-six-page report that recommended a quadrupling of U.S. defense spending in order to globalize the policy of containment first outlined in the Truman Doctrine. Designed as a strategic game plan for winning the Cold War, NSC-68 called for rapid development of thermonuclear weapons, a psychological offensive against communism both at home and abroad, and the establishment of anti-Soviet regional defense groupings modeled on the recently created North Atlantic Treaty Organization (NATO). Although they mentioned Iran, Turkey, and Greece only in passing, the drafters of NSC-68 emphasized that "Soviet efforts are now directed toward the domination of the Eurasian land mass" and warned that the Kremlin might be preparing "to drive toward the oil-bearing areas of the Near and Middle East."[29]

How to strengthen the strategically positioned and economically important Arab states without fueling a Middle East arms race and jeopardizing Israeli security was the principal dilemma U.S. officials confronted during the spring of 1950 as they reviewed American policy toward the region. In NSC-65, a top secret study of security requirements in the Middle East completed just ten days before NSC-68, White House advisers welcomed Whitehall's plans to provide arms to Egypt as part of an "Anglo-Egyptian military partnership to assist the defense of the Near East in case of Soviet aggression." But to prevent the emergence of a regional arms imbalance that might tempt the Arabs to attack Israel, the drafters of NSC-65 recommended that Washington work closely with London to regulate tightly the influx of military hardware into the area.[30] Truman, who reviewed NSC-65 at a cabinet meeting on 14 April, "was much interested in this idea."[31] Broadening the scope of the proposal to include both British war matériel earmarked for the Arabs and French arms destined for Israel, U.S. diplomats unveiled a multilateral scheme in early May designed to minimize the danger of a regional conflagration. On 25 May 1950 Britain, France, and the United States signed the Tripartite Declaration, under which all three powers pledged to uphold the principles of arms control and territorial integrity in the Middle East.[32]

The eruption of the Korean War one month later galvanized support on Capitol Hill for the expensive national security programs laid out in NSC-68 and sparked renewed concern at the White House about potential Soviet aggression from the Persian Gulf to the Eastern Mediterranean. Having just witnessed the Kremlin's clients launch a surprise attack on South Korea, one of the most pro-American regimes in Asia, the Truman administration suspected that something more substantive than the Tripartite Declaration would be required to ensure peace and security in the Middle East, where anti-Western sentiment was spreading. By late October U.K. and U.S. policymakers were discussing an anti-Soviet regional defense initiative that would eventually come to be known as the Middle East Command (MEC). Pointing out that "whoever controls the Middle East controls access to three continents," Sir Oliver Franks, the British ambassador, and Field Marshall William J. Slim, chief of the Imperial General Staff, sought U.S. help in bringing Egypt aboard as a junior partner in a three-way alliance that would create an unbreachable barrier to Soviet expansion.[33] General Omar Bradley, chairman of the U.S. Joint Chiefs of Staff (JCS), expressed considerable interest in Whitehall's Egypt-centered plan for regional security. But with one eye on the escalating conflict in Korea and the other on rising tensions in Europe, General Lawton Collins, the army chief of staff, reiterated that from the Pentagon's point of view, "the Middle East is a British responsibility in case of a hot war."[34]

British and U.S. officials met again in early 1951 to discuss a MEC modeled on NATO. The MEC was to be composed of an "inner ring" consisting of Egypt and other Arab states led by a British supreme commander and linked to an "outer ring" stretching along Russia's southern flank from Greece to Iran. Convinced that this U.K. initiative would serve "to build up the will of the area to resist Communism" by working "to strengthen the whole Near Eastern will to defend itself and to join with the West," the Truman administration agreed to provide modest amounts of U.S. military assistance to key Arab states under the auspices of America's new Mutual Security Program.[35]

Despite the establishment of an Anglo-American working group in June charged with breathing life into the new regional security organization, the MEC was dead on arrival in December. The fatal blow was inflicted in mid-October by the Egyptians, who regarded the dire U.S. and U.K. concerns about the Soviet menace as a rhetorical fig leaf designed to conceal a far graver threat to Arab independence: British imperialism. Egypt's flat rejection of the MEC and its blunt demand that Whitehall evacuate the huge British military complex that straddled the Suez Canal, the NSC staff concluded two days before Christmas, was evidence of "the rapidly declining ability of the U.K. to maintain and defend Western interests in parts of the Middle East," which signaled "the decline of the U.K. as a world power" sooner rather than later. "Doubtful that . . . the U.S. or the U.K., or both together [could] maintain and defend Western interests in the area in the 19th century fashion," Truman's advisers believed that "the West must work toward . . . a new kind of relationship" with the nations of the Middle East.[36]

The new year, however, would bring only old wine in new bottles. Hoping to soothe a sore spot with Arab leaders for whom the word "command" evoked ugly memories of British imperialism, U.S. officials rechristened the MEC in

June 1952 as the Middle East Defense Organization (MEDO).[37] Semantics and nomenclature notwithstanding, the primary objective for MEDO, as for its predecessor, was the containment of the Soviet Union, something which rang increasingly hollow in the ears of Arabs who believed that they had more to fear from Whitehall than from the Kremlin. Later that summer top U.S. officials privately acknowledged that the security of Western interests in the Middle East would probably require not only a change in names but also an Anglo-American reversal in roles. Noting that "some parts of the area reminded me too much of the China situation for comfort," Assistant Secretary of State Henry Byroade warned Harry Truman on 8 August that "there was a great chance . . . that we would see a general withdrawal of the British from the Middle East" before the new defense organization had come into being. "If this happened," Byroade added, "the United States would be faced with some very fundamental decisions as to what we could do to help fill the vacuum thus created and maintain and strengthen the U.S. position in the area." Troubled by signs of instability from the Nile Delta to the Persian Gulf, Truman "agreed with this general analysis, indicating that he thought the United States would soon face just such a set of circumstances."[38]

Since he had already decided not to seek reelection in November, the Missouri Democrat doubtless took comfort from the knowledge that someone else would be responsible for filling the vacuum in the Middle East. Yet for the man who had promulgated the Truman Doctrine in March 1947, there must also have been much concern. A little more than five years after moving boldly to contain the Kremlin in Greece, Turkey, and Iran, Washington seemed destined to assume London's responsibilities for preventing Soviet expansion into the Arab world as well. By 1960 the United States would succeed Great Britain as the senior member of the Anglo-American partnership in the Middle East.

The Rise and Fall of the Eisenhower Doctrine, 1953–1960

Highly critical of the Truman administration for its oversolicitousness of British initiatives in the Middle East and its insufficient response to the Soviet threat, Dwight Eisenhower and John Foster Dulles entered office in early 1953 eager to establish America's role as the senior Western partner in the region. They initially believed that this objective could be achieved most easily by pursuing more aggressively the regional defense program developed by their predecessors. But Egypt's Gamal Abdel Nasser let it be known in mid-May that the Arabs regarded MEDO as a nonstarter. Reporting that only Pakistan and Turkey seemed interested in a British-led Middle Eastern NATO, Dulles told Eisenhower on 1 June 1953 that "the old MEDO concept was certainly finished" and recommended "a new concept for defense" grounded in "the contribution of the indigenous peoples."[39]

During the next eighteen months the Eisenhower administration worked to persuade Whitehall to shift its regional security policy away from defense in depth with an Arab core toward a perimeter defense along the "Northern Tier" extending from Turkey to Pakistan. But Sir Winston Churchill, who had returned as Britain's prime minister in late 1951, was far less interested in fortifying Turkey or Pakistan than in hanging on to British imperial outposts farther south in the Persian Gulf and the isthmus of Suez. Foreign Secretary Anthony Eden likewise confirmed that Britain would never relinquish its military installations in Egypt without ironclad assurances from Nasser regarding its residual right to defend the Suez Canal.[40]

By the time Churchill and Eden arrived at the White House in June 1954, however, a change in Whitehall's strategic doctrine had persuaded them to consider a slow-motion liquidation of Britain's position in Egypt. Earlier that spring U.K. military planners had concluded that the development of the hydrogen bomb made large strategic bases such as the one at Suez so vulnerable to devastating attack that they were, in effect, obsolete. "Our strategic needs in the Middle East," Churchill informed the Cabinet on the eve of his departure for Washington, "had been radically changed by the development of thermonuclear weapons."[41] Yet the British, he cautioned Eisenhower on 25 June, were not simply going to cut and run. "The situation must be avoided," he thundered, "in which people would think that the United States had driven the UK out of Egypt."[42] In short order Eisenhower and Churchill hammered out a face-saving arrangement whereby Britain would "withdraw all military forces" from Suez within twenty-four months provided that the Egyptians agreed to the "continued maintenance of the Base by civilian contractors" employed by British firms. This eleventh-hour compromise proved to be the key ingredient in the Suez Base agreement initialed by British and Egyptian negotiators at Cairo on 27 July 1954 and ratified four months later.[43]

The Anglo-Egyptian settlement came as welcome news at the White House, where Eisenhower and Dulles hoped that Whitehall's agreement to pull its troops out of Suez would help pave the way for a U.S-backed system of regional defense. The first concrete step in this direction had come on 2 April 1954, when Turkey and Pakistan signed a vaguely worded bilateral mutual security treaty. "The Turk-Pakistani agreement provides a new basis for development of a Western-oriented defense grouping in the Middle East," U.S. intelligence analysts concluded on 22 June, that "would be less subject to the stigma of being under direct Western control than were the Middle East Command and Middle East Defense Organization."[44] This insight was not lost on the drafters of NSC-5428, a top secret review of U.S. policy that Eisenhower approved one month later. According to NSC-5428 the best regional defense strategy was based on "the 'northern tier', which would include Turkey, Pakistan, Iran and Iraq."[45]

Although the locally controlled perimeter defense system outlined in NSC-5428 seemed in theory an extremely effective way to shore up Western interests in the Middle East, tactical disagreements between Britain and the United States and bitter rivalries among the Turks, the Iranians, and the Arabs made implementing the northern tier scheme a diplomatic nightmare. Seeking ways to reassert their presence and rebuild their prestige in the area in the wake of the decision to relinquish their military base at Suez, the British ignored American advice to remain at arm's length and edged instead toward formal membership in the emerging regional security organization.[46] The Iraqis, with quiet encouragement from London, soft-pedaled the northern tier concept during the autumn of 1954 and gravitated toward a freestanding pan-Arab collective security pact directed against Israel, not against Russia.[47] The shah of Iran, whose realm constituted the only available geopolitical land bridge that could "close [the] Turk-Pakistani gap" stretching from the Indian Ocean to the Caspian Sea, told Washington on 15 December that he could not even think about joining a regional defense grouping unless he received a multimillion-dollar U.S. military aid package.[48]

Despite pan-Arab skullduggery and royal blackmail, during 1955 the Eisenhower administration managed to sell most of America's friends in the Middle East on the northern tier concept. The U.S. proposal assumed concrete form on 24 February when Turkey and Iraq signed an anti-Soviet mutual defense agreement known as the Baghdad Pact. Pakistan followed suit seven months later after receiving promises of increased U.S. military assistance, as did Iran, which became a formal part of the new regional security scheme on 3 November in exchange for Washington's commitment to help upgrade the shah's arsenal. But there were also complications. Among the biggest was Whitehall's decision to join the Baghdad Pact on 5 April 1955, a move that top U.S. policymakers interpreted as Britain's not very subtle attempt to reaffirm its traditional role as the senior Western partner in the Middle East. The Eisenhower administration saw at least two implications in such high-profile U.K. involvement in regional security. "In the first place, the British desired to assure themselves of command responsibility in the area in the event of difficulties," Undersecretary of State Herbert Hoover Jr. told the NSC on 5 May. "Secondly, the British expected the United States to foot the bill required to place the area in some posture of defense."[49]

A third and far more momentous implication was that Whitehall's membership in the Baghdad Pact effectively ruled out any participation by Egypt's

Nasser, whose abiding mistrust of the British and whose mounting suspicion of the Israelis were propelling him toward the Kremlin. Despite some increasingly strident pro-Arab rhetoric, down through Stalin's death in March 1953 Soviet policymakers, like their U.S. counterparts, had accorded the Middle East a lower priority than Central Europe or Northeast Asia. Although Nikita Khrushchev, Russia's new leader, vowed to launch an anti-Western ideological and diplomatic offensive among the newly emerging nations from North Africa to Southeast Asia, as late as the summer of 1955 the Soviets could claim few converts to communism in the Muslim world and could count not a single Middle Eastern regime in their small stable of Third World client states.[50] U.S. support for and British participation in the Baghdad Pact, however, triggered a nationalist backlash in Damascus and Cairo, where Kremlin propagandists spread word that "Western-backed defense arrangements represent a disguised form of imperialism which involves Middle East countries in provocations against the Soviet Union."[51] This antiimperialist rationale served as the catalyst for the $86 million arms-for-cotton deal that Khrushchev and Nasser concluded with the help of Czech middlemen in September 1955.

The Soviet decision to provide Egypt with military hardware suggested that the Kremlin intended to leapfrog over the northern tier into the heart of the Arab world, an action that would call into question the concept of perimeter defense on which the Baghdad Pact and America's approach to regional security in the Middle East was predicated. U.S. and U.K. policymakers hoped to counter Khrushchev's bold move by offering the Egyptians economic and technical assistance in December 1955 for the construction of the High Dam at Aswan on the Upper Nile. But this Anglo-American initiative merely convinced Nasser that he could play the East against the West, a tactic that embittered anticommunist members of the Baghdad Pact, who complained repeatedly during the first half of 1956 that Cairo's flirtation with Moscow was paying bigger dividends in Washington than was their own ideological faithfulness. Having inadvertently strained America's relations with the nations of the northern tier without arresting Egypt's drift toward the Kremlin, top U.S. officials blamed Whitehall, whose diplomatic machinations had backfired, undermining rather than bolstering regional defense. "The trouble was that the British have taken [the Baghdad Pact] over and run it as an instrument of British policy," Dulles complained on 7 April, and "pushed Egypt into the deal with the Russians."[52]

That U.S. and British leaders no longer saw eye to eye regarding how best to promote regional security and prevent further Soviet inroads into the Middle East would become painfully obvious before the year was over. After conferring with U.K. officials, on 20 July 1956 the Eisenhower administration withdrew its offer to help Egypt finance the Aswan Dam. Six days later Nasser retaliated by wresting control of the Suez Canal from its British and French owners. Despite Eisenhower's insistence that a negotiated settlement to the Suez crisis was feasible, Anthony Eden, who had succeeded Churchill as prime minister a year earlier, moved inexorably during the autumn on 1956 toward British armed intervention to retake the canal with French and Israeli help. Stunned by Eden's decision to bomb Cairo and airlift U.K. troops into the Suez in early November, Eisenhower employed U.S. diplomatic and financial leverage against the British, who reluctantly withdrew from Egypt once United Nations peacekeepers arrived to take their place a month later.

The implications of Washington's diplomatic coup against London were obvious to policymakers on both sides of the Atlantic. In late November Undersecretary of State Hoover wondered whether "it might be necessary for us to approach the British and say that it looks as though they are 'through' in the area, and ask if they want us to pick up their commitments."[53] U.K. officials wasted little time answering Hoover's loaded question. Bitter over what he regarded as monumental U.S. bad faith and on the verge of a nervous breakdown, in late November Prime Minister Eden flew to Jamaica, where he contemplated further British retrenchment in the Middle East. Meanwhile Chancellor of the Exchequer Harold Macmillan, whom many in Washington regarded as Eden's heir apparent, frankly interpreted the outcome of the Suez crisis as meaning that Britain had passed the torch to the United States. "The British action was the last gasp of a declining power," Macmillan told Dulles on 12 December. "Perhaps in two hundred years the United States 'would know how we felt.'" In the meantime he urged the Americans "to think up some big, imaginative plan for the Middle East."[54]

The Eisenhower administration was already contemplating several possible lines of action to fill the vacuum likely to be created by Britain's impending retreat from the Middle East. "There were three alternatives," Dulles had advised Eisenhower as early as 8 December: the United States could "join the Baghdad Pact," it could "try to create a new grouping under the [United Nations] charter," or it could "deal on a nation to nation basis 'under authority that would be granted'" by Congress. Both men dismissed the second alternative as too cumbersome and debated the merits of the other options. Eisenhower "thought we could proceed carrying 'two strings to our bow'—namely #1 and #3 proposals." Dulles reminded the president, however, that "there would be Congressional hostility to the Baghdad Pact," particularly from New York's Jacob Javits and like-minded senators on both sides of the aisle "who wanted us to give assurances to Israel." Unwilling to offer such assurances, Eisenhower concluded that "we will probably have to go along with the third choice."[55] As the year drew to a close, Eisenhower and his senior advisers hammered out the details of a new U.S. strategic doctrine that would require,

Dulles was quick to point out, "going to Congress and asking for a resolution" allowing the president to use both military force and up to $400 million in economic aid "as a means of building our position in the Middle East."[56]

On New Year's Day 1957 Eisenhower ushered a bipartisan group of twenty-nine congressional leaders into the Cabinet Room for an unprecedented four-hour briefing on the Middle East. While Iowa trounced Oregon State in the Rose Bowl and an Alberta clipper chilled most of the northern plains, the president and his secretary of state painted a grim picture of a troubled region that required the urgent attention of the United States. The Suez crisis had destroyed Britain's traditional influence in the Muslim world, Eisenhower explained, stimulating radical Arab nationalism and opening the door to fresh Soviet inroads. Given "traditional Russian ambitions" in the region and "the present impossibility of France and Britain acting as a counterweight," Eisenhower insisted that "the United States just cannot leave a vacuum in the Middle East and assume that Russia will stay out." Having outlined the gravity of the situation, Ike said that he would be asking Congress for "a special economic fund and authorization for the use of military force if necessary." To avoid "suffering loss of that area to Russia," Eisenhower concluded, "the United States must put the entire world on notice that we are ready to move instantly."[57]

During secret testimony before the Senate Committee on Foreign Relations the next day, Dulles elaborated more fully on the rationale for what would soon be known as the Eisenhower Doctrine. America's current problems in the Middle East were "primarily due to the collapse of British power and influence in the area," he told his listeners. "To keep Russia out has been British policy for the last hundred years, and they have succeeded pretty well up to the present time," Dulles explained. "Now they are finished, and it is a good deal like the situation was in Greece and Turkey" ten years earlier. Unless the United States assumed important new commitments, "the area will probably fall under Soviet control, and that will be a very great disaster." Authorizing Eisenhower in advance to use military force, Dulles pointed out, would help "deter open armed attack" by the Soviets and would reassure jittery American friends in Iran, Iraq, and Turkey. Furthermore, he added, providing U.S. financial aid would help "build up the economies of the free countries there" and prevent communist subversion.[58]

Despite Dulles's theatrics, several senators expressed grave doubts about the Eisenhower Doctrine. Citing "the horrible example of Korea," Richard Russell, the Georgia Democrat who chaired the Senate Armed Services Committee, worried that the White House was about to undertake another open-ended military commitment without having assessed the consequences. Hubert Humphrey agreed and chided Dulles for "asking us for a predated declaration of war." It would be wiser, the Minnesota Democrat insisted, to reassure America's Muslim allies by simply joining the Baghdad Pact.[59] After spending much time massaging lawmakers who, like Russell and Humphrey, questioned the wisdom of the United States assuming Britain's role in the Middle East, Dulles and Ike won grudging approval for the Eisenhower Doctrine in early March. By margins of 72 to 19 in the Senate and 350 to 60 in the House, Congress authorized the president to use military force and $200 million in economic aid to support any nation in the Middle East "requesting assistance against armed aggression from any country controlled by international communism."[60]

James P. Richards, a South Carolina Democrat who had chaired the House Foreign Affairs Committee before becoming Ike's troubleshooter for the Middle East, soon learned that the Eisenhower Doctrine evoked even more ambivalence in Muslim capitals than it did on Capitol Hill. During a whirlwind tour of fifteen countries in March and April 1957, Richards found the Turks, the Iranians, and the Lebanese eager for more direct U.S. support for regional security.[61] In Jordan, on the other hand, anti-American and pro-Nasser demonstrations forced Richards to cancel his meeting with King Hussein. In Libya, Saudi Arabia, and Yemen, Arab conservatives kept their distance to avoid being tarred as U.S. stooges. The radical regimes in Egypt and Syria refused even to extend Richards an invitation.[62]

Four months after Richards returned to Washington, Syria shocked the Eisenhower administration by announcing a wheat-for-weapons deal with the Kremlin. Damascus and Washington traded ugly charges of political conspiracy and diplomatic bad faith in mid-August. There was "evidence in Syria of the development of a dangerous and classic pattern," Dulles warned Eisenhower on 20 August, a pattern that virtually guaranteed "that the country will fall under the control of International Communism and become a Soviet satellite, whose destinies are directed from Moscow."[63] Convinced that he must act quickly or "lose the whole Middle East to Communism," the president ordered the Pentagon to prepare for possible military action and reassured Syria's neighbors that he stood ready to invoke the Eisenhower Doctrine and "come to the assistance of any of them in the event of Syrian or Russian aggression."[64]

Eisenhower's actions received mixed reviews from America's friends and allies. In Ankara, for example, Prime Minister Adnan Menderes saw a "real danger that Syria might become a Soviet satellite" and informed U.S. officials that "Turkey would be prepared if necessary [to] enter [the] picture" to prevent this.[65] In London, on the other hand, policymakers believed that Washington had overreacted. The Americans, Prime Minister Macmillan grumbled, were "interpreting the new 'Eisenhower Doctrine' with all the enthusiasm of recent converts" to justify "the most drastic measures—Suez in reverse."[66] Dulles, however, regarded the Syrian crisis as "another Munich," not a second

Suez, and insisted that Nikita Khrushchev was "more like Hitler than any Russian leader we have previously seen."[67] Although Eisenhower did "not want to repeat the type of pressures that were used on Czechoslovakia to force them to accept Hitler's demands" in 1938, neither did he wish to repeat the mistakes that had transformed a smoldering crisis in the Eastern Mediterranean into a global cataclysm in 1914.[68] Surprised by British second-guessing and chastened by a nasty warning from the Soviets, who had just tested the world's first intercontinental ballistic missile, the White House began to edge away from invoking the Eisenhower Doctrine in Syria as the summer drew to a close.[69]

Although the president had resisted the temptation to equate events in Damascus in 1957 with those in Prague nineteen years earlier, many in Washington expected that the waning of Britain's influence and the waxing of Russia's would eventually force him to invoke the Eisenhower Doctrine to avert a Middle Eastern Munich. "The long-run hope," Dulles told Macmillan on 19 September, "must be that the Russians will to some extent moderate their ambitions." But because there were at present so few signs of such moderation, Dulles believed that "we need what, in Middle East discussions, we have come to call 'containment plus,'" a strategy designed to halt and reverse recent Soviet gains in the Arab world.[70] Privately, however, U.S. policymakers suspected that Britain's contribution to this endeavor might well be a net minus. "The British are the first to recognize that they no longer have a paramount position in the area," the State Department's Policy Planning Staff pointed out on 30 October 1957. "The obstacles to the attainment of our objectives are so great and the forces working to weaken the U.S. position in the area are so strong that we cannot exclude the possibility of being faced with a set of circumstances which put up to us squarely the choice of either using force to maintain our position in the area or seeing it disappear entirely."[71]

Nine months later a left-wing revolution in Iraq, an abortive coup in Jordan, and a nasty civil war in Lebanon would present the Eisenhower administration with what amounted to a Hobson's choice in the Middle East. On 14 July 1958 anti-Western officers seized power in Baghdad while like-minded conspirators nearly toppled the monarchy next door in Amman. Faced with escalating sectarian strife between Muslims and Christians and convinced that pro-Western elements in Lebanon would soon meet the same fate as their brethren in Iraq, Lebanese president Camille Chamoun asked Eisenhower to send American troops to Beirut to restore order and prevent chaos. Meanwhile, Jordan's King Hussein was clamoring for U.S. or U.K. help to save his throne. The top State Department, Pentagon, and CIA officials who hurried to the Oval Office for a Bastille Day meeting with Eisenhower believed that the United States must respond swiftly.[72] So did Ike. Noting that the Iraqi revolution had badly shaken America's friends along the northern tier, "the President said we must act or get out of the Middle East entirely" and prepared to send U.S. marines ashore in Lebanon at a moment's notice.[73]

Well aware of lingering doubts on Capitol Hill about the wisdom of the Eisenhower Doctrine, the president invited thirty congressional leaders to the White House a few hours later. Insisting that "this is not a matter of a decision already taken," the president asked Dulles to lay out the rationale for intervention. Dulles stressed that the Lebanese crisis was a symbolic test of U.S. credibility, not merely in the Middle East but throughout the Third World. "Turkey, Iran and Pakistan would feel—if we do not act—that our inaction is because we are afraid of the Soviet Union," he explained. "Elsewhere, the impact of not going in—from Morocco to Indo-China—would be very harmful to us." Some of the lawmakers questioned this latest White House prescription for regional defense and worried that the United States was meddling in a civil war. A few, like Senator J. William Fulbright, an Arkansas Democrat, insisted that unless the president could provide real evidence of communist subversion, the Eisenhower Doctrine was probably not applicable to Lebanon. "The crucial question is what the victims believe," Ike retorted; "Chamoun believes it is Soviet Communism that is causing him his trouble."[74]

After Fulbright and the others filed out, Eisenhower confirmed his earlier decision to send in the marines and called Britain's Harold Macmillan with the news. "You are doing a Suez on me," Macmillan joked. Of course Britain would support the U.S. move in Lebanon, he added more seriously. But Macmillan also saw an opportunity to turn the tables on U.S. officials, who for more than a year had been hinting that Whitehall must reconcile itself to a much smaller role in the Middle East.[75] Noting that King Hussein had just renewed his request for British troops and that Kuwaiti leaders might soon turn to Whitehall for military help as well, Macmillan pressed the White House for what Dulles called "a blank check" to support U.K. intervention in Jordan and the Persian Gulf.[76] Reluctant at first, Washington did agree to "give *moral* and *logistical* support" after British troops arrived in Amman on 16 July.[77] "Whatever happens in Iraq and other parts of the area," Eisenhower cabled Macmillan two days later, Britain and the United States must work together in places such as Lebanon, Jordan, and Kuwait to ensure that the Middle East "stays within the Western orbit."[78]

By late July, however, few in Washington believed that invoking the Eisenhower Doctrine was the most effective way to keep the region inside the Anglo-American gravitational field. To be sure, Turkey, Iran, and Pakistan had interpreted Eisenhower's "gratifying decision" to intervene in Lebanon as what Turkish foreign minister Fatin Zorlu called "a guarantee of our own defense, in [the] event it should become necessary."[79] U.S. marines did succeed in restoring order in Beirut without firing a shot, and British paratroopers did prevent an anti-Western coup in Amman.[80] But none of this changed a simple truth that Eisenhower himself had recognized as the marines waded ashore in Lebanon. "The trouble is that we have a campaign of hatred against us, not by the governments but by the people," he had told Vice-President Richard Nixon on 15 July. "The people are on Nasser's side."[81]

While Dulles flew to London at the end of the month to reassure Washington's friends inside the Baghdad Pact, Eisenhower instructed the NSC staff to reevaluate America's approach to the Middle East. The new policy that emerged during the autumn of 1958 did not mark a complete break with the past. The United States remained more determined than ever to prevent the Soviets from overrunning the northern tier. When word arrived from Dulles, for example, that the Iraqi revolution had doomed the Baghdad Pact, Eisenhower swiftly approved a series of executive agreements with Iran, Turkey, and Pakistan that laid the foundations for a new regional defense system, the Central Treaty Organization.[82] But by early October the White House task force examining the situation in the Middle East had concluded that the Eisenhower Doctrine "must now be regarded as out of date" and that, as a result, some major changes were in order.[83] As Ike thumbed through NSC-5820, "U.S. Policy toward the Near East," he found a powerful argument for establishing "an effective working relationship with Arab nationalism" that highlighted Washington's "opposition to external domination and infringement of local sovereignty." This meant that the United States must distance itself from Britain and must "reserve the right to act alone" whenever U.S. and U.K. objectives proved incompatible.[84]

The policies embodied in NSC-5820 were bound to strain Washington's relations with its junior partner in London. When Christian Herter, who had recently succeeded the dying Dulles as secretary of state, reviewed America's new approach with British officials in April 1959, Foreign Secretary Selwyn Lloyd "said his main anxiety was that the United Kingdom and the United States should not drift apart in their policies towards the Middle East."[85] Fourteen months later Eisenhower approved a pair of policy papers suggesting that Lloyd's anxiety was not unfounded. The first prophesied that Britain's decline as a power in the Middle East would soon accelerate. "Over a period of time, Arab nationalism may be expected to bring increasing pressure on the British position in the various U.K. dependencies on the Arabian Peninsula," the drafters of NSC-6011 pointed out on 17 June 1960.[86] The second identified a leading candidate to succeed Britain as America's junior partner in the Middle East. According to NSC-6010, a review of Iranian-American relations completed in early July, "Iran is deeply disturbed by pan-Arabism . . . as a possible barrier to Iranian aspirations in the Persian Gulf" and "considers itself the logical heir to present British influence in the area."[87] During the decade ahead Eisenhower's successors would work hard to convert Iran and other conservative Muslim regimes into America's regional proxies.

Pillars and Proxies: The Making of the Nixon Doctrine, 1961–1972

By the time Ike left office, the Eisenhower Doctrine, a policy designed to defend the Middle East by combining U.S. military muscle with U.K. political savoir faire, had become strategically irrelevant thanks to the rise of Nasser's brand of Arab nationalism and the fall of Britain's informal empire. Although Middle East defense was far down John F. Kennedy's list of priorities during the spring of 1961, the Massachusetts Democrat had been highly critical of the Eisenhower Doctrine during his stint on the Senate Foreign Relations Committee in the late 1950s. Convinced that Dulles's anticommunist pactomania and Ike's gunboat diplomacy had sparked a backlash among Arab nationalists who regarded U.S. intervention as merely the reincarnation of British imperialism, the Kennedy administration hoped that the shah of Iran or the House of Saud would fill the vacuum created by Whitehall's eventual departure from the region.

Any doubts regarding the importance of filling that vacuum sooner rather than later disappeared early that summer, when Britain's decision to shut down its military installations in Kuwait led Iraq to resurrect its long-standing claim to London's oil-rich protectorate. "If Persian Gulf shaikhdoms were going to break loose from their traditional association with the U.K.," Parker Hart, America's new ambassador to Saudi Arabia, warned Kennedy in late June, "in a sense it became 'open season' for larger neighboring powers to assert such claims that they might have."[88] In the short run Kennedy had little choice but to encourage Britain to reassert its military presence in the Middle East. The United States, he assured U.K. officials on 29 June 1961, would "give full political and logistic support" to British troops deployed in the Persian Gulf "to forestall any Iraq attempt to take over Kuwait by force."[89] Over the long haul, however, U.S. policymakers preferred an "Arab solution" to the crisis and applauded Saudi Arabia's decision in mid-July to put several hundred of its own troops at the disposal of the Kuwaiti government. As the summer drew to a close, Riyadh's plans for "replacing [the] British with troops from Arab League member states" bore fruit with the arrival of a Saudi-led multilateral force in Kuwait that enabled Whitehall to bring its soldiers home on 19 September.[90]

Although the Kennedy administration was grateful for Saudi help in forging an Arab solution to the crisis in Kuwait, most U.S. officials questioned whether the House of Saud was sufficiently strong or reliable to fill by itself the vacuum resulting from Britain's eventual withdrawal from the Persian Gulf. King Saud, the eldest son of the dynasty's founder, Abdul Aziz Ibn Saud, had "projected a bad image" in Washington, Parker Hart recalled long afterward, because of his "extravagance, particularly the extravagance of his sons, his unwillingness or inability to control them, the enormous amount of wastage of funds."[91] Worse than the king's profligacy was his fickleness, symbolized as early as March 1961 by his cancellation of the Pentagon's lease on the Dhahran airfield, an important transit facility that had linked U.S. military operations in Western Europe with those in East Asia for fifteen years.[92]

Unwilling to rely solely on the corrupt and unpredictable House of Saud to shore up sagging Western interests in the Middle East, the architects of Kennedy's national security policy included in their blueprint a second pillar: Iran. To be sure, prospects for grooming the shah of Iran to succeed John Bull as one of Uncle Sam's sentinels in the Persian Gulf seemed bleak during JFK's first year in office. The forty-two-year-old absolutist who sat atop the Peacock Throne in Tehran was every bit as autocratic and temperamental as his counterpart in Riyadh, and his realm was as badly in need of reform as the Saudi monarchy. Despite its chronic internal political problems, however, Iran remained an active member of the Central Treaty Organization, possessed one of the largest armies in the area, and proved eager to play an expanded role in regional defense. With the British "revamping their military planning, and gravitating south of Suez" toward the Indian Ocean, the shah assured Secretary of State Dean Rusk in April 1962 that Iran stood ready to step into the breach provided that the United States delivered enough guns and dollars under the auspices of Kennedy's Military Assistance Program.[93]

Fearful that the shah's regional ambitions might slow the pace of long-overdue reforms and divert resources from badly needed development projects, Kennedy asked Vice-President Lyndon B. Johnson to visit Tehran during his trip to the Middle East four months later. Johnson, who also made stops in Athens and Ankara, confirmed that the Greeks, the Turks, and the Iranians "remain vigilant and faithful, despite communist threats and abuse" and recommended more U.S. economic aid to ensure that "these rimland states" were able to "maintain their armed forces along the underbelly of the [Soviet] Bloc." He believed that much of the aid should find its way to the man on the Peacock Throne. "In Iran, we must accept the Shah, with his shortcomings, as a valuable asset," Johnson advised Kennedy on 10 September 1962. "We should carefully determine the real military potential, present and future, of the Shah's military forces and allocate [military assistance] to them in a context of global U.S. security interests."[94]

Yet in a global context, sorting out America's relationships with Iran or

Saudi Arabia did not rank high on Kennedy's list of priorities during his final year in office. Indeed, most of JFK's time and energy through November 1963 were devoted to handling far more acute problems: the nuclear test ban treaty with Russia, the diplomatic grudge match with French president Charles de Gaulle over the future of NATO, and the military quagmire emerging in Vietnam. Nevertheless, in the months before his death Kennedy seriously considered a plan "to beef up our capabilities in the Indian Ocean/Persian Gulf/Red Sea area" proposed by White House Middle East expert Robert Komer. "We have traditionally left the defense of this region to the British," Komer pointed out on 19 June 1963, "yet their strength is waning at a time when we face a potential show of force or actual combat needs ranging from Saudi Arabia to the Persian Gulf and Iran through India and Burma to Malaysia." By redeploying a naval task force from the Western Pacific to the Indian Ocean, Kennedy could "give quite a fillip" to America's friends and "lend more credibility to our statements we could support them effectively if the need arose."[95] Intrigued by Komer's proposal, JFK passed it along to the Pentagon with a chit asking, "What about this?"[96] The U.S. Navy liked the idea of an Indian Ocean squadron, Komer informed his boss on 6 September, because it "buys us credibility in Red Sea, Persian Gulf, Iran, Pakistan, India, Burma, Malaysia, Indonesia—all for one price."[97]

It was, however, a price that not everyone at the Pentagon was eager to pay. Preoccupied with the rapidly deteriorating situation in Vietnam during the autumn of 1963, Secretary of Defense Robert McNamara balked at assuming additional military burdens in the Middle East and had yet to respond to the White House proposal when Kennedy left for Dallas in mid-November. Although Lyndon B. Johnson shared McNamara's fixation on Vietnam, in March 1964 the new president approved periodic naval deployments in the Indian Ocean, hoping thereby to thicken the thin Western defense perimeter that stretched east from the Persian Gulf to Singapore.[98]

Despite LBJ's best efforts, that perimeter showed signs of growing even thinner at the end of the year, when Britain's new Labour government began to reassess all U.K. military commitments in the Middle East. Convinced that "the British position in the area will continue to erode," by late 1965 State Department planners were urging that "greater attention should thus be given to the provision of other capabilities 'over the horizon' to meet the continuing need for the West to be able to react quickly with small forces in local crises in the oil rich Persian Gulf and elsewhere in the region."[99] One of the most attractive of these capabilities lay in the Indian Ocean 2,500 miles south of the Straits of Hormuz at Diego Garcia, a tiny island controlled by the British, who in short order agreed to allow the Pentagon to establish a naval base on the V-shaped atoll.[100]

On 22 February 1966, however, Whitehall unveiled a White Paper that suggested that something more substantial than a base at Diego Garcia would be required to fill the vacuum created by Britain's inexorable decline as a regional power. A rising budget deficit and a falling pound sterling, Prime Minister Harold Wilson had informed LBJ during an Oval Office meeting two months earlier, would necessitate "readjustments in the British defense posture East of Suez." Although Wilson insisted that "the British world-wide role would be maintained," he made it clear that U.K. retrenchment in the Middle East was unavoidable. The Labour government, he told Johnson, was preparing to abandon the crown colony at Aden in southwestern Arabia and was also seeking ways "to lighten the British presence in the [Persian] Gulf."[101] Once Whitehall's decisions became public knowledge in early 1966, U.S. officials in London wasted little time spelling out the implications for American policy in the region. "There is no denying that British power and influence have relatively run down," Chargé d'Affaires Philip Kaiser advised Foggy Bottom on 23 May. "The accelerated rate of contraction of British interests in the Middle East," Kaiser added, had already triggered "many nagging difficulties connected with 'bits and pieces' of a dissolving British colonial domain which affect us in a number of direct and indirect ways."[102]

By the summer of 1966 the Johnson administration had begun to address some of those nagging difficulties by adopting a "two pillars" policy in the Persian Gulf that called for Saudi Arabia and Iran to assume many of Britain's responsibilities for defending the region. When King Faisal visited the White House in June, for example, Johnson sought Saudi help "to fill the gap the British will leave in South Arabia and the Persian Gulf." After Faisal hinted that this would require his kingdom to upgrade its arsenal, LBJ approved the sale of $100 million in nonlethal military hardware—mostly trucks and jeeps—to strengthen America's emerging partnership with the House of Saud.[103]

The most enthusiastic candidate to succeed John Bull as the region's policeman, however, was the shah of Iran, who dreamed of combining his nation's fabulous oil wealth with high-tech U.S. weaponry to recapture the ancient grandeur of Cyrus the Great. In the wake of Whitehall's February 1966 White Paper the shah, like King Faisal and LBJ, "worried that the British may eventually withdraw from the Persian Gulf," where the Soviets and their Arab clients were always eager to fish in troubled waters. By mid-July the Iranian monarch was insisting that Washington sell him a squadron of F-4 Phantom jets comparable to the MIG-21s that Moscow had recently promised to Cairo and Baghdad. Although the supersonic squadron's $50 million price tag threatened to bust Iran's budget, national security adviser Walt W. Rostow reminded President Johnson that "with the British pulling out of South Arabia and retrenching in the Persian Gulf" and with U.S. military involvement in Vietnam escalating rapidly, beefing up the shah's arsenal was the most cost-effective method of promoting Middle East defense. Not only did Johnson approve the sale of the Phantoms in early August; he also provided $200 million in revolving credit to finance future Iranian arms purchases.[104]

The new year brought fresh indications that Saudi Arabia and Iran might have to assume their new roles as regional policemen sooner rather than later. While most eyes were riveted on the Egyptian-Israeli showdown that culminated in the Six Day War in June, throughout the spring of 1967 and into the summer, U.S. Middle East experts watched Whitehall fight a losing battle against shadowy Soviet-backed guerrilla movements such as the Front for the Liberation of South Yemen and the Popular Front for the Liberation of the Occupied Arab Gulf. Plagued by acute imperial overstretch from the Persian Gulf to Southeast Asia and afflicted by chronic underemployment at home, Britain's Labour government edged ever closer to liquidating what remained of the empire east of Suez. Convinced that such drastic action would merely reinforce the growing impression in Washington of "a Little England" important chiefly for "thatched cottages and Beefeaters or mini-skirts and Beatles," British ambassador Patrick Dean warned his superiors in late October that a policy of scuttle from Bahrain to Singapore would produce "a qualitative change in the Anglo-American relationship."[105]

Despite Dean's words of caution, the British government took a series of increasingly drastic actions during the following three months. On 18 November Whitehall devalued the pound sterling by 15 percent in a bid to cure Britain's deepening balance of payments problems. On 20 December Chancellor of the Exchequer Roy Jenkins stunned the Cabinet by declaring that unless they sliced £300 from the defense budget, "we had come to the point of defeat on the economic road." On 3 January 1968 Harold Wilson and Foreign Secretary George Brown agreed that the only way to make such large cuts was for Britain to cut its losses east of Suez. Convinced that "we could not stay in the [Persian] Gulf after we had withdrawn from the Far East," the Cabinet concluded that "an early announcement was absolutely necessary" in order to prepare "the local administrations concerned to protect foreign oil installations."[106]

A week later George Brown crossed the Atlantic to break the bad news to the Johnson administration, which did not react well to the prospect of Britain withdrawing from the Persian Gulf and the Far East, except Hong Kong, within three years. "I had a bloody unpleasant meeting in Washington this morning," Brown cabled Whitehall on 11 January, "with [Dean] Rusk," who grumbled that "we had got our priorities wrong" and pleaded, "For God's sake, be Britain."[107] What was being proposed here was "tantamount to British withdrawal from world affairs," Rusk thundered, and Brown should know that "the

US could not and would not fill the vacuum."[108] Echoing his secretary of state, Johnson insisted that "accelerated British withdrawal both from its Far Eastern bases and from the Persian Gulf would create most serious problems . . . for the security of the entire free world," and he implored Harold Wilson to "postpone any irrevocable steps" east of Suez "until other stable arrangements can be put in place."[109]

Ambassador David Bruce, who relayed Johnson's concerns to London, doubted that the Labour government had any interest in postponement. Whitehall's "calamitous, destructive, selfish, [and] myopic" decisions in the Persian Gulf and the Far East, Bruce cabled Washington on 15 January, showed "the most deplorable resolve, except for Munich, that any British Government has taken during the last 150 years."[110] Within hours LBJ received a poignant "Dear Lyndon" letter from Harold Wilson describing the abandonment of empire east of Suez as "the most difficult and the heaviest" decision that he and most other Britons could remember. "This does not mean," Wilson insisted, "a British withdrawal from world affairs" but, rather, that "the British people were sick and tired of being thought willing to eke out a comfortable existence on borrowed money." Only by bringing its commitments more closely into line with its resources, Wilson concluded, "can Britain find the new place on the world stage that I firmly believe the British people ardently desire."[111]

Later that evening on the other side of the Atlantic David Bruce's old friend Averell Harriman, who had served every Democratic president since Franklin Roosevelt as a diplomatic troubleshooter, had a blunt chat with Harold Wilson's representative in Washington. Nicknamed "the Crocodile" because he never minced words, Harriman told Ambassador Patrick Dean, "We cannot accept this decision as final. It must be reversed." The British diplomat retorted, "Well, it's been made." Insisting that "the U.S. cannot be the only world power on the Free World side," Harriman testily reminded Dean that "your government has fantastic interests in the Middle East" and that U.K. retrenchment "opens the door for an easier way for the Russians to take your place and push us still further out."[112]

While the Crocodile snapped at Ambassador Dean, Walt Rostow, who wielded immense influence on LBJ's foreign policy, sprang into action. Adopting as his motto "Don't Mourn, Organize," Rostow informed Johnson on 16 January that the NSC staff had begun to consider "how nations in the Middle East and in Southeast Asia can fill the gap left by the British, with our encouragement." Although Rostow expected the defense perimeter along the Pacific rim to remain extremely fluid, he prophesied that Australia, Indonesia, and Japan would eventually assume Whitehall's strategic role from the Malaca Straits to the China Sea. The situation in the Persian Gulf, on the other hand, already seemed clear. Iran and Saudi Arabia—"both rich and increasingly confident"—were eager to play expanded roles in regional defense but were "uncertain as to how to proceed." If the United States could "give them both encouragement and sell them arms," Rostow believed that the Iranians and the Saudis would fill the vacuum created by Britain's departure from the Middle East.[113]

Lyndon Johnson saw the beauty of Rostow's scheme at once. In short order Washington approved King Faisal's request for an arms package including jet aircraft, agreed to expedite the shah's latest appeal for U.S. military hardware, and mediated a complex dispute over drilling rights for offshore oil in the Persian Gulf that threatened to poison relations between Saudi Arabia and Iran.[114] Later that spring Johnson invited both the shah and Saudi crown prince Khalid, Faisal's heir apparent, to the White House to review Persian Gulf security issues.[115] "Close cooperation between Shah and Faisal [is] of greatest importance," State Department officials emphasized in their briefing materials, "in assuring stability in Gulf after British withdrawal."[116] To be sure, Johnson's advisers continued to worry that Saudi Arabia and Iran might not be up to the task and told U.K. officials in September 1968 that "if the situation really began to deteriorate the U.S. and everyone else concerned would look to the British."[117] But when LBJ departed the White House four months later, the foundations of America's new strategy for assuring stability in the Middle East were in place. By early 1969 the U.S. Navy had begun preliminary work on its new over-the-horizon facility at Diego Garcia, Saudi Arabia and Iran were edging toward agreement regarding their mutual responsibilities in the Persian Gulf, and modest amounts of U.S. weaponry were on their way to Riyadh and Tehran.

Although the Johnson administration had drafted the blueprint, Richard Nixon gave the new U.S. strategic doctrine in the Middle East its name. Attributing his narrow victory in the November 1968 elections to mounting popular frustration with LBJ's costly but ineffective war in Vietnam, the California Republican entered office on 20 January hoping to reduce the risk of military involvement in the Third World by relying on pro-Western proxies to be armed and bankrolled by the United States. The earliest and best example of this approach surfaced in Asia under the guise of "Vietnamization." On the eve of a midsummer minisummit meeting with South Vietnamese president Nguyen Van Thieu on Guam, Nixon announced that America's "Asian friends" were going to have to assume more of the initiative and also bear more of the burden for promoting regional security than they had in the past. When it came to "military defense, except for the threat of a major power involving nuclear weapons," Lyndon Johnson's successor told reporters on 25 July 1969 in words that quickly became known as the Nixon Doctrine, "the

United States is going to encourage and has a right to expect that this problem will be increasingly handled by, and the responsibility for it taken by, the Asian nations themselves."[118]

While the Pentagon moved gradually to Vietnamize the ground war in Southeast Asia by beginning to withdraw the half-million GIs that Johnson had sent to Indochina, the White House moved swiftly to apply the Nixon Doctrine to the Middle East. Two weeks before Nixon flew to Guam, he had approved National Security Study Memorandum 66, which established an interdepartmental task force to determine how best to handle "the problems created by withdrawal from the [Persian] Gulf of the British presence." In September 1969 the task force confirmed that the most attractive option was to rely increasingly on oil-rich Saudi Arabia and Iran as America's sentinels in the area.[119] Eager to expand its strategic role in the Persian Gulf, between 1969 and 1972 the House of Saud used its burgeoning oil revenues to double its defense spending from $700 million to $1.4 billion and used its diplomatic influence to help persuade six tiny sheikdoms in Southeast Arabia formerly controlled by the British to establish a pro-Western federation, the United Arab Emirates (UAE). With the Nixon administration's blessing, King Faisal also set up an elite military academy to provide state-of-the-art training for Saudi officers and pilots and purchased a broad range of Western military hardware, including American F-5E fighter-bombers.[120]

The most enthusiastic proponent of the new Nixon Doctrine in the Middle East, however, remained the shah of Iran, whose grandiose scheme to transform his realm into a great power coincided nicely with Washington's desire to shift the costs of regional defense from the U.S. taxpayer to stable and well-armed proxies in the Third World. As early as October 1969 the shah had outlined for U.S. officials his plans to use his rising reservoir of petrodollars to finance a military buildup that would dwarf parallel Saudi efforts that were just getting under way across the Persian Gulf.[121] By September 1970 the CIA was touting the shah as "a confident powerful autocrat" who seemed "determined to ensure for Iran a position of power and leadership in the Persian Gulf after the British withdrawal."[122] Six months later Secretary of State William P. Rogers termed the shah "statesmanlike," called his realm "a constructive force in the region," and "urged Iran, Saudi Arabia, and the other Gulf States to cooperate in fostering stability and progress" throughout the area.[123] "In effect," Assistant Secretary of Defense James Noyes, a Middle East specialist who helped Foggy Bottom lay the groundwork for the Nixon Doctrine during 1971, recalled long afterward, "Iran and Saudi Arabia were to receive U.S. support for the sake of their own strength and for keeping peace in the region."[124]

On 30 May 1972 Air Force One banked high over the Caspian Sea and swooped down just outside Tehran. Fresh from their summit meeting in Moscow with Soviet premier Leonid Brezhnev, Richard Nixon and his national security adviser, Henry Kissinger, hoped that "one of America's closest allies, the Shah of Iran," could help prevent the Kremlin from taking advantage of Whitehall's "historic withdrawal of its forces and military protection from the Persian Gulf."[125] The president, State Department briefers had suggested three weeks earlier, should "commend the Shah for his farsighted recognition of Iran's responsibilities as a regional power and say this was precisely what you had in mind when you enunciated the Nixon Doctrine."[126]

The shah's visitors were determined that Iran should assume its role as America's proxy sooner rather than later. According to one U.S. official then in a position to know, Nixon looked his host in the eye and said simply, "Protect me."[127] Well aware that "there was no possibility of assigning any American military forces to the Indian Ocean in the midst of the Vietnam war and its attendant trauma," Nixon and Kissinger were relieved that "Iran was willing to play this role." What the Iranians expected in return, however, was access to all nonnuclear hardware in America's arsenal, including F-14 and F-15 supersonic jets. Because "the Shah was willing to pay for the equipment out of his oil revenues" and because he was "a vital ally carrying burdens which otherwise we would have had to assume," Nixon promised to sell the aircraft to Iran and "added a proviso that in the future Iranian requests should not be second-guessed."[128]

Upon their return to Washington Nixon and Kissinger swiftly showed that they meant what they said. In short order the White House approved an arms package that included supersonic aircraft, laser-guided bombs, and helicopter gunships, which the Pentagon was to deliver "as promptly as possible." To expedite delivery, "decisions on the acquisition of military equipment should be left primarily to the government of Iran."[129] Never known for restraint when it came to shopping lists, during the next five years the shah would shell out $16.2 billion—nearly seven times what he had spent during the preceding two decades—for U.S. planes, tanks, warships, and other sophisticated weapons systems. He wasted little time demonstrating his eagerness to promote Western interests in the Persian Gulf. When the sultan of Oman needed help snuffing out a Soviet-backed uprising in Dhofar province in early 1973, the shah delighted the Nixon administration by using his recently acquired U.S. helicopters to ferry 1,200 Iranian commandos to Southeast Arabia. "We are trying to checkmate Soviet influence wherever it appears and to exhaust them in any adventures they may pursue," Kissinger told the shah in July. Iran would help the United States fulfill these objectives in Oman before the year was over.[130]

Thanks to the enthusiastic support of America's friends in Riyadh and Tehran, then, by the mid-1970s the Nixon Doctrine actually seemed to be more effective in the Middle East than in Southeast Asia, the site of its first application. Unlike Washington's client regime in South Vietnam, which collapsed like a house of cards in April 1975, two years after the last GI flew out of Than Son Nhut airport, Saudi Arabia and Iran stood firm as America's twin pillars in the Muslim world. Indeed, as Gerald Ford and Henry Kissinger prepared for a White House meeting with the shah just two weeks after the fall of Saigon, they took considerable comfort that U.S. policy in the Persian Gulf seemed anchored in far safer waters than the Tonkin Gulf. "There is no doubt that the Shah, should he survive a sufficient number of years, will have a key, if not the controlling, role among the regional powers in helping to assure stability in the Persian Gulf area," Kissinger assured his boss in the Oval Office on 13 May 1975. "It has been a cardinal point in our policy over the past several years to encourage Iran to intensify its cooperation with other moderate anti-communist states in the Gulf region, particularly Saudi Arabia."[131]

By late 1976 U.S. strategic interests in the Middle East seemed more secure than they had at any time since the British had commenced their slow-motion retreat thirty years earlier. Well-armed pro-American Muslim sentinels were standing guard on both sides of the Persian Gulf, and U.S. Navy Seabees were completing work on a $100 million port and communications facility over the horizon on Diego Garcia. Despite recent Russian arms deliveries to Iraq and South Yemen, U.S. intelligence took heart that "increased wealth has permitted a new self-assertiveness on the part of the major local states, Saudi Arabia and Iran, which are determined to prevent Soviet encroachment." Thanks to "its rapidly expanding military strength," CIA experts pointed out one month after Gerald Ford failed in his bid to become president in his own right, Iran in particular "has expressed a commitment to police the Gulf and exclude foreign intrusions." The principal danger to America's clients, the intelligence analysts concluded, came not from external intervention but, rather, from internal instability. However remote the possibility, a radical takeover in Riyadh or Tehran would mean that "doors now shut would open to the Soviets elsewhere in the Gulf, and they would quickly enlarge their presence."[132] Although Ford, Kissinger, and other high-ranking U.S. officials remained confident that the Nixon Doctrine had contained the Kremlin and laid a solid foundation for order and progress in the Middle East, their successors would see the CIA's worst-case scenario come to pass.

America Stands Alone: The Carter Doctrine

Jimmy Carter was elected president in November 1976 largely because the voting public perceived him as far more honest than Richard Nixon and far more intelligent than Gerald Ford. Carter had reinforced these perceptions during his campaign by promising not only to clean up domestic political corruption symbolized by Nixon's Watergate scandal but also to clear up the ambiguities surrounding Soviet-American détente symbolized by Ford's election-year foreign policy gaffes. One area where the Georgia Democrat did not distance himself from the policies of his predecessors, however, was the Persian Gulf. He embraced the Nixon Doctrine and continued to rely on the shah of Iran to promote political stability and prevent Kremlin inroads. But the shah's seemingly limitless appetite for U.S. military hardware soon gave the new president pause. The anti-Western revolution that rocked Iran and toppled the Pahlavi dynasty in early 1979 sent U.S. policymakers scrambling for a new strategy in the region. After the Soviets sent troops into Afghanistan at the end of the year, the White House unveiled the Carter Doctrine, signaling that, at long last, the United States was reluctantly willing to assume the lonely burden of protecting Western interests in the Persian Gulf that Great Britain had shouldered through the early 1970s.

The policies that the Carter administration inherited from Nixon and Ford seemed, at first glance, to constitute low-risk, cost-effective tactics for preventing trouble in a strategically important part of the world. U.S. efforts "to assist and encourage Iran to become a regional power which would assume limited security responsibilities and play a generally more active role supportive of our mutual interests," a State Department transition briefing paper pointed out on 3 January 1977, had largely succeeded. "Iran has accepted this role—for it was consistent with the Shah's view of Iran's key position in the area—and has used its military power (in Oman), its financial strength (loans to India, Pakistan, Afghanistan, Egypt, Jordan and Syria) and its general influence to help resolve regional disputes."[133] Cyrus Vance, who moved into the seventh floor at Foggy Bottom three weeks later, saw a certain logic to recent U.S. policy in the region. "The Shah's determination that Iran must assume more responsibility in the gulf coincided with the adoption of the 'Nixon Doctrine' which envisioned key regional states as surrogates for American military power in preserving order and blocking Soviet inroads," Vance recalled in his memoirs, and the Carter administration "recognized the importance of Iran in Persian Gulf security matters."[134]

National security adviser Zbigniew Brzezinski, who second-guessed Cyrus Vance on just about everything from human rights to nuclear disarmament, shared the secretary of state's faith in the Nixon Doctrine in the Persian Gulf. Praising Carter's predecessors for "building up" Iran and Saudi Arabia "as the two American-backed pillars of regional security," Brzezinski agreed that the shah had become "our major strategic asset in the wake of the British disengagement from 'east of Suez'" during the Nixon and Ford years. "Recognizing Iran's strategic centrality," he remarked several years later, "we chose to continue that policy, approving major sales of arms" to the shah, whose realm was the "pivot of a protected tier shielding the crucial oil-rich region of the Persian Gulf from possible Soviet intrusion."[135] Gary Sick, a holdover from the Ford administration who quickly emerged as the chief Iran specialist in the Carter White House, confirmed that "the Nixon-Kissinger policy of placing U.S. security interests in the Persian Gulf almost exclusively in the hands of the shah had been fully absorbed by the bureaucracy and the U.S. power structure." But for Sick the downside to the Nixon Doctrine was obvious. "The United States now lay strategically naked beneath the thin blanket of Iranian security," he observed long afterward. "By the time President Carter arrived in the White House," Sick added, "whether one liked it or not, Iran was the regional tail wagging the superpower dog."[136]

By all accounts Jimmy Carter liked it less and less the longer he was in office. Worried that continued U.S. arms sales to the shah and other autocratic Third World clients under the auspices of the Nixon Doctrine would divert resources from economic development, weaken respect for human rights, and, in the long run, undermine political stability, Carter sent Secretary of State Vance to Tehran in May 1977 in hopes of developing "a better way of determining Iran's future military needs and how they could best be met." Vance assured the shah that the Carter administration still wished to work closely with him on a plan "for denying the Soviets opportunities to increase their influence" in the Persian Gulf. He confirmed that Washington would deliver the F-16 jet fighters and AWACS electronic surveillance aircraft that Iran had ordered earlier, but not high-performance F-18 fighter-bombers. He gently reminded the shah that the Georgia Democrat regarded "the primacy of human rights as a national goal."[137]

Although Vance returned from Tehran convinced that the visit had gone reasonably well, in almost no time the tail tried to wag the dog. The shah, Iranian ambassador Ardeshir Zahedi complained on 28 May, was finding Carter's more stringent controls on arms sales "disappointing" in light of Iran's informal alliance with the United States and was privately asking himself, "Was this a special relationship?" Vance replied that Washington fully intended to continue providing Tehran with "advanced weaponry to offset quantitative and other disadvantages in order to maintain a regional balance." Indeed, he reminded Zahedi, "our [arms] sales to Iran this year will be larger than to any other country and about one half of the total." In short, Zahedi's boss could rest assured that "there is and will continue to be a special relationship between the U.S. and Iran."[138]

When Mohammed Reza Pahlavi visited the United States six months later, however, there were signs that the relationship was becoming less and less special. As he stepped onto the south lawn of the White House on 15 November with President Carter at his side, the shah was taunted by thousands of jeering Iranian exchange students who had poured into Washington from college and university campuses across the country to vent their frustration over autocratic rule in their homeland. Before long, jittery police tried to disperse the huge crowd with tear gas, which wafted toward the two heads of state, who beat a watery-eyed retreat indoors. Once inside, a dry-eyed shah dazzled Carter and his top advisers with "an excellent analysis of the troubled situation around the Persian Gulf," where Iran was using its U.S. military hardware to promote Western interests. But when Carter remarked that mullahs and middle-class students were making human rights a front-page issue in Iran and asked the shah to consider "easing off on some of the strict police policies," he was greeted with stony silence. "There is nothing I can do," the shah replied somewhat sadly. "I must enforce the Iranian laws, which are designed to combat communism." Dissidents such as those chanting "Death to the Shah" outside the White House, he insisted, were "really just a tiny minority, and have no support among the vast majority of [the] Iranian people."[139]

Despite his own suspicion that the shah's heavy-handed policies would eventually backfire, Carter continued to hope for the best. At a White House dinner later that evening, for example, he made light of the ugly incident earlier in the day, joking that "there's one thing I can say about the Shah—he knows how to draw a crowd" and hailing the guest of honor as "a stabilizing influence . . . throughout the Persian Gulf, the Indian Ocean, and with a growing degree of influence, in the Western World."[140] Six weeks later during a New Year's Eve gala in Tehran hosted by Pahlavi, the Georgia Democrat toasted the Persian king as a staunch ally and firm friend. "Iran, because of the great leadership of the Shah," Carter gushed in words that would soon ring hollow, "is an island of stability in one of the more troubled areas of the world."[141]

Even as Islamic revolution rocked the Peacock Throne during the first half of 1978, few U.S. officials were willing to admit that one of the central pillars of the Nixon Doctrine was about to crumble. "American security strategy for the Persian Gulf, the Indian Ocean and ultimately all of Southwest Asia had, over a period of more than a decade, come to be based squarely on the premise that Iran was and would continue to be a strong, stable regional power whose interests coincided with those of the United States," the NSC's Gary Sick recalled. As Ayatollah Khomeini brought the Iranian revolution to a crescendo in early 1979, Carter's advisers were asking themselves, "How can U.S. policy interests be preserved if the shah falls?"[142]

Before the year was over, the Soviet invasion of Afghanistan would make answering that question far more difficult—and also far more important. An arid, landlocked, and mountainous kingdom, Afghanistan had always been a buffer state, first between the expanding British and Russian empires and then, after 1945, between the Free World and the Soviet bloc. As was the case next door in Tehran, rapid modernization generated serious political turmoil in Kabul, where Afghan communists seized power in a bloody coup in April 1978. Although the upheaval in Afghanistan came as welcome news at the Kremlin, Cyrus Vance recalled long afterward that "we had no evidence of Soviet complicity in the coup."[143] Neither Vance nor his colleagues, however, were pleased by the communist takeover in Kabul. "Afghanistan as Finland is probably inevitable," Gary Sick remarked shortly after the April revolution, "but an Afghan Hungary is a positive danger to the long-term stability of the entire region."[144]

By the spring of 1979, however, the news from Afghanistan sounded more like something out of Budapest than Helsinki. Mired in a nasty war with Islamic guerrillas, the left-wing regime in Kabul sought help from Moscow, which dispatched several hundred military advisers in March. Three months later at a summit meeting with Leonid Brezhnev in Vienna, Jimmy Carter hinted that further Russian intervention in Afghanistan would jeopardize Soviet-American détente. "We have certain areas of vital interest . . . in the Persian Gulf and the Arabian Peninsula," Carter pointed out on 17 June, and "there are many problems in Iran and Afghanistan." For its part, "the United States has not interfered in the internal affairs of those nations," he told Brezhnev. "We expect the Soviet Union to do the same." Brezhnev was not amused. "Don't blame the Soviet Union for changes taking place in the world," he growled. "Soviet leaders are very careful not to categorize the United States as 'adversary' or 'foe,' and we want the same treatment from you."[145]

Before the end of the year, relations between Washington and Moscow would become downright adversarial. While Carter and Brezhnev traded barbs over how best to verify the SALT II agreement and how much importance to place on a Soviet combat brigade in Cuba, the situation in Afghanistan went from bad to worse. With factional infighting among Afghan communists undermining the war against the Islamic radicals and weakening Moscow's influence, on Christmas Eve the Kremlin airlifted thousands of Russian commandos into Afghanistan, where they installed a staunchly pro-Soviet regime. "In this extremely difficult situation, which has threatened the gains of the April revolution and the interests of maintaining our national security," Brezhnev's top advisers told the Politburo a week later, "a decision has been made to send the necessary contingent of the Soviet army to Afghanistan." Although evidence to the contrary may well remain locked inside the Russian archives, materials released thus far suggest that Moscow's military intervention in Kabul was probably a defensive maneuver and not the first step in a Kremlin master plan to drive the United States out of the Persian Gulf.[146]

The situation looked different from Washington's end of the telescope, however. For more than a year national security adviser Zbigniew Brzezinski had been warning Jimmy Carter about an "arc of crisis" stretching from the Horn of Africa to the Persian Gulf, where Britain's departure, the fall of the shah, and Russian meddling threatened U.S. interests. "If the Soviets succeed in Afghanistan," Brzezinski informed his boss a few hours after the Red Army arrived in Kabul, "the age-long dream of Moscow to have direct access to the Indian Ocean will have been fulfilled" at America's expense. "Historically, the British provided the barrier to that drive and Afghanistan was their buffer state," he concluded. "We assumed that role in 1945, but the Iranian crisis has led to the collapse of the balance of power in Southwest Asia, and it could produce Soviet presence right down on the edge of the Arabian and Oman Gulfs."[147] Carter had to move decisively to create "a new 'security framework,'" Brzezinski insisted in the waning days of 1979, not only "to reassert U.S. power and influence in the region" but also "to demonstrate his genuine toughness."[148] Secretary of State Cyrus Vance, on the other hand, counseled restraint. "My view was that Moscow had acted as it did . . . to protect Soviet political interests in Afghanistan which they saw endangered," he recalled in his memoirs. "They feared that the regime would be replaced by a fundamentalist Islamic government and that this would, in turn, be followed by a spread of 'Khomeini fever' to other nations along Russia's southern border."[149]

Preoccupied with events in Tehran, where Iranian radicals held fifty-two American hostages, and confronted with polling data showing that the public regarded him as too weak to warrant reelection in November, Jimmy Carter sided with his national security adviser. "This is deliberate aggression that calls into question détente and the way we have been doing business with the Soviets for the past decade," he told White House chief of staff Hamilton Jordan on 27 December.[150] "This was the first time they had used their troops to expand their sphere of influence since they had overthrown the government of Czechoslovakia in February 1948," Carter observed in his memoirs, with a bow to Harry Truman. "A successful take-over of Afghanistan would give the Soviets a deep penetration between Iran and Pakistan and pose a threat to the rich oil fields of the Persian Gulf area."[151]

On 2 January 1980 the embattled Georgia Democrat and his NSC adopted a hard-line response to what they saw as an unprecedented act of Soviet aggression. The United States would embargo all grain exports to Russia, withdraw from the Summer Olympics to be held in Moscow, and create a "Rapid Deployment Force" capable of airlifting U.S. troops to the Persian Gulf at a moment's notice. The president made the new Carter Doctrine the centerpiece of his annual state of the union address three weeks later. "The implications of the Soviet invasion of Afghanistan could pose the most serious threat to the peace since the Second World War," Carter told the nation on 23 January. Echoing the Missouri Democrat who had stood in the same spot a generation earlier, he issued a call to arms. "Let our position be absolutely clear," Carter remarked solemnly. "An attempt by any outside force to gain control of the Persian Gulf region will be regarded as an assault on the vital interests of the United States of America, and such an assault will be repelled by any means necessary, including military force."[152]

The allusions to the Truman Doctrine were hardly a coincidence. "You have the opportunity to do what President Truman did on Greece and Turkey," Zbigniew Brzezinski had reminded Jimmy Carter in early January. "You might want to think of a 'Carter Doctrine.'"[153] Although Carter avoided drawing explicit comparisons between himself and Truman during the 1980 election campaign, "Give 'Em Hell Harry's" get-tough policy toward the Kremlin in the Middle East was implicit every time "Give 'Em Heck Jimmy" mentioned Afghanistan, new U.S. strategic bases in Somalia and Oman, or the Pentagon's proposed Rapid Deployment Force. Brzezinski removed any remaining doubts about the matter several years later when he stated categorically in his memoirs, "The Carter Doctrine was modeled on the Truman Doctrine."[154]

Those memoirs also hinted that there was a covert side to the Carter Doctrine in Afghanistan. Nine months before the Red Army rolled into Kabul, Brzezinski had expressed "concern over the Soviets' creeping intervention in Afghanistan" and insisted that Washington must be "more sympathetic to those Afghans who were determined to preserve their country's independence."[155] The Pentagon's Walter Slocombe agreed and wondered whether clandestine U.S. support for Muslim guerrillas might succeed in "sucking the Soviets into a Vietnamese quagmire."[156] On 6 April 1979 the Special Coordination Committee, an interagency group chaired by Brzezinski, instructed the CIA to develop a comprehensive plan for a secret war in Afghanistan backed by the United States, ranging from "indirect financial assistance to the insurgents" to "weapons support." Three months later President Carter signed a finding authorizing the agency to begin helping the Afghan mujahadeen, as the Muslim rebels now called themselves, with propaganda, cash, and nonmilitary supplies. In short order Pakistani president Mohammed Zia al-Haq, whose nation shared a long and porous border with Afghanistan, put his Inter-Services Intelligence Agency (ISI) to work running guns to anti-Soviet guerrillas next door.[157] Thanks to this covert help from Pakistan and the United States, by December 1979 the mujahadeen stood ready to resist the Soviet takeover.[158]

Over the next decade the Carter and Reagan administrations would funnel nearly $3 billion into Afghanistan to help the Muslim resistance fight pro-Soviet president Babrak Karmal, his like-minded successor Mohammed Najibullah, and a 100,000-man Russian expeditionary force. By July 1980 Washington was providing the mujahadeen with everything from captured Soviet AK-47 assault rifles to Chinese rocket-propelled grenade launchers via a CIA-ISI arms pipeline running through Peshawar, a Pakistani frontier town near the Khyber Pass. After the Soviet occupation of Afghanistan became a hot-button campaign issue later that fall for Republicans who eventually succeeded in making Jimmy Carter a one-term president, CIA director Stansfield Turner let it be known that his agency "was pushing everything through the pipeline that the Pakistanis were willing to receive."[159]

Ronald Reagan and his director of central intelligence, William Casey, wasted little time devising increasingly ingenious ways to provide funds, weapons, and advice to the Afghan guerrillas. In late 1982, for example, deputy national security adviser Robert McFarlane asked Prince Bandar bin Sultan, the House of Saud's representative in Washington, whether his government might be willing to help finance the mujahadeen's war against the Soviets. "The Saudis understood that our interests in rolling back Marxism coincided closely with their own," McFarlane noted long afterward, and over time they, too, would channel almost $3 billion into the CIA's covert crusade in Afghanistan. Among the first to put those dollars to good use against the Red Army was Osama bin Laden, a Saudi engineer in his late twenties.[160] Meanwhile, in early 1983 the White House issued National Security Decision Directive 75, a blueprint for destabilizing "the Evil Empire" that made the Afghan war the centerpiece of what came to be known as the Reagan Doctrine. America's principal objective in Afghanistan, the drafters of the directive emphasized, was "to keep maximum pressure on Moscow for withdrawal and to ensure that the Soviets' political, military, and other costs remain high while the occupation continues."[161]

As the decade wore on, the Soviets and their Afghan clients realized that they were fighting a losing battle against the mujahadeen. By 1986 the Reagan administration had infiltrated sixty U.S. Green Berets into Afghanistan, where they coordinated the flow of supplies to a guerrilla army whose ranks had swelled to 30,000 and taught the rebels how to use high-tech weapons such as shoulder-launched Stinger antiaircraft missiles that made sitting ducks of Soviet helicopter gunships. Once the Kremlin decided to cut its losses and sued for peace three years later, it was only a matter of time before President Najibullah's pro-Soviet regime disintegrated in April 1992. "It was the CIA's war," Charles Cogan, the former chief of the agency's Middle Eastern division, observed in a recent postmortem. "There were no American military forces involved and no American soldiers killed."[162]

During the early 1990s Cogan and his colleagues downplayed the length and cost of the war in order to emphasize its success. Few would deny that Washington's clandestine triumph in Afghanistan helped trigger the collapse of the Soviet Union or that it helped accelerate the end of the Cold War. Yet the revelation that the Muslim terrorists who bombed New York City's World Trade Center in early 1993 and the Taliban extremists who established a bitterly anti-American Islamic republic in Kabul in late 1996 had learned their craft while helping the CIA defeat the Red Army in Afghanistan made the agency's most successful covert operation ring hollow in many ears.[163] To be sure, some Cold Warriors insisted that the "blowback" from the Afghan battlefield was a small price to pay for defeating the Kremlin. "For almost ten years, Moscow had to carry on a war . . . that brought about the demoralization and finally the breakup of the Soviet empire," Zbigniew Brzezinski remarked in early 1998 when asked whether he had any regrets about having supported the mujahadeen. "What is most important in the history of the world? The Taliban or . . . the liberation of Central Europe and the end of the cold war?"[164] For most Americans, however, the answer to this rhetorical question seemed far less obvious after 11 September 2001, when the Taliban's friend Osama bin Laden attacked New York City and Washington, than when Brzezinski first unveiled the Carter Doctrine two decades earlier.

American strategic doctrine had come full circle since the United States reluctantly began to assume Great Britain's burdens east of Suez after the Second World War. How to contain the Soviet Union and promote regional security, or more metaphorically, how to develop a Monroe Doctrine for the Middle East was a riddle that had bedeviled U.S. policymakers for more than fifty years. Preoccupied with a series of crises in Central Europe and East Asia, Harry Truman hoped to prevent fresh Kremlin encroachments in the Middle East by blending U.S. dollars with British ingenuity to launch collective security organizations such as MEC and MEDO. Once Britain's high-profile role tainted such initiatives with the scent of colonialism, Dwight Eisenhower pressed Whitehall to limit its responsibilities to the Persian Gulf and embraced a policy of unilateral U.S. military intervention to block Soviet gains elsewhere in the region. After the Eisenhower Doctrine tarred the United States itself with the brush of imperialism, John Kennedy and Lyndon Johnson turned toward regional proxies such as Iran and Saudi Arabia to thwart Russian-backed radicals, laying the groundwork for what became the Nixon Doctrine. When Islamic upheavals jeopardized those proxies and provoked Soviet intervention in Afghanistan, Washington invoked the Carter Doctrine and stood alone against Moscow in Southwest Asia.

At one level the tale of four doctrines seemed to have ended happily, with the United States cast in Britain's role and with the Persian Gulf safely outside the Kremlin's reach. Throughout the 1980s and into the 1990s Jimmy Carter's successors refined his strategic approach to the Middle East. The Reagan Doctrine extended clandestine U.S. support to anti-Soviet "freedom fighters" in Afghanistan. The Powell Doctrine, perfected by George Bush and his chairman of the JCS in 1991, put teeth in Carter's strategy for defending the Persian Gulf. The so-called Clinton Doctrine brought Washington into the post–Cold War era with a policy of "dual containment" directed at Iran and Iraq, two rogue states that American officials identified as most likely to succeed Moscow as the chief threat to U.S. interests in the region. By the late 1990s, however, it was clear that a fixation with combating the Soviet threat had led a generation of U.S. policymakers to neglect the appeal of revolutionary nationalism and radical Islam among the peoples of the Muslim world. In short, the doctrines that contained international communism after 1945 proved largely ineffective, not only against the nationalist upheavals that swept east from Cairo through Baghdad to Tehran during the last half of the twentieth century, but also against devilish terrorists such as Osama bin Laden who stunned the United States during the early years of the twenty-first.

Although the Americans are constantly modifying or abrogating some of their laws, they by no means display revolutionary passions. It may be easily seen from the promptitude with which they check and calm themselves when public excitement begins to grow alarming, and at the very moment when passions seem most roused, that they dread a revolution as the worst of misfortunes, and that every one of them is inwardly resolved to make great sacrifices to avoid such a catastrophe.—Alexis de Tocqueville, 1831

I believe that in the perspective of history the Egyptian revolution will be to the Middle East what the French Revolution was to Europe. It, too, had its self-seeking leaders, its power cliques, its political nationalism; but it let loose forces that finally changed the pattern of social life in most of Europe. That is what the Egyptian revolution has begun to do in the Middle East and why it strikes fire in some form in every country.—John S. Badeau, 1958

Sympathy for the Devil?

America, Nasser, and Arab
Revolutionary Nationalism

5

Every administration from Truman's to Reagan's openly embraced some variant of the doctrine of containment that defined Soviet expansion as the principal threat to U.S. interests in the Middle East. Behind closed doors, however, policymakers wondered whether the wave of revolutionary nationalism that swept the Muslim world after 1945 posed an even greater challenge. Americans have always harbored ambivalent attitudes toward revolution. Although statesmen from Thomas Jefferson to John F. Kennedy publicly hoped that the Spirit of 1776—republicanism, anticolonialism, and moderation—would guide other revolutions in other lands, privately they dreaded that it would not. Indeed, foreign revolutionaries seldom lived up to U.S. expectations, and their movements were often marked by socialism, xenophobia, and terror. The violent social upheavals that rocked France after 1789, Russia after 1917, and

Cuba after 1959 suggested that the American Revolution was largely irrelevant for societies polarized between rich and poor, landlord and peasant, or colonizer and colonized. Well into the 1990s this same ambivalence haunted Americans as they pondered the wave of Eastern European revolutions that ended the Cold War.

Yet when the peoples of Asia, the Balkans, and the Middle East launched struggles for national self-determination in the aftermath of the First and Second World Wars, they were inspired in no small measure by the Spirit of 1776, as updated by Woodrow Wilson and Franklin D. Roosevelt. That spirit was especially appealing to Arab radicals, many of whom adopted the Fourteen Points or the Atlantic Charter as sacred texts in their struggle to liberate their nations from European imperialism. For most U.S. policymakers, however, anticolonial revolutions in the Middle East were a mixed blessing. More often than not, hope for U.S.-style evolutionary change competed with fear of a Russian-style cataclysm.

Nowhere would this prove more accurate than in Egypt, where the United States would find itself on a collision course with Gamal Abdel Nasser, the Arab world's leading revolutionary. After seizing power in a palace coup in July 1952, Nasser issued a call for revolutionary social and economic change that echoed throughout the region and bedeviled U.S. policy for nearly two decades. "The Egyptian revolution will be to the Middle East," John S. Badeau prophesied three years before he became John F. Kennedy's ambassador to Egypt, "what the French Revolution was to Europe."[1] The unanswered question was whether Americans should greet this news with sympathy or with dread.

Loaded with Dynamite: Self-Determination and Arab Nationalism

For Woodrow Wilson and most other Americans, the second decade of the twentieth century was synonymous with war—and revolution. While the European empires staggered toward stalemate in the First World War, radical movements seeking to redistribute wealth and power exploded in Mexico, China, and almost every corner of the globe. America's most disturbing encounter with revolution, however, came in war-weary Russia, where in March 1917 Alexander Kerensky and his Constitutional Democrats toppled the Romanov dynasty and won Wilson's praise for establishing a provisional republic and promising free elections. But six months later Vladimir Ilyich Lenin and a small band of bolshevik revolutionaries backed by peasants and workers demanding bread, peace, and land overthrew Kerensky, proclaimed a dictatorship of the proletariat, and called for national liberation movements in "the semi-colonial countries, such as China, Persia and Turkey, and all the colonies."[2]

Determined to counteract Lenin's call for world revolution, Wilson incorporated the principle of national self-determination into the Fourteen Points that he unveiled in January 1918. Point 12, which stipulated that "other nationalities which are now under Turkish rule should be assured an undoubted security of life and an absolutely unmolested opportunity of autonomous development," was of particular interest to the Arabs, who had recently launched a revolt against the Ottoman Turks.[3] The nationalist upheaval that rocked the Arab world during the First World War was the product of powerful internal and external currents that had been eroding Ottoman rule for more than a generation. The revival of Arabic as a literary language during the late nineteenth century generated not only an outpouring of poetry in the drawing rooms of Cairo but also a growing awareness in the coffeehouses of Damascus of past Arab political accomplishments. Having watched first the Germans, then the Italians, and finally in 1909 the Turks themselves undergo nationalist revolutions, Arab intellectuals embraced an ideology of national liberation. When Turkey declared war on Britain and France in 1915, British agents enlisted the support of Sharif Hussein, keeper of the holy places in Mecca, by pledging independence for the Arabs. In short order Hussein and his son, Emir Feisal, wrested control of western Arabia from the Turks and helped liberate Syria, a nationalist stronghold, from Ottoman control.[4]

Once the shooting stopped, Hussein sent Feisal to Versailles in early 1919 to make the case for Arab self-determination with the peacemakers face-to-face. "The Allies had now won the war, and the Arabic speaking peoples thought themselves entitled to independence and worthy of it," Feisal told U.K. and U.S. officials on 6 February. "It was in accord with the principles laid down by President Wilson and accepted by all the Allies." Wilson, however, had begun to have second thoughts about self-determination and urged Feisal to consider allowing the new League of Nations to establish a system of mandates designed to prepare the Arabs for independence under European tutelage.[5] Wilson's concerns stemmed in part from the embarrassing discovery that two years before he had issued the Fourteen Points, Britain and France had secretly signed the Sykes-Picot agreement, which carved out a British sphere of influence in Iraq and Palestine and a French sphere in Syria and Lebanon.[6]

Yet these diplomatic complications were probably less important in America's decision to edge away from Arab independence than philosophical reservations about self-determination. Robert Lansing, Wilson's secretary of state, had spelled out the nature of those reservations on the eve of the Versailles conference. "The more I think about the President's declaration as to the right of 'self-determination,' the more convinced I am as to the danger of putting such ideas into the minds of certain races," Lansing grumbled on 30 December 1918. "Will it not breed discontent, disorder and rebellion? Will not the Mohammedans of Syria and Palestine, and possibly of Morocco and Tripoli rely on it?" The concept of self-determination, Lansing concluded, "is simply loaded with dynamite."[7] Although Wilson remained far more optimistic than Lansing, he, too, worried about the explosive appeal of revolutionary nationalism and reluctantly agreed to strike all explicit references to the principle of national self-determination from the Versailles Treaty in February 1919.[8]

Five weeks later Wilson secured British and French approval for the creation of a special Inter-Allied Commission headed by two Americans, Henry King and Charles Crane, who were to visit the Middle East, survey popular sentiment, and ascertain whether the Arab peoples were ready for self-government. After six months of travel and intensive study the King-Crane Commission concluded that full independence for the Arabs would be premature and recommended instead that the United States assume a League of Nations mandate for Syria and Palestine.[9] Shortly after the King-Crane report landed on Wilson's desk in the autumn of 1919, however, the president was felled by a near-fatal stroke that paralyzed his foreign policy and enabled Britain and France to establish their own system of mandates (British in Palestine and Iraq, French in Syria and Lebanon), dashing Arab hopes for independence.[10]

Unlike most Americans, who were quick to consign the concept of self-determination to the scrap heap of Wilsonian idealism, Arab radicals developed an ideology of national liberation during the 1920s to challenge British and French imperialism. In Iraq, Syria, and Palestine sporadic uprisings prompted Britain and France to employ scorched-earth tactics to crush the rebels. The most dynamic nationalist movement in the Arab world, however, emerged in Egypt, where the British had held a protectorate over the entire Nile Valley from the Sudan to the Mediterranean coast since 1882. After Whitehall refused to permit an Egyptian delegation to make its case for independence at Versailles in early 1919, Saad Zaghlul, a fiery critic of imperialism, pleaded for U.S. help. The desire for "a democratic and durable peace" based on the principle of self-determination was "deep-rooted in the hearts of the whole Egyptian people," whose "absolute faith in the fourteen points," Zaghlul assured Woodrow Wilson on 6 June, "was unshakable." When Wilson's faith proved far less absolute and far more pro-British than expected, Zaghlul founded the Wafd Party and waged a nationalist crusade until his death in 1927. Nine years later Whitehall signed a treaty promising sixteen-year-old King Farouk and Zaghlul's Wafdist successors that Britain would withdraw from Egypt within two decades.[11]

Farouk and the Wafd used their symbolic victory over Britain to divert attention from more pressing problems closer to home. By the late 1930s most Egyptians were packed into the fertile but densely populated Nile Valley, where two-thirds of the arable land was owned by a few thousand wealthy pashas and tended by several million landless fellahin. A handful of Egyptian-owned factories had sprung up to produce shoes, textiles, and cigarettes, but the key sectors of the economy—railroads, banks, and public utilities—were dominated by British firms. Ignoring the country's socioeconomic woes, Wafd leaders devoted themselves to rigging elections, shuffling cabinets, and lining their pockets, while Farouk grew fat and dissolute on a steady diet of French cuisine and Nubian concubines. Although Egypt's tiny communist underground made modest inroads among students and workers, the only serious challenge to the established order came from the Ikhwan al-Muslimin, or Muslim Brotherhood, a secret society whose half-million members were determined to purge the country of Western corruption in order to make way for an Islamic state.[12]

The eruption of the Second World War in September 1939 highlighted the strategic importance of Farouk's realm, bisected by the Suez Canal and buffeted by the winds of nationalism. Eager to prevent the Nazis from exploiting anti-imperialist sentiment among Egyptians and other colonial peoples in Asia and Africa, Franklin D. Roosevelt moved to resurrect national self-determination as a guiding principle for the United States on the eve of its entry into the global conflict. To this end Roosevelt insisted that the Atlantic Charter, a joint statement of Anglo-American war aims issued on 14 August 1941, include a commitment to "respect the right of all peoples to choose the form of government under which they will live."[13]

During the following four years the Roosevelt administration paid only lip service to self-determination in the Middle East. When, for example, King Farouk attempted to declare Cairo's diplomatic independence from London in February 1942 by refusing to appoint a staunchly anti-Nazi cabinet, U.K. officials ringed the royal palace with tanks and forced him to capitulate while U.S. policymakers affirmed that Egypt was "clearly within the British sphere of influence."[14] Few Americans believed that the Iraqis were any better prepared for self-government than the Egyptians. Fewer still could imagine anything other than a British protectorate in strife-torn Palestine. Almost nobody in Washington shared the enthusiasm of General Patrick Hurley, Franklin Roosevelt's roving ambassador in the Middle East, for exporting "the American pattern of self-government" to Iran, a non-Arab land where U.K. influence remained paramount.[15] Hurley's proposal was "messianic globaloney," Assistant Secretary of State Dean Acheson sneered on 28 January 1944. "The military, political and commercial security of the United States requires stability and order in the vast belt of territory, from Casablanca to India and beyond, which constitutes the Mohammedan and Hindu world." If the United States wished to avoid political chaos and a military vacuum, Acheson concluded, it must work with Britain to channel Middle Eastern nationalism in constructive directions.[16]

During the weeks after V-J Day the nationalist tide swelled almost to flood stage. "It seems vital to recognize that the whole Arab world is in ferment, that its peoples are on the threshold of a new renaissance, [and] that each of them wants forthrightly to run its own show," George Wadsworth, the American ambassador to Lebanon, told Harry Truman in November 1945. "If the United States fails them, they will turn to Russia and will be lost to our civilization."[17] Despite tight budgets and more pressing problems in Europe and Asia, the president eventually promulgated the Truman Doctrine and signaled his intention to help Whitehall stabilize the Middle East. In September 1947 high-ranking U.S. and U.K. officials met in Washington and reached a grim conclusion about the Arab world: "If the rising nationalism of the peoples of the Middle East should harden in a mould of hostility to the West," then "great power ambitions and rivalries and local discontents and jealousies . . . might eventually lead to a third World War."[18]

The war that exploded in Palestine eight months later threatened to trigger just such a chain reaction and strained relations between Washington and London. The British insisted that U.S. support for the Jewish state was sparking an anti-Western backlash among Arab radicals who, with Soviet help, might make the Middle East into "another China."[19] Americans, on the other hand, believed that a century of European imperialism had done more than a decade of Zionist state-building to unleash the wave of Arab nationalism that the Kremlin was riding.[20] Only by assisting the Arabs "to acquire self-respect and their proper place among the nations of the world," Assistant Secretary of State George McGhee told U.K. officials in the autumn of 1949, could Britain and the United States hope "to align the forces of nationalism in the Middle East against communism and to guide them into channels friendly to the Western powers."[21]

Guiding Arab nationalism into calmer waters, however, was risky business during the early 1950s. With impatient Arab radicals blaming the region's woes on "colonial and imperialistic practices," a White House staff study pointed out in late 1951, "social revolution may be impossible to prevent."[22] In April 1952 the State Department's Harold B. Hoskins confirmed that Western interests in the Middle East were being swamped by a "rising tide of *nationalism*." Having lobbied hard for the Atlantic Charter a decade earlier as FDR's special emissary to the region, Hoskins insisted that the United States should offer cautious support for Arab self-determination. "We cannot afford to give even tacit backing to varying degrees of 19th century imperialism frequently linked to reactionary elements still in power in many countries in the area," Hoskins concluded. "Nor, on the other hand, can we afford to give indiscriminate support to all forms of nationalism especially of the extreme type that combines a demand for complete and immediate freedom with xenophobic opposition to every form or vestige of 'foreign' interest."[23] Three months later a revolution in Egypt would confront the United States with precisely this dilemma.

Like Niagara in a Rowboat: America and the Egyptian Revolution

Just before dawn on 23 July 1952 a band of self-styled "Free Officers" led by thirty-four-year-old Gamal Abdel Nasser seized power in Cairo and swept Egypt toward the cataract of social revolution and national liberation. Tension had been mounting for more than two years between the British, who hoped that King Farouk would permit them to retain their vast military base at Suez beyond the 1956 deadline spelled out by treaty, and Egyptian nationalists, who pressed the wobbly monarch to shut it down sooner rather than later. While Farouk dithered, closed-door talks produced agreement on neither the fate of the Suez base nor the future of the Sudan, where both Britain and Egypt were maneuvering to control the headwaters of the Nile. Then on 8 October 1951 Prime Minister Mustafa Nahas, who headed Zaghlul's old Wafd Party, unilaterally abrogated the 1936 Anglo-Egyptian treaty, insisted that Britain withdraw from Suez immediately, and unknowingly lit the fuse for revolution. Before the month was over, nationalist guerrillas had begun to stage hit-and-run raids against U.K. positions along the Suez Canal while Egyptian police looked the other way. Meanwhile on the banks of the Thames, Prime Minister Winston Churchill set the tone for a get-tough policy toward the Egyptians in mid-December when, after one too many whiskeys, he growled to Foreign Secretary Anthony Eden, "Tell them that if we have any more of their cheek we will set the Jews on them and drive them into the gutter, from which they should never have emerged."[24]

U.S. policymakers began to prepare for the worst. Ambassador Jefferson Caffery, a veteran diplomat who had helped the French government weather a communist challenge in 1947 before he departed for Cairo two years later, warned Foggy Bottom just after Thanksgiving 1951 that Egypt might "explode at no distant date, an explosion with a potential chain reaction of occupation, revolution, [and] eventual Commie domination."[25] When Churchill and Eden visited Washington early in the new year, Caffery's boss emphasized that the Egyptian crisis was symptomatic of a more fundamental Western dilemma in the Middle East. "Here we had a situation which might have been devised by Karl Marx," Secretary of State Dean Acheson told Harry Truman and his British guests on 5 January as they cruised the Potomac on the presidential yacht *Williamsburg*: "Vast masses of people in a state of poverty; practically no middle class . . . ; a small owning and governing class, incompetent and corrupt; and foreign influences, against which agitators could arouse the population, which, after being aroused and destroying foreign influences, could be used to bring about a communist regime." If Britain and the United States continued "merely sitting tight," Acheson warned, "we would be like two people locked in loving embrace in a rowboat which was about to go over Niagara Falls." The time had come, he concluded, to "break the embrace and take to the oars."[26]

Before British and U.S. leaders could heed Acheson's advice, however, they were swept into a revolutionary vortex in Egypt. The crisis deepened throughout January amidst Egyptian charges that Britain would never agree to withdraw from Suez and Whitehall's countercharges that members of Egypt's auxiliary police were encouraging anti-British guerrillas. After two Tommies were killed by a bomb just outside Ismailia on 25 January, the British sent an armored column into the heart of Egypt's third largest city to disarm the policemen. When the shooting stopped in Ismailia, forty-two Egyptians and four British soldiers lay dead. After the news reached Cairo, angry mobs swept through the capital on "Black Saturday," 26 January, burning Shepheards Hotel and other symbols of British domination and killing twenty-six Westerners, including eleven Britons. Holding Mustafa Nahas and the Wafd responsible for the violence, King Farouk shook up the cabinet and named Ali Mahir, a political reformer popular with the army, as Egypt's new prime minister.[27]

Although top U.S. officials were shocked by the events of Black Saturday, they believed that Britain must eschew gunboat diplomacy and strike a quick deal with Prime Minister Mahir to avoid making a bad situation terrible. "The 'splutter of musketry,'" Dean Acheson informed a British diplomat on 27 January, "apparently does not stop things as we had been told from time to time that it would."[28] Echoing his boss, Ambassador Jefferson Caffery cabled Washington a month later that "this is not one the British can win by stalling," because "reoccupation, revolt, [and] revolution . . . are all visible on the cards in Egypt today."[29] Unwilling to admit that they held a losing hand, however, in early March the British encouraged Farouk to sack Ali Mahir and replace him with Neguib Hilali, a rank political opportunist who seemed more amenable than his predecessor to long-term U.K. control over the Suez base.[30]

Few Americans saw any grounds for optimism. Prime Minister Hilali and King Farouk were "sitting on a volcano," Egyptian ambassador Mohammed Rahim warned State Department officials in early March, "with the possibility of an imminent eruption of which the riots of January 26 were but a minor foretaste." Signs mounted during the next four months that lava was indeed about to flow. "The pressures of social discontent, economic hardship and cultural insecurity," Caffery observed on 14 April, were generating a "romantic vision of an heroic national struggle for 'liberation'" among student radicals and Muslim extremists. The word from Cairo by mid-June was that even the peasantry was responding to "the mouthings of Communist promisers who raise false hopes." It was clear, Dean Acheson recalled in his memoirs, that "the old order was passing and [that] new xenophobic ferment, fanned from Moscow, grew daily."[31]

The passing of the old order came with dramatic suddenness. In late June, Farouk forced Hilali to resign and replaced him with court favorite Hussein Sirry, who predictably showed little interest in cleaning up political corruption. "The new government," Caffery reported on 3 July, "is by far the weakest yet and is made up almost entirely of second-drawer politicians and technicians."[32] From the standpoint of Gamal Abdel Nasser, Anwar Sadat, and other Egyptian Free Officers, this placed the new prime minister and his colleagues at least one drawer too high. After Sirry's third-rate cabinet collapsed two weeks later, Nasser staged a bloodless coup on 23 July; installed General Mohammed Naguib, a senior officer well known for his liberal ideas, as prime minister; and established a nine-man Revolutionary Command Council (RCC). When the king panicked and sought British and U.S. help in reversing the coup, neither Whitehall nor the White House would lift a finger. On 26 July the Free Officers placed Farouk on a slow boat to Naples and turned to the daunting task of "cleaning out corruption."[33]

The initial U.S. reaction to these developments was quite favorable. "The present movement," Caffery predicted on 18 August, might "forestall the chaos and, perhaps, Communist take-over toward which the country seemed hypnotically drifting."[34] Acheson likewise exuded optimism, telling reporters in early September that there had been "some encouraging developments in Egypt" in recent weeks and wishing the leaders of the new regime "every success in their efforts to solve the internal problems of their country."[35] Before the end of the year, however, top U.S. officials began to find fault with the more radical aspects of Nasser's blueprint for change: rapid land reform, the postponement of free elections, and prolonged one-party rule. Indeed, Acheson evidently detected parallels between events in Cairo during 1952 and those in Moscow thirty-five years earlier. The Egyptian coup, he recalled in his memoirs, "appeared to us as mildly encouraging, somewhat as did the February 1917 Russian Revolution to President Wilson." But in the end, Acheson noted, "the colossal ignorance and inexperience of the military junta and the deep skepticism of the British Foreign Office" had made progress toward peaceful change extremely difficult.[36]

Yet ignorant and inexperienced though the Free Officers might have been, Acheson realized that they were the only alternative to complete chaos. This being so, he tried to persuade Harry Truman early in the new year to approve an $11 million arms package requested by General Naguib, who was widely regarded as a moderating influence on Nasser and the RCC. Acheson understood, of course, that the Israelis were bound to object, as were the British. He insisted, however, that the security of the entire region "would be greatly threatened by the collapse of the Naguib regime and the rise of uncontrollable nationalism in Egypt." Unimpressed by Acheson's line of reasoning, on 7 January Truman vetoed any military assistance for Egypt.[37] Two weeks later he turned the Oval Office over to Dwight Eisenhower, whose new secretary of state, John Foster Dulles, saw most Third World revolutionaries as Soviet stooges and regarded Mohammed Naguib as little more than an Egyptian Kerensky.

Kerensky with a Fez: Naguib, Nasser, and John Foster Dulles

Dulles arrived in Cairo on 11 May 1953 to size up the Egyptian revolution. He had a cordial three-hour meeting with Prime Minister Naguib, who insisted that Britain's "master-slave relationship" with Egypt must end but emphasized that the "Russians [are] not our friend[s]."[38] When Dulles met Nasser, the chairman of the RCC, the next day, however, sparks flew. Asserting that "the US wants to see Egypt free," Dulles suggested that the Soviets posed a far greater threat to Egyptian freedom than did the British. "The population of Egypt," Nasser retorted, "would think crazy anybody saying this." The RCC and the Egyptian people, he added, were united on one principle: "British influence must *entirely disappear*."[39] The two men resumed their geopolitical debate later that evening over dinner at the American embassy. Unperturbed by the specter of a Russian-dominated Middle East that haunted Dulles, Nasser insisted that British imperialism, not Soviet subversion, posed the greatest threat to the region's stability. "I think you are complicating the football game," he told Dulles. "Colonialism is played out and now the match is between two teams—communism and nationalism. And if you insist on playing, you are going to spoil the game for others."[40]

Dulles flew home in late May and warned his boss that unless Washington moved swiftly to broker an Anglo-Egyptian agreement on the Suez base, Nasser seemed certain to change the rules of the game. "General Naguib had turned out not to be the 'strong man' in Egypt," Dulles told Eisenhower on 1 June, "but merely a front behind which four military members of the Revolutionary Command Council exercised real power."[41] Naguib's elevation to the

Egyptian presidency three weeks later and Nasser's simultaneous appointment as deputy prime minister confirmed that the Egyptian revolution stood at a crossroads. Naguib was "sitting on a lid that covers a seething desire to throw out every foreigner in the country," Ike warned British prime minister Churchill on 6 July, an eventuality that could be averted only if Britain agreed to withdraw from the Suez base sooner rather than later.[42]

While British and Egyptian negotiators edged toward a compromise on Suez during late 1953, Naguib and Nasser prepared for their showdown. Seeking to curb the power of the RCC and to increase his own authority, early in the new year the Egyptian president called for a plebiscite, parliamentary elections, and an end to military rule. After Nasser rejected these proposals out of hand, Naguib resigned on 25 February 1954, touching off a political crisis.[43] To avert civil strife and to avoid derailing the Suez talks with Britain, the RCC reluctantly agreed to permit Naguib to return as president in early March. But "a definitive show-down with Naguib at some future date is probably inevitable," Nasser told U.S. diplomats on 23 March, because the RCC "did not intend to sit by and allow opposition elements to undo what the present regime has accomplished."[44]

One of Nasser's greatest accomplishments came seven months later on 19 October 1954, when he and Britain's Anthony Nutting initialed the Heads of Agreement and broke the deadlock over the Suez base. Whitehall pledged to withdraw from the huge military facility within twenty months, and the Egyptians agreed that for seven years, U.K. forces could return any time that the British deemed the security of the canal zone to be in jeopardy. When the Muslim Brotherhood angrily denounced the compromise as a betrayal of Egyptian nationalism, the RCC cracked down not only on Islamic extremists but on its other critics as well, including General Naguib, who was unceremoniously stripped of his powers and placed under house arrest in mid-November.[45] Once Nasser moved into the vacant presidency, phase one of Egypt's revolution drew to a close. Most U.S. observers expected the second phase to be even stormier than the first. Cyrus L. Sulzberger of the *New York Times* may have put it best on 17 November when he likened Naguib to "Kerensky with a fez" and warned that, as in Russia a generation earlier, "the revolution on the Nile may devour others of its children." Convinced that "Naguib is the Kerensky of the Egyptian revolution," Sulzberger prophesied that Nasser was almost certain to be its Lenin.[46]

Gamal Abdel Nasser had first revealed the full scope of his brand of radical Arab nationalism in August 1954 when he published *Egypt's Liberation: The Philosophy of the Revolution*, an incendiary pamphlet with which both Sulzberger and top U.S. policymakers became quite familiar. A postman's son, a career officer, and a self-made man, Nasser insisted that only the army could free

Egypt from political corruption, economic underdevelopment, and foreign domination. By triumphing over "feudalism" and "imperialism," the Egyptian revolution would serve as a model for newly emerging nations from the Persian Gulf to the Cape of Good Hope. With Nasser at the helm, a strong and fully independent Egypt would stand at the hub of three concentric circles—the Arab world, Africa, and Muslim civilization—each of which was to be transformed by revolutionary nationalism.[47] An abridged version of Nasser's treatise reached a much wider American audience in January 1955 when "The Egyptian Revolution" appeared in the journal *Foreign Affairs*. Although Nasser did not quote Lenin and although he distanced himself from the Kremlin, he chided Americans, who tended to rebuff Third World nationalists "for fear of annoying some colonial power."[48]

Egypt and the United States drifted steadily apart during 1955, largely because Nasser's actions struck the Eisenhower administration as increasingly unreasonable. First, Nasser refused to participate in a secret Anglo-American peace initiative that called for Israel to make territorial concessions in exchange for Arab recognition of the Jewish state's right to exist.[49] Second, he irritated Ike and Anthony Eden, who had recently succeeded Winston Churchill as prime minister, by opposing U.S. and U.K. efforts to promote the Baghdad Pact. Third, Nasser polished his reputation as an antiimperialist revolutionary in April 1955 by attending a conference of nonaligned nations at Bandung, Indonesia, where he rubbed elbows with neutralists like Yugoslavia's Jozef Tito and communists such as China's Zhou En-lai. Fourth and most important, in late September Nasser accepted the Kremlin's offer to swap $86 million worth of Soviet military hardware for 100,000 tons of Egyptian cotton.[50]

Although policymakers on both sides of the Atlantic were well aware that Soviet and Egyptian diplomats had been discussing an arms-for-cotton deal for months, U.S. and U.K. officials evidently believed that Nasser was bluffing. A few hours after receiving the stunning news on 26 September 1955 that Egypt had accepted the Kremlin's proposal, John Foster Dulles sat down with British foreign secretary Harold Macmillan at the United Nations in New York City to ponder what to do next. Rather than punishing Nasser, the two diplomats hoped to persuade him to rescind the arms deal in exchange for Western economic assistance. By late October Dulles and Macmillan were considering offering Egypt $200 million to help finance the Aswan Dam, a $1.3 billion project that would expand irrigated cropland, ensure flood control, and provide badly needed hydroelectric power.[51] Like Dulles and Macmillan, Eisenhower feared that if Britain and the United States declined to help, Nasser would simply turn to Russia. Determined to limit the Kremlin's influence, Ike approved the first phase of the Aswan project on 1 December 1955. America's share was to be $56 million and Britain's was to be $14 million, with the World Bank providing $130 million.[52]

Nasser was interested in the $200 million aid package until he learned early in the new year that the release of U.S. funds was contingent on a peace settlement with Israel. Such an arrangement was out of the question, Nasser thundered, because his followers would conclude that he had "sold out to the Western powers."[53] By the time Eden and his new foreign secretary, Selwyn Lloyd, arrived at the White House in late January, few in Washington or London were optimistic. "What kind of fellow is Nasser?" Ike asked. "He is ambitious," Lloyd responded, and he "dreams of an Arab empire from [the] Atlantic to [the] Persian Gulf."[54] Ambition "was a healthy thing that could be played upon," Dulles observed. Should Nasser actually "become a tool of the Russians," however, "we might have to consider a revision of our whole policy."[55]

Eisenhower, Dulles, and their British counterparts soon agreed that the time had arrived for just such a revision. For Whitehall the moment of truth came on 1 March in Amman, where King Hussein caved in to pro-Nasser demonstrators; expelled Sir John Glubb, Britain's de facto proconsul; and turned control of the British-trained Arab Legion over to Jordanian officers. "It is utter illusion," Eden snapped shortly afterward, "to think that Nasser can be appeased."[56] For the White House it came a few days later in Cairo, where Nasser rejected Eisenhower's appeal to begin peace talks with Israel. "It looks as if Egypt, under Nasser, is going to make no move whatsoever to meet the Israelites," Ike confided in his diary on 8 March. "Moreover, the Arabs, absorbing major consignments of arms from the Soviets, are daily growing more arrogant and [are] disregarding the interests of Western Europe and of the United States in the Middle East."[57]

During the next three weeks U.S. and U.K. officials developed plans for a tough new anti-Nasser strategy. "Like Mussolini before him," Lloyd advised Dulles on 21 March, Nasser had "become beholden to a ruthless power," leaving Britain and the United States little choice but to "withdraw our offer of financial support over the Aswan Dam."[58] There could no longer be any doubt that "Nasser had reached the point of no return," U.K. Middle East experts told their U.S. counterparts in London that same day. His "usual pro-Moslem, anti-British line" had recently been infused with "a new and insidious note of attack on the entire Western position, with reference particularly to oil, i.e. the suggestion that the oil of the Arab countries should be exploited by the people of the area and not by foreigners."[59]

When Eisenhower and his top advisers met on 28 March to review the situation in the Middle East, concerns about Nasser, oil, and Arab nationalism were foremost in their minds. "Near Eastern resources are so vital to the security interests of the United States and the West generally," Assistant Secretary of State William Rountree noted, "that we could not accept a situation in which access to those resources would be subject to hostile control." As the meeting drew to a close, Eisenhower agreed that Britain and the United States should begin exerting political and economic pressure against Egypt, including a de facto freeze on funds for the Aswan project.[60] "A fundamental factor in the problem," Ike noted in his diary, "is the growing ambition of Nasser, the sense of power he has gained out of his association with the Soviets, [and] his belief that he can emerge as a true leader of the entire Arab world."[61]

Tensions mounted between Washington and Cairo during the weeks that followed. "Egypt is taking a bad turn," Eisenhower remarked on 3 April, thanks mainly to Nasser, who was creating "an Arab 'bloc' extending from Pakistan to Dakar, with weak and unstable governments and institutions, and resulting vulnerability to Soviet penetration" and Kremlin influence.[62] "We were going to wake up some morning," Eisenhower grumbled five weeks later, "and find that Egypt, for instance, had slipped behind the Iron Curtain."[63] On 17 May 1956 the Eisenhower administration awoke to the news that Nasser's Egypt had recognized the People's Republic of China. Few actions could have disturbed that arch anticommunist John Foster Dulles more. "Everything Egypt says and does is a slap in the face of the United States," he told Ahmed Hussein, Nasser's representative in Washington. "Recognition of Communist China has brought about an almost impossible situation." Many Americans, Dulles continued, "honestly believed Nasser had made a bargain with the Devil with the hope of developing his own power and establishing an empire stretching from the Persian Gulf to the Atlantic Ocean." Unless Nasser changed his ways, Dulles warned Hussein, the friends of Israel, the cotton lobby, and hard-line Cold Warriors would join forces on Capitol Hill to block funds for the Aswan Dam.[64]

Whitehall was no more enamored of Nasser's ways than the White House. With the approach of summer, Eden's special Middle East Committee wondered whether the time had come publicly to pull the plug on all Western aid for Egypt. "Nasser's conduct became so obviously hostile," the committee reminded the Cabinet on 11 June, "that we agreed with the Americans not to help him anymore, and specifically, to let the Aswan Dam negotiations 'languish,' without telling him so yet." Convinced that Washington and London were stalling, the Egyptians were pressing hard for a straight answer, and this created a dilemma. "If we are forced to declare ourselves against carrying out our undertaking, Nasser is better placed to take his revenge on us than on the Americans," particularly "in the Suez Canal and in the Persian Gulf," the Middle East Committee pointed out. This being so, "it will be a good thing to get the Americans to take the lead."[65]

One step ahead of the Americans and the British, Nasser invited Soviet Foreign Minister Dmitri Shepilov to Cairo in mid-June to discuss Russian funding for the project. According to CIA sources, on 17 June Shepilov offered Nasser a $400 million interest-free Soviet loan to be repaid in cotton over a period of sixty years.[66] Before accepting this "frighteningly good" Soviet proposal to construct the dam, however, Nasser instructed Ambassador Ahmed Hussein to ask John Foster Dulles point-blank whether the United States, Britain, and the World Bank were still prepared to make good on their earlier $200 million offer.[67] The consensus in Washington was that the answer should be a resounding no. The State Department's George Allen may have put it best in a terse memorandum he prepared for Dulles in mid-July. "Our quarrel with Egypt is not that it is following a 'neutral' course in declining to align itself with either the East or West," Allen observed. "Nasser is not guided by 'cold war' considerations but by his own vision of . . . Egyptian preponderance first in the Arab world, next in Africa and then in the Moslem world as a whole." The most effective way to combat such revolutionary ambitions, Allen concluded, was to withdraw the Western offer to finance the Aswan Dam, forcing Nasser to turn to the Kremlin and exposing him throughout the Middle East as a Soviet stooge.[68]

The formal announcement that Washington was pulling out came on 19 July 1956. Just after breakfast Dulles conferred with Eisenhower, who agreed that "we should withdraw the U.S. offer." An hour later Dulles advised British ambassador Roger Makins that the United States now felt that "the project was no longer feasible" and was about to say so publicly.[69] Neither Makins nor his superiors were surprised by the U.S. move. "Mr. Dulles has taken the decision for us," Whitehall's Archibald Ross remarked after hearing the news. "We were not absolutely in step at the last moment but the difference between us was no more than a nuance: refusal outright or refusal implied."[70]

Late that afternoon Dulles informed Ahmed Hussein that Egypt's strident anti-Western policies and its mounting economic woes had forced the United States to retract its earlier offer of assistance. "No single project," Ike's secretary of state explained, "was as unpopular today as the Aswan Dam" was on Capitol Hill.[71] No single political phenomenon, he might have added, evoked as much suspicion and mistrust inside the White House as the Egyptian revolution. "You have heard the news?" Nasser asked Henry Byroade, Jefferson Caffery's successor as U.S. ambassador to Egypt, early the next morning. "I have," came the reply. "We are going to have a lot to talk about," Nasser observed, his mind already riveted on the Suez Canal.[72]

Walking a Tightrope: The Suez Crisis

A few minutes before dusk on 26 July 1956, the fourth anniversary of King Farouk's abdication, Gamal Abdel Nasser strode into Menshiyeh Square in the heart of Alexandria. In a fiery two-hour speech he denounced Western imperialism in general and America's withdrawal of its offer to finance the Aswan Dam in particular. "We shall all of us defend our nationalism and Arabism," Nasser thundered, "and we shall all work so that the Arab homeland may extend from the Atlantic Ocean to the Persian Gulf." To this end, he told the cheering crowd, Egypt would nationalize the Suez Canal Company and use the tolls to finance the Aswan Dam and other badly needed development projects.[73] Although Nasser promised to compensate the firm's British and French shareholders for their losses at book value and although he pledged to keep the canal open, U.K. officials greeted news of the Egyptian takeover with shock, disbelief, and rage. During an emergency meeting of the British Cabinet that went on well after midnight, Prime Minister Anthony Eden and his colleagues quickly "agreed that our essential interests in this area must, if necessary, be safeguarded by military action" against Egypt. "Failure to hold the Suez Canal would lead inevitably to the loss one by one of all our interests and assets in the Middle East."[74]

Nasser's stunning move was greeted more with chagrin than with rage on the other side of the Atlantic. John Foster Dulles, who just a week earlier had gloated that the retraction of U.S. aid for the Aswan Dam was "as big a chess move as US diplomacy has made in a long time," now sputtered that Egypt's "reckless attempt to confiscate a great international investment" confirmed the wisdom of canceling America's offer to help finance the dam.[75] Britain was not likely to stand idly by with Egypt poised to stop the flow of the "two-thirds of Middle Eastern oil [that] passes through the Canal," Undersecretary of State Herbert Hoover Jr. advised Eisenhower on 27 July.[76] Four days later the CIA warned that Egypt's seizure of the Suez Canal would not only "have an intoxicating effect on Arab nationalist sentiment" but might also "encourage future moves toward early nationalization or other action against foreign-owned pipelines and petroleum facilities."[77]

Eisenhower did not doubt for a moment that if Nasser succeeded in mixing Suez with oil and Arab nationalism, there would be explosive consequences. Should Nasser retain control over the Suez Canal, Ike prophesied on 31 July, he would soon be able to "array the world from Dakar to the Philippine Islands against us." John Foster Dulles agreed that "Nasser must be made to disgorge his theft." The challenge for the United States, however, was to accomplish this without resorting to Western military intervention and without "inflaming the whole Arab world." To this end the president instructed Dulles to fly to London for talks with top U.K. officials.[78]

During the long flight across the Atlantic, Dulles put the finishing touches on a plan calling for Britain and the other maritime powers to sit down at the conference table with Egypt and hammer out a peaceful solution to the crisis. British policymakers were hardly enthusiastic about this U.S. proposal. "Nasser was a paranoiac and had the same type of mind as Hitler," Selwyn Lloyd told Dulles on 1 August. Should Britain prove foolish enough to accept prolonged negotiations over the future of the canal, "our economy would then be slowly strangled."[79] Prime Minister Eden was equally blunt when he met with Dulles later that same day. "Prompt forcible action was necessary," Eden explained, because "if Nasser 'got away with it', it would mean disaster for British interests in the whole Middle East, and France felt the same way with respect to their interests in North Africa." Dulles, however, worried that "a military venture by Britain and France . . . could be plausibly portrayed as motivated by imperialist and colonialist ambitions" and could easily create a situation where "all the Arab, and parts of the Moslem world would be arrayed against the United Kingdom." Eden reluctantly agreed, "after considerable discussion, pro and con," that Britain "would be willing to give a try to the conference method, if it could be pushed ahead quickly."[80]

Eden's reluctance proved well founded, for before the week was out, Nasser announced that Egypt would not participate in the conference of Suez Canal users to be held in London in mid-August. "Egypt had gone too far," Eisenhower complained during an NSC meeting on 9 August. How could Europe, he thundered, "be expected to remain at the mercy of the whim of a dictator?" A careful reading of *The Philosophy of the Revolution*, Dulles pointed out, revealed that Nasser had been "dreaming of a great buildup of Arab power and a corresponding diminution of the power of the West" for several years. Nodding, Eisenhower warned that "Nasser's prestige would be so high if he got away with the Canal seizure" that "there will be chaos in the Middle East for a long time."[81]

While Eisenhower and his top advisers fumed, however, conditions halfway around the world were surprisingly unchaotic. Well aware that Britain and France were likely to point to any turmoil in the Eastern Mediterranean as the pretext they needed to send in troops, Nasser took pains to ensure that the Suez Canal continued to operate smoothly and that tankers laden with Persian Gulf oil passed through the contested waterway unimpeded on their way to Western Europe. This was good news for British and French drivers and homeowners, but bad news for U.S. policymakers, who found it increasingly difficult to sell a hard-line anti-Nasser approach on Capitol Hill.[82]

When a bipartisan congressional delegation called at the White House on 12 August to discuss the Suez crisis, Democrats such as Speaker of the House Sam Rayburn and Republicans like California's Senator William Knowland posed the same question. Now that the Egyptians had proved capable of running the canal themselves, why was there any need for Britain or France to contemplate reversing Nasser's nationalization decree? Pointing once again to Nasser's *Philosophy of the Revolution*, Eisenhower argued that "Nasser's aggressive statements . . . seemed much like Hitler's in 'Mein Kampf,' a book no one believed." The British and the French, Dulles added, were convinced that "Nasser is a wild man brandishing an axe and that they do not have to wait for the blow to fall."[83]

Nevertheless, when Dulles arrived in London three days later to attend the eighteen-nation conference on the Suez crisis, he cautioned Prime Minister Eden and French Foreign Minister Christian Pineau not to act on that conviction. Publicly, British and French officials now seemed less determined to attack Egypt and more aware of "the magnitude of the task of military intervention," Dulles cabled Eisenhower on 16 August. Privately, however, they abhorred the prospect of prolonged Egyptian control over the flow of oil from the Persian Gulf and placed little faith in a negotiated settlement.[84] Unimpressed by the decision of the London conference to send an international delegation headed by Australian prime minister Robert Menzies to Cairo for talks with Nasser, Eden predicted that Whitehall would soon "be faced with the choice of accepting a slow strangulation of our economy or taking action which might be unwelcome to some of our friends."[85] Eden's friend in the Oval Office, of course, continued to counsel restraint. Should Britain resort to military intervention in Egypt, Eisenhower warned Eden on 2 September, "the peoples of the Near East and of North Africa and, to some extent, of all of Asia and all of Africa, would be consolidated against the West to a degree which, I fear, could not be overcome in a generation and, perhaps, not even in a century particularly having in mind the capacity of the Russians to make mischief."[86]

Yet even as he wrote, Eisenhower was well aware that hope for a diplomatic solution to the Suez crisis was fading fast. The Menzies delegation arrived in Cairo in early September for two days of desultory talks, during which Nasser reminded his visitors that maritime traffic had continued to pass through the Suez Canal without interruption since the Egyptian takeover six weeks earlier. Why, he wondered on 5 September, was there any need even to consider international control of the waterway? Because, Menzies replied, those who used the canal did not trust Egypt. "Trust is a two-way traffic," Nasser retorted. "I don't trust the proposed users' committee." Nor, he added, did he trust Anthony Eden or John Foster Dulles. "If there is an attempt to impose a solution, it will mean trouble."[87]

Few in Washington were surprised that Menzies made so little headway in Cairo, but nearly everyone worried that his failure would sorely tempt White-hall to commence military operations in the near future. "The British feel that if Nasser gets away with it, it will start a chain of events in the Near East that will reduce the U.K. to another Netherlands or Portugal," John Foster Dulles observed on 6 September. "Our problem in the long run," however, "was how to guide the new nations from colonialism to independence in an orderly way." For Dulles the prescription seemed clear: "We must have evolution, not revolution." Accomplishing this would require a painful process, with the United States "destined to play a mediating role between the powers of Western Europe and the new nations of Asia and Africa; a most unpopular position but one essential to orderly transition."[88]

Dulles shuttled back to London in mid-September for a second conference of maritime powers, where he intended to redouble his efforts at mediation. Amidst rumors of war, Eisenhower's secretary of state won grudging British approval for a Suez Canal Users Association, which would be authorized to collect tolls from all vessels passing through the waterway until Nasser accepted a system of international control. Although Dulles returned to Washington on 22 September touting the association as the best way to resolve the crisis peacefully, Chancellor of the Exchequer Harold Macmillan made it clear when he arrived at Foggy Bottom three days later that the British saw things differently. Because Whitehall could not afford to allow Nasser to control the Suez Canal indefinitely, Macmillan explained, military intervention was fast becoming a possibility. According to Macmillan, Dulles "quite realised that we might have to act by force" and "thought our threat of force was vital, whether we used it or not, to keep Nasser worried." Then, after noting "that at present Suez was not playing much part in the [1956 presidential] election," Eisenhower's secretary of state asked Macmillan for a favor. "Could we not," Dulles wondered, "try and hold things off until after November 6th?"[89]

In just a little more than one month it would become clear that the short answer was no. With no evidence that the Suez Canal Users Association, the United States, or the United Nations could persuade the Egyptians to accept international control of the Suez Canal, Anthony Eden's options began to narrow rapidly in early October. Convinced that open-ended military mobilization would bankrupt Britain without intimidating Nasser, right-wing Conservatives both inside and outside the Cabinet insisted that their prime minister must act forcibly, sooner rather than later. Across the English Channel in Paris, Premier Guy Mollet and his Socialist colleagues echoed Eden's Tory critics. Outraged by Nasser's support for Muslim rebels seeking to liberate Algeria from French rule and resolved that he must never be allowed to control the waterway through which France imported three-quarters of its oil, Mollet and Foreign Minister Pineau secretly contacted Israeli leaders to propose re-taking the Suez Canal by force. Hoping to deliver a knockout blow to the Nasser regime before the Egyptians had fully integrated their recently acquired Soviet planes and tanks into their arsenal, Prime Minister David Ben Gurion agreed to meet Selwyn Lloyd and Christian Pineau at Sevres, a fashionable suburb just outside Paris, on 23 October.[90]

The next day Israel, Britain, and France approved a complicated plan for military intervention. Under the terms of the Sevres protocol, within a week Israel was to attack Egypt without warning and march through the Sinai Desert to the banks of the Suez Canal. Britain and France would then issue an ultimatum calling for both Israel and Egypt to pull back at least ten miles from the waterway. By prior agreement the Israelis would comply at once. Nasser, however, was certain to reject the ultimatum as a gross infringement of Egyptian sovereignty, providing Eden and Mollet with the pretext they needed to send in British and French troops to protect the canal. Neither Britain nor France was willing to risk informing the United States in advance and preferred instead to present the Eisenhower administration with a fait accompli on the eve of the 1956 elections.[91]

News of Israel's lightning strike across the Sinai reached Washington on Monday afternoon, 29 October, just as Eisenhower was completing a hectic day of campaigning. During an Oval Office meeting a few hours later, the furious chief executive expressed outrage that the Israelis had ignored his personal eleventh-hour appeal not to initiate hostilities. "Foster, you tell 'em, goddamn it," Ike roared. "We're going to apply sanctions, we're going to the United Nations, we're going to do everything that there is so we can stop this thing."[92] Eisenhower grew even angrier as evidence mounted of British complicity. "We should let them know at once," he growled, "that we recognize that much is on their side in this dispute with the Egyptians, but that nothing justifies double-crossing us."[93]

For weeks Ambassador Roger Makins had been warning that America's long-standing opposition to colonialism would make it extremely difficult for the Eisenhower administration to support an imperial display of armed force in Egypt. "As regards military action," Makins cautioned Lloyd on 9 September, "to attempt it without full American moral and military support could easily lead to disaster."[94] A month later Makins told Eden that "I have noticed before this deep seated feeling about colonialism, which is common to so many Americans, occasionally welling up inside Foster [Dulles] like lava in a dormant volcano."[95] To be sure, some Americans had believed all along that Western military intervention was the best way to resolve the Suez crisis. Dean Acheson, for example, had nothing but contempt for Nasser, whom he would later describe as "a male Cleopatra playing off the two superpowers." Never bashful about expressing his European-centered view of the world, Truman's secretary of state told Cyrus Sulzberger over dinner in Georgetown on 17 October 1956 that "Britain and France should have invaded Egypt within two weeks instead of dawdling on the Suez Canal issue."[96]

Nevertheless, it was the volcanic Dulles and not the stolidly Anglophilic Acheson who occupied the top post at Foggy Bottom. And it was Dulles who had the direct line to the furious occupant of the Oval Office when Britain and France stopped their dawdling two weeks later. Convinced that the French and the British "might well be considered the aggressors in the eyes of the world, engaged in an anti-Arab, anti-Asian war," Dulles and Eisenhower worked desperately throughout the morning of 30 October to arrange an Israeli-Egyptian cease-fire before Eden and Mollet could send in their troops.[97] Early that afternoon, however, Dulles telephoned Eisenhower with terrible news. Britain and France had just delivered "a 12-hour ultimatum to Egypt that is about as crude & brutal as anything he has ever seen." This meant, Dulles added, "that of course by tomorrow they will be in."[98] Because that was almost certain to lead to the cutoff of all oil from the Persian Gulf, Eisenhower sat down with Arthur Flemming, the director of the Office of Defense Mobilization, to discuss whether to reallocate petroleum supplies from the Western Hemisphere to Western Europe. "Extremely angry with both the British and the French for taking this action unilaterally," the president did not mince words. "Those who began this operation," he told Flemming, "should be left to work out their own oil problems — to boil in their own oil, so to speak."[99]

Eisenhower's actions soon showed that he meant what he said. Just after dusk on 31 October, British *Canberra* bombers based in Malta and Cyprus leveled Egyptian fortifications in the canal zone and destroyed Nasser's air force. "The White House," one observer recalled afterward, "crackled with barrack-room language," mostly Eisenhower's. "Bombs by God," Ike thundered. "What does Anthony think he's doing?"[100] In a nationally televised address to the American people later that evening, Eisenhower scarcely concealed his anger with the British for blocking a cease-fire resolution favored by the United Nations Security Council and vowed to bring a similar proposal before the General Assembly, where there was no great power veto. "There can be no peace — without law," Eisenhower concluded. "And there can be no law — if we were to invoke one code of international conduct for those who oppose us — and another for our friends."[101]

To a great degree Ike's vow to resolve the Suez crisis under the auspices of international law despite the objections of America's friends was designed to seize the moral high ground from America's chief opponent, the Soviet Union, which was invoking the law of the jungle in the streets of Budapest. For nearly a year Premier Nikita Khrushchev had been pursuing "de-Stalinization," a bold attempt at political liberalization inside Russia. News of Khrushchev's program touched off a revolution of rising expectations among the Kremlin's Eastern European satellites. While the rest of the world was mesmerized in August and September by the slow-motion crisis unfolding at Suez, Imre Nagy, a sixty-year-old apparatchik, led a grassroots movement for reform and national self-determination in Hungary. After Nagy became prime minister in late October, he abolished one-party rule and persuaded the Kremlin to withdraw all Soviet troops stationed inside Hungary at once. Eisenhower received the good news from Budapest just before the speech in which he would condemn British, French, and Israeli aggression against Egypt. Likening de-Stalinization in Eastern Europe to "the time of the American Revolution," he drew an implicit parallel between the minutemen of 1776 and Nagy's freedom fighters in 1956 and praised "this brave people" who had "offered their very lives for independence from foreign masters."[102]

The next morning, as Eisenhower prepared for an NSC meeting that would decide U.S. policy at Suez, Hungary's foreign masters executed an abrupt about-face and sent their armored columns clanking back toward Budapest for a showdown with Nagy. With bombs falling on Egypt, with tanks rolling into Hungary, and with elections just a week away, an angry and frustrated John Foster Dulles wasted little time summing up America's dilemma. "It is nothing less than tragic that at this very time, when we are on the point of winning an immense and long-hoped-for victory over Soviet colonialism in Eastern Europe," he observed on 1 November, "we should be forced to choose between following in the footsteps of Anglo-French colonialism in Asia and Africa, or splitting our course away from their course." For more than a decade "the United States has been walking a tightrope between the effort to maintain our old and valued relations with our British and French allies on the one hand, and on the other trying to assure ourselves of the friendship and understanding of the newly independent countries who have escaped from colonialism." Unless Washington could persuade London and Paris to withdraw from Suez, Dulles warned his colleagues, "we will be looked upon as forever tied to British and French colonialist policies," and the new nations of Asia and Africa "will turn from us to the USSR" for world leadership. "Win or lose," he concluded, "we will share the fate of Britain and France."[103]

Not everyone sitting around the cabinet table was as eager to step off the tightrope as Dulles. Treasury secretary George Humphrey, for example, thought that it might be wiser to rely on United Nations mediation to resolve the crisis. Secretary of Defense Charles Wilson worried that a falling out between the United States and its longtime allies would seriously weaken NATO. Presidential adviser Harold Stassen actually suggested that Eisenhower look the other way while Eden and Mollet finished Nasser off. A little amazed by Stassen's hawkish position, the president asked, "How could we possibly support Britain and France if in doing so we lose the whole Arab world?" Admitting that there were risks either way, Eisenhower said that "his idea was to do what was decent and right, but still not condemn more furiously than we had to." After all, Eisenhower added as the meeting broke up, "he had told Anthony Eden a week ago that if the British did what they are now doing and the Russians got into the Middle East, the fat would really be in the fire."[104]

On several occasions during the next four days the fat in the fire seemed on the verge of flaring into a global inferno. In the wee hours of 2 November the United Nations General Assembly passed a resolution calling for an immediate cease-fire and a speedy withdrawal of all Israeli troops from Egyptian territory. Refusing to comply, Britain and France sought to divert attention from their own impending airborne and amphibious assault on Egypt by calling for prompt U.N. action to prevent a Soviet crackdown against Hungary. Dulles was furious with the British and the French. "It is a mockery for them to come in with bombs falling over Egypt," he told U.S. ambassador to the United Nations Henry Cabot Lodge, "and denounce the SU for perhaps doing something that is not quite as bad."[105]

Thirty-six hours later, however, Dulles and Eisenhower learned that the Kremlin had done something far worse. Just before dawn on 4 November, Soviet tanks opened fire on lightly armed anticommunist militiamen in central Budapest, Russian jets strafed the Hungarian parliament building, and Nikita Khrushchev ordered the arrest of Imre Nagy, who was secretly transported to Moscow and executed early in the new year. By the time the shooting stopped at the end of the month, 4,000 Hungarians lay dead, a half-million had fled across the border into neutral Austria, and Janos Kadar, Nagy's successor as prime minister, had reestablished a Stalinist police state backed by the Red Army.[106]

While the world reeled from news of the awful carnage in the streets of Budapest, 600 British paratroopers, the first contingent of what was to become a 22,000-man Anglo-French invasion force, landed silently along the banks of the Suez Canal on 5 November. Hoping Eisenhower might acquiesce at the last moment, Anthony Eden tried to place the assault on Egypt in the context of containing Arab revolutionary nationalism. "If we had allowed things to drift," he cabled Ike, "Nasser would have become a kind of Moslem Mussolini and our friends in Iraq, Jordan, Saudi Arabia, and even Iran would gradually have been brought down."[107] There was no disagreement in Washington that Nasserism posed a serious threat to pro-Western regimes throughout the area. Indeed, Eisenhower was secretly delighted that Britain's airborne assault had left the Napoleon of the Arabs in a "hopeless" position. "Tell Nasser," Eisenhower joked, "we'll be glad to put him on St. Helena and give him a million bucks."[108]

The message that Eisenhower had received from Soviet president Nikolai Bulganin a few hours earlier, however, was no laughing matter. Bulganin proposed a joint Soviet-American peacekeeping operation in the Middle East and implied that, should the United States decline to participate, the Kremlin might act unilaterally. "The Soviets," Ike told his top aides, "seeing their position and their policy failing so badly in the satellites, are ready to take any wild adventure." In light of all this, Eisenhower concluded, Britain and France must be persuaded to accept the United Nations cease-fire at once in order to prevent the Suez crisis from escalating into a full-blown superpower confrontation. Then, he frowned, U.S. officials should ask the Arabs, "Do you want the Soviets in the Middle East doing what they are now doing in Hungary?"[109]

Tuesday, 6 November, was election day, but Eisenhower was less concerned about ballots in Middle America than about bullets in the Middle East. The news that both Britain and France had accepted a cease-fire just after noon was greeted with great relief at the White House. The president immediately telephoned Anthony Eden to emphasize the importance of speedy British and French withdrawal from Suez. Dragging matters out, Ike explained, would "give Egypt an opportunity to quibble" and invite further Soviet meddling in the Arab world. Eden promised to withdraw just as soon as a United Nations peacekeeping force, preferably composed mostly of U.S. troops, was in place to ensure the security of the canal. Worried that the Kremlin would use such an arrangement as a pretext for dispatching Soviet "peacekeepers" to the Middle East, Eisenhower preferred to see "none of the great nations in it." Otherwise, he warned Eden, "I am afraid the Red boy is going to demand the lion's share."[110]

Convinced that a precipitous U.K. withdrawal so soon after invading Egypt would mean the fall of his own government, Eden balked, forcing Eisenhower reluctantly to employ economic leverage—steady pressure on the pound sterling and an informal embargo on Western Hemisphere oil—against Britain in mid-November. With British gold and petroleum reserves dwindling rapidly and with Eden considering resignation, Chancellor of the Exchequer Harold Macmillan took the lead in hammering out a bargain with the Eisenhower administration at the end of the month. Once U.K. troops began to withdraw from Suez on 3 December, dollars and oil once again began to flow into Britain from the United States.[111]

Eager to patch up its relations with Whitehall, the Eisenhower administration emphasized that its commitment to anticolonialism should not be misconstrued as an endorsement of revolutionary nationalism, Arab style. Irritated by Nasser's "great undependability and unreliability" and suspicious of his "overweening ambitions," top U.S. officials worried that if the Egyptian revolution remained unchecked, it might, like its French precursor a century and a half earlier, disrupt the regional balance of power and trigger a wider conflict.[112] On 12 December Dulles arrived in Paris for a NATO meeting with instructions from Eisenhower to remind America's allies that "we regard Nasser as an evil influence" whose radical ideology threatened Western interests throughout the Middle East. "We have made it abundantly clear that while we share in general the British and French opinions of Nasser," Ike added, "they chose a bad time and incident on which to launch corrective measures."[113] Choosing a good time to undertake such measures was a question that would bedevil Washington right down through Nasser's death in September 1970.

Dining with the Devil: America and Nasser, 1957–1970

If Eisenhower's handling of the Suez crisis showed that the United States regarded European colonialism as a relic of the past, the policies that Ike and his successors pursued during the next fifteen years confirmed that America did not view nationalist revolution as the wave of the future. For every occupant of the White House from Eisenhower to Nixon, dealing with Nasser was tantamount to dining with the devil. By combining economic rewards with military threats, they hoped to exorcise the demon of Nasserism and shield pro-Western regimes from revolutionary change.

Nasser's categorical rejection of the Eisenhower Doctrine in early 1957 suggested that the exorcism was likely to be long and painful. Claiming that "there was no danger from Soviet aggression" in the Muslim world, Nasser insisted on 10 January that the real target of Eisenhower's new policy was Arab nationalism, not international communism.[114] Dulles begged to differ. "There is ample evidence of Communist infiltration into certain areas," he assured the Senate Foreign Relations Committee four days later, and the Egyptians were deluding themselves if they thought otherwise.[115] "We were not opposed to nationalism but supported it," Eisenhower's secretary of state insisted on 5 February. "We did not, however, support the type of nationalism which would lead to a loss of independence, especially," he emphasized, "in the Middle East." Countries pursuing an ideology "dependent upon Communism" would soon "isolate themselves and die," Dulles concluded. "Nasser's philosophy would have this result."[116]

During the months ahead, however, Eisenhower and Dulles detected numerous signs that Nasserism, far from expiring, was about to infect Syria. Despite U.S. support for Syrian independence immediately after the Second

World War, the political climate in Damascus had become poisonously anti-American by the Eisenhower era, thanks mainly to the rise of the Ba'ath Party, whose leaders praised Nasser, preached "Unity, Socialism, and Freedom," and promoted closer ties with Moscow.[117] By the summer of 1957 Syria was being run by a Ba'athist revolutionary command council modeled on Egypt's and headed by Abdel Hamid al-Sarraj, a friend of Nasser and a foe of the Eisenhower Doctrine. News that the Syrians intended to swap surplus wheat for Russian military hardware in late July prompted the CIA to step up its covert political action in Damascus. Insisting that "we could not afford to have exist a Soviet satellite not contiguous to the Soviet border and in the midst of the already delicate Middle East situation," in mid-August Dulles actually urged Ike to consider overt military intervention.[118] Although Eisenhower stopped short of sending in the marines, he believed that the Sarraj regime "was far more vulnerable to Communist penetration than was Egypt" and moved secretly in early September to arm several of Syria's anticommunist and anti-Nasser neighbors.[119]

Convinced that Arab unity constituted the best antidote for Western intimidation, Colonel Sarraj flew to Cairo in January 1958 for talks with Nasser regarding the creation of a Syro-Egyptian confederation to be called the United Arab Republic (UAR). Well aware that nationalism, Cairo style, was not universally popular in Damascus and that Syria's laissez-faire economy was not likely to mesh well with Egyptian state socialism, Nasser nevertheless believed that the creation of the UAR would confirm his emergence as the true leader of the Arab world and demonstrate his intention to keep his distance from both Moscow and Washington. Persuaded that the potential pluses outweighed the obvious minuses, Nasser announced that the new confederation would come into being in February.[120]

State Department experts regarded these developments as a mixed blessing. In the short run Nasser's latest move would probably mean the "complete elimination [of] Communist influence from Syria." But in the long run the formation of the UAR seemed certain to "facilitat[e] Egyptian domination [of the] Arab world," something that might have revolutionary consequences for America's friends in the region.[121] From his perch in Cairo, Ambassador Raymond Hare retorted that Egypt's complicated merger with Syria would force Nasser to turn his attention from exporting revolution and toward managing internal affairs.[122] Although few in Washington were as confident as Hare that Nasser's preoccupation with consolidating the UAR would lead him to scale back his pan-Arab aspirations, the Eisenhower administration did recognize the UAR on 25 February 1958, despite much grumbling from Iraq and other pro-Western regimes.[123]

During the next two years U.S. relations with the UAR slowly began to warm up. Radio Cairo, of course, continued to brand pro-Western leaders such as Lebanon's Camille Chamoun and Jordan's King Hussein as American stooges, and U.S. policymakers continued to blur the distinction between Nasserism and communism. But after Nasser condemned the Kremlin for meddling in Iraq and jailed Egyptian communists in early 1959, the Eisenhower administration offered him $150 million worth of surplus U.S. wheat under the auspices of Public Law 480 (PL-480), the Food for Peace program. To be sure, Ike would still tell Britain's new prime minister, Harold Macmillan, that "Nasser was not a character that we respected." He would still nod when Britain's old foreign secretary, Selwyn Lloyd, remarked that "dining with the devil called for a long spoon."[124] He would still cringe when Nasser supported Congolese revolutionaries in their unsuccessful bid to topple the pro-Western conservatives who ruled the newly independent former Belgian colony during the summer of 1960. But Eisenhower would also smile when the Arab world's leading revolutionary made his only visit to the United States later that same year. Indeed, after Nasser confessed in September 1960 that "he had wanted good relations with the U.S. ever since 1952 when he came to power," Eisenhower replied that the feeling was mutual.[125]

After taking up residence at 1600 Pennsylvania Avenue, John F. Kennedy hoped to expand his predecessor's modest rapprochement with Nasser through a blend of personal diplomacy and economic aid. "Nasser's got his problems. I've got my problems," JFK told White House aide Richard Goodwin in early 1961. "I'm not going to persuade him to act against his interests. I won't even try. But it can't hurt down the line if we understand each other a little better."[126] To this end Kennedy tapped John Badeau, the Arabic-speaking former president of the American University in Cairo, as his new ambassador to the UAR. A longtime Nasser-watcher, Badeau was convinced that with U.S. help, the Egyptian revolution could transform the Middle East, just as the French revolution had transformed Europe two centuries earlier. To this end Badeau used the promise of more PL-480 wheat during the last half of 1961 to convince Nasser to put hot-button issues such as Palestine "in the ice box" and to put simmering problems like Egyptian economic development on the front burner.[127]

By early 1962 Egyptian-American relations were better than they had been in a decade. After a five-day visit to Cairo, Chester Bowles, JFK's roving ambassador to the Third World, confirmed that Nasser's Egypt stood at a crossroads. "If Nasser can gradually be led to forsake the microphone for the bulldozer," Bowles cabled the White House on 21 February, "he may assume a key role in bringing the Middle East peacefully into our modern world." Four months later U.S. and UAR officials initialed a three-year, $500 million PL-480 wheat agreement in Washington. All smiles, Bowles, Badeau, and other Egypt-watchers inside the Kennedy administration hoped that Nasser was finally ready to shed his revolutionary regalia and don his work boots.[128]

During the autumn of 1962, however, the leader of the Egyptian revolution would make it clear that he still preferred tanks to bulldozers. For almost a year Nasser had been nursing an ego badly bruised by Syria's secession from the UAR after a right-wing coup in Damascus in September 1961. When a left-wing coup rocked Yemen, a backward land at the mouth of the Red Sea, a year later, Nasser saw a chance to recapture his lost charisma. After pro-Nasser officers in San'a, the Yemeni capital, abolished the monarchy, proclaimed the Yemen Arab Republic (YAR), and appealed for Egyptian assistance, the president of the UAR sent troops, tanks, and jet fighters to his revolutionary comrades in Southwest Arabia in October 1962.[129]

Unwilling to jeopardize America's promising new relationship with Egypt, the Kennedy administration at first downplayed Nasser's role in the Yemeni revolution and recognized the YAR just before Christmas. Privately, however, U.S. policymakers confessed that YAR president Abdallah al-Sallal reminded them of Nasser in the wake of his coup against King Farouk. "Yemen had been ripe for revolution," State Department Middle East specialist Rodger Davies told a reporter on 3 January 1963. "It was one of the most primitive countries in the world, a theocratic state and an anachronism even in the Arab world." Nasserism was bound to appeal to Sallal and other YAR leaders, who were eager to modernize their own country. "What was occurring in Egypt," Davies explained, "was the nearest thing to a social revolution in the area."[130]

The possibility that social revolution might spread from Yemen to Saudi Arabia next door, however, did not sit well with Crown Prince Faisal, the House of Saud's foreign minister. Deeply troubled by the presence of Egyptian troops and fighter-bombers in Yemen, Faisal funneled aid to royalist guerrillas and complained bitterly that Nasser had interpreted Washington's tilt toward Cairo "as a hunting license to go after Saudi Arabia."[131] Whitehall, whose Aden protectorate had become the target of pro-Nasser radicals backed by the YAR, echoed Faisal's complaints. Kennedy tended to be sympathetic. "The big risk as we see it is that Nasser and his little brother Sallal will in their frustration adopt more extremist lines," JFK wrote British prime minister Harold Macmillan in late January. "If Nasser escalates and the Saudis then hit back with mercenary pilots, we may have the Near East aflame," Kennedy added. "I'm sure this will suit the Soviets, but you and I would surely be the losers."[132]

Although it never escalated to a full-scale conflagration, the Saudi-Egyptian proxy war in Southwest Arabia dragged on for more than five years and eventually helped destroy America's rapprochement with Nasser's Egypt. Throughout the spring of 1963 and into the summer, the Kennedy administration pressed both sides to implement a United Nations plan calling for the House of Saud to halt its aid to the Yemeni royalists and for Nasser gradually to bring his troops, his tanks, and his warplanes home. Despite the best efforts of U.S. and U.N. diplomats, however, the fighting in Yemen continued. By early autumn JFK was convinced that the root of the problem lay in Cairo, not in Riyadh, and he told Nasser so. Egypt's meddling in Yemen, Kennedy pointed out on 19 October, was "inevitably complicating, not least in the Congress, my own effort to carry forward our policy of friendly collaboration in areas of mutual interest with the UAR."[133] What JFK meant became clear in short order. On 7 November both the House and the Senate amended the annual foreign aid bill and banned economic assistance for any nation "engaging in or preparing for aggressive military efforts" against the United States or its friends. Although the White House pledged to honor the final two years of its PL-480 commitment to Egypt, within days Nasser was "speaking bitterly and at length against the U.S. tactic of using aid to put pressure on him."[134]

Lyndon Johnson had always regarded Kennedy's opening to Nasser as a fool's errand doomed to fail because of Egyptian duplicity and U.S. naïveté. LBJ's skepticism stemmed not only from his own sympathy for Israel but also from Nasser's support for revolution in the Middle East and elsewhere in the Third World. The prophet of Egypt's liberation was little more than a tin-pot colonel who spent too much time "trying to dominate the Arab world," Johnson grumbled many years later, and too little "improving the lot of his own people."[135] By the summer of 1964 State Department officials had confirmed that Nasser was still firmly entrenched in Yemen and still calling for the "Export of Revolution" to Libya, Jordan, Saudi Arabia, and other "traditional tribal and monarchic regimes" in the region.[136] Furthermore, Nasser's promise in early September to help the newly created PLO train a guerrilla army and his pledge in mid-October to continue helping Congolese radicals battle Western imperialism left little doubt that he intended to export his revolution even more widely.[137]

Before the year was over, angry African exchange students chanting anti-American slogans stormed the USIA library in Cairo and burned it to the ground. When Nasser declined to apologize, Johnson resorted to economic leverage. "How can I ask Congress for wheat," he snapped at Egyptian ambassador Mustapha Kamel just before Christmas, "when you burn our library?"[138] Johnson answered his own question early in the new year by tabling plans to renew the PL-480 Food for Peace deal that JFK had struck with Egypt. Nasser and other Third World radicals such as Indonesia's Achmed Sukarno and Ghana's Kwame Nkrumah must be taught not to bite the hand that feeds, LBJ told congressional leaders on 22 January. Echoing his boss, Dean Rusk agreed that the time had come to send the unmistakable message that there would be "no new agreements with Nasser."[139]

By resorting to economic leverage during 1965, however, the Johnson administration merely tempted Nasser to step up his revolutionary jeremiads. In February he invited Che Guevara, who was in the process of injecting Cuban-style revolution into the heart of Africa, to Cairo to discuss how best to topple the pro-American regime in the Congo.[140] U.S. policymakers were even more disturbed later that spring when Nasser unveiled a "Blueprint for the Liberation of Palestine" that called for "Arab revolutionary action" against Israel.[141] These developments caused considerable concern for Lyndon Johnson, who must have bristled in September 1965 when Foggy Bottom reported that "the Near East is not yet at the Viet-Nam stage of anti-Western insurgency, but Soviet advisors have already infiltrated the inner circles of the Arab military in Egypt, Syria, and Yemen."[142]

Egyptian-American relations grew even chillier during the spring of 1966. In April Nasser permitted the Viet Cong to open an office in Cairo, a gesture that confirmed his "sympathy if not support for [the] insurgents . . . as [a] progressive, nationalist and not necessarily communist movement."[143] A month later Johnson learned that the Egyptians were stirring up more trouble in the Middle East. "Nasir has attacked the Shah [of Iran] directly in recent speeches," the CIA reported on 21 May, and "is actively engaged in subversive activity in the Persian Gulf sheikdoms."[144] The agency also suspected that the Kremlin was "preparing to work somewhat more closely with [Nasser] than in the past in espousing his kind of Arab nationalism, socialism, and opposition to Western influence."[145]

With the approach of summer, some top U.S. policymakers were inclined to write Nasser off as a lost cause. Walt Rostow, who had recently become Johnson's national security adviser, gradually emerged as a particularly staunch critic of the UAR, less because of his private affection for Israel than because of his very public distaste for Soviet-backed wars of national liberation in the Third World. There was no point, Rostow told his boss on 18 June, in resuming Food for Peace aid to Egypt. "We recommend this line with some regret," he explained, "but Nasser has left us little choice." The list of Nasser's sins was predictable. "He has almost dared us publicly not to renew our agreement. He has lambasted us on Vietnam," Rostow reminded LBJ, and "he continues to stir things up in Yemen and South Arabia."[146]

The news elsewhere in the Middle East was no more encouraging. In Damascus, where the Ba'ath Party had staged a coup in February, ruthless young Syrian officers such as Hafez al-Assad were challenging Nasser for leadership of the Arab world and calling for war with Israel. "A new radical government in Syria increased terrorist raids against Israel, sending Arab guerrillas across the borders," Johnson recalled in his memoirs, in a "flagrant violation of international law" reminiscent of Viet Cong attacks on U.S. troops in South

Vietnam. When LBJ requested "a special study of Soviet penetration in the Middle East" in late 1966, his advisers confirmed "a pattern of serious Soviet advances," not only in Damascus but also in Cairo, where Nasser was busily substituting rubles for dollars.[147]

To assess the threat that Nasser and the Soviet Union presented for the United States and its friends, the White House sent NSC Middle East expert Harold Saunders to Tel Aviv and several Arab capitals in early 1967. His report makes gloomy reading even thirty years after it landed on LBJ's desk in mid-May. Noting that Soviet-backed wars of national liberation were shaping up from the West Bank to Aden, Saunders was particularly disturbed by *"the deepening political cleavages"* in the Middle East, not just between Arabs and Israelis, but also "between moderate (Saudi Arabia, Jordan, Lebanon) and pro-Nasser states." Both sets of cleavages intersected in Cairo. For the Israelis, Nasser was little more than Hitler on the Nile. For Saudi Arabia's King Faisal, "Nasser is the agent of Communism and is out to topple moderate regimes throughout the area" with Soviet help. "If Egypt ever gets over revolutionary phobias and inferiority complexes, its 30 million people, its economic inheritance, its drive to lead, its pride of achievement and its military power make it unquestionably the Arab power," Saunders concluded on 16 May. But at present, "one is almost forced to agree with many of our Israeli and Arab friends that the only language Nasser understands is firmness backed by unmistakable military power and the willingness to apply it."[148]

Almost before the ink was dry on this grim forecast, Nasser took steps that would prompt his enemies to speak to him in the language that he seemed to know best. In quick succession he forced United Nations peacekeepers to evacuate their outposts in the Sinai Desert, positioned Egyptian troops along the border with Israel, and closed the Straits of Tiran at the mouth of the Gulf of Aqaba to Israeli shipping.[149] In late May 1967 Johnson and his NSC pondered how best to persuade Nasser to back down. "The main issue in the Middle East today is whether Nasser, the radical states and their Soviet backers are going to dominate the area," Walt Rostow observed with characteristic bluntness. "A related issue is whether the US is going to stand up for its friends, the moderates, or back down as a major power in the Near East" at a time when the Kremlin was probing for weak spots. "Two weeks ago, we expected South Arabia to provide that test," Rostow concluded. "The current Arab-Israeli crisis has brought the test sooner than we expected."[150]

Nasser's left-wing adventurism was deeply disturbing for America's friends in the Middle East, who seemed by early June increasingly eager to lay low the leading revolutionary in the Arab world. The Israelis could not be expected to wait forever for Nasser to come to his senses and reopen the Straits of Tiran, Walt Rostow advised Johnson just fifteen hours before the shooting started. Equally important, from Beirut to Tehran moderate Muslims were growing tired of Nasser's pan-Arab rabble-rousing. "Just beneath the surface is the potentiality for a new phase in the Middle East of moderation; a focusing on economic development; regional collaboration; and an acceptance of Israel as part of the Middle East," Rostow told his boss on 4 June. "But all this depends on Nasser's being cut down to size."[151]

This kind of thinking seems to have guided Johnson's policies, and those of his Middle Eastern friends, during the Six Day War and its immediate aftermath. Almost everyone in Israel, of course, hoped that Nasser would be cut down to size, preferably sooner rather than later.[152] So did his Muslim enemies like the shah of Iran. Indeed, during a meeting with Undersecretary of State Averell Harriman in Paris just a few hours after the war erupted, the shah said that he "considered the long-range objective of both the United States and Iran to be 'how Nasser could be destroyed.'"[153] During a White House lunch with ambassadors from six conservative Arab states, Johnson provided his answer four months after the shooting stopped. While LBJ was trying to convince his guests that U.S. policy in the Middle East was not so much pro-Israel as anti-Nasser, one of the White House beagles wandered into the Fish Room to beg for table scraps. According to one of the guests, Johnson called the dog over and began talking to it. "What can I do? One man was so nasty to his neighbor that his neighbor was not able to stand it any more," he drawled. "So his neighbor took hold of him and gave him a good beating. What can I do to him?"[154] For LBJ the lesson seemed clear. With America's blessing, Israel had finally exposed the bankruptcy of Arab revolutionary nationalism.

Although the beagle's thoughts that day went unrecorded, Nasser would spend the final eighteen months of his life trying to show LBJ's successor that the Texas Democrat was wrong. Like Lyndon Johnson, Richard Nixon had long regarded Nasserism with a mixture of fear and loathing. The California Republican had begun monitoring the Arab radicals a decade earlier, when he had used his limited influence as Eisenhower's vice-president to plump for a hard line against the Egyptian revolution at the height of the Suez crisis. A July 1963 visit to Egypt, where Soviet engineers were just completing work on the Aswan Dam, left citizen Nixon more convinced than ever that Nasser was a garden-variety Third World revolutionary. "Like Sukarno and Nkrumah, Nasser had devoted the best of his energies to revolution," Nixon recalled in his memoirs. "Now he was more interested in a grandiose crusade for Arab unity than he was in the vital but less glamorous task of managing and improving Egypt's economic, political, and social structure."[155]

Nixon's dealings with Nasser after January 1969 merely reinforced the misgivings he had expressed after his visit to Egypt five and a half years earlier.

While the new president was still settling into the Oval Office, Egyptian artillery began to pound Israeli positions along the Suez Canal in the first phase of what by the end of the year would become a bloody "War of Attrition." Nasser's decision to escalate the conflict with Israel reflected his own frustration with the Nixon administration. "It has become obvious to us that America's attitude toward the Arabs . . . is gradually going from bad to worse and that the US has finally reached total partiality for Israel," he told his cabinet on 28 June 1969. "I can see no hope with the Americans until they have become completely convinced that we are capable of both steadfastness and confrontation."[156]

By early 1970 the Israeli air force was flying "deep penetration" raids against Egyptian military positions and the Arab world's leading revolutionary was receiving shiploads of Soviet surface-to-air missiles. Stunned by Nasser's latest deal with Moscow, the White House sent Joseph Sisco, a seasoned troubleshooter, to Cairo in early April. Nasser, however, greeted Nixon's emissary coolly, blasted U.S. policy as pro-Israel, and "speaking for all the Arabs," vowed to liberate Palestine. "He said in very straightforward and plain language he does not trust us," Sisco cabled Washington, "and he feels he has no alternative but to rely on the Soviet Union."[157]

Nixon and his national security adviser, Henry Kissinger, regarded Egypt's latest flirtation with Russia as further evidence that Nasser preferred revolution over realpolitik. "He gloried in his radicalism, which he thought essential to his Pan-Arab ambitions, and for this he must have felt compelled to remain in perpetual confrontation with us in the Middle East," Kissinger observed nine years after Nasser suffered a fatal heart attack in September 1970. "Nasser could not make the choice between his rhetorical ambitions and his intuition of the limits of Egypt's ability to achieve those ambitions" and had "died without ever making the choice."[158]

Notwithstanding the stinging epitaph offered by Henry Kissinger, Gamal Abdel Nasser did, in fact, choose at the end of his life to reaffirm the revolutionary pan-Arab ideology that he had first unveiled nearly two decades earlier. "Every people on earth goes through two revolutions," he had written in *The Philosophy of the Revolution* in 1955, one political and the other social. "For us, the terrible experience through which our people are going is that we are having both revolutions at the same time." Because "it was not within our power to stand on the road of history like a traffic policeman and hold up the passage of one revolution until the other had passed by," Nasser concluded, "the only thing possible to do was act as best we could and try to avoid being ground between the millstones."[159]

Fifteen years after he wrote those words, Nasser reminisced about how he had prevented the Egyptian revolution from being pulverized. "When thinking about practical ways of protecting the revolution, you have first to define its friends and its enemies," he observed in February 1970. Then "you must pay attention to reforming the economy and you must avoid creating any economic recession." As for foreign affairs, the successful revolutionary must always remember that "the United States will attempt to contain you in order to protect its strategic and economic interests, while the Soviet Union will work to support and back you." Nasser, however, had few illusions about the motives of the Kremlin. "The Soviet Union's attitude towards us is not inspired by love for our dark eyes," he laughed, "but is based on our endeavours to eliminate Western colonialism in the region." When Nasser died seven months later, his commitment to those revolutionary endeavors remained as strong as ever.[160]

Nasser's steadfast antiimperialism certainly came as no surprise to John Badeau, who had returned from his brief stint as Washington's emissary in Cairo during the early 1960s to write an inside account of his errand among the Arabs. In the spring of 1968 the ambassador-turned-professor published *The American Approach to the Arab World*, a diplomatic primer about the "political and ideological cold war" raging in the Middle East between those who favored change and those wedded to the status quo. Radical nationalists such as Nasser were trumpeting the virtues of revolution, while conservatives from Rabat to Riyadh were preaching the value of tradition. "New men" inspired by a "new nationalism," Badeau explained, had sparked "a revolt of middle and lower classes against the traditional elite," first in Egypt and then in Syria and Yemen. Nasser and his comrades saw no reason why their prescription for radical change would not work its magic in other Arab lands. "If the revolutionary leaders are right," Badeau warned his readers, "the traditional rulers might ultimately lose their thrones and possibly their heads."[161]

Eighteen months before Badeau's primer appeared in Capitol Hill bookstores, J. William Fulbright, the Arkansas Democrat who chaired the Senate Foreign Relations Committee, had offered some similar words to a much wider audience. In his best-selling book *The Arrogance of Power*, Fulbright traced America's ambivalent encounter with social upheavals in the Third World and argued that, for a variety of reasons, Americans were "emotionally and intellectually handicapped" in dealing with revolutionaries like Fidel Castro, Mao Zedong, and by implication, Gamal Abdel Nasser. Although most Americans were loath to admit it, they lived in "an unrevolutionary society" frightened by the prospect of radical change and unwilling to admit that the peoples of Africa, Asia, and the Middle East were likely to pursue a path to the future very different from the one traveled by the United States. The concept of "peaceful revolution," Fulbright insisted, was a political oxymoron. Although violent change might not be inevitable, in certain societies it was quite probable. In any case, Americans could do very little to alter the odds. "It is important, therefore," Fulbright concluded, "that we set aside false analogies and recognize the social revolutions of the 'third world' as alien phenomena, as phenomena to which American experience has little relevance but which warrant nonetheless our sympathy and support."[162]

Long before Fulbright or Nasser was born, however, Alexis de Tocqueville questioned whether Americans would ever accept such advice. The heirs of the first great anticolonial upheaval of the modern era might embrace reform, the French aristocrat had observed with more than a trace of irony in 1831, but they were not likely to sympathize with something as alien as social revolution.[163] Indeed, Tocqueville's adage that Americans love change but dread revolution helps make sense of the policies of Woodrow Wilson and Franklin Roosevelt, who preached national self-determination to Arab sheiks while acquiescing in European imperialism. It helps explain why Cyrus Sulzberger regarded Mohammed Naguib as Kerensky with a Fez and why Dwight Eisenhower regarded Nasser as an evil influence. And it helps us understand why Lyndon Johnson and Richard Nixon showed so little sympathy when dining with the devil in Cairo.

Since Nasser's death his successors have evoked a more sympathetic response from Washington because they were willing to eschew revolutionary romanticism and embrace peace, progress, and pragmatism, qualities that Tocqueville regarded as quintessentially American. By the late 1970s Anwar Sadat, who in an earlier life helped Nasser topple King Farouk, had become a Nobel peacemaker, a frequent White House dinner guest, and America's favorite Arab. Throughout the 1980s Hosni Mubarak cracked down on the extremist Gama'at al-Islamiyya, or Islamic Group, responsible for Sadat's assassination; distanced himself from the Arab radicals; and reaped a multibillion-dollar harvest of U.S. aid. As the twentieth century drew to a close, however, some Egypt-watchers saw an "impending crisis" fueled by a revolution of rising frustrations, with the aging Mubarak cast in Farouk's role. The House Committee on International Relations, for example, prophesied in April 1997 that despite Mubarak's relentless campaign against Islamic radicals, the wave of xenophobia and anti-Semitism sweeping Egypt would become more and more violent.[164]

This prophecy was fulfilled before the end of the year. On 17 November gunmen from the Egyptian Islamic Jihad, a terrorist group led by Ayman al-Zawahiri, a pediatrician-turned-revolutionary with close ties to Osama bin Laden, murdered fifty-eight European tourists at Luxor. During the following nine months Zawahiri helped bin Laden plan and carry out the deadly truck-bombings at the U.S. embassies in Kenya and Tanzania. To no one's great surprise, on the eve of the new millennium the State Department issued warnings that Egyptian terrorists, now firmly allied with al-Qaeda, were "threatening anti-US action" throughout the Middle East. As one could easily predict, Mohammed Atta, the Cairo-born hijacker who crashed the first Boeing 767 into the World Trade Center on 11 September 2001, had ties to both the Egyptian Islamic Jihad and the Islamic Group. "We don't have feelings of hatred toward the U.S. people," Montasser al-Zayyat, a spokesman for the Islamic Group, told a reporter a few days after Atta's suicide mission, "but feelings of hatred toward the government of the U.S. have developed," in part because of America's close ties with Hosni Mubarak but also "because you support Israel so blindly."[165] A half-century after the Free Officers seized power on the banks of the Nile, Mubarak was trapped between the legacy of Gamal Abdel Nasser and the specter of Osama bin Laden. Sooner rather than later he would have to choose between repression and revolution, a choice from which, according to Alexis de Tocqueville, Americans had always recoiled.

Tocqueville sheds light not merely on the ambivalent U.S. response to Nasser's brand of revolutionary nationalism but also on America's complex relations with more traditional regimes in the Middle East. He helps explain both Washington's eagerness to prescribe political reform as the best antidote to Nasserism and American support for economic modernization in Iraq, Libya, and Iran that inadvertently triggered anti-Western revolutions. He helps solve a riddle that has bedeviled U.S. policymakers for more than a generation: Why has America's quest for the Muslim equivalent of Thomas Jefferson been met so often by the likes of Saddam Hussein, Muammar al-Qaddafi, and Ayatollah Khomeini?

We live at a very special moment in history. The whole southern half of the world—Latin America, Africa, the Middle East, and Asia—are caught up in the adventures of asserting their independence and modernizing their old ways of life. . . .

The fundamental task of our foreign aid program in the 1960's is not negatively to fight Communism: Its fundamental task is to help make a historical demonstration that in the twentieth century, as in the nineteenth—in the southern half of the globe as in the north—economic growth and political democracy can develop hand in hand.—John F. Kennedy, 22 March 1961

It is not always by going from bad to worse that a society falls into revolution. It happens most often that a people, which has supported without complaint, as if they were not felt, the most oppressive laws, violently throws them off as soon as their weight is lightened. The social order destroyed by a revolution is almost always better than that which immediately preceded it, and experience shows that the most dangerous moment for a bad government is generally that in which it sets about reform.—Alexis de Tocqueville, *L'Ancien Regime* (1856)

6

Modernizing the Middle East

*From Reform to Revolution
in Iraq, Libya, and Iran*

Having labored long and hard to put the genie of Nasserism back into the bottle in Egypt, U.S. policymakers hoped to keep the stopper in place elsewhere in the Muslim world by reciting the magic words: reform, development, and modernization. Always skeptical of any Third World radical who deviated from a Jeffersonian trajectory, America's national security managers believed that by combining Yankee ingenuity with Middle East petrodollars, the United States could nudge traditional societies such as Iraq, Libya, and Iran down the road toward evolutionary change, thereby making revolutionary change impossible. To this end Washington would offer pro-Western leaders such as Iraqi prime minister Nuri Said, Libya's King Idris, and the shah of Iran enough military and economic assistance to buy time for long-overdue political and social reforms.

Prescribing reform as an antidote to radical change in the Muslim world, however, frequently produced unpleasant side effects. Eisenhower's policies in Iraq, for example, helped accelerate a revolution of rising expectations that culminated in July 1958 when Colonel Abdel Karim Qassim toppled the Hashemite monarchy and tilted Baghdad toward Moscow. The specter of bolshevism in Iraq prompted U.S. officials to redouble their efforts to bring reform to Libya and Iran before Nasser, Qassim, or the Kremlin brought revolution. U.S. efforts to engineer peaceful evolution in Tripoli notwithstanding, King Idris was overthrown in September 1969 by Colonel Muammar al-Qaddafi, who drew his ideology from the preachings of the Prophet Mohammed, not from the teachings of Vladimir Ilyich Lenin.

The explosive potential of revolutionary Islam, however, would become most painfully apparent to the American public and its leaders during the late 1970s not in thinly populated Libya but, rather, 2,000 miles to the east in Iran. Despite mounting evidence that previous U.S. efforts to inoculate Iraq and Libya against radical change had backfired, during the fifteen years after 1963 Washington nevertheless endorsed the shah's White Revolution, an ambitious program of westernization and economic growth designed to avert a political cataclysm in Tehran. Ironically, the very reforms that the shah and his U.S. supporters had hoped would make Iran safe from left-wing revolution eventually played into the hands of Ayatollah Ruhollah Khomeini, whose electrifying tirades persuaded 35 million Iranians during 1978 that their monarch had betrayed traditional Islamic values and sold out to the West.

Having insisted for twenty years that economic development and political reform would contain Nasserism and bring stability to Iraq, Libya, and Iran, U.S. policymakers were stunned when modernization brought xenophobic nationalism and revolutionary Islam instead. They should not have been surprised. After all, more than a century earlier Alexis de Tocqueville had observed that "the most dangerous moment for a bad government is generally that in which it sets about reform."[1]

Modernization: Making Bad Governments Better?

The wave of revolutionary nationalism in the Middle East that crested with Nasser's seizure of the Suez Canal helped persuade U.S. leaders and the academic experts who frequently advised them that the restless societies of the Third World were likely to become the principal battlegrounds for the Cold War during the decades ahead. Throughout the late 1940s and well into the 1950s the Council on Foreign Relations sponsored a series of study groups in New York City, where experts from inside and outside the U.S. government sat down together to analyze the social and economic problems facing the newly emerging nations of Asia, Africa, and the Middle East.[2] Harry Truman had acknowledged the connection between foreign aid, economic modernization, and political stability as early as January 1949, when he unveiled his Point Four Program, which by the end of his second term was funneling $500 million a year in technical and financial assistance to developing nations, mostly in Asia.[3]

Dwight Eisenhower, on the other hand, was a fiscal conservative who believed that trade, not aid, was the best antidote for what ailed the Third World. As a result he switched the focus of America's billion-dollar Mutual Security Program from economic to military assistance and shifted the balance of the foreign aid budget from grants to loans. By 1956 the growth of U.S. investment in and trade with developing nations seemed to confirm that private enterprise was ready to fill the vacuum created by cutbacks in the public sector. The political upheavals that rocked the Middle East, Latin America, and Africa during Eisenhower's second term, however, sparked criticism from liberals, both inside and outside the Republican Party, who charged that his tight-fisted approach to foreign aid was penny wise but pound foolish.[4]

Chief among the Republican critics was New York governor Nelson Rockefeller, whose incurable case of Potomac fever led him to ask Harvard political scientist Henry Kissinger in early 1956 to coordinate a series of wide-ranging studies on the challenges likely to confront the United States at home and abroad. Before the decade was over, Kissinger would publish a pair of reports that highlighted the "revolution of rising expectations" sweeping the Third World, where "the overthrow of the colonial rule involves at the same time the collapse of the existing political framework and often the social framework as well." Stressing that "America cannot stand aloof from this revolution," Kissinger and his colleagues on the Rockefeller Panel insisted that whoever took over the White House in 1961 must either "assist these states in becoming economically and socially viable" or watch them drift into the Kremlin's orbit.[5]

Walt Rostow, whom Kissinger had recruited for the Rockefeller project, outlined how the nations of the Third World might achieve viability in *The Stages of Economic Growth*, a collection of essays published in 1960 with the eye-catching subtitle, "A Non-Communist Manifesto." Defining communism as "a kind of disease which can befall a transitional society if it fails . . . to get on with the job of modernization," Rostow prescribed an antidote—large doses of U.S. foreign aid—to ensure that the developing nations of Asia, Africa, and Latin America could mobilize the resources necessary to achieve an "early take-off" into self-sustained economic growth.[6]

Among those most fascinated by these ideas was John F. Kennedy, who brought Rostow to Washington to help lay the foundations for the New Frontier. Echoing *Stages of Economic Growth*, Kennedy labeled the 1960s "the crucial 'Decade of Development'" during which Africans, Asians, and Latin Americans must begin "modernizing their old ways of life" by showing that "economic growth and political democracy can develop hand in hand." U.S. financial assistance would be critical during the take-off phase, but so would enlightened political leadership inside the less-developed nations themselves, where "self-help and internal reform—including land reform, tax reform and improved education and social justice" were the chief orders of the day.[7] Kennedy and Rostow's line of reasoning not only persuaded Congress to expand U.S. aid for less-developed countries by 80 percent during the early 1960s; it also provided the intellectual rationale for a more aggressive program of "nation building" designed to cure the economic and political woes afflicting transitional societies in Africa, Latin America, and Southeast Asia.[8]

By the time Walt Rostow completed his stint as Lyndon Johnson's national security adviser five years later, however, the Third World seemed destined not for a takeoff into self-sustained economic growth but, rather, for a crash landing into political chaos. Rostow attributed the revolutionary turmoil sweeping Africa, Latin America, and Asia to Soviet subversion and stubbornly insisted that making bad governments better remained a good objective.[9] But Henry Kissinger, who soon emerged as Richard Nixon's Rostow, probably came closer to the truth when he confessed in his memoirs that the American experience, based as it was on a liberal political tradition, a mature industrial economy, and a strong middle class, was "not entirely relevant" for Third World societies "taking the wrenching first steps toward modernization" during the Kennedy and Johnson years. "Nation-building depended crucially on the ability to establish political authority," Kissinger recalled. "Economic aid, by accelerating the erosion of the traditional (frequently feudal) order, often made political stability even harder to achieve."[10]

The paradoxes of modernization did not escape the notice of Zbigniew Brzezinski, the Columbia University Sovietologist who would become Jimmy Carter's Kissinger. In *Between Two Ages*, a trendy screed about the emerging computer-dominated "technetronic era" published during Nixon's second year in office, Brzezinski likened the nations of the Third World to "Global Ghettos" wracked by "active explosions of undirected anger" and "insatiable aspirations" for the good life available only on television. Strong leadership, perhaps even "personal dictatorship," capable of "imposing social-economic modernization from above" was the only way to save the neighborhood. Otherwise, Brzezinski prophesied, "the peoples of the developed world may well take refuge in the self-serving argument that the irrational fanaticism of the leaders of the global ghettos precludes cooperation."[11]

Preoccupied as they were with the quagmire in Southeast Asia, Rostow, Kissinger, and Brzezinski seldom had much to say about modernization in the Middle East. Farther down the bureaucratic food chain, however, other academics had been saying quite a lot. As early as 1949, for example, Bayard Dodge, president of the American University in Beirut, had cautioned a Council on Foreign Relations study group that modernization was likely to be a mixed blessing in the Muslim world, where "change has been too rapid to be healthy." Indeed, he feared that the rise of "violent nationalism" and "a craving for whatever is most modern" might easily "prepare the way for the exceedingly active Communist agitation." In short, Dodge believed that "the Middle East was on the whole like a man who has shifted gear in his automobile but who has not yet decided which way he is to turn."[12]

James Landis, formerly one of FDR's roving emissaries in the Middle East and now chair of the study group, felt that it was up to the United States to provide the necessary driver's education. "Unfortunately," he told Dodge, "the United States cannot support revolution in this century as it did in the last." But neither should Washington support "what is" and embrace the status quo. "To someone really interested in preserving American interests in the Middle East," Landis concluded, "the best way is not to support the existing governments which may blow up in his face at any moment, but instead to gradually change what is in order to avert Communist revolt."[13]

During the following two decades academic experts on the Muslim world endorsed Landis's prescription for reform as the best antidote for revolution. By 1958 MIT sociologist Daniel Lerner had drafted a blueprint for U.S.-backed evolutionary change in his widely read book *The Passing of Traditional Society: Modernizing the Middle East*. A onetime colleague of Walt Rostow at MIT's Center for International Studies, Lerner insisted that "Middle Easterners more than ever want the modern package" whose delivery hinged on U.S. encouragement and aid. "What America is—to condense a rule more powerful than its numerous exceptions—the modernizing Middle East seeks to become," he concluded, and the prospects for exporting the American dream to Iran and other Middle Eastern lands seemed quite good.[14]

Five years later Princeton University political scientist Manfred Halpern offered a more sophisticated but less cheerful assessment of prospects for modernization in *The Politics of Social Change in the Middle East and North Africa*. A veteran of the State Department's Division of Research and Intelligence who had returned to the ivory tower at the dawn of the Kennedy era, Halpern had few illusions that his former colleagues could find a quick fix for the "revolution of rising expectations" that was sweeping the Muslim world. His diagnosis and prescription were blunt. Because "the Middle Eastern states still lack the strength and skill to solve the problems of peace, stability, and welfare unassisted," the United States must help them to "succeed in establishing their changing society on a new and stable base." Lest policymakers assume that treating "nationalism and its discontents" would be either quick or cheap, Halpern cautioned that "it will cost much to attain modest results."[15]

For U.S. officials to achieve the highest return on their political and economic investment, Halpern believed that they must construct their portfolio carefully. "The majority of Middle Eastern countries belong to the domain of Alice's Red Queen," he pointed out, "where everyone will have to run very fast if he is merely to stand still." In places like Egypt and Syria, Halpern noted ruefully, "discontent breeds more quickly than economic opportunities— faster even than people." Among the handful of candidates for successful modernization were Iran, Iraq, and Libya, whose oil revenues, if invested wisely, might yield higher standards of living. All three, however, "lacked primarily the political will to dare to face the far reaching structural changes in politics and society which economic development entails." As a result, Halpern prophesied, the principal question facing his friends at Foggy Bottom during the 1960s would be how to persuade traditional leaders from Tehran to Tripoli to modernize their societies before it was too late.[16]

As the decade drew to a close, the answer remained as elusive as ever. Just a few months before LBJ turned the Oval Office over to Richard Nixon, however, John Badeau, JFK's man in Cairo, reiterated the importance of Halpern's question in *The American Approach to the Arab World*. In a section titled "Modernizing the Traditional Middle East," Badeau argued that if U.S. officials wished to prevent "a revolutionary onslaught on the forms and institutions of the past," then they must work with Arab moderates such as Jordan's King Hussein to launch "progressive movements and liberal institutions" essential for "a gradual evolution to modernity." In more conservative states like Libya, Americans must seek to identify "progressive-traditional rulers" who could "demonstrate that an Arab country can pass into the modern world and solve its basic problems without the destructive upheaval of revolution." Washington was already doing this in Iran, a non-Arab Muslim land where, with U.S. help, the shah was embracing modernization. But lest there be any doubt that doing something entailed almost as many risks as doing nothing, Badeau could point to what had happened a decade earlier in Iraq, where pro-Western moderates had sowed reform only to reap revolution.[17]

America and the Iraqi Revolution

The muezzin's rhythmic chant calling Baghdad's faithful to morning prayers on 14 July 1958 was interrupted shortly after dawn by the crackle of machine-gun fire and the whine of tanks. Before the day was over, troops led by Colonel

Abdel Karim Qassim, a forty-four-year-old career officer, had overthrown the Iraqi monarchy, slaughtered dozens of pro-Western political figures, and stunned the Eisenhower administration. Top U.S. officials had regarded Iraq, with its conservative leadership and its alliance with Britain, as an island of stability in a sea of turmoil. Alone among the Arab states, Iraq had joined the Baghdad Pact, the U.S.-backed regional defense organization. Alone among Arab leaders, Iraqi prime minister Nuri Said had worked openly to help channel the tide of Nasser-style radical nationalism sweeping the region in directions safer for Western interests. And alone among Arab armies, Iraq's officer corps had seemed impervious both to Nasser's left-wing authoritarianism and to Ba'athism, that curious blend of socialism and nationalism that had taken root inside the armed forces next door in Syria.[18]

Beneath Iraq's veneer of pro-Western stability, however, revolutionary pressures had been mounting for more than a generation. Most of Iraq's 5 million inhabitants had known nothing but abject poverty since 1920, when Whitehall had welded together three very different Ottoman provinces—Kurdish Mosul in the north, Sunni Baghdad in the center, and Shi'ite Basra in the south—into a British mandate headed by the Emir Feisal, the Hashemite prince who had spearheaded the Arab revolt against Turkish rule during the First World War. For twelve years Great Britain helped King Feisal fashion a governing coalition composed of crafty political insiders such as Nuri Said and wealthy landlord sheiks backed by a small British-trained army and bankrolled by the British-dominated IPC. Although Whitehall terminated the mandate and granted Iraq formal independence in 1932, the British continued to exercise an informal protectorate, retaining air bases at Habbaniyah and Shaiba and working with Nuri Said, who would serve as prime minister thirteen times, to suppress nationalist outbursts such as the Wathbah, a communist-led protest that left 350 dead in early 1948.[19]

Haunted by the Wathbah, Nuri Said and his British patrons developed an autocratic program of modernization during the early 1950s. With Whitehall's blessing Nuri channeled oil revenues into an ambitious plan that addressed Iraq's irrigation, transportation, and other long-term infrastructural needs without touching its remarkably hierarchical political and social structures. U.S. ambassador Waldemar Gallman, who arrived in Baghdad in 1954, was soon waxing optimistic about the situation. Insisting that Iraq's heavy-handed anticommunist policies were a small price to pay for economic progress, Gallman recalled that "toward the end of Nuri's life the Ottoman Empire's neglected province was beginning to take on the aspects of biblical Mesopotamia."[20]

Many in Washington, however, were beginning to suspect that the Bible story most relevant for Nuri's Iraq was actually Noah's Babylonia on the eve of the great flood. Although Eisenhower's advisers were delighted by Iraq's willingness to funnel its burgeoning oil revenues into long-term infrastructural projects during the spring of 1955, as the year drew to a close, they worried that the "miserably poor, depressed and politically apathetic" Iraqi people "could be exploited by communist agents" unless the Hashemite monarchy undertook more "short-term immediate impact projects."[21] By early 1956 even Ambassador Gallman was becoming worried about the situation in Baghdad. Although Nuri Said remained the "most effective friend [that the] West can expect in Iraq in [the] near future," Gallman admitted on 15 January that the irrepressible prime minister was "somewhat less strong than a year ago."[22] Wesley Nelson, a U.S. economist who sat on the Iraqi Development Board, made no secret of his own growing concern. "When Nuri drops out of the picture," he told a reporter on 3 April, "the country may be in for trouble."[23] Two months later the CIA reported that the fate of the Hashemite kingdom lay in the hands of Iraq's 53,000-man army, widely regarded as loyal, well trained, and apolitical. "There is no evidence," the agency concluded, "of a revolutionary-minded military clique among Iraqi officers—such as that which overthrew King Farouk in Egypt."[24]

The aftershocks from the Suez crisis that rattled Baghdad later that year, however, made parallels between Farouk's Egypt and Hashemite Iraq seem less far-fetched. Anti-Western demonstrations had erupted from Mosul in the north to Najaf in the south, where students and workers chanted pro-Nasser slogans, battled police, and called for revolution. Matters seemed likely to get much worse. "Dissatisfaction is reported in the Iraqi army," CIA director Allen Dulles noted ominously on 22 November, "particularly among the junior officers."[25] By late 1956 Colonel Abdel Karim Qassim and a small group of anti-Hashemite and anti-British Free Officers were meeting secretly in Baghdad. Inspired by Nasser, the conspirators embraced national self-determination and radical social change, goals that required the overthrow of the Hashemite monarchy, the expulsion of Britain from its air bases at Habbaniyah and Shaiba, and the establishment of a fully independent Arab republic. By early 1958 Qassim could count some 200 supporters inside the Iraqi officers corps, including the commanders of several key garrisons just outside the capital.[26]

During the nineteen months between the Suez crisis and Qassim's coup, the Eisenhower administration hoped to avert revolution by encouraging Nuri to upgrade his internal security apparatus and accelerate economic development and social reform. When James Richards, Ike's special emissary in the Middle East, arrived in Baghdad in April 1957, he reported that "Iraq is booming, Texas fashion," in part because the Hashemites seemed "to be making really effective use of oil revenues for [the] benefit [of the] country as [a] whole" but mainly because Nuri understood the "importance of guarding against internal subversion."[27] Two months later, however, Eisenhower received a national intelligence estimate warning that urban discontent, peasant agitation, and military impatience had begun to generate explosive pressures for radical political change that threatened to overwhelm Nuri, the Hashemites, and the narrow elite that surrounded them. "Over the longer run," the CIA concluded, "the natural development of factors already present in Iraqi society will probably confront the present tightly controlled system of rule with increasingly forceful challenges by elements demanding a broadening of the base of public participation in governmental affairs." Only by encouraging reform could the United States hope to make Iraq safe from revolution.[28]

Yet by the summer of 1957 U.S. officials inside Iraq were beginning to worry that the reformist approach favored by Washington would have revolutionary implications in Baghdad. The radical redistribution of land, Ambassador Gallman warned Foggy Bottom on 6 July, might benefit thousands of sharecroppers and tenant farmers, but it would also undermine hundreds of tribal sheiks, "who constitute [an] important political stabilizing factor" in Iraq.[29] With the approach of winter, the nature of America's dilemma would emerge in sharper focus. Although "the present regime lacks widespread popular support," State Department Middle East experts confessed on 30 October, "a change of regime or a period of chronic instability brought about by successful civil commotion could only greatly endanger our interests." Under these circumstances the Eisenhower administration had no choice but to shore up Nuri's autocratic rule while working behind the scenes for "peaceful change" and "a more broadly-based, moderate, and progressive government."[30]

The formation of the UAR in February 1958 was an especially painful blow for Nuri Said, whose oil had long flowed west across Syria to the Mediterranean through a pipeline that would now be controlled by Gamal Abdel Nasser, his leading rival for the leadership of the Arab world. British foreign secretary Selwyn Lloyd, who visited Baghdad in early March, "found Iraqi leaders in [a] very jittery state" and told Secretary of State John Foster Dulles that the Hashemites were "acting as though they expected to be gone in six months."[31] Most of Dulles's Middle East experts, however, remained confident that by fostering "a climate for economic development" in highly stratified Arab states like Iraq, the United States could help generate higher standards of living that would, "over the long run, lead to evolutionary reforms and to a broader base of support for the government."[32]

U.S. diplomats stationed in Arab capitals, on the other hand, painted a far gloomier picture and peppered the State Department with warnings of palace revolutions or other political upheavals. By June the most likely flash point seemed to be not Iraq but Lebanon, where chronic Christian-Muslim tensions had flared into outright civil war in previous weeks, or Jordan, where rumors had begun to fly that King Hussein was about to be toppled by pro-Nasser military officers. Convinced that the pro-Western government in Baghdad was much less vulnerable than its counterparts in Beirut or Amman, the CIA insisted as late as 3 July 1958 that the Iraqi opposition had no contacts inside the army and "lack[ed] the immediate capacity to overthrow the regime."[33] Eleven days later Iraq was rocked by a bloody revolution that showed how wrong Eisenhower's experts had been.

After learning that Abdel Karim Qassim and his Free Officers had toppled the Hashemite monarchy on 14 July, both the White House and Whitehall moved swiftly to isolate the Iraqi revolution to prevent other Arab conservatives from meeting similar fates. Within seventy-two hours of the coup in Baghdad, Eisenhower would send U.S. marines to Lebanon and Prime Minister Harold Macmillan would airlift U.K. paratroopers to Jordan to reassure nervous pro-Western leaders in Beirut and Amman.[34] By the end of the month, however, U.S. policymakers believed that the best way to "exert constructive influence upon the new regime" was to recognize it "without delay," something that Eisenhower did on 30 July.[35] A similar line of reasoning led Whitehall to extend formal recognition to republican Iraq a few hours later.[36]

Throughout the autumn of 1958 and into the winter of 1959 Iraq underwent profound and often bloody social and political changes that led many in Washington and London to express second thoughts about recognizing the new republic. Committed to dismantling the oligarchy of pro-Hashemite tribal sheiks who had supported Nuri Said, Qassim expropriated hundreds of large estates and distributed small plots to the landless peasants who had welcomed the 14 July coup. Determined to destroy the muscular internal security apparatus through which the old regime had upheld the repressive status quo for more than a generation, Qassim authorized a series of show trials that were frequently punctuated by public executions of former Iraqi officials linked to Britain and the United States. In developments that surprised the Eisenhower administration, which had assumed that Iraq's Free Officers intended to make their country the third member of the UAR, Qassim distanced himself from Nasser, jailed those who advocated union with Egypt, and legalized the Communist Party as a counterweight to pan-Arab Iraqi radicals.[37]

Viewed from Washington, republican Iraq seemed to be teetering on the brink of a bolshevik cataclysm. Undersecretary of State Robert Murphy, who had visited Baghdad in August 1958 in an effort to secure Iraqi support for a negotiated settlement in Lebanon, believed that Qassim and his followers "may prove to be a transitory Kerensky type element."[38] After Qassim announced arms and trade agreements with the Kremlin in early October, some State Department officials feared that "the point of no return may be reached in a few months," after which Iraq would become a Soviet satellite.[39] The situation eventually grew so bleak that the Eisenhower administration considered secretly encouraging Nasser to intervene. When some of Ike's advisers proposed using Iraq's small Ba'ath Party (whose leaders preached pan-Arabism and anticommunism) to reverse the Kremlin's recent inroads into Baghdad, the man in the Oval Office had a simpler idea. "It might be good policy," Eisenhower observed shortly before Christmas, "to help the UAR take over in Iraq."[40]

Having long regarded Iraq as the principal obstacle to Egyptian leadership of the Arab world, Nasser required little prompting from Washington to encourage Qassim's foes. On 8 March 1959 Ba'athist officers in Mosul, Iraq's most northerly province, launched a revolt designed to root out communism and to bring their country into Nasser's UAR. After three days of bloody street fighting, troops loyal to Qassim, assisted by the communist-controlled provincial militia, put down the uprising, killing 200 rebels and wounding 300 more. In the weeks that followed, Qassim purged the army of all Ba'athist and pro-Nasser elements, Iraqi Communist Party membership swelled to 25,000, and a half-million peasants and workers joined radical anti-Western labor organizations. John J. Jernegan, who had just succeeded Waldemar Gallman as U.S. ambassador to Iraq, relayed the gloomy news to Washington on 26 March. With Qassim "too far along [the] road to communism to turn back," Jernegan concluded, "it looks as if 1959 will be [the] year of the bear in Iraq."[41]

Undaunted by Jernegan's bleak forecast, Eisenhower moved swiftly to contain the revolution in Baghdad. Hoping to avert "the complete loss of Iraq to the Communists," he set up a secret Inter-Agency Group on 2 April to examine a broad array of options ranging from covert action to military intervention.[42] Two weeks later he reviewed "the grave situation in Iraq" with his top advisers. Never one to mince words, Treasury Secretary Robert Anderson, a Texas oil executive who had earlier served as Ike's secret emissary to Egypt and Israel, warned that "the whole of the Middle East is likely to go down the drain" unless the United States acted decisively. "We do not want another Dienbienphu," Anderson pointed out, alluding to the situation in Vietnam five Aprils earlier. "Much of Indochina was lost to the Communists while we were here talking and planning about saving it," he reminded his listeners. "We must not now repeat this error in the Middle East." Despite the specter of a Middle Eastern Dienbienphu, however, Eisenhower preferred a policy of watchful waiting to afford Qassim "the opportunity to stand up to the Communists."[43] The Iraqi leader would seize that opportunity in July 1959, crushing a communist uprising in Kirkuk, an oil center in Mosul province 180 miles north of Baghdad, and purging pro-Soviet elements in the armed forces.[44]

Notwithstanding Iraq's uncertain future, officials on both sides of the Atlantic took some comfort that "a residual stability" had begun to reassert itself in Baghdad just twelve months after the July 1958 revolution. The "lesson to be learned" from Qassim's sudden crackdown against the communists, Assistant Secretary of State Lewis Jones told his British counterpart, Sir Roger Stevens, on 28 August 1959, was that "a bad situation had tended to right itself in the absence of any capability by the U.S. and U.K. to influence events." Noting that Whitehall had always been relatively confident that nationalism would eventually triumph over communism in Baghdad, Stevens believed that patience should be the watchword for both British and U.S. policies toward Iraq. "We should keep our fingers crossed," he told Jones, "and *out*."[45]

The confusing and at times chaotic situation in Baghdad between late 1959 and early 1963 made it increasingly difficult for U.S. policymakers to control their itchy fingers. Targeted for assassination both by left-wing Ba'athist militants and by right-wing extremists inside the army, the enigmatic and charismatic Qassim proclaimed himself "Sole Leader" during the winter of 1960 and edged toward a "clearly messianic" cult of personality. By the end of the year Iraqis from across the political spectrum were complaining that, despite having received nearly $400 million in technical and military assistance from the Kremlin, their Sole Leader, like the old regime he had overthrown in July 1958, had "fail[ed] to make a convincing show of social and economic progress."[46] The greatest source of popular disenchantment was Qassim's ill-fated program of agrarian reform, which by breaking up large estates had inadvertently reduced agricultural productivity, creating food shortages and triggering huge price hikes for staples such as wheat and rice. As the Eisenhower administration drew to a close, some U.S. Middle East experts worried that the "continued sluggishness of Iraq's economy" and the rising expectations of Iraqi peasants and workers might tempt Qassim to seek greater control over the production of Persian Gulf oil.[47]

Although Iraq was hardly among the most critical foreign policy issues confronting John F. Kennedy in January 1961, it surely ranked among the most complex. Qassim's threat to occupy Kuwait after Britain terminated its protectorate in June evoked private assurances from the White House that the United States stood ready to assist Whitehall in the event that "the Iraqis should be sufficiently stupid" to invade the sheikdom.[48] Too smart to risk war with the great powers over a claim that most of his neighbors regarded as specious, in the autumn of 1961 Qassim turned his attention to a target reviled by nationalists throughout the Arab world: IPC, the Anglo-American consortium that controlled his country's most valuable natural resource. For more than a year Qassim hinted that expropriation was just around the corner and imposed taxes that most U.S. and U.K. executives regarded as confiscatory. JFK's Middle East experts were not amused. "It would appear that Iraqi leadership intends to play a game of brinksmanship in its efforts to gain control of Kuwait and to obtain at least part ownership of IPC," Foggy Bottom's Phillips

Talbot growled in late 1961. "The situation in Iraq, therefore, appears to be returning to something like the post-revolutionary period in 1958 and 1959, during which there was great alarm that Iraq was going communist."[49]

Preoccupied with the IPC imbroglio and ever more dependent on Russian diplomatic support, Qassim began to rely more and more heavily on the well-organized Communist Party to keep his domestic rivals and his foreign critics off guard. Iraqi anticommunists delivered their knockout counterpunch on 8 February 1963, when Ba'athist officers seized power in Baghdad, executed Qassim and hundreds of his followers, and moved the country out of the Soviet orbit. The bill of attainder that the Ba'athists unveiled against Qassim consisted of three main charges. First, the Sole Leader had jeopardized Arab unity by his flirtation with the Kremlin and Iraqi communists. Second, he had weakened the army by rewarding loyalty rather than competence and by filling key posts with his cronies. Third, Qassim, like Nuri Said before him, had overpromised and underdelivered when it came to political reform and economic development. Determined to reverse course as swiftly as possible, Prime Minister Ahmed Hassan al-Bakr and his Ba'athist comrades rounded up thousands of communists, resumed negotiations with IPC, and put out feelers for Western aid.[50]

U.S. policymakers shed few tears for Abdel Karim Qassim. "While it's still early, [the] Iraqi revolution seems to have succeeded," NSC staffer Robert Komer told JFK shortly after the coup. "It is almost certainly a net gain for our side."[51] Kennedy agreed and recognized the new regime on 11 February. Four days later Foggy Bottom confirmed that the Ba'athists were willing "to bargain on relatively reasonable terms" with IPC and that "the pace of modernization and reform [was] to be speeded."[52] Bakr and his comrades "appeared to be intelligent and systematic, radical in their approach to certain problems but not irrational, [and] proponents of statism while leaving room for private enterprise," the State Department's Robert Strong assured a representative of Chase Manhattan Bank on 25 February. The word out of Baghdad was far less measured. The Ba'athist regime "from our perspective is certainly the best we could have hoped to have emerge after the Qasim nightmare," U.S. chargé d'affaires Roy Melbourne gloated at the end of the month. "The Russians give every sign of knowing what we do, namely, that they have received a serious defeat in the Middle East."[53]

Throughout the spring and into the summer of 1963 Washington worked hard to take maximum advantage of Moscow's defeat. When Kennedy asked "what we're doing for the new Iraqi regime" on 2 April, his NSC staff replied that "we're being as helpful as possible without getting into an unwarranted big new aid program." To this end the Agency for International Development favored offering Baghdad economic assistance "to help justify its crackdown on the Communists." For its part the Pentagon was willing to sell the Bakr regime twelve helicopters for use against pro-Qassim insurgents and was also "considering civic action possibilities" to beef up Iraq's system of internal security. By mid-April Foggy Bottom confirmed that Iraq was continuing "to reduce its present dependence on the Soviet Union" and might "gradually come to rely primarily on the West for economic development and technology." Two months later U.S. and Iraqi officials were discussing possibilities for U.S. assistance ranging from surplus wheat available through the Food for Peace program to an Export-Import Bank loan to purchase three Boeing 727 jets. The United States, White House Middle East expert Robert Komer assured Kennedy on 10 July, was "making [the] most of [this] Iraqi opportunity."[54]

Before the year was out, however, America's Iraqi opportunity had evaporated. To be sure, Ahmed Hassan al-Bakr welcomed U.S. economic support, which he hoped would facilitate his plans for land reform, irrigation, and industrialization. He assured the business community that he would "cooperate with private capital," and he purged "Commie officers" from the army.[55] But Bakr could not quell factionalism inside the Ba'ath Party. As a result he became the odd man out after a military coup in November 1963 that ushered in an era of vicious political infighting during which expressions such as "social reform" and "economic development" were seldom uttered. When Bakr finally regained control in July 1968, he was able to do so only with the help of a ruthless anti-Western Ba'ath zealot named Saddam Hussein, for whom modernization was subordinated to something far more traditional in Baghdad: the quest for power.[56]

Ten weeks after Saddam's patron had come to power the first time, the CIA had warned that what had happened to the Iraqi Hashemites could easily happen to monarchies elsewhere in the Middle East. Although U.S. intelligence suggested that "Soviet and local Communist opportunities in the conservative Arab states—Jordan, Saudi Arabia, Libya, Kuwait—are slight," Ba'athists and other Muslim radicals posed a real threat. "Some conservative states have attempted to prevent revolution by gradual reform," the CIA prophesied on 24 April 1963, "but it is probable that they will not be able to prevent some kind of revolutionary upheaval in the years ahead."[57] By the end of the decade this prophecy would be fulfilled in Libya.

King Idris, Colonel Qaddafi, and the Libyan Revolution

U.S. policymakers hoped that by pondering the unpleasant lessons they had learned in Iraq, they might spare themselves a painful education in other Arab lands such as Libya, where by the mid-1960s an oil boom had spawned demands for social change and political reform that King Idris was hard pressed to meet. Although U.S. officials calibrated their prescription for modernization more carefully in Tripoli than in Baghdad, Libya was rocked by a nationalist upheaval in 1969 that soon posed a far graver threat to American interests than revolutions led by Nasser or Qassim. Embracing an ideology powered less by pan-Arab socialism than by radical Islam, Colonel Muammar al-Qaddafi sought to use Libya's burgeoning oil revenues to purge the Muslim world of all traces of Western influence and to launch a revolution that seemed at times to have more in common with seventeenth-century religious warfare than with twentieth-century class conflict.[58]

In 1945 most Americans would probably have recognized Libya as the site of ferocious fighting between Allied troops and Hitler's Afrika Korps, but very few could have imagined that the thinly populated no-man's-land would be transformed in just four decades into one of the richest and most volatile nations on earth. Modern Libya was the creation of empire builders in Italy, who by 1911 had fused three desert provinces nominally under Ottoman rule—Cyrenaica in the east, Tripolitania in the west, and Fezzan in the south—into a single colony that served as an Italian bridgehead in North Africa. Unwilling to accept the Italian takeover without a fight, Arab nationalists led by Omar Mukhtar launched an armed liberation movement during the 1920s. Benito Mussolini's Italy retaliated with brutal, scorched-earth tactics to demoralize the Libyans. When the shooting stopped in 1931, Mukhtar and 25,000 of his followers—some were guerrillas but most were noncombatants—lay dead, and Libya lay squarely under Italian rule.[59]

Despite help and encouragement from Nazi Germany, Mussolini's Libyan empire crumbled rapidly. By the end of the Second World War, U.S. and U.K. forces had taken over strategically important air bases near Tripoli and Tobruk, enabling the newly created United Nations to begin the daunting task of preparing Libya for independence. Because Italy's former colony was divided into three zones of allied occupation, it was not until 1951 that United Nations officials succeeded in crafting a workable formula for self-government calling for Libya to become a hereditary monarchy headed by the sixty-one-year-old Emir Idris, who led the Sanussi brotherhood, a tightly knit clan of religious activists committed to the purification of Islam. Idris permitted Britain and the United States to retain military facilities inside his new kingdom in exchange for modest U.K. and U.S. subsidies.[60]

Early in his reign King Idris clearly needed all the economic help he could get. Three times the size of Texas, his realm was a vast desert wasteland whose leading export during the 1950s was scrap metal gathered from the burned-out tanks and half-tracks that littered the Libyan landscape. "Libya was just a tray of sand in 1951," Abdul Hamid Bakoush, one of the king's confidants, recalled long afterward. "It had an income of £3 million a year, and that came from Britain and the United States in rent for the bases on Libyan territory."[61] For U.S. officials $1 million seemed a small price to pay for the use of Wheelus Field, a sprawling complex outside Tripoli where the U.S. Air Force stationed dozens of long-range bombers laden with nuclear weapons. "It is an extremely important base . . . from the standpoint of a strategic air operation," John Foster Dulles told the Senate Foreign Relations Committee on 3 June 1953, "which is a quiet way of saying atomic bombing of Russia."[62]

King Idris could not have agreed more. Indeed, he persuaded Dulles and Eisenhower a year later that Wheelus Field was important enough for the Pentagon to sign a seventeen-year lease that would bring Libya $4 million per year through 1960 and $1 million annually thereafter.[63] By the summer of 1956 U.S. intelligence was convinced that the multimillion-dollar agreement would provide Idris with the resources necessary "to maintain a precarious political stability" in the short run. "Unless current and projected oil explorations prove[d] extraordinarily successful," however, Libya's economic plight would deepen and, over the long run, U.S. and U.K. military facilities would become convenient targets for nationalists who shared "the anticolonial and anti-Western feelings of the Arab world."[64]

The pro-Nasser and anti-Western demonstrations that rocked Tripoli in November 1956 following Britain's intervention next door in Egypt highlighted the importance of addressing Libya's economic woes sooner rather than later. "Libyan public opinion has veered toward [the] Soviets on the basis [of] recent events," John Tappin, the U.S. ambassador in Tripoli, warned Washington on New Year's Day 1957. A modest increase in U.S. economic aid could reverse recent Russian gains and help make Libya a pro-Western "show-window" in North Africa. "Can't we get away from the penny pinching and the delay?" he grumbled. "Can't we snatch a bargain when we see one?"[65] To judge from the unpleasant exchange in late March between top Libyan officials and James Richards, Eisenhower's Middle Eastern troubleshooter, the short answer seemed to be no. Although King Idris and Prime Minister Mustafa Ben Halim professed to be leaning "firmly to [the] West," Richards saw them as fair-weather friends and offered only a 5 percent increase in the $4 million aid package that Washington had already earmarked for Libya.[66]

Britain's decision later that spring sharply to scale back its subsidy to Idris placed an even greater premium on sweetening the U.S. aid package. Being penny wise and pound foolish, Foggy Bottom's Robert Murphy pointed out on 26 April, might permit the Kremlin to "open the gateway to all of North Africa and the NATO flank."[67] A week later Eisenhower confessed that "the United States would be 'in an awful fix' if we ever lost Libya."[68] To help avert such an eventuality, the White House announced a $2.5 million increase in the Pentagon's Libyan aid package in early May. This modest show of support strengthened Washington's grip on Wheelus Field and left King Idris "more determined than ever to support pro-Western policies."[69]

As Ike thumbed through a top secret review of U.S. policy toward Libya completed in June 1957, however, he saw few grounds for complacency. According to NSC-5716 the most effective way for the United States to ensure the existence of a "stable and independent" Libya "free of anti-Western (particularly Egyptian and Soviet) influence" was to "take primary responsibility for developing over a period of years a Libyan army trained and equipped to maintain internal security and to resist guerrilla raids."[70] Eisenhower remained confident through June 1958 that King Idris was already receiving sufficient U.S. help "successfully [to] forestall the possibilities of Libya falling under communist domination."[71] The sudden overthrow of the Iraqi Hashemites in mid-July, however, led many at the White House and the State Department to wonder whether the Sanussi dynasty would be next. So long as the king's opponents remained "poorly organized," U.S. officials did not expect serious trouble in Libya. But "much of the present regime's strength depends upon the longevity of King Idris," who had "not groomed a successor" and who was "isolating himself from political reality at remote palaces."[72]

After U.S. and U.K. multinationals located a huge pool of oil 200 miles southeast of Tripoli in late 1958, Western concerns about Libya escalated dramatically. Noting that Nasserism had begun to exert "a strong popular appeal" among Idris's subjects, Eisenhower and his top aides agreed in mid-December that U.S. oil executives and diplomats must work hard to "assure that the Libyan people would profit from these natural resources and not merely the King and a few people around him."[73] Although U.S. petroleum experts expected Libya to be producing 300,000 barrels of crude oil per day within five years, in the short run King Idris faced serious cash flow problems compounded by increasingly strident calls for economic development and political reform from pro-Nasser forces. Determined to cure his financial ills sooner rather than later, Idris stunned Washington in May 1959 by requesting a whopping elevenfold increase in the $4 million annual fee the United States paid Libya for the use of Wheelus Field.[74]

By the autumn of 1959 it was clear that King Idris was not the only Libyan whose political and economic expectations had been raised by the oil boom. Skilled workers, junior officers, and other "emergent elite groups" were "embarrassed and resentful at Libya's dependence on the West for assistance," U.S. intelligence analysts noted on 28 August, and were "likely to become more politically restive as Libyan oil revenues grow."[75] Libya was "a 'weak reed' politically," NSC staffer Karl Harr told Ike and his key advisers two months later, "a country which had been plagued by poverty" that "was now facing the prospect of being moderately embarrassed with riches."[76]

To ensure that the transition from indigence to opulence was as smooth as possible, Eisenhower requested a review of U.S. policy toward the Sanussi kingdom. Completed in March 1960, NSC-6004 confirmed that substantial oil revenues were likely to solve Libya's chronic financial woes in short order. Over the longer haul, however, the influx of petrodollars would "stimulate commercial and industrial activities, which in turn will attract migration to the cities, and thus create fertile ground for political agitation" among Libyans influenced by the preachings of Radio Cairo. To check the growth of left-wing nationalism and to bolster U.S. interests in Libya, NSC-6004 recommended that Washington help Idris undertake "rational and well-directed planning for the use of available capital" and provide him with increased military aid in order "to maintain internal security." Convinced that the demise of the Sanussi dynasty seemed certain to "precipitate a chaotic free-for-all," the Eisenhower administration bequeathed John Kennedy a set of policies that wedded the United States squarely to the Libyan status quo.[77]

The oil revenues that began surging through the Libyan economy during the early 1960s, however, stimulated a revolution of rising expectations that made it much harder for Idris and his American friends to stand pat. "The Libyans had become politicized in terms of Arab nationalism," Harrison Symmes, who spent the Kennedy years at the U.S. embassy in Tripoli, recalled long afterward. Libyans outside the king's inner circle "were concerned about what was going to be done with the oil money and what it meant for them."[78] Unless the petroleum boom meant higher living standards and political modernization, U.S. officials feared that the Sanussi dynasty was doomed. "Libya, ruled by an aged and ailing king, rich in oil, and geographically accessible," CIA analysts pointed out in March 1962, was "a tempting target" for Arab radicals like Nasser.[79] If the United States wished to prevent anti-Western elements from gaining the upper hand, State Department experts advised Kennedy three months later, it must encourage the Libyans to pursue "the orderly economic development of the country."[80]

Foggy Bottom's reformist agenda in Libya struck a responsive chord at the White House. Troubled by signs that the Libyan oil boom was spawning "uncontrolled spending (and grafting)" and "sheer financial chaos," in October 1962 JFK reminded Crown Prince Hasan, Idris's nephew and heir apparent, just how important "the achievement of progress and prosperity" was for the Sanussis and their subjects.[81] Idris, Hasan, and Prime Minister Mohieddine Fekini, however, continued to channel most of Libya's petrodollars into their own pockets and hoped to finance their country's economic development by extracting higher payments from Washington for the use of Wheelus Field. This did not sit well with JFK, who reminded Fekini in September 1963 that King Idris was "swimming in oil" and insisted that "what Libya needs is not money but technical help in learning to use wisely all the money it's already getting (and squandering)."[82]

Kennedy's words rang hollow, however, and wisdom was still in short supply when Lyndon B. Johnson turned his attention to Libya in 1964. Troubled by recent anti-American outbursts in Africa, LBJ had sent Undersecretary of State Averell Harriman on a fact-finding trip early in the new year. Although conditions south of the Sahara did not bode well for U.S. interests, Harriman regarded Libya as the "most difficult and urgent immediate problem of the countries he had visited." Nasser was stepping up his anti-Western propaganda, Harriman told Johnson on 3 April, fueling "'super Arabism' and anti-Israeli sentiment" that might soon force Washington to abandon Wheelus Field and that might ultimately "jeopardize US oil investment in Libya."[83]

By the time Harriman visited the Sanussi kingdom in 1964, Libya did not figure as prominently in U.S. Cold War strategy as it had a decade earlier. Because the United States had shifted the focus of its nuclear deterrent from long-range bombers to intercontinental missiles in the late 1950s, the Pentagon no longer stationed B-52s at Wheelus Field and used the air base mainly for fuel storage and target practice during the Johnson years.[84] As Libya's strategic significance gradually declined, however, its economic importance increased dramatically. By 1965 Libya was exporting 1.2 million barrels of sulfur-free crude oil to Western Europe each day. Because those exports did not pass through the Suez Canal, the Sanussi kingdom constituted a far more dependable and far cheaper source of supply than Saudi Arabia or Iran.[85]

So long as Idris retained power, America's huge stake in the Libyan petroleum industry and its military installations at Wheelus Field seemed secure. Despite occasional anti-American outbursts, U.S. interests were "safe under the present government," Ambassador David Newsom reported from Tripoli in December 1966.[86] Washington's diplomatic support for Israel during the June 1967 Six Day War, however, sparked a fresh wave of anti-American demonstrations in Libya that nearly cost the seventy-seven-year-old monarch his crown. Galvanized into action by Nasser's specious claims that U.S. jets stationed at Wheelus Field had secretly assisted Israel in its devastating air raids on Egypt, Libyan radicals taunted U.S. diplomats, marched on the air base armed with dynamite and Molotov cocktails, and briefly forced King Idris to suspend oil exports to Western Europe.[87]

U.S. officials doubted that the king would nationalize the petroleum industry, but they did expect fresh demands for both the United States and Britain to abandon their military facilities in Libya. Such demands, national security adviser Walt Rostow warned LBJ on 17 June 1967, raised the frightening prospect of "a Nasser takeover of Libya after U.S.-U.K. bases are withdrawn," something that "would put Nasser on easy street with oil." Although U.S. diplomats were working hard to "buy time," Rostow emphasized that "a good deal depends on whether the King can sweat it out."[88] Top officials on both sides of the Atlantic, however, believed that Idris would soon lose his nerve. "The British," CIA experts reported a week later, "doubt that the king's pace will be fast enough to keep ahead of a deteriorating internal security situation." Undersecretary of State Eugene Rostow, Walt Rostow's older brother and Foggy Bottom's point man on the Middle East, likewise held out little hope that the aging King Idris could exert firm leadership or that Nasser could be persuaded to "leave Libya alone."[89]

Thanks to rising Libyan oil revenues and modest amounts of U.S. military aid, the Johnson administration nevertheless managed to keep King Idris in power until Richard Nixon moved into the White House in January 1969. But LBJ's advisers expected the new administration to encounter serious trouble in Tripoli sooner rather than later. "I have been as much concerned about Libya as about Israel in this whole period," Eugene Rostow confessed shortly before leaving the State Department. "Libya is just as rich as can be, unbelievable oil there," he told an interviewer in late 1968. But "a very weak society and a very small population right next door to Egypt" had produced "a very dangerous situation" in Tripoli, where "Nasserite mob pressure" might bring King Idris and his pro-Western regime down.[90]

Just after sunrise on 1 September 1969 a small band of officers led by twenty-seven-year-old Colonel Muammar al-Qaddafi overthrew the rickety Sanussi dynasty. Although Qaddafi's bloodless coup apparently stunned King Idris, who was vacationing with his entourage in the Aegean, the Libyan military takeover came as no surprise to Eugene Rostow's successors at Foggy Bottom. David Newsom, who had left his post as U.S. ambassador in Tripoli for a State Department position just three months before Qaddafi took over, believed that "the situation politically in Libya was not healthy" and told senior U.S. policymakers so in the summer of 1969.[91] "The Idris regime was certainly one of the most corrupt in the area and probably one of the most corrupt in the world," State Department oil expert James Akins confessed several years later. "It was overthrown with surprising ease and there was almost no resistance."[92] The CIA evidently corroborated these assessments by monitoring the activities of Qaddafi and his followers on the eve of the coup.[93] But the Nixon administration made no attempt to help Idris save his throne. "Despite close U.S. ties with the Libyan monarchy," David Newsom told the Senate Foreign Relations Committee in July 1970, "there was no question of the United States intervening on its behalf when the coup occurred in September 1969."[94]

U.S. policymakers, however, were nonetheless deeply troubled by the implications of Qaddafi's revolution, which combined elements of Libyan nationalism, pan-Arab socialism, and Islamic revivalism. A true son of the desert whose father had joined Omar Mukhtar's nationalist crusade against the Italians a generation earlier, Muammar al-Qaddafi was also a devout Muslim who believed that the regeneration of the Arab peoples would come only through rejecting the West and returning to the fundamentals of Islam. Although as a teenager Qaddafi had been a self-proclaimed Nasserite, Egypt's overwhelming defeat in the 1967 Six Day War led him to conclude that the Arab predicament stemmed at least in part from Nasser's focus on secular reform and his neglect of religious tradition. Because the youthful Libyan firebrand saw himself as better suited to lead the Arab world than his Egyptian neighbor and because Islam seemed incompatible with communism, many observers in Washington hoped that the new regime in Tripoli would keep its distance from Cairo and Moscow.[95]

Revolutionary nationalism Libyan style, however, soon proved as dangerous to Western interests in the Middle East as the Egyptian variety. Qaddafi wasted little time serving notice that both the United States and Britain must abandon their military installations in Libya as soon as possible. "We accept no bases, no foreigner, no colonialist, no intruder," he told a cheering crowd in Tripoli on 16 October 1969, and "we will liberate our territory . . . whatever the cost."[96] Convinced that a protracted struggle to retain U.K. military facilities at Tobruk would only jeopardize British access to Libyan oil, Whitehall struck a quick deal and turned its base over to Qaddafi on 28 March 1970. Hoping to prevent friction between Tripoli and Washington, the Nixon administration followed suit ten weeks later and evacuated Wheelus Field on 11 June, eighteen months ahead of the timetable that Eisenhower and Idris had approved sixteen years earlier.[97]

Regaining control of Tobruk and Wheelus Field proved but the opening volley in Qaddafi's campaign to transform Libya's role in the world. Although Washington expected further trouble from the "militant Arab nationalist regime" in Tripoli, through the summer of 1970 top U.S. officials believed that the "essentially Islamic and religious . . . character" of the Libyan revolution would prevent Kremlin inroads.[98] In late July, however, "Libya began to receive significant amounts of tanks and other ground equipment from the Soviet Union," which worried Richard Nixon and William Rogers, his secretary of state.[99] More bad news arrived two months later when Qaddafi took aim at U.S. petroleum firms operating in Libya, touching off a three-year tug-of-war over output, prices, and profits. He delivered the coup de grâce on 1 September 1973, the fourth anniversary of his coup d'état, by revoking all foreign concessions and nationalizing the entire Libyan petroleum industry.[100]

More troubling than Qaddafi's expropriation of America's $1.5 billion stake in Libyan oil was his vow to use his petrodollars to finance an Islamic revival designed to undermine Western influence throughout the Middle East. In April 1973 Qaddafi issued the three-part *Green Book* outlining his plans for a Muslim "cultural revolution." Much of Qaddafi's ideology—his critique of imperialism, his focus on Arab socialism, and his calls for direct democracy— was all too familiar to U.S. policymakers who had been struggling to contain revolutionary nationalism in the Muslim world for two decades. What stood out in the *Green Book*, however, was the "Third Universal Theory," which claimed that by returning to the fundamentals of Islam, Libyans could lead Muslims everywhere along a "Third Way" toward economic development and political change that rejected both capitalism and communism.[101] By the late 1970s Qaddafi had begun to put theory into practice, expelling Italian settlers and other non-Muslims from Libya, championing Islamic wars of national liberation next door in Chad and halfway around the world in the Philippines, and bankrolling Palestinian terrorism.[102]

By the time Jimmy Carter entered the Oval Office, many U.S. policymakers regarded the unpredictable Qaddafi as public enemy number one. In 1977 the State Department included Libya, with Cuba and North Korea, on its short list of outlaw states suspected of supporting international terrorism. Two years later Islamic militants supporting Ayatollah Khomeini's revolution in Iran ransacked the U.S. embassy in Tripoli and burned it to the ground. By the end of the Carter administration, top U.S. officials were deeply concerned "about the potential for foreign troublemaking provided by [Qaddafi's] oil revenues," State Department policy planning director Anthony Lake recalled long afterward, and also about "his appeal to Islamic revolutionaries beyond his borders." On 2 May 1980 President Carter severed diplomatic relations with the Qaddafi regime, setting the stage for a series of nasty military skirmishes during the Reagan era.[103]

Just a decade and a half after Eisenhower and Kennedy had set out to transform the Sanussi kingdom from a fragmented desert wasteland into a prosperous, pro-Western nation-state, peaceful reform in Libya had given way to violent anti-Western revolution. Long convinced that secular Soviet-backed radicals such as Nasser and Qassim posed the most serious threat to American interests in the Middle East, U.S. policymakers had been ill-prepared to cope with Qaddafi's brand of revolutionary Islam. Washington's frustrating attempt to sort out religion and politics in Libya after 1969 was a harbinger of a far more explosive American encounter with Islamic extremism in Iran ten years later.

Reform from Above: The Shah
and Iran's White Revolution

Nowhere in the Middle East did the United States push more consistently for reform and modernization after 1945 than in Iran, and nowhere did America fail more spectacularly. A mountainous land slightly larger than Alaska blessed with enormous oil reserves and a commanding position along the northern shore of the Persian Gulf, Iran had since the nineteenth century attracted the attention of British and Russian expansionists. Determined to retain control over the exclusive petroleum concession that U.K. firms had secured from the Qajar dynasty in 1902, Whitehall built a huge oil refinery at Abadan, a boomtown on the Iranian side of the Shatt-al-Arab. Frustrated by twenty years of British informal empire in Tehran, Reza Khan, an illiterate cavalry officer, overthrew the Qajars in 1921 and proclaimed himself Reza Shah Pahlavi four years later. To counterbalance the powerful influence of Great Britain, Iran's newest monarch signed a treaty of friendship with the Soviet Union, which coveted a warm water port on the Persian Gulf. During the late 1930s, however, Reza Shah swung to the right and embraced the blend of Aryan supremacy and anticommunism first popularized in Nazi Germany.[104]

By the summer of 1941 Reza Shah had few admirers either in Moscow, where Josef Stalin worried that Tehran's flirtation with Berlin would help the Nazis turn Russia's southern flank, or in London, where Winston Churchill suspected that the Pahlavi regime, with German encouragement, might nationalize AIOC. On 25 August British and Russian troops occupied Iran, deposed the troublesome shah, and replaced him with his twenty-one-year-old son, Mohammed Reza Pahlavi. To prevent this Anglo-Soviet power play from compromising Iranian independence and territorial integrity, the United States helped the young shah consolidate his position in Tehran and insisted that both Britain and Russia agree to withdraw from Iran after the Second World War. Whitehall honored its promise; but the Kremlin did not, and the Red Army remained in northern Iran until May 1946.[105]

Despite considerable anxiety in Tehran about the Soviet menace, top U.S. policymakers believed that the most critical challenges confronting Iran during the late 1940s were economic modernization and land reform. Notwithstanding their country's obvious oil wealth, most of the shah's 20 million subjects were impoverished peasants whose fate lay in the hands of a narrow, landowning elite that dominated the Majlis, the Iranian parliament. When the shah visited Washington in the autumn of 1949 seeking a hefty increase in U.S. military aid, Secretary of State Dean Acheson "emphasized the fundamental necessity of giving priority to economic and social development" and pointed out that U.S. arms for Chiang Kai-shek had not prevented Mao Zedong from seizing power in Beijing a few weeks earlier. Without economic development and political modernization, the JCS warned six months later, Iran would remain "an incipient China."[106]

While the Truman administration stumbled toward undeclared war with the real China in the snows of Korea in late 1950, the shah's opponents flocked to the National Front, a broad coalition calling for social reform to be financed by oil revenues generated by expropriating AIOC. Early in the new year anti-Western radicals gunned down Prime Minister Ali Razmara, who had opposed nationalization of the giant British oil firm. "Frustration and hopelessness among the mass of the people," White House Iran-watchers concluded on 14 March 1951, "is now seriously threatening the internal stability of the country." Unless Washington could find ways to "foster social reform and an expanding economy," the Pahlavi regime might be swept away by revolutionaries with ties to Moscow.[107]

U.S. officials had grave doubts about Mohammed Mossadegh, the mercurial leader of the National Front whom the shah reluctantly named prime minister in April 1951. Despite belonging to one of the wealthiest landholding families in Iran, the sixty-nine-year-old Mossadegh was a longtime member of the Majlis well known for supporting agrarian reform and for opposing foreign oil interests. After AIOC refused to revise its concession, Mossadegh drafted a nationalization decree that the Majlis passed unanimously on 15 March 1951. Ignoring the shah's objections, Mossadegh moved swiftly to expropriate AIOC, prompting Whitehall to organize an international embargo on Iranian oil. A White House study completed at the end of the year confirmed that the nationalization of AIOC "has heightened popular desire for promised economic and social betterment and has increased social unrest." By "wresting the political initiative from the Shah, the landlords and other traditional holders of power" and reaching out to the left-leaning Tudeh Party, Mossadegh had unleashed revolutionary forces so potent that "Iran could be effectively lost to the free world."[108]

By the time Dwight Eisenhower turned his attention to Iran in early 1953, most U.S. policymakers felt that drastic action was required to save the shah's throne. "A Communist takeover is becoming more and more likely," U.S. intelligence warned Ike as the Iranian oil crisis dragged into its third year. "If Iran succumbed to the Communists," CIA director Allen Dulles reminded Eisenhower on 4 March 1953, "there was little doubt that in short order the other areas of the Middle East, with some 60% of the world's oil reserves, would fall into Communist control."[109] The crisis deepened in early June when Mossadegh, his treasury nearly empty thanks to the effects of the Western oil embargo, signed a trade agreement with the Soviet Union. A month later rumors flew that Mossadegh, with the help of the Tudeh Party, would force the shah to abdicate, leaving the septuagenarian nationalist and his left-wing supporters "in unchallenged and absolute control" in Tehran. "If present trends persist over a period of time whereby each step Mossadegh takes gradually increases his dependence on [the] Tudeh," U.S. embassy officials warned Washington in late July, the "results [would be] too obvious to need elaboration."[110] With covert encouragement from the United States, the Iranian army staged a pro-Western coup d'état on 19 August 1953. General Fazlollah Zahedi and fellow officers loyal to the Pahlavi dynasty arrested Mossadegh, restored full authority to the shah, and abruptly shifted Iran's political compass from left to right.[111]

Having helped overthrow Mossadegh in order to stem the tide of revolutionary nationalism in Iran, the Eisenhower administration worried that the shah's reactionary policies constituted a prescription for further turmoil. Although Prime Minister Zahedi had "put a good many of the leaders of the Tudeh party in jail," Allen Dulles warned Ike on 30 December 1953, he had made "little or no progress in the crucial area of social and economic reforms."[112] Moscow's generous military assistance for Egypt and Syria and its persistent harassment of Iran and other pro-Western Muslim regimes made it difficult during the mid-1950s for Washington to insist that the shah reallocate his resources from national defense to economic development. Yet many in Washington regarded Qassim's takeover in Baghdad in July 1958 as a preview of what lay in store next door in Tehran. "We still take a gloomy view of the Shah's future unless he can be persuaded to undertake some dramatic reforms," Dulles told Eisenhower on 21 August 1958. "The problem is very much like that earlier in Iraq, and we should try to persuade the Shah to undertake reforms while there was yet time."[113]

Persuasive though Eisenhower could be, he and his administration made little headway with their reformist agenda in Tehran during his final two years in office. After the State Department succeeded in pulling together a $125 million package drawn from the U.S. Development Loan Fund and the World Bank to stimulate Iranian economic growth in late 1958, for example, the shah countered with a fresh request for more U.S. military assistance to meet the danger posed by Iraq, which he claimed was "about to become a base for new Tudeh (Communist) Party activities designed against the regime in Iran."[114] Because of his fixation on external threats and his neglect of internal problems, U.S. intelligence analysts found it "unlikely that [the shah] will effect such a fundamental reform program as would satisfy rising popular demand and broaden the base of his support sufficiently to insure the stability of his regime."[115] To be sure, Eisenhower had "a good discussion with the Shah on the subject of land reform" during a December 1959 visit to Tehran, sparking hope that the Pahlavi regime would "take measures of major importance very

shortly which should have a great impact on this problem."[116] But the land reform law that the shah pushed through the Majlis in early 1960 was too little
for the peasants and too much for the landlords. "The Shah's reform measures,"
the CIA advised Ike on 7 April, "have alienated new groups of people without
causing any groups already opposed to the Shah to come over to his side."[117]

Shortly afterward Eisenhower instructed his NSC staff to undertake a thorough reevaluation of U.S. policy toward Iran. The end product, NSC-6010, did
not make for pleasant reading. "Without internal reform," the drafters of the
document concluded, "the monarchy is likely to be overthrown." The diagnosis of what ailed Iran seemed clear: "Current dissatisfaction is based in part on
awakening popular expectations for reform of Iran's archaic social, economic
and political structure and concomitant disillusionment with the Shah's limited efforts to date to move in this direction with resolution and speed." NSC-
6010 prescribed few options, however, for dealing with those ills. "Despite the
weaknesses of the Shah's regime, the absence of any constructive, pro-Western
alternative at present makes U.S. support of the regime the best hope of fur-
thering U.S. interests in Iran." Only by accelerating Iranian economic growth
and strengthening the shah's internal security apparatus could the United States
hope to control the revolution of rising expectations in Tehran and buy time
for peaceful reform.[118]

Eisenhower would reluctantly approve NSC-6010 in early July. Complaining
that "all our aid merely perpetuates the ruling class of many countries and in-
tensifies the tremendous differences between the rich and the poor," Ike wondered how "could we continue to support governments which could not carry
out land reform and which would not lay out any constructive program for
the betterment of the situation?" Yet withdrawing U.S. aid from pro-Western
autocrats risked creating a situation where "we could only stand by and watch
a wave of revolution sweeping around the world." Although the shah was
"slow in undertaking the necessary reforms in his country," Eisenhower kept
the dollars flowing and left John Kennedy to sort out the Iranian mess in January 1961.[119]

JFK staffed his administration with a cadre of self-styled action intellectuals
whose fascination with modernization theory virtually guaranteed that the new
president would not stand idly by while the shah was swept away by a rising
tide of revolutionary nationalism. Just four months after he entered the White
House, Kennedy set up a special task force to assess deteriorating conditions in
Tehran, where a fresh wave of disorders was rapidly undermining the authority of the Pahlavi dynasty. To minimize the "growing chance of domestic strife
leading to chaos, or coups by rightist or leftist cliques, or Soviet-managed
subversion," the task force recommended redoubling U.S. efforts to foster
economic development and social reform in Iran.[120] The first step was to per-

suade the shah to appoint Ali Amini, a pro-Western technocrat with a reputation as a "strong reformist," as prime minister in late May. If Amini succeeded in stimulating growth, redistributing land, and cleaning up corruption, Assistant Secretary of State Phillips Talbot expected to see "a stronger, more broadly based Government in Iran."[121]

The shah, however, had serious reservations about the blueprint for change drafted by Amini and his American patrons. Effective land reform, for example, would require breaking up many large estates whose owners were more often than not leading supporters of the Pahlavi regime. Fomenting economic development would mean squeezing the shah's military budget at a time when he believed Iran was on the verge of becoming a dominant force in the Persian Gulf.[122] JFK raised both issues directly with the shah himself during an Oval Office meeting in April 1962. Praising Amini's efforts to spur economic growth and social change, Kennedy insisted that "the main problem in Iran was internal" and that "a very large Iranian army was not needed." Pointing out that Washington had recently approved a big military aid package for its NATO allies in Ankara, the shah complained that "America treats Turkey like a wife, and Iran like a concubine." JFK, whose taste in concubines ran in other directions, retorted that the United States stood ready to protect Iran from external aggression, provided the shah did not stand in the way of modernization and reform at home.[123]

Still bristling over Kennedy's patronizing attitude, in May Mohammed Reza Pahlavi returned home, where he quarreled repeatedly with Amini. Interpreting his prime minister's preference for land reform over national defense as American-inspired insubordination, the shah forced Amini to resign on 18 July 1962 and replaced him with Asadollah Alam, a longtime Pahlavi crony.[124] Determined to prevent a return to business as usual, the White House sent Vice-President Lyndon B. Johnson to Tehran later that summer in an effort "to steer [the] Shah on to our desire [that] he continue pressing internal development and reform."[125] The Kennedy administration, LBJ told the shah on 24 August, was convinced that "the ultimate strength, prosperity and independence of Iran would be in the progress made in the fields of economic well-being of the population and in social justice." If the shah wished to receive further "moral and material assistance," he must embrace Washington's reformist agenda.[126]

After pondering Washington's message for several months, the shah unveiled an ambitious program of social reform and economic modernization in January 1963. Rather than permitting pressure for change to bubble up from the grass roots as during the Amini era, he proposed instead a tightly controlled top-down White Revolution designed to transform Iranian society without reducing his own authority. Relieved to have "got the Shah onto the wicket of running a 'white revolution instead of a red one,'" the Kennedy administration began to develop "an overall strategy for moving Iran toward more effective solutions to its crucial internal problems" later that spring.[127] On 20 April Secretary of State Dean Rusk handed JFK a pair of reports that outlined a two-pronged American approach. First, the United States must continue "encouraging the Shah in his 'White Revolution' on a course fast enough to maintain lower class support of the regime but slow enough to avoid social and/or economic collapse." Second, U.S. advisers must work with the Iranians on "improving the counter-insurgency capacity of the military and of rural and urban police forces." By adopting such a strategy, the United States should be able to preserve an Iran "free from all foreign domination, with a stable government oriented toward the West and an economy capable of self-sustaining economic growth."[128]

But Kennedy's Iran-watchers also sounded a note of caution. Although "the U.S. is strongly identified with the regime and the reform program," American policymakers must be aware of the "Pitfalls of Direct Involvement" in "implementing land reform and other thorny aspects of the Shah's program." The United States must understand that "this is an Iranian revolution which will evolve at a Persian tempo and produce Persian results" and that "like any revolution, these events bring with them great problems which perhaps we can help the Iranians solve or meet but which we cannot solve by ourselves." Then JFK's Middle East experts offered a prophecy that would reverberate through the streets of Tehran fifteen years later. "The success of the [shah's] program over the long run may well rest on the extent to which it is identified an an indigenous effort." In short, the White House should remember "that the Shah's greatest liability may well be his vulnerability to charges by both reactionary and radical opposition elements that he is a foreign puppet."[129]

On 3 June 1963 Ayatollah Ruhollah Khomeini, a sixty-four-year-old cleric with fiery dark eyes and a flowing white beard, strode from his mosque in the holy city of Qom and denounced the man on the Peacock Throne as an American puppet. Outraged by the shah's recent characterization of Iran's clergy as "parasitic" agents of "Black Reaction" for whom progress was synonymous with blasphemy, Khomeini posed a simple question for which there was no simple answer: "What do you mean [by] a White Revolution?" Branding such American-backed initiatives as secular education, women's rights, and land reform as affronts to Islamic tradition, the relatively unknown ayatollah quickly became the leading symbol of opposition to the Pahlavi dynasty for the restless students, oil workers, and shopkeepers who surged into the streets of Iran's major cities. With the support of U.S. diplomats, the shah ordered a brutal crackdown that left more than 1,000 Iranians dead and then placed Khomeini and dozens of other clerics under house arrest.[130] Undaunted,

Khomeini resumed his Islamic jeremiads sixteen months later. "I don't know where this White Revolution is that they are making so much fuss about," he thundered in October 1964, but the shah's policies seemed to have "reduced the Iranian people to a level lower than that of an American dog." Determined to rid himself of this querulous ayatollah as quickly as possible, Mohammed Reza Pahlavi would send Khomeini into exile before the year was out, first to Turkey and then to Iraq.[131]

Misreading the implications of Khomeini's movement, the Kennedy administration and its successors encouraged the shah to press on with his White Revolution. Dismissing the recent disorders as the product of "demagogic discontent" that would fade away in the face of a concerted program of land reform, women's suffrage, and public education, the State Department's Phillips Talbot told a congressional panel on 17 July 1963 that the shah's initiatives "truly constitute a peaceful revolution."[132] Increasingly preoccupied with the deteriorating situation in Vietnam that he had inherited from Kennedy, by the summer of 1964 Lyndon Johnson regarded the shah's White Revolution as one of the few bright spots for U.S. foreign policy. "What is going on in Iran," LBJ told a visitor on 16 June, "is about the best thing going on anywhere in the world."[133] Two years later Armin Meyer, Johnson's ambassador in Tehran, confirmed that the "Shah is making Iran [a] show-case of modernization in this part of the world."[134] Indeed, by late 1968 the Johnson administration believed that Iran's rapid economic growth accompanied by social reform had provided the shah with a strong foundation for his bid to succeed Great Britain as the chief pillar of pro-Western stability in the Persian Gulf.

Humpty Dumpty Meets the Ayatollah: The Iranian Revolution

Richard Nixon, who had known and admired the shah since the Eisenhower era, hoped that the Pahlavi regime would become America's partner in the Middle East. The Iranian monarch's steadfast support for U.S. policy in Southeast Asia and his adamant refusal to join the Arabs in embargoing oil exports to the United States reflected a level of personal loyalty Nixon always demanded but seldom received. According to William Safire, a full-time Nixon speechwriter and part-time confidant, by the early 1970s "the Shah was about the President's favorite statesman in the world."[135] Like his boss in the Oval Office, national security adviser Henry Kissinger regarded the shah as "a pillar of stability in a turbulent and vital region" who, "despite the travesties of retroactive myth," was really "a dedicated reformer." The White Revolution, Kissinger recalled in 1979, had yielded remarkable achievements in areas such as land redistribution and women's rights while generating an economic boom that saw annual growth rates approach 10 percent, but the shah was simply "not farsighted enough to create new political institutions or to enlist new loyalties to sustain political stability."[136]

Although Kissinger was loath to admit it, the shah's problems were exacerbated by the diplomatic myopia of the Nixon administration, which believed that as Iran modernized, it would become America's surrogate in the Middle East. A national intelligence estimate on Iran prepared during the summer of 1970 captured the ebullient mood in Nixon's Washington. "The Shah is determined to ensure for Iran a position of power and leadership in the Persian Gulf after the British withdrawal," CIA analysts pointed out on 3 September, and his ambitious program of modernization—"land reform, industrialization, and wide-scale education"—had given him "great confidence that he is master in his own house."[137] Two years later the man in the Oval Office got a firsthand look at America's new partner in the Persian Gulf, and he liked what he saw. During a two-day visit to Tehran in May 1972 Nixon toasted the shah for his "progressive actions in everything from land reform to education" and praised "Iran's impressive record in the development of a strong economy and the successful implementation of His Imperial Majesty's 'White Revolution.'"[138] Convinced that these modernization schemes would bring Iran progress and prosperity and delighted that the shah was eager to help shore up Western interests in the region, Nixon and Kissinger promised to sell the Iranian monarch anything he wanted from the Pentagon's arsenal, except nuclear weapons.[139]

While the shah flexed his newfound military muscle, his multibillion-dollar spending spree spawned inflation at home that eroded the earnings of tenant farmers, oil workers, and shopkeepers. Moreover, his close ties with Washington left him vulnerable to charges leveled by middle-class students and disgruntled mullahs that he was fast becoming an American stooge. The Pahlavi regime responded with a fresh round of repression, jailing its leading critics and stepping up surveillance by its secret police.[140] Few in Washington appreciated the explosive potential building beneath the surface. Henry Kissinger, for example, continued to accentuate the positive when he briefed Gerald Ford, Nixon's successor, on the eve of the shah's visit to the White House in the spring of 1975. Stressing that "the Iranian economy is booming, having enjoyed GNP increases at the average rate of 15 per cent annually for a number of years," Kissinger praised the shah for having launched "land reform and a variety of other development programs designed to bring the benefits of . . . the 'White Revolution' to the population." Equally enthusiastic, Ford hailed the shah on 15 May for "wise leadership" that had enabled Iran to make "extraordinary strides in its economic development and in its relationships with other countries of its region."[141] Ten months later he vowed to strengthen "the special relationship we enjoy with Iran."[142]

Indeed, Ford and Kissinger were so enamored with the shah's White Revolution that they evidently encouraged him to export it next door to Afghanistan. In July 1973 Mohammed Daoud Khan, a high-ranking Afghan military officer committed to westernization, had staged a bloodless coup against his neutralist cousin, King Zahir, and established a republic. With Washington's blessing the shah offered Daoud a $400 million loan to encourage political reform, strengthen Afghanistan's economic infrastructure, and accelerate Kabul's tilt toward the West. The Iranian-backed reform program, however, was unpopular with landowners and clerics, who began to mobilize against modernization. When violent protests erupted in 1975, Daoud drove his Islamic opponents across the border into Pakistan, where during the next two decades they helped spawn the mujahadeen and, eventually, the Taliban.[143]

During the mid-1970s, however, Iranian and U.S. officials were far more concerned about the Soviet menace in Kabul than the specter of militant Islam. In March 1976 the shah "expressed great concern over the situation in Afghanistan," telling Nelson Rockefeller, Gerald Ford's vice-president and a long-time fan of the Pahlavis, "that Daoud Khan's position is under threat and that a group of communist army officers are in the ascendant."[144] Seventeen months later the CIA confirmed that the Iranian monarch regarded the Afghan president as "a country cousin, unsophisticated, backward and likely to be taken by the city slicker, in this case, the USSR."[145] Heeding his figurative cousin's advice, Daoud purged anti-Western elements from the Afghan army in early 1978 and attempted to arrest the leaders of the pro-Soviet People's Democratic Party of Afghanistan. But on 27 April Daoud was overthrown and killed by left-wing officers loyal to the People's Democratic Party in a bloody shootout. With the approach of summer an atmosphere of crisis enveloped Kabul, Tehran, and Washington.[146]

Jimmy Carter, the Georgia Democrat who had defeated Gerald Ford in November 1976, was initially less inclined than his Republican predecessor to embrace the shah's top-down model for modernization in Iran and Afghanistan. A State Department transition briefing paper that landed on Carter's desk in January 1977 highlighted the contradictions inherent in the White Revolution. "For thirty years, especially in the last fifteen, a very traditional society has been going through as massive a social and economic change as any country in the world," Foggy Bottom's Iran-watchers pointed out, and such rapid modernization had produced "rising expectations in all sectors of national life." Opposition to the shah's revolution from above was spreading, not only among the intellectuals but also among the ayatollahs, who "do not accept the present monarchy or its reform policies."[147] Eight months later the CIA confirmed that the principal challenge facing the Carter administration in Iran would be "Making a Silk Purse out of a Shah's Ear." Despite the fanfare associated with the White Revolution, more and more Iranians were dismissing their monarch's "reforms" as little more than "a long series of artificial creations to give the appearance but not the reality of political freedom." CIA analysts believed that sooner or later the shah's opponents were going to demand the real thing.[148]

A staunch advocate of human rights and democracy abroad, Carter quietly encouraged the Iranian monarch throughout the summer and into the autumn of 1977 to ease his authoritarian rule. Well aware that "the Shah's single-minded pursuit of his own goals had engendered opposition from the intelligentsia and others who desired more participation in the political process," Carter asked him during a White House meeting in mid-November to consider employing less repressive measures against his critics. Yet when Carter visited Tehran six weeks later, he had changed his tune. Like Nixon and Ford before him, the Georgia Democrat toasted the shah as a firm friend of the West, praised the White Revolution, and "acknowledged the value of the good relationship between our two nations."[149]

Carter could not utter such a toast a year later. When students and mullahs loyal to the exiled Ayatollah Khomeini gathered in Qom on 8 January 1978 to protest the shah's autocratic pro-Western policies, government forces opened fire, killing two dozen demonstrators and sparking a wave of anti-Pahlavi outbursts across the country. After one particularly bloody episode in late February, White House Middle East expert Gary Sick warned Zbigniew Brzezinski, Carter's national security adviser, that the reforms accomplished by the shah's White Revolution seemed to have backfired. "Although the government is making reference to Communist support and outside involvement," Sick pointed instead toward "what may be the true threat to the Shah's regime—the reactionary Muslim right wing which finds his modernization program too liberal and moving too fast away from the traditional values of Iranian society."[150]

The accuracy of Sick's diagnosis was quickly confirmed during the spring and summer of 1978 by a wave of street demonstrations inspired by Khomeini's recorded jeremiads and orchestrated by Muslim clerics eager to establish an Islamic republic. On 8 September troops loyal to the shah fired on 20,000 pro-Khomeini protesters gathered in Tehran's Jaleh square, killing 400 and wounding 4,000. Angry students, shopkeepers, and mullahs responded by organizing even bigger protests against Pahlavi rule. By end of the month William Sullivan, the U.S. ambassador in Tehran, was insisting that the "massive firestorm directed against the Shah" had been "brought on to a considerable extent by the frustrations, inequities, corruption, and rising expectations engendered by the shah's program of economic development and westernized social reform since 1963."[151]

The political inferno raging in Tehran set off alarms in Washington, where high-ranking U.S. policymakers worried that Iran's escalating cycle of violence was taking on a life of its own. The shah deserved praise for seeking "aggressively to establish democratic principles in Iran" and for adopting "a progressive attitude toward social questions [and] social problems," Jimmy Carter told reporters on 10 October, but "he may not be moving fast enough for some [and] he may be moving too fast for others." The White Revolution, Carter confided in his diary two weeks later, "has alienated a lot of powerful groups, particularly the right wing religious leaders who don't want any changes made in the old ways of doing things." With few other options, however, the Georgia Democrat urged the shah in early November "to hang firm and to count on our backing."[152]

Halfway around the world in Tehran, Ambassador William Sullivan had begun "Thinking the Unthinkable." Ever more certain that Khomeini's supporters were going to topple the Pahlavi dynasty, Carter's representative in Iran hoped to patch together a reformist coalition of pro-Western military officers, middle-class professionals, and religious moderates capable of reining in the Islamic extremists. "If the Shah should abdicate," Sullivan cabled Washington on 9 November, perhaps Khomeini could be persuaded to accept "some sort of Gandhi-like position in the political constellation," while the day-to-day affairs of state remained in the hands of "someone acceptable to the military rather than a Nasser-Qadhafi type that might be the Ayatollah's preferred candidate." This might seem like a "rather Pollyannish scenario," but Sullivan insisted that "we need to think the unthinkable at this time in order to give our thoughts some precision should the unthinkable contingency arise."[153]

Few inside the Carter administration, however, found Sullivan's thoughts thinkable. "The president and his top advisers were far from concluding that the shah was doomed," the NSC's Gary Sick pointed out several years later, "and they wished to avoid at all costs the appearance or reality of abandoning a close ally." As a result, throughout November and into early December the White House continued "directing all its efforts toward bolstering the shah and persuading him to act with more decisiveness."[154] Indeed, only after George Ball, a Democratic "wise man" with close ties to Jimmy Carter, paid a ten-day visit to Tehran just after Thanksgiving did U.S. policymakers fully appreciate the gravity of the crisis in Iran. "I reluctantly concluded that the Shah was on the way to a great fall," Ball recalled in his memoirs, "and that, like Humpty Dumpty, his regime could not be put together again." Ball explained why in a hard-hitting report that he handed to Carter on 11 December. "We made the Shah what he has become. We nurtured his love for grandiose geopolitical schemes and we supplied him with the hardware to indulge his fantasies," Ball concluded. "Once we had anointed him as protector of our nation's interests in the Persian Gulf, we became dependent on him. Now that his regime is coming apart under the pressure of imported modernization, we have so committed ourselves as to have no ready alternative."[155]

When Carter's senior advisers reviewed Ball's report two days later, they agreed that time was rapidly running out. "At this point," Undersecretary of State Warren Christopher remarked, "the shah had less than a fifty-fifty chance of survival." Zbigniew Brzezinski agreed and wondered whether "it would be useful to put in motion a process of political change" calculated to produce a caretaker regime composed of pro-Western officers and moderate elements among the shah's opponents.[156] But before the year was over, most U.S. policymakers realized that the clashes between pro-shah and pro-Khomeini forces had become so bitter and so bloody that no compromise was possible. Hoping to avert civil war in Iran, President Carter rejected last-minute calls for an American-backed military takeover in Tehran and quietly encouraged the shah to leave the country instead. The end came with dramatic suddenness. On 16 January 1979 Mohammed Reza Shah Pahlavi bid his unruly subjects farewell and departed for exile in Egypt. "Iran was likely to shift piecemeal to an orientation similar to that of Libya or into anarchy," an unhappy Brzezinski warned the man in the Oval Office two days later, "with the result that our position in the [Persian] Gulf would be undermined."[157]

At the end of the month Ayatollah Khomeini returned from his own exile in triumph. Demonizing the United States as "the Great Satan," he denounced the shah as "a vile traitor" and dismissed the White Revolution as an affront to Muslim tradition. Noting that the shah had promised economic development and then squandered Iran's oil revenues on U.S. military hardware, Khomeini told a huge crowd just outside Tehran on 2 February that "Muhammad Riza enacted his so-called reforms in order to create markets for America and to increase our dependence upon America."[158] Vowing to change all that, the ayatollah set about laying the groundwork for an Islamic republic that would pose a far graver threat to U.S. interests in Iran than had Mohammed Mossadegh's nationalist regime a generation earlier. By late 1979 pro-Khomeini gunmen had taken fifty-two Americans hostage at the U.S. embassy in Tehran and the ayatollah's government had begun channeling Iran's oil revenues into the hands of anti-American terrorists from Saudi Arabia to Lebanon.[159] As they had done earlier in Iraq and Libya, U.S. policymakers had sown the winds of reform in Iran only to reap the whirlwind of revolution.

Wedded to the belief that economic development and westernization would bring political stability to pro-American regimes from Tehran to Tripoli, every administration from Eisenhower's to Carter's embraced a reformist agenda that had unintended revolutionary consequences. More often than not, U.S.-backed programs such as the shah's White Revolution, which were designed to raise living standards and to prevent communist inroads, inadvertently raised popular expectations to unrealistic levels and triggered a violent backlash. In a postmortem explaining America's failure in Tehran and, by implication, in places like Afghanistan as well, Gary Sick confessed that "the emergence in Iran of a coalition of non-Communist, non-fanatic Islamic and pro-Western moderates operating within a responsible constitutional framework was profoundly to be preferred to the virulently anti-Western theocracy that ultimately assumed power."[160]

By the summer of 1980, however, nonfanatic, pro-Western moderates were in short supply in the Persian Gulf. Ironically, when U.S. policymakers surveyed the region for someone capable of containing Islamic extremism, one of the most likely suspects was Saddam Hussein, the fiercely secular Iraqi strongman who had helped overthrow the anti-Western Qassim regime in Baghdad two decades earlier. While no hard evidence has surfaced indicating that the Carter administration actively encouraged Ba'athist Iraq to attack theocratic Iran in early September, U.S. officials clearly hoped that Khomeini's difficulties on the battlefield would make him more interested in improving relations with the United States, which controlled the supply of spare parts for most weapons in the Iranian arsenal.

After Ronald Reagan took over in January 1981, Washington tilted steadily toward Baghdad, providing Saddam Hussein with a half-billion dollars in agricultural credits and dual-use technology having both civilian and military applications. "It wasn't that we wanted Iraq to win the war, we did not want Iraq to lose," Reagan NSC staffer Geoffrey Kemp recalled a few years later. "We knew [Saddam Hussein] was an S.O.B., but he was our S.O.B."[161] Viewed through the looking glass of modernization, the Iraq-Iran war might be construed as a confrontation between the future and the past, between the twentieth century and the fourteenth. Shortly after the shooting stopped, however, America's thoroughly modern S.O.B. would resort to some thoroughly traditional smash-and-grab tactics next door in Kuwait.

Our failure in Vietnam still casts a shadow over U.S. intervention anywhere, and other setbacks — notably those we suffered in Lebanon — have left some predisposed to pessimism about
our ability to promote U.S. interests in the Third world. . . .

If this cumulative effect cannot be checked or reversed in the future, it will gradually undermine America's ability to defend its interests in the most vital regions, such as the Persian Gulf,
the Mediterranean, and the Western Pacific. — Report of the Commission on Integrated Long-
Term Strategy, January 1988

By God, we've kicked the Vietnam syndrome once and for all. — George Bush, 1 March 1991

Kicking the Vietnam Syndrome

*Waging Limited War from the
Mediterranean to the Persian Gulf*

National security managers and action intellectuals might insist that modernization would stabilize the Middle East and make military intervention unnecessary, but for two centuries the United States had demonstrated a willingness to use armed force to protect its interests from the Straits of Gibraltar
to the Persian Gulf. America's burgeoning commercial and cultural presence in
the Mediterranean basin during the nineteenth century prompted Thomas Jefferson and his successors to deploy U.S. warships from the Barbary Coast to
Asia Minor. The subsequent discovery of black gold in the Middle East ignited
an oil boom that heightened the strategic importance of North Africa, which
was an early battleground for U.S. troops during the Second World War.

America's Cold War confrontation with the Soviet Union along the northern tier convinced the Truman administration to flex some naval muscle in the Eastern Mediterranean by establishing the U.S. Sixth Fleet in 1949. During the following forty years American warships shadowed the Soviet navy, showed the flag from the Dardanelles to the Straits of Hormuz, and hovered just over the horizon to support friends such as Jordan's King Hussein and to subdue foes such as Libya's Muammar al-Qaddafi.

In the early going such military ventures in the Middle East seemed relatively effective. Not a single American soldier died, for example, when Dwight Eisenhower sent U.S. troops to stamp out a brushfire war in Lebanon in 1958. But America's efforts were disastrous in Vietnam, where limited involvement escalated rapidly into a bloody stalemate and raised doubts about armed intervention elsewhere. During the Carter years some Americans began to wonder whether the costs of their country's expanding military commitments in the Middle East outweighed the benefits, as in Southeast Asia. Those doubts deepened during the 1980s after a truck bomb reduced U.S. military headquarters at the Beirut airport to a smoldering mass grave for a battalion of U.S. Marine "peacekeepers" and after an Iraqi warplane accidentally attacked a U.S. frigate patrolling the Persian Gulf.

Iraq's sudden invasion of Kuwait in August 1990 confirmed that Saddam Hussein was on a collision course with the United States, and that it was no accident. George Bush responded swiftly and sent a half-million U.S. troops to the Persian Gulf to spearhead a broad anti-Iraq military coalition that included many NATO members and several Arab states. Rejecting gradual escalation as a sure route to a desert quagmire, the Pentagon launched a high-tech aerial bombardment of Iraq in early 1991 before unleashing a multinational juggernaut that outgunned, outnumbered, and outwitted Saddam Hussein's army. By demonstrating that the United States could still plan and win a major ground war, Operation Desert Storm seemed to cure Americans of the debilitating Vietnam syndrome that had flared up any time Washington contemplated armed intervention in the Third World.

Whether or not victory in the Persian Gulf truly reversed a generation of Vietnam-induced American self-doubt, it did confirm that the ingredients for military success in the Middle East in the 1990s were the same as those that had spelled triumph along the Barbary Coast 200 years earlier: overwhelming technological superiority and the broadest possible array of weaponry. Having the right hardware matters little, of course, if one relies on the wrong tactics. Although Pentagon planners learned this lesson the hard way in places like Saigon and Beirut, they seem also to have learned an important corollary in other places such as Tripoli and Baghdad. U.S. intervention in the Middle East has been successful only when technology and tactics have meshed with objectives that are focused and finite. That corollary seemed more important than ever by the autumn of 2001 as George W. Bush launched an open-ended crusade against al-Qaeda and Islamic terrorism that some feared would become a Central Asian Vietnam.

From the Shores of Tripoli to the Sixth Fleet

Separated by 3,000 miles of ocean from the military conflicts of the Old World and preoccupied with the challenges of nation building in the New, most Americans saw no compelling reason for their country to upgrade its puny arsenal until Algiers and the other Barbary states began to wage war on the U.S. carrying trade in North African waters during the late 1780s. Congress responded by appropriating funds for America's first three men-of-war, which soon patrolled the shores of Tripoli as part of a new Mediterranean squadron, the U.S. Navy's first sustained venture outside territorial waters. After 1801 the Jefferson and Madison administrations waged undeclared war against the Barbary states, whose autocratic rulers had become accustomed to sinking U.S. merchant ships, seizing cargoes bound from Boston and New York to Barcelona and Naples, and holding American sailors for ransom. Thanks more to tribute paid than to battles won, the United States held the upper hand until 1812, when war erupted with Britain, enabling the Barbary states to resume their depredations confident that the U.S. Navy was otherwise engaged. Once peace was restored between Washington and London, President James Madison sent Commodore Stephen Decatur into the Mediterranean to settle some old scores. After bombarding Algiers in June 1815 to secure the release of two dozen American captives, Decatur's squadron sailed 1,000 miles east to Tripoli, where a show of force prompted Pasha Yusuf suddenly to see the wisdom of respecting freedom of the seas.[1]

Although immortalized in the words of the marine corps hymn as a tremendous victory, America's twenty-year confrontation with the Barbary states actually highlighted the high costs associated with military intervention in the Muslim world. As a result the U.S. Navy adopted a lower profile in the Mediterranean after 1815, maintaining a tiny squadron based at Port Mahon on Minorca, the smallest of the Balearic Islands, and occasionally showing the flag farther east when trouble flared in places such as Crete or Lebanon. The United States continued to make its military presence felt in the Middle East, however, by providing arms and advisers to Turkey and Egypt. As early as the 1830s Sultan Mahmud hired U.S. shipbuilders to construct a modern Turkish navy to replace the one sent to the bottom at the Battle of Navarino, and forty years later Khedive Ismail appointed Colonel Charles Stone, a Civil War veteran and soldier of fortune, as the Egyptian army's chief of staff and de facto minister of defense. Occasional efforts to reverse the flow by incorporating Middle Eastern tactics into America's arsenal, on the other hand, were much less successful. Indeed, the War Department's ill-advised decision to import 300 camels in 1855 as part of an experimental dromedary corps charged with taming the American Southwest became for the U.S. cavalry a legendary example of the wrong idea in the wrong place at the wrong time.[2]

With Washington increasingly content to treat the Middle East as a British and French sphere of influence, U.S. military involvement in the region continued to decline throughout the first four decades of the twentieth century. By the late 1930s the U.S. naval presence in the Mediterranean had sunk so low that months went by without a U.S. warship passing through the Suez Canal. All that would change in September 1939, however, when Nazi Germany plunged the world into another war that would eventually make Algiers, Tripoli, and Suez household words in the United States for the first time in a hundred years. With his accomplice Benito Mussolini already firmly in control of an Italian desert empire in Libya, Adolf Hitler regarded the swift Nazi triumph over France in June 1940 as a golden opportunity to gain access to French North Africa, to consolidate the Axis partnership between Germany and Italy, and to sever Britain's imperial lifeline by invading Egypt and seizing the Suez Canal.[3]

Although Tokyo's sneak attack on Pearl Harbor in December 1941 brought calls for a war of revenge in the Pacific, Franklin Roosevelt and British prime minister Winston Churchill quickly agreed that defeating Germany should be a higher priority than settling old scores with Japan. Convinced that the first blow should come in North Africa, U.S. and U.K. military planners worked feverishly to complete preparations for Operation Torch, an amphibious assault designed to wrest control of Algeria from Hitler's Vichy French puppets and halt the Nazi drive toward Alexandria, the Nile Delta, and the isthmus of Suez. On 8 November 1942 a U.S. armada that included everything from 350-ton landing craft to 35,000-ton battleships loomed into view off Algiers and its sister port Oran, shelled Vichy French shore installations, and landed 84,000 GIs. By Christmas Allied troops held sway in Algeria and were taking aim at Axis armies farther east. With U.S. and U.K. forces firmly in control from Tunisia to Libya by May 1943, it was clear that Hitler's high-stakes bid to conquer the Middle East had failed. Moreover, the momentum generated by this desert victory helped accelerate Allied plans to invade Sicily later that summer and the Italian mainland early in the new year, two key stepping stones along the path to V-E Day in May 1945.[4]

Once the Second World War ended, public pressure mounted for the rapid demobilization of U.S. armed forces and for a sharp reduction in America's military involvement in peripheral ports of call in the Middle East, a region that remained terra incognita for most of Main Street. By December 1945 90 percent of the U.S. fleet was stationed in the Pacific, and the Truman administration fully expected the Royal Navy to promote stability and to project Western seapower from Gibraltar to the Persian Gulf. But increasingly heavy-handed Soviet pressure on Turkey to grant the Red Navy free passage through the Dardanelles and disturbing indications that Britain lacked both the financial resources and the political will to fulfill its military obligations in the Eastern Mediterranean soon prompted U.S. policymakers to rethink their low-profile tactics in the region. Chief among the advocates of a more forceful U.S. approach was Secretary of the Navy James Forrestal, an anticommunist zealot who sent the battleship *Missouri* to Athens and Istanbul, as Constantinople was now known, in April 1946 and shortly thereafter dispatched the aircraft carrier *Franklin D. Roosevelt* on a Mediterranean odyssey.[5]

Such sporadic shows of force notwithstanding, Forrestal believed that only by establishing a permanent and formidable U.S. naval presence in the area could Washington prevent Moscow from fishing in troubled waters. Unhappy that U.S. seapower from Gibraltar to Suez was "stripped down as a result of our rapid demobilization to a dangerously low point of efficiency," Forrestal secured White House and State Department approval for a 1 October 1946 navy press release affirming that "units of the American Fleet have been in the Mediterranean and will continue to be there in the future."[6] Truman's decision to make Forrestal America's first secretary of defense a year later signaled a deepening commitment to Cold War projects such as upgrading the U.S. Navy's capabilities in the Middle East. On 4 August 1947, only a few days after Forrestal took over at the Pentagon, he was asked by Secretary of State George Marshall, perhaps Truman's most trusted diplomatic adviser, "to explore the possibility of stepping up gradually our naval forces in the Mediterranean."[7]

Long convinced that the Kremlin could be contained only by superior military force, Forrestal quietly began to redeploy U.S. warships from Brooklyn and Newport News to Athens and Istanbul. Rechristened the Sixth Task Fleet in June 1948, the navy's burgeoning Mediterranean squadron now included one aircraft carrier, three cruisers, nine destroyers, and a marine battalion based in Naples, Italy. Forrestal's nervous breakdown and suicide in May 1949 prevented him from overseeing plans for further expansion. Nine months later, however, his brainchild completed its metamorphosis into the U.S. Sixth Fleet, which by the mid-1950s had grown into an armada of more than fifty vessels whose frequent centerpiece was the uss *Forrestal*, a 60,000-ton supercarrier loaded with 100 fighter-bombers that would have made Stephen Decatur's day.[8]

Up the Down Escalator: Of Brushfire
Wars and Flexible Response

Created during the late 1940s as part of a Cold War call to arms to deter the Kremlin, Forrestal's Sixth Fleet would spend its first two decades quelling crises and rebellions rather than containing the Soviet navy, which did not begin to make regular visits to Middle Eastern waters until the mid-1960s. Throughout the late 1950s the U.S. Navy's Mediterranean squadron repeatedly engaged in "show of force" operations to demonstrate support for pro-Western regimes in the Middle East. When Jordan's King Hussein appealed for U.S. help to thwart a pro-Nasser coup in April 1957, for example, Dwight Eisenhower moved a carrier task force built around the *Forrestal* within striking distance of Amman. According to its commander, Admiral Charles R. Brown, the Sixth Fleet was the "steel-grey stabilizer" that saved Hussein's throne.[9] When a left-wing coup in Damascus four months later unnerved America's friends in Amman, Beirut, and Ankara, Eisenhower ordered U.S. warships to stand by off the Syrian coast.[10]

The highest-profile Middle Eastern episode involving the Sixth Fleet during the Eisenhower years, however, was Operation Blue Bat, which saw 14,000 U.S. Marines wade ashore at Beirut on 15 July 1958 to prop up a pro-American regime under fire from anti-Western radicals. Half Christian and half Muslim, Lebanon was by the mid-1950s a sectarian powderkeg waiting to explode. President Camille Chamoun, a Maronite warlord with close ties to Washington, had lit the fuse by rigging the 1957 parliamentary elections in order to secure an unprecedented second term. The explosion came in the spring of 1958, when his Sunni and Shi'ite opponents launched an uprising that threatened to bring a pro-Nasser Muslim government to power in Beirut. For months Chamoun had been telling U.S. officials that "it would be comforting if some elements of the Sixth Fleet might be moved to [the] eastern Mediterranean."[11] Hoping to avoid military intervention, the Eisenhower administration offered nebulous assurances that the United States would stand by its friends while working quietly behind the scenes to broker a peaceful settlement to the Lebanese strife. But the bloody coup that rocked Baghdad on 14 July 1958 sent shock waves rippling all the way to Beirut, where Chamoun asked Eisenhower to send in the marines.[12]

Although Chamoun's request came more suddenly than many in Washington expected, top Pentagon officials had been anticipating just such an eventuality for nearly a year. As early as November 1957 the JCS had begun to develop "on an urgent basis, a plan for possible combined U.S.-U.K. military intervention in the event of an imminent or actual coup d'etat in Jordan and/or Lebanon."[13] By May 1958 the White House and Whitehall were putting the finishing touches on Operation Blue Bat, which called for U.K. paratroopers based in Cyprus and U.S. Marines aboard the Sixth Fleet to secure the Beirut area in the event of a crisis.[14]

Despite thorough Anglo-American contingency planning and despite Eisenhower's well-deserved reputation for carefully correlating military means with geopolitical ends, Operation Blue Bat threatened to spiral out of control once it got under way. A few hours after Chamoun's call for help, British prime minister Harold Macmillan telephoned Eisenhower to suggest that rather than "sitting in this [half-penny] place" in Lebanon, U.K. and U.S. forces should "carry this thing on to the Persian Gulf" and undertake "a big operation running all the way through Syria and Iraq." Worried that this would mean "opening Pandora's box" without really knowing "what's at the bottom of it," Eisenhower insisted that, for the time being, intervention should be limited to Lebanon, where U.S. Marines were about to go ashore, and to Jordan, where a jittery King Hussein was on the verge of requesting U.K. troops to prevent an anti-Western uprising.[15]

Notwithstanding Eisenhower's determination to keep Operation Blue Bat within strict limits, avoiding wider war in the Middle East owed as much to good luck as to wise crisis management. Even before their boots were dry, U.S. Marines had very nearly stumbled into a shooting match with Muslim militiamen, who briefly surrounded the beachhead at Beirut until the warships of the Sixth Fleet and the warnings of U.S. diplomats persuaded Chamoun's foes to back off. When British flying boxcars ferrying 3,700 Tommies from Cyprus to Jordan flew through Israeli airspace three days later without securing prior approval, Whitehall nearly found itself in a high-altitude shootout with the Jewish state. Even more ominous were rumblings from the Persian Gulf suggesting that the revolutionary regime in Iraq was about to take over oil-rich Kuwait. Eisenhower moved to deter the Iraqis by ordering the U.S. Seventh Fleet to steam from Okinawa to the Indian Ocean while Secretary of State John Foster Dulles advised British officials that "we should not exclude the possibility of early military action to secure Kuwait, even if the Kuwait authorities were not at this stage willing to invite us in."[16] In the end this nightmare scenario never materialized, and the U.S. and U.K. troops departed from Beirut and Amman on schedule in the autumn of 1958 without having suffered a single casualty. The landings in Beirut, U.S. ambassador to Lebanon Robert McClintock remarked on 4 November, were "an eminently successful exercise in limited war."[17] Ike himself echoed these views. "It had been the kind of intervention," he told Harold Macmillan in March 1959, "which had not left a nasty aftertaste."[18]

In memoirs published six years later as one of his successors prepared to plunge into the quagmire of Vietnam, Eisenhower continued to insist that Blue

Bat was an excellent example of how to intervene successfully in the Third World. "The operation in Lebanon," Ike observed with an eye on Southeast Asia, "demonstrated the ability of the United States to react swiftly with conventional armed forces to meet small scale, or 'brush fire' situations" like the one unfolding in Indochina.[19] Although in the short run Eisenhower managed to douse the Lebanese brushfire in 1958 by deploying the Sixth Fleet and the U.S. Marines, over the longer haul Operation Blue Bat added to the tinder that would fuel an inferno in Vietnam and ignite a firestorm in the Persian Gulf a generation later. By employing globalist ideology, anticommunist rhetoric, and heavy firepower to combat a regional threat rooted in Third World nationalism, Ike helped place Uncle Sam's foot on the lowest rung of the ladder of escalation first tested in Beirut by a new breed of military bureaucrats and national security managers who would soon quantify and incrementalize their way to disaster in Saigon.

John F. Kennedy used foreign policy as a blunt instrument with which to attack Eisenhower's vice-president and heir apparent, Richard M. Nixon, during the 1960 elections. As a result Ike's success in Lebanon was overshadowed in the eyes of many Americans by his spectacular failures in places such as Cuba and the Congo, where left-wing radicals fanned smoldering brushfires into blazing anti-Western infernos.[20] Having won the hearts and votes of an electorate frankly worried that the United States was rapidly losing ground to the Soviets in the Third World, JFK wasted little time upgrading America's capacity to wage limited war in trouble spots from Southeast Asia to Southwest Arabia. For advice on how to extinguish brushfires sparked by anti-American guerrillas, Kennedy relied on military mavericks such as General Maxwell D. Taylor, action intellectuals like national security adviser McGeorge Bundy, and number-crunching systems analysts like Secretary of Defense Robert McNamara.

Maxwell Taylor had first caught JFK's eye during 1960 with the publication of *The Uncertain Trumpet*, a best-seller that challenged Eisenhower's doctrine of massive retaliation and advocated more unorthodox tactics for handling Third World trouble spots. A thinking person's paratrooper who spent most of Eisenhower's second term as U.S. army chief of staff, Taylor discounted the loose talk about thermonuclear Armageddon and insisted that the military conflicts of the future were more likely to be limited wars similar to Operation Blue Bat in Lebanon. Although he admitted that Eisenhower had handled that crisis reasonably well, Taylor pointed out that "the size of our landing in Lebanon was controlled by the capacity of the single airfield and port at Beirut." Unless the Pentagon upgraded its "strategic mobility" and modernized its "counterattrition forces," the next crisis in the Third World might not have such a happy ending. In short, given America's global responsibilities, the next president should give high priority to "extending the scope of our potential military reaction across the entire spectrum of possible challenge in accordance with a strategy of Flexible Response." Five months after moving into the Oval office, JFK would appoint Maxwell Taylor as White House military representative.[21]

Among those most delighted to see Taylor join the New Frontier was McGeorge Bundy, who had left his post as dean of the faculty at Harvard University to become Kennedy's national security adviser in January 1961. JFK was much impressed by Bundy's blend of bureaucratic savoir faire and intellectual toughness. Dubbed "Harry Hopkins—with hand grenades" by a *New York Times* reporter who evidently detected parallels between the New Frontier and the New Deal, Bundy quickly emerged as one of the most outspoken advocates of flexible response in Kennedy's Washington.[22] Meeting the military challenges of the coming decade would require "flexibility of all sorts," Bundy told White House counsel Theodore Sorensen in March 1961, including "increased capabilities in the area of limited war" in places like Southeast Asia. In particular, "we need to have a much more varied set" of tactics, Bundy insisted, "for guerrilla and anti-guerrilla efforts."[23]

Across the Potomac at the Pentagon, Bundy and Taylor found another staunch proponent of flexible response in Secretary of Defense Robert McNamara. A mathematical wizard who earned an MBA from Harvard before joining the U.S. strategic bombing survey during the Second World War, by 1960 McNamara had become president of the Ford Motor Company, where he relied on cost-benefit analysis to maximize profits and earned a reputation as the thinking person's auto executive. Intrigued by the combination of managerial acumen, sharp intellect, and liberal Republicanism, JFK wanted McNamara to shake up the Department of Defense.[24] The businessman-turned-policymaker did not disappoint. "Our preliminary evaluation convinced us," McNamara recalled shortly after leaving the Pentagon for the World Bank in 1968, "that we and our allies would have to make a much greater effort toward a force structure which could cope with limited aggression . . . ranging from small-scale guerrilla and subversive activities to overt attacks by sizable military units." Determined "to strengthen our limited war capabilities," he worked closely with Bundy and Taylor during the Kennedy years to develop an arsenal mobile enough and tactics flexible enough to escalate the level of U.S. military involvement incrementally.[25]

The laboratory in which JFK and his New Frontiersmen staged their earliest experiments with military escalation was South Vietnam, where 850 U.S. military advisers were helping America's client Ngo Dinh Diem battle communist guerrillas in January 1961. During the next thousand days Taylor, Bundy, and McNamara prepared a blueprint for escalation with an ever widening set of tactical options and an ever improving array of military hardware that were supposed to ensure a speedy victory in Vietnam. This blueprint, however, would prove as useless for the 17,500 U.S. advisers Kennedy had stationed in Saigon by November 1963 as for the half-million U.S. combat troops Lyndon Johnson would ship to Indochina over the following four years. In the rice paddies along the Mekong River, in the waters of the Tonkin Gulf, and in the skies over North Vietnam, incremental escalation seemed only to beget further escalation and rising American casualties.[26]

Despite their growing preoccupation with the escalating war in Southeast Asia, both the Kennedy and the Johnson administrations remained ready and willing to flex U.S. military muscle in the Middle East whenever American interests there seemed in jeopardy. The best example of JFK's willingness to escalate U.S. involvement in the region came in Saudi Arabia, where the Pentagon had maintained a small airfield and fuel depot outside Dhahran for nearly twenty years. When left-wing officers next door in Yemen overthrew Imam Mohammed al-Badr in September 1962 and invited Nasser to send Egyptian troops to help them consolidate their power, U.S. diplomats and military advisers in Riyadh worried that King Saud might be next. So did Saudi Arabia's foreign minister and Saud's heir apparent, Crown Prince Faisal, whose decision to run guns to pro-Badr guerrillas in northern Yemen prompted Egyptian retaliation against royalist base camps just inside Saudi territory at Najran. Claiming that the Najran raid proved that Nasser intended to use armed force to extend his UAR across the Red Sea, on New Year's Eve Faisal demanded concrete signs of U.S. support, including the "dispatch of USAF planes to Saudi Arabia."[27]

U.S. officials quickly reaffirmed America's commitment to the territorial integrity of Saudi Arabia, but none of JFK's advisers was eager to send air force jets. As the Saudi-Egyptian proxy war in Yemen heated up in early 1963, however, Washington moved to assuage Faisal's anxieties. "We've already done a lot to deter the UAR from escalating," White House Middle East expert Robert Komer told Kennedy on 21 February. "We've had destroyers visit Saudi port, bombers flying in, now a Special Forces Team is there. We've warned Nasser again not to step on our toes." Yet unless Egypt pulled out its troops and planes, Komer warned, the House of Saud was likely to ask JFK to do still more.[28] Four days later Kennedy approved National Security Action Memorandum 227, which provided Faisal with the tangible evidence of U.S. military support that he had been seeking for months. Under the terms of NSAM 227, JFK authorized the "temporary stationing of a token air defense squadron with associated ground environment in western Saudi Arabia to deter UAR air operations," contingent on Faisal's pledge "to suspend aid simultaneously to the Yemeni royalists."[29]

After several months of haggling with the Saudis and the Pentagon over the rules of engagement, the White House gave the go-ahead for Operation Hard Surface, as the U.S. Air Force mission to Saudi Arabia was now known, in July 1963. Billed as a fifteen-week "training mission," Hard Surface soon saw U.S. jets patrolling the skies within sight of Yemen, raising the disturbing possibility of a high-altitude Egyptian-American shootout. This did not sit well with General Curtis LeMay, the U.S. Air Force chief of staff, who wanted to authorize his pilots to shoot on sight and insisted that unless the rules of engagement were broadened by 15 October, he would terminate Hard Surface.[30] One week before LeMay's deadline, President Kennedy decided gradually to phase out the token U.S. air unit at Dhahran and to station two tactical fighter wings, a second Sixth Fleet carrier task force, and a squadron of B-47 bombers in the Eastern Mediterranean and the Red Sea. "The express purpose of such a prepositioning," Kennedy acknowledged, "is to assist in the stabilization of the situation in Saudi Arabia and to reduce the reaction time should the use of such forces be required."[31]

Although JFK did not live long enough to see his decisions carried out, the Pentagon moved quietly during the final weeks of 1963 to enhance America's over-the-horizon naval and air capabilities in the Middle East so that the F-100s could be pulled out of Saudi Arabia early in the new year. The State Department continued to fight a rearguard action against "deserting our Saudi friends." But Maxwell Taylor, who had recently become chairman of the JCS, won the debate by arguing that "with Hard Surface in place, the United States will be forced to respond militarily or risk loss of credibility of its military power, not only in the Middle East, but world-wide."[32] Shortly after Christmas Lyndon Johnson agreed to follow his predecessor's lead and terminate Operation Hard Surface on 31 January 1964 while simultaneously moving the Sixth Fleet into the Eastern Mediterranean. He broke the bad news to Crown Prince Faisal a few days in advance, softening the blow by promising to sell him early warning radar and other antiaircraft defense systems.[33]

One unspoken reason why the Johnson administration decided to terminate Hard Surface and limit America's role in Southwest Arabia to selling war matériel was that preparations were already under way during the spring of 1964 to escalate dramatically U.S. military involvement in Southeast Asia. When North Vietnamese torpedo boats attacked two U.S. destroyers patrolling the Gulf of Tonkin in early August, Lyndon Johnson approved retaliatory raids against enemy shore facilities and secured overwhelming support on Capitol Hill for a resolution granting a congressional "blank check" to wage presidential war in Indochina. By late 1965 a U.S. Air Force bombing campaign code-named Rolling Thunder was pounding North Vietnam while nearly 200,000 American GIs were fighting Viet Cong guerrillas in the south.[34]

The rapid escalation of the war in Southeast Asia during 1965 seemed to confirm the wisdom of limiting U.S. military involvement in the Middle East to modest arms sales. Ever since the Truman administration had signed the Tripartite Declaration in 1950, U.S. policymakers had striven to preserve a rough balance between Arab and Israeli arsenals by regulating the flow of American, British, and French weapons to the region. After Egypt, Syria, and Iraq began to receive large amounts of Russian military hardware during the late 1950s, Washington moved to ensure Israeli security by providing the Jewish state with jeeps and recoilless rifles in 1958 and Hawk antiaircraft missiles in 1962.[35] As the decade wore on, however, the Arab-Israeli arms race threatened to spiral out of control. Seeking to preserve the fragile balance between Israel and Jordan, Washington agreed in February 1965 to sell each side more than 200 M-48 tanks. Infuriated by fresh evidence of U.S. support for his Jewish enemies and his Arab rivals, Nasser pressed the Kremlin, which had already provided him with nearly a billion dollars in weapons over the preceding decade, to expedite delivery of still more military hardware, including guided-missile boats and medium-range bombers. Nasser's moves in turn created new anxieties for the Israelis, who accelerated their own missile program and renewed their request for U.S. jet fighters to counteract the mounting Egyptian threat.

By the spring of 1967 this escalating arms spiral would confront U.S. policymakers with the prospect of being dragged into a full-blown war in the Middle East at a time when the military situation in Southeast Asia was rapidly going from bad to terrible. Should the Johnson administration suddenly find itself bogged down in two wars, there would be hell to pay on Capitol Hill. "The problem of 'Tonkin Gulfitis,'" Secretary of State Dean Rusk and Robert McNamara reminded LBJ in late May, "remains acute."[36] Nasser's expulsion of United Nations peacekeepers from their outposts in the Sinai, his closure of the Straits of Tiran to Israeli vessels, and his defensive pact with Jordan's King Hussein made that second war look more and more likely. On Monday, 5 June 1967, Israeli fighter-bombers struck military targets throughout Egypt while Israeli M-48 tanks roared across the River Jordan, knocking out King Hussein's M-48s, seizing most of the West Bank, and occupying Arab East Jerusalem in just twenty-four hours. American professions of strict neutrality struck most Arabs as hypocritical. "You are not neutral at all," Egyptian foreign minister Mahmoud Riad snapped at U.S. officials in Cairo. "If Egypt had been the aggressor, the Sixth Fleet would now be on the shore of Egypt."[37]

Even as Riad spoke, the USS *Liberty*, an unescorted navy intelligence vessel, was lumbering into position just thirteen miles off the Sinai coast on a reconnaissance mission that would very nearly draw the Sixth Fleet into the Six Day War. After monitoring the *Liberty* for several hours, Israeli jets and patrol boats attacked the floating surveillance platform on the afternoon of 8 June with rockets, napalm, and torpedoes, killing 34 U.S. sailors and wounding 171 others. Before Israeli pilots shot away the *Liberty's* five-by-eight-foot American flag and distinctive satellite communications dish, its captain radioed for help from the Sixth Fleet, which was cruising 400 miles to the northwest off Crete.[38]

Fearing that the Russians or their Arab clients were behind the attack, the fleet's commander authorized the carrier *America* to launch four nuclear-equipped F-4 fighters to assist the *Liberty*. When this news reached Washington, top Pentagon officials went ballistic. "Tell Sixth Fleet to get those aircraft back immediately," Secretary of Defense McNamara barked. Admiral David McDonald, chief of naval operations, relayed McNamara's orders to the *America's* skipper, one sailor to another: "You get those fucking airplanes back on deck, and you get them back *now!*" By the time the F-4s made their U-turns and flew back to the *America* to be refitted with conventional bomb racks, the Israelis had broken off their attack, which they explained as a tragic case of mistaken identity, and allowed the badly damaged *Liberty* to limp to Malta for repairs.[39]

Few observers in Washington were willing to accept this Israeli explanation at face value. "[Three] strafing passes [and] 3 torpedo boats" made it "inconceivable it was [an] accident," Clark Clifford, the longtime friend of the Jewish state who chaired Lyndon Johnson's intelligence advisory board, growled on 9 June. "Handle as if Arabs or USSR had done it."[40] Although the Israelis apologized profusely and eventually agreed to pay a $3.3 million indemnity, some U.S. officials continued to suspect that a high-ranking Israeli policymaker—perhaps even Minister of Defense Moshe Dayan himself—had authorized the attack.[41] "I was never satisfied with the Israeli explanation. Their sustained attack to disable and sink *Liberty* precluded an assault by accident or by some trigger-happy local commander," Dean Rusk observed in his memoirs. "I didn't believe them then, and I don't believe them to this day. The attack was outrageous."[42]

Because even thirty years after the fact most of the documents relating to the *Liberty* episode remain classified, explaining either America's rationale for placing the vessel in harm's way or Israel's motives for inflicting harm requires a fair amount of informed speculation. When asked long afterward what the *Liberty* was doing in the Eastern Mediterranean in the midst of the Six Day War, Walt Rostow, LBJ's national security adviser, replied frankly, "We were eavesdropping on everybody—the Israelis, the Egyptians. The Soviet navy was there too."[43] In any event, U.S. intelligence clearly was monitoring Israeli military frequencies, perhaps for indications that warhawks such as Moshe Dayan might force Prime Minister Levi Eshkol to widen the conflict. Israeli officials did subsequently confirm that shortly after the *Liberty* arrived in the war zone on 8 June, they temporarily postponed their plans to seize the Golan Heights from Syria, which had unaccountably remained on the sidelines during the first days of the war. Whether Israel's leaders feared that the *Liberty* might provide Washington with enough advance warning to prevent their invasion of Syria or whether, as the CIA suspected, the vessel's high-tech surveillance equipment "was having the effect of jamming Israeli military communications," it seems more than mere coincidence that Dayan sent his troops into the Golan Heights just fifteen hours after the U.S. Navy's electronic eyes and ears had been snuffed out.[44]

By the evening of 9 June Israeli troops were within striking distance of Damascus, raising the disturbing possibility that the Kremlin might come to the aid of its Syrian client and trigger a chain-reaction superpower showdown. "The Soviets [had] hinted," Dean Rusk recalled many years later, "that if the Israelis attacked Syria, they would intervene with their own forces."[45] To prevent such an eventuality, the Johnson administration pressed for an immediate cease-fire and warned the Russians to stay out. When the Kremlin hinted on 10 June that Russian military action might be imminent, LBJ decided to "turn the Sixth Fleet around to sail toward the eastern Mediterranean," a move that "Soviet submarines monitoring the Fleet's operations would report immediately" to Moscow. Ultimately, NSC Middle East expert Harold Saunders noted afterward, the Soviets backed down, the Israelis accepted the cease-fire, and "everyone relaxed a bit as it became clear that the fighting was petering out."[46]

The uneasy state of "no war/no peace" that descended on the Middle East in late June 1967 escalated so rapidly six years later that it nearly triggered U.S. military intervention. Anwar Sadat, who had become president of Egypt after Nasser died in September 1970, was determined to reverse the outcome of the Six Day War by diplomacy if possible but by armed force if necessary. Frustrated that neither the United States nor Israel seemed interested in peace talks, Sadat secretly contacted Syrian president Hafez al-Assad in early 1973 to prepare for war.[47] On 6 October 1973, while most Israelis were celebrating Yom Kippur, the Egyptian army shot its way across the Suez Canal and drove into the Sinai Desert while Syrian troops stormed the Golan Heights. During the first days of the October War, the Israelis fell back along both fronts, taking heavy casualties and losing dozens of planes and hundreds of tanks. In the wee hours of 9 October, Prime Minister Golda Meir pleaded with the Nixon administration to begin replenishing her arsenal at once. After trying unsuccessfully to patch together an airlift relying exclusively on commercial aviation, the president decided to have the Pentagon handle the resupply mission on 13 October. "I want every last goddamn airplane. We are going to be condemned by the Arabs one way or the other. It's going to be a mess, but we are supporting Israel on this," Nixon snapped at national security adviser Henry Kissinger. "Get your ass out of here and tell those people to move." Within twenty-four hours the first U.S. Air Force C-5A transport laden with tanks and other military hardware had put down just outside Tel Aviv.[48]

The U.S. airlift turned the tide decisively in Israel's favor, prompting the Arab members of OPEC to impose an oil embargo on the United States and tempting the Kremlin to intervene during the final days of the October War. Buoyed by the Nixon administration's concrete show of support, the Israelis retook the initiative on both fronts. Hoping to recoup Moscow's dwindling influence in Cairo and other Arab capitals while Washington was preoccupied with the fallout from the Watergate scandal, Soviet premier Leonid Brezhnev warned the White House on 24 October that unless Israel agreed to an immediate cease-fire, he was prepared to airlift troops into Egypt to assist Sadat's beleaguered armed forces. "All you had to do was read the ultimatum to know we had World War III in the making," General Alexander Haig, Nixon's chief of staff, recalled years later. Determined to keep the Kremlin out of the Middle East, the White House responded by placing U.S. strategic forces at DEFCON 3, the highest state of nuclear alert before all-out war, "to convey to the Russians that we meant business." Meanwhile, Henry Kissinger was persuading the Israelis to halt their offensive by promising them $2.2 billion in military aid. The guns finally fell silent on 26 October without either superpower having fired a shot in anger.[49]

Although rattling the Pentagon's nuclear sabers evidently helped prevent Soviet armed intervention, flexing America's conventional military muscle seemed unlikely to persuade Arab oil producers to rescind the embargo on Persian Gulf crude imposed following the U.S. airlift to Israel. To be sure, the JCS did begin to develop contingency plans for taking over the region's petroleum reserves, and hawkish intellectuals such as Robert Tucker did float bizarre scenarios calling for U.S. troops to seize a 400-mile oil-rich strip stretching from Kuwait to Qatar.[50] In a well-publicized interview granted several months after OPEC's Arab members had agreed to resume exports to the United States, Henry Kissinger hinted that Washington was prepared to intervene militarily if necessary to preserve access to Persian Gulf oil. "We should have learned from Vietnam that it is easier to get into a war than to get out of it," he told a *Business Week* reporter in January 1975. Then resorting to one of the triple negatives for which he became famous, Kissinger delivered the punch line: "I am not saying that there's no circumstance where we would not use force," especially if "there's some actual strangulation of the industrial world."[51]

Despite Kissinger's bluster, however, Pentagon officials were well aware of the limits of U.S. military power in the Middle East during the post-Vietnam era. After reading a 1974 U.S. Navy study titled "Direct Economic/Military Actions in Response to Arab Oil Leverage," for example, Admiral James L. Holloway, chief of naval operations, scrawled, "It becomes evident that there is little we can effectively accomplish in M.E." Jimmy Carter moved to address this vulnerability four years later by signing Presidential Directive 18, which called for the creation of a "deployment force of light divisions with strategic mobility" for use in trouble spots such as Korea or the Persian Gulf. During the next fifteen months the Pentagon developed an ambitious blueprint for a powerful Rapid Deployment Force equipped with helicopter gunships and amphibious assault craft, manned by marine commandos and supported by a new U.S. Fifth Fleet to be based in the Indian Ocean.[52]

Although all this looked good on paper, the tumultuous events of 1979 revealed that in practice the Carter administration was powerless to thwart an anti-American revolution in Iran or to prevent Soviet troops from occupying Afghanistan. Notwithstanding the belligerent rhetoric of the Carter Doctrine in January 1980, it was the failure of Operation Eagle Claw three months later that symbolized America's military limitations in the Middle East. In the early hours of 24 April 1980, eight U.S. Navy *Sea Stallion* helicopters rendezvoused with three U.S. Air Force C-130 transports just outside Tehran for the last leg of a mission to rescue fifty-two Americans held hostage by Iranian revolutionaries. When sand clogged the engines of three helicopters, Carter had to abort the operation at the last minute. In the ensuing confusion two aircraft collided and eight U.S. sailors were killed.[53] With the public still reeling from a debacle in Vietnam that had seen 57,000 GIs die in an unsuccessful attempt to prevent a communist takeover in Saigon, Carter's failure in Iran constituted for most Americans a microcosm of their country's diminished capacity for armed intervention overseas.

During the twenty-odd years since Dwight Eisenhower had first waged limited war in Lebanon, White House advocates of flexible response and Pentagon devotees of incremental escalation had pressed for deeper U.S. involvement not only in Southeast Asia but also in the Middle East. Fiascos like the assault on the uss *Liberty* or the crash-landing of Eagle Claw confirmed that armed intervention often carried a high price. Even successful displays of deterrence such as Operation Hard Surface in 1963 or the DEFCON 3 nuclear alert a decade later led many critics to claim that the risks of escalation far exceeded the benefits. By the time Jimmy Carter returned to Georgia in January 1981, the United States was in the grips of a Vietnam Syndrome whose chief symptom seemed to be an instinctive aversion to military intervention anywhere. For the Midwestern lifeguard-turned-B-movie-actor who succeeded

Carter, the simplest cure seemed at times to be military intervention almost everywhere, including the Persian Gulf.

Risky Business: Reagan and Armed Neutrality

Ronald Reagan was elected president in November 1980 largely because he offered simple solutions to the complicated problems that bedeviled the United States both at home and abroad. The cure for stagflation—high unemployment and even higher inflation triggered by recent OPEC price hikes—was lower taxes, the California Republican assured voters with a chuckle and a smile that could melt glaciers. The cure for the Vietnam Syndrome, Reagan insisted with wistful tenacity, first on the campaign trail and then in the White House, was a stronger will to win and higher military spending.[54]

The key players on the new foreign policy team agreed that by resuscitating the country's martial spirit and restocking its arsenal with high-tech weapons systems, the Reagan administration could once again make America Number One. Secretary of State Alexander Haig, a West Point graduate who bore the scars of Vietnam and Watergate, vowed never to lose again and reveled in tough talk about firing warning shots across other people's bows. Caspar Weinberger, who had headed one of the nation's biggest defense contractors before taking over at the Pentagon in early 1981, could be a staunch proponent of armed intervention, provided the United States possessed well-defined objectives and the right military hardware.[55] Robert McFarlane, the ambitious Naval Academy alumnus who worked his way up from counselor in Haig's State Department to White House national security adviser, had shown a preference for shooting first and asking questions later ever since he had masterminded the 1975 *Mayaguez* rescue mission, the sole bright spot during the Ford administration's darkest hour in Southeast Asia.[56]

While Reagan and his top advisers worked to provide the will and the hardware necessary to rebuild America's military prowess, Colonel Harry Summers, a veteran of both the Korean and Vietnam wars, was busy developing the strategy. Convinced that limited war, incremental escalation, and other concepts popularized by Kennedy's and Johnson's action intellectuals had been a prescription for military disaster in Southeast Asia, Summers focused on the "Three S's": security, surprise, and simplicity. In *On Strategy*, a 1982 bestseller, he emphasized the importance of setting objectives that were clearly linked to U.S. national interests, of employing unpredictable tactics more akin to a roller-coaster than an escalator, and of streamlining the Pentagon's cumbersome top-down bureaucracy in order to establish a more straightforward and unified chain of command where decisions could also flow from the bottom up.[57] An early example of the effectiveness of Summers's approach to military intervention came in Grenada, where Reagan sent 5,000 marines ashore in October 1983 to reverse a left-wing coup and to protect nearly 1,000 U.S. tourists and students basking on the beaches of the nutmeg capital of the eastern Caribbean at a cost of just 19 American dead and 115 wounded.[58]

Just two days before the first GIs had arrived in Grenada, however, a horrible explosion halfway around the world in Lebanon had demonstrated that, in the Middle East, military intervention seldom went as planned. American soldiers had been in harm's way in that part of the world since the summer of 1982, when Reagan proposed sending a contingent of U.S. troops to Beirut as part of a Multinational Force to help restore a modicum of order in the wake of Israel's invasion of Lebanon. Secretary of Defense Weinberger and JCS chairman John Vessey saw a Vietnam-in-the-making and "argued that we should not be one of the participants."[59] But Reagan disregarded the Pentagon's misgivings at the behest of George Shultz, the Princeton-educated ex-marine who had succeeded the power-hungry Alexander Haig as secretary of state six weeks earlier. By escorting Yasser Arafat and the PLO out of Beirut and by safeguarding the Palestinian noncombatants left behind in the refugee camps just outside the Lebanese capital, Shultz argued, U.S. troops would pave the way for a speedy Israeli withdrawal and place both sides on the path to a lasting peace. On 25 August Reagan sent 800 U.S. Marines ashore in Lebanon, where they linked up with French and Italian contingents of the Multinational Force.[60]

It did not take long for all hell to break loose. Never happy about U.S. participation in the Multinational Force, Weinberger insisted that the marines had accomplished their mission with the departure of the PLO and convinced Reagan to redeploy them offshore aboard the vessels of the Sixth Fleet on 10 September. Within days a fresh round of sectarian violence erupted in Beirut, culminating in the massacre of nearly 1,000 Palestinians at the Sabra and Shatila refugee camps by Lebanese Christian extremists linked to Israel. Horrified by the mass killings, Reagan reversed himself and announced on 20 September that he was sending the marines back to Lebanon to rejoin the Multinational Force.[61]

During the following thirteen months the size of the U.S. force at Beirut grew to 1,200, and its activities escalated from passive peacekeeping to sporadic involvement in the Lebanese civil war. Throughout the autumn of 1982 top Pentagon officials grew ever more doubtful that the token U.S. military presence in Lebanon could prevent further bloodshed. "I don't think anybody had any expectation we could turn it around," General Vessey recalled years later. "The guilt feeling affected us all. Still, we could see it's the wrong place to be."[62] Once U.S. Marines began to exchange fire with Muslim militiamen in the spring of 1983, Weinberger resumed his crusade to terminate the operation. "My own feeling was that we should not commit American troops to any situation unless the objectives were so important to American interests that we had to fight," he observed in his memoirs. If that point were ever reached, "then we had to commit, as a last resort, not just token forces to provide an American presence, but enough forces to win and win overwhelmingly."[63] But with Shultz insisting that an abrupt pullout would undermine U.S. credibility in the Middle East and with opinion polls showing that the American public had no stomach for further escalation, Reagan attempted to muddle through. By the end of the summer, however, sporadic mortar and sniper attacks had claimed the lives of six U.S. Marines, prompting the president to order the USS *New Jersey* to begin lobbing two-ton shells into anti-American strongholds in the snow-capped Shouf Mountains overlooking Beirut.[64]

Any hope that gunboat diplomacy might lessen the danger to U.S. forces stationed in Lebanon disappeared just after dawn on 23 October 1983, when a huge truck bomb reduced the U.S. Marine compound at the Beirut airport to a mountain of twisted rubble, killing 241 GIs and injuring more than 100 others. In short order U.S. intelligence confirmed that the bombing was the work of Islamic Jihad, a band of anti-American fanatics bankrolled by Iran and based in Lebanon's Beka'a Valley, where they plotted their campaign of terror while Syria's occupying army looked the other way. Having vowed before a national television audience that "those who directed this atrocity must be dealt justice, and they will be," Ronald Reagan ordered U.S. Navy jets from the Sixth Fleet to launch air strikes in early December against selected targets in Baalbek, the Beka'a Valley town that housed Islamic Jihad's high command.[65]

As 1983 drew to a close, pressure was mounting both outside and inside the Reagan administration to halt the air strikes against Baalbek, pull the marines out of Beirut, and scale back U.S. intervention in Lebanon before it escalated into something far more serious. While no one in Washington could be certain that the continued display of U.S. naval air power in the skies over the Beka'a Valley would deter Islamic Jihad, everyone saw real danger for inadvertent involvement in a wider war, especially after Soviet-built Syrian surface-to-air missiles downed a pair of American planes on 4 December. Reagan tried to make the best possible case for the Lebanese operation in a report he delivered to Congress ten days later. "Premature withdrawal of the [Multinational Force] would damage seriously the international credibility of the United States and its partners," he explained, "and call into question the resolve of the West to carry out its responsibilities to help the free world defend itself."[66]

But with the release of a Pentagon postmortem on the Beirut bombing highly critical of the entire mission in Lebanon, advocates of an early withdrawal gained the upper hand. Increasingly frustrated by what he called "the nonsensical emphasis on quite inadequate military options as a tool of influence when, in fact, the Lebanese political landscape was cracking beneath our feet," early in the new year Secretary of Defense Weinberger began "pursuing aggressively the arguments that we must get our men out of the impossible situation that had contributed so much to the tragedy."[67] Weinberger's arguments were seconded by his senior military adviser, a savvy and ambitious forty-six-year-old colonel named Colin Powell. "America [was] sticking its hand into a thousand-year-old hornet's nest with the expectation that our mere presence might pacify the hornets," Powell recalled in his memoirs. The White House needed to learn, he added, that "to provide a 'symbol' or a 'presence' is not good enough" in a charnel house like Lebanon.[68] After a six-week search for a face-saving way out of the quagmire, on 7 February 1984 Reagan announced the "redeployment of the Marines from the Beirut Airport to their ships offshore" as soon as possible.[69] "We're not bugging out," he assured reporters two weeks later; "we're just going to a little more defensible position."[70] Reagan's national security adviser, however, offered a far grimmer appraisal of the debacle in Lebanon. "It was," Robert McFarlane remembered long afterward, "one of the worst defeats of the Reagan administration."[71]

Although the last U.S. Marine departed from Beirut on 26 February 1984, the intervention in Lebanon served as a cautionary tale whenever American policymakers contemplated renewed military involvement in the Middle East during Reagan's second term. Weinberger and Powell spent much of the next nine months developing "six major tests to be applied when we are weighing the use of U.S. combat forces abroad." Among the most important considerations, Weinberger told the National Press Club in November 1984, were "clearly defined political and military objectives," a willingness "to commit the forces and resources necessary to achieve our objectives," and "some reasonable assurance we will have the support of the American people" and their representatives on Capitol Hill.[72] "Clausewitz would have applauded," Powell remarked long afterward. "And in the future, when it became my responsibility to advise Presidents on committing our forces to combat, Weinberger's rules turned out to be a practical guide."[73]

Weinberger's first opportunity to apply his rules in the Middle East would come during the spring of 1986, when Libyan support for terrorist attacks on American tourists and soldiers in Europe prompted the Reagan administration to retaliate against Muammar al-Qaddafi. In late March Reagan moved the U.S. Sixth Fleet into the disputed Gulf of Sidra, international waters that Qaddafi had recently designated a "Zone of Death" in which all U.S. military and commercial vessels would be subject to attack. After U.S. Navy jets sank four of his guided-missile boats and knocked out most of his Soviet-built shore-based surface-to-air missile batteries, Qaddafi called "for confrontation—for war" and vowed "to expand the struggle . . . all over the world."[74] In short order, bombs exploded onboard a TWA jetliner loaded with Americans bound for Athens and outside a West Berlin discotheque frequented by U.S. GIs, leaving six dead and dozens injured. Once the CIA confirmed that both incidents were the work of Libyan intelligence, the White House gave the green light for Operation El Dorado Canyon. "The purpose of our plan was to teach Qaddafi and others the lesson that the practice of terrorism would not be free of cost to themselves," Weinberger observed in his memoirs, "that indeed they would pay a terrible price for practicing it."[75]

Just before dawn on 15 April 1986 eighteen F-111 fighter-bombers based in England and dozens of F-16 jets from the Sixth Fleet swept in from the Gulf of Sidra, demolished most of Qaddafi's Soviet-built air force, and leveled his official residence. Although Qaddafi escaped with his life, dozens of other Libyans died, including his fifteen-month-old adopted daughter. American losses were limited to one F-111 and its two-man crew.[76] Noting that "nothing was heard from Qaddafi for many months after the attack," Weinberger regarded the raid on Libya as "all the vindication that anyone should need of our correctness in rebuilding our military strength and in deciding when to use it." Operation El Dorado Canyon was a textbook example of successful intervention, Weinberger insisted several years later, largely because, in sharp contrast to Lebanon, top Pentagon officials had insisted that "we assemble sufficient forces, and act decisively and effectively, to achieve all of the President's objectives."[77]

Applying Weinberger's rules against Qaddafi in a computerized reenactment of the Barbary Wars, however, was far easier than applying them 2,000 miles away on the other side of the Middle East, where six years of bloody conflict between Iraq and Iran had by the summer of 1986 begun to threaten U.S. national interests in the Persian Gulf. The reasons for Iraqi dictator Saddam Hussein's sudden attack on Ayatollah Khomeini's Iran had not been complicated. A festering dispute between Baghdad and Tehran over the Shatt-al-Arab waterway at the head of the Persian Gulf, growing misgivings among Iraq's Sunni ruling elite about Shi'ite fundamentalism next door in Iran, and Saddam's own burgeoning pan-Arab ambitions made war seem an attractive option in September 1980.[78] The anticipated Iraqi blitzkrieg victory over an Iranian regime still in the throes of revolution, however, never materialized, and the two nations became locked in a ghastly war of attrition in which the more populous Iran seemed to have the upper hand. Convinced that a victory for Ayatollah Khomeini would spell disaster for the West, the Reagan administration secretly provided Saddam Hussein with satellite photos of Iranian troop deployments in 1982, offered Baghdad agricultural credits in 1983, and funneled black market arms to the beleaguered Iraqi army in 1984.[79]

To be sure, this tilt toward Baghdad did waver during the Iran-Contra Affair of 1985–86. Hoping to win the release of seven Americans kidnapped by pro-Iranian Hizbollah extremists in Beirut and raise several million dollars in cash for Nicaraguan counterrevolutionaries fighting the Sandinista regime in Managua, NSC staffer Oliver North secretly arranged to sell the Iranians 500 U.S. antitank missiles for use against the Iraqis. When Israeli middlemen failed to deliver all the missiles, however, Hizbollah refused to release the American captives and Oliver North's "neat idea" proved not so neat after all. By the autumn of 1986 House and Senate Democrats were outraged by the Reagan administration's violation of a legislative ban on U.S. aid for the Contras, Saddam Hussein had launched another offensive against Iran, and Ayatollah Khomeini had stepped up his "Tanker War" designed to disrupt the flow of oil through the Persian Gulf to Western consumers.[80]

Between 1984 and 1986 Iranian mines and torpedoes damaged sixty-seven oil tankers, including eight registered in Kuwait, and nudged gasoline prices and maritime insurance rates toward the pain threshold. On 13 January 1987 the government of Kuwait asked whether U.S. officials were willing to permit eleven Kuwaiti tankers to fly the Stars and Stripes. After learning that the Kuwaitis were also approaching the Kremlin with a similar request, the Reagan administration approved the reflagging proposal on 29 January and announced five weeks later that the U.S. Navy would escort the reflagged tankers through the Persian Gulf war zone.[81] Unless the United States granted Kuwait's request, Caspar Weinberger reminded critics second-guessing Reagan's decision, "we would be accepting Iran's right to close the international waters of the Gulf" and, even worse, opening the door to the Kremlin, which "would be more than happy to become the sole guarantor of the security of the small Gulf states."[82]

The possibility that the reflagging operation would draw Washington into a shooting war in the Persian Gulf, however, did not seem far-fetched after an errant Iraqi missile struck the USS *Stark* on 7 May 1987 and killed thirty-seven sailors. "Too many times, we have gotten into very serious situations abroad and exposed our military people to grave dangers," Sam Nunn, the Georgia Democrat who chaired the Senate Armed Services Committee, complained in early June, "without, in my opinion, having thought through, from a leadership point of view, the implication of those steps." Before the United States became more deeply involved in the Persian Gulf, Nunn wanted answers to "some fundamental questions," such as, "Does this initiative to protect Kuwaiti tankers increase the possibility that the United States will be drawn directly into the war between Iran and Iraq?"[83] In testimony before Nunn's committee on 5 June, Admiral William Crowe, who had recently succeeded John Vessey as JCS chairman, insisted that "we have the capability to keep the oil line to Kuwait open, to assure our Arab friends of our commitment, and to keep the risks low." Nevertheless, the admiral had to admit that "there are no absolute guarantees that such an operation will be casualty-free or that Iran will not escalate the sea war, which will present us with further difficult choices."[84]

During the next two weeks Reagan administration officials worked hard to persuade Nunn and other doubters on Capitol Hill that the reflagging operation was prudent. Insisting that "our intent is to deter, . . . not to provoke," Undersecretary of State Michael Armacost stressed that "this is not an open-ended kind of commitment to a lot of other countries."[85] America's adversaries in Tehran and Moscow, Assistant Secretary of Defense Richard Armitage told the Armed Services Committee on 16 June, would be the big winners if Reagan were forced to cancel Operation Earnest Will, as the reflagging operation was now known. Cancellation would mean "either emboldening the Iranians more to try to intimidate Kuwait or to have the Soviets step in an area of vital interest to us, which eight Presidents over 40 years have been successful in keeping them out," Armitage concluded in syntax almost as convoluted as U.S. policy in the Persian Gulf.[86] Although the Senate heeded Armacost's and Armitage's words and did not terminate Operation Earnest Will, a November 1987 Foreign Relations Committee report pointed out that U.S. objectives remained "dangerously nebulous" and warned that "the United States seriously risks being drawn into war."[87]

As the prophets on Capitol Hill had expected, the reflagging operation eventually drew the U.S. Navy into its largest surface engagement since the Second World War. During late 1987 and early 1988 the Pentagon doubled the U.S. naval presence in the Persian Gulf from six to thirteen warships and authorized nearly 100 escort missions under the auspices of Earnest Will. Tehran responded by sowing more mines along the tanker routes, shelling convoys from Iranian offshore oil platforms, and deploying Chinese-built Silkworm missiles along the Straits of Hormuz at the mouth of the Persian Gulf. After a U.S. frigate escorting a Kuwaiti tanker struck a mine in mid-April and nearly sank, the Pentagon launched Operation Praying Mantis. On the morning of 18 April 1988 U.S. warplanes and warships put half of the Iranian navy—two frigates and six high-speed torpedo boats—out of action, demolished two of Tehran's floating oil rigs, and pounded Iran's Silkworm batteries. The United States lost only one reconnaissance helicopter and its two-man crew.[88]

Bitten by Praying Mantis, the Iranians gradually wound down their tanker war. Meanwhile, the U.S. Navy stepped up its patrols in the Persian Gulf. At daybreak on 3 July American warships detected a large unidentified aircraft headed straight for them. Determined not to meet the same fate as the USS *Stark*, the commander of the guided-missile cruiser *Vincennes* fired two heat-seeking missiles and destroyed an Air Iran jetliner, killing all 290 passengers aboard. Claiming that, far from being accidental, the Air Iran tragedy showed just how far the United States would go to assist Iraq, Ayatollah Khomeini announced on 18 July 1988 that his government was willing to accept a United Nations–backed cease-fire in the Persian Gulf in order to spare the lives of other innocent civilians. Khomeini's humanitarian rhetoric notwithstanding, however, the final casualties in the Iran-Iraq war may well have been the planeload of 270 innocent civilians, mostly Americans, who died when Libyan terrorists heeded the ayatollah's calls for revenge and blew a Pan American 747 out of the sky over Lockerbie, Scotland, five months later.[89]

In short, not all of the Reagan administration's risky business in the Middle East paid off. As always, armed intervention had cost lives, some military and some civilian, some Muslim and some American. The marines would certainly never forget the Beirut airport, and the navy would always remember the *Stark*. But as the most popular president in a generation completed his second term, he firmly believed that Americans were finally putting the Vietnam debacle behind them. Twelve months before he left the Oval Office, Ronald Reagan received a report from his Commission on Integrated Long-Term Strategy confirming that the United States was gradually regaining its capacity for "discriminate deterrence" and for waging brushfire wars. Yet Zbigniew Brzezinski, Henry Kissinger, and the other strategic luminaries who sat on the panel delivered a mixed verdict. "Our failure in Vietnam still casts a shadow over U.S. intervention anywhere, and other setbacks—notably those we suffered in Lebanon—have left some predisposed to pessimism about our ability to promote U.S. interests in the Third world," the commissioners concluded. "If this cumulative effect cannot be checked or reversed in the future, it will gradually undermine America's ability to defend its interests in the most vital regions, such as the Persian Gulf, the Mediterranean, and the Western Pacific."[90] Checking that cumulative effect once and for all would be the principal order of business for Reagan's successor after August 1990.

Kicking the Vietnam Syndrome: George Bush and the Gulf War

Although Ronald Reagan was largely responsible for rebuilding America's military arsenal and rekindling the nation's martial spirit, George Bush made good use of that legacy to win a smashing victory in the Persian Gulf that promised to reverse the Vietnam Syndrome. During the eight years that he played second fiddle to Reagan, Bush had worked closely with George Shultz, Robert McFarlane, and CIA director William Casey to beef up America's military presence in the Middle East. He applauded the Pentagon's virtuoso display of air and sea power during Operations El Dorado Canyon and Praying Mantis, he backed Reagan's risky decision to reflag Kuwaiti tankers, and he pulled strings in Washington to help ensure that Saddam Hussein had access to U.S. dual-use technology that gave Iraq the military edge over Ayatollah Khomeini's Iran.[91]

When President George Bush and his secretary of state, James Baker, assumed control of U.S. foreign policy on 20 January 1989, they evidently believed that America's recent military clash with Iran and Saddam Hussein's need for Western help in rebuilding Iraq's war-torn economy would ensure better relations between Washington and Baghdad. Preoccupied with ending the Cold War, preserving strong ties with Soviet president Mikhail Gorbachev, and encouraging democracy in Eastern Europe, neither Bush nor Baker gave much thought to the Middle East during their first year in office. But what few decisions they did hand down regarding the Persian Gulf were based on the assumption that it was possible to reach an accommodation with Saddam Hussein. As early as January 1989 a State Department transition team had suggested that "the lessons of war [with Iran] may have changed Iraq from a radical state challenging the system to a more responsible, status-quo state working within the system, and promoting stability in the region."[92] These ideas were translated into policy nine months later when Bush signed National Security Directive 26 (NSD-26) on 2 October. Largely unnoticed at the time, NSD-26 instructed U.S. policymakers to devise "economic and political incentives for Iraq to moderate its behavior and to increase our influence with Iraq."[93]

Indeed, the Bush administration's most noteworthy initiative in the Third World during 1989 did not occur in the Persian Gulf but in Panama, where on 20 December the Pentagon unleashed Operation Just Cause. In the most massive display of U.S. military force since Vietnam, 22,500 GIs stormed ashore to secure the Panama Canal, protect American lives and property, and arrest Panamanian president Manuel Noriega, whom General Colin Powell, the new JCS chairman, described as "a dope-sniffing, voodoo-loving thug."[94] Although he mourned the 23 Americans and the 300 Panamanians who died, Powell confessed that Operation Just Cause "confirmed all my convictions over the preceding twenty years, since the days of doubt over Vietnam." The lessons of Panama seemed obvious. "Have a clear political objective and stick to it. Use all the force necessary, and do not apologize for going in big if that is what it takes," Powell observed in his memoirs. "Decisive force ends wars quickly and in the long run saves lives. Whatever threats we faced in the future, I intended to make these rules the bedrock of my military counsel."[95]

Iraq's invasion of Kuwait on 2 August 1990 showed Powell and the president he served exactly what kind of threat the United States would face in the future. The rapid buildup of Operation Desert Shield during the following three months confirmed that both Powell and Bush agreed on one bedrock rule of engagement: If the United States were to intervene in the Persian Gulf, it must go in even bigger and more decisively than it had in Panama. In the clear light of hindsight Saddam Hussein's assault on Kuwait was as predictable as his attack on Iran a decade earlier. Having wasted nearly a half-trillion dollars and a quarter-million Iraqi lives to achieve a military stalemate with Iran, Saddam made no secret during the spring of 1990 that he expected the Kuwaitis and the other oil-rich Gulf Arabs to help rebuild his arsenal and his economy by forgiving almost $100 billion in war debts and by raising the price of Persian Gulf crude to $25 per barrel. With the approach of summer, he turned up the heat by placing a pair of simmering territorial disputes with Kuwait, a state many Iraqis regarded as a lost province, on the front burner. Unless the sheikdom granted Iraq full control over both the Rumaila oil field that straddled the border between the two nations and the offshore islands of Warba and Bubiyan that impeded Baghdad's access to the Persian Gulf, Saddam warned Jabir al-Ahmed al-Sabah, the emir of Kuwait on 18 July 1990, there would be serious trouble.[96]

By late July top U.S. policymakers were finally expressing concern about Saddam Hussein's increasingly belligerent antics. Ever hopeful that Iraq could be fully integrated into the family of nations through economic incentives such as those outlined in NSD-26 ten months earlier, State Department officials worked well into the summer to block congressional legislation canceling $400 million in U.S. agricultural credits because of Saddam's human rights abuses. But the Bush administration did seek to signal its abiding commitment to Iraq's jittery neighbors on 21 July by authorizing U.S. participation in joint maneuvers in the Persian Gulf with the armed forces of the UAE. Irritated by this modest display of American military muscle, Saddam Hussein summoned Ambassador April Glaspie to the Iraqi Ministry of Foreign Affairs four days later for what would prove to be one of the most controversial diplomatic exchanges in recent history.[97]

According to the Iraqi transcript of the 25 July 1990 meeting, Saddam told Ambassador Glaspie that the United States should steer clear of inter-Arab disputes. "So what can it mean when America says it will now protect its friends?" he thundered. "This stance plus maneuvers and statements which have been made has encouraged the U.A.E. and Kuwait to disregard Iraqi rights." Glaspie, an Arabic-speaking career foreign service officer who had first been posted to the Persian Gulf during the late 1960s, evidently took a conciliatory line, assuring the Iraqi dictator that "we have no opinion on the Arab-Arab conflicts, like your border dispute with Kuwait."[98] After she returned to Washington, however, the embattled ambassador dismissed the Iraqi account as "a fabrication, disinformation" and claimed that she had told Saddam "that we would insist on settlements being made in a nonviolent manner, not by threats, not by intimidation, and certainly not by aggression." The partially declassified text of Glaspie's own account of the 25 July meeting confirms that she did inform Iraq's president that "we can never excuse settlement of disputes by other than peaceful means" and that he did assure her that "nothing will happen" before early August. But when Congressman Lee Hamilton, an Indiana Democrat who chaired the House Subcommittee on the Middle East, asked months later whether she had ever told Saddam Hussein that "if you go across the line into Kuwait, we are going to fight," Glaspie replied with a twinge of regret, "No, I did not."[99]

In the days immediately after Glaspie's momentous meeting with Saddam Hussein, U.S. intelligence detected unmistakable signs that the Iraqi dictator was about to plunge across that line. On 30 July Patrick Lang, a Defense Intelligence Agency analyst monitoring the Persian Gulf, warned his boss that Iraq had massed more than 100,000 troops plus hundreds of howitzers, tanks, and helicopters along its southern border, giving Baghdad "the capability to overrun all of Kuwait and all of Eastern Saudi Arabia" with dramatic suddenness. "In short, Saddam Hussein has moved a force disproportionate to the task at hand, if it is to bluff," Lang concluded. "Then there is only one answer: he intends to use it."[100] This ominous news prompted Colin Powell to summon General Norman Schwartzkopf, whose Central Command (CENTCOM) was responsible for America's rapid deployment capability in the Middle East, to the Pentagon on 1 August.[101] A few hours after Schwartzkopf finished briefing the JCS on Operations Plan 90-1002, which required thirty days' advance warning to begin deploying U.S. troops to the Persian Gulf, Saddam Hussein's army invaded Kuwait.[102]

It was a somber lot of bureaucrats, diplomats, and soldiers who attended the NSC meeting that George Bush convened in the Cabinet Room at 8:00 A.M. on 2 August 1990. The Iraqis were in complete control of Kuwait and were moving troops toward the Saudi border. "If Saddam stays where he is, he'll own twenty percent of the world's oil reserves. And a few miles away he can seize another twenty percent," CIA director William Webster grimaced. "We've got to make a response," NSC adviser Brent Scowcroft snapped, "and accommodating Saddam is not an option." Secretary of Defense Richard Cheney agreed. "You can't separate Kuwait from Saudi Arabia," he explained. "When the Iraqis hit the Saudi border, they're only forty kilometers from the Saudi oil fields. We have the potential here for a major conflict." Pinch-hitting for Secretary of State Baker, who was en route to Washington after cutting short a visit to several Asian capitals, Foggy Bottom's Lawrence Eagleburger suggested that the Bush administration work through the United Nations and seek Security Council authorization for economic sanctions and, ultimately, for military intervention. President Bush agreed that "we've got to get the international community behind us" and noted that he had already contacted Egypt's Hosni Mubarak, Jordan's King Hussein, and Saudi Arabia's King Fahd, all of whom "still tell me they can find an Arab solution."[103]

Skeptical about prospects for a diplomatic solution, Bush turned to Colin Powell for an assessment of the military options. Convinced that the time had come for "laying down a line in the sand concerning Saudi Arabia," the JCS chairman reviewed CENTCOM's ponderous contingency plan 90-1002. Although Powell was certain that the Iraqis "did not relish a war with the United States," he was equally certain that even the appearance of U.S. inaction would serve "to embolden Saddam further." Therefore "it's important," Powell concluded, "to plant the American flag in the Saudi desert as soon as possible, assuming we can get their okay." His listeners nodded in agreement. "We're committed to Saudi Arabia," Bush replied, and the Pentagon "could start alerting units to be prepared to defend the country."[104]

Then Powell posed what he later termed "a Clausewitzian question," which produced "a chill in the room" and some frowns from his colleagues. "Was it worth going to war," the JCS chairman asked, "to liberate Kuwait?" The question, Powell admitted in his memoirs, was probably premature and should in any case have come from one of Bush's diplomatic advisers, not from America's highest-ranking military officer. But the debacle in Indochina two decades earlier still cast a long shadow. "I had been appalled at the docility of the Joint Chiefs of Staff," Powell explained long afterward, "fighting in Vietnam without ever pressing the political leaders to lay out clear objectives for them." When the NSC meeting broke up shortly before noon, President Bush had not replied to "Colin von Clausewitz."[105]

When the president reconvened the NSC thirty hours later, however, his answer was becoming clearer. Insisting that Saddam's smash-and-grab tactics in Kuwait threatened the stability of the emerging post–Cold War order, Brent Scowcroft, who was fast emerging as Bush's alter ego, argued that "the stakes in this for the United States are such that to accommodate Iraq should not be a policy option." Keeping Saddam out of Saudi Arabia, Colin Powell retorted, would be far easier than expelling him from Kuwait. "Looking at this option, . . . this is harder than Panama and Libya," the JCS chairman explained. "This would be the NFL, not a scrimmage," and the Iraqi strongman was "a professional and a megalomaniac," not a tinpot dictator like Noriega or Qaddafi. Yet precisely because George Bush agreed that Saddam Hussein was indeed Hitler on the Euphrates, he was not willing to accept "another Munich" in the Persian Gulf.[106] This became clear two days later when he stepped off a helicopter onto the White House lawn after a working weekend at Camp David. "This will not stand," Bush told reporters, jabbing his finger in the air for emphasis, "this aggression against Kuwait."[107] Colin Powell, who had been watching Bush's remarks live on CNN at home in his study on the other side of the Potomac, bolted upright. "Had the President," Powell asked himself, "just committed the United States to liberating Kuwait?"[108] Within three months it would be very clear that the answer to that question was a resounding yes.

The first phase of America's military intervention in the Persian Gulf, Operation Desert Shield, called for the Pentagon to deploy approximately 200,000 U.S. troops in Saudi Arabia within ninety days to deter an Iraqi invasion. At the outset the biggest obstacle to Desert Shield was King Fahd, who had repeatedly refused to permit the Pentagon to stockpile weapons or to deploy logistical personnel inside his kingdom. Because Kuwait, the UAE, and the other Arab sheikdoms were quick to follow the Saudi lead, the Defense Department had been forced in early 1983 to establish the headquarters for the newly created CENTCOM not in the Persian Gulf but, rather, halfway around the world in Tampa, Florida.[109] Nevertheless, once Secretary of Defense Cheney and CENTCOM's Norman Schwartzkopf arrived in Jiddah, King Fahd's royal capital, on 6 August with satellite photos showing that the vanguard of Saddam Hussein's million-man army, the fourth largest in the world, was poised in Kuwait to strike Saudi Arabia, the House of Saud had a sudden change of heart. "We have to do this," King Fahd said after hearing Cheney and Schwartzkopf describe plans for Operation Desert Shield. "The most important thing is to proceed to protect our country, together with the Americans."[110]

Once King Fahd gave the green light on 8 August, President Bush sent the U.S. Army's 82nd Airborne and two U.S. Air Force tactical fighter wings to Dhahran and ordered three U.S. Navy carrier battle groups into the Persian Gulf. During the next ten weeks the Pentagon would airlift and sealift almost 250,000 American GIs and nearly 2 million tons of military hardware and war supplies to Saudi Arabia.[111] Meanwhile, Secretary of State James Baker worked overtime to patch together the broadest possible anti-Iraq coalition. By late October U.S. forces in the Persian Gulf had been joined by troops, tanks, or planes from Britain, France, Italy, Saudi Arabia, Egypt, and nearly two dozen other countries. This stunning display of international solidarity plus the tough economic sanctions maintained under the auspices of United Nations Security Council Resolution 661 seemed certain by mid-autumn to prevent Saddam Hussein from attempting to make the House of Saud his next victim.[112]

But as top U.S. policymakers had suspected ever since George Bush had vowed on the White House lawn that Saddam's aggression would not stand, once Desert Shield was firmly in place in Saudi Arabia, the man in the Oval Office would be tempted to unleash a desert storm strong enough to blow the Iraqi army out of Kuwait. The president had begun to push hard for an offensive option as early as 24 September, wondering whether General Powell believed America's overwhelming advantage in the air could ensure a quick and clean victory without a long and messy ground war. Powell, however, recommended that "we continue preparing a full-scale air, land, and sea campaign," hoping in the meantime to defeat Iraq by "strangling her into withdrawal through sanctions" before the U.S. offensive was ready early in the new year. "It's good to consider all angles," Bush told Powell as the meeting drew to a close. "But I really don't think we have time for sanctions to work."[113]

With time running out, General Powell boarded a plane on 22 October for Saudi Arabia, where he and Schwartzkopf put the finishing touches on a bold plan to drive Saddam Hussein out of Kuwait. Their blueprint for what would eventually become Operation Desert Storm was breathtakingly simple. First, the U.S. Air Force would destroy Iraq's military and economic infrastructure with laser-guided missiles and smart bombs. Then the U.S. Navy would position itself as though it were about to launch an amphibious assault on Iraqi forces dug in at Kuwait City. When Baghdad rushed reinforcements to the coast, the U.S. Army and Marines would execute a swift "left hook" flanking maneuver far to the west in the desert no-man's-land between Iraq and Saudi Arabia, trapping and smashing Saddam Hussein's army in Kuwait. This air-land plan of battle, however, would mean doubling the size of the U.S. expeditionary force in the Persian Gulf to nearly 500,000. Having experienced as young officers the pain and frustration of an ever escalating military stalemate in Indochina, neither Powell nor Schwartzkopf was interested in half-measures. "We had learned a lesson in Panama. Go in big and end it quickly," Powell recalled in his memoirs. "We could not put the United States through another Vietnam."[114]

The JCS chairman flew back to Washington at the end of the month to brief President Bush and Secretary of State Baker on plans for Operation Desert Storm. Baker, a Texas-born and Princeton-educated ex-marine whose street-smart advice usually found favor in the Oval Office, believed that his boss would reap big political dividends from embracing Schwartzkopf and Powell's big bang theory. "New world order—Have to be principled & stand up to aggression," Baker remembered telling Bush in late October. "Don't make [the] same mistake we did in 30s; *nor* same as in Vietnam—uncertain, tentative, etc.—if we go in we have to have *massive* force."[115] The ex–navy pilot in the White House needed little persuading. After listening to Powell lay out the tactical details and the awesome new manpower requirements, Bush took a deep breath on 30 October and said simply, "Okay, do it." A week later the White House announced that America's military presence in the Persian Gulf would be expanded to a half-million men and women before the end of the year. "We would go to war in three months," Powell thought to himself, "if sanctions did not work and the Iraqis were still in Kuwait."[116]

Conflicting lessons of the past were foremost in the minds of the Bush administration and its critics as the countdown proceeded inexorably toward war with Iraq during the final weeks of 1990. Secretary of Defense Cheney, for example, evoked memories of Hitler, Munich, and appeasement during testimony before the Senate Armed Services Committee. "Saddam Hussein has operated as sort of your traditional dictator," Cheney told the lawmakers on 3 December. With his blitzkrieg against Kuwait, the Iraqi strongman had "put himself in the position to dominate the Persian Gulf, to dominate the Middle East, and obviously also [to] put a choke-hold on the world's economy." Like Hitler after his conquest of the Sudetenland, Saddam Hussein "would be in a position to blackmail any nation which chose not to do his bidding," Cheney concluded.[117]

Seconding the secretary of defense, Colin Powell insisted that the lessons of Vietnam showed that "removing the Iraqi army from Kuwait" could not be done on the cheap. "Many experts, amateurs and others in this town believe that this can be accomplished by such things as surgical air strikes or . . . other, nice, tidy, alleged low-cost, incremental, may work options," he observed acidly. "Such strategies are designed to hope to win; they are not designed to win." To avert a replay of the disaster in Southeast Asia, the Bush administration intended to prepare a "combined, overwhelming, air/land/sea campaign" designed to seize the initiative and bring swift victory. "I know the deserts of Kuwait and Iraq are quite different from the triple canopy jungles of Vietnam or the forests of Germany," Powell admitted, but unless the massive military buildup already under way in the Persian Gulf were completed, the United States would run the risk of repeating its earlier mistakes: overestimating the effectiveness of air power and underestimating the enemy's will to win.[118]

Many senators, however, had learned different lessons. Sam Nunn insisted on holding hearings because Republican trigger-happiness in recent clashes with Libya and Panama had led him to believe that an impatient Bush administration might not allow sufficient time for economic sanctions to do their job against Iraq. Astronaut-turned-solon John Glenn likewise questioned what he called Bush's "Chicken Little approach" toward Iraq. "The sky is falling in and there is only one option, and that is war," the Ohioan complained. Edward Kennedy was outraged to hear the secretary of defense say that President Bush could use the 500,000 U.S. troops stationed in Saudi Arabia against Saddam Hussein whether Congress liked it or not. "We are not talking about Libya, not about Grenada, not about Panama," the Massachusetts Democrat thundered. "We are talking about a major American military involvement." Was George Bush really prepared to claim that "he and he alone can bring this country to war?" Citing the president's constitutional powers as commander in chief, Cheney retorted that Bush indeed was "within his authority at this point to carry out his responsibilities" in the Persian Gulf.[119]

It remained for Albert Gore Jr., one of the few Vietnam veterans sitting in the Senate, to draw the parallel between the Gulf of Tonkin and the Persian Gulf. "This is not Vietnam. It is not Panama either. . . . But some of the lessons of past experience do apply," the Tennessee Democrat pointed out. "One of the lessons from Vietnam is that an undeclared war waged with progressively more opposition from the American people reduces the chance of success in the undertaking and divides the country." Urging that sanctions be permitted to run their course, Gore insisted that if war did become necessary, "the country is better off if the President formally asks for a declaration." Yet like many others who had served in Indochina, Gore seemed to take comfort from the knowledge that George Bush had "assembled a much larger force than was assembled for the assault on the continent of Europe at Normandy on D-Day." Remembering all too well the high price of limited war in Vietnam, Gore had only one concern. "If we decide to launch an offensive action," he asked Secretary of Defense Cheney, "do we go just partway?"[120]

The answers to Gore's question and to those of his colleagues came gradually into focus early in the new year. Convinced that economic sanctions would have little effect on the Hitler of the Euphrates, George Bush set a 15 January 1991 deadline for an Iraqi withdrawal from Kuwait and sent Secretary of State Baker to Geneva at the eleventh hour to tell Tariq Aziz, Saddam Hussein's foreign minister, that "that's the only solution we'll accept." Reminding the Iraqi diplomat that the Bush administration had pulled together an impressive coalition composed of NATO members and moderate Arab states, Baker warned that if what Aziz's boss liked to call "the mother of all battles" erupted, it would "not be a war of attrition like you fought with Iran" during the 1980s. "This will not be another Vietnam," Baker informed Aziz. "Should war begin, God forbid, it will be fought to a swift, decisive conclusion."[121]

While Aziz relayed Baker's warning to Baghdad, a resolution endorsing Bush's plans for war in the Persian Gulf was making its way up Capitol Hill. Although the White House continued to insist that the president could send U.S. troops into combat against Iraq without formal congressional approval, Bush's allies in the House and the Senate believed that they could secure the votes necessary to authorize him to resort to deadly force. After three days of fierce debate, Congress passed a joint resolution on 12 January supporting the use of the U.S. armed forces to liberate Kuwait, provided that "all appropriate diplomatic and other peaceful means to obtain compliance by Iraq" had been exhausted. The vote was 52 to 47 in the Senate and 250 to 183 in the House. Ninety-eight percent of the Republicans on Capitol Hill voted for the resolution, but because the Democrats controlled Congress, they held the critical swing votes.[122]

As the roll was called, key Democrats crossed the aisle. Some, like Senator Gore, did so because they believed that economic sanctions would never work, that the Iraqi army was simply digging in deeper with each passing week, and that fewer GIs would die if war came sooner rather than later.[123] Others, like Representative Stephen Solarz, a liberal New Yorker who had been an antiwar activist a quarter-century earlier, did so because they believed that the United States must "resist the Saddamization of the Middle East." Well aware that many Democrats were drawing parallels between the Persian Gulf and Southeast Asia, Congressman Solarz rejected the analogy with Vietnam in the pages of the *New Republic*. "In Indochina the cost in blood and treasure was out of all proportion to the expected gains," but Iraq's invasion of Kuwait posed "a challenge not only to fundamental American interests, but to essential American values." Moreover, Solarz predicted that the outcomes of the two conflicts were likely to be very different. "The war in Vietnam dragged on for years and ended in an American defeat," he pointed out. "A war in the Gulf, if it cannot be avoided, is likely to end with a decisive American victory in months, if not in weeks." With an eye to the Tonkin Gulf, the New York Democrat concluded that "sometimes you are condemned to repeat the past if you *do* remember it—that is, if you draw the wrong lessons from it, and let the memory of the past distort your view of the present."[124]

Three days after Gore, Solarz, and ninety-four other Democrats cast their ballots for the joint resolution, the deadline that George Bush had imposed on Saddam Hussein expired. Just before 3:00 A.M. on 17 January 1991, U.S. Tomahawk cruise missiles smashed into selected military targets in and around Baghdad, signaling that Desert Shield had become Desert Storm. The war unfolded just as Bush, Powell, and Solarz had foreseen. For more than a month high-tech F-117 Stealth jet fighters, aging B-52 bombers, and warplanes from other members of the coalition pounded Saddam Hussein's army and air force and pulverized much of Iraq's economic infrastructure. While the air war raged, the Pentagon methodically prepared for the ground war to follow. "Our strategy in going after this army is very simple," Colin Powell told reporters on 23 January. "First we are going to cut it off, and then we are going to kill it."[125] At 4:00 A.M. on 24 February, General Norman Schwartzkopf launched the blitzkrieg that Powell had promised, ordering 30,000 U.S. marines to storm Kuwait City and sending the 82nd and 101st Airborne and two U.S. armored divisions knifing across the desert 300 miles to the west in a brilliant flanking maneuver that blocked the Iraqi army's line of retreat. When the shooting stopped four days later, coalition forces controlled Kuwait; Iraqi tanks, trucks, and corpses littered the "highway of death" leading north toward the Euphrates; and U.S. troops stood poised to march on Baghdad.[126]

In just 100 hours in the Persian Gulf the Pentagon had accomplished what it could not in 100 months in Southeast Asia. "By God," a jubilant President Bush told visiting state government officials on 1 March, "we've kicked the Vietnam syndrome once and for all."[127] Indeed, his administration had achieved its principal objective—the liberation of Kuwait from Saddam Hussein—at a surprisingly low cost. While Iraqi casualties numbered in the tens of thousands, Operation Desert Storm saw just 148 Americans killed in action and another 467 wounded. To be sure, U.S. casualties would have been much higher had the White House heeded the maximalist advice of some pundits and attempted to conquer Baghdad and depose Saddam Hussein. Colin Powell, however, persuaded Bush that it would be far easier to get into Iraq than to get out. "The President," Powell emphasized in his memoirs, "had promised the American people that Desert Storm would not become a Persian Gulf Vietnam, and he kept his promise." Although both George Bush and his chief military adviser despised Saddam Hussein, neither was willing to dissipate the fruits of victory in Kuwait by plunging into a quagmire next door in Iraq. "After the stalemate in Korea and the long agony in Southeast Asia, the country was hungry for victory," Powell observed in the afterglow of Desert Storm. "We had given America a clear win at low casualties in a noble cause, and the American people fell in love again with their armed forces."[128]

Strategists such as Harry Summers agreed. A decade after writing his critique of the debacle in Indochina, Summers published *On Strategy II*, a glowing appraisal of Operation Desert Storm dedicated to his former classmate at Fort Leavenworth, Colin Powell. By relying on the Three S's—surprise, security, and simplicity—and by embracing the newly developed "AirLand Battle Doctrine," the Pentagon had engineered a smashing triumph. "If you would understand America's victory in the Persian Gulf war you must first understand America's defeat in Vietnam," Summers told his readers. "Seen as a loser that had been defeated by a ragtag peasant army in Vietnam, plagued by a series of mishaps at Desert One in Iran and the Marine barracks in Beirut, their successes in Grenada and Panama overshadowed by reports of things gone wrong," the U.S. military was "ridiculed in the media as 'the gang that couldn't shoot straight.'" But Desert Storm changed all that. "As events were to dramatize," Summers concluded, "the notion that America was a paper tiger, fierce in appearance but toothless in reality was (to use H. L. Mencken's words) 'neat, plausible . . . and wrong.'"[129]

While few Iraqis regarded Uncle Sam any longer as a paper tiger, the Gulf War did not lay to rest all questions concerning U.S. armed intervention in the Middle East or, more generally, in the Third World. To be sure, ten years after Operation Desert Storm, Washington maintained a formidable military presence in the Persian Gulf. A squadron of U.S. Air Force jets based in Turkey continued to enforce a "no-fly zone" over northern Iraq. The Pentagon had designated Manama, Bahrain, as the home port for the recently created U.S. Fifth Fleet, whose twenty-one warships patrolled the sea lanes from the Shatt-al-Arab to the Straits of Hormuz. And 5,000 GIs were stationed at Dhahran as part of Operation Desert Falcon, which symbolized ongoing U.S. support for the House of Saud.[130]

But despite much talk about America's central role in building a global order at the end of the twentieth century, both the Pentagon and the U.S. public blanched when faced with the prospect of sending troops to the remote corners of what seemed to be the same old disorderly world. When some in the media claimed that the United States had a moral obligation to intervene in Yugoslavia's civil war in late 1992, for example, General Powell retorted that "I get nervous when so-called experts suggest that all we need is a little surgical bombing or a limited attack," because "history has not been kind to this approach."[131] When Bill Clinton briefly considered military intervention in Bosnia to halt a bloody wave of ethnic cleansing in early 1993, worried Pentagon officials reportedly informed the White House that "we do deserts, we don't do mountains."[132] Memories of the nightmare in Indochina simply could not be put to rest. "The lesson drawn from Vietnam," former U.S. ambassador to Yugoslavia Warren Zimmermann explained, "was that even a minimum injection of American forces could swell into a major commitment and produce a quagmire" in the Balkans. "Vietnam," Lawrence Eagleburger, George Bush's last secretary of state, remarked ruefully in 1994, "never goes away."[133] Indeed, when Bush's successor finally decided to send 12,500 GIs to Bosnia two years later as part of the Dayton Accords, his military advisers warned that it would be a lot easier to get in than to get out.[134]

The men and women on Main Street were no more eager than the four-star generals at the Pentagon to see the United States become bogged down in another Vietnam. Few Americans favored using U.S. troops to restore order in Haiti in the autumn of 1993. Fewer still saw any reason to risk American lives to stop the gruesome ethnic strife that pitted Hutu against Tutsi in Rwanda the following spring. For most Americans the perils of military intervention in the Third World were best captured by a single horrifying image: a color photo of a dead GI—one of eighteen killed in a shootout with Somali guerrillas—being dragged through the streets of Mogadishu in October 1993, ten months after George Bush had sent in U.S. troops to restore order.[135]

This popular reluctance to send in the marines also extended to the Middle East. During Clinton's first term there were disturbing reminders that military intervention often carried a terrible price. In April 1994 friendly fire from a pair of F-15s downed two U.S. helicopters in the Iraqi no-fly zone, and fifteen Americans died. In January 1996 Bahrain was rocked by a series of bombings that threatened the safety of U.S. soldiers and sailors. Four months later an enormous truck bomb exploded outside Khobar Towers in Dhahran, leaving nineteen GIs dead and raising fresh doubts about Saudi security practices.[136]

The debate over how best to thwart Saddam Hussein's quest for biological weapons during Bill Clinton's second term showed that there was still no consensus regarding armed intervention in the Persian Gulf. While the White House prepared to unleash the U.S. Air Force against Iraqi weapons facilities in February 1998, anonymous Pentagon officials whispered that this would be merely "putting holes in the desert."[137] When Osama bin Laden's operatives bombed the U.S. embassies in Kenya and Tanzania six months later, killing 250 and injuring 5,500, the Clinton administration launched cruise missiles at al-Qaeda base camps in Afghanistan and put holes in the mountains but stopped well short of dispatching troops to root out the terrorist infrastructure.[138]

The best indication on Clinton's watch that the Vietnam syndrome was still alive and well, however, came in the spring of 1999 in Kosovo. As the United States and its NATO allies prepared to intervene in the rugged no-man's-land in southern Yugoslavia, where Serbian paramilitary forces loyal to Slobodan Milosevic were practicing ethnic cleansing against the Albanian majority, the White House and the Pentagon worried that a ground war was quite likely to become a Balkan Vietnam. To avert such an eventuality the Clinton administration kept American GIs out of harm's way and relied instead on overwhelming air power, which did eventually drive the Serbs out of Kosovo, but not before they butchered thousands of Albanians. Although the intensive bombing campaign forced Milosevic to reverse course, some U.S. officials heard echoes of Operation Rolling Thunder in Indochina a generation earlier. "I don't want you to take this personally, sir," one junior officer told General Michael Short as wave after wave of U.S. warplanes pounded Belgrade, "but it seems to me that what we are doing is randomly bombing military targets with no coherent strategy." Finding it hard to disagree, Clinton's number two man in the Balkans could only reply, "You wiseass, you're absolutely right."[139]

During his first months in office George W. Bush seemed no more inclined than his predecessor to use ground troops to supplement air power in protecting U.S. national security. The merest hint that the United States should send peacekeepers to quell the violence on the West Bank, for example, was greeted with stony silence from the Oval Office. In the wake of the terrorist attacks of 11 September 2001, however, the Texas Republican readied plans to uproot al-Qaeda and destroy its Taliban hosts. After deploying 10,000 marines aboard U.S. carrier groups in the Arabian Sea just outside the Straits of Hormuz and after airlifting 1,500 army special forces into Uzbekistan just across the Afghan frontier, the Pentagon launched Operation Enduring Freedom on 7 October, with cruise missiles and B-52 bombers filling the skies over Kabul and with U.S. shadow warriors ready to track down Osama bin Laden at a moment's notice.[140]

"Can you avoid being drawn into a Vietnam-like quagmire in Afghanistan?" a reporter asked George W. Bush four days later. "We learned some very important lessons in Vietnam," America's forty-third president replied. "Perhaps the most important lesson that I learned is that you cannot fight a guerrilla war with conventional forces." Although he insisted that "we're smoking al Qaeda out of their caves so that we can bring them to justice," Bush admitted that this "may take a year or two."[141] With the approach of winter, however, Americans could be excused for wondering whether Bush's estimate might be too optimistic. Noting that the Pentagon had already exhausted its list of military targets, Senator Joseph Biden, a Delaware Democrat with a mild case of Potomac fever, warned that the continued bombing of Afghanistan was making the United States look like "a high-tech bully." Admitting that air power was unlikely by itself to topple the Taliban or thwart bin Laden, an unnamed Defense Department official pointed out that "we bombed the North Vietnamese for 15 years and didn't bring them to their knees." The United States should be ready for a long war against the Taliban and al-Qaeda, the Pentagon's John Stufflebeem told reporters on 24 October. "The entire world needs to recognize that terrorism and terrorists are a much different kind of threat than we have ever faced before."[142]

To be sure, the Taliban regime did collapse with dramatic suddenness several weeks later, thanks to the relentless U.S. air war that tilted the balance on the ground toward the American-backed Northern Alliance. For Americans old enough to remember Vietnam, however, Stufflebeem's comments seemed ominously reminiscent of the early 1960s, when Washington prepared to use unlimited resources to wage a limited war against elusive guerrillas in forbidding terrain. For more than two centuries, Afghanistan has been a graveyard for outsiders, a sad and enduring truth confirmed by the trickle of aluminum coffins that the Pentagon began to airlift out of Kabul and Kandahar shortly after Christmas. As the White House prepared the public for a long battle against shadowy terrorists like Osama bin Laden, the key question for Senator Biden and other skeptics was not "Were American troops brave?" or "Were American policymakers tough?" but, rather, "Were the American people and their leaders wise?" With more than 50,000 GIs in harm's way from the deserts of Saudi Arabia to the mountains of Afghanistan, there was no clear answer by early 2002. But if the jury was still out as to whether Operation Enduring Freedom would finally enable George W. Bush to kick the Vietnam Syndrome, there was no doubt that his father's splendid little victory over Iraq in the 1991 Gulf War had helped break the Israeli-Palestinian deadlock and set in motion negotiations that promised to produce a long-awaited peace settlement early in the new millennium.

The Palestinians have never missed an opportunity to miss an opportunity.—Abba Eban, 1986

We were young and fragile in those early days and our prospect of survival was a matter more of faith than of reason. But we were sustained by a clear and lucid vision. . . . We understood that our task was not only to assert our own rights, but also to bring our rights into harmony with the rights and interests of others. . . . And so, in our first decades, we gave a new impulse and direction to Jewish history and set Israel on a path in which the opportunities transcended the dangers.—Abba Eban, *Personal Witness* (1992)

8

Opportunities Lost and Found

The United States and the Arab-Israeli Peace Process

Eight months after President George Bush announced that the United States had kicked the Vietnam Syndrome in the Hundred Hours War, a Middle East peace conference opened inside the Crystal Pavilion in the heart of Madrid. Seldom had hopes for an Arab-Israeli settlement been higher than in October 1991. The Cold War was over, the Soviet Union was crumbling, and the Arab radicals could no longer count on the Kremlin to sell them arms. Israel was showing signs of flexibility, the PLO was edging away from its anti-Zionist crusade, and for the first time, Israeli and Palestinian representatives were sitting across from each other at the negotiating table. The United States, the world's sole remaining superpower, was committed to creating a New World

Order grounded in a neo-Wilsonian faith in national self-determination, a principal tenet of both Israeli and Palestinian political cosmology. Although the path to peace would prove more winding than most U.S. policymakers anticipated, the Israelis and the Palestinians would eventually find their way from the plains of Castile through the fjords of Norway to Bill Clinton's White House in the autumn of 1993.

The Oslo Accords that Israeli prime minister Yitzhak Rabin and PLO chairman Yasser Arafat signed in the Rose Garden on 13 September 1993 were at bottom based on a simple formula: peace for land. For the Israelis the accords meant not only permitting the establishment of Arab-controlled enclaves in the Gaza Strip and the West Bank that might, over time, evolve into a Palestinian ministate, but also limiting Jewish settlements in those same occupied territories. For the Palestinians the accords meant not only accepting Israel's right to live in peace with its Arab neighbors behind secure borders, but also renouncing the terrorist tactics for which the PLO had become notorious. For both sides the three-word principle behind the Oslo Accords meant transcending short-term dangers in order to seize long-term opportunities for a more peaceful Middle East. Predictably, attempts to put the peace-for-land formula into practice sparked bitter recriminations between Israeli and Palestinian leaders, who seemed unable by the late 1990s to agree on such essential matters as which lands and what kind of peace. Indeed, as the deadline for a final settlement loomed early in the new millennium, neither Yasser Arafat nor Ariel Sharon, Yitzhak Rabin's longtime rival, seemed able to summon sufficient courage or imagination to secure a lasting peace.

Over the years, of course, the Israelis and the Palestinians have never been bashful about dragging their feet, raising their voices, or brandishing their weapons whenever they believed that the peace process was headed in the wrong direction. In the early days, it was the Arabs who constituted the biggest obstacle to peace in the Middle East. After rejecting the United Nations partition plan for Palestine in 1947, the Arab states refused to negotiate with the Israelis for two decades and waged war—usually with words but sometimes with guns and bombs—against a Jewish state whose leaders seemed, at least until June 1967, interested in trading land for peace. Israeli statesman Abba Eban may have put it best when he remarked that the Arabs have never missed an opportunity to miss an opportunity. Ironically, the fruits of Israel's victory in the Six Day War made many Israelis more interested in land than peace. For the past thirty years the West Bank, the Golan Heights, and Arab East Jerusalem have loomed ever larger in the mind's eye of Israeli expansionists such as Menachem Begin, Yitzhak Shamir, and Benjamin Netanyahu.

Not all Israelis, however, saw eye to eye with advocates of a Greater Israel. Convinced by the words and deeds of Anwar Sadat, King Hussein, and Yasser

Arafat that the Arabs were finally ready for peace, Abba Eban worried that Israel might be about to make the same mistake that the Arabs had made a generation earlier. "Our task was not only to assert our own rights, but also to bring our rights into harmony with the rights and interests of others," Eban reminded readers of his memoirs in 1992. Those still committed to accomplishing that task, he added, must once again "set Israel on a path in which the opportunities transcended the dangers."[1] Setting both the Arabs and the Israelis on such a path has preoccupied the men in the Oval Office and their Middle Eastern experts since the late 1940s.

Balfour in Reverse?: Truman, Israel, and the Palestinians

Harry Truman may have been the midwife who eased the birth of the Jewish state at the end of his first term, but during his second term he looked more like a family therapist frustrated by his inability to arrange a reconciliation between the Israelis and the Palestinian Arabs whom they had displaced. During the 1948 war and its aftermath 750,000 Palestinians fled their homes inside what would become Israel, establishing themselves in what they hoped would be temporary quarters in southern Lebanon or on the West Bank.[2] Some of the refugees were pressured to uproot themselves by the Arab Liberation Army, a 16,000-man force of Palestinian irregulars and "volunteers" from Syria and Iraq, which had been terrorizing Jewish farmers and bullying Arab villagers since early 1948. But most of the refugees chose exile to avoid living under Jewish rule or to escape intimidation and death at the hands of extremist groups like Menachem Begin's Irgun, whose commandos slaughtered 250 Palestinian men, women, and children at Deir Yassin, an Arab village just west of Jerusalem, on the eve of Israeli independence.[3]

Zionist pioneers such as Prime Minister David Ben Gurion had long insisted that their new nation must be a peaceable commonwealth inside which Jews and Arabs would coexist. But the escalating wave of terror that the Arab Liberation Army and the Irgun unleashed during March and April and the three-sided invasion of Israel that the Arab states launched in May and June convinced the leaders of the Jewish state that there could be no compromise with the Palestinians. With Israeli troops poised to secure a strategically important corridor linking Tel Aviv with Jerusalem, General Yigal Allon met with Ben Gurion on 12 July 1948. "What shall we do with the Arabs?" Allon asked. "Expel them," came the prime minister's reply.[4]

Neither the Truman administration nor Count Folke Bernadotte, the Swedish statesman whom the United Nations had recently tapped to mediate between Arab and Jew, was pleased by Ben Gurion's decision. The Jewish state was "showing signs of [a] swelled-head," the mediator complained in early August after Israeli foreign minister Moshe Sharett refused even to discuss repatriation of some Arab refugees to their former homes. A month later Secretary of State George Marshall worried that the "hatred of Arabs for Israel engendered by [the] refugee problem" was fast becoming "a great obstacle to those peace negotiations" that both Sharett and Ben Gurion said they desired. "Arab refugee problem is one involving life and death," Marshall concluded on 1 September. "The leaders of Israel would make a grave miscalculation if they thought callous treatment of this tragic issue could pass unnoticed by world opinion." Israeli extremists sent a message to Marshall and the rest of the world by ruthlessly gunning down Count Bernadotte in broad daylight as he drove through Jerusalem on 17 September 1948. But far from resolving the refugee question in Israel's favor, Bernadotte's assassination merely prompted United Nations officials to step up their efforts to assist the thousands of Palestinians huddled in makeshift camps on the West Bank.[5]

Although humanitarian concerns weighed heavily on U.S. policymakers, Cold War considerations were paramount in Washington's handling of the Palestinian tragedy. For months the State Department had been peppered with warnings that the refugees were, in the words of the U.S. ambassador to Syria, "unquestionably ripe for Communist indoctrination."[6] Convinced that a just and lasting peace was the best antidote to Soviet subversion in the Middle East and that such a peace hinged on reversing the Palestinian diaspora, the Truman administration helped secure passage of U.N. Resolution 194 on 11 December 1948. Based largely on Bernadotte's ideas, Resolution 194 affirmed that "the refugees wishing to return to their homes and live in peace with their neighbors should be permitted to do so at the earliest practicable date" and established a three-member Palestine Conciliation Commission, composed of representatives from France, Turkey, and the United States, to achieve that end.[7]

Once they began to meet regularly in early 1949, the commissioners discovered that implementing Resolution 194 would be no easy task. By mid-April Mark Ethridge, the White House insider who served as the U.S. representative on the commission, was complaining to Harry Truman that "this is by far the toughest assignment you have ever given to me." For their part, "the Arabs are shocked and stupefied by their defeat and have great bitterness toward the UN and the United States," Ethridge reported, while the Israelis "still feel too strongly that their security lies in military might instead of in good relations with their neighbors." Stressing that "the absence of peace plays into Russia's hands," Ethridge pushed for Israeli concessions and urged Truman to "keep the pressure up." The Missouri Democrat evidently tried to do just that when he sat down for lunch with Israeli president Chaim Weizmann on 25 April. Weizmann made it clear, however, that Israel's policy on

Palestinian refugees would not change. "The answer lies, as I stated, not in repatriation but in resettlement," he wrote Truman two days later. The Arabs who had fled Israel should be transplanted in "the underpopulated and fertile acres" of southern Iraq, northern Syria, or western Jordan.[8]

The more Truman and his advisers thought about Weizmann's resettlement scheme, the better it looked. The Jewish state obviously could not reabsorb all of the Arab refugees, whose ranks had swelled to 950,000. But if Israel would agree to repatriate up to 200,000, State Department experts believed that U.S. dollars could help meet the needs of the remainder "through reintegration of the refugees on a self-sustaining basis" into the neighboring Arab states. Ben Gurion and Sharett, of course, insisted that the return of even 200,000 refugees was asking far too much, but by early May they were quietly furnishing Washington with "information on early repatriation of families of Arabs now residing in areas under Israeli control."[9]

The Truman administration hoped that continued evidence of Israeli flexibility would evoke a positive response from the Arabs. On 29 July Ambassador Eliahu Epstein personally assured Truman that Israel "was anxious to make progress on the refugee question" and was willing to repatriate up to 100,000 displaced Palestinians if they could not find suitable homes in the neighboring Arab states.[10] But when U.S. officials presented Epstein's idea to Arab representatives at the Palestine Conciliation Commission armistice talks in Lausanne, Switzerland, a week later, "instant rejection" ensued. Emphatically dismissing the Israeli proposal as a "mere propaganda scheme," one Syrian diplomat snarled that the "Jews [are] either at your feet or throat." Few in Washington or Lausanne expected a diplomatic breakthrough any time soon.[11]

Convinced that the only way to break the deadlock was to shift the focus from diplomacy to development, Harry Truman asked Gordon Clapp, the chairman of the Tennessee Valley Authority (TVA), to head an Economic Survey Mission to the Middle East in late August 1949. After a three-week tour of the Holy Land, Clapp concluded that a Jordan River development project modeled on the TVA and administered by the United Nations would make it economically feasible to settle most of the Palestinian refugees on the West Bank and reduce the pressure to repatriate them to Israel. By building dams and other public works projects and by expanding the amount of water available for irrigation, U.S. engineers could increase both the number of jobs and the supply of land available to Palestinians, who would become less likely to brood over their lost homes and farms inside the Jewish state. In early December the General Assembly passed U.N. Resolution 302 establishing the United Nations Relief and Works Agency (UNRWA) with a budget of $55 million and a mandate to implement the projects outlined by the Clapp mission.[12]

Although the Israelis were interested in Clapp's proposals and UNRWA's activities, the Arabs kept their distance. Pointing out that an economic approach ignored the political aspirations of the Palestinians, Lebanese foreign minister Charles Malik, normally a voice of moderation in a region where anti-Americanism was spreading rapidly, warned that the Truman administration was creating the impression that "the US does not give a damn about the Arabs." To dispel the notion that "every election year the United States Government will yield to Zionist pressure," Malik suggested in August 1950 that Washington issue a "Balfour Declaration in reverse" committing itself to the establishment of a Palestinian homeland.[13] With border skirmishes between Syria and Israel escalating ominously and with armed Palestinians raiding Jewish settlements in the no-man's-land around Jerusalem, however, few U.S. policymakers regarded Malik's proposal as realistic. By October 1951 impatient State Department officials grumbled that Malik and other Arabs should "face existing realities" and help resettle the Palestinian refugees outside Israel. When Truman turned the Oval Office over to Dwight Eisenhower fifteen months later, the peace process remained stalemated, thanks in large measure to the unwillingness of the Arabs to accept a new reality: Israel was there to stay.[14]

Two Strikes for Ike: The Johnston Plan and Operation Alpha

Eisenhower and his foreign policy team entered office convinced that by adopting a more evenhanded approach to the Palestine question than that of their predecessors, they could broker an Arab-Israeli settlement based on economic development, modest boundary changes, and a modicum of justice for the refugees. In short order, however, these ambitious plans met stiff resistance not merely from the Israelis, who regarded any territorial concessions as suicidal, but also from the Arab radicals, who denied Israel's right to exist and refused even to negotiate with its representatives. Secretary of State John Foster Dulles learned just how bitter the Palestinians had become in May 1953 during a visit to Jordan, where he listened to refugees describe life in the hardscrabble camps that dotted the West Bank. "The Democracies have been treating the refugee problem during the last five years as if it were an academic problem which could be solved by rehabilitation of the refugees in the Arab countries, and the payment of monies," the Palestinians bitterly informed their visitor. Insisting that the problem was not economic or humanitarian but political, the refugees bluntly warned Dulles that "any amount of money, no matter how large, . . . would not lead to the solution of the problem, nor would it stem the tide of communism which is about to sweep the Near East."[15]

Dulles returned to Washington convinced that unless the Arab-Israeli deadlock was resolved swiftly, the Kremlin would make giant inroads throughout the region. "Some of these refugees could be resettled in the area presently controlled by Israel," Dulles told a national radio audience on 1 June. "Most, however, could more readily be integrated into the lives of the neighboring Arab countries."[16] During a closed-door Senate hearing two days later, Dulles insisted that "any real solution" to the Palestinian problem lay in the "cooperative development" of the region's water resources, not only in the Jordan Valley but also in the Euphrates and Tigris basins, where "it would be possible to develop a good deal more land on which these refugees could be absorbed."[17]

Persuaded that economic development was the key to a broader political settlement, Eisenhower agreed to consider a $66 million TVA-like project for the Jordan Valley and appointed Eric Johnston, a West Coast businessman who headed the Motion Picture Association of America, as his personal emissary. Full of optimism, in mid-October Johnston flew to the Middle East, where he shuttled between Amman, Tel Aviv, Damascus, and Beirut. The Israelis, Johnston informed Eisenhower on 17 November, were "essentially receptive" to the U.S. proposal. Although the Arabs were publicly calling for "resistance to collaboration with Israel," privately Jordan's King Hussein and Lebanon's Camille Chamoun were willing at least to consider an economic development package.[18] By the time Johnston returned to the Middle East seven months later, however, Jordanian and Lebanese ambivalence toward his initiative had hardened into outright opposition. State Department experts had few doubts about who was responsible. In the words of one position paper prepared in November 1954, "consistent Arab trouble makers" like Ahmed Shukairy, a high-ranking Arab League official and Palestinian firebrand who would found the PLO a decade later, were sabotaging the Johnston Plan.[19]

Dulles did not disagree. The Arab states, he complained on 9 December, "were keeping the problem alive as a political weapon against Israel and against the West."[20] To be sure, Dulles did persuade Eisenhower to send Johnston back to the Middle East twice during 1955 in search of Arab support for a Jordan Valley TVA. Both times, however, he returned empty-handed. After four visits to Arab capitals in just two years, Hollywood was evidently beginning to look better and better. Frustrated by the endless wrangling with Arab troublemakers, the movie-mogul-turned-diplomat confessed that the Johnston Plan was not likely to win an Oscar any time soon and headed back to the West Coast as Ike's first term drew to a close.[21]

The top secret peace initiative that Eisenhower and Prime Minister Anthony Eden launched in late 1954 would fare no better at the hands of the Arabs than had the unilateral U.S. approach embodied in the Johnston Plan. Four days before Christmas Eisenhower and Eden agreed to set up an Anglo-American working group code-named Operation Alpha. A month later a rough outline of what would eventually become the Alpha initiative had begun to emerge. The Israelis would be pressed to allow a small number of displaced Palestinians to return, but the vast majority of the refugees would be permanently resettled in the neighboring Arab states. Israel would be expected to make modest territorial concessions in the Negev Desert to permit the creation of a land bridge connecting Egypt and Jordan, in exchange for which the Arabs would be expected formally to recognize the Jewish state's right to exist behind secure borders. To make these arrangements more palatable for the Arabs, there would also be a multimillion-dollar development package for projects from the Aswan Dam to the Jordan Valley. Once accepted by both the Arabs and the Israelis, this comprehensive settlement would be backed by explicit security guarantees from both Britain and the United States.[22]

Impressed with the working group's handiwork, Eisenhower and Dulles hoped to convince Egypt's Gamal Abdel Nasser to accept Operation Alpha before next year's presidential campaign moved into full swing. "The Arabs should be told that unless they make peace with Israel now they will miss their best opportunity," Dulles observed on 27 January 1955.[23] Although Ike "felt somewhat appalled" by the $1 billion price tag attached to Operation Alpha, he agreed in mid-February to "make an all-out effort to get a settlement if possible, before the elections of '56." Before the month was over, however, Israel attacked an Egyptian garrison in the Gaza Strip, prompting Nasser to put Operation Alpha on hold for six months while he sought arms abroad.[24]

As Nasser shopped for tanks and planes, first in Washington and then in Moscow, U.S. and U.K. policymakers worked behind the scenes to push their ambitious Arab-Israeli initiative back on track. With prospects for peace apparently fading fast, Prime Minister Eden "compared the Israelis and Arabs to the Hatfields and the McCoys in Tennessee" and preferred to proceed with caution.[25] Eisenhower, on the other hand, wanted action before the summer was over and authorized John Foster Dulles to float the Alpha proposal during a well-publicized speech in New York City. The United States, with Israel's help, was ready to take the lead in developing arable land, creating real jobs, and finding decent homes for the Palestinians, Dulles told the Council on Foreign Relations on 26 August 1955, provided that the Arabs accepted "fixed permanent boundaries" and formal treaties.[26]

The peace-for-land formula that won praise at the Council on Foreign Relations evoked only scorn in Arab capitals. One month after Dulles unveiled Operation Alpha, the Kremlin agreed to provide Nasser with arms through Czech intermediaries, leaving him less interested than ever in buying the peace plan that Washington and London were selling. The Israelis, by contrast, proved eager to participate in Alpha and were even willing to consider repatriating some Palestinian refugees or making minor territorial concessions in the Negev in order to initiate face-to-face talks with the Egyptian leader. Seeking to salvage something from the stalled peace process before election-year politics made progress impossible, Eisenhower asked former deputy secretary of defense Robert Anderson to undertake a secret mission to the Middle East in early 1956.[27]

Anderson flew to Cairo in mid-January, but it soon became clear that his host was in no mood for compromise. Direct negotiations with the Israelis, Nasser insisted, were "impossible" unless and until they agreed "to repatriate all of the refugees" and to cede the entire Negev Desert to Egypt.[28] When Anderson countered by proposing a complicated system of overpasses and underpasses in the southern Negev designed to give Egypt a land bridge to Jordan without shutting off Israel's access to the Gulf of Aqaba, Nasser was amused. "So, we are to have the overpass?" he chuckled. "But supposing . . . one of our soldiers wanted to piss, and did so from the overpass and onto some Israelis in the underpass—wouldn't that start a war?"[29] Prime Minister David Ben Gurion, by contrast, was at least willing to discuss the Alpha proposal when Anderson arrived in Israel in late January. Heartened by fresh evidence of continued Israeli interest, Ike's emissary flew back to Washington to compare notes with Francis Russell, Foggy Bottom's chief Middle East expert. Irritated by Nasser's "attitude of cockiness and overconfidence" in his dealings with Anderson, Russell warned Dulles in late February that the prospects for a peace settlement were now "less than fifty-fifty."[30]

Despite the long odds, Anderson made a second trip to Cairo in early March. As before, however, Nasser rejected the idea of face-to-face talks with Ben Gurion, insisted that Israel must give up most of the Negev, and welcomed "growing restiveness among the refugees," who had no interest in a compromise with the Jewish state.[31] None of this came as a surprise to Eisenhower. "The chances for peaceful settlement seem remote," he confided in his diary following a debriefing session with a weary Robert Anderson on 13 March, largely because "Nasser proved to be a complete stumbling block." Thanks to Arab intransigence, Operation Alpha, like the Johnston Plan, was dead.[32]

The futile efforts of Eric Johnston and Robert Anderson to broker peace between the Hatfields and the McCoys of the Middle East were soon overshadowed by the Suez crisis and its aftermath, which received much higher priority than the refugee problem during Eisenhower's second term. To be sure, top U.S. officials continued to insist that "every effort should be made to whittle down the refugee rolls as rapidly as possible by the development of economic opportunities" through such agencies as UNRWA so that the Palestinians might "become self supporting." By late 1959, however, Congress was "increasingly reluctant" to bankroll UNRWA, which had received nearly $250 million from U.S. taxpayers during the preceding decade, "unless there could be the glimmer of a possible solution." With time running out, Ike's Middle East experts could only hope that another "Bob Anderson type mission" would be launched "after the new administration is installed."[33]

From Evenhanded to Empty-handed:
JFK and the Johnson Plan

Seven months after installing himself at 1600 Pennsylvania Avenue, John F. Kennedy quietly launched a new quest to solve the refugee problem, with Joseph Johnson, the president of the Carnegie Endowment for International Peace, cast in the role of Robert Anderson. JFK's views on the Arab-Israeli conflict had been forged during a pair of visits to the Holy Land in 1939 and 1951 that revealed both the amazing fertility of the soil and the ferocious hatred between the Arabs and the Jews who tilled it. Although his admiration for the Zionist experiment and his own presidential ambitions made the Massachusetts Democrat an early supporter of Israel, candidate Kennedy never lost sight of the plight of the Palestinian Arabs. The refugee problem "has lain like a naked sword between Israel and the Arab States," JFK reminded diners at a B'nai Zion banquet in New York City in February 1959. If elected, he vowed to break the deadlock through "negotiation, resettlement, and outside international assistance."[34]

President Kennedy wasted little time making good on that vow. In early May 1961 he sent letters to Nasser and five other Arab leaders urging them to work for "an honorable and humane settlement" to the "tragic Palestine refugee problem."[35] JFK also pressed Prime Minister Ben Gurion to rethink Israel's position on refugees when the two men met at New York City's Waldorf Astoria at the end of the month. Ben Gurion was understandably more interested in resettlement than in repatriation of refugees, which he said the Arab states regarded "as the best weapon at hand" for destroying Israel from within. Nevertheless, he told Kennedy that Israel would do what it could.[36]

In early August Kennedy and Secretary of State Dean Rusk arranged for United Nations Secretary General Dag Hammarskjöld to appoint Joseph Johnson as his special representative in the Middle East. Johnson, for whom Rusk had worked fifteen years earlier at Foggy Bottom's Division of United Nations Affairs, proved quite adept at juggling his overlapping responsibilities to Hammarskjöld and Kennedy.[37] Indeed, Johnson returned from his inaugural round of shuttle diplomacy in late September convinced that his dual status as a United Nations representative and an informal U.S. emissary actually strengthened his hand. To be sure, neither the Arabs nor the Israelis had been enthusiastic at first, but once they learned that "the US will foot the bill," both sides warmed up considerably. "The 'hunch' is that Israel might accept somewhere up to 10,000 refugees per year for an initial period of 2 or 3 years," Johnson advised State Department officials on 29 September. "In the end, of course, any solution may be rejected by the Arabs on political grounds, as was Eric Johnston's Jordan waters plan," he added. "Still, the effort is worth a try."[38]

Despite nasty clashes between Palestinian and Israeli villagers in late 1961 and bloody border skirmishes between Syria and Israel early in the new year, Johnson continued his shuttling throughout the spring of 1962. In late July Dean Rusk sat down with his old boss to go over the details of a peace-for-land deal that soon came to be known as the Johnson Plan. Under the terms of Johnson's proposal, UNRWA would confidentially poll the refugees, Israel would repatriate those who wanted to return to their old homes, and the Arab states would permanently resettle those who wanted to start new lives elsewhere. Although the Johnson Plan included no specific ceiling on how many Palestinians might be repatriated to Israel, its author expected that number to be less than 100,000, or fewer than one in ten. To sweeten what was sure to be a bitter pill for Israel, Johnson believed that the United States must be prepared to cover a sizable portion of the estimated $1 billion cost of the repatriation and resettlement scheme over the next ten years.[39] Fearful that "in the absence of progress, extremist elements in the Arab states might seek to use the refugees to 'Algerianize' the Arab-Israeli dispute," Rusk forwarded the Johnson Plan to JFK on 7 August 1962.[40]

Kennedy invited Joseph Johnson to the White House a week later to review the Palestinian stalemate with Dean Rusk and several other senior advisers, including Myer "Mike" Feldman, the presidential liaison with the American Jewish community. The key to the plan, Johnson told Kennedy and his aides, was to provide the refugees a real choice between repatriation and resettlement and then prevent the Israelis and the other Arabs from meddling in the process. If the Palestinians were presented with these two options, "few will choose to return" to Israel, which could in any event veto, on a case-by-case basis, those troublemakers who did. While it was true that "the Arabs have missed many trains," Johnson believed that at least some of the refugees would take seats aboard his West Bank Limited once it became clear that the United States would provide compensation.[41]

Kennedy was far less optimistic than Johnson. The man in the Oval Office feared that Arab radicals "would use propaganda" to compel "all the refugees to go back to Israel." He blanched at the U.S. share of the cost of the plan, which Johnson estimated at $700 million over ten years. He worried that unless there were some firm ceiling on the total number of Palestinians to be repatriated, the Israelis would put up "a costly fight," something he wished to avoid "because of [off-year] elections" in November. Could the Israelis, JFK wondered, ever be persuaded to accept the open-ended repatriation provisions of the Johnson Plan? Myer Feldman, who had spent much of the summer pressing the Pentagon to sell surface-to-air missiles to Israel, thought there was a chance. "If we could tie in the Hawk [missiles]," he told his boss, "it might work."[42]

The next morning Feldman boarded a plane bound for Tel Aviv. In his pocket he carried a letter from Kennedy to Ben Gurion gently linking the U.S. sale of Hawk missiles to Israeli acquiescence to the Johnson Plan. "I found Israel receptive to the Plan," Feldman recalled long afterward. "Both Ben Gurion and Golda Meir accepted its terms."[43] Things fell apart, Feldman insisted, only after State Department officials persuaded Johnson to accept sixty-two amendments designed to "make the plan slightly more favorable to the Arabs."[44] Armin Meyer, one of the leading proponents of the Johnson Plan at Foggy Bottom, remembers things a bit differently. "Mike [Feldman] went out and talked to BG and BG said, no," Meyer recently told an interviewer. Although "the Israelis would have [had] veto power over every single Arab who considered returning," Ben Gurion had been "worried about a stampede effect."[45]

Despite his friendship with Joseph Johnson and Armin Meyer, Dean Rusk sided with Myer Feldman and blamed the Arabs, not the Israelis, for the ultimate demise of the refugee scheme. The Johnson Plan "failed primarily because the Arabs were unwilling to agree to any figure for the return of Palestinian refugees that was within Israel's capacity to accept," Rusk noted in his memoirs. Permanent resettlement outside Israel was simply anathema for the "Arab extremists," he added, who "threatened to tell the camp refugees that if they elected anything other than to stay where they were, they risked having their throats cut."[46]

If Feldman, Meyer, and Rusk could not agree on why the Johnson Plan failed, all three regretted the consequences. "We came a millimeter away from having Israel and Egypt both accept the Plan, resolve the refugee question, and obviate the rise of the PLO," Feldman remarked sadly. "If we could have gotten those refugees out of those camps and made them productive members of society," Meyer confessed three decades later, "we could have, to use Joe Johnson's phraseology, 'dissolved' the refugee problem, thus thwarting what has since become the formidable 'Palestinian problem.'" But Dean Rusk may have expressed it best. "I still think this approach—allowing each refugee a private and secret choice as to where he wants to live—has promise for an eventual settlement," JFK's secretary of state wrote in 1990. The Johnson Plan, however, was "buried somewhere in the archives of lost hopes for the Middle East," along with, he might have added, the Clapp Report, Johnston Plan, and Operation Alpha.[47] Kennedy, then, like Truman and Eisenhower before him, left office empty-handed, his evenhanded approach scuttled by Israeli insecurity and Arab intransigence.

Rube Goldberg Meets Huck Finn: LBJ, the PLO, and United Nations Resolution 242

The smoldering refugee problem that Lyndon Johnson inherited from JFK in November 1963 would eventually explode into a full-scale Arab-Israeli war in June 1967. Less tolerant of the Arab radicals than his predecessor and more preoccupied with deepening U.S. involvement in Southeast Asia, LBJ could only shake his head when Nasser embraced the Viet Cong's struggle against U.S. imperialism and exhorted the Palestinians to launch their own war for national liberation. The new president was still settling into the Oval Office when Nasser unveiled plans in January 1964 for a vague "Palestinian entity" to be headed by Ahmed Shukairy, long a burr under America's saddle.[48] Three months later in Jerusalem, Shukairy and several other Palestinian firebrands, including Yasser Arafat, founded the PLO, which would take as its principal goal the destruction of Israel.[49]

By the time Arafat became one of the founding fathers of the PLO in May 1964, he and a small band of Palestinian radicals had been staging hit-and-run raids against Israel for nearly a decade. Arafat was an eighteen-year-old engineering student serving in the Egyptian militia when he fired his first shots at Israeli troops in May 1948. By the mid-1950s he was leading guerrilla attacks against Israeli installations from bases inside the refugee camps in Gaza. After the Suez debacle Arafat fled to Kuwait, where in 1959 he founded Fatah— a reverse acronym for Harakat al-Tahrir al-Filastini—the Palestine National Liberation Movement. Fatah put out pamphlets publicizing the Palestinian cause, built up a small but loyal following among the refugees in Gaza and on the West Bank, and sought support from Nasser, Algerian president Ahmed Ben Bella, and other Arab radicals. But with no Palestinian homeland in sight by the summer of 1964, Arafat and his restless followers were ready to resume their guerrilla campaign against Israel and vowed to make Fatah the action arm of the new PLO.[50]

At first Washington did not take Fatah or the PLO seriously. When Shukairy announced the creation of an Egyptian-trained "Palestine Army" in September 1964, for example, U.S. diplomats predicted that this merely meant that Nasser would be "issuing new badges to [the] Palestine Brigade presently in Sinai" to further the myth of national liberation.[51] Few Americans noticed Fatah's "Military Communiqué Number One," which announced a fresh round of raids against the Jewish state on New Year's Day 1965. But once Palestinian fedayeen based on the West Bank began dynamiting power plants and terrorizing villages inside Israel later that spring, Secretary of State Dean Rusk had to admit that Fatah's tactics had "created a more explosive atmosphere in the Near East" than at any time in recent memory.[52]

Nasser soon made matters worse by seconding Fatah's call for a Palestinian war of national liberation. During a fiery address to the second annual Palestine National Congress in May 1965, he vowed to "mobilize four million men if necessary" to defeat Israel. "Since Palestine was usurped by the sword," Nasser thundered, "it must be regained by the sword." The State Department's assessment of Nasser's remarks made grim reading at the White House: "His words were blunt, stripped of the customary Arab rhetoric, and—we think—spoken in deadly earnest."[53]

Gratified to find such strong support for their direct action tactics in Cairo, Fatah and the PLO would receive even more encouragement from Damascus and Moscow during 1966. After a left-wing coup rocked Syria in February, White House Middle East expert Harold Saunders recalled, anti-Western officers embraced the PLO and "openly endorsed the 'war of liberation' as the proper way for the Palestinians to regain their 'homeland.'"[54] Not to be outdone by these Syrian radicals, the Soviets soon proclaimed their own support for a "progressive revolutionary" front among the Arabs, whose chief instrument was to be the PLO.[55] Emboldened by the Syrians and the Soviets, the PLO escalated its guerrilla war against Zionism and imperialism. Israel retaliated on 13 November with a devastating assault on Samu, a West Bank village suspected of housing a Fatah base camp.[56] Far from intimidating the Palestinians, however, the Samu raid provoked even greater Arab hostility, which the CIA predicted would mean more "Syrian support of the Fatah terrorist organization in its commando raids into Israeli territory." When PLO guerrillas based in the Golan Heights launched one too many attacks in April 1967, Israeli jets streaked toward Damascus and lit the fuse for the Six Day War, whose roots lay to a great degree in the unresolved question of the Palestinian refugees.[57]

As the war clouds loomed, Washington blamed the Arabs, whose intransigence made compromise impossible. Following a whirlwind visit to the Middle East, Harold Saunders confirmed that "among the *Palestinians* on Jordan's West Bank, there is no sign of resignation to [the] loss of their homes in Israel." Having brooded for nearly two decades in squalid shacks and tents, their hatred of Zionism knew no bounds. "Don't make the mistake of thinking that time will solve the refugee problem," Saunders had been told over and over. "From the bitterest of these refugees," he reminded his superiors on 16 May 1967, "the Fatah terrorist group sends its saboteurs into Israel."[58]

If Fatah and its bitter followers hoped to regain their lost homeland on the battlefield, they were sorely mistaken. Israel's stunning victory in June 1967 brought Gaza, the West Bank, and Arab East Jerusalem under Israeli control, territorial changes that U.S. policymakers did not expect to be easily reversed. "Israel was riding high," Dean Rusk warned LBJ as early as 7 June, "and its demands will be substantial." Well aware of Israel's territorial ambitions, Johnson nevertheless hoped "to develop as few heroes and as few heels as we can."[59] Harold Saunders agreed. "Refugees must be the nub of a settlement," he pointed out later that same day. The Israelis, however, were likely to insist on formal peace treaties with the Arabs and "will not give up the West Bank or Sharm al-Sheikh easily."[60]

Even before the shooting stopped, thousands of Palestinian refugees fled across the Jordan River onto the East Bank. After the cease-fire went into effect on 10 June, Israeli troops evicted Palestinian families and leveled Palestinian dwellings in East Jerusalem and other strategically important West Bank towns. Touting "self-determination" as a better option than Israeli expansionism, Rusk warned Johnson on 14 June that "Israel's keeping territory w[ou]ld create a revanchism for the rest of the 20th c[entury]."[61] But as the month drew to a close, the CIA confirmed that "the exodus of refugees—130,000 so far according to [Jordan's] King Husayn—from the West Bank continues," partly because of "fear of what the Israelis might do" and partly because "Israeli soldiers forced them to leave."[62]

Hoping to prevent Arab intransigence and Israeli expansionism from unleashing yet another cycle of terror, retaliation, and war, Lyndon Johnson laid out his own blueprint for peace on 19 June 1967. There must be a "recognized right of national life" for both the Arab states and Israel, LBJ insisted, and "political independence and territorial integrity for all." But there must also be "justice for the refugees," he hastened to add, for "there will be no peace for any party in the Middle East unless this problem is attacked with new energy."[63] During the next five months Johnson's advisers struggled to transform his blueprint into diplomatic bricks and mortar at the United Nations. They initially expected the most resistance from the Arabs, who obliged in late August by issuing their famous "Three Noes"—no recognition of, no negotiations with, and no peace for Israel—at their summit in Khartoum, Sudan. Privately, however, both Nasser and King Hussein let it be known that they were willing to pursue their goals "by political rather than by military means." This was an opportunity that the United States could not afford to miss, Walt Rostow advised LBJ on 3 October, because "the longer Israel sits on occupied territory, the harder it will be to convince friendlier Arabs that we're not reneging on our commitment to territorial integrity."[64]

Just how difficult it would be to secure Israeli support for the peace-for-land formula that U.S. diplomats were peddling at the United Nations soon became crystal clear. "Israel is pursuing a policy that's more likely to lead to another explosion than to a peace settlement," Walt Rostow warned LBJ on the eve of Foreign Minister Abba Eban's visit to Washington. The time had come to press Eban and other Israeli leaders "to settle the refugee problem once and for all" by permitting "some of those poor people . . . to go back and live in Israel if they want to."[65] Although he did not go so far as to insist that the refugees be permitted to go back to their homes inside the Jewish state, Johnson did remind Eban in late October that "the Israelis should not forget what we had said about territorial integrity and boundaries." With an eye to the occupied territories, he warned the Israeli foreign minister that "the further away from June 5 you get, the further you are getting away from peace."[66]

Judging from Israel's acquiescence in the peace-for-land formula endorsed by the United Nations Security Council a month later, Lyndon Johnson had gotten his points across. After conferring with King Hussein and other Arab moderates in New York City, Ambassador Arthur Goldberg and Lord Caradon, his British colleague at the United Nations, hammered out the language for what would become Resolution 242 in mid-November. Goldberg and Caradon's wording was truly ingenious. Without mentioning Israel by name, their draft acknowledged "the sovereignty, territorial integrity and political independence of every State in the area." Without condemning the Israelis as aggressors, their draft emphasized "the inadmissibility of the acquisition of territory by war." Without clarifying all the details, their draft called for "a just settlement of the refugee problem."[67]

The most controversial part of Goldberg and Caradon's diplomatic handiwork, however, was a twelve-word sentence that dealt with the future of the West Bank and other real estate that Israel had acquired during the Six Day War. In what seemed like relatively straightforward language, their draft called for the "withdrawal of Israeli armed forces from territories occupied in the recent conflict." Convinced that Israel would never accept a return to the prewar status quo, Arab leaders proposed inserting "all" or "the" before the word "territories," something to which Israeli officials objected strenuously. With just a couple of three-letter words holding up the peace process, Goldberg and Caradon hit upon a solution that, in retrospect, would prove too clever by half. First, they saw to it that the French translation, which in accordance with United Nations procedures carried the same weight as the English version, read as follows: "Retrait des forces armées israeliennes des territoires occupés lors du recent conflit." This would enable the Arabs to claim that the French word "des" implied the presence of the missing "the" in the English text. Second, Goldberg privately assured Jordan's King Hussein that the ambiguous clause would permit only "minor reciprocal border rectifications" and that "the United States did not conceive of any substantial redrawing of the map." When the king questioned whether the Israelis would accept this interpretation, Goldberg replied, "Don't worry. They're on board."[68]

Not long after Lord Caradon won unanimous approval from the U.N. Security Council for Resolution 242 on 22 November 1967, however, British and U.S. officials discovered that the Israelis had stepped off the train. Shortly before Christmas Gunnar Jarring, the Swedish diplomat whom Secretary General U Thant had appointed as U.N. mediator, arrived in the Middle East to oversee the implementation of the peace-for-land formula. While the Arabs were eager to move ahead, the Israelis were not and told Jarring so. When Lyndon Johnson sought assurances "that the Israelis aren't going to sit themselves tight right into a 'fortress Israel,'" Prime Minister Levi Eshkol replied that Fatah's guerrilla campaign proved that the Arabs were not really committed to peace.[69] As Israel tightened its grip on the occupied territories, LBJ wondered "whether there was any chance that Jarring would succeed." Shaking his head, Secretary of Defense Robert McNamara concluded on 26 February 1968 that the Swede's chances were no better than "one in four."[70]

The odds against Jarring grew considerably longer a month later when Fatah commandos inflicted heavy losses on Israeli troops in the Battle of Karameh. Hoping to capture Yasser Arafat and other PLO leaders, Israel raided a refugee camp outside the East Bank village of Karameh on 21 March. Jordanian officials had urged Arafat to cut and run, but he refused. "After the Arab defeat of 1967," he explained, "there must be some group who can prove that there are people in our Arab nation who are ready to fight and to die." Fatah was such a group. "We will not withdraw," Arafat vowed. "We will fight and we will die." When Israeli tanks and troops rolled into the Palestinian stronghold at dawn, Arafat and 300 fedayeen fought back with machine guns, rocket-propelled grenades, and dynamite. In short order Jordanian troops stationed nearby joined the fray. When the shooting stopped a few hours later, 28 Israelis, 93 Palestinians, and 128 Jordanians lay dead. Surveying the burned-out hulks of the 18 tanks that the Israelis left behind, Arafat and his comrades claimed to have won an impressive moral victory.[71]

In the aftermath of Karameh the Israelis became even less interested in returning the occupied territories and ever more insistent that the Arabs agree to formal peace treaties before any land changed hands. Israel, Walt Rostow complained on 17 May, was becoming "too theological" on these matters. The United States did not favor a return to the "Rube Goldberg chewing gum and tape" arrangements that had existed prior to the Six Day War, he told Israeli ambassador Yitzhak Rabin. But Rostow thought it was unrealistic "to have the Arabs 'like Huck Finn prick their fingers and sign in blood' before talks could begin that they would sign a big peace treaty at the end of it."[72] Like Tom Sawyer standing before Jim the slave, however, the Israelis continued to bar the door to a peace-for-land settlement throughout the spring and into the summer. "What we hear from Egyptians, what we hear from Jarring, and what we hear from Israelis," one U.S. diplomat reported in mid-June, "adds up to a pretty depressing picture of stalemate."[73]

With the approach of autumn few U.S. policymakers had any hope for the

Jarring mission, and many held Israel more responsible for the stalemate than the Arabs. Undersecretary of State Eugene Rostow, like his younger brother Walt, insisted that the Jewish state must take risks for peace. "Failure of effort under SC Nov22 resolution would be catastrophe for USG and for GOI as well," he told Ambassador Rabin on 17 August. "Emergence [of] intense Palestinian personality throughout area focussed on fedayeen activity is threat to political stability [of] many governments." The situation was no better at the end of the year, Walt Rostow advised Lyndon Johnson as the two men prepared for a transition briefing session with president-elect Richard Nixon on 12 December 1968. "Israel appears to intend to retain some of [the] territory occupied [in] June 1967," Walt explained, and was digging itself deeper into the West Bank. "Meantime," he concluded, "terrorism and cease-fire violations continue with danger of escalation."[74] By the time that Nixon moved into the White House five weeks later, most U.S. officials agreed that Israel had become as big an obstacle to a peace-for-land settlement as the Arabs.

Nixon, Kissinger, and the Rogers Plan

Richard Nixon had become intimately familiar with the Arab-Israeli conflict and the centrality of the Palestinian question while he was vice-president. Late in Eisenhower's second term Nixon had reminded Prime Minister David Ben Gurion that "the Arabs were effectively using the refugee problem as a political weapon" and emphasized "the importance to Israel of finding some means to offset this."[75] During eight years in the political wilderness following his painful loss to John F. Kennedy in November 1960, Nixon passed through the Middle East several times and came away ever more convinced that the best way for Washington to neutralize that "refugee weapon" was to adopt a more evenhanded policy.[76]

Both of President Nixon's senior foreign policy advisers were less familiar with the Arab-Israeli dispute than was their new boss. William P. Rogers, a corporate lawyer who had served as Eisenhower's attorney general, became secretary of state largely because of Nixon's respect for his "intellect, negotiating skill, and judgment," qualities that were to be sorely tested by both the Arabs and the Israelis.[77] Henry Kissinger, the Harvard professor and student of realpolitik whom Nixon appointed as national security adviser, had visited Israel several times but had no real grasp of the complicated issues that had bedeviled the region for a generation. "When I entered office," Kissinger confessed in a rare moment of modesty a decade later, "I knew very little of the Middle East."[78]

Although these appointments gave no hint that the new administration would pay much attention to the region, president-elect Nixon made it perfectly clear that breaking the Arab-Israeli impasse and solving the refugee problem would be a central objective of his foreign policy. Six weeks before he took the oath of office, Nixon sent William Scranton, a Pennsylvania Republican who had recently turned down the job that William Rogers subsequently accepted, on a fact-finding mission to the Middle East. After nine days of closed-door talks about the Jarring mission and Resolution 242 with Arab and Israeli leaders, Scranton told reporters during an impromptu West Bank press conference on 9 December 1968 that "America would do well to have a more evenhanded policy" in the Middle East.[79] Fearing that Scranton's comments signaled a radical shift in the U.S. approach to the region, Israel and its friends in Washington clamored for Nixon to clarify matters. "Those were Scranton remarks," Ronald Ziegler, the president-elect's press secretary, observed tersely the next day, "not Nixon remarks."[80]

Despite such high-profile backpedaling, however, Nixon's initial policies remained closer to Scranton's remarks than he cared to admit. Secretary of State Rogers wasted little time confirming that the Nixon administration, like its predecessor, regarded U.N. Resolution 242 as the best blueprint for an Arab-Israeli settlement. "That resolution," he told the Senate Foreign Relations Committee on 27 March 1969, "will be the bedrock of our policy." Achieving "a state of peace" would require the Arabs to accept Israel's right to exist behind secure borders and to end their state of war. But it would also require Israel to withdraw from the occupied territories and to address the needs of the Palestinian refugees.[81] "Israel's standpat policy is detrimental to both U.S. and Israeli interests," Rogers told Nixon six months later. "The settlement we envisage must be based on a map not very different from the one that existed before the 1967 war."[82]

On 9 December 1969 the secretary of state unveiled a blueprint for a settlement that would eventually be known as the Rogers Plan. Reaffirming America's commitment to a "balanced and fair" policy based on U.N. Resolution 242, he pledged not only "to encourage the Arabs to accept a permanent peace based on a binding agreement and to urge the Israelis to withdraw from occupied territory," but also to seek a "just settlement" of the refugee question. "There is a new consciousness among the young Palestinians who have grown up since 1948," Rogers concluded, "which needs to be channelled away from bitterness and frustration toward hope and justice."[83]

The Rogers Plan got a frosty reception in Israel, where Levi Eshkol's sudden death in February 1969 had made seventy-year-old Golda Meir prime minister. Born in Kiev but raised in Milwaukee, in 1921 Meir had boarded a steamer bound for Tel Aviv, where for nearly a half-century she worked closely with David Ben Gurion, with whom she shared an implacable commitment to Israeli security and an abiding mistrust of the Palestinians. Upon learning what the Nixon administration had in mind for the Middle East, Meir flew to Washington in September 1969. She vowed never to accept a peace-for-land formula—whether imposed by the United States, the United Nations, or the superpowers—that might lead to the creation of a Palestinian state.[84] Reading the Rogers Plan three months later finally brought the volatile Meir to a full boil. "Nobody in the world can make us accept it," she thundered on 22 December. "We didn't survive three wars in order to commit suicide." Israel's American friends echoed Meir's concerns. AIPAC in particular urged Jewish leaders to inundate the White House and Congress with protests. By February 1970, 70 senators and 280 representatives had joined the rising chorus urging the Nixon administration to stop twisting Israel's arm at the peace table and start selling Israel arms for use on the battlefield.[85]

Nixon backed quickly away from the Rogers Plan, not merely because the peace-for-land formula at its core was unpopular with Golda Meir and the Israel lobby, but also because the comprehensive settlement favored by Foggy Bottom ran counter to the step-by-step diplomacy preferred by his national security adviser. When it came to what he called "the liturgy of Middle East negotiations," Henry Kissinger was a self-proclaimed agnostic. "Someone invoked the sacramental language of United Nations Security Council Resolution 242, mumbling about the need for a just and lasting peace with secure and recognized borders," Kissinger confessed in his memoirs, and "I thought the phrase so platitudinous that I accused the speaker of pulling my leg." Kissinger knew, of course, that someday the Israelis would have to trade land for peace, but that moment had not arrived yet. The Rogers Plan "cannot produce a solution without massive pressure on Israel," Kissinger warned his boss in late 1969. "It is more than likely going to wind up antagonizing both sides. It may produce a war."[86] Nixon agreed and asked Kissinger to work with Leonard Garment, the informal White House liaison to the American Jewish community, to secure Golda Meir's help in torpedoing the State Department initiative. "Tell her wherever she goes," Kissinger told Garment in early 1970, "we want her to slam the hell out of Rogers and his plan." Meir had just one word for Garment when he caught up with her at LaGuardia Airport on the eve of a cross-country speaking tour: "Fine."[87]

While Golda Meir slammed the Rogers Plan from New York to Los Angeles, Assistant Secretary of State Joseph Sisco flew to the Middle East in April 1970. He was received coolly but correctly by the Israelis, who were relieved to learn that the Rogers Plan was dead on arrival. Sisco was forced to cancel his stop in Jordan, however, when angry Palestinians stormed the USIA office and set it on fire. After the tongue-lashing he received in Cairo on 12 April, Sisco probably wished he had canceled that stop as well. Complaining bitterly that the United States remained "entirely on Israel's side," Nasser told Sisco that he was "prepared to do what Res 242 calls for—to recognize Israel," but "he could not close his eyes to [the] Palestinians as Golda Meir had said" he must. "How many lost opportunities there had been" over the past two decades, Sisco remarked wistfully as he prepared to return to Washington, and yet "there would now be another lost opportunity." Nasser agreed but vowed nonetheless that "there will be no peace without solution of Palestine problem."[88]

Indeed there was no peace and no solution. By the summer of 1970 the Palestinians were resorting to ever more ruthless tactics to gain attention for their cause. They hijacked airliners, bombed schools, and attempted to assassinate Jordan's King Hussein, whom they regarded as insufficiently anti-Israel. After Hussein sent his troops into the refugee camps outside Amman with Nixon's and Kissinger's blessing in early September, bloody fighting erupted that left 1,500 Palestinians dead, 2,500 in jail, and another 5,000 in exile in Lebanon. Bitter members of the PLO and nearly a dozen alphabet-soup splinter groups responded by unleashing a wave of terror, assassinating Jordanian prime minister Wasfi al-Tal in Cairo in November 1971, murdering eleven Israeli Olympic athletes in Munich in September 1972, and executing three U.S. diplomats in Khartoum six months later. It is not surprising that when Yasser Arafat offered in mid-1973 to open a secret dialogue based on the premise that "Israel is here to stay," no one in Nixon's Washington took him seriously.[89]

The Arab-Israeli war that erupted that autumn dramatically transformed the political landscape of the Middle East but did not alter Nixon's and Kissinger's disdain for the Palestinians. Egypt's new president, Anwar Sadat, and Syria's Hafez al-Assad attacked Israel in October 1973 not to achieve Palestinian self-determination but, rather, to regain the Sinai and the Golan Heights. Ironically, however, the October War eventually paid bigger dividends for the PLO than for the Egyptians or the Syrians. While Sadat could claim only modest territorial gains and Assad none at all, on 29 October 1974 Arafat persuaded Arab leaders at their summit in Rabat, Morocco, to designate the PLO as "the sole legitimate representative of the Palestinian people."[90]

By that time Richard Nixon had been forced to resign over the Watergate scandal, but his successor, Gerald Ford, had little reason to regard Arafat as legitimate. Ford's reservations about the PLO were echoed by Henry Kissinger, who had replaced William Rogers as secretary of state on the eve of the October War. Reading Kissinger's recent account of the hard bargaining with Israel over territorial concessions during 1975, one has to wonder whether the professor-turned-diplomat ever regretted torpedoing the Rogers Plan, with its peace-for-land proviso, five years earlier. To secure even a partial Israeli withdrawal from the Sinai in September 1975, not only did the Ford administration have to provide the Jewish state with nearly $2 billion in arms and oil; it also had to pledge not to negotiate with the PLO until Arafat's organization recognized Israel's right to exist.[91]

Yet just two months later, Harold Saunders, a holdover from the Johnson administration who had become one of Kissinger's most trusted lieutenants, cautioned Congress that the United States could no longer afford to ignore the Palestinian question. "The legitimate interests of the Palestinian Arabs must be taken into account in the negotiation of an Arab-Israeli peace," he told the House Committee on Foreign Affairs on 12 November. This would mean, Saunders added, clarifying the future of the occupied territories under the auspices of U.N. Resolution 242.[92]

Saunders's remarks shocked Israel's friends on Capitol Hill and angered Yitzhak Rabin, who had succeeded Golda Meir as prime minister in the aftermath of the October War. The Ford administration, Rabin warned U.S. diplomats, was playing into the hands of the PLO and jeopardizing Israeli security. But when Israel announced plans to establish permanent settlements on the West Bank in early 1976, William Scranton, Nixon's onetime evenhanded envoy and now Ford's ambassador to the United Nations, protested loudly. Invoking the spirit of Resolution 242, Scranton told the Security Council on 23 March that the United States agreed that "substantial resettlement of the Israeli civilian population in occupied territories, including East Jerusalem, is illegal" under international law.[93] When Gerald Ford, Henry Kissinger, and the other survivors from the Nixon era slipped quietly out of office ten months later, they left a tattered copy of the Rogers Plan, a pile of debris from the October War, and a laundry list of complaints that contained as many entries about Israel as about the Arabs.

Carter, Camp David, and the Quest for Palestinian Autonomy

The little bit that Jimmy Carter said about peace in the Middle East during his remarkable odyssey from Plains to the Potomac left little doubt that the Georgia Democrat would be at least as tough with Israel as the Michigan Republican whom he replaced. Shortly after tossing his hat into the ring, Carter had endorsed a controversial December 1975 Brookings Institution blueprint for an Arab-Israeli settlement based on the principle of peace for land. Without mentioning U.N. Resolution 242, the Brookings report stated that the Arabs must accept Israel's right to exist behind secure borders, that the Israelis must withdraw from the occupied territories, and that both sides must work to solve the refugee problem. Then the Brookings Institution spelled out what would eventually become one of the cornerstones of Carter's policy in the Middle

East: "There should be provision for Palestinian self-determination subject to Palestinian acceptance of the sovereignty and integrity of Israel within agreed boundaries."[94]

Watergate, not the Middle East, was the decisive issue during the 1976 presidential campaign. One week before Election Day, however, candidate Carter received an 11,000-word foreign policy game plan touching on everything from Argentina to Zaire. The report was prepared by Cyrus Vance, the Yale-educated Washington insider who would become secretary of state in the new administration. In just five brief paragraphs on the Arab-Israeli dispute, Vance confirmed that the peace-for-land formula was the key to any lasting settlement, reminded Carter of the domestic political considerations involved, and urged him "not [to] take any strong initiative" but, rather, to "nudge the situation along."[95] During the days after his narrow victory at the polls on 2 November, the president-elect became convinced that the complicated dispute between Arab and Jew boiled down to three simple issues: "Israeli security; who owned the land; and Palestinian rights."[96]

Addressing those issues was a high priority for President Carter during the spring of 1977. When he raised the possibility of swapping land for peace during a 7 March Oval Office meeting with Israeli prime minister Rabin, however, Carter was greeted with stony silence. When Carter remarked almost casually at a town meeting in Clinton, Massachusetts, nine days later that "there has to be a homeland provided for the Palestinian refugees who have suffered for many, many years," he outraged many of Israel's American supporters. Carter's remarks could not have come at a worse time for Yitzhak Rabin, who faced a stiff challenge from Menachem Begin in Israeli elections scheduled for 17 May. Declaring that "Palestinian" was merely a synonym for "terrorist," Begin made Carter and Arafat his whipping boys, and when the ballots were counted, Israel had a different prime minister.[97]

An arch expansionist who advocated Jewish settlements throughout the occupied Arab territories, Begin informed Carter three months later that, as far as he was concerned, the peace-for-land formula in Resolution 242 was a dead letter. The existing Israeli settlements on the West Bank were permanent, Begin declared in early August, and more would be built.[98] When Moshe Dayan, Begin's foreign minister, visited the White House in September, Carter complained that Israel's "gratuitous endorsement of a new group of settlements" in the occupied territories and its refusal to discuss Palestinian rights were creating "almost insuperable obstacles" to peace.[99]

The Israeli-American impasse was broken neither by Carter nor by Begin but by Anwar Sadat, whose unprecedented visit to Jerusalem in November 1977 set in motion a peace process that would lead to the Camp David Accords ten months later. One of the chief architects of the October War, Sadat now realized that he was more likely to achieve his goals at the bargaining table. "I have come to you," he told the Israeli Knesset on 20 November, "so that together we should build a durable peace based on justice to avoid the shedding of a single drop of blood by both sides." What would this mean? "The answer," Sadat replied, "would be that Israel lives within her borders, among her Arab neighbors in safety and security, within the framework of all the guarantees she accepts and that are offered to her." For its part, Egypt was ready to negotiate a peace treaty based on U.N. Resolution 242, provided that Israel addressed the problem of Palestine. "It is no use to refrain from recognizing the Palestinian people and their right to statehood as their right of return," Sadat confessed. "We, the Arabs, have faced this experience before with you." Together, he told the Knesset, Israel and Egypt must break the cycle of violence and "seize this opportunity today of a durable peace based on justice."[100]

Sadat's speech won a warmer reception in Washington, however, than in Jerusalem. Having worked for a decade to implement Resolution 242, U.S. officials could finally see a peace-for-land deal taking shape that might settle the refugee question once and for all. Israeli leaders, however, remained convinced that self-rule would eventually trigger a Palestinian jihad and tried to maneuver Sadat into accepting a separate peace that would have returned the Sinai to Egypt while leaving Israel firmly in control of the West Bank and Gaza. Jimmy Carter attributed the deepening diplomatic stalemate mainly to Begin's inflexibility and said so on 21 March. "The obstacle to peace was Israel's obvious intention to retain perpetual control over the West Bank," he declared bluntly, and if Begin "did not seize the opportunity for peace, it would soon be lost."[101]

Following several months of increasingly frustrating palaver, Carter seized that opportunity himself by inviting both Begin and Sadat to a Middle East summit to be held at Camp David. The Egyptian and Israeli delegations arrived on 5 September 1978 to begin nearly two weeks of grueling negotiations that sorely tested both Carter's faith and his patience. Carter quickly got the two sides to hammer out a bilateral deal calling for Israel to withdraw completely from the Sinai in exchange for a formal peace treaty with Egypt. But the summit very nearly collapsed because of a bitter disagreement about the future of the West Bank, which Sadat argued must become a Palestinian homeland. Begin, however, insisted that "the War of 1967 gives Israel the right to change frontiers" and balked at discussing Palestinian autonomy. "What you say convinces me that Sadat was right—what you want is land!" Carter exploded on 10 September. "If you had openly disavowed United Nations Resolution 242, I would not have invited you to Camp David."[102]

Begin shied away from repudiating Resolution 242, but he would not agree to dismantle the settlements that Israel had established on the West Bank or to accept the principle of Palestinian self-determination. Sensitive to PLO charges that Egypt would eventually sell out the Palestinians at Camp David, Sadat packed his bags and prepared to fly home to Cairo. Hoping to avert a monumental diplomatic fiasco, U.S. officials drafted tough new peace-for-land language regarding the West Bank and East Jerusalem that placated Sadat but nearly sent Begin packing. For a brief moment even Carter seemed ready to pack up and come down from the mountain empty-handed. "The best thing for us to do, to salvage what we could, would be to refuse to sign any document with either country," he told Cyrus Vance on 15 September, "just to terminate the talks and announce that we had all done our best and failed."[103]

Thirteen days after the summit began, however, Carter managed to broker an eleventh-hour compromise that appeared to send everyone home relatively happy. Sadat and Begin reluctantly accepted a framework for peace that called for the Israelis to withdraw from the Sinai, for the Egyptians to negotiate a formal treaty ending hostilities with Israel, and for both sides to work for "the resolution of the Palestinian problem in all its respects" during a five-year transitional period. Without using words such as "homeland" or "autonomy," Carter's compromise language did "recognize the legitimate rights of the Palestinian people" and did provide "for the elected representatives of the inhabitants of the West Bank and Gaza to decide how they shall govern themselves."[104] Carter believed that he had resolved the most controversial matter—whether or not the Israelis would continue to expand their presence on the West Bank— through bilateral negotiations with Begin. According to William Quandt, a key member of the U.S. negotiating team, Begin agreed to send Carter a side letter on the West Bank confirming that "after the signing of the framework and during the negotiations, no new Israeli settlements will be established in this area."[105]

The ink was hardly dry on the Camp David Accords, however, before Carter had a sinking feeling that the Israelis had not bargained in good faith. During the weeks after the summit meeting, Begin moved swiftly toward a formal peace agreement with Sadat but backtracked on Palestinian autonomy. "It is obvious," Carter observed as early as 8 November 1978, "that the Israelis want a separate treaty with Egypt; they want to keep the West Bank and Gaza permanently." Once Israel and Egypt had signed their peace treaty on 26 March 1979, Begin resumed building Jewish settlements and refused to discuss autonomy until the Palestinians recognized Israeli sovereignty over the West Bank. This did not sit well with the chief architect of the Camp David Accords. "We were opposed to any Israeli settlements in the occupied territories," Carter recalled in his memoirs. "We considered them to be illegal and an obstacle to peace."[106]

Far from halting the growth of Jewish settlements in the occupied territories, Carter's complaints merely sparked charges from members of his own party that he was selling Israel out, never good news during an election year. By the time Begin paid his last visit to the Carter White House in April 1980, a peace-for-land deal between the Israelis and the Palestinians seemed as remote as ever. "The Camp David accords had now become almost like the Bible, with the words and phrases taking on a special importance," Carter observed several years later. "The problem was that the actual words—such as 'autonomy,' 'security,' Palestinian rights,' and even 'West Bank'—had different meanings for each of us and those we represented."[107] Disheartened that these words seemed to mean so little to his visitor, Carter must have been tempted during his last year in office ruefully to paraphrase Abba Eban, one of the Israeli prime minister's most outspoken critics: Menachem Begin never missed an opportunity to miss an opportunity.

Teaching Yasser to Say Uncle: Reagan, Shultz, and the PLO

Israel's staunchest supporters in the United States did not miss the opportunity to defeat Jimmy Carter in November 1980 by casting their ballots for Ronald Reagan. As the California Republican positioned himself for a run at the White House during the late 1970s, he had made it no secret that he regarded the creation of Israel as the fulfillment of a biblical prophecy and as atonement for the monstrous crimes of the Holocaust. Nor did Reagan conceal his doubts about Palestinian autonomy, which he worried might enable "bloodthirsty fanatics" inside the PLO and its splinter groups to escalate their terrorist crusade against the Jewish state.[108]

During his first eighteen months in office Reagan implicitly repudiated Carter's commitment to Palestinian autonomy on the West Bank. When reporters asked Reagan on 2 February 1981 how he felt about Israeli settlements in the occupied territories, for example, he replied, "I disagreed when the previous Administration referred to them as illegal, they're not illegal." Insisting that U.N. Resolution 242 "leaves the West Bank open to all people—Arab and Israeli alike," Reagan dismissed Arafat's call for Israel's withdrawal by remarking that "I never thought that the P.L.O. had ever been elected by the Palestinians." Convinced that neither Reagan nor Begin would ever implement those sections of the Camp David Accords calling for Palestinian self-determination, terrorists such as Abu Nidal spilled still more blood during the autumn of 1981 while Muslim extremists assassinated Anwar Sadat on 6 October for betraying the Arab cause and accepting a separate peace with Israel.[109]

These developments merely strengthened the hand of Alexander Haig, Reagan's gruff and opinionated secretary of state, who regarded Israel as America's strongest asset in the battle against international terrorism. Haig likened radical Palestinian groups to "so many political time bombs" that, thanks to the Kremlin, "possessed the means to destabilize through terror" the entire Middle East. Eager to bring the Israelis into an anti-Soviet strategic consensus with Arab moderates, Haig acquiesced to Begin's plans for more settlements on the West Bank and did little to discourage Ariel Sharon, Israel's ultraexpansionist minister of defense, from invading Lebanon in June 1982 to root out the PLO infrastructure.[110]

While Haig and Reagan hoped that Israel would succeed in decapitating the PLO and demolishing its network of terrorist bases in Lebanon, they also worried that the size and scope of the Israeli invasion would convince Arab leaders that Begin and Sharon were more interested in the spoils of war than the fruits of peace. Washington began to press the Israelis to turn their attention from the battlefield to the peace table in mid-July, when George Shultz replaced Secretary of State Haig, who had sent Reagan one too many letters of resignation during a turf battle with the NSC staff. Shultz had little sympathy for the PLO, whose bargaining tactics were "all too vague and slippery." But he was no more enamored of the Israelis, whose adventure in Lebanon had left them "in tough shape around the world" and whose leaders needed to approach the Palestinian issue in a manner "consistent with the Camp David Accords."[111]

The nature of the approach that Washington preferred came more clearly into focus once Yasser Arafat and 8,500 of his followers departed Beirut for Tunis in late August. "With the shooting stopped," Ronald Reagan recalled in his memoirs, "I regarded this moment in the explosive history of the Middle East as a possible golden opportunity to make a fresh start toward achieving a long-term settlement of the region's problems."[112] George Shultz agreed wholeheartedly. "When the last ship sails out of the port of Beirut with the last PLO fighter on board," he told his senior advisers, "we must be ready to move on the larger Palestinian issue."[113] Convinced that "peace would never come to the Middle East as long as the occupied territories remained under the permanent political control of Israel," Reagan and Shultz unveiled a "land for peace" proposal on 1 September 1982. Combining elements of U.N. Resolution 242 and the Camp David Accords, the Reagan Plan called for Israel to withdraw its troops from the occupied territories and freeze its settlements there in exchange for PLO recognition of the Jewish state's right to exist. As for the sensitive matter of Palestinian autonomy, the Reagan Plan proposed that the Arabs of the West Bank and Gaza be granted self-government "in association with Jordan."[114]

The reaction to the Reagan Plan was decidedly mixed. "The Saudis, Egyptians, Moroccans and PLO all were reported to be positive and upbeat," Shultz recalled a decade later. Although the Jordanians, who had the most at stake among the Arabs, were publicly noncommittal, privately they were ecstatic. "King [Hussein] is very interested," Assistant Secretary of State Nicholas Veliotes assured Shultz; "it's just that he has to cover his ass."[115] The Israelis, on the other hand, were negative and up in arms. "We have wiped the PLO from the scene," Israeli ambassador Moshe Arens told U.S. officials after getting wind of the Reagan Plan in late August. "Don't you Americans now pick the PLO up, dust it off, and give it artificial respiration."[116] A few days later Menachem Begin sent Reagan a blistering "Dear Ron" letter rejecting the land-for-peace formula as sacrilege. "What some call the West Bank, Mr. President, is Judea and Samaria," Begin thundered. Fifteen years ago "we liberated with God's help that portion of our homeland," he added, and it "will never again" be part of any state but Israel.[117]

Within a fortnight the consequences of Begin's rejection of the Reagan Plan and his demonization of the Palestinians were manifested in gruesome fashion, not on the West Bank but, rather, in the Sabra and Shatilla refugee camps in West Beirut. Home to thousands of Palestinians who had fled Jordan in September 1970, the camps had been hotbeds of PLO activity before Arafat and his commandos departed for Tunis in August 1982. Suspect in the eyes of Begin and Sharon, whose troops ringed the camps, the refugees were despised by the Lebanese Phalangists, right-wing Christian extremists who were loosely allied with Israel. On 17 September Israeli officers permitted 1,500 Phalangists to enter Sabra and Shatilla, where they butchered 800 to 1,000 unarmed Palestinians, many of whom were women and children. U.S. diplomat Morris Draper pleaded with Ariel Sharon to restrain the Phalangists, but to no avail. "They can kill the terrorists," Sharon replied coldly. "But if they don't, we will." Once word of the massacre spread, however, Israeli officials disclaimed any responsibility for the killings and warned Washington that any American claims to the contrary "will be a shadow across the U.S.-Israeli relationship."[118]

Appalled by the carnage at Sabra and Shatilla and stunned by Israel's disclaimer, Secretary of State Shultz did not mince words when he met with Moshe Arens two days later. "Face the facts," he growled at the Israeli ambassador. "You bear responsibility."[119] Although Begin branded such remarks "a blood libel," the judicial commission that investigated the massacre ultimately agreed with Shultz. Likening the killings to anti-Semitic pogroms, Israeli chief justice Yitzhak Kahan, who headed the commission, reminded Begin in February 1983 that "the Jewish public's stand has always been that the responsibility for such deeds falls not only on those who rioted and committed atrocities but also on those who were responsible for safety and public order, who could have prevented the disturbances and did not." Insisting that Israeli officials should have known "that the Phalangists would commit massacres and pogroms against inhabitants of the camps," the Kahan commission recommended that Ariel Sharon step down as minister of defense.[120]

Despite Sharon's departure from the cabinet in mid-February and Begin's own resignation seven months later, the Reagan Plan was dead and the Israeli-Palestinian peace process remained in suspended animation throughout 1983 and for several years thereafter. The stalemate stemmed in part from the stubbornness of Israel's new prime minister, Yitzhak Shamir, who was more adamantly opposed to trading land for peace than was his predecessor. But even had Shamir been open to compromise, the Reagan administration would have balked at pleading the Palestinian case during the mid-1980s, when terrorists such as Abu Nidal were hijacking airliners and cruise ships and bombing airports and discos with as little remorse as the Phalangist militiamen at Sabra and Shatilla. Indeed, when Israeli warplanes bombed PLO headquarters in Tunis in October 1985 to retaliate for recent terrorist incidents, George Shultz privately confessed that Yasser Arafat and his comrades had finally gotten what they deserved.[121]

In the end, however, neither Yitzhak Shamir nor Yasser Arafat rekindled Washington's interest in the stalled peace process but, rather, a nameless band of Palestinian teenagers who hurled stones and Molotov cocktails at Israeli troops in the Gaza Strip on 8 December 1987, igniting the "Intifada," an Arabic word that means "shaking off." Twenty years after tanks marked with the Star of David had first rolled into the occupied territories, restless students and shopkeepers from Gaza to the West Bank bypassed the PLO and launched their own grassroots struggle to shake off Israeli rule. "The uprising was not 'led,'" George Shultz remarked in his memoirs, "but seemed rather to 'explode' in a kind of spontaneous combustion." Thanks to satellite technology, Israel's brutal attempts to control the explosion soon became the lead story on the nightly news.[122]

As the death toll from the Intifada approached 500, the Reagan administration pressed both sides to stop fighting and start talking about a peace-for-land deal. Insisting that "Israel's brutal crackdown was doing great damage to its own interests," George Shultz privately urged Shamir in January 1988 to "halt expansion of settlements in the occupied territories" and to hold free elections on the West Bank for a "Palestinian self-governing authority" within one year. Insisting that "the PLO has a reality problem," he warned two leaders of the Intifada later that same month that the Palestinians must also be prepared to compromise. "Until the PLO accepts Israel's right to exist and Resolution 242, and until the PLO renounces the use of terrorism," Shultz declared that the United States would never recognize Arafat's organization as a legitimate negotiating partner.[123]

Although neither side was eager at first to embrace the "formula of territory for peace," as the Intifada dragged on from weeks to months, the Israelis and the PLO were once again overtaken by events that gradually made Shultz's proposal look more attractive. During the spring of 1988 the Israelis reported that the Palestinian uprising seemed stronger and better organized, which they attributed to the emergence of the homegrown Islamic Resistance Movement, or Harakat al-Muqawama al-Islamiyya, better known by its acronym Hamas, the Arabic word for "zeal." Inspired by Egypt's Muslim Brotherhood, the leaders of Hamas condemned Israel as the mortal enemy of Islam; denounced the PLO as corrupt, secular, and out of touch with the situation in the occupied territories; and vowed to wage a jihad against both. Deeply troubled by the spread of militant Islam among his many Palestinian subjects, King Hussein suddenly relinquished all Jordanian claims to the West Bank on 31 July 1988, dashing Israeli hopes that the Arab thirst for self-determination might be slaked by defining Jordan as Palestine. Once Hamas unveiled a charter proclaiming that "giving up any part of the homeland is like giving up part of the religious faith itself," some Israelis and many Americans began to regard Arafat's PLO as the lesser of two evils.[124]

Over the objections of the ever suspicious Yitzhak Shamir, George Shultz dealt the United States into a game of "high stakes poker with the PLO" during the final months of the Reagan administration. With Hamas challenging the PLO's leadership inside the occupied territories and with the Israelis curbing his options on the outside, Yasser Arafat informed Shultz through Swedish intermediaries that in exchange for direct negotiations with the United States, the PLO would agree to Shultz's peace-for-land formula and would also accept Israel's right to exist. Getting the slippery Arafat to acknowledge this publicly and renounce that part of the PLO's charter calling for the destruction of Israel took the better part of six weeks. "In one place Arafat was saying, 'Unc, unc, unc' and in another he was saying, 'cle, cle, cle,'" Shultz told Reagan twelve days before Christmas, "but nowhere will he yet bring himself to say, 'Uncle.'"[125]

On 14 December 1988, however, Yasser Arafat finally said the magic word. During a press conference in Geneva, Switzerland, he confirmed that the PLO "undertakes to live in peace with Israel" and that "it condemns individual, group and State terrorism in all its forms." Shultz was "glad to have forced some important words out of Arafat's mouth" and was hopeful that the new U.S. dialogue with the PLO would yield a peace-for-land settlement. So was Vice-President George Bush, who had been monitoring the State Department's poker game with the PLO closely since hitting the political jackpot himself on election day. "It's terrific progress," Bush told Shultz during the waning days of the Reagan administration. "I will support a dialogue. I'm all for it."[126]

But Yitzhak Shamir and Moshe Arens, Israel's new foreign minister, charged that George Shultz was dealing from the bottom of the deck. Blunt as ever, Shamir had warned Shultz in mid-December that "there will be great difficulty in our relationship if the U.S. moves to open dialogue with the PLO."[127] Arens, an Israeli hawk who had cultivated close ties with AIPAC during his brief stay in Washington five years earlier, rejected the idea of "land for peace" on the West Bank as appeasement of the Arabs.[128] Like Begin and Sharon before them, Shamir and Arens had no interest in territorial compromise with the Palestinians, whether under the guise of U.N. Resolution 242, the Reagan Plan, or the Shultz initiative. The Intifada merely prompted expansionists like Shamir to create more Jewish settlements in Judaea and Samaria as the surest way to promote security in the land of Israel. Having labored long and hard to win PLO acceptance of Israel's right to exist, however, by late 1988 and early 1989 top U.S. policymakers regarded Israel's quest for more land on the West Bank as the biggest single obstacle to peace.

From Madrid to Oslo: Bush, Clinton, and the Path to Peace

During George Bush's single term in office, the end of the Cold War and America's triumph in the Persian Gulf seemed to clear the way for peace between Arab and Jew. Bush's first encounter with the Palestinian-Israeli problem had come in 1971 when, during a brief stint as Nixon's ambassador to the United Nations, he condemned Jewish settlements in Arab East Jerusalem and warned that "an Israeli occupation policy made up of unilaterally determined practices cannot help promote a just and lasting peace."[129] According to one Israeli diplomat, Vice-President Bush "seemed very reserved about Israel's positions and policies," was "extremely critical" of its invasion of Lebanon in 1982, and actually favored imposing sanctions unless Begin and Sharon withdrew their troops immediately.[130] During his first months in the Oval Office, President Bush broadened the U.S. dialogue with the PLO and pressed for a comprehensive peace settlement based on "security for Israel, the end of the occupation, and achievement of Palestinian political rights."[131]

The most vocal advocate of such a settlement inside the Bush administration, however, was Secretary of State James Baker, who complained that the Israelis were far more interested in land than peace. "Today, the rocks are flying and the blood is flowing—bad blood—between the Palestinians and the Israelis," he remarked during Senate confirmation hearings on 17 January.[132] Once Baker settled in at Foggy Bottom, he and Bush would struggle to prevent Israel's territorial ambitions from knocking the peace process off track. "We both believed there would never be peace in the Middle East," Baker recalled several years later, "until Israel was willing to accept the principle of exchanging territory for peace as embodied in United Nations Resolution 242."[133] Secretary of State Baker signaled the Bush administration's mounting displeasure with Israel during a well-publicized speech on 22 May. "For Israel, now is the time to lay aside once and for all the unrealistic vision of a Greater Israel," Baker told 1,200 AIPAC members at their annual political conference in Washington. "Forswear annexation. Stop settlement activity. Allow schools to reopen," he pleaded, and "reach out to the Palestinians as neighbors who deserve political rights." Baker's remarks were greeted by months of stony silence from both Israel and its American friends.[134]

Convinced that U.S. diplomatic leverage would never produce the desired changes in Israel's policies, the Palestinians took matters into their own hands during the spring of 1990. On 30 May two boatloads of Palestine Liberation Front terrorists, longtime rivals of the PLO, were intercepted by Israeli naval forces patrolling the coast near Tel Aviv. After Arafat refused to condemn the operation, Bush reluctantly suspended the U.S.-PLO dialogue on 20 June. The PLO's ill-advised support for Saddam Hussein's Persian Gulf adventure later that summer gave U.S. policymakers an additional incentive not to resume the dialogue. Dismissing comparisons between Iraq's invasion of Kuwait and Israel's occupation of the West Bank as specious, Bush reminded reporters in the wake of Operation Desert Storm that Arafat and his followers had "bet on the wrong horse for the wrong reasons."[135]

Once the Bush administration was able to turn its attention from waging war in the Persian Gulf to forging peace in the Holy Land, it did not bet on the PLO but, rather, on West Bank Palestinian moderates such as Hanan Ashrawi. A middle-aged professor of English literature at Bir Zeit University on the West Bank, Ashrawi had sprung to prominence during the Intifada as an outspoken advocate of Palestinian rights and a vociferous critic of Palestinian terrorism.[136] When Jim Baker arrived in East Jerusalem in July 1991, he asked whether Ashrawi would be willing to serve on a joint Palestinian-Jordanian delegation to the Middle East peace conference he hoped to convene in the fall. She balked at first, pointing out that most Arabs still recognized the PLO as the sole legitimate representative of the Palestinian people. The Israelis were not yet ready to sit down with the PLO, Baker replied, but they might be willing to talk with West Bank Palestinian leaders, which would be a major breakthrough. "You know as well as I do that people have said that Palestinians never pass up an opportunity to pass up an opportunity," Baker reminded Ashrawi. "Please don't pass up this one."[137]

While Ashrawi pondered Baker's proposal, Baker drove to West Jerusalem to make his pitch to Yitzhak Shamir. Negotiating a peace-for-land settlement with Palestinians was almost as unthinkable for the Israeli prime minister in

July 1991 as it had been two years earlier. "There's a lot of suspicion in Israel that the U.S. is determined to force Israel from the territories," Shamir observed. "There's a lot of suspicion in the United States," Baker retorted, "that you aren't serious about negotiating peace." Emphasizing that, for the first time, all of Israel's neighbors, including its longtime nemesis Syria, were willing to begin face-to-face peace talks in the absence of Yasser Arafat's PLO, Baker told Shamir that recent developments in the Middle East were "nothing short of the breakthrough that you have sought for decades."[138] After carefully reviewing their options, in late July the Israelis agreed to attend Baker's peace conference, the West Bank Palestinians followed suit in early August, and three months later both sides took their seats across from each other at Madrid.

In substantive terms the Madrid Conference proved anticlimactic. One by one the Arab and Israeli delegates stood and delivered stock speeches staking out their respective negotiating positions. George Bush uttered a ritual incantation endorsing security for Israel and justice for the Palestinians and reminded both sides that "territorial compromise is essential for peace." But no deals were struck, no wrongs were righted, and no land changed hands. Yet in symbolic terms the proceedings at Madrid were breathtaking, for they placed the Palestinian question squarely at the center of the peace process. In just a half-hour on 31 October, Palestinian delegate Haidar Abdel-Shafi managed to humanize his people in the eyes of the world in an emotional speech drafted by Hanan Ashrawi. "We, the people of Palestine," Abdel-Shafi began, "have long harbored a yearning for peace and a dream of justice and freedom." Insisting that "the settlements must stop now," he stressed that "peace cannot be waged while Palestinian land is confiscated in myriad ways and the status of the occupied territories is being decided each day by bulldozers and barbed wire." Whether the Israelis wanted to admit it or not, Abdel-Shafi thundered, the Palestinians had a right to self-determination. "My homeland is not a suitcase," he declared in the words of the Palestinian poet Mahmoud Darwish, "and I am no traveler."[139]

Eight months after Abdel-Shafi recited Darwish's words in Madrid, *National Geographic* carried a thirty-page photoessay titled "Who Are the Palestinians?" that brought the poet's message into U.S. living rooms. Although a few of the photographs were in keeping with the magazine's earlier tradition of presenting Arabs as exotic orientals, most of them depicted the Palestinians as disturbingly familiar: a PLO leader dressed in a double-breasted business suit, a teenager sporting a Philadelphia Phillies tee shirt, and a distraught young mother in an appliquéd blouse and knit skirt fainting at the feet of an Israeli soldier who resembled one of Darth Vader's imperial stormtroopers. Moreover, the text cataloged the enormous human costs of the Israeli occupation: forced relocation, widespread unemployment, and since the eruption of the Intifada, torture and deportation. "You know we Palestinians are civilized people," an old man told *National Geographic*, "but we are treated like aborigines." Yet even as the magazine gently made the case for a just and lasting peace based on territorial compromise, it reminded readers that the Palestinians were partially responsible for their own predicament. "With immaculate hindsight," Hanan Ashrawi confessed to a *National Geographic* writer, "the worst blunder we made was not to accept the partition of Palestine" four decades earlier, when the Israelis were ready to accept a "two state solution."[140]

By the spring of 1992 the Bush administration was worried that Israel might be on the verge of making the same kind of blunder. After learning in January that Yitzhak Shamir intended to construct 5,500 units of new housing in the occupied territories, Jim Baker recommended that the White House block legislation granting Israel $10 billion in loan guarantees needed to accommodate the recent influx of Soviet Jews. When Israel's friends on Capitol Hill floated a compromise in March that would have freed up $2 billion for 1992, Baker complained that this would enable Shamir "to keep building settlements at an expanded rate for at least another year," a development that "would drive the Arabs from the peace table."[141] George Bush agreed. "Settlements are counterproductive to peace," he told reporters on St. Patrick's Day, "and everybody knows that."[142] Privately the president "vowed to veto any loan guarantees legislation that did not include a freeze on all new settlements." Despite some last-minute maneuvering by AIPAC in the House and Senate, the foreign aid bill that Bush signed into law in mid-April contained no loan guarantees for Israel.[143]

Two months later Israeli voters weary of Yitzhak Shamir's feud with Washington voted his Likud coalition out of office and made Yitzhak Rabin prime minister. Labor's warrior-statesman soon proved far more open to territorial compromise than his predecessor had been. In mid-July Jim Baker flew to Israel, where Prime Minister Rabin agreed to suspend all new Jewish settlements in Gaza and the West Bank. He told Baker that "3.9 million Israeli Jews and a million Israeli Arabs should not have to mortgage their future because of the 100,000 settlers in the territories." The effect on Baker was electric. "I have just visited a different Israel," he told Bush on 21 July. Rabin was "reordering Israel's priorities away from the territories and to revitalizing Israel's economy." Although Rabin was not willing to consider wholesale Israeli withdrawal from the West Bank, he personally assured Bush during a mid-August meeting at the summer White House in Maine that "Arab lands in the territories would no longer be expropriated for settlements."[144]

Bush's pleasure at having kept the peace process on track was tempered, of course, when U.S. voters derailed his plans for a second term later that fall. The Republican incumbent's handling of the Israeli-Palestinian imbroglio, however, seems to have played almost no role in an election whose most memorable slogan was "It's the economy, stupid." In any case President Bill Clinton saw no reason to reverse course in the Middle East after he moved from the governor's mansion in Little Rock to the White House in January 1993. During Clinton's first months in office, Palestinian and Israeli negotiators continued to meet in Washington. Both sides, however, quickly concluded that the talks were going nowhere fast, in part because intense media attention inside the Beltway made secrecy impossible and in part because U.S. officials seemed to be afflicted with what one Palestinian diplomat later called "a Pygmalion complex" that did not sit well with either of America's headstrong pupils.[145]

Unpersuaded that the United States knew best, early in the new year Yitzhak Rabin and Yasser Arafat quietly set up their own secret back channel in Norway. By June and July Israel and the PLO were quietly edging toward a peace-for-land deal in the land of the midnight sun. Then, on 20 August 1993, Norwegian foreign Minister Johann Jurgen Holst confirmed that the two sides had reached a tentative agreement calling for the PLO officially to recognize Israel and renounce terrorism and for the Israelis to turn over the Gaza Strip and the West Bank town of Jericho to the new Palestinian Authority by the end of the year. Once full recognition and partial withdrawal were completed, Israel and the Palestinian Authority would commence negotiations on the final status of the rest of the West Bank, including the fate of the Jewish settlements and the future of Jerusalem. Three weeks later Prime Minister Rabin, Israeli foreign minister Shimon Peres, and PLO chairman Arafat signed the Oslo Accords in the White House Rose Garden.[146]

What stood out most during the ceremony on 13 September was not Arafat's stilted vow of reconciliation or Clinton's flowery benediction but, rather, Rabin's emotional prayer for peace. Israel and the PLO stood "on the eve of an opportunity, opportunity for peace and perhaps end of violence and war," the man whose troops had conquered the West Bank a quarter-century earlier declared to the world. Because "we are destined to live together on the same soil in the same land," Rabin told Arafat, "we who have fought against you, the Palestinians—we say to you today, in a loud and a clear voice: enough of blood and tears. Enough." Reminding everyone that too many Israelis and too many Palestinians had known the heartbreaking costs of war, Rabin declared that "we are today giving peace a chance."[147]

Sadly, not everyone heard Rabin's prayer or heeded his plea to trade land for peace as an act of faith. Claiming that Arafat had sold out at Oslo, Islamic extremists inside Hamas launched a holy war in late 1993 against both Israel and the fledgling Palestinian Authority, leaving a trail of bombs, blood, and broken bodies. Claiming that Rabin had sold out on the West Bank, Israeli extremists unleashed their own brutal campaign of terror against Palestinians from Hebron to Jerusalem in early 1994. When, against long odds, Israeli and Palestinian negotiators struck a deal eighteen months later that would have placed most but not all of the West Bank under control of the Palestinian Authority, still more blood flowed. On the evening of 4 November 1995 Yitzhak Rabin made his final plea for peace. "I waged war as long as there was no chance for peace," he told a huge crowd in downtown Tel Aviv, but somewhere between Madrid and Oslo "we found a partner for peace among the Palestinians—the P.L.O., which used to be an enemy." Emphasizing that "violence erodes the basis of Israeli democracy," Rabin expressed the hope that this rally would show the world "that the people of Israel want peace." Moments later he was shot dead by Yigal Amir, a twenty-five-year-old right-wing Israeli law student who evidently wanted something else.[148]

Rabin's assassination stunned most Israelis, shocked U.S. policymakers, and saddened many Palestinians. "We lost a great man who made the peace of the brave with us," Yasser Arafat wrote Rabin's widow, Leah, a few days later. "He was our partner."[149] Shimon Peres, who succeeded Rabin as prime minister, vowed to preserve and even to expand Israel's partnership with the PLO, but extremists on both sides thought otherwise. Advocates of Greater Israel, for whom any withdrawal from the West Bank was tantamount to treason, whispered that Rabin had been a traitor to Zionism, shouted that the Oslo Accords constituted nothing less than appeasement of the Arabs, and vowed to defeat Peres at the polls in the spring of 1996. Smelling blood, the underground Hamas movement saw to it that the election campaign was punctuated by bombs and bullets. They created a climate of fear and insecurity that prompted many voters to abandon Peres and his land-for-peace policy and to embrace instead Benjamin Netanyahu, a flamboyant expansionist who had succeeded Yitzhak Shamir as head of the Likud Party. When the votes were counted in late May, Netanyahu won a narrow victory that he interpreted as a mandate to slow down the peace process.[150]

Most Palestinians and many Americans watched and listened to Prime Minister Netanyahu closely, for they questioned whether he was committed to the principle of peace for land. Netanyahu's actions during his first year in office certainly did nothing to dispel those doubts. In September 1996 he agreed to open a tunnel for Jewish pilgrims under a sacred Muslim shrine in Jerusalem. Rioting erupted, and seventy Palestinians died. Then in March 1997 Netanyahu announced plans to build 6,500 units of new housing in what had once been Arab East Jerusalem. Hamas responded with a fresh wave of terror, bombing buses and sidewalk cafes and killing schoolgirls and tourists. Despite some harsh words from Bill Clinton, however, Netanyahu proved unwilling to accelerate Israel's withdrawal from the West Bank or to discuss the future of the

Holy City that both Israelis and Palestinians have claimed as their capital as long as anyone can remember.[151]

By the spring of 1998 Clinton and his inner circle were bracing for a diplomatic showdown with Netanyahu. With the White House insisting that Israel must return more of the West Bank to the Palestinians to keep the peace process alive, Hillary Clinton launched a trial balloon via satellite. "I think that it will be in the long-term interest of the Middle East," she told Arab and Israeli schoolchildren gathered in Switzerland on 5 May, "for Palestine to be a state." Emboldened by the First Lady's endorsement, Yasser Arafat used the fiftieth anniversary of "al-Nakba," the Arabic term for "catastrophe" that was for all Palestinians a code word for the creation of Israel, to press his claims for statehood. "We are not asking for the moon," he told a huge radio audience on 14 May. "We are asking to close the chapter of nakba once and for all, for the refugees to return, and build an independent Palestinian state on our land . . . just like other peoples." Ultimately, Arafat concluded, "we want to celebrate in our capital, holy Jerusalem."[152]

Netanyahu was not amused by what Secretary of State Madeline Albright termed Clinton's "wake-up call." Implying that the fate of the West Bank and the future of Jerusalem were nonnegotiable, he bluntly invited Washington to butt out. "I would not presume to tell the United States," Netanyahu observed on 15 May, "how to defend their bases in the Philippines or Europe at the height of the Cold War."[153] A month later he announced that Israel would extend its control over Har Homa and other disputed communities on the outskirts of Jerusalem. When Albright remarked tersely that this "was not helpful to the peace process," Netanyahu did not mince words. "Write this down," he told reporters on 21 June 1998: "You will see houses at Har Homa, many houses, by the year 2000."[154] Although Netanyahu insisted that "we are not trying to unravel the Oslo Accords," his repudiation of the peace-for-land concept that lay at the heart of the Israeli-Palestinian dialogue led many to worry that the new millennium would bring more war.[155]

To be sure, Netanyahu did sit down with Arafat four months later at the minisummit that Bill Clinton hosted on Maryland's Eastern Shore, and he did sign the Wye Memorandum pledging to turn another 13 percent of the West Bank over to the Palestinians by the end of the year. But Netanyahu's right-wing supporters greeted the new concessions with noisy vituperation, while his critics on the left insisted that he would never follow through on his pledge. "The state is mired in mud," Ehud Barak, who had succeeded Shimon Peres as head of the Labor Party, told reporters on 25 October 1998. "It's time to act toward early elections and establish a government that will start pulling us out."[156] Bristling at Barak's words, Netanyahu responded by "freezing" Israeli compliance with the Wye Memorandum six weeks later, setting the stage for a bitter electoral battle over whether or not to implement the peace-for-land formula.

When the ballots were counted on 23 May 1999, Ehud Barak won by a landslide, mainly because most Israelis seemed to want peace sooner rather than later and were willing to trade land to get it. A seasoned warrior with a pragmatic streak like his martyred mentor, Yitzhak Rabin, Prime Minister Barak did some hard bargaining with Lebanon and Syria during his first year in office. As it had for more than a half-century, however, the central issue remained how to engineer a just and equitable settlement between Israel and the Palestinians. Sensing an opportunity to resolve the matter once and for all, Clinton invited Barak and Arafat to Camp David in July 2000. Although Barak irritated U.S. officials by constantly haggling over details, he was at least willing to consider swapping land, including even a slice of Jerusalem, for peace. Arafat, on the other hand, refused to endorse any peace-for-land formula unless Israel agreed beforehand to return to its pre-1967 borders.[157]

When the summit talks deadlocked, both the United States and Israel blamed the Palestinians. "If the Israelis can make compromises and you can't, I should go home," Clinton snapped at Arafat. "You have been here fourteen days and said no to everything." Warning that "failure will mean the end of the peace process," the Arkansas Democrat threw up his hands and shouted, "Let's let hell break lose and live with the consequences."[158] Barak and his advisers shared Clinton's frustrations. "The ball is now in Arafat's court," Israeli cabinet secretary Yitzhak Herzog told reporters on 20 July. "My uncle Abba Eban once said that the Palestinians never miss a chance to miss a chance, and I hope and pray for all our children that they don't miss this one."[159] But White House Arab-Israeli specialist Robert Malley, who rode shotgun with Clinton at Camp David, contends that things were far more complicated. Refusing to hold Arafat solely responsible for the stalemate, Malley blames both sides and recently described the failed summit as "an opportunity that was missed by all, less by design than by mistake, more through miscalculation than through mischief."[160]

As Bill Clinton had feared, ten weeks after the mistakes and miscalculations at Camp David, all hell did break lose. On 28 September Ariel Sharon, who had succeeded Netanyahu as the leader of the Likud coalition, and 1,000 heavily armed Israeli police paid a well-publicized visit to the Jerusalem's Temple Mount hard by the Dome of the Rock and the Al-Aqsa mosque, among the holiest sites in Islam. The next day riots rocked the West Bank, and Israeli troops opened fire on Palestinian demonstrators, killing 4 and injuring 200. With the death toll spiraling ever upward, Bill Clinton sought to quell the violence during the waning days of his presidency by establishing a fact-finding commission headed by former senator George Mitchell, who had earlier helped broker a truce in Northern Ireland. After Israeli voters made Ariel Sharon their prime minister early in the new year, most U.S. policymakers agreed that the fact-finders faced some very long odds.

On 30 April 2001 the Mitchell commission handed Clinton's successor a report endorsing the peace-for-land formula so central to U.S. policy for a half-century. Noting that more than 500 people had died and more than 10,000 had been injured since the start of the "Al-Aqsa Intifada," the report concluded that the bloodshed would never stop unless both sides took bold steps to rebuild mutual confidence. The Palestinian Authority must "make a 100 percent effort to prevent terrorist operations and to punish perpetrators," Mitchell and his colleagues insisted, and Israel must "freeze all settlement activity, including the 'natural growth' of existing settlements."[161] George W. Bush and his top advisers were quietly pushing ahead with such confidence-building measures when Osama bin Laden launched his airborne attack on the United States on 11 September in the name of Islamic salvation and Palestinian liberation. Despite loud protests from Ariel Sharon, U.S. officials remained committed to the principle of peace for land. "If we ever get into the Mitchell process where we can start discussing a political solution in the Middle East," Bush told reporters during a press conference one month after the destruction of the World Trade Center, "I believe there ought to be a Palestinian state . . . [that] recognizes the right of Israel to exist and will treat Israel with respect, and will be peaceful on her borders."[162]

Although the cycle of Palestinian protests and Israeli crackdowns degenerated during late 2001 into a bloody spiral of terror and reprisal, many Arabs and Jews continued to hope that, with America's help, they could resolve their differences and achieve a lasting agreement. In the end, of course, real peace will depend on the willingness of both Israelis and Palestinians to make further diplomatic acts of faith, but the two sides would never have come this far without U.S. prodding. Every administration from Harry Truman's to George W. Bush's has insisted that trading peace for land offered the best opportunity for a lasting settlement. From 1947 to 1967 it was the Arabs who never missed an opportunity to miss an opportunity, rejecting the partition of Palestine; dismissing initiatives such as the Clapp mission, Operation Alpha, and the Johnson Plan; and vowing to drive the Jews into the sea. After the Six Day War, however, it was the Israelis who proved increasingly unwilling to trade land for peace, whether under the guise of U.N. Resolution 242, the Camp David Accords, or the Reagan Plan.

Only with the opening of a direct dialogue at Oslo did both sides seize the opportunity that had seemed so obvious to so many for so long. Benjamin Netanyahu's born-again expansionism nearly derailed the peace process during the late 1990s and helped stimulate the born-again PLO rejectionism that led to stalemate at Camp David, violence on the West Bank, and terror in the streets of Jerusalem early in the new millennium. Unless Ariel Sharon and Yasser Arafat can put that process back on track and implement the peace-for-land formula in all its complex simplicity, the children of Isaac and the children of Ishmael will surely continue to lay down their lives.

Did not the Pope send all the Princes of Christendom upon a Fool's Errand to gain the Holy Land?
—Edmund Hickergill, *Priestcraft* (1721)

I [have] told the American people many times . . . that this is a struggle that's going to take a while, that it's not one of these Kodak moments. There is no moment to this; this is a long struggle and a different kind of war.—George W. Bush, 7 November 2001

Fool's Errand or Kodak Moment?

America and the Middle East at the Dawn of the Twenty-first Century

Six weeks into 1945 the uss *Murphy* peeled away from picket duty in the Red Sea and made a beeline for the sleepy Arabian port of Jidda, where King Ibn Saud clambered aboard, accompanied by his sons, his favorite servants, and seven of his sheep. While the Saudis lounged under a tent pitched beneath the forecastle, the U.S. destroyer headed north to the Egyptian coast, glided quietly into the Suez Canal, and made its way to the Great Bitter Lake at the waterway's midpoint. There the *Murphy* slid alongside the uss *Quincy*, a heavy cruiser whose most important passenger, Franklin D. Roosevelt, was returning from a summit meeting at Yalta with Josef Stalin and Winston Churchill and had stopped in Egypt expressly to pay his respects to the patriarch of the House of Saud. Moored amidst sand dunes and still water, FDR and Ibn Saud dined on fresh mutton, traded stories about their physical infirmities, and chatted for five hours about oil, Palestine, and the fate of empires, subjects that would preoccupy their successors for decades to come.

Fifty-five years later and 1,500 miles to the south-southeast, the USS *Cole* pulled into the bustling harbor at Aden, a Yemeni port that had once been a British crown colony. Just after breakfast on 12 October 2000, while the captain and crew were refueling for the final leg of their voyage to the Persian Gulf, two terrorists steered a small boat filled with high explosives alongside and detonated their cargo, killing seventeen U.S. sailors and nearly sending the guided-missile frigate to the bottom. No group claimed responsibility, but U.S. intelligence gradually narrowed the list of likely suspects. After ruling out Palestinian radicals unhappy with the American-backed peace process and Iraqi operatives dispatched by Saddam Hussein to settle old scores, the CIA zeroed in on Islamic extremist Osama bin Laden, whose al-Qaeda would become synonymous with terrorism after 11 September 2001.

Separated by a half-century, these two episodes at opposite ends of the Red Sea symbolized how much had changed in America's relations with the Middle East from the day FDR welcomed Ibn Saud aboard the USS *Quincy* to the day al-Qaeda's boatload of bombs tore through the hull of the USS *Cole*. A region that had figured only marginally in U.S. strategic calculations in February 1945 was the center of national attention by late 2001. How could Ibn Saud's realm, for so long the home of some of America's staunchest friends in the Arab world, also prove to be the birthplace of America's blood enemy Osama bin Laden and almost all the hijackers who destroyed the World Trade Center and attacked the Pentagon? Why were Uncle Sam's good intentions in the Middle East so often repaid in the currency of evil? Over the years many Americans came to suspect that their country had set off on a fool's errand whose principal outcome was a Kodak moment.

Given the relatively low U.S. profile from the Eastern Mediterranean to the Persian Gulf at the end of the Second World War, few Americans could have dreamed that the United States would have so much at stake there in the decades ahead. Yet within ten years of V-J Day the nature of U.S. interests in the Middle East had come into sharp focus, as had the policies that U.S. officials deemed necessary to promote and protect them. The black gold that lay beneath Ibn Saud's realm and neighboring lands was critical for the political and economic well-being of America's Western European allies. The birth of the Jewish state—democratic and pro-Western but militarily vulnerable— evoked strong support among key segments of the American public and posed diplomatic dilemmas for U.S. policymakers. The emerging Cold War rivalry with the Soviet Union highlighted the importance of the doctrine of containment for the security of the Middle East as Britain reluctantly began its slow-motion retreat from empire east of Suez. Given this constellation of U.S. interests, the national aspirations of Arabs and Iranians were usually dismissed in Truman's and Eisenhower's Washington as manifestations of oil-inspired economic arrogance, anti-Semitic rabble-rousing, or oriental affinity for revolutionary despotism of the sort made infamous by the Kremlin. More often than not, the best antidote for nationalist revolutions from Cairo to Tehran seemed to be a blend of covert action and modernization theory, occasionally punctuated by military intervention.

The series of Middle East crises that began at Suez in 1956 and stretched into the 1990s, however, slowly forced U.S. officials to reevaluate all of their assumptions and, eventually, their policies as well. Gamal Abdel Nasser's seizure of the Suez Canal simultaneously exposed the hollowness of Britain's power in the Muslim world and the folly of America's belief that Arab nationalism could be handled most effectively by manipulation and modernization. Although the Eisenhower administration openly criticized British colonialism during the mid-1950s, Ike was also skeptical of Nasser, whom he regarded as one part Hitler and one part Saladin. Yet by the end of the decade the Egyptian leader looked better and better, in part because other Arab radicals, particularly Iraq's Abdel Karim Qassim, looked worse and worse, but mainly because Nasser's call for nonalignment in the Cold War suggested that he was not a Soviet stooge. The Kennedy administration took Nasser's neutralism seriously enough to wager a half-billion dollars in U.S. aid that he would eventually abandon the locomotive of revolution for the bulldozer of economic development. John F. Kennedy and his successor, Lyndon Johnson, ultimately lost that bet in 1967 when Nasser veered back toward the Kremlin on the eve of the Six Day War.

Nasser's change of heart came as no surprise to the Israelis, who set out to cut him down to size and emerged from the 1967 crisis as the big winners. Israel's stunning victory in the Six Day War marked the turning point in its relations with the United States. Prior to June 1967 U.S. policymakers regarded the Jewish state as a liability, partly because of the complicated situation on Capitol Hill, where Israel had powerful friends on both sides of the aisle who believed that disputes over foreign policy did not stop at the water's edge, and partly because of the complicated situation in the Middle East, where Israel had implacable Arab foes on all sides who believed that "the friend of my enemy is my enemy." By defeating three Arab armies and seizing Gaza, the West Bank, and the Golan Heights, the Israelis positioned themselves to become a strategic asset at precisely the moment when the debacle in Southeast Asia was tempting the United States to limit its involvement in the Middle East and elsewhere in the Third World. Richard Nixon and Henry Kissinger embraced this special relationship after the Jewish state helped them help King Hussein save his throne during the 1970 Black September crisis in Jordan. As the new decade unfolded, Nixon's America had cast its lot with Israel, a staunch opponent of revolutionary Arab nationalism whose arsenal was reported to include nuclear weapons.

That America's Israeli asset also carried strategic liabilities became obvious in the wake of the 1973 October War, when angry Arab members of OPEC embargoed oil shipments to the United States and touched off an energy crisis. During the quarter-century since FDR had greeted Ibn Saud at the Great Bitter Lake, America's energy policy had been predicated on the availability of a seemingly inexhaustible supply of low-cost petroleum made available via sweetheart deals between U.S. multinationals and friendly Muslim states such as Saudi Arabia. Although U.S. policymakers at first assumed that most Persian Gulf crude would flow to Western Europe, U.S. consumption skyrocketed during the 1960s, and demand soon outstripped supply. The 1973 Middle East crisis merely provided OPEC with a convenient occasion to do something that America's growing energy dependence was making ever more likely: wrest control of both price and output from the Western oil firms. Despite some brash talk about storming the oil fields, in the end U.S. policymakers acquiesced and subsidized exploration for new sources of crude outside OPEC's orbit, chasing the pipe dream of synthetic fuels and ratcheting thermostats down and miles per gallon up.

Americans had just about resigned themselves to paying more for less when a political earthquake rocked Iran, the only Persian Gulf producer to defy the OPEC embargo and ship oil to the United States after the October War. The Iranian crisis of 1978 stunned Washington, where the Nixon, Ford, and Carter administrations had applauded the shah's efforts to modernize his realm through a top-down White Revolution financed by petrodollars. Although the most obvious short-term impact of the Islamic upheaval that swept the shah from power in January 1979 was another quadrupling of oil prices, over the long haul the most lasting consequence was the rejection of modernization and westernization by Ayatollah Khomeini, whose theocratic worldview was antithetical to the secular democratic creed that the United States had been preaching in the Third World for more than a generation. Because free elections, free markets, and free people had long been articles of faith among U.S. policymakers and the social scientists who frequently advised them, their rejection by Islamic radicals constituted a fundamental challenge to the core beliefs that shaped American relations with the Middle East. By the late 1980s the conflict between traditional Islam and modern America had become so intense that some pundits spoke of "a clash of civilizations."

Meanwhile, the Kremlin was enduring its own version of the clash of civilizations a thousand miles to the northwest in the mountains of Afghanistan, where the Red Army battled Muslim guerrillas seeking to overthrow the pro-Soviet government of Mohammed Najibullah. Although both the Carter and the Reagan administrations feared that Afghanistan would become a launching pad for a Russian drive to the Persian Gulf, Moscow had intervened in Kabul for the same reason that Washington had meddled in Tehran: an aversion to radical Islam. The result was the same: absolute chaos. The costs of the Afghan adventure as measured in blood, rubles, and prestige eventually grew so high that Soviet premier Mikhail Gorbachev pulled out in early 1989 and abandoned the feckless Najibullah. The Kremlin's about-face in Afghanistan did not go unnoticed inside the Soviet bloc. By the end of the year the Berlin Wall had come down; the peoples of Poland, Hungary, and Romania had risen up; and the Muslim population of Russia's Central Asian empire had embraced resurgent Islam. The global implications of the crisis of 1989 would only become apparent in the autumn of 1991, when the Soviet Union collapsed like a house of cards, ending more than forty years of Cold War and severing Russian ties with Arab radicals such as Syria's Hafez al-Assad and Iraq's Saddam Hussein.

The crisis in the Persian Gulf that began with the Iraqi invasion of Kuwait in August 1990 and ended with America's smashing victory in Operation Desert Storm seven months later would almost certainly have played out very differently had it occurred during the height of the Cold War. Whether Kremlin leaders undistracted by multiple crises closer to home could have restrained Saddam Hussein is an open question, but few analysts doubt that the Bush administration would have had far fewer options had the Soviets chosen to station advisers in Baghdad or to resupply the Iraqi army. While snatching Kuwait back from the grasp of a tinpot dictator played well on Main Street, what mattered most to the policymaking elite inside the Beltway was, as George Bush put it just a few hours after the shooting stopped in February 1991, that the United States had kicked the Vietnam Syndrome once and for all. To be sure, military intervention still carried enormous risks, as the botched Operation Restore Hope in Somalia proved in 1993, and Bill Clinton remained more reluctant than his predecessor to put American GIs in harm's way. But the hundred days' war that the United States and its NATO allies waged in the spring of 1999 to drive Serbia's Slobodan Milosevic out of Kosovo seemed to confirm the lessons learned eight years earlier in the Persian Gulf: go in big, quick, and dirty.

In short, a series of military confrontations, nationalist revolutions, and cultural upheavals extending from the Suez crisis through the Gulf War altered the political and diplomatic topography of the Middle East profoundly. To be sure, the basic outline of U.S. interests in the region (oil, Israel, and containment) remained relatively unchanged from the 1940s through the 1990s. But the policies that flowed from those interests at the end of the twentieth century would have been largely unrecognizable not only to Franklin Roosevelt and Harry Truman but probably to Lyndon Johnson and Richard Nixon as well. Consider oil. From the Roosevelt through the Nixon eras the center of gravity for the global petroleum order had been the Middle East, where U.S. diplomats and business executives worked together to ensure that a steady stream of cheap oil flowed to Western consumers. The rise of OPEC turned the tables during the 1970s and tilted the balance of economic power from the multinational oil firms to the producing states. By the mid-1990s, however, OPEC's clout was waning and the world was awash in petroleum, thanks not only to steadily rising output from the North Sea to West Africa but also to a flood of crude from the Transcaucasian oil fields, where post-Soviet regimes in the Caspian Basin undersold their Persian Gulf competitors and drove real prices back toward pre-1973 levels. While the oil of the Middle East was still important, it was far less crucial for U.S. national security in the eyes of most American policymakers.

Israel likewise remained an important factor in U.S. policy toward the Middle East, but the relationship between Washington and Tel Aviv looked very different at the end of the century than it had fifty years earlier. For Harry Truman and Dwight Eisenhower, and even for JFK and LBJ, Israel was cast as David surrounded by a gang of Arab Goliaths bent on his destruction. During the three decades after the Six Day War, however, Israel itself began to take on certain aspects of Goliath, digging in on the West Bank, ignoring Jimmy Carter's appeals for Palestinian self-determination, and cracking heads when civil disturbances erupted inside the occupied territories in late 1987. From Intifada to Oslo and back to Intifada, Israel's longtime relationship with the United States looked less and less special. Yitzhak Rabin or Ehud Barak could occasionally rekindle the old magic, but Menachem Begin, Yitzhak Shamir, and Benjamin Netanyahu were usually quick to snuff it out. Ariel Sharon's election as Israel's prime minister in February 2001 close on the heels of George W. Bush's inauguration as America's forty-third president did not bode well, either for the peace process or for U.S. relations with the Jewish state. With the Israelis unwilling to negotiate from a position of strength and the Arabs unwilling to negotiate from a position of weakness, the possibility that Bush and his secretary of state Colin Powell might redress the imbalance by endorsing a Palestinian state did not seem far-fetched.

If the significance of Israel and oil for America's strategic calculations about the Middle East in 2001 was noticeably different from what it had been in 1945, the meaning of containment had shifted dramatically during those fifty-six years as well. Designed to galvanize the American public for an open-ended crusade against international communism at the dawn of the Cold War, containment was predicated on the belief that the United States and the Soviet Union were locked in a zero-sum game in which for every winner there must be exactly one loser. In the Middle East this geopolitical logic was translated into the Eisenhower and Nixon Doctrines, and from the 1950s through the 1970s Russia's foes in the Middle East became, almost by definition, America's friends, and vice versa. Once the end of the Cold War confirmed the intellectual bankruptcy of the Soviet experiment, one might reasonably have expected that containment would have outlived its usefulness. By the mid-1990s, however, Islamic and Arab radicalism had replaced international communism as the mother of all threats to U.S. civilization, and the Clinton administration embraced a strategy of "dual containment" directed against Saddam Hussein's Iraq and the theocratic regime in Iran.

Containment may have been the best way to handle rogue states like the one based in Baghdad, but the Cold War–style focus on containing America's mortal enemies soon became an ideological straitjacket that made it much more difficult for the Clinton administration to deal with positive developments across the Shatt-al-Arab in Tehran. During the ten years following the death of Ayatollah Khomeini in 1989, there was much pushing and shoving between militant proponents of an Islamic republic and advocates of a more secular regime. After a generation of fiercely theocratic rule, Iran held a presidential election in the summer of 1997, and by a wide margin the voters chose Mohammed Khatami, a reformer interested in limiting the power of the mullahs and improving relations with the United States. Ever the pragmatist, Khatami deferred to the clergy on matters of religion and shied away from embracing modernization Pahlavi style, but he also let it be known through back channels that the United States was no longer dealing with the ayatollah's Iran. This news, however, seemed to make little difference in Bill Clinton's Washington. Wedded to his strategy of dual containment, the Arkansas Democrat declined to lift U.S. sanctions on Iran and focused instead on brokering a legacy-saving peace settlement between Israel and the Palestinians during his final months in office.

That peace, however, proved as elusive in 2001 as it had in 1946, when Bill Clinton was born. To be sure, there have been some extraordinary changes over the years. Conservation and innovation have lessened U.S. reliance on Persian Gulf oil, while the end of the Cold War has reduced the geopolitical importance of the Middle East in Washington's eyes. But two things have remained relatively constant. First, Palestinians and Israelis continue to harbor a mutual mistrust so abiding and so visceral that neither can resist the temptation to demonize the other. This reciprocal demonization accelerated rapidly after the Oslo peace process deadlocked during the late 1990s. Precisely because there were real-life demons — suicide bombers trained by Hamas and trigger-happy settlers backed by the Likud — a bad situation seemed ever more likely to go from worse to terrible. Once violent clashes erupted on the Temple Mount during the autumn of 2000, the Clinton administration's behind-the-scenes efforts to persuade both sides to stop shooting and start talking looked more and more like a fool's errand to the Holy Land.

The second constant that continues to make U.S. relations with the Middle East problematic has been American orientalism, a tendency to underestimate the peoples of the region and to overestimate America's ability to make a bad situation better. Although there is greater appreciation for the complexities of the Muslim world than a generation ago, most Americans still view radical Islam as a cause for instant alarm. Having been fed a steady diet of books, films, and news reports depicting Arabs as demonic anti-Western others and Israelis as heroic pro-Western partners and having watched in horror the events of 11 September 2001, the American public understandably fears Osama bin Laden and cheers Aladdin.

In the winter of 1998 an obscure Arabic newspaper in London published a *fatwa*, or spiritual call to arms, in which bin Laden announced a jihad against the United States. The bill of attainder drafted by the forty-one-year-old Saudi financier-turned-terrorist demonized America in much the same way that America subsequently demonized him. "For more than seven years the United States is occupying the lands of Islam in the holiest of its territories, Arabia," bin Laden wrote on 23 February, "plundering its riches, overwhelming its rulers, humiliating its peoples, threatening its neighbors, and using its bases in the peninsula as a spearhead to fight against the neighboring Islamic peoples." By blockading Iraq and bankrolling Israel, he thundered, the United States was seeking "the continuation of the calamitous Crusader occupation" of the Arab world. Bin Laden's punch line was chilling: "To kill Americans and their allies, both civil and military, is an individual duty of every Muslim who is able, . . . until their armies, shattered and broken-winged, depart from all the lands of Islam, incapable of threatening any Muslim." The bombings at the U.S. embassies in Nairobi and Dar es-Salaam six months later merely signaled that bin Laden and his followers in al-Qaeda were both well organized and deadly serious.[1]

In many ways the suicide attacks on New York City and Washington three summers later marked the culmination of America's uneasy encounter with the Middle East during the preceding 200 years. The image of an alien and barbaric Islam that was so deeply ingrained in U.S. popular culture from nineteenth-century ballads to Disney's *Aladdin* came to life in the autumn of 2001 as CNN beamed into America's living rooms video of al-Qaeda guerrillas training for jihad in their Afghan base camps and small but jubilant groups of Palestinians in Gaza cheering news of the carnage at ground zero in lower Manhattan. When bin Laden extended his *fatwa* in early November to include the United Nations for supporting the U.S. air war in Afghanistan, Toby Gati, the former head of the State Department's intelligence bureau, worried that the terrorists would succeed in igniting a battle between Islam and the West. "This reinforces my belief that we are doing the right thing in bombing him," Gati told the *New York Times*, "because if we don't want this to be a war of civilizations, we have really got to get rid of a person who is intent on making it that way."[2]

By engaging in civilizational warfare, Osama bin Laden has embraced what might be called occidentalism, a tendency to demonize the West in ways that ironically mirror American orientalism. For some Americans, of course, the demonic events of 11 September 2001 seemed to vindicate the dire warnings of action intellectuals like Samuel Huntington, who had been prophesying a bloody "clash of civilizations" between Islam and the West since the early 1990s.[3] But in their recent essay "Occidentalism," Ian Buruma and Avishai Margalit have downplayed civilizational conflict and interpreted al-Qaeda's Islamic extremism as merely the latest variant in a long line of fanatically anti-Western ideologies whose proponents have included Mao's China, Hitler's Germany, and Hirohito's Japan. Outraged by the triumph of modernity and the decline of patriarchy and appalled by secularization and urbanization, occidentalists like bin Laden are calling for a no-holds-barred holy war against westernization as symbolized by the United States.[4] "The Crusader spirit that runs in the blood of all Occidentals," Sayyid Qutb, an Islamic firebrand whose writings helped inspire al-Qaeda, observed nearly forty years ago, "is responsible for their imperialistic fear of the spirit of Islam and for their efforts to crush the strength of Islam." In his *fatwa* against America, bin Laden echoed Qutb, denouncing Americans as crusaders, Zionists, and enemies of God in tones that have resonated with the battle cries of Hamas, Islamic Jihad, and other radical Muslim groups.[5]

The intensity of the occidentalist impulse, however, may have been captured best in an eerily prophetic poem titled "The Funeral of New York," written in 1971 by Syrian-born Ali Ahmed Said, who is known from Baghdad to Benghazi as Adonis. "Call it a city on four legs heading for murder," the poet laureate of the Arab world told his readers. "New York is a woman holding, according to history, a rag called liberty with one hand and strangling the earth with the other." Then Adonis offered a bitter warning whose occidentalist punch line would reverberate across America thirty years later. "New York, you will find in my land . . . the stone of Mecca and the waters of the Tigris. In spite of all this, you pant in Palestine and Hanoi. East and west you contend with people whose only history is fire."[6]

Although bin Laden's fiery crusade against the United States is deeply rooted in his occidentalism, the attack on the World Trade Center was also a product of the unintended consequences of five decades of U.S. policy in the Middle East. Like many Arabs, bin Laden believes that the United States has adopted a double standard in its dealings with Israel, easing the birth of the Jewish state in 1948 and then casting a blind eye to the sufferings of the Palestinians. Yet even if George W. Bush could jawbone Ariel Sharon into delivering a just and lasting peace embraced by Yasser Arafat and his people, al-Qaeda would not go away. For bin Laden, America's special relationship with Israel symbolizes a threat far greater than the loss of some choice territory between the River Jordan and the Mediterranean. In his eyes rapid modernization and westernization are destroying the very foundations of the fundamentalist brand of Islam to which he and his Taliban allies are deeply committed. As in Iraq, Libya, and Iran, so, too, in Saudi Arabia and Afghanistan political reform, social change, and economic development produced a violent Islamic backlash that brought down the World Trade Center and may eventually topple Pervez Musharraf's pro-American regime in Pakistan.

That the Pakistani and U.S. intelligence services helped stoke the fires of radical Islam among bin Laden and the Afghan mujahadeen during the 1980s is one of the cruelest ironies of the Cold War. The strategies of containment perfected by Truman, Eisenhower, Nixon, and Carter may have enabled the Reagan administration to use Muslim guerrillas to drive the Soviet Union out of Kabul, but those doctrines were based on the questionable principle that "the enemy of my enemy is my friend." By the late 1980s, Saudi intelligence was, with America's blessing, using bin Laden as a conduit to channel millions of petrodollars to the mujahadeen, while by the mid-1990s the Pakistani ISI was running guns to the Taliban, who were locked in a bloody civil war with Afghan factions that early in the new millennium would coalesce into the Northern Alliance. In short, both bin Laden and the Taliban were to some degree Frankenstein's monsters created by U.S. and Pakistani political experiments that were too clever by half.[7]

Should those monsters gain control over the oil of Saudi Arabia or Central Asia, the United States would face an energy crisis worse than the one that produced stagflation during the Ford and Carter years. By the autumn of 2001, policymakers and oil executives in George W. Bush's Washington privately acknowledged that if bin Laden ever toppled the House of Saud, neither OPEC nor the multinational petroleum giants could prevent the price of Middle East crude from spiking beyond $100 per barrel.[8] Although there was no oil or natural gas in Afghanistan, during the late 1990s the Taliban were calling for Islamic revolution in places such as Turkmenistan and Azerbaijan, where there was. As a result several multinational oil firms spent millions of dollars "romancing the Taliban" in an effort to prevent the radical regime in Kabul from blocking the construction of pipelines to carry oil and natural gas from Central Asia to the Eastern Mediterranean and the Persian Gulf.[9]

From the perspective of a twenty-first century rocked by ethnic wars and terrorized by Islamic extremists, Americans could be forgiven for growing nostalgic about some of the secular nationalists who had given the United States such fits in the Middle East during the last half of the twentieth century. The contrast between Mohammed Mossadegh, who merely wanted Iran to control its own oil and its own destiny, and Ayatollah Khomeini, who wanted to destroy the Great Satan, was obvious from the moment Islamic militants seized the U.S. embassy in Tehran in November 1979. Likewise, the contrast between the relatively westernized Gamal Abdel Nasser, whose quest for self-determination during the 1950s and 1960s stopped well short of a clash of civilizations, and extremists such as Egypt's Islamic Group, who rejected Nasserism and hoped to trigger an anti-Western upheaval by assassinating Anwar Sadat in 1981, was plain to see as U.S. officials worked to ensure that Hosni Mubarak avoided a similar fate. In short, greater sympathy for the devil of revolutionary nationalism after 1945 might have helped to prevent America's hellish confrontation with Osama bin Laden and Islamic extremism early in the new millennium.

Five months after al-Qaeda's assault on the United States, the Bush administration faced huge military and diplomatic challenges in the Middle East. Although the air war over Afghanistan did topple the Taliban, Osama bin Laden remained at large, the U.S. public remained fearful of new terrorist attacks, and American special forces remained in harm's way high in the Hindu Kush. Amidst mounting concern about a widening war in the Muslim world, George W. Bush insisted that Uncle Sam was not perched once again atop a slippery slope to another Vietnam. He also hinted that the silver lining in the battle against terrorism might be an opportunity to "get into the Mitchell process" and resume the Israeli-Palestinian dialogue about peace. Nevertheless, he was careful to point out that "we fight a new kind of war" that could last for months or years on battlefields that stretched "beyond just Afghanistan" to as many as sixty other countries. "It's not one of these Kodak moments," Bush had told reporters on 7 November 2001. "There is no moment to this; this is a long struggle and a different kind of war."[10] The more important question, however, was whether it was a fool's errand.

Because Mark Twain had spent the summer of 1867 watching Americans make fools of themselves in the Holy Land, this question would not have surprised him. From the moment that the *Quaker City* steamed through the Straits of Gibraltar and into the Eastern Mediterranean, most Americans have assumed that their country's wealth and power would provide the moral authority necessary to control the Middle East. During the last half of the twentieth century the United States would finally have the opportunity to test the validity of that assumption. Although the author of *Innocents Abroad* would have understood the peculiarly American brand of expansionism that propelled the United States into the Middle East, he would probably have questioned the wisdom of stepping between the Arabs and the Israelis. He would likely have viewed corporate solutions for tapping oil from the Persian Gulf, White Revolutions in Mohammed Reza Pahlavi's Iran, and United Nations resolutions designed to bring peace to the Holy Land as well-intended but misguided. He would certainly have regarded an orientalist crusade against Iraq, Iran, and other members of what George W. Bush was calling "an axis of evil" as foolish yet predictable. For as Mark Twain prophesied more than 130 years ago, whenever the peoples of the Middle East have challenged U.S. interests, America has usually borne down on them with its greatness in an effort to crush them. His insight helps explain the crushing tragedy, irony, and loss of innocence that confronted America on 11 September 2001.

NOTES

Abbreviations

In addition to the abbreviations used in the text, the following appear in the notes.

AWF	Ann Whitman Files
cirtel	circular telegram
DDE	Dwight D. Eisenhower
DDEL	Dwight D. Eisenhower Presidential Library, Abilene, Kans.
DDRS	*Declassified Documents Reference System* (microfiche) (Arlington, Va.: Carrollton Press, 1975–96)
DOS	Department of State
DOSB	*Department of State Bulletin*
FRUS	*Foreign Relations of the United States*
JFD	John Foster Dulles
JFKL	John F. Kennedy Presidential Library, Boston, Mass.
LBJL	Lyndon B. Johnson Presidential Library, Austin, Tex.
memcon	memorandum of conversation
NA	National Archives II, College Park, Md.
NIE	National Intelligence Estimates
NSF	National Security Files
OCB	Operations Coordinating Board

POF   President's Office Files
PPP   *Public Papers of the President* (Washington, D.C.:
         Government Printing Office, 1946–2000)
PRO   Public Record Office, Kew, Surrey, England
tel.   telegram
telcon   telephone conversation

Introduction

1. To avoid confusion, the current occupant of the Oval Office will be referred to as George W. Bush. His father, who was president from 1989 to 1993, will be referred to as George Bush.

2. "Text of President Bush's Address," *New York Times*, 21 Sept. 2001.

3. Painter, *Oil and the American Century*; David Schoenbaum, *United States and Israel*; Bill, *Eagle and the Lion*.

4. Hahn, *United States, Great Britain, and Egypt*; Kunz, *Economic Diplomacy of the Suez Crisis*; Neff, *Warriors for Jerusalem*; Freedman and Karsh, *Gulf Conflict*.

5. Fraser, *USA and the Middle East since World War 2*; Lenczowski, *American Presidents and the Middle East*; Brands, *Into the Labyrinth*. An exception to this rule is Tillman, *United States in the Middle East*, whose topical approach combines the depth of a monograph with the breadth of a survey.

Chapter One

1. Hunt, *Ideology and U.S. Foreign Policy*, 79, 163, 177.

2. Said, *Orientalism*, 31–49, 284–328. For an interesting discussion of Said's analytical approach, see Rotter, "Saidism without Said."

3. Lutz and Collins, *Reading National Geographic*, 11–14, 119–53.

4. On the earliest English translations, see the introductory essay in Haddawy, *Arabian Nights*, xv–xvii.

5. Allison, *Crescent Obscured*, xiv–xviii, 190–92.

6. Ibid., 204–6.

7. "Affairs of Greece," *North American Review*, 41 (Oct. 1823): 420.

8. Field, *America and the Mediterranean World*, 154–65.

9. Diary entry, 6 Jan. 1839, in Charles Francis Adams, *Memoirs of John Quincy Adams*, 10:90–91.

10. Sachar, *History of the Jews in America*, 48–51, 72–75.

11. Field, *America and the Mediterranean World*, 274–85.

12. "The Dead Sea, Sodom, and Gomorrah," *Harper's New Monthly Magazine*, Jan. 1855, quoted in Davis, *Landscape of Belief*, 5.

13. Sha'ban, *Islam and Arabs in Early American Thought*, xiii–xxi.

14. Davis, *Landscape of Belief*, 101–48.

15. Edwards, *Noble Dreams, Wicked Pleasures*, 12–18, 31–34, 77–82.

16. Twain, *Innocents Abroad*, 516.

17. Ibid., 101, 431, 433, 499.

18. For the impact of Twain's *Innocents Abroad* and other nineteenth-century travel literature on U.S. popular culture, see Christison, *Perceptions of Palestine*, 16–25.

19. Quoted in Field, *America and the Mediterranean World*, 311.

20. Ibid., 345–59.

21. Lawrence, *Seven Pillars of Wisdom*, 45.

22. Pearson to DOS, 12 Aug. 1906, *FRUS 1906*, 2:1216–17.

23. Leishman to DOS, 8 Aug. 1908, *FRUS 1908*, 747–48, and 15 Apr. 1909, *FRUS 1909*, 563–65.

24. Roosevelt to Spring Rice, 1 July 1907, and to Silas McBee, 27 Aug. 1907, in Morison, *Letters of Theodore Roosevelt*, 5:698–99, 774–75. On Roosevelt's orientalized views of Egypt and the Arabs, see Brands, *Last Romantic*, 33–36, 660–61.

25. Roosevelt to Lyman Abbott, 29 May 1908, in Morison, *Letters of Theodore Roosevelt*, 6:1042–43. For more on Roosevelt and Jews, see Blum, *Republican Roosevelt*, 37–38.

26. Roosevelt to Lioubomir Michailovitch, 11 July 1918, and to Julian H. Miller, 16 Sept. 1918, in Morison, *Letters of Theodore Roosevelt*, 8:1350, 1372.

27. Sanders, *Shores of Refuge*, 116–17.

28. Morris, *Righteous Victims*, 20–26, 56–59. For the 85,000 figure, see Hourani, *History of the Arab Peoples*, 288–89, and Tessler, *History of the Israeli-Palestinian Conflict*, 145.

29. Grose, *Israel in the Mind of America*, 46–71.

30. Balfour to William Wiseman, 6 Oct. 1917, and Wilson to Edward House, 13 Oct. 1917, in Link, *Papers of Woodrow Wilson*, 44:324–25, 371; Lebow, "Wilson and the Balfour Declaration," 507–13.

31. Sanders, *High Walls of Jerusalem*, 594–613.

32. Fromkin, *Peace to End All Peace*, 396–98; Howard, *King-Crane Commission*, 36–51, 270–75.

33. James Harbord, "Report of the American Military Mission to Armenia," 16 Oct. 1919, *FRUS 1919*, 2:849–50, 859–60, 865, 874.

34. Michalek, "Arab in American Cinema"; Edwards, *Noble Dreams, Wicked Pleasures*, 99–117.

35. Lawrence, *Revolt in the Desert*. On the reaction to Lawrence's two books, see Liddell Hart, *T. E. Lawrence*, 403, and Jeremy Wilson, *Lawrence of Arabia*, 782–90.

36. *National Geographic Magazine*, May 1923, 568. For an account of the discovery of King Tut's tomb and its impact on the popular imagination, see John A. Wilson, *Signs and Wonders upon Pharaoh*, 159–66.

37. Williams, "East of Suez," 737.

38. Harnet Chalmers Adams, "Cirenaica," 692, 714–15.

39. Van Der Meulen, "Into Burning Hadhramaut," 387.

40. Whiting, "Among the Bethlehem Shepherds" and "Bethlehem and the Christmas Story"; Keith-Roche, "Pageant of Jerusalem."

41. Keith-Roche, "Changing Palestine," 521, 527.

42. Simpich, "Change Comes to Bible Lands," 708, 710, 730, 748.

43. Grose, *Israel in the Mind of America*, 93–104.

44. Zionist Organization of America membership figures are from David Schoen-

baum, *United States and Israel,* 19. See also Grose, *Israel in the Mind of America,* 225–31.

45. Murray to Acting Secretary of State R. Walton Moore, and Moore memcon, 18 Nov. 1936, *FRUS 1936,* 3:455–59.

46. Burleigh and Wippermann, *Racial State,* 77–86.

47. Cohen, *Palestine: Retreat from the Mandate,* 66–87.

48. Quoted in Grose, *Israel in the Mind of America,* 134.

49. FDR to Hull, 17 May 1939, *FRUS 1939,* 4:757–58.

50. Baram, *Department of State in the Middle East,* 249–54.

51. Wyman, *Abandonment of the Jews,* 19–41.

52. Grose, *Israel in the Mind of America,* 169–76; Wyman, *Abandonment of the Jews,* 157–77.

53. Quoted in David Schoenbaum, *United States and Israel,* 29.

54. FDR to Wagner, 15 Oct. 1944, *FRUS 1944,* 5:615–16. This letter was evidently drafted by Stephen Wise. See Halperin and Oder, "United States in Search of a Policy," 335.

55. Edward Stettinius phone call to Stephen Wise, 15 Nov. 1944, and Stettinius memcon, 23 Nov. 1944, "ERS Calendar Notes and Records of Phone Conversations, 11/15/44–11/27/44," box 243, Stettinius Papers; FDR to Wagner, 3 Dec. 1944, in Roosevelt, *F.D.R.,* 2:1559.

56. William Eddy memcon, 14 Feb. 1945, *FRUS 1945,* 8:2–3.

57. Diary entry, 14 Mar. 1945, in Berle and Jacobs, *Navigating the Rapids,* 475–76.

58. Wise, *Challenging Years,* 232.

59. Murray to Acting Secretary of State Joseph Grew, 20 Mar. 1945, *FRUS 1945,* 8:694–95.

60. Unsigned account of liberation of Buchenwald, n.d. [probably late May 1945], in Hackett, *Buchenwald Report,* 331–34. See also Abzug, *Inside the Vicious Heart,* 45–60.

61. Simpich, "Americans Help Liberated Europe Live Again," 748, 755, 757.

62. Chase, "Palestine Today," 501, 504, 507, 509.

63. Ibid., 511, 516.

64. Villiers, "Sailing with Sindbad's Sons," 679, 686.

65. Glueck, "Archaeologist Looks at Palestine," 740–43, 751.

66. "Arab Lands beyond the Jordan."

67. Clark, "Yemen," 632, 644, 672.

68. Truman to Bess, 14 Aug. 1946, in Ferrell, *Dear Bess,* 531.

69. Clifford to Truman, 8 Mar. 1948, *FRUS 1948,* 5:695.

70. McClintock to Dean Rusk, 1 July 1948, ibid., 1173.

71. Kennan, *Memoirs,* 184, 380.

72. CIA Report SR-13, "Arab World," 27 Sept. 1949, Office of Privacy Coordination, CIA.

73. Coon quoted in Kaplan, *Arabists,* 110.

74. Diary entry, 13 Aug. 1952, in Berle and Jacobs, *Navigating the Rapids,* 607.

75. Troutbeck to Eden, 31 Oct. 1952, quoted in Louis, "British and the Origins of the Iraqi Revolution," 35.

76. Ike to Mamie, 27 Nov. 1942, in John S. D. Eisenhower, *Letters to Mamie,* 66.

77. Dwight D. Eisenhower, *The White House Years: Mandate for Change,* 150.

78. Eisenhower quoted in Goodpaster memcon, 31 July 1956, *FRUS 1955–57*, 16:64.

79. Eisenhower quoted in Goodpaster memcon, 23 July 1958, *FRUS 1958–60*, 12:99.

80. Eisenhower quoted in the minutes of the 410th NSC meeting, 18 June 1959, ibid., 16:101.

81. John Foster Dulles to Walter Bedell Smith, tel., 13 May 1953, and minutes of the 147th NSC meeting, 1 June 1953, *FRUS 1952–54*, 9:25–26, 383–384.

82. Dulles quoted in Heiss, *Empire and Nationhood*, 180.

83. Murphy, *Diplomat among Warriors*, 394, 412–13, 418.

84. Villard to DOS, tel., 12 June 1954, *FRUS 1952–54*, 11:588.

85. Byroade to Foster Dulles, tel., 14 Mar. 1956, "Briefing for Cairo Visit, 3rd Anderson Visit," box 34, Alpha Files, lot 59D 518, NA.

86. NSC-6011, "U.S. Policy toward the Near East," 19 July 1960, *FRUS 1958–60*, 12:269.

87. On the rapid transformation of Israelis from "feminized" victims to "hypermasculine" Cold Warriors in U.S. popular culture during the 1950s, see Mart, "Tough Guys and American Cold War Policy."

88. For the script of the play, see Goodrich and Hackett, *Diary of Anne Frank*.

89. Raviv and Melman, *Every Spy a Prince*, 114–18. For a best-selling contemporary account of Eichmann's arrest, trial, and execution, see Arendt, *Eichmann in Jerusalem*.

90. Shor, "Crusader Road to Jerusalem," "Conquest of the Holy City," and "Holy Land Today."

91. Abercrombie, "Behind the Veil of Troubled Yemen," 402–5, 407, 416.

92. Scofield, "Israel," 396.

93. CIA, NIE 36-61, "Nasser and the Future of Arab Nationalism," 27 June 1961, "36 Arab World," box 6, NIE, NSF, LBJL.

94. Komer to JFK, 28 Nov. 1962, *FRUS 1961–63*, 18:238.

95. Komer memcon, 14 Nov. 1963, ibid., 782–83.

96. Glidden quoted in Robert Estabrook to *Washington Post*, tel., 23 May 1963, "Cabled Materials," folder 3, box 5, Estabrook Papers.

97. LBJ toast, 14 Apr. 1964, *PPP, Lyndon B. Johnson, 1963–64*, 1:462.

98. B. K. Smith memcon, 22 Jan. 1965, "Miscellaneous Meetings," vol. 1, box 18, Bundy Files, NSF, LBJL.

99. Heikal, *Cairo Documents*, 229–30.

100. Johnson, *Vantage Point*, 289.

101. Roche to LBJ, 22 May 1967, "Middle East Crisis," vol. 1, box 17, NSC History Files, NSF, LBJL.

102. Rusk cirtel, 3 June 1967, quoted in Quandt, *Peace Process*, 519 n. 83.

103. Badeau, *American Approach to the Arab World*, 177–78.

104. "CIA Post-Mortem," n.d. [autumn 1973], quoted in Pike, *CIA*, 146 n. 293.

105. Suleiman, *Arabs in the Mind of America*, 119–22.

106. Michener, *The Source*, 882. The first Fawcett paperback edition of *The Source* appeared in January 1967.

107. Harbutt, "Eyewitness to War in the Holy Land," 786.

108. Diary entry, 5 Sept. 1972, in Haldeman, *Diaries*, 501; Nixon remarks to reporters, 5 Sept. 1972, *PPP, Richard M. Nixon, 1972*, 857–58.

109. Kissinger, *Years of Upheaval*, 202–3.

110. Nixon, *RN*, 1011–12.

111. Ford, *Time to Heal*, 290–91. For Ford's gaffe, see his toast, 27 Oct. 1975, *PPP, Gerald R. Ford, 1975*, 2:1728.

112. Carter, *Keeping Faith*, 328.

113. Arden, "Eternal Sinai," 453–56.

114. Diary entry, 6 Oct. 1981, in Carter, *Keeping Faith*, 269.

115. Carter, *Blood of Abraham*, 170.

116. Glidden, "Arab World."

117. Patai, *Arab Mind* (1973), 1–5, 30–32, 129, 312–13.

118. Laffin, *Arab Mind Considered*, 15, 22–23, 106–8.

119. Brown, *Last Crusade*, 30–31.

120. Said, *Orientalism*, 287, 291.

121. Said, *Culture and Imperialism*, 260–61.

122. Patai, *Arab Mind* (1983), 356.

123. Pryce-Jones, *Closed Circle*, 16–18.

124. Bernard Lewis, "Roots of Muslim Rage," 50, 52, 59, 60.

125. Table of contents, *Atlantic Monthly*, Sept. 1990, 2; Esposito, *Islamic Threat*, 3–5.

126. Shaheen, *TV Arab*, 59–60.

127. Ibid., 61–62.

128. Stockton, "Ethnic Archetypes and the Arab Image," 133–34, 139, 140, 148. See also Lendenmann, "Arab Stereotyping in Contemporary Political Cartoons."

129. Interview with Jim Hoaglund, in Ghareeb, *Split Vision*, 227–28.

130. Interview with John Cooley, in ibid., 210–11.

131. Interview with Peter Jennings, in ibid., 105–6.

132. Interview with Jim Lehrer, in ibid., 259–60.

133. Ibid. For a critique of PBS coverage of the Iranian revolution and the hostage crisis, see Said, *Covering Islam*, 89–91.

134. Interview with Anthony Lewis, in Ghareeb, *Split Vision*, 199–200.

135. Uris, *The Haj*, 81. For a fuller examination of these orientalist themes in other novels, see Christison, "Arab in Recent Popular Fiction."

136. For an discussion of the "jihad" themes implicit in *True Lies* and other Hollywood fare, see Rahme, "Ethnocentric and Stereotypical Concepts in the Study of Islamic and World History."

137. Ray Hanania, "My Turn: One of the Bad Guys?," *Newsweek*, 2 Nov. 1998, 14. See also "Again, Islam Is an Easy Villain," *New York Times*, 10 Nov. 1998.

138. Chafets, *Double Vision*, 177–78; Karetzky, *Media's War against Israel*, 16–23, 85–89.

139. Arens, *Broken Covenant*, 59.

140. "Islamic Nations Move to Keep Out 'Schindler's List,'" *New York Times*, 7 Apr. 1994.

141. "'Aladdin' Bows to a Protest," *New York Times*, 11 July 1993; "It's Racist, but Hey, It's Disney," *New York Times* editorial, 14 July 1993. For more on the reaction to *Aladdin*, see Schrag and Javidi, "Through a Glass Darkly," 216–20.

142. Bush remarks, 17 Sept. 2001, and address, 20 Sept. 2001, http://www.whitehouse.gov/news.

143. Bush address, 20 Sept. 2001, http://www.whitehouse.gov/news. On the fallout from the events of 11 September among Arab Americans, see Singer, "Home Is Here."

Chapter Two

1. Alfred Hippisley to W. W. Rockhill, 25 July 1899, quoted in Griswold, *Far Eastern Policy of the United States*, 65–66.
2. Yergin, *Prize*, 108–13.
3. Gibb and Knowlton, *History of Standard Oil*, 359–408; Yergin, *Prize*, 134–57, 233–37; Sampson, *Seven Sisters*, 59–69, 78–79.
4. John W. Davis to Lord Curzon, 12 May 1920, and Colby to Curzon, 20 Nov. 1920, *FRUS 1920*, 2:651–52, 669–73.
5. Gibb and Knowlton, *History of Standard Oil*, 284–91.
6. Stivers, *Supremacy and Oil*, 110–12.
7. Yergin, *Prize*, 201–4.
8. Sampson, *Seven Sisters*, 80–84; Yergin, *Prize*, 204–5.
9. Anderson, *Aramco*, 22–29.
10. Yergin, *Prize*, 295–98.
11. FDR to Jesse Jones, 18 July 1941, *FRUS 1941*, 3:642–43.
12. Barnhart, *Japan Prepares for Total War*, 165–69; Yergin, *Prize*, 334–38.
13. James A. Moffett (CASOC) to FDR, 16 Apr. 1941, *FRUS 1941*, 3:624–25.
14. Anderson, *Aramco*, 46–49.
15. Yergin, *Prize*, 400–402.
16. Anderson, *Aramco*, 95–107; Sampson, *Seven Sisters*, 112–19.
17. Feis to Hull, 22 Mar. 1943, quoted in Hull, *Memoirs*, 2:1517.
18. DeGolyer quoted in Stoff, *Oil, War, and American Security*, 135–36.
19. FDR to Churchill, tel., 22 Feb. 1944, in Kimball, *Churchill and Roosevelt*, 2:744–45; Yergin, *Prize*, 407.
20. Pew quoted in Stoff, *Oil, War, and American Security*, 182.
21. Painter, *Oil and the American Century*, 66–69.
22. Loftus to John Linebaugh, 31 May 1945, *FRUS 1945*, 8:51–54.
23. Murray to DOS, 25 Sept. 1945, ibid., 417–19.
24. Forrestal quoted in Yergin, *Prize*, 407.
25. Loftus, "Oil in United States Foreign Policy." On the relationship between U.S. consumption and reserves during the 1940s, see Painter, *Oil and the American Century*, 97.
26. Bonnet to Byrnes, 4 Jan. 1947; DOS memcon, 9 Jan. 1947; and Acheson to Bonnet, 10 Apr. 1947, *FRUS 1947*, 5:627–31, 657–60.
27. Anderson, *Aramco*, 154–59; Stoff, *Oil, War, and American Security*, 205–6.
28. Justice Department ruling quoted in Yergin, *Prize*, 416.
29. Forrestal testimony, 29 Jan. 1948, in U.S. Congress, Senate, Special Committee Investigating the National Defense Program, *Investigation of the National Defense Program*, 25290–91.
30. Diary entry, 16 Jan. 1948, box 4, James Forrestal Diaries, Forrestal Papers.
31. Little, "Pipeline Politics," 261–68.

32. DOS, "Current Economic Developments," 23 May 1949, *FRUS, Current Economic Developments, 1945–54* (microfiche ed.), fiche 40; Little, "Pipeline Politics," 277–81.

33. Shwadran, *Middle East, Oil, and the Great Powers*, 343–45.

34. McGhee quoted in Yergin, *Prize*, 447.

35. DOS memcon, 6 Nov. 1950, *FRUS 1950*, 5:106–9.

36. Yergin, *Prize*, 446–47; Painter, *Oil and the American Century*, 165–71.

37. Quoted in Engler, *Politics of Oil*, 211–12.

38. Kaufman, "Mideast Multinational Oil," 946–49.

39. "Security and International Issues Arising from the Current Situation in Petroleum," 6 Jan. 1953, *FRUS 1952–54*, 9:637–48.

40. Department of Justice, "The Grand Jury Investigation of the International Oil Cartel," 6 Jan. 1953, ibid., 650–55.

41. Charles Bohlen, "National Security Council Meeting," 9 Jan. 1953, and Truman to McGranery, 12 Jan. 1953, ibid., 655–56.

42. Engler, *Politics of Oil*, 203; Heiss, *Empire and Nationhood*, 45–76.

43. Acheson, *Present at the Creation*, 503.

44. Yergin, *Prize*, 464.

45. Heiss, *Empire and Nationhood*, 188–201; Shwadran, *Middle East, Oil, and the Great Powers*, 142–49.

46. Minutes of the 180th NSC meeting, 14 Jan. 1954, *FRUS 1952–54*, 10:897–98.

47. Heiss, *Empire and Nationhood*, 203.

48. Kyle, *Suez*, 314–70; minutes of the 303rd NSC meeting, 8 Nov. 1956, *FRUS 1955–57*, 16:1075.

49. Yergin, *Prize*, 486–95; minutes of the 303rd NSC meeting, 8 Nov. 1956, *FRUS 1955–57*, 16:1077–78.

50. On alternative pipeline routes, see DOS memcon, 25 Jan. 1957, *FRUS 1955–57*, 12:443–44.

51. Fraser Wilkins (NEA) to Ike, "Outline of Short Term and Long Term United States Plans in the Middle East," 21 Nov. 1956, 611.80/11-2156, State Department Central Decimal File, RG59, NA.

52. DOS Policy Planning Staff, "United States Objectives with Respect to the Near East," 30 Oct. 1957, *FRUS 1955–57*, 12:646.

53. DOS, INR Report 8091, "Economic and Political Significance of North African Discoveries," 27 Aug. 1959, in *OSS/State Department Intelligence and Research Reports*, pt. 12, reel 3.

54. Terzian, *OPEC*, 42–44.

55. Dulles phone call to John J. McCloy, 2 Jan. 1958, *FRUS 1958–60*, 12:1–2.

56. NSC briefing note, 25 July 1958, "Middle East, 1957–59 (1)," box 13, Records of the Office of the Special Adviser for National Security Affairs, DDEL.

57. DOS memcon, 18 Mar. 1959, *FRUS 1958–60*, 12:214–15.

58. Walter Schwinn (Dhahran) to DOS, tel., 23 Apr. 1959, 886A.2553/4-2359, State Department Central Decimal File, RG59, NA.

59. Yergin, *Prize*, 513–18.

60. Tariki quoted in Engler, *Politics of Oil*, 186.

61. Minutes of the 406th NSC meeting, 13 May 1959, *FRUS 1958–60*, 4:595–606, 610–16.

62. Jones to DOS legal adviser Eric Hager, 20 Apr. 1960, ibid., 12:251–53.

63. Minutes of the 444th NSC meeting, 9 May 1960, and NSC Action 2233, 13 May 1960, ibid., 257–58.

64. Minutes of the 451st NSC meeting, 15 July 1960, ibid., 260–62.

65. Rodger Davies (Baghdad) to DOS, tel., 15 Sept. 1960, and minutes of the 460th NSC meeting, 21 Sept. 1960, ibid., 274, 276.

66. DOS memcon, 19 Oct. 1960, ibid., 277–79.

67. NIE 30-60, "Middle East Oil," 13 Dec. 1960, *FRUS 1958–60*, 4:674–77.

68. Qassim quoted in Skeet, *Opec*, 1.

69. Stork, *Middle East Oil and the Energy Crisis*, 102–4; Yergin, *Prize*, 535.

70. Talbot to George Ball, 18 Dec. 1961, *FRUS 1961–63*, 17:364–66.

71. Jernegan Oral History, 19–20.

72. Robert Komer to McGeorge Bundy, 29 Dec. 1961, *FRUS 1961–63*, 17:378–80.

73. Stork, *Middle East Oil and the Energy Crisis*, 105–7.

74. For oil production figures for the early 1960s, see United Nations, Department of Economic and Social Affairs, *United Nations Statistical Yearbook*, 207.

75. DOS memcon, 13 Jan. 1965, "Near East," vol. 1, box 116, Country Files, NSF, LBJL.

76. Harold Saunders to LBJ, 24 May 1967, *FRUS 1964–68*, 34:419.

77. Ahmed Zaki Yamani to ARAMCO, 7 June 1967, "Middle East Crisis," vol. 4, Memos (1 of 2), box 116, Country Files, NSF, LBJL.

78. Yergin, *Prize*, 555; Brenchley, *Britain and the Middle East*, 150.

79. Rostow to LBJ, 29 May 1967, "Rostow," vol. 2, Memos to the President, box 16, NSF, LBJL.

80. Yergin, *Prize*, 554–56.

81. CIA, "Arab-Israeli Situation Report," 3 July 1967, "Middle East Crisis," vol. 11, box 21, NSC History Files, NSF, LBJL; Little, "Choosing Sides," 179–80.

82. For an excellent discussion of the impact of the 1959 quota on U.S. energy consumption and the pattern of oil imports, see Blair, *Control of Oil*, 169–84.

83. Yergin, *Prize*, 590–94.

84. Terzian, *OPEC*, 108–10.

85. Yergin, *Prize*, 639–42.

86. Sampson, *Seven Sisters*, 248–73.

87. Terzian, *OPEC*, 118–20; Yergin, *Prize*, 577–80.

88. McCloy to Jerome Levinson, 12 July 1974, in U.S. Congress, Senate Committee on Foreign Relations, Subcommittee on Multinational Corporations, *Multinational Corporations and United States Foreign Policy*, pt. 8, 767–68.

89. Testimony of Deputy Secretary of State John Irwin, 31 Jan. 1974, in ibid., pt. 5, 145–51.

90. Yergin, *Prize*, 580–85.

91. McCloy memcon, 21 Jan. 1972, in U.S. Congress, Senate Committee on Foreign Relations, Subcommittee on Multinational Corporations, *Multinational Corporations and United States Foreign Policy*, pt. 6, 303–4.

92. Terzian, *OPEC*, 151–57.

93. Yamani quoted in Yergin, *Prize*, 584.

94. Akins, "Oil Crisis," 467.

95. Exxon officials quoted in Sampson, *Seven Sisters*, 293. See also Terzian, *OPEC*, 166.

96. Faisal quoted in Terzian, *OPEC*, 167.

97. Transcript of 5 Sept. 1973 press conference, *PPP, Richard M. Nixon, 1973*, 735–36.

98. John J. McCloy, "Meeting at Auditorium (Exxon)," 10 Oct. 1973, "Correspondence 1973," folder 15, Oil, box 3, McCloy Papers; Terzian, *OPEC*, 169; Yergin, *Prize*, 639–42.

99. Terzian, *OPEC*, 170, 184–85.

100. Kissinger, *Years of Upheaval*, 854–58.

101. Ibid., 854.

102. Yergin, *Prize*, 657–58; McCloy to Church, 25 Mar. 1974, in U.S. Congress, Senate Committee on Foreign Relations, Subcommittee on Multinational Corporations, *Multinational Corporations and United States Foreign Policy*, pt. 6, 290–93.

103. Church to McCloy, 11 Apr. 1974, in U.S. Congress, Senate Committee on Foreign Relations, Subcommittee on Multinational Corporations, *Multinational Corporations and United States Foreign Policy*, pt. 6, 293–94.

104. Piercy quoted in U.S. Congress, Senate Committee on Foreign Relations, Subcommittee on Multinational Corporations, *Multinational Oil Corporations and U.S. Foreign Policy*, 15.

105. McCloy to Church, 30 May 1974, in U.S. Congress, Senate Committee on Foreign Relations, Subcommittee on Multinational Corporations, *Multinational Corporations and United States Foreign Policy*, pt. 6, 294–96.

106. U.S. Congress, Senate Committee on Foreign Relations, Subcommittee on Multinational Corporations, *Multinational Oil Corporations and U.S. Foreign Policy*, 17–18.

107. Yergin, *Prize*, 592, 615, 622, 625–26, 681–98.

108. Ibid., 703–14.

109. For an inside account of the impact of growing competitive forces on the Arab oil-producing states, see Chalabi, "World Oil Price Collapse of 1986." Chalabi served as OPEC's deputy secretary general from 1978 to 1989.

110. Freedman and Karsh, *Gulf Conflict*, 180–88.

111. George Bush, "Address to Joint Session of Congress," 11 Sept. 1990, *PPP, George Bush, 1990*, 2:1219.

112. Gause, "Saudi Arabia over a Barrel"; "Oil Price Exceeds $30 a Barrel for First Time since 1991," *New York Times*, 15 Feb. 2000.

113. Hersh, "Annals of National Security," 39. See also "Fears, Again, of Oil Supplies at Risk," *New York Times*, 14 Oct. 2001.

Chapter Three

1. John Winthrop lay sermon, in Merrill and Paterson, *Major Problems in American Foreign Relations*, 30–31.

2. Melville, *White Jacket*, 189.

3. Zahniser, *Uncertain Friendship*, 17–53.

4. For the text of Washington's "Farewell Address," see Merrill and Paterson, *Major Problems in American Foreign Relations*, 74–76.

5. For a concise account of the Anglo-American reconciliation during the early twentieth century, see Hathaway, *Great Britain and the United States*, 1–8.

6. Wise, *Challenging Years*, 232; Wallace Murray to Joseph Grew, 20 Mar. 1945, and FDR to Ibn Saud, 5 Apr. 1945, *FRUS 1945*, 8:694–95, 698.

7. Cohen, *Palestine and the Great Powers*, 56–58.

8. "Report of Earl G. Harrison."

9. Truman, *Years of Trial and Hope*, 138–40; Truman to Attlee, 31 Aug. 1945, *FRUS 1945*, 8:737–39.

10. Stettinius to Truman, 18 Apr. 1945, ibid., 704–5.

11. Truman, *Years of Trial and Hope*, 136–37.

12. Louis, *British Empire in the Middle East*, 397–419.

13. Cohen, "Zionist Perspective," 82–93; Silver, *Begin*, 81–87.

14. Truman quoted in Eddy, *F. D. R. Meets Ibn Saud*, 37.

15. Grose, "President versus the Diplomats," 39; Cohen, *Truman and Israel*, 130–31.

16. Diary entry, 30 July 1946, in Blum, *Price of Vision*, 606–7.

17. Baruch quoted in Ganin, *Truman, American Jewry, and Israel*, 101 (ellipsis in original).

18. Goldmann quoted in ibid., 90; Truman statement, 4 Oct. 1946, *PPP, Harry S. Truman, 1946*, 442–44.

19. Bevin to Marshall, n.d., attached to Henderson to Acheson, 17 Feb. 1947; Marshall to Truman, 17 Apr. 1947; "Report of the First Committee on a Special Committee on Palestine," 13 May 1947; and Marshall to Truman, 16 May 1947, *FRUS 1947*, 5:1051–53, 1070–73, 1083–84, 1085–86. The eleven members of UNSCOP were Australia, Canada, Czechoslovakia, Guatemala, India, Iran, the Netherlands, Peru, Sweden, Uruguay, and Yugoslavia.

20. Cohen, *Truman and Israel*, 149–59.

21. Grose, *Israel in the Mind of America*, 244–54.

22. Macatee to DOS, 31 Dec. 1947, *FRUS 1947*, 5:1322–28; PPS/19, 19 Jan. 1948, attached to George Kennan to George Marshall, 20 Jan. 1948, *FRUS 1948*, 5:545–54; Cohen, *Palestine and the Great Powers*, 301–6, 312–13.

23. Forrestal, 2 memcons, 21 Jan. 1948, "Correspondence: Lovett," box 80, Forrestal Papers.

24. Marshall to Ambassador Warren Austin (USUN), tel., 16 Mar. 1948, *FRUS 1948*, 5:728–29; Truman, *Years of Trial and Hope*, 161; Cohen, *Truman and Israel*, 179–87.

25. Diary entry, 20 Mar. 1948, in Ferrell, *Off the Record*, 127; McCullough, *Truman*, 610–11.

26. Clifford, *Counsel to the President*, 8–9.

27. Clifford quoted in Cohen, *Truman and Israel*, 193.

28. Ibid., 90–91, 195–210. The quote by Dean Alfange is at 208–9.

29. George M. Elsey memcon and DOS memcon, both 12 May 1948, *FRUS 1948*, 5:972–76.

30. Clifford quoted in Daniels, *Man of Independence*, 319.

31. Clifford, *Counsel to the President*, 15.

32. DOS memcon, 12 May 1948, *FRUS 1948*, 5:975.

33. Clifford, *Counsel to the President*, 16–17.

34. Ibid., 21.

35. Lovett memcon, 17 May 1948, *FRUS 1948*, 5:1005–7.

36. Ibid.

37. Quoted in McCullough, *Truman*, 601.

38. Truman to Dean Alfange, 18 May 1948, quoted in Cohen, *Truman and Israel*, 209.

39. Cohen, *Palestine and the Great Powers*, 301–12; Consul General John MacDonald (Jerusalem) to DOS, 17 Sept. 1948, *FRUS 1948*, 5:1412–13; Stanger, "Haunting Legacy," 264–66.

40. Lovett to Marshall, tel., 29 Oct. 1948; Truman to Ben Gurion, in DOS to Special Representative James G. McDonald (Tel Aviv), tel., 30 Dec. 1948, *FRUS 1948*, 5:1528, 1704–5.

41. Ben Gurion quoted in McDonald to DOS, tel., 1 Jan. 1949, *FRUS 1949*, 6:594–95.

42. Kenen, *Israel's Defense Line*, 66–91. Kenen was one of the chief architects of AIPAC.

43. DOS memcon, 14 May 1953, *FRUS 1952–54*, 9:36–40.

44. Dulles, "Report on the Near East"; minutes of the 153rd NSC meeting, 9 July 1953, and NSC-155/1, "U.S. Objectives and Policies with Respect to the Near East," 14 July 1953, *FRUS 1952–54*, 9:397–98, 401–2.

45. DOS to Francis Russell (Tel Aviv), tel., 8 Sept. 1953; Acting Secretary of State Walter Bedell Smith to Eisenhower, 21 Oct. 1953; and DOS memcon, 21 Oct. 1953, *FRUS 1952–54*, 9:1303, 1371–73.

46. DOS memcon, 26 Oct. 1953, and DOS press release, "Aid to Israel," 28 Oct. 1953, ibid., 1384–87, 1390–91.

47. Green, *Taking Sides*, 107–14.

48. Minutes of the 239th NSC meeting, 3 Mar. 1955, and Ambassador Edward Lawson (Tel Aviv) to DOS, 4 Mar. 1955, *FRUS 1955–57*, 14:81–82, 83–86.

49. Neff, *Warriors at Suez*, 112–14; Shlaim, "Conflicting Approaches to Israel's Relations with the Arabs," 191–98 (Sharett quote on 195–96). On the planning for Operation Omer, see Bar-On, *Gates of Gaza*, 48–52. Bar-On served as Dayan's private secretary.

50. Goodpaster memcon, 27 Oct. 1956, and Eisenhower to Ben Gurion, tel., 27 Oct. 1956, *FRUS 1955–57*, 16:793–95.

51. Hughes, *Ordeal of Power*, 211–12.

52. Eisenhower to Ben Gurion, tel., 28 Oct. 1956, and Goodpaster memcon, 29 Oct. 1956, *FRUS 1955–57*, 16:801, 833–34.

53. Goodpaster memcon, 29 Oct. 1956, ibid., 833–39.

54. Eisenhower to Ben Gurion, tel., 7 Nov. 1956, ibid., 1063–64; Eisenhower phone call to Herbert Hoover Jr., 7 Nov. 1956, "Israel (4)," box 29, International Series, AWF, DDEL.

55. Ben Gurion to Eisenhower, 8 Nov. 1956, *FRUS 1955–57*, 16:1095–96.

56. DDE to Ben Gurion, 3 Feb. 1957, "Israel (3)," International Series, AWF, DDEL.

57. Ben Gurion quoted in Bar-Zohar, *Ben-Gurion*, 254.

58. Kenen, *Israel's Defense Line*, 133–37; Knowland to JFD, phone calls, 14, 16, 18 Feb. 1957, and LBJ to JFD, phone call, 14 Feb. 1957, Memoranda of Telephone Calls, Dulles Papers, DDEL.

59. JFD memcon, 16 Feb. 1957, White House Memoranda Series, Dulles Papers, DDEL.

60. Minnich, "Minutes of Bipartisan Legislative Meeting," 20 Feb. 1957, "Feb. 57 Misc. (3)," DDE Diary Series, AWF, DDEL; Sherman Adams, *Firsthand Report*, 280–81.

61. Eisenhower address, 20 Feb. 1957, *Department of State Bulletin* 36 (11 Mar. 1957): 387–90.

62. Eban, *Autobiography*, 244–46; JFD to Lodge, phone call, 24 Feb. 1957, Memoranda of Telephone Calls, Dulles Papers, DDEL.

63. JFD to Hammarskjöld, two phone calls, 25 Feb. 1957, and Lodge to JFD, phone call, 1 Mar. 1957, Dulles Papers, DDEL; Eban, *Autobiography*, 249–53; Rafael, *Destination Peace*, 62–67.

64. Little, "Puppet in Search of a Puppeteer?," 525–28.

65. Eban, *Autobiography*, 263–64; Ben Gurion to Eisenhower, 24 July 1958, "Middle East July 1958 (4)," box 36, International Series, AWF, DDEL.

66. Dulles to Ben Gurion, 1 Aug. 1958, *FRUS 1958–60*, 13:77–79. See also Rountree to Dulles, 22 Aug., 10 Sept. 1958, 784A.56/8-2258 and /9-1058, State Department Central Decimal File, RG59, NA. For the sandbag analogy, see Herzog, *People That Dwells Alone*, 249–50. Herzog was Israel's deputy chief of mission in Washington.

67. Rountree to Dulles, 22 Aug. 1958, and Rountree, "U.S. Response to Israel's Arms Request," 26 Aug. 1958, 784A.56/8-2258 and /8-2658, State Department Central Decimal File, RG59, NA.

68. Eban, *Autobiography*, 263–64.

69. Kenen, *Israel's Defense Line*, 66, 110, 144.

70. Rountree to Herter, 21 Apr. 1959, 784A MSP.5/4-2159, State Department Central Decimal File, RG59, NA. See also Kenen, *Israel's Defense Line*, 148–53.

71. OCB report on the Near East, 3 Feb. 1960, *DDRS 1984*, item 2567.

72. State Department memcon, 10 Mar. 1960, "Israel (2)," box 8, International Series, White House Office of the Staff Secretary, DDEL; "Considerations Bearing on Israel's Request for Hawk Missiles," n.d. [July 1960], *DDRS 1989*, item 187; Herter to Ben Gurion, 4 Aug. 1960, *DDRS 1987*, item 1462.

73. Eban, *Autobiography*, 272.

74. On the background to the Dimona imbroglio, see Clifton to JFK, "Ben Gurion's Resignation," 8 Feb. 1961, *DDRS 1979*, item 352A; Quester, "Nuclear Weapons and Israel," 548–49; Hersh, *Samson Option*, 47–81.

75. Herter testimony, 6 Jan. 1961, in U.S. Congress, Senate Committee on Foreign Relations, *Executive Sessions*, 13:7; Eisenhower's message and Ben Gurion's rejoinder are quoted in Bar-Zohar, *Ben-Gurion*, 271–72.

76. Memo for the record, 6 Dec. 1960, "Memos of the Staff re Change of Administration," box 1, Transition Series, AWF, DDEL.

77. Bundy to Kennedy, 29 May 1961, *FRUS 1961–63*, 17:132–33.

78. DOS memcon, 30 May 1961, ibid., 134–41.

79. Talbot to Feldman, 9 Aug. 1962; Feldman to JFK, 10 Aug. 1962; JFK to Ben Gurion, 15 Aug. 1962; and Feldman to JFK and Rusk, 19 Aug. 1962, all in Countries: Israel, box 119, NSF, JFKL.

80. Bundy, *Danger and Survival*, 510. Feldman confirmed the link between the Hawks and the Dimona reactor six years after he visited Tel Aviv. See *New York Times*, 16 June 1968.

81. DOS cirtel, 31 Oct. 1962, *FRUS 1961–63*, 18:196–98.

82. State Department memcon, "Conversation with Foreign Minister Meir," 27 Dec. 1962, Countries: Israel, box 119, NSF, JFKL. See also Hersh, *Samson Option*, 118.

83. DOS, "Near East Tour d'Horizon," 2 Apr. 1963, Countries: Israel, box 119, NSF, JFKL; Sherman Kent (CIA), "Consequences of Israel Acquisition of Nuclear Capability," 6 Mar. 1963, *FRUS 1961–63*, 18:398–401. On the disarmament task force, see Talbot to Rusk, 14 May 1963, Countries: Israel, box 119, NSF, JFKL.

84. JFK to Ben Gurion, tel., 4 May 1963, *FRUS 1961–63*, 18:511–14; DOS cirtel, 9 May 1963, Countries: Israel, box 119, NSF, JFKL.

85. Komer to McGeorge Bundy, 6 May 1963, box 322, Meetings and Memoranda: Komer, and Komer, "Memorandum for the Record," 14 May 1963, Countries: Israel, box 119, NSF, JFKL; Komer Oral History, 75–76.

86. Talbot to Rusk, 14 May 1963, and Rusk to JFK, 16 May 1963, both in Countries: Israel, box 119, NSF, JFKL.

87. Burns, *Economic Aid and American Policy toward Egypt*, 141–43; remarks by Hermann Eilts at the New England Historical Association Conference, 21 Oct. 1989, Smith College, Northampton, Mass.

88. Komer to McGeorge Bundy, 14 May 1963, Meetings and Memoranda: Komer, box 322, and Glenn Seaborg to Bundy, 1 July 1963; Barbour to Rusk, tel., 16 Aug. 1963; and Read to Bundy, 24 Sept. 1963, Countries: Israel, box 119, all in NSF, JFKL.

89. Rodger Davies (NEA), "U.S. Security Guarantee for Israel," 11 Sept. 1963, Countries: Israel, box 119, NSF, JFKL.

90. JFK to Eshkol, 2 Oct. 1963, and Komer memcon, 21 Nov. 1963, *FRUS 1961–63*, 18:720–22, 797–801.

91. Talbot memcon, 25 Nov. 1963, in *Lyndon B. Johnson National Security Files*, reel 1, frame 44.

92. On pro-Israel sentiment among LBJ's advisers and friends, see Spiegel, *Other Arab-Israeli Conflict*, 128–29; Neff, *Warriors for Jerusalem*, 83–84, 110–11; and Tivnan, *Lobby*, 59–60.

93. Rusk to LBJ, 25 Feb. 1964, Country Files: UAR, box 158, NSF, LBJL.

94. Feldman to LBJ, 14 Mar. 1964; Komer to LBJ, 4 Mar. 1964; and McGeorge Bundy to LBJ, 12 May 1964, Memos to the President, box 1, NSF, LBJL; Peres, *David's Sling*, 103–7.

95. Deputy Assistant Secretary of Defense for International Security Affairs Peter Solbert to McGeorge Bundy, 8 Mar. 1965, in *Lyndon B. Johnson National Security Files*, reel 3, frames 150–56.

96. "U.S. Draft Memorandum of Understanding," n.d. [late Mar. 1965], and Rusk to Talbot, tel., 21 Apr. 1965, in *Lyndon B. Johnson National Security Files*, reel 1, frames 239–44, 378–80.

97. Rusk to Barbour, tel., 14 Oct. 1965; Barbour to Rusk, tel., 29 Oct. 1965; and Benjamin Read (State Department Secretariat) to Walt Rostow, 30 Apr. 1966, all in *Lyndon B. Johnson National Security Files*, reel 1, frames 282, 353–54, 513–15.

98. "U.S. Arms Sale to Israel," n.d., attached to Rusk to LBJ, 29 July 1966, in *Lyndon B. Johnson National Security Files*, reel 3, frames 318, 336–37.

99. Spiegel, *Other Arab-Israeli Conflict*, 136–37; Neff, *Warriors for Jerusalem*, 40–46, 57–58; Dann, *King Hussein and the Challenge of Arab Radicalism*, 154–57.

100. Harold Saunders, "The President's Stake in the Middle East," 16 May 1967, Memos to the President, box 16, NSF, LBJL.

101. Ibid.

102. Johnson, *Vantage Point*, 290–93.

103. "United States Policy and Diplomacy in the Middle East Crisis, May 15–June 10, 1967," vol. 1, appendix P, box 20, NSC History Files: 1967 Middle East Crisis, NSF, LBJL, 34–35.

104. Miller, *Lyndon*, 478–79.

105. Minutes of the NSC Meeting, 24 May 1967, vol. 4, tab. 52, ME Crisis, box 2, NSC Meeting File, NSF, LBJL.

106. For the latest sanitized account of this meeting, see DOS memcon, 26 May 1967, *DDRS 1993*, item 546.

107. Miller, *Lyndon*, 480.

108. "United States Policy and Diplomacy in the Middle East Crisis, May 15–June 10, 1967," vol. 1, appendix P, box 20, NSC History Files: 1967 Middle East Crisis, NSF, LBJL, 97.

109. Quandt, "Lyndon Johnson and the June 1967 War," 221.

110. Eban, *Personal Witness*, 405.

111. Evron quoted in Melman and Raviv, *Friends in Deed*, 119–20.

112. Rusk to Gromyko, tel., 5 June 1967, 72D 192, box 927, Rusk Papers.

113. Johnson, *Vantage Point*, 303–4.

114. Rusk and Eban are quoted in Thomas J. Schoenbaum, *Waging Peace and War*, 463. For further evidence of Rusk's concerns about Israeli territorial and nuclear ambitions, see Rusk, *As I Saw It*, 343, 389.

115. Saunders to Rostow, "Rough Sketch of Package for Eshkol," 29 Dec. 1967, Country Files: Israel, box 144, NSF, LBJL.

116. Rostow to LBJ, "The Issues for Eshkol," 5 Jan. 1968, and "Notes on Meeting between LBJ & Eshkol," 7–8 Jan. 1968, both in Country Files: Israel, box 143, NSF, LBJL.

117. Bick, "Ethnic Linkages and Foreign Policy," 166–67.

118. Rusk to Hart, tel., 19 Sept. 1968, Country Files: Israel, box 142, NSF, LBJL.

119. LBJ to Eshkol, 23 Oct. 1968, *DDRS 1996*, item 1719.

120. Warnke, "Negotiations with Israel: F-4 and Advanced Weapons," 4 Nov. 1968, Country Files: Israel, box 142, NSF, LBJL.

121. Warnke to author, 12 Sept. 1989, in author's possession. On AIPAC's role in the Phantom negotiations, see Spiegel, *Other Arab-Israeli Conflict*, 161–64.

122. Safire, *Before the Fall*, 565.

123. NSSM 2, "Middle East Policy," 21 Jan. 1969, Information Policy Directorate, National Security Memoranda, NSC.

124. Nixon news conference, 27 Jan. 1969, *PPP, Richard M. Nixon, 1969*, 18.

125. Nixon quoted in Kissinger, *White House Years*, 372–73.

126. Rabin, *Memoirs*, 156.

127. Rogers, "Lasting Peace in the Middle East."

128. Rabin, *Memoirs*, 158–62. Meir is quoted on 158.

129. Kenen, *Israel's Defense Line*, 238.

130. Nixon, *RN*, 479–81.

131. Ibid., 481.

132. Kissinger, *White House Years*, 571.

133. Spiegel, *Other Arab-Israeli Conflict*, 195; Quandt, *Decade of Decisions*, 112.

134. Kissinger, *White House Years*, 625.

135. Kissinger quoted in Rabin, *Memoirs*, 189.

136. Quandt, *Decade of Decisions*, 143–47; Cockburn and Cockburn, *Dangerous Liaisons*, 170–73.

137. Nixon quoted in Sulzberger, *World and Richard Nixon*, 185.

138. For the details on the airlift, see Quandt, *Decade of Decisions*, 185 n. 46.

139. Nixon, *RN*, 923–24; Kenen, *Israel's Defense Line*, 300–303.

140. Schlesinger interview, 25 Apr. 1989, quoted in Hersh, *Samson Option*, 230, 330.

141. Spiegel, *Other Arab-Israeli Conflict*, 251–55.

142. Kissinger, *Years of Upheaval*, 1136–37.

143. Nixon, *RN*, 1017–19.

144. Ford quoted in Golden, *Quiet Diplomat*, 314–15. Max Fisher was Ford's liaison with the American Jewish community.

145. Ford to Rabin, 21 Mar. 1975, quoted in Rabin, *Memoirs*, 256; David Schoenbaum, *United States and Israel*, 233–34.

146. Minutes of the NSC meeting, 28 Mar. 1975, *DDRS 1996*, item 506.

147. Ford, *Time to Heal*, 308.

148. Rabin, *Memoirs*, 261.

149. NSC, "Middle East Interim Agreement," 4 Sept. 1975, *DDRS 1996*, item 1042.

150. Carter remarks at Clinton, Mass., 16 Mar. 1977, *PPP, Jimmy Carter, 1977*, 1:387.

151. Rabin, *Memoirs*, 298–300.

152. Carter, *Keeping Faith*, 288, 292–93.

153. Brzezinski, *Power and Principle*, 247–49; Tivnan, *Lobby*, 124–29.

154. David Schoenbaum, *United States and Israel*, 260–73; Spiegel, *Other Arab-Israeli Conflict*, 361–79.

155. Reagan, *American Life*, 410; Spiegel, *Other Arab-Israeli Conflict*, 406.

156. Haig, *Caveat*, 165–71, 325–28; "U.S.-Israel Memorandum of Understanding," 30 Nov. 1981, in Laqueur and Rubin, *Israel-Arab Reader*, 420–21.

157. Begin quoted in Haig, *Caveat*, 328–29. On Reagan, Begin, and the battle over AWACS, see Tivnan, *Lobby*, 138–61, and Samuel Lewis, "United States and Israel," 233–36.

158. Sharon and Habib quoted in Schiff and Ya'ari, *Israel's Lebanon War*, 65–66.

159. Haig, *Caveat*, 335.

160. Lewis and Tanter quoted in Melman and Raviv, *Friends in Deed*, 218–19.

161. *New York Times*, 21, 26 Jan. 1983.

162. On NSDD-111 and the Eagleburger mission, see Gwertzman, "Reagan Turns to Israel," 62–64.

163. On the Shamir government's involvement in the Pollard case, see Blitzer, *Territory of Lies*, 289–92. On Israel's role in the Iran-Contra affair, see Draper, *Very Thin Line*, 137–54, 181–82.

164. Melman and Raviv, *Friends in Deed*, 381–91, 406–15.

165. James A. Baker, *Politics of Diplomacy*, 556.

166. Clinton remarks to the Israeli news media, 13 Sept. 1993, *PPP, William J. Clinton, 1993*, 2:1481.

167. Rabinovich quoted in Remnick, "Letter from Jerusalem," 95. Netanyahu quoted in Schmemann, "Outside In," 59.

168. Netanyahu, *Place among Nations*, 391.

169. Nagourney, "Sound Bites over Jerusalem," 44–47; *New York Times*, 16, 19 July 1999; *Washington Post*, 20 July 1999.

170. Malley and Agha, "Camp David," 60.

171. *New York Times*, 6, 7 Oct. 2001.

Chapter Four

1. Monroe, "Annual Message to Congress," 2 Dec. 1823, in Richardson, *Compilation of the Messages and Papers of the Presidents*, 2:209–220.

2. Crabb, *Doctrines of American Foreign Policy*, 37–38.

3. Mahan, "Persian Gulf and International Relations," 234–37.

4. FDR to Churchill, tel., 9 Mar. 1942, in Kimball, *Churchill and Roosevelt*, 1:399.

5. Hurley to FDR, 13 May 1943, *FRUS 1943*, 4:368–69.

6. OSS Research Report 1749, "Communist and Pro-Russian Trends in the Near East," 23 May 1944, in *OSS/State Department Intelligence and Research Reports*, pt. 7, reel 1, item 11.

7. DOS, "American Economic Policy in the Middle East," 2 May 1945, *FRUS 1945*, 8:38.

8. DOS, "Draft Memorandum for President Truman," n.d., attached to Dean Acheson to Secretary of State James F. Byrnes, 9 Oct. 1945, ibid., 45–48.

9. Henderson, "The Present Situation in the Near East: A Danger to World Peace," n.d. [28 Dec. 1945], *FRUS 1946*, 7:1–6.

10. Truman, *Years of Trial and Hope*, 94. For the text of the protest, see Byrnes to Molotov, 5 Mar. 1946, *FRUS 1946*, 7:340–42.

11. Byrnes quoted in Edwin M. Wright, "Events Relative to the Azerbaijan Issue, March 1946," 16 Aug. 1945, printed in editorial note, *FRUS 1946*, 7:346–48.

12. Kennan to DOS, tel., 22 Feb. 1946, ibid., 699–702. For the background to and implications of Kennan's then unprecedented 8,000-word telegram, see Kennan, *Memoirs*, 290–307.

13. Acheson to Byrnes (Paris), tel., 15 Aug. 1946, *FRUS 1946*, 7:840–42.

14. Ambassador Edwin Wilson (Ankara) to DOS, tels., 15, 18 Aug. 1946; DOS to Byrnes (Paris), tel., 17 Aug. 1946; Acheson to Orekhov, 19 Aug. 1946; and Bevin to the Soviet chargé d'affaires, 21 Aug. 1946, ibid., 842, 845, 846–48, 850–51.

15. DOS, "Memorandum on Turkey," 21 Oct. 1946, ibid., 894–97.

16. British Embassy to DOS, 21 Feb. 1947, *FRUS 1947*, 5:35–37.

17. Ethridge to DOS, tel., 17 Feb. 1947, ibid., 23–25.

18. Acheson, "Crisis and Imminent Possibility of Collapse in Greece," 21 Feb. 1947, ibid., 29–31.

19. Marshall quoted in Forrestal Diaries, 24 Feb. 1947, in Wittner, *American Intervention in Greece*, 67–68.

20. Acheson, *Present at the Creation*, 219.

21. Truman, *Years of Trial and Hope*, 103.

22. Truman address, 12 Mar. 1947, *PPP, Harry S. Truman, 1947*, 176–80.

23. Leffler, *Preponderance of Power* 142–64, 174–79.

24. Foreign Office Steering Brief, n.d. [Oct. 1947], quoted in Louis, *British Empire in the Middle East*, 111.

25. DOS, "The British and American Positions," n.d. [Oct. 1947], *FRUS 1947*, 5:511–14.

26. DOS, "The American Paper," n.d., and Foreign Office, "Memorandum on Policy in the Middle East and the Eastern Mediterranean," n.d. [both Nov. 1947], ibid., 575–76, 580–82.

27. "Statement by the U.S. and U.K. Groups," 14 Nov. 1949, *FRUS 1949*, 6:61–64.

28. Truman to Acheson, 31 Jan. 1950, *FRUS 1950*, 1:141–42.

29. NSC-68, 7 Apr. 1950, ibid., 234–92. The quoted passage is on 249.

30. NSC-65, "U.S. Policy toward Arms Shipments to the Near East," 28 Mar. 1950, ibid., 5:131–35.

31. Memorandum by Lucius Battle, 14 Apr. 1950, ibid., 135 n. 6.

32. Acheson to Undersecretary of State James Webb, 12 May 1950, and DOS cirtel, 20 May 1950, ibid., 161–62, 167–68; "The Tripartite Declaration," *DOSB*, 5 June 1950, 886.

33. DOS, "Minutes of the U.S.-U.K. Political Military Conversations," 26 Oct. 1950, *FRUS 1950*, 5:233–38.

34. Ibid.

35. DOS memcon, 17 May 1951, and editorial note, *FRUS 1951*, 5:134–39, 3:522–24.

36. Draft Study by the National Security Council, 27 Dec. 1951, ibid., 5:257–64.

37. Acheson to Ambassador Walter Gifford (London), tel., 21 June 1952, and Acheson (London) to DOS, tel., 27 June 1952, *FRUS 1952–54*, 9:247–49, 251–54.

38. Byroade memcon, 8 Aug. 1952, ibid., 262–66.

39. Minutes of the 147th NSC meeting, 1 June 1953, ibid., 383–86.

40. Eden quoted in Theodore Achilles (Paris) to DOS, tel., 16 Dec. 1953, ibid., 2174–75.

41. Churchill quoted in Louis, "Anglo-Egyptian Settlement of 1954," 69.

42. Eisenhower-Churchill memcon, 25 June 1954, *FRUS 1952–54*, 6:1081–83.

43. DOS memcon, "Egypt," 26 June 1954, ibid., 1104–7.

44. NIE 30-54, "Prospects for Creation of a Middle East Defense Grouping," 22 June 1954, *FRUS 1952–54*, 9:518.

45. NSC-5428, "U.S. Objectives and Policies with Respect to the Near East," 23 July 1954, ibid., 525–30; minutes of the 207th NSC meeting, 22 July 1954, box 5, NSC Series, AWF, DDEL.

46. Ashton, "Hijacking of a Pact," 125–28.

47. Foster Dulles to Ambassador Avra Warren (Ankara), tel., 7 Oct. 1954, *FRUS 1952–54*, 9:549–50.

48. Robert Murphy memcon, 15 Dec. 1954, and DOS to Ambassador Loy Henderson (Tehran), tel., 15 Dec. 1954, ibid., 10:1074–76.

49. Minutes of the 247th NSC meeting, 5 May 1955, *FRUS 1955–57*, 12:54.

50. On Stalin's and Khrushchev's differing approaches to the Arab world, see Smolansky, *Soviet Union and the Arab East under Khrushchev*, 15–17, and Golan, *Soviet Policies in the Middle East from World War II to Gorbachev*, 29–43.

51. NIE 30-55, "Middle East Defense Problems and Prospects," 21 June 1955, *FRUS 1955–57*, 12:79–80, 91–92.

52. Eisenhower-Dulles telcon, 7 Apr. 1956, ibid., 270.

53. Goodpaster memcon, 25 Nov. 1956, *FRUS 1955–57*, 16:1194–95.

54. Dulles-Macmillan memcon (Paris), 12 Dec. 1956, ibid., 27:677–78.

55. Eisenhower-Dulles telcon, 8 Dec. 1956, "Dec. 1956 Phone Calls," DDE Diary Series, AWF, DDEL.

56. Goodpaster memcon, 20 Dec. 1956, "Dec. 1956 Diary," ibid.

57. "Minutes of the Bipartisan Congressional Leadership Meeting," 1 Jan. 1957, "Jan. 1957, Misc (3)," ibid.

58. Dulles testimony, 2 Jan. 1957, in U.S. Congress, Senate Committee on Foreign Relations, *Executive Sessions*, 9:10–12, 21–22, 25.

59. Dulles's exchanges with Russell and Humphrey are in ibid., 18, 19, 22.

60. "Joint Congressional Resolution to Promote Peace and Stability in the Middle East," 9 Mar. 1957, U.S. Department of State, *United States Policy in the Middle East*, 44–46. For the vote, see editorial note, *FRUS 1955–57*, 12:452.

61. On Turkey, see Richards to DOS, tel., 22 Mar. 1957, *FRUS 1955–57*, 24:710–12. On Iran, see Bill, *Eagle and the Lion*, 118. On Lebanon, see Richards to DOS, tel., 15 Mar. 1957, *FRUS 1955–57*, 13:208–9. On Iraq, see Gallman, *Iraq under General Nuri*, 79–81.

62. Minutes of the Intelligence Advisory Committee, 23 Apr. 1957; DDE to JFD, phone call, 24 Apr. 1957; and JFD memcon, 24 Apr. 1957, *FRUS 1955–57*, 13:102–3.

63. Dulles to Ike, 20 Aug. 1957, "Dulles, Aug. 1957 (1)," Dulles-Herter Series, AWF, DDEL.

64. Dwight D. Eisenhower, *The White House Years: Waging Peace*, 199; Dulles to Henderson, tel., 23 Aug. 1957, *FRUS 1955–57*, 13:650–51.

65. Henderson to JFD, tel., 26 Aug. 1957, *FRUS 1955–57*, 13:656–57.

66. Macmillan, *Riding the Storm*, 277–81.

67. Dulles to Macmillan, 5 Sept. 1957, *FRUS 1955–57*, 13:681–82.

68. Goodpaster memcon, 7 Sept. 1957, ibid., 685–89.

69. Lesch, *Syria and the United States*, 152–65; Little, "Cold War and Covert Action," 72–74.

70. Dulles to Macmillan, 19 Sept. 1957, "Dulles, Aug. 1957 (2)," box 7, Dulles-Herter Series, AWF, DDEL.

71. PPS, "U.S. Objectives and Policies with Respect to the Near East," 30 Oct. 1957, *FRUS 1955–57*, 12:626, 642.

72. "Meeting re Iraq," 14 July 1958, *DDRS: Retrospective Collection*, item 628H.

73. Eisenhower quoted in "Timetable of Events of Week of July 14–19," n.d., "Mideast, July 1958 (7)," International Series, AWF, DDEL. See also Cutler, *No Time for Rest*, 362–63.

74. Goodpaster memcon, 14 July 1958, *DDRS 1984*, item 1391.

75. Eisenhower to Macmillan, phone call, 14 July 1958, "Mideast, July 1958 (8)," International Series, AWF, DDEL; Macmillan, *Riding the Storm*, 504–5, 512; Dulles to Ike, 21 Oct. 1957, and Dulles to Whitney, tel., 9 Dec. 1957, *FRUS 1955–57*, 13:510 n. 2, 511–12.

76. Macmillan, *Riding the Storm*, 513, 523; Dulles to Eisenhower, phone call, 15 July 1958, "Telephone Calls, July 1958," DDE Diary Series, AWF, DDEL.

77. Diary entry, 16 July 1958, in Macmillan, *Riding the Storm*, 516–17 (emphasis in original).

78. Reinhardt memcon, 17 July 1958, and Eisenhower to Macmillan, appended to Dulles to Whitney, tel., 18 July 1958, "Mideast, July 1958 (2)," International Series, AWF, DDEL.

79. Hall (Ankara) to JFD, tel., 16 July 1958, "Iran, 1953–59 (4)," ibid.

80. Little, "His Finest Hour?"; Johnston, *Brink of Jordan*, 101–4. Johnston was the British ambassador to Jordan in 1958.

81. Staff notes, 15 July 1958, "Mideast, July 1958 (8)," International Series, AWF, DDEL.

82. DDE to JFD, tel., n.d. [27 July 1958], "Middle East, July 1958 (4)," and "Declaration," 28 July 1958, "Mideast," ibid.

83. Annex A, "General Considerations Affecting U.S. Policy toward the Near East," NSC-5820, 3 Oct. 1958, *DDRS 1988*, item 388.

84. NSC-5820/1, "U.S. Policy toward the Near East," 4 Nov. 1958, *FRUS 1958–60*, 12:187–89.

85. Lloyd-Herter memcon, 29 Apr. 1959, V1074/5, vol. 141841, FO371, PRO.

86. NSC-6011, "U.S. Policy toward the Near East," 17 June 1960, *Documents of the National Security Council*, reel 3.

87. NSC-6010, "Statement of U.S. Policy toward Iran," 6 July 1960, *FRUS 1958–60*, 12:685.

88. Hart memcon, 29 June 1961, *FRUS 1961–63*, 17:169–71.

89. Minutes of the 486th NSC meeting, 29 June 1961, and Rusk to Foreign Secretary Douglas Home, tel., 29 June 1961, ibid., 172, editorial note 73.

90. Talbot memcon, 24 July 1961, ibid., 197–99.

91. Hart Oral History, 4–5.

92. Lucius Battle to Ralph Dungan, 21 Mar. 1961, *FRUS 1961–63*, 17:51–53.

93. DOS memcon, 13 Apr. 1962, "Iran Subjects: Shah Visits 4/16/62–5/14/62," Countries, box 116/117, NSF, JFKL.

94. LBJ to JFK, 10 Sept. 1962, "Middle East Memos," box 10, Vice Presidential Security Series, LBJL.

95. Komer to JFK, 19 June 1963, Subject File: Komer, box 481, JFK-LBJ Series, Harriman Papers.

96. Komer to Harriman, 10 Aug. 1963, ibid.

97. Komer to Bundy and Harriman, 6 Sept. 1963, ibid.

98. For a discussion of NSAM 289, "Western Pacific and Indian Ocean Base Study," 19 Mar. 1964, see Stivers, *America's Confrontation with Revolutionary Change in the Middle East*, 43–44, 53, 114.

99. Walt W. Rostow, "Alternatives for the US in the Persian Gulf–Arabian Sea Area Stemming from UK Defense Review," 4 Oct. 1965, quoted in Pieragostini, *Britain, Aden, and South Arabia*, 167.

100. Stivers, *America's Confrontation with Revolutionary Change in the Middle East*, 51–53.

101. DOS memcon, "Visit of Prime Minister Wilson, December 15–19, 1965," n.d., *DDRS 1995*, item 210.

102. Kaiser to DOS, "A View of US-UK Policy Relations," 23 May 1966, *DDRS 1995*, item 891.

103. Rostow to LBJ, 20, 22 June 1966, "Saudi Arabia, Faisal Trip," box 155, Country Files, NSF, LBJL; Safran, *Saudi Arabia*, 119, 121–22, 198, 200–201.

104. Walt Rostow to LBJ, 19 July 1966, *DDRS 1991*, item 457; Walt Rostow to LBJ, 10 Aug. 1966, "Iran," vol. 2, box 136, Country Files, NSF, LBJL.

105. Dean to Paul Gore Booth, 25 Oct. 1967, vol. 771, FCO 7, PRO.

106. Minutes of a Meeting in the Foreign Secretary's Room, House of Commons, 20 Dec. 1967, vol. 1999, PREM 13, and Cabinet Minutes, 4 Jan. 1968, CC1(68), CAB 128/143, PRO.

107. Brown to Wilson, tel., 11 Jan. 1968, vol. 1999, PREM 13, PRO.

108. Undersecretary of State Nicholas Katzenbach to LBJ, 11 Jan. 1968, *DDRS 1995,* item 895.

109. LBJ to Wilson, 12, 15 Jan. 1968, vol. 63, Bruce Diary, Bruce Papers.

110. Bruce to William Bundy, tel., 15 Jan. 1968, ibid.

111. Wilson to LBJ, tel., 15 Jan. 1968, vol. 1999, PREM 13, PRO.

112. Harriman memcon, 16 Jan. 1968, Subject File: Macmillan, box 486, JFK-LBJ Series, Harriman Papers.

113. Rostow to LBJ, 16 Jan. 1968, "Rostow Memos," box 7, Name File, NSF, LBJL.

114. Rusk to LBJ, "Release of Arms for Saudi Arabia," 19 Jan. 1968, and Consul Dhahran to Rusk, tel., 31 Jan. 1968, "Saudi Arabia," vol. 2, box 155, and Meyer to Rusk, tel., 9 Feb. 1968, and Eugene Rostow to Meyer, tel., 8 Mar. 1968, "Iran," vol. 2, box 136, all in Country Files, NSF, LBJL.

115. Rusk to Meyer, 12 June 1968, "Iran," vol. 2, box 136, and "Briefing Paper," n.d., attached to Read to Rostow, 22 June 1968, "Saudi Arabia," vol. 2, box 155, ibid.

116. State Department cirtel, 18 June 1968, "Saudi Arabia," vol. 2, box 155, ibid.

117. FO memcon, 13 Sept. 1968, vol. 37, FCO 8, PRO.

118. Nixon, "Informal Remarks on Guam with Newsmen," 25 July 1969, *PPP, Richard M. Nixon, 1969,* 549.

119. NSSM 66, "Policy toward the Persian Gulf," 12 July 1969, in National Security Archive, *Iran,* fiche 319, item 1375; Litwak, *Detente and the Nixon Doctrine,* 140.

120. Safran, *Saudi Arabia,* 182–83, 196–205.

121. Litwak, *Detente and the Nixon Doctrine,* 139–40.

122. CIA, SNIE 34-70, "Iran's International Position," 3 Sept. 1970, CIA, Office of Information and Privacy Coordination.

123. Rogers, *United States Foreign Policy,* 85, 89.

124. Noyes, *Clouded Lens,* 54–55.

125. Kissinger, *White House Years,* 1262–64.

126. DOS briefing paper, "Iran's Role in Regional Security," May 1972, attached to Rogers to Nixon, 12 May 1972, in National Security Archive, *Iran,* fiche 123, item 767.

127. Nixon quoted in Sick, *All Fall Down,* 14. Sick's source (344 n. 14) was "an individual in the Nixon administration who was personally familiar with the events of the Tehran visit."

128. Kissinger, *White House Years,* 1263–64.

129. Kissinger to William Rogers and Melvin Laird, 15 June, 25 July 1972, in National Security Archive, *Iran,* fiche 124, item 778, and fiche 126, item 782.

130. On Oman, see Saikal, *Rise and Fall of the Shah,* 178–79, and Bill, *Eagle and the Lion,* 202–7. For the checkmate analogy, see Kissinger, *Years of Renewal,* 582–83.

131. Kissinger to Ford, "Strategy for Your Discussions with the Shah of Iran," 13 May 1975, in National Security Archive, *Iran,* fiche 154, item 955.

132. CIA, "The Soviets in the Persian Gulf/Arabian Peninsula: Assets and Prospects," Dec. 1976, in ibid., fiche 185, item 1127.

133. DOS, "Iran," 3 Jan. 1977, in ibid., fiche 187, item 1138.

134. Vance, *Hard Choices,* 314–16.

135. Brzezinski, *Power and Principle,* 356–57.

136. Sick, *All Fall Down,* 18, 21.

137. Vance, *Hard Choices,* 317–19.

138. Vance to Embassy Tehran, tel., 29 May 1977, in National Security Archive, *Iran*, fiche 195, item 1184.

139. Carter, *Keeping Faith*, 433–37; Sick, *All Fall Down*, 28–29.

140. Carter toast, 15 Nov. 1977, *PPP, Jimmy Carter, 1977*, 2:2029–30.

141. Carter toast, 31 Dec. 1977, ibid., 2220–21; Sick, *All Fall Down*, 29–31.

142. Sick, *All Fall Down*, 34–35, 38–41.

143. Vance, *Hard Choices*, 384; Hammond, *Red Flag over Afghanistan*, 49–55.

144. Sick, *All Fall Down*, 36.

145. Carter, *Keeping Faith*, 254–55.

146. Gromyko-Andropov-Ustinov-Ponomarev Report, 31 Dec. 1979, *Cold War International History Project Bulletin*, 160–61. For more on Soviet motives, see Garthoff, *Détente and Confrontation*, 1034–43.

147. Brzezinski to Carter, 26 Dec. 1979, in Westad, *Fall of Détente*, 329.

148. Brzezinski, *Power and Principle*, 429–30, 446–47.

149. Vance, *Hard Choices*, 388.

150. Jordan, *Crisis*, 98–99.

151. Carter, *Keeping Faith*, 471–72.

152. Carter, "State of the Union Address," 23 Jan. 1980, *PPP, Jimmy Carter, 1980–81*, 1:196.

153. Brzezinski to Carter, 3, 9 Jan. 1980, *DDRS 1997*, items 460, 1672.

154. Brzezinski, *Power and Principle*, 444–45.

155. Ibid., 426–27.

156. Slocombe quoted in Gates, *From the Shadows*, 144–45.

157. Ibid., 143–44. For an inside account of the ISI's relationship with the CIA during the Afghan war, see Yousaf with Adkin, *Bear Trap*, 78–112.

158. Gates, *From the Shadows*, 145–47. On the origins of the Special Coordination Committee, see Brzezinski, *Power and Principle*, 59–62.

159. Gates, *From the Shadows*, 147–49. For a firsthand account of activities in Peshawar during early 1980, see Brzezinski, *Power and Principle*, 449.

160. McFarlane with Smardz, *Special Trust*, 69. On Saudi financial assistance to the mujahadeen, see Weaver, "Children of the Jihad," 41. On bin Laden's activities in Afghanistan during the 1980s, see Bodansky, *Bin Laden*, 12–15, and Rashid, *Taliban*, 131–33.

161. NSDD-75, "U.S. Relations with the USSR," 17 Jan. 1983, in McFarlane, *Special Trust*, 372–80.

162. Cogan, "Partners in Time," 76–79.

163. See Weiner, "Blowback from the Afghan Battlefield"; Weaver, "Blowback"; "In Afghanistan, Triumph of Fundamentalism," *New York Times*, 26 May 1997.

164. Brzezinski quoted in "The CIA's Intervention in Afghanistan," http://globalresearch.ca/articles/BRZ110A.html, posted 15 Oct. 2001. For the original interview, see *Le Nouvel Observateur*, 15–21 Jan. 1998.

Chapter Five

1. Badeau, "Middle East," 240.

2. Wilson address to joint session of Congress, 2 Apr. 1917, *FRUS 1917, Supplement 1*, 200; V. I. Lenin, "The Socialist Revolution and the Right of Nations to Self-Determi-

nation," in Lenin, *National Liberation, Socialism, and Imperialism,* 118–19. On Wilson's rivalry with Lenin, see McFadden, *Alternative Paths,* 50–54.

3. Wilson, "The Final Draft of the Fourteen Points Address," 7 Jan. 1918, in Link, *Papers of Woodrow Wilson,* 45:528. For a more general discussion of Wilson's views on these matters, see Heater, *National Self-Determination.*

4. On the intellectual origins of Arab nationalism, see Dawn, *From Ottomanism to Arabism,* 122–79, and Haddad, "Rise of Arab Nationalism Reconsidered." For a classic account of the Arab revolt, see Antonius, *Arab Awakening,* 164–215.

5. Minutes of the Council of Ten Meeting, 6 Feb. 1919, *FRUS: Paris Peace Conference 1919,* 3:888–94.

6. Fromkin, *Peace to End All Peace,* 188–96, 389–402.

7. Lansing, *Peace Negotiations,* 97–98.

8. For a discussion of Wilson's second thoughts, see Buchheit, *Secession,* 63–66, 113–15.

9. Howard, *King-Crane Commission,* 31–43.

10. Fromkin, *Peace to End All Peace,* 435–54.

11. Zaghlul to Wilson, 6 June 1919, in Noble, "Voice of Egypt"; Manela, "Friction from the Sidelines," 42–53; Eran, "Negotiating the Anglo-Egyptian Relationship between the World Wars."

12. Gordon, *Nasser's Blessed Movement,* 17–20; Raymond William Baker, *Egypt's Uncertain Revolution,* 5–9.

13. For the background and the text of the Atlantic Charter, see Undersecretary of State Sumner Welles, two memcons, 11 Aug. 1941, and Joint Statement by Roosevelt and Churchill, 14 Aug. 1941, *FRUS 1941,* 1:356–69.

14. Sumner Welles to Wallace Murray, 5 Feb. 1942, *FRUS 1942,* 4:70. See also Hahn, *United States, Great Britain, and Egypt,* 11–18.

15. Hurley to FDR, 21 Dec. 1943, *FRUS 1943,* 4:420–26.

16. Acheson to Undersecretary of State Edward R. Stettinius, 28 Jan. 1944, "NEA (Mr. Murray, Jan 1944)," box 217, Stettinius Papers.

17. Wadsworth quoted in Henderson to Byrnes, 13 Nov. 1945, *FRUS 1945,* 8:11–18.

18. NEA position paper, "The British and American Positions," n.d. [late Sept. 1947], *FRUS 1947,* 5:513.

19. Chargé d'Affaires Julius Holmes (London) to DOS, tel., 22 Dec. 1948, *FRUS 1948,* 5:1680–85.

20. DOS, OIR Report #4904.4, "Potentials of World Communism: Middle and Near East," 1 Aug. 1949, *OSS/State Department Intelligence and Research Reports,* pt. 7, reel 1; CIA, SR-13, "The Arab States," 27 Sept. 1949, CIA, Office of Privacy Coordination.

21. McGhee, "Introductory Discussions on the Middle East between US and UK Groups," 14 Nov. 1949, *FRUS 1949,* 6:62–63.

22. NSC, "Position Paper on the Middle East," 27 Dec. 1951, *FRUS 1951,* 5:257–64.

23. Hoskins to Byroade, 7 Apr. 1952, *FRUS 1952–54,* 9:204–8 (emphasis in original). On Hoskins, FDR, and the Atlantic Charter, see Cordell Hull to John Winant (London), 2 tels., 27 Aug. 1942; Winant to Hull, tel., 15 Sept. 1942; and Sumner Welles to Alexander Kirk (Cairo), tel., 20 Nov. 1942, *FRUS 1942,* 4:26–33, 35–36.

24. Churchill quoted in diary entry, 16 Dec. 1951, in Shuckburgh, *Descent to Suez,* 28–29. On the Anglo-Egyptian impasse, see Hahn, *United States, Great Britain, and Egypt,* 132–39, and Louis, *British Empire in the Middle East,* 691–735.

25. Caffery to DOS, tel., 7 Dec. 1951, 641.74/12-751, State Department Central Decimal File, RG59, NA.

26. Acheson memcon, 5 Jan. 1952, *FRUS 1952–54*, 6:737–38.

27. Gordon, *Nasser's Blessed Movement*, 27–34; Hahn, *United States, Great Britain, and Egypt*, 138–41.

28. Acheson telcon, 27 Jan. 1952, *FRUS 1952–54*, 9:1755.

29. Caffery to DOS, tel., 21 Feb. 1952, 774.00/2-2152, State Department Central Decimal File, RG59, NA.

30. Gordon, *Nasser's Blessed Movement*, 34–37.

31. DOS memcon, 7 Mar. 1952, 774.00/3-752; Caffery to DOS, 14 Apr. 1952, 774.00/4-1452; and C. Robert Payne (Cairo) to DOS, 16 June 1952, 774.00/6-1652, State Department Central Decimal File, RG59, NA; Acheson, *Present at the Creation*, 566.

32. Caffery to DOS, tel., 3 July 1952, 774.00/7-352, State Department Central Decimal File, RG59, NA.

33. Alta F. Fowler (NEA), "Weekly Summary of Events, Egypt and the Sudan," 28 July 1952, *FRUS 1952–54*, 9:1844–47. For details on Nasser's coup, see Raymond William Baker, *Egypt's Uncertain Revolution*, 18–31, and Gordon, *Nasser's Blessed Movement*, 39–57.

34. Caffery to DOS, 18 Aug. 1952, 774.00/8-1852, State Department Central Decimal File, RG59, NA.

35. Acheson's remarks of 3 September quoted in *DOSB*, 15 Sept. 1952, 406.

36. Acheson, *Present at the Creation*, 566.

37. Acheson memcon, 7 Jan. 1953, *FRUS 1952–54*, 9:1954–55.

38. Dulles-Naguib memcon, 11 May 1953, ibid., 8–18.

39. Dulles-Nasser memcon, 12 May 1953, ibid., 19–25 (emphasis in original).

40. Nasser quoted in Heikal, *Cairo Documents*, 41.

41. Dulles to Bedell Smith, tel., 13 May 1953; Dulles to Ike, tel., 17 May 1953; and Dulles quoted in the minutes of the 147th NSC meeting, 1 June 1953, *FRUS 1952–54*, 9:25–26, 88–89, 380–81.

42. Caffery to DOS, tel., 22 June 1953, and Ike to Churchill, 6 July 1953, ibid., 2104, 2110.

43. Caffery to DOS, tels., 25, 26 Feb. 1954, ibid., 2221–23.

44. Caffery to DOS, 9, 23 Mar. 1954, ibid., 2226, 2242–44.

45. Gordon, *Nasser's Blessed Movement*, 175–87.

46. C. L. Sulzberger, "Foreign Affairs," *New York Times*, 17 Nov. 1954.

47. Nasser, *Egypt's Liberation*, 98–114.

48. Nasser, "Egyptian Revolution," 210–11.

49. William Burdett (NEA), "Measures to Counter Communist Threat in Arab Countries," 28 Jan. 1955, Alpha Files, lot 518D, RG59, NA; Byroade to DOS, tel., 21 Mar. 1955, *FRUS 1955–57*, 14:117.

50. Donald Neff, *Warriors at Suez*, 74–93; Hahn, *United States, Great Britain, and Egypt*, 180–210.

51. Dulles-Macmillan memcons, 26 Sept., 26 Oct. 1955, *FRUS 1955–57*, 14:516–17, 655.

52. Minutes of the 267th NSC meeting, 21 Nov. 1955, box 7, NSC Series, AWF, DDEL; minutes of the 268th NSC meeting, 1 Dec. 1955, ibid., 812–17.

53. Anderson to DOS, tel., 19 Jan. 1956, *FRUS 1955–57*, 15:28–36.

54. Ike and Lloyd quoted in diary entry, 30 Jan. 1956, in Shuckburgh, *Descent to Suez*, 229.

55. Dulles quoted in DOS memcon, 30 Jan. 1956, *FRUS 1955–57*, 12:244.

56. Eden to Lloyd, tel., 7 Mar. 1956, V1075/61A, vol. 121271, FO371, PRO.

57. Diary entry, 8 Mar. 1956, "Diary, March 1956," box 13, DDE Diary Series, AWF, DDEL. For Ike's appeal, see Eisenhower to Nasser, 27 Feb. 1956, *FRUS 1955–57*, 15:243.

58. Lloyd to Dulles, n.d., attached to Makins to Dulles, 21 Mar. 1956, *FRUS 1955–57*, 15:384–87.

59. Chargé Evan Wilson (London) to DOS, 21 Mar. 1956, ibid., 389–91.

60. Rountree memcon, 28 Mar. 1956, ibid., 421–23.

61. Eisenhower diary entry, 28 Mar. 1956, ibid., 425.

62. Goodpaster memcon, 3 Apr. 1956, ibid., 446–48.

63. Minutes of the 284th NSC meeting, 10 May 1956, NSC Series, AWF, DDEL.

64. Dulles-Hussein memcon, 17 May 1956, *FRUS 1955–57*, 15:645–50.

65. Middle East Committee, "High Aswan Dam," 11 June 1956, vol. 119055, FO371, PRO.

66. Allen Dulles to Foster Dulles, "Shepilov's Visit to Egypt," 27 June 1956, *FRUS 1955–57*, 15:751–54.

67. Heikal, *Cutting the Lion's Tail*, 110; Russell to Foster Dulles, 19 July 1956, *FRUS 1955–57*, 15:865.

68. George Allen to Foster Dulles, 17 July 1956, *FRUS 1955–57*, 15:849–51.

69. Dulles-Eisenhower memcon, 19 July 1956, and Dulles-Makins memcon, 19 July 1956, ibid., 861–64.

70. Minute by Ross, 20 July 1956, JE1422/243A, vol. 119056, FO371, PRO.

71. Dulles-Hussein memcon, 19 July 1956, *FRUS 1955–57*, 15:867–73.

72. Nasser and Byroade quoted in Heikal, *Cutting the Lion's Tail*, 116.

73. Nasser quoted in Neff, *Warriors at Suez*, 270–71.

74. Cabinet Minutes, 27 July 1956, CM(56)54, CAB 128/30, PRO. See also Chargé Andrew Foster (London) to DOS, tel., 27 July 1956, *FRUS 1955–57*, 16:3–5. Foster attended the Cabinet meeting at Eden's invitation.

75. Dulles phone call to C. D. Jackson, 20 July 1956, quoted in Kyle, *Suez*, 130; Dulles to DOS, tel., 27 July 1956, *FRUS 1955–57*, 16:6 n. 3.

76. Hoover quoted in Goodpaster memcon, 27 July 1956, *FRUS 1955–57*, 16:6–7.

77. CIA, SNIE 30-3-56, "Nasser and the Middle East Situation," 31 July 1956, ibid., 79, 89.

78. Goodpaster memcon, 31 July 1956, ibid., 62–68.

79. Lloyd-Dulles memcon, 1 Aug. 1956, folder 1098, PREM 11, PRO.

80. Dulles-Eden memcon, 1 Aug. 1956, *FRUS 1955–57*, 16:98–100.

81. Minutes of the 292nd NSC meeting, 9 Aug. 1956, ibid., 165–76.

82. Kyle, *Suez*, 249–52.

83. Arthur Minnich, "Minutes of the Bipartisan Meeting," 12 Aug. 1956, *FRUS 1955–57*, 16:188–96.

84. Dulles to DOS, tel., and Dulles to Ike, 16 Aug. 1956, ibid., 203–5, 210–11.

85. Minutes of the 21st meeting of the Egypt Committee, 24 Aug. 1956, E.C.(56), CAB 143/1216, PRO.

86. Eisenhower to Eden, 2 Sept. 1956, *FRUS 1955–57*, 16:355–58.

87. Heikal, *Cutting the Lion's Tail*, 149–51.

88. Dulles memcon, 6 Sept. 1956, *FRUS 1955–57*, 16:396–98.

89. Dulles-Eisenhower memcon, 22 Sept. 1956, ibid., 566; Macmillan memcon, 25 Sept. 1956, folder 1102, PREM 11, PRO.

90. Kyle, *Suez*, 291–331; Lucas, *Divided We Stand*, 227–56.

91. Neff, *Warriors at Suez*, 341–48; Kyle, *Suez*, 332–47.

92. Dwight D. Eisenhower, *The White House Years: Waging Peace*, 68–74; Eisenhower to Ben Gurion, tel., 28 Oct. 1956; Dulles-Eban memcon, 28 Oct. 1956; and Goodpaster memcon, 29 Oct. 1956, *FRUS 1955–57*, 16:801, 808–10, 833–39. Eisenhower's angry remarks to Dulles are quoted in Love, *Suez*, 503.

93. Goodpaster memcon, 29 Oct. 1956, *FRUS 1955–57*, 16:833–39.

94. Makins to Lloyd, 9 Sept. 1956, quoted in Kyle, *Suez*, 229.

95. Makins to Eden, tel., 4 Oct. 1956, quoted in Louis, "Dulles, Suez, and the British," 133–34.

96. Acheson, *Present at the Creation*, 567; Acheson quoted in diary entry, 17 Oct. 1956, in Sulzberger, *Last of the Giants*, 331.

97. Goodpaster memcon, 30 Oct. 1956, 10:06 A.M., *FRUS 1955–57*, 16:851–55.

98. Dulles-Eisenhower telcon, 30 Oct. 1956, 2:17 P.M., ibid., 863.

99. Goodpaster memcon, 30 Oct. 1956, 4:25 P.M., ibid., 873–74.

100. Ike quoted in Cooper, *Lion's Last Roar*, 171. See also Divine, *Eisenhower and the Cold War*, 85–86, and Love, *Suez*, 504.

101. Eisenhower address, 31 Oct. 1956, *PPP, Dwight D. Eisenhower, 1956*, 1060–66.

102. Annex to NSC-5608, "U.S. Policy toward the Soviet Satellites in Eastern Europe," 6 July 1956; Chargé Spencer Barnes (Budapest) to DOS, 30 Aug. 1956; and Barnes to DOS, tel., 23 Oct. 1956, *FRUS 1955–57*, 25:198–210, 231–41, 263–65; Eisenhower address, 31 Oct. 1956, *PPP, Dwight D. Eisenhower, 1956*, 1061.

103. "Notes on the 42nd Meeting of the Special Committee on Soviet and Related Problems," 1 Nov. 1956, and Minutes of the 302nd NSC meeting, 1 Nov. 1956, *FRUS 1955–57*, 25:359–60, 16:902–16.

104. Minutes of the 302nd NSC meeting, 1 Nov. 1956, ibid., 16:902–16.

105. Dulles-Lodge telcon, 2 Nov. 1956, ibid., 938.

106. Békés, "New Findings on the 1956 Hungarian Revolution."

107. Eden to Eisenhower, tel., 5 Nov. 1956, *FRUS 1955–57*, 16:984–86.

108. Eisenhower quoted in Hughes, *Ordeal of Power*, 223–24.

109. Goodpaster memcon, 5 Nov. 1956, *FRUS 1955–57*, 16:1000–1001.

110. Ike-Eden telcon, 6 Nov. 1956, 12:55 P.M., ibid., 1025–27.

111. Kunz, *Economic Diplomacy of the Suez Crisis*, 138–62; Neff, *Warriors at Suez*, 424–29.

112. MacArthur to Hoover, 20 Nov. 1956, and DOS cirtel, 24 Nov. 1956, *FRUS 1955–57*, 16:1165, 1191–92.

113. Ike to Dulles, 12 Dec. 1956, ibid., 1296–98.

114. Hare to DOS, tel., 10 Jan. 1957, *FRUS 1955–57*, 17:16–19.

115. Dulles testimony, 14 Jan. 1957, in U.S. Congress, Senate Committee on Foreign Relations, 85th Cong., 1st sess., *President's Proposal on the Middle East*, 5.

116. DOS memcon, 5 Feb. 1957, *FRUS 1955–57*, 13:202.

117. OCB, "Analysis of Internal Security Situation in Syria," 7 July 1955, ibid., 530–31. See also Lesch, *Syria and the United States*, 17–56.

118. DOS memcon, 19 Aug. 1957, *FRUS 1955–57*, 13:640–41; Dulles to Ike, 20 Aug. 1957, "Dulles, Aug. 1957 (1)," box 7, Dulles-Herter Series, AWF, DDEL. For a more detailed discussion of this episode, see Little, "Cold War and Covert Action," 69–74.

119. Dwight D. Eisenhower, *The White House Years: Waging Peace*, 196–97.

120. DOS memcon, "US-Syrian Relations," 7 Nov. 1957, *FRUS 1955–57*, 13:740–44. The two best accounts of the formation of the UAR remain Seale, *Struggle for Syria*, 307–26, and Kerr, *Arab Cold War*, 7–19.

121. Herter to Dulles, tel., 25 Jan. 1958, *FRUS 1958–60*, 13:408.

122. Hare to DOS, tel., 10 Feb. 1958, ibid., 422–25.

123. DOS cirtels, 15, 21 Feb. 1958, ibid., 425–26, 430–32.

124. Eisenhower and Lloyd quoted in DOS memcon, 22 Mar. 1959, ibid., 12:217. On Eisenhower and Nasser, see Burns, *Economic Aid and American Policy toward Egypt*, 108–20.

125. Goodpaster memcon, 26 Sept. 1960, "United Arab Republic," box 49, International Series, AWF, DDEL.

126. JFK quoted in Goodwin, *Remembering America*, 135.

127. Burns, *Economic Aid and American Policy toward Egypt*, 121–31; Little, "New Frontier on the Nile," 504–7.

128. Bowles to JFK, Rusk, and Hamilton, tel., 21 Feb. 1962, *FRUS 1961–63*, 17:482, 486; Burns, *Economic Aid and American Policy toward Egypt*, 131–34.

129. Little, "From Even-Handed to Empty-Handed," 167–70.

130. Davies memcon, 3 Jan. 1963, 780.00/1-363, State Department Central Decimal File, RG59, NA.

131. Faisal quoted in Hart Oral History, 18.

132. JFK to Macmillan, 26 Jan. 1963, *FRUS 1961–63*, 18:324–25.

133. JFK to Nasser, enclosed in DOS to Badeau, tel., 19 Oct. 1963, ibid., 752. See also Little, "New Frontier on the Nile," 523–25.

134. Bundy to Fulbright, 11 Nov. 1963, *FRUS 1961–63*, 18:775.

135. Johnson, *Vantage Point*, 289–90.

136. "Major Issues in U.S.-U.A.R. Relations," n.d., attached to Rusk to LBJ, 21 Aug. 1964, "UAR Memos," vol. 2, box 159, Country Files, NSF, LBJL.

137. Embassy Cairo to DOS, tel., 12 Sept. 1964, ibid.; Heikal, *Cairo Documents*, 226–27.

138. Heikal, *Cairo Documents*, 229–30.

139. "President's Meeting with Congressional Leaders," 22 Jan. 1965, "Misc. Meetings," vol. 1, box 18, Bundy Files, NSF, LBJL.

140. Heikal, *Cairo Documents*, 348–49.

141. Nasser quoted in Read to Bundy, 5 June 1965, "UAR Cables," vol. 4, box 159, Country Files, NSF, LBJL.

142. "Protection of American Interests in the Near East," n.d., attached to Rusk to LBJ, 23 Sept. 1965, "UAR Memos," vol. 4, ibid.

143. Battle to DOS, tel., 13 May 1966, "UAR Cables," ibid.

144. CIA, "The Arab Threat to Iran," 21 May 1966, "UAR Memos," ibid.

145. CIA, "Egyptian-Soviet Relations," 28 May 1966, ibid.

146. Rostow to LBJ, 18 June 1966, ibid.

147. Johnson, *Vantage Point*, 288.

148. Saunders to Rostow, 16 May 1967, attached to Rostow to LBJ, 17 May 1967, "Saunders Memos," box 7, Name File, NSF, LBJL (emphasis in original).

149. Little, "Choosing Sides," 174–76.

150. Walt Rostow to LBJ, "NSC Discussion: South Arabia," 23 May 1967, "Briefing Papers NSC Mtgs," box 1, Meeting Notes File, NSF, LBJL.

151. Walt Rostow to LBJ, 4 June 1967, 11:30 A.M., *DDRS 1995*, item 1143.

152. Ambassador Walworth Barbour to DOS, tel., 7 June 1967, "Middle East Crisis, Cables," vol. 4, box 107, Country Files, NSF, LBJL.

153. Shah quoted in "U.S. Policy and Diplomacy in the Middle East Crisis, May 15–June 10, 1967," box 20, NSC History Files: 1967 Middle East Crisis, NSF, LBJL, 115.

154. Heikal, *Cairo Documents*, 249.

155. Nixon, *RN*, 179, 249.

156. Nasser quoted in minutes of cabinet meeting, 8 June 1969, in Farid, *Nasser*, 137.

157. Sisco to Nixon and Rogers, tel., 12 Apr. 1970, "ORG 7 NEA," State Department Alpha-Numeric File, RG59, NA; Parker, *Politics of Miscalculation in the Middle East*, 125–47; Quandt, *Peace Process*, 85–91.

158. Kissinger, *White House Years*, 361.

159. Nasser, *Egypt's Liberation*, 39–40.

160. Nasser memcon, 14 Feb. 1970, in Farid, *Nasser*, 168–69.

161. Badeau, *American Approach to the Arab World*, 45–46, 53–55.

162. Fulbright, *Arrogance of Power*, 69–73.

163. Tocqueville, *Democracy in America*, 2:270.

164. Cassandra [pseud.], "Impending Crisis in Egypt"; U.S. Congress, House Committee on International Relations, *U.S. Policy toward Egypt*, 1–17.

165. Bodansky, *Bin Laden*, 210–12, 236–37, 247–49; U.S. Department of State, *Patterns of Global Terrorism 1999*; Goldberg, "Letter from Cairo," 53–55.

Chapter Six

1. Tocqueville, *L'Ancien Regime*, 186.

2. For a general account of the council's activities during the Truman and Eisenhower years, see Schulzinger, *Wise Men of Foreign Affairs*, 135–41, 145–48, 165–73. Materials relating to the study groups, which covered topics such as "Non-Self-Governing Territories," "Emerging African Problems," and "The Middle East and Modern Islam," are available in Council on Foreign Relations, Archives, Records of Groups.

3. Truman, "Inaugural Address," 20 Jan. 1949, *PPP, Harry S. Truman, 1949*, 114. On Truman, Point Four, and foreign aid for developing countries, see Packenham, *Liberal America and the Third World*, 35–49.

4. On Eisenhower's approach to foreign aid, see Kaufman, *Trade and Aid*, 12–33, 95–112, 207–11, and Packenham, *Liberal America and the Third World*, 49–58.

5. Rockefeller Brothers Fund, *Prospect for America*, 54–56, 165–71. On Kissinger's role in the Rockefeller study, see Schulzinger, *Henry Kissinger*, 13–14.

6. Rostow, *Stages of Economic Growth*, 164–66.

7. JFK, "Special Message on Foreign Aid," 22 Mar. 1961, *PPP, John F. Kennedy, 1961*,

208; Rostow, *Diffusion of Power*, 185–88. For an excellent account of the impact of modernization theory on the New Frontier, see Latham, "Ideology, Social Science, and Destiny."

8. On the Peace Corps in Africa, see Cobbs Hoffman, "Diplomatic History and the Meaning of Life." On the Kennedy administration's efforts to modernize Latin America, see Latham, "Ideology, Social Science, and Destiny," 207–19. For an inside account of early attempts at nation building in Vietnam, see Rostow, *Diffusion of Power*, 264–76.

9. On America's good intentions and bad results in the Third World during the Johnson years, see Rostow, *Diffusion of Power*, 406–34.

10. Kissinger, *White House Years*, 69.

11. Brzezinski, *Between Two Ages*, 9, 35–36, 50–51.

12. Dodge quoted in "Discussion Meeting Report: The Moslem World," 9 May 1949, vol. 28, Council on Foreign Relations, Archives, Records of Groups.

13. Landis quoted in ibid. On Landis's activities during the war, see Baram, *Department of State in the Middle East*, 164–65, 191–92.

14. Lerner, *Passing of Traditional Society*, vii–viii, 44–45, 78–79, 399–400.

15. Halpern, *Politics of Social Change in the Middle East*, vii, 415, 418, 420. For Halpern's discussion of his ties with the State Department, see xvii–xviii and 55 n. 4. For a critique of Halpern's and Lerner's thinking, see Said, *Orientalism*, 310–11.

16. Halpern, *Politics of Social Change in the Middle East*, 357–58, 420.

17. Badeau, *American Approach to the Arab World*, 53–56, 108–9.

18. On Qassim and the coup, see Khadduri, *Republican Iraq*, 38–61; Batatu, *Old Social Classes and Revolutionary Movements of Iraq*, 778–79, 783–88, 800–807; and Thacher, "Reflections on US Foreign Policy towards Iraq in the 1950s."

19. Simon, *Iraq between the World Wars*, 1–7, 45–57, 145–65; Louis, *British Empire in the Middle East*, 331–44; Batatu, *Old Social Classes and Revolutionary Movements of Iraq*, 545–66.

20. Louis, "British and the Origins of the Iraqi Revolution"; Gallman, *Iraq under General Nuri*, xi–xiii, 92–93.

21. OCB Report, 14 Dec. 1955, *FRUS 1955–57*, 12:979–86.

22. Gallman to DOS, tel., 15 Jan. 1956, ibid., 988–92.

23. Nelson quoted in Sam Pope Brewer Diary entry, 3 Apr. 1956, box 24, Brewer Papers.

24. SNIE 36.2-56, "Outlook for Iraq's Stability," 17 July 1956, *FRUS 1955–57*, 12:997–1010.

25. Allen Dulles to Herbert Hoover Jr., 22 Nov. 1956, ibid., 1012–14.

26. Batatu, *Old Social Classes and Revolutionary Movements of Iraq*, 749–57, 776–83, 788.

27. Richards to DOS, tel., 9 Apr. 1957, *FRUS 1955–57*, 12:1044–47.

28. SNIE 36.2-57, "The Outlook for Iraq," 4 June 1957, ibid., 1048–58.

29. Gallman to DOS, 6 July 1957, ibid., 1062–63.

30. DOS Staff Study, "U.S. Objectives and Policies with Respect to the Near East," 30 Oct. 1957, ibid., 639–40.

31. Dulles to DOS, tel., 11 Mar. 1958, *FRUS 1958–60*, 12:294–96.

32. Stuart Rockwell (NEA) to Rountree, 26 Mar. 1958, ibid., 11:282–86.

33. Dulles memcon, 15 June 1958, and Frank Wisner (CIA) to Hugh Cumming (DOS), 3 July 1958, ibid., 11:136–37, 12:304–5.

34. Ovendale, "Great Britain and the Anglo-American Invasion of Jordan and Lebanon"; Tal, "Britain and the Jordan Crisis of 1958"; Little, "His Finest Hour?"

35. John Foster Dulles–Allen Dulles phone call, 25 July 1958, and Foster Dulles to Ike, 30 July 1958, *FRUS 1958–60*, 12:333–34, editorial note 131.

36. Ambassador Michael Wright (Baghdad) to FO, tel., 27 July 1958, and FO cirtel, 30 July 1958, folder 2368, PREM 11, PRO.

37. Farouk-Sluglett and Sluglett, *Iraq since 1958*, 51–66; Batatu, *Old Social Classes and Revolutionary Movements of Iraq*, 832–60.

38. Murphy memo, 15 Aug. 1958, *FRUS 1958–60*, 12:146.

39. Minutes of the 383rd NSC meeting, 16 Oct. 1958, *DDRS 1990*, item 332.

40. Minutes of the 391st NSC meeting, 18 Dec. 1958, *FRUS 1958–60*, 12:363–64.

41. Jernegan to DOS, tel., 26 Mar. 1959, ibid., 395–98. On the Mosul rebellion, see Batatu, *Old Social Classes and Revolutionary Movements of Iraq*, 866–89.

42. Minutes of the 401st NSC meeting, 2 Apr. 1959, and Gray, "Iraq," 3 Apr. 1959, *FRUS 1958–60*, 12:402–6, 410.

43. Anderson quoted in minutes of the 402nd NSC meeting, 17 Apr. 1959, and John Eisenhower, "Synopsis of State and Intelligence Material," 14 May 1959, ibid., 423–37, 450.

44. Jernegan to DOS, tel., 9 Aug. 1959, ibid., 474–77.

45. Stevens memcon, 29 Aug. 1959, vol. 141841, FO371, PRO.

46. Jernegan to DOS, tel., 26 Feb. 1960, and NIE 36.2-60, "Outlook for Iraq," 1 Nov. 1960, *FRUS 1958–60*, 12:502–6, 516–23.

47. OCB, "Operations Plan for Iraq," 14 Dec. 1960, ibid., 524–30.

48. Jernegan Oral History, 13–15.

49. Talbot to Ball, 18 Dec. 1961, *FRUS 1961–63*, 17:364–65. For the background to Qassim's assault on IPC, see Stork, *Middle East Oil and the Energy Crisis*, 102–8, and Blair, *Control of Oil*, 80–90.

50. Khadduri, *Republican Iraq*, 188–200; Batatu, *Old Social Classes and Revolutionary Movements of Iraq*, 974–94; Farouk-Sluglett and Sluglett, *Iraq since 1958*, 82–84.

51. Komer to JFK, 8 Feb. 1963, *FRUS 1961–63*, 18:342 n. 1.

52. DOS cirtel, 10 Feb. 1963, ibid., 345 n. 3; William Brubeck to McGeorge Bundy, 15 Feb. 1963, POL 26 IRAQ, State Department Alpha-Numeric File, RG59, NA.

53. Strong memcon, 25 Feb. 1963, POL 26 IRAQ, State Department Alpha-Numeric File, RG59, NA; Melbourne to Jernegan, 28 Feb. 1963, "Iraq: Misc," Subject File, box 10, Henderson Papers.

54. Saunders to Bundy, 2 Apr. 1963; DOS cirtel 18 Apr. 1963; Brubeck to Bundy, 19 July 1963; and Komer to JFK, 10 July 1963, *FRUS 1961–63*, 18:445–46, 470–73, 595–96, 638.

55. Ambassador Robert Strong (Baghdad) to DOS, tel., 17 July 1963, POL 15-4 IRAQ, and Strong to DOS, tel., 3 Sept. 1963, POL 26 IRAQ, State Department Alpha-Numeric File, RG59, NA.

56. Miller and Mylroie, *Saddam Hussein and the Crisis in the Gulf*, 85–105; Sciolino, *Outlaw State*, 62–63, 87–88; Karsh and Rautsi, *Saddam Hussein*, 22–50.

57. CIA, NIE 11-6-63, "The Soviet Role in the Arab World," 24 Apr. 1963, Office of Privacy Coordination, CIA.

58. The best account of Qaddafi's coup remains Cooley, *Libyan Sandstorm*, 1–20.

59. Khadduri, *Modern Libya*, 10–27; First, *Libya*, 45–55; John Wright, *Libya*, 25–43.

60. Louis, *British Empire in the Middle East*, 265–306; First, *Libya*, 56–74. For a detailed but very narrow account of great power rivalry over Libya during the late 1940s, see Bills, *Libyan Arena*.

61. Bakoush quoted in Blundy and Lycett, *Qaddafi and the Libyan Revolution*, 39.

62. DOS memcon, 28 May 1953, and minutes of the 147th NSC meeting, 1 June 1953, *FRUS 1952–54*, 9:162–66, 383; Dulles testimony, 3 June 1953, in U.S. Congress, Senate Committee on Foreign Relations, *Executive Sessions*, 5:437–38.

63. Ambassador Henry Villard to DOS, tel., 12 June 1954, and DOS to Villard, tels., 20, 29 July 1954, *FRUS 1952–54*, 11:588–94.

64. NIE 36.5-56, "Outlook for US Interests in Libya," 19 June 1956, *FRUS 1955–57*, 18:454–55.

65. Tappin to DOS, tel., 22 Nov. 1956, and to Joseph Palmer (NEA), 1 Jan. 1957, ibid., 456–57, 459–61.

66. Richards to DOS, tel., 21 Mar. 1957, and Tappin to DOS, tel., 22 Mar. 1957, *FRUS 1955–57*, 12:472–79.

67. Murphy memo, 26 Apr. 1957, ibid., 18:482 n. 7.

68. Minutes of the 321st NSC meeting, 2 May 1957, ibid., 481–85.

69. Richards to DOS, tel., 4 May 1957, ibid., 478 n. 5; "Staff Notes," 18 May 1957, "May 57 Diary: Staff Memos," box 24, DDE Diary Series, AWF, DDEL.

70. NSC-5716/1, "U.S. Policy toward Libya," 25 June 1957, *FRUS 1955–57*, 18:490–95.

71. DOS memcon, 23 June 1958, "Staff Notes (2), June 1958," box 33, DDE Diary Series, AWF, DDEL.

72. DOS, INR Report 7792, "Moderate Leadership on the Defensive in North Africa," 28 Aug. 1958, *OSS/State Department Intelligence Reports*, reel 6.

73. Minutes of the 390th NSC meeting, 11 Dec. 1958, *FRUS 1958–60*, 13:727–29.

74. Douglas Dillon to Neil McElroy, 22 May 1959, ibid., 731–33.

75. DOS, INR Report 8091, "Economic and Political Significance of North African Oil Discoveries," *OSS/State Department Intelligence Reports*, reel 6.

76. Minutes of the 422nd NSC meeting, 29 Oct. 1959, *FRUS 1958–60*, 13:733–34.

77. NSC-6004/1, "U.S. Policy toward Libya," 15 Mar. 1960, ibid., 740–49.

78. Symmes Oral History.

79. SNIE 36.1-62, "Prospects for Nasser," 28 Mar. 1962, "36.1 United Arab Republic," box 6, National Intelligence Estimates, NSF, LBJL.

80. DOS memo, "Libya," June 1962, "Libya, 1961–63," Countries, box 121A, POF, JFKL.

81. Komer to JFK, 16 Oct. 1962, and "Kennedy-Hasan Joint Communiqué," 17 Oct. 1962, ibid.

82. Benjamin Read to Bundy, 27 Sept. 1963, and Komer to JFK, 28 Sept. 1963, ibid.

83. William Brubeck memcon, 3 Apr. 1964, "Memos of Meetings with the President," vol. 1, box 19, Bundy Files, NSF, LBJL.

84. Robert Komer to JFK, 30 Sept. 1963, "Libya 1961–63," Countries, box 121A, POF, JFKL; Symmes Oral History.

85. Cooley, *Libyan Sandstorm*, 42–58; Yergin, *Prize*, 527–30.

86. Newsom quoted in Bruce Diary entry, 15 Dec. 1966, vol. 58, Bruce Papers.

87. First, *Libya*, 81–86; Little, "Choosing Sides," 177–79.

88. Newsom to DOS, tel., 16 June 1967, and Rostow to LBJ, 17 June 1967, "Rostow," vol. 3, Memos to the President, box 17, NSF, LBJL.

89. CIA, Arab-Israeli Situation Report, 29 June 1967, "Middle East Crisis," vol. 11, appendix Q (V), box 21, NSC History Files, and Eugene Rostow, "UAR Pressure on Libya," 30 June 1967, UAR, vol. 5, box 60, Country Files, ibid.

90. Eugene Rostow Oral History.

91. Newsom testimony, 20 July 1970, in U.S. Congress, Senate Committee on Foreign Relations, *U.S. Security Agreements and Commitments Abroad*, 2002. On the last days of Idris's rule and Qaddafi's takeover, see First, *Libya*, 99–113.

92. Akins testimony, 11 Oct. 1973, U.S. Congress, Senate Committee on Foreign Relations, Subcommittee on Multinational Corporations, *Multinational Corporations and United States Foreign Policy*, pt. 5, 1–2.

93. Seale and McConville, *Hilton Assignment*, 174–75; Cooley, *Libyan Sandstorm*, 83–86; Blundy and Lycett, *Qaddafi and the Libyan Revolution*, 55.

94. Newsom testimony, 20 July 1970, in U.S. Congress, Senate Committee on Foreign Relations, *U.S. Security Agreements and Commitments Abroad*, 1993.

95. First, *Libya*, 13–26; Cooley, *Libyan Sandstorm*, 8–15.

96. Qaddafi speech, 16 Oct. 1969, in "The Libyan Revolution in the Words of Its Leaders."

97. Newsom testimony, 20 July 1970, in U.S. Congress, Senate Committee on Foreign Relations, *U.S. Security Agreements and Commitments Abroad*, 1990–93.

98. Ibid., 2004.

99. Rogers, *United States Foreign Policy*, 145–46.

100. Yergin, *Prize*, 577–85; Cooley, *Libyan Sandstorm*, 62–79.

101. Qaddafi, *Green Book*, 83–103.

102. Burgat and Dowell, *Islamic Movement in North Africa*, 153–60; Cooley, *Libyan Sandstorm*, 134–57, 188–218, 223–27; First, *Libya*, 119–40.

103. Lake, *Third World Radical Regimes*, 22–23.

104. Keddie, *Roots of Revolution*, 86–112; Rubin, *Paved with Good Intentions*, 3–18; Yergin, *Prize*, 134–49, 269–71, 450.

105. Lytle, *Origins of the Iranian-American Alliance*, 120–55; Bill, *Eagle and the Lion*, 18–41.

106. DOS memcon, 18 Nov. 1949, *FRUS 1949*, 6:574–79; JCS to Louis Johnson, "Iran," 2 May 1950, quoted in Poole, *History of the Joint Chiefs of Staff*, 354. See also Goode, *United States and Iran*, 52–60.

107. NSC Staff Study, "The Position of the United States with Respect to Iran," n.d. [14 Mar. 1951], and NSC-107, "Iran," 14 Mar. 1951, *FRUS 1952–54*, 10:11–23.

108. NSC-136/1, "Present Situation in Iran," 20 Nov. 1952, ibid., 529–34; Heiss, *Empire and Nationhood*, 15–44, 107–34.

109. CIA to Eisenhower, "The Iranian Situation," 1 Mar. 1953, and minutes of the 135th NSC meeting, 4 Mar. 1953, *FRUS 1952–54*, 10:689–93.

110. Gordon Mattison to DOS, tel., 25 July 1953, ibid., 738–39.

111. The best accounts of the events of August 1953 remain Gasiorowski, "The 1953 Coup d'Etat in Iran," and Bill, *Eagle and the Lion*, 86–97.

112. Minutes of the 178th NSC meeting, 30 Dec. 1953, box 5, NSC Series, AWF, DDEL.

113. Minutes of the 377th NSC meeting, 21 Aug. 1958, *DDRS 1990*, item 352.

114. DOS memcon, "Iranian Budgetary Situation," 9 Dec. 1958, and minutes of the 394th NSC meeting, 22 Jan. 1959, *FRUS 1958–60*, 12:619–21, 625–26.

115. NIE 34-59, "The Outlook for Iran," 3 Mar. 1959, ibid., 643–45.

116. Eisenhower-Shah memcon, 14 Dec. 1959, ibid., 658–59.

117. John Eisenhower, "Synopsis of State and Intelligence Material," 22 Mar. 1960, and minutes of the 440th NSC meeting, 7 Apr. 1960, ibid., 671.

118. NSC-6010, "Statement of U.S. Policy toward Iran," 6 July 1960, ibid., 680–88.

119. Minutes of the 449th NSC meeting, 30 June 1960, and James Lay memo, 6 July 1960, ibid., 676–78, 681.

120. "A Review of Problems in Iran and Recommendations for the National Security Council," 15 May 1961, "Iran, 5/15/61," box 115, Countries, NSF, JFKL; "Study Group Report: Iran," 25 Oct. 1961, vol. 84, Council on Foreign Relations, Archives, Records of Groups; Goode, "Reforming Iran during the Kennedy Years."

121. Talbot testimony, 12 June 1961, in U.S. Congress, Senate Committee on Foreign Relations, *International Development and Security*, 499–500.

122. Chester Bowles to JFK, Rusk, and Fowler, tel., 17 Feb. 1962, "White House Correspondence: JFK, Jan.–Mar. 1962," folder 497, box 297, Bowles Papers.

123. JFK-Shah memcon, 12 Apr. 1962, "Iran: Shah Visit, 1962," box 117, Countries, NSF, JFKL.

124. Komer Oral History, 10–11.

125. "Substantive Points to Make to the Shah," n.d. [early Aug. 1962], "Middle East Trip 1962," box 2, Vice Presidential Security Series, LBJL.

126. Ambassador Julius Holmes (Tehran) to DOS, tel., 25 Aug. 1962, ibid.

127. JFK to State, Defense, and CIA, 14 Mar. 1963, "NSAM 228, Review of the Iranian Situation," box 340, Meetings and Memoranda, NSF, JFKL.

128. "Our Current Policy toward Iran," n.d., and "U.S. Strategy for Iran," n.d., both enclosed in Rusk to JFK, 20 Apr. 1963, "NSAM 228, Review of the Iranian Situation, May 1963," ibid.

129. "U.S. Strategy for Iran," n.d., enclosed in ibid.

130. Khomeini speech, 3 June 1963, in Algar, *Islam and Revolution*, 178–79. On Khomeini's meteoric rise during the summer of 1963, see Bill, *Eagle and the Lion*, 152–53.

131. Khomeini speech, 27 Oct. 1964, in Algar, *Islam and Revolution*, 181–85; Bill, *Eagle and the Lion*, 154–61.

132. Talbot testimony, 17 July 1963, in U.S. Congress, House Committee on Appropriations, Subcommittee on Foreign Operations, *Foreign Operations Appropriations for 1964*, 1137–38.

133. LBJ quoted in Bill, *Eagle and the Lion*, 178.

134. Meyer to LBJ, tel., 23 May 1966, "Iran," vol. 2, box 136, Country Files, NSF, LBJL.

135. Safire, *Before the Fall*, 458.

136. Kissinger, *White House Years*, 1259–60.

137. CIA, "Iran's International Position," SNIE 34-70, Office of Privacy Coordination, CIA.

138. Nixon toast, 30 May 1972, and Nixon-Shah Joint Communiqué, 31 May 1972, *PPP, Richard M. Nixon, 1972,* 646, 651–52.

139. Bill, *Eagle and the Lion,* 200–15; Rubin, *Paved with Good Intentions,* 158–89.

140. Saikal, *Rise and Fall of the Shah,* 182–201; Hunt, *Crises in U.S. Foreign Policy,* 365–73.

141. Kissinger to Ford, 13 May 1975, in National Security Archive, *Iran,* fiche 154, item 955; Ford toast, 15 May 1975, *PPP, Gerald R. Ford, 1975,* 1:675.

142. Ford to Shah, 21 Feb. 1976, quoted in Rubin, *Paved with Good Intentions,* 154.

143. On Afghanistan under Daoud, see Garthoff, *Détente and Confrontation,* 982–85; Hammond, *Red Flag over Afghanistan,* 35–45; and Rashid, *Taliban,* 12–13.

144. Diary entry, 24 Mar. 1976, in Alam, *Shah and I,* 477. Alam served as the shah's minister of court from 1969 to 1977.

145. CIA, "Iran in the 1980s," Aug. 1977, in National Security Archive, *Iran,* fiche 199/200, item 1210.

146. Vance, *Hard Choices,* 384; Hammond, *Red Flag over Afghanistan,* 49–55.

147. DOS, "Iran Briefing Paper," 3 Jan. 1977, in National Security Archive, *Iran,* fiche 187, item 1138.

148. CIA, "Iran: New Political Activity—Making a Silk Purse out of a Shah's Ear," 12 Aug. 1977, in ibid., fiche 200, item 1213.

149. Carter, *Keeping Faith,* 435–37.

150. Sick, *All Fall Down,* 34–35.

151. Sullivan to DOS, tel., 21 Sept. 1978, in National Security Archive, *Iran,* fiche 254, item 1538.

152. Carter remarks at press conference, 10 Oct. 1978, *PPP, Jimmy Carter, 1978,* 2:1750; Carter diary entries for 25 Oct., 2 Nov. 1978, in Carter, *Keeping Faith,* 438–39.

153. Sullivan to DOS, tel., 9 Nov. 1978, in National Security Archive, *Iran,* fiche 279, item 1711.

154. Sick, *All Fall Down,* 86–87.

155. Ball, *Past Has Another Pattern,* 455–59.

156. Sick, *All Fall Down,* 116–17. See also Brzezinski, *Power and Principle,* 372–74, and Ball, *Past Has Another Pattern,* 460–62.

157. Brzezinski, *Power and Principle,* 385–86.

158. Khomeini speech, 2 Feb. 1979, in Algar, *Islam and Revolution,* 254–57.

159. Bill, *Eagle and the Lion,* 261–97; Keddie, *Roots of Revolution,* 258–72.

160. Sick, *All Fall Down,* 83.

161. Kemp quoted in Miller and Mylroie, *Saddam Hussein and the Crisis in the Gulf,* 143.

Chapter Seven

1. Bryson, *Tars, Turks, and Tankers,* 2–5; Irwin, *Diplomatic Relations of the United States with the Barbary Powers,* 171–86; Allen, *Our Navy and the Barbary Corsairs,* 281–302.

2. Bryson, *Tars, Turks, and Tankers,* 35–38; Field, *America and the Mediterranean World,* 165–75, 219, 238, 244–45, 313–22, 389–409.

3. Bryson, *Tars, Turks, and Tankers*, 43–46, 52–55, 60–61.

4. Howe, *Northwest Africa*, 35, 487–90, 548–56; Bryson, *Tars, Turks, and Tankers*, 62–85.

5. Bryson, *Tars, Turks, and Tankers*, 86–97; Hoopes and Brinkley, *Driven Patriot*, 293–95.

6. Diary entries for 22 Aug., 30 Sept. 1946, in Millis, *Forrestal Diaries*, 196, 211; Hoopes and Brinkley, *Driven Patriot*, 295.

7. Diary entry, 4 Aug. 1947, in Millis, *Forrestal Diaries*, 301–2.

8. Bryson, *Tars, Turks, and Tankers*, 100–4. On Forrestal's suicide, see Hoopes and Brinkley, *Driven Patriot*, 446–68.

9. Brown to chief of naval operations, 5 Sept. 1959, quoted in Bryson, *Tars, Turks, and Tankers*, 125. On the background to the crisis in Jordan, see Little, "Puppet in Search of a Puppeteer?," 523–25.

10. Little, "Cold War and Covert Action," 71–73.

11. Ambassador Robert McClintock to DOS, tel., 30 Jan. 1958, *FRUS 1958–60*, 11:8–9.

12. On the background to the Lebanese crisis, see Little, "His Finest Hour?," and Gendzier, *Notes from the Minefield*, 264–304.

13. Assistant Secretary of Defense John Irwin to Undersecretary of State Robert Murphy, 6 Feb. 1958, *FRUS 1958–60*, 11:9–10.

14. E. M. Rose (Eastern Department), "Lebanon," 9 May 1958, vol. 134156, FO371, PRO; JCS 2293/1, "Review of Actions Related to U.S. Military Intervention in Lebanon (U)," 23 Oct. 1958, *DDRS 1983*, item 2324.

15. "Conversation between the President and Prime Minister," 10:30 P.M., 14 July 1958, vol. 134159, FO371, PRO. For the White House version of the conversation, which also contains the reference to Pandora's box, see *FRUS 1958–60*, 11:231–34.

16. Lloyd to Macmillan, 17 July 1958, PREM 11, folder 2380, and Lloyd memcon, 19 July 1958, vol. 133823, FO371, PRO.

17. McClintock to DOS, tel., 4 Nov. 1958, *FRUS 1958–60*, 11:626–27.

18. Eisenhower quoted in DOS memcon, "Middle East," 22 Mar. 1959, ibid., 12:218.

19. Dwight D. Eisenhower, *The White House Years: Waging Peace*, 290.

20. For Kennedy's critique of Republican foreign policies during his campaign for the presidency, see "Conventional Forces in the Atomic Age," 16 Oct. 1959, in Kennedy, *Strategy of Peace*, 183–86, and Matthews, *Kennedy and Nixon*, 57–69.

21. Taylor, *Uncertain Trumpet*, 92–93, 151–53. On Taylor's background, see Halberstam, *Best and Brightest*, 162–65. On JFK's interest in Taylor's ideas, see Kinnard, *Certain Trumpet*, 56–58, and Taylor, *Swords and Ploughshares*, 204–6.

22. For Bundy's background and an early assessment of his role in the Kennedy administration, including the Harry Hopkins metaphor, see Hyman, "When Bundy Says"; Gardner, "Harry Hopkins with Hand Grenades?," 204–10; and Halberstam, *Best and Brightest*, 47–63.

23. Bundy to Sorensen, 13 Mar. 1961, *FRUS 1961–63*, 8:66–67. On the need for limited war options in Southeast Asia, see Bundy to JFK, 31 Jan. 1961, ibid., 18. Nearly thirty years later Bundy confirmed that "improved conventional readiness was a first clear objective" for Kennedy's military strategists. See Bundy, *Danger and Survival*, 352.

24. On McNamara's background, see Shapely, *Promise and Power*, 28–44, 52–74, and Halberstam, *Best and Brightest*, 213–39.

25. McNamara, *Essence of Security*, 78–81.

26. On JFK and Vietnam, see Bassett and Pelz, "Failed Search for Victory." For an excellent discussion of the debate over escalation inside the Pentagon during the Johnson years, see Buzzanco, *Masters of War*.

27. DOS to Ambassador Parker Hart (Riyadh), tel., 31 Dec. 1962, *FRUS 1961–63*, 18:290.

28. Komer to JFK, 21 Feb. 1963, ibid., 352–53.

29. NSAM 227, "Decisions Taken at the President's Meeting on Yemen Crisis, 25 February 1963," 27 Feb. 1963, ibid., 366–67.

30. Minutes of DOS-JCS Staff Meeting, 16 Aug. 1963, ibid., 675–80.

31. DOD memcon, 8 Oct. 1963, ibid., 726–27.

32. DOS, "Appraisal and Recommended Course of Action Regarding Yemen," 11 Dec. 1963, and Taylor to McNamara, 12 Dec. 1963, ibid., 837–40, 856–58.

33. Johnson's 19 January 1964 letter to Faisal is summarized in Komer to LBJ, 31 Jan. 1964, "Yemen," vol. 1, box 161, Country Files, NSF, LBJL. On the antiaircraft equipment, see "Summary of Recommendations of the U.S. Air Defense Survey Team to Saudi Arabia," January 1964, "Saudi Arabia," vol. 1, "Memos and Cables, 12/63–1/69," box 155, ibid.

34. For the text of the Gulf of Tonkin Resolution, see *DOSB*, 24 Aug. 1964, 268. For a detailed examination of the "structural dynamics of escalation," see Gibson, *Perfect War*, 320–56.

35. Little, "Making of a Special Relationship."

36. Rusk and McNamara to LBJ, 30 May 1967, "Middle East Crisis," vol. 3, tabs. 81–95, box 18, NSC History Files, NSF, LBJL.

37. Riad quoted in Neff, *Warriors for Jerusalem*, 221.

38. Ibid., 253–60.

39. Ennes, *Assault on the Liberty*, 61–103. McNamara and McDonald are quoted on 78.

40. Clifford quoted in Harold Saunders, "Minutes of NSC Special Committee, 9 June 1967," in "Middle East Crisis," vol. 7, appendix I (1–3), box 19, NSC History Files, NSF, LBJL.

41. Confidential Israeli sources informed the CIA in November 1967 "that Dayan personally ordered the attack on the ship and that one of his generals adamantly opposed the action and said, 'This is pure murder'" (CIA intelligence report, 9 Nov. 1967, quoted in Bamford, *Puzzle Palace*, 293. For Bamford's latest thinking on the *Liberty* episode, see his *Body of Secrets*, 187–239).

42. Rusk, *As I Saw It*, 388.

43. Walt W. Rostow Interview.

44. On the jamming, see CIA information cable, 22 June 1967, "Israel/Turkey/USA," in Kesaris, *CIA Research Reports*, reel 3.

45. Rusk, *As I Saw It*, 386.

46. Harold Saunders, "Hot Line Meeting, June 10, 1967," 22 Oct. 1968, "Middle East Crisis," vol. 7, box 19, NSC History Files, NSF, LBJL.

47. On the origins of the October War, see Neff, *Warriors against Israel*, 43–47, 82–90, 99–109, and Quandt, *Peace Process*, 117–47.

48. Nixon quoted by White House counsel Leonard Garment in Strober and Strober, *Nixon*, 152–53.

49. Haig quoted in ibid., 154–55. On the endgame of the October War, see Kissinger, *Years of Upheaval*, 591–611.

50. Palmer, *Guardians of the Gulf*, 97–99; Tucker, "Oil."

51. "Kissinger on Oil, Food, and Trade," *Business Week*, 13 Jan. 1975, 69.

52. Holloway and Carter quoted in Palmer, *Guardians of the Gulf*, 100–101.

53. Carter, *Keeping Faith*, 506–22, and Palmer, *Guardians of the Gulf*, 108–9, 285–86 n. 84.

54. For a brief discussion of Reagan's campaign rhetoric about U.S. intervention in Vietnam, which he called "a noble cause," see Barrett, *Gambling with History*, 40–42.

55. Cannon, *President Reagan*, 77–82; Haig, *Caveat*, 9–15; Weinberger, *Fighting for Peace*, 23–39.

56. McFarlane with Smardz, *Special Trust*, 161–63.

57. Summers, *On Strategy*, 196–206.

58. McFarlane with Smardz, *Special Trust*, 257–67. For two brief accounts of U.S. intervention in Grenada, see Spector, *U.S. Marines in Grenada*, 1–12, and Pastor, "United States and the Grenada Revolution."

59. Weinberger, *Fighting for Peace*, 143–44.

60. Shultz, *Turmoil and Triumph*, 62–84; Cannon, *President Reagan*, 389–406.

61. McFarlane with Smardz, *Special Trust*, 209–13; Shultz, *Turmoil and Triumph*, 78–84, 107–12.

62. Vessey quoted in Martin and Walcott, *Best Laid Plans*, 96.

63. Weinberger, *Fighting for Peace*, 159–60.

64. McFarlane with Smardz, *Special Trust*, 248–53.

65. For Reagan's vow, see "Address to the Nation on Events in Lebanon and Grenada," 27 Oct. 1983, *PPP, Ronald Reagan, 1983*, 2:1519.

66. "Lebanon Report," 12 Dec. 1983, attached to Reagan to Speaker of the House Thomas P. O'Neill, 14 Dec. 1983, "Misc. Reagan: Lebanon," box 10, Miscellaneous Documents, Records of the National Security Council, RG273, NA.

67. Weinberger, *Fighting for Peace*, 163–64.

68. Powell, *My American Journey*, 281.

69. Reagan statement, 7 Feb. 1984, *PPP, Ronald Reagan, 1984*, 1:185.

70. Reagan remarks at news conference, 22 Feb. 1984, ibid., 1:247.

71. McFarlane with Smardz, *Special Trust*, 273.

72. For the text of Weinberger's remarks, see Weinberger, *Fighting for Peace*, 433–45. On Powell's role, see his *My American Journey*, 292.

73. Powell, *My American Journey*, 293.

74. Martin and Walcott, *Best Laid Plans*, 274–85. Qaddafi is quoted on 284.

75. Weinberger, *Fighting for Peace*, 188–89. See also Martin and Walcott, *Best Laid Plans*, 285–88.

76. Martin and Walcott, *Best Laid Plans*, 297–311; Hersh, "Target Qaddafi."

77. Weinberger, *Fighting for Peace*, 199–201.

78. Claudia Wright, "Behind Iraq's Bold Bid."

79. Jentleson, *With Friends Like These*, 31–56.

80. The definitive account of these events remains Draper, *Very Thin Line*, 129–46, 164–83, 272–283. North's "neat idea" quote is on 274. See also Prados, *Keepers of the Keys*, 530–45.

81. For the sequence of events leading to Reagan's decision, see Richard Armitage testimony, 16 June 1987, in U.S. Congress, Senate Committee on Armed Services, *U.S. Military Forces to Protect "Re-Flagged" Kuwaiti Oil Tankers*, 89.

82. Weinberger, *Fighting for Peace*, 387–89.

83. Nunn statement, 5 June 1987, in U.S. Congress, Senate Armed Services Committee, *U.S. Military Forces to Protect "Re-Flagged" Kuwaiti Oil Tankers*, 3.

84. Crowe testimony, 5 June 1987, in ibid., 18.

85. Armacost testimony, 11 June 1987, in ibid., 31, 56–57. For a critique of the Reagan administration's attempt to deter Iran with the reflagging operation, see Stein, "Wrong Strategy in the Right Place."

86. Armitage testimony, 16 June 1987, in U.S. Congress, Senate Armed Services Committee, *U.S. Military Forces to Protect "Re-Flagged" Kuwaiti Oil Tankers*, 95.

87. U.S. Congress, Senate Committee on Foreign Relations, *War in the Persian Gulf: The U.S. Takes Sides*, vii.

88. Palmer, *Guardians of the Gulf*, 138–44.

89. Ibid., 144–48. On Iranian involvement in the bombing of Pan American flight 103, see Rubin, *Cauldron of Turmoil*, 108–9.

90. Commission on Integrated Long-Term Strategy, *Discriminate Deterrence*, 13.

91. On military intervention against Libya, see Bush, "Unity against Terrorism." On dual-use technology, see Jentleson, *With Friends Like These*, 60–61.

92. DOS, "Guidelines for U.S.-Iraq Policy," n.d. [probably January 1989], quoted in Jentleson, *With Friends Like These*, 98.

93. NSD-26, 2 Oct. 1989, quoted in ibid., 94.

94. Powell quoted in Woodward, *Commanders*, 191.

95. Powell, *My American Journey*, 420–21.

96. On Saddam Hussein's relations with Kuwait, see Freedman and Karsh, *Gulf Conflict*, 19–63.

97. Miller and Mylroie, *Saddam Hussein and the Crisis in the Gulf*, 149–52; Woodward, *Commanders*, 205–10.

98. "Excerpts from Iraqi Transcript of Meeting with U.S. Envoy," *New York Times*, 23 Sept. 1990.

99. Glaspie and Hamilton quoted in Jentleson, *With Friends Like These*, 170–71.

100. Lang quoted in Woodward, *Commanders*, 216–17.

101. Powell, *My American Journey*, 444–45.

102. Woodward, *Commanders*, 220–21.

103. All quotes are from Powell, *My American Journey*, 450–51. See also Woodward, *Commanders*, 225–27.

104. Powell, *My American Journey*, 451.

105. Ibid.

106. Bush and Scowcroft, *World Transformed*, 322–26.

107. Bush remarks to reporters, 5 Aug. 1990, *PPP, George Bush, 1990*, 2:1102.

108. Powell, *My American Journey*, 453.

109. On the establishment of CENTCOM, see Palmer, *Guardians of the Gulf*, 113–17.

110. Woodward, *Commanders*, 266–71.

111. Palmer, *Guardians of the Gulf*, 170–74.

112. James A. Baker, *Politics of Diplomacy*, 275–99.

113. Powell, *My American Journey*, 466–67.

114. Ibid., 473–74.

115. James A. Baker, *Politics of Diplomacy*, 303 (emphasis in original).

116. Powell, *My American Journey*, 474–76.

117. Cheney testimony, 3 Dec. 1990, in U.S. Congress, Senate Committee on Armed Services, *Crisis in the Persian Gulf Region*, 639, 643–44.

118. Powell testimony, 3 Dec. 1990, in ibid., 662–63.

119. Nunn, Glenn, Kennedy, and Cheney remarks in ibid., 681, 701–2, 718.

120. Gore remarks, 3 Dec. 1990, in ibid., 722–23.

121. James A. Baker, *Politics of Diplomacy*, 358–59.

122. Freedman and Karsh, *Gulf Conflict*, 283–95; *New York Times*, 13 Jan. 1991.

123. See Gore's remarks, 12 Jan. 1991, quoted in *New York Times*, 13 Jan. 1991.

124. Solarz, "Stakes in the Gulf."

125. Powell, *My American Journey*, 495.

126. Schwartzkopf, *It Doesn't Take a Hero*, 451–61.

127. Bush remarks, 1 Mar. 1991, *PPP, George Bush, 1991*, 1:197.

128. Powell, *My American Journey*, 512, 518.

129. Summers, *On Strategy II*, vii, 1–3, 139–49.

130. "U.S. Struggles to Clarify Policy on Persian Gulf," *New York Times*, 20 Apr. 1997; "At a Saudi Base, U.S. Digs in, Gingerly, for Longer Stay," ibid., 29 Dec. 1997; Kagan, "Benevolent Empire."

131. Colin Powell, "Why Generals Get Nervous," *New York Times*, 8 Oct. 1992.

132. Quoted in Newhouse, "No Exit, No Entrance," 46.

133. Zimmermann and Eagleburger are quoted in Danner, "America and the Bosnia Genocide," 58.

134. Danner, "Slouching toward Dayton."

135. For an excellent analysis of the perils of meddling in ethnic strife from the Balkans to Africa, see Callahan, *Unwinnable Wars*. On Clinton's decision not to intervene in Rwanda, see Power, "Bystanders to Genocide," 90–98. For a detailed account of the botched intervention in Somalia and the impact of media coverage, see Bowden, *Black Hawk Down*.

136. "U.S. Jets over Iraq Attack Own Helicopters in Error," *New York Times*, 26 Apr. 1994; "Bahrain Rulers Say They're Determined to End Village Unrest," ibid., 28 Jan. 1996; "Saudi Kingdom Shows Cracks, U.S. Aides Fear," ibid., 30 June 1996.

137. Pentagon sources quoted in Bernard Trainor, "Force May Not Achieve U.S. Goal in Iraq," ibid., 13 Feb. 1998.

138. Bodansky, *Bin Laden*, 231–32, 283–87.

139. Halberstam, *War in a Time of Peace*, 444–51.

140. "A Month in a Difficult Battlefield: Assessing U.S. War Strategy," *New York Times*, 8 Nov. 2001.

141. Bush remarks, 11 Oct. 2001, http://www.whitehouse.gov/news.

142. "Pentagon Says Taliban Is Ready for Long Fight," *Washington Post*, 25 Oct. 2001.

Chapter Eight

1. Eban, *Personal Witness*, 656.

2. At the end of the year State Department officials placed the total number of Palestinian refugees at between 650,000 and 750,000. See DOS cirtel, 29 Dec. 1948, *FRUS 1948*, 5:1696.

3. On Deir Yassin and the brutal struggle between the Irgun and the Arab Liberation Army, see Morris, *Birth of the Palestinian Refugee Problem*, 111–18.

4. Allon and Ben Gurion quoted in ibid., 207.

5. Bernadotte quoted in Jefferson Patterson (Cairo) to DOS, tel., 7 Aug. 1948; Marshall to James McDonald (Jerusalem), tel., 1 Sept. 1948; and McDonald to Truman, 17 Oct. 1948, *FRUS 1948*, 5:1295, 1367, 1486.

6. Ambassador James Keeley to DOS, tel., 24 Aug. 1948, 890D.00/8-2448, State Department Central Decimal File, RG59, NA.

7. U.N. Resolution 194 (III), 11 Dec. 1948, quoted in editorial note, *FRUS 1948*, 5:1661–62.

8. Ethridge to Truman, 11 Apr. 1949; Acheson memcon, 25 Apr. 1949; and Weizmann to Truman, 27 Apr. 1949, *FRUS 1949*, 6:905, 943–44, 947–48.

9. George McGhee, "Palestine Refugee Problem," 22 Apr. 1949, and Acheson to Ethridge, tel., 12 May 1949, ibid., 934–37, 1004–5.

10. Acheson, "Conference with the President, July 29," 1 Aug. 1949, ibid., 1272.

11. Paul Porter (Lausanne) to DOS, tel., 5 Aug. 1949, and Stuart Rockwell (Lausanne) to DOS, tel., 11 Aug. 1949, ibid., 1287, 1300.

12. DOS, "Interim Report of the Economic Survey Mission to the Near East," 9 Nov. 1949, and editorial note, ibid., 1476–79, 1529–30; Truman statement, 30 Dec. 1949, *PPP, Harry S. Truman, 1949*, 592–93.

13. Malik quoted in DOS memcon, 1 Aug. 1950, *FRUS 1950*, 5:1104–5.

14. DOS position paper, "The Palestine Question," 12 Oct. 1951, *FRUS 1951*, 5:894.

15. DOS memcon, 15 May 1953, *FRUS 1952–54*, 9:51–54.

16. Dulles, "Report on the Near East," 832–34.

17. Dulles testimony, 3 June 1953, in U.S. Congress, Senate Committee on Foreign Relations, *Executive Sessions*, 5:445–47.

18. Eisenhower to Johnston, 7 Oct. 1953; DOS cirtel, 11 Oct. 1953; Dulles to Johnston, 13 Oct. 1953; and Johnston, "Report to the President on Near East Mission," 17 Nov. 1953, *FRUS 1952–54*, 9:1348 n. 1, 1345–46, 1348–53, 1418–23.

19. DOS position paper, 10 Nov. 1954, ibid., 1690.

20. DOS memcon, 9 Dec. 1954, ibid., 1706–7.

21. Johnston to Dulles, tel., 20 Feb. 1955; Dulles to Mallory (Amman), tel., 3 June 1955; Dulles phone call to Johnston, 18 Aug. 1955; and Johnston to DOS, tel., 7 Oct. 1955, *FRUS 1955–57*, 14:65–66, 218–19, 363–64, 565–67. For an account of the rise and fall of the Johnston Plan more critical of Israel, see Gerner, "Missed Opportunities and Roads Not Taken," 84–86.

22. Russell to Walter Butterworth (London), 21 Dec. 1955, *FRUS 1952–54*, 9:1732; DOS memcon, 27 Jan. 1955, *FRUS 1955–57*, 14:24–28.

23. Dulles quoted in Shuckburgh diary entry, 27 Jan. 1955, in Shuckburgh, *Descent to*

Suez, 247. For a less colorful version of Dulles's remarks, see DOS memcon, 27 Jan. 1955, *FRUS 1955–57*, 14:30–32.

24. Dulles memcon, 14 Feb. 1955, *FRUS 1955–57*, 14:53–54.

25. National Security Advisor Dillon Anderson to Herbert Hoover Jr., 26 July 1955, ibid., 322–23.

26. Dulles, "Middle East."

27. Dulles memcon, 11 Jan. 1956, and Eisenhower diary entry, 11 Jan. 1956, *FRUS 1955–57*, 15:20–23.

28. Anderson to DOS, tel., 21 Jan. 1956, ibid., 43–47.

29. Nasser quoted in Heikal, *Cutting the Lion's Tail*, 93.

30. Anderson to DOS, tel., 25 Jan. 1956, and Russell to Dulles, 20 Feb. 1956, *FRUS 1955–57*, 15:68–70, 189–91.

31. Anderson to DOS, tel., 7 Mar. 1956, ibid., 320–22.

32. Ike diary entry, 13 Mar. 1956, "Diary, March 1956," box 13, DDE Diary Series, AWF, DDEL.

33. Villard to Herter, 28 Apr. 1959, and DOS memcons, 10 Nov. 1959, 25 May 1960, *FRUS 1958–60*, 13:54, 217, 323–25.

34. Kennedy, *Strategy of Peace*, 118, 121.

35. JFK to Nasser, in Bowles to Badeau (Cairo), tel., 11 May 1961, *FRUS 1961–63*, 17:110–13; 110 n. 1 describes the five other letters.

36. JFK-Ben Gurion memcon, 30 May 1961, ibid., 139–40.

37. On Johnson's background and appointment, see Meyer Oral History, 34; Rusk, *As I Saw It*, 125; and DOS to Rusk, tel., 9 Aug. 1961, *FRUS 1961–63*, 17:221.

38. DOS memcon, 29 Sept. 1961, *FRUS 1961–63*, 17:264–66.

39. DOS memcons, 7 June, 28, 31 July, 6 Aug. 1962, ibid., 17:707–10, 18:17–19.

40. "The Johnson Plan: Considerations for the United States," n.d., attached to Rusk to JFK, 7 Aug. 1962, ibid., 18:33–39.

41. "White House Conference on the Johnson Plan," 14 Aug. 1962, ibid., 54–58.

42. Ibid.

43. Feldman to author, 20 Aug. 1985, in author's possession.

44. Feldman Oral History.

45. Meyer Oral History, 35.

46. Rusk, *As I Saw It*, 382–83.

47. Feldman to author, 20 Aug. 1985, in author's possession; Meyer Oral History, 35; Rusk, *As I Saw It*, 383.

48. Benjamin Read to McGeorge Bundy, "U.S. Influence on the Arab Summit Conference," 12 Feb. 1964, "UAR Cables," vol. 1, Nov. 1963–May 1964, box 158, Country Files, NSF, LBJL.

49. Dann, *King Hussein and the Challenge of Arab Radicalism*, 137, 140–42; Nutting, *Nasser*, 364–65; Tessler, *History of the Israeli-Palestinian Conflict*, 372–74.

50. On Arafat and the rise of Fatah, see Hart, *Arafat*, 67–80, 106–30, and Quandt, Jabber, and Lesch, *Politics of Palestinian Nationalism*, 55–56.

51. Boswell (Cairo) to DOS, tel., 12 Sept. 1964, "UAR Cables," vol. 2, June–Dec. 1964, box 159, Country Files, NSF, LBJL.

52. Rusk quoted in DOS memcon, 28 May 1965, *Lyndon B. Johnson National Security*

Files, reel 1, frame 408. By the spring of 1965 Fatah commandos were calling themselves "fedayeen," an Arabic word meaning "self-sacrificer." On early fedayeen raids, see Neff, *Warriors for Jerusalem,* 31–36; Khouri, "Policy of Retaliation in Arab-Israeli Relations," 448–50; and Quandt, Jabber, and Lesch, *Politics of Palestinian Nationalism,* 157–59.

53. Read to Bundy, 5 June 1965, "UAR Memos," vol. 4, June 1965–June 1966, box 159, Country Files, NSF, LBJL.

54. Saunders, "Terrorist Origins of the Present Crisis," n.d. [mid-June 1967], "Middle East Crisis," vol. 1, tabs. 1–10, box 17, NSC History Files, NSF, LBJL.

55. Stephens, *Nasser,* 459–60.

56. Saunders, "Terrorist Origins of the Present Crisis," n.d. [mid-June 1967], "Middle East Crisis," vol. 1, tabs. 1–10, box 17, NSC History Files, NSF, LBJL. On the Samu raid, see Mutawi, *Jordan in the 1967 War,* 79–84, and Mackey, *Passion and Politics,* 199.

57. CIA Report, "Syria: A Center of Instability," 24 Mar. 1967, "Syria," vol. 1, box 156, Country Files, NSF, LBJL; CIA National Intelligence Estimate, "The Arab-Israeli Dispute: Current Phase," 13 Apr. 1967, Office of Information and Privacy Coordination, CIA. On Nasser's actions, see Parker, *Six Day War,* 17–19.

58. Saunders to Rostow, "The President's Stake in the Middle East," 16 May 1967, attached to Rostow to LBJ, 17 May 1967, "Saunders Memos," box 7, Name File, NSF, LBJL (emphasis in original).

59. Saunders, "NSC Meeting, Wednesday, June 7, 1967," 7 Jan. 1969, vol. 4, tab. 53, "Middle East War," box 2, NSC Meeting File, NSF, LBJL.

60. Saunders to Bundy, 7 June 1967, "Middle East Crisis, Cables," vol. 4, box 116, Country Files, NSF, LBJL.

61. Neff, *Warriors for Jerusalem,* 289–300; Rusk quoted in Saunders, "Minutes of the NSC Special Committee," 14 June 1967, "Middle East Crisis," vol. 7, appendix I (1–3), box 19, NSC History Files, NSF, LBJL.

62. CIA, "Arab-Israeli Situation Report," 23 June 1967, "Middle East Crisis," vol. 11, appendix Q (V), box 21, NSC History Files, NSF, LBJL. See also DOS/CIA, "Comprehensive Picture of Refugee Situation in Jordan," 3 July 1967, "Memos to NSC Committee, July 1967," "NSC Meeting Files, 1966–1970," box 1, Top Secret Records of the Assistant Secretary of State, RG59, NA.

63. LBJ address, 19 June 1967, *PPP Lyndon B. Johnson, 1967,* 1:633–34.

64. Rostow to LBJ, 3 Oct. 1967, *DDRS 1991,* item 499.

65. Rostow to LBJ (2 memos), 17 Oct. 1967, "Rostow," vol. 46 (2 of 2), Memos to the President, box 24, NSF, LBJL.

66. DOS memcon, 24 Oct. 1967, "Israel," vol. 7, Aug.–Dec. 1967, box 140, Country Files, and George Christian memcon, 24 Oct. 1967, "Mtg. with Abba Eban," box 2, Meeting Notes File, NSF, LBJL. On the Palestinian refugees from the Six Day War, see Day, *East Bank/West Bank,* 31–32.

67. Neff, *Warriors for Jerusalem,* 335–40; Spiegel, *Other Arab-Israeli Conflict,* 155–57. For the English and French texts of Resolution 242, see Moore, *Arab-Israeli Conflict,* 3:1034–35.

68. Rostow to LBJ, 8 Nov. 1967, "Rostow," vol. 50 (2 of 2), Memos to the President, box 25, NSF, LBJL; Goldberg and Hussein quoted in Neff, *Warriors for Jerusalem,* 341–43.

69. Rostow to LBJ, "Issues for Eshkol," 5 Jan. 1968, "Israel: Eshkol Visit Briefing Book," box 144, Country Files, NSF, LBJL.

70. Harold Saunders, Minutes of NSC Meeting, 26 Feb. 1968, *DDRS 1988*, item 390.

71. Hart, *Arafat*, 254–63. (The Arafat quote is on 260).

72. Rostow quoted in Saunders memcon, 17 May 1968, "Israel Memos," vol. 10, June–Nov. 1968, box 142, Country Files, NSF, LBJL.

73. Donald Bergus (Cairo) to DOS, tel., 15 June 1968, "UAR Cables," vol. 6, box 160, ibid.

74. Eugene Rostow to Barbour, tel., 17 Aug. 1968, "Israel Cables," vol. 10, box 142, Country Files, NSF, LBJL; Walt Rostow to LBJ, "Notes for 5:30 Briefing of Mr. Nixon," 12 Dec. 1968, *DDRS 1996*, item 1798.

75. DOS memcon, 13 Mar. 1960, *FRUS 1958–60*, 13:295.

76. Nixon, *RN*, 249–50.

77. Nixon notes, 9 Dec. 1968, quoted in Safire, *Before the Fall*, 108–9.

78. Kissinger, *White House Years*, 341.

79. Scranton quoted in Lenczowski, *American Presidents and the Middle East*, 120. On Scranton declining Nixon's offer to become secretary of state, see Parmet, *Richard Nixon and His America*, 538.

80. Ziegler quoted in Thomas, "From Orientalism to Professionalism," 522.

81. Rogers remarks, 27 Mar. 1969, in *DOSB*, 14 Apr. 1969, 305–6.

82. Rogers to Nixon, "Suggested Position to Take with Israeli Prime Minister," 16 Sept. 1969, and "Scope and Objectives," n.d. [probably 16 Sept. 1969], "Top Secret 1969," box 1, Top Secret Records of the Assistant Secretary of State, RG59, NA.

83. Rogers, "A Lasting Peace in the Middle East," *DOSB*, 5 Jan. 1970, 7–11.

84. Meir, *My Life*, 389–90.

85. Kenen, *Israel's Defense Line*, 237–40. Meir quoted on 238.

86. Kissinger, *White House Years*, 341, 356, 374.

87. Garment, *Crazy Rhythm*, 192–93.

88. Sisco to DOS, tel., 14 Apr. 1970, "ORG 7 NEA," State Department Alpha-Numeric File, RG59, NA.

89. Kissinger, *White House Years*, 626.

90. Arab League Summit Communiqué, 29 Oct. 1974, in Lukacs, *Documents on the Israeli-Palestinian Conflict*, 223–24.

91. Kissinger, *Years of Renewal*, 422–59; "U.S.-Israeli Memorandum of Understanding," 1 Sept. 1975, in Sheehan, *Arabs, Israelis, and Kissinger*, 253–57.

92. Saunders, *Other Walls*, 9.

93. Scranton remarks, 23 Mar. 1976, in Lukacs, *Documents on the Israeli-Palestinian Conflict*, 30–32.

94. Brookings Institution Study Group, *Toward Peace in the Middle East*, 1–12. The quotation is on 2. On Carter's endorsement of the Brookings study, see Brzezinski, *Power and Principle*, 84–85, and David Schoenbaum, *United States and Israel*, 246.

95. "Overview of Foreign Policy Issues and Positions," 24 Oct. 1976, in Vance, *Hard Choices*, 443, 447–48.

96. Carter, *Keeping Faith*, 279.

97. Ibid., 279–81; Carter remarks, 16 Mar. 1977, *PPP, Jimmy Carter, 1977*, 1:386–87. On the Israeli elections, see Rabin, *Memoirs*, 291–97, 315–18.

98. Vance, *Hard Choices*, 188–90.

99. Carter, *Keeping Faith*, 292–93.

100. Sadat address to the Knesset, 20 Nov. 1977, in Quandt, *Camp David*, 351–53.

101. Vance, *Hard Choices*, 208–11.

102. Carter, *Keeping Faith*, 374–75.

103. Ibid., 391–93.

104. "Camp David Accords," 17 September 1978, in Quandt, *Camp David*, 376–83.

105. Ibid., 247–48.

106. Carter, *Keeping Faith*, 409, 492.

107. Ibid., 495.

108. Cannon, *President Reagan*, 288–89, 391; Reagan, *American Life*, 408–9.

109. "Excerpts from Interview with President Reagan," *New York Times*, 3 Feb. 1981; Neff, *Fallen Pillars*, 119–24, 159–61.

110. Haig, *Caveat*, 123, 171–72. On Haig, Sharon, and the invasion of Lebanon, see Schiff, "Green Light," 77–83.

111. Shultz, *Turmoil and Triumph*, 49–51.

112. Reagan, *American Life*, 430.

113. Shultz, *Turmoil and Triumph*, 86.

114. Reagan, *American Life*, 430–31; Shultz, *Turmoil and Triumph*, 96–98.

115. Shultz, *Turmoil and Triumph*, 92–93, 98. Veliotes is quoted on 92.

116. Arens quoted in ibid., 91, 95–96.

117. Begin to Reagan, n.d. [early Sept. 1982], quoted in Reagan, *American Life*, 432–34.

118. Shultz, *Turmoil and Triumph*, 104–7, 110. Sharon is quoted on 105. The best accounts of the Sabra and Shatilla massacres are Schiff and Ya'ari, *Israel's Lebanon War*, 250–85, and Friedman, *From Beirut to Jerusalem*, 160–66.

119. Shultz, *Turmoil and Triumph*, 110.

120. Kahan commission report quoted in ibid., 111–13.

121. Ibid., 457–58.

122. Ibid., 949.

123. Ibid., 1017–20.

124. Abu-Amr, "Hamas," 10–14.

125. Shultz, *Turmoil and Triumph*, 1034–35, 1043.

126. Ibid., 1040–45.

127. Ibid., 1043.

128. Arens, *Broken Covenant*, 30–31, 38–39.

129. Bush statement, 25 Sept. 1971, *DOSB*, 25 Oct. 1971, 469–70. See also Bush statement, 10 Dec. 1971, *DOSB*, 17 Jan. 1972, 72.

130. Arens, *Broken Covenant*, 28.

131. Bush remarks, 3 Apr. 1989, *PPP, George Bush, 1989*, 1:348.

132. "Secretary-Designate's Confirmation Hearings," 17 Jan. 1989, *DOSB*, Apr. 1989, 15.

133. James A. Baker, *Politics of Diplomacy*, 118.

134. James A. Baker, "Principles and Pragmatism: American Policy toward the Arab-Israeli Conflict," 22 May 1989, *DOSB*, July 1989, 24–27.

135. James A. Baker, *Politics of Diplomacy*, 129–30; Bush remarks, 10 Mar. 1991, *PPP, George Bush, 1991*, 1:233–34.

136. For sympathetic portraits of Ashrawi, see Victor, *Voice of Reason*, and Shlaim, "Woman of the Year."

137. James A. Baker, *Politics of Diplomacy*, 491. For Ashrawi's version of the meeting, see Ashrawi, *This Side of Peace*, 80–87.

138. James A. Baker, *Politics of Diplomacy*, 493.

139. "Excerpts of Haidar Abdel-Shafi's Remarks," *New York Times*, 1 Nov. 1991. On Ashrawi's authorship, see Ashrawi, *This Side of Peace*, 145–48.

140. Tad Szulc, "Who Are the Palestinians?" The quotations are on 94 and 98.

141. James A. Baker, *Politics of Diplomacy*, 553–54.

142. Bush remarks, 17 Mar. 1992, *PPP, George Bush, 1992–93*, 1:467.

143. James A. Baker, *Politics of Diplomacy*, 554–55.

144. Ibid., 555–57.

145. "Interview with Nabil Shaath." Shaath was the chief Palestinian negotiator in Washington. For a critical account of Clinton's handling of the peace process, see Neff, "Clinton Administration and UN Resolution 242."

146. For two inside accounts of the Oslo negotiations, see Peres, *New Middle East*, 18–32, and Savir, "Why Oslo Still Matters."

147. For the full text of the remarks of the three men on 13 September, see *Middle East Policy*, 2, no. 3 (1993): 183–88.

148. "Rabin's Last Speech," *New York Times*, 5 Nov. 1995. On Amir and the Israeli right, see Amos Elon, "Israel's Demons."

149. Arafat to Leah Rabin, 9 Nov. 1995, in Arzt, *Refugees into Citizens*, vii.

150. Peretz and Doron, "Israel's 1996 Elections."

151. For three excellent analyses of Netanyahu's hard-line approach to the peace process, see Elon, "Israel and the End of Zionism," 24–25; Schmemann, "Outside In," 55–59, 74–77; and Remnick, "Letter from Jerusalem."

152. "Hillary Clinton Says Palestinians Deserve an Independent State," *Jerusalem Post*, 8 May 1998. Arafat quoted in "9 Palestinians Killed, Scores Wounded by Israelis," *New York Times*, 15 May 1998.

153. Albright quoted in "Israel Torn by Competing Israeli Concerns on Settlements," *New York Times*, 14 May 1998. Netanyahu quoted in "Netanyahu Expresses Newfound Optimism on Peace Talks," ibid., 16 May 1998.

154. Albright and Netanyahu quoted in Serge Schmemann, "Plan to Expand Jerusalem's Municipal Control Is Approved," ibid., 22 June 1998.

155. Netanyahu quoted in "PM Raps Albright," *Jerusalem Post*, 22 June 1998.

156. Barak quoted in "Returning Home, Netanyahu Faces the Real Battle As Settlers Stage Protests," *New York Times*, 26 Oct. 1998.

157. "Quest for Mideast Peace: How and Why It Failed," *New York Times*, 26 July 2001.

158. Clinton quoted in Malley and Agha, "Camp David," 62–63.

159. Herzog quoted in "Stalled but Alive, Peace Talks on the Mideast Reach 10th Day," *New York Times*, 21 July 2000. See also "'Unique Opportunity' Lost at Camp David," *Washington Post*, 30 July 2000.

160. Malley and Agha, "Camp David," 65.

161. U.S. Department of State, *Report of the Sharm El-Sheikh [Mitchell] Fact-Finding Committee*.

162. Bush remarks, 11 Oct. 2001, http://www.whitehouse.gov/news.

Conclusion

1. Bernard Lewis, "License to Kill," 14–15; Bodansky, *Bin Laden*, 185–204.

2. Gati quoted in "As U.N. Meets, Bin Laden Tape Sets Off Alarms," *New York Times*, 9 Nov. 2001.

3. Huntington, *Clash of Civilizations and the Remaking of World Order*, 109–21, 246–58. On Huntington and his critics, see Kaplan, "Looking the World in the Eye," 68–70, 81–82.

4. Buruma and Margalit, "Occidentalism."

5. Doran, "Somebody Else's Civil War," 27–38. Qutb is quoted on 30.

6. Adonis is quoted in ibid., 22, 42. For an excellent analysis of the background and the poetry of Adonis, see Ajami, *Dream Palace of the Arabs*, 114–24.

7. Gates, *From the Shadows*, 143–44; Yousaf with Adkin, *Bear Trap*, 78–112; Marsden, *Taliban*, 128–29; Rashid, *Taliban*, 89–92.

8. "Fears, Again, of Oil Supplies at Risk," *New York Times*, 14 Oct. 2001.

9. Rashid, *Taliban*, 156–82.

10. Bush remarks, 7 Nov. 2001, http://www.whitehouse.gov/news.

BIBLIOGRAPHY

Primary Sources

Private Papers

Acheson, Dean G. Harry Truman Presidential Library, Independence, Mo.
Ball, George W. Telephone Notes File. Lyndon B. Johnson Presidential Library, Austin, Tex.
Bowles, Chester W. Sterling Library, Yale University, New Haven, Conn.
Brewer, Sam Pope. Wisconsin State Historical Society, Madison.
Bruce, David K. E. Virginia Historical Society, Richmond.
Council on Foreign Relations. Archives, Records of Groups. Pratt House, New York, N.Y.
Dulles, John Foster. Dwight D. Eisenhower Presidential Library, Abilene, Kans.
Estabrook, Robert. Wisconsin State Historical Society, Madison.
Forrestal, James A. Firestone Library, Princeton University, Princeton, N.J.
Fulbright, J. William. University of Arkansas Library, Fayetteville.
Harriman, W. Averell. Library of Congress, Washington, D.C.
Henderson, Loy W. Library of Congress, Washington, D.C.
Herter, Christian A. Dwight D. Eisenhower Presidential Library, Abilene, Kans.
Humphrey, Hubert H. Minnesota Historical Society, St. Paul.
McCloy, John J. Amherst College, Amherst, Mass.

Rusk, Dean. Office of Freedom of Information, Privacy, and Classification, U.S. Department of State, Washington, D.C.

Stettinius, Edward R., Jr. University of Virginia Library, Charlottesville.

Unpublished Government Documents

Central Intelligence Agency, Office of Information and Privacy Coordination, Washington, D.C.
  National Intelligence Estimates
Dwight D. Eisenhower Presidential Library, Abilene, Kans.
  John Foster Dulles Papers
  Records of the Office of the Special Adviser for National Security Affairs
  White House Office of the Staff Secretary, Records, 1952–61
  Ann Whitman Files
    Dulles-Herter Series
    Dwight D. Eisenhower Diary Series
    International Series
    National Security Council Series
    Transition Series
Lyndon B. Johnson Presidential Library, Austin, Tex.
  National Security Files
    McGeorge Bundy Files
    Country Files
    Meeting Notes File
    Memos to the President
    Name File
    National Intelligence Estimates
    National Security Council History Files
    National Security Council Meeting File
  Vice Presidential Security Series
John F. Kennedy Presidential Library, Boston, Mass.
  National Security Files
    Countries
    Meetings and Memoranda
    Meetings and Memoranda: Robert Komer
  President's Office Files
National Archives II, College Park, Md.
  RG59
    Alpha Files, Lot 59D 518
    State Department Alpha-Numeric File
    State Department Central Decimal File
    Top Secret Records of the Assistant Secretary of State for Near Eastern and South Asian Affairs, 1965–73, Lot 80D234
  RG273
    Records of the National Security Council
National Security Council, Washington, D.C.
  Information Policy Directorate, National Security Memoranda

Public Record Office, Kew, Surrey, England
  CAB 128, Cabinet Minutes
  CAB 143, Records of the Egypt Committee
  FCO 7, Records of the Foreign and Commonwealth Office: American and Latin
    American Departments, 1967–
  FCO 8, Records of the Foreign and Commonwealth Office: Arabian Department,
    1967–
  FO 371, General Correspondence of the Foreign Office, 1906–66
  PREM 11, Records of the Prime Minister's Office: Correspondence and Papers,
    1951–64
  PREM 13, Records of the Prime Minister's Office: Correspondence and Papers,
    1964–70

Oral Histories and Interviews

Feldman, Myer. Oral History. John F. Kennedy Presidential Library, Boston, Mass.
Hart, Parker T. Oral History. John F. Kennedy Presidential Library, Boston, Mass.
Jernegan, John. Oral History. John F. Kennedy Presidential Library, Boston, Mass.
Komer, Robert. Oral History. John F. Kennedy Presidential Library, Boston, Mass.
Meyer, Armin. Foreign Service Oral History Project. Georgetown University, Wash-
  ington, D.C.
Rostow, Eugene. Oral History. Lyndon B. Johnson Presidential Library, Austin, Tex.
Rostow, Walt W. Interview with author, 25 July 1991, Austin, Tex.
Symmes, Harrison. Foreign Service Oral History Project. Georgetown University,
  Washington, D.C.

Published Documents

Brookings Institution Study Group. *Toward Peace in the Middle East.* Washington,
  D.C.: Brookings Institution, 1975.
Cold War International History Project Bulletin 8/9 (winter 1996/97).
Commission on Integrated Long-Term Strategy. *Discriminate Deterrence.* Washington,
  D.C.: Government Printing Office, 1988.
Declassified Documents Reference System (microfiche). Arlington, Va.: Carrollton
  Press, 1975–96.
Declassified Documents Reference System: Retrospective Collection (microfiche). Ar-
  lington, Va.: Carrollton Press, 1976.
Documents of the National Security Council, 2nd Supplement (microfilm). Frederick,
  Md.: University Publications of America, 1983.
Kesaris, Paul, ed. *CIA Research Reports: The Middle East, 1946–1976* (microfilm).
  Washington, D.C.: University Publications of America, 1980.
Lukacs, Yehuda, ed. *Documents on the Israeli-Palestinian Conflict, 1967–1983.* New
  York: Cambridge University Press, 1984.
Lyndon B. Johnson National Security Files: Israel (microfilm). Fredericktown, Md.:
  University Publications of America, 1982.
Moore, John Norton, ed. *The Arab-Israeli Conflict.* 4 vols. Princeton: Princeton Uni-
  versity Press, 1975.

National Security Archive. *Iran: The Making of U.S. Policy, 1977–80* (microfiche). Alexandria, Va.: Chadwyck Healey, 1990.

OSS/State Department Intelligence and Research Reports. Pt. 7, *The Middle East, 1941–1976*. Washington, D.C.: University Publications of America, 1977.

OSS/State Department Intelligence and Research Reports. Pt. 12, *The Middle East, 1950–1961, Supplement*. Washington, D.C.: University Publications of America, 1980.

OSS/State Department Intelligence Reports. Pt. 13, *Africa, 1941–1961*. Washington, D.C.: University Publications of America, 1980.

Pike, Otis. *CIA: The Pike Report*. Nottingham, England: Bertrand Russell Peace Foundation, 1977.

Public Papers of the President. Washington, D.C.: Government Printing Office, 1946–2000.

Richardson, James D., ed. *A Compilation of the Messages and Papers of the Presidents, 1789–1897*. 10 vols. Washington, D.C.: Bureau of National Literature, 1911.

United Nations. Department of Economic and Social Affairs. *United Nations Statistical Yearbook, 1968*. New York, 1969.

U.S. Congress. House. Committee on Appropriations. Subcommittee on Foreign Operations. *Foreign Operations Appropriations for 1964*. Washington, D.C.: Government Printing Office, 1963.

U.S. Congress. House. Committee on International Relations. *U.S. Policy toward Egypt*. Washington, D.C.: Government Printing Office, 1997.

U.S. Congress. Senate. Committee on Armed Services. 101st Cong., 2d sess. *Crisis in the Persian Gulf Region: U.S. Policy Options and Implications*. Washington, D.C.: Government Printing Office, 1990.

———. *U.S. Military Forces to Protect "Re-Flagged" Kuwaiti Oil Tankers*. Washington, D.C.: Government Printing Office, 1987.

U.S. Congress. Senate. Committee on Foreign Relations. *Executive Sessions of the Senate Foreign Relations Committee (Historical Series)*. 18 vols. Washington D.C.: Government Printing Office, 1976–97.

———. *International Development and Security: Hearings on Senate Resolution 1983*. Washington, D.C.: Government Printing Office, 1961.

———. 85th Cong., 1st sess. *The President's Proposal on the Middle East*. Washington, D.C.: Government Printing Office, 1957.

———. *U.S. Security Agreements and Commitments Abroad*. Pt. 9, *Morocco and Libya*. Washington, D.C.: Government Printing Office, 1969.

———. *War in the Persian Gulf: The U.S. Takes Sides*. Washington, D.C.: Government Printing Office, 1987.

U.S. Congress. Senate. Committee on Foreign Relations. Subcommittee on Multinational Corporations. *Multinational Corporations and United States Foreign Policy*. Washington, D.C.: Government Printing Office, 1974.

———. *Multinational Oil Corporations and U.S. Foreign Policy*. Washington, D.C.: Government Printing Office, 1975.

U.S. Congress. Senate. Special Committee Investigating the National Defense Program. *Investigation of the National Defense Program*. Pt. 41, *Petroleum Arrangements with Saudi Arabia*. Washington, D.C.: Government Printing Office, 1948.

U.S. Department of State. *Foreign Relations of the United States*. Washington, D.C.: Government Printing Office, 1908–2001.

———. *Patterns of Global Terrorism, 1999*. Washington, D.C.: Government Printing Office, 2000. www.state.gov/www/globalterrorism/1999report.

———. *Report of the Sharm El-Sheikh [Mitchell] Fact-Finding Committee*, 30 April 2001. http://usinfo.state.gov/regional/nea/mitchell.htm.

———. *United States Policy in the Middle East, September 1956–June 1957*. Washington, D.C.: Government Printing Office, 1957.

Published Memoirs, Reports, Letters, and Papers

Acheson, Dean G. *Present at the Creation: My Years in the State Department*. New York: Norton, 1969.

Adams, Charles Francis, ed. *The Memoirs of John Quincy Adams*. 12 vols. 1874–77. Reprint, New York: AMS Press, 1970.

Adams, Sherman. *Firsthand Report: The Story of the Eisenhower Administration*. New York: Harper and Row, 1961.

Alam, Asadollah. *The Shah and I: The Confidential Diary of Iran's Royal Court, 1969–1977*. Edited and translated by Alinagh Alikhani. London: I. B. Tauris, 1991.

Algar, Hamid, ed. and trans. *Islam and Revolution: Writings and Declarations of Imam Khomeini*. 1981. Reprint, London: KPI, 1985.

Arens, Moshe. *Broken Covenant: American Foreign Policy and the Crisis between the U.S. and Israel*. New York: Simon and Schuster, 1995.

Ashrawi, Hanan. *This Side of Peace: A Personal Account*. New York: Simon and Schuster, 1995.

Badeau, John S. *The American Approach to the Arab World*. New York: Harper and Row, 1968.

Baker, James A. *The Politics of Diplomacy: Revolution, War, and Peace, 1989–1992*. New York: Putnam, 1995.

Ball, George W. *The Past Has Another Pattern: Memoirs*. New York: Norton, 1982.

Bar-On, Mordechai. *The Gates of Gaza: Israel's Road to Suez and Back, 1955–1957*. New York: St. Martin's Press, 1994.

Berle, Beatrice Bishop, and Travis Beal Jacobs, eds. *Navigating the Rapids, 1918–1971: From the Papers of Adolf A. Berle*. New York: Harcourt Brace Jovanovich, 1973.

Blum, John Morton, ed. *The Price of Vision: The Diary of Henry A. Wallace*. Boston: Houghton Mifflin, 1973.

Brown, William R. *The Last Crusade: A Middle East Negotiator's Handbook*. Chicago: Nelson-Hall, 1980.

Brzezinski, Zbigniew. *Power and Principle: Memoirs of the National Security Adviser, 1977–1981*. New York: Farrar, Straus and Giroux, 1983.

Bush, George. "Unity against Terrorism." *Department of State Bulletin* 87 (April 1987): 3–5.

Bush, George, and Brent Scowcroft. *A World Transformed*. New York: Knopf, 1998.

Carter, Jimmy. *The Blood of Abraham*. Boston: Houghton Mifflin, 1985.

———. *Keeping Faith: Memoirs of a President*. New York: Bantam, 1982.

Clifford, Clark. *Counsel to the President: A Memoir*. New York: Random House, 1991.

Cutler, Robert. *No Time for Rest*. Boston: Little, Brown, 1966.

Dulles, John Foster. "The Middle East." *Department of State Bulletin* 33 (5 September 1955): 378–80.

———. "Report on the Near East." *Department of State Bulletin* 28 (15 June 1953): 831–35.

Eban, Abba. *An Autobiography*. New York: Random House, 1977.

———. *Personal Witness: Israel through My Eyes*. New York: Putnam, 1992.

Eisenhower, Dwight D. *The White House Years: Mandate for Change, 1953–1956*. Garden City, N.Y.: Doubleday, 1963.

———. *The White House Years: Waging Peace, 1956–1961*. Garden City, N.Y.: Doubleday, 1965.

Eisenhower, John S. D., ed. *Letters to Mamie*. Garden City, N.Y.: Doubleday, 1978.

Ennes, James M., Jr. *Assault on the Liberty*. New York: Random House, 1979.

Ferrell, Robert, ed. *Dear Bess: Letters from Harry to Bess Truman, 1910–1959*. New York: Norton, 1983.

———. *Off the Record: The Private Papers of Harry Truman*. New York: Harper and Row, 1980.

Ford, Gerald R. *A Time to Heal*. New York: Harper and Row, 1979.

Gallman, Waldemar J. *Iraq under General Nuri: My Recollections of Nuri al-Said, 1954–1958*. Baltimore: Johns Hopkins University Press, 1964.

Garment, Leonard. *Crazy Rhythm*. New York: Times Books, 1997.

Gates, Robert M. *From the Shadows: The Ultimate Insider's Story of Five Presidents and How They Won the Cold War*. New York: Simon and Schuster, 1996.

Goodwin, Richard N. *Remembering America: A Voice from the Sixties*. Boston: Little, Brown, 1988.

Haig, Alexander M., Jr. *Caveat: Realism, Reagan, and Foreign Policy*. New York: Macmillan, 1984.

Haldeman, H. R. *The Haldeman Diaries: Inside the Nixon White House*. New York: Putnam, 1994.

Herzog, Yaacov. *A People That Dwells Alone: Speeches and Writings of Yaacov Herzog*. Edited by Misha Louvish. London: Weidenfield and Nicolson, 1975.

Hughes, Emmet John. *The Ordeal of Power: A Political Memoir of the Eisenhower Years*. New York: Atheneum, 1963.

Hull, Cordell. *Memoirs*. 2 vols. New York: Macmillan, 1948.

Johnson, Lyndon B. *The Vantage Point: Perspectives on the Presidency, 1963–1969*. New York: Holt, Rinehart and Winston, 1971.

Johnston, Charles. *The Brink of Jordan*. London: Hamish Hamilton, 1972.

Jordan, Hamilton. *Crisis: The Last Year of the Carter Presidency*. New York: Putnam, 1982.

Kennan, George F. *Memoirs, 1925–1950*. Boston: Atlantic, Little, Brown, 1967.

Kennedy, John F. *The Strategy of Peace*. New York: Harper and Brothers, 1960.

Kimball, Warren F., ed. *Churchill and Roosevelt: The Complete Correspondence*. Princeton: Princeton University Press, 1984.

Kissinger, Henry. *White House Years*. Boston: Little, Brown, 1979.

———. *Years of Renewal*. New York: Simon and Schuster, 1999.

———. *Years of Upheaval*. Boston: Little, Brown, 1982.

Lansing, Robert. *The Peace Negotiations: A Personal Narrative.* Boston: Houghton Mifflin, 1921.

Laqueur, Walter, and Barry Rubin, eds. *The Israel-Arab Reader: A Documentary History of the Middle East Conflict.* 5th ed. New York: Penguin, 1995.

Lenin, V. I. *National Liberation, Socialism, and Imperialism: Selected Writings.* New York: International Publishers, 1968.

Link, Arthur S. *Papers of Woodrow Wilson.* 67 vols. Princeton: Princeton University Press, 1966–94.

McFarlane, Robert C., with Zofia Smardz. *Special Trust.* New York: Cadell and Davies, 1994.

Macmillan, Harold. *Riding the Storm, 1956–1959.* New York: Harper and Row, 1971.

McNamara, Robert S. *The Essence of Security: Reflections in Office.* New York: Harper and Row, 1968.

Meir, Golda. *My Life.* New York: Putnam, 1975.

Millis, Walter. *The Forrestal Diaries.* New York: Viking, 1951.

Morison, Elting B., ed. *The Letters of Theodore Roosevelt.* 8 vols. Cambridge: Harvard University Press, 1952.

Murphy, Robert. *Diplomat among Warriors.* Garden City, N.Y.: Doubleday, 1964.

Nasser, Gamal Abdel. "The Egyptian Revolution." *Foreign Affairs* 33 (January 1955): 199–211.

————. *Egypt's Liberation: The Philosophy of the Revolution.* Washington, D.C.: Public Affairs Press, 1955.

Netanyahu, Benjamin. *A Place among Nations: Israel and the World.* New York: Bantam, 1993.

Nixon, Richard. *RN: The Memoirs of Richard Nixon.* New York: Grosset and Dunlap, 1978.

Peres, Shimon. *David's Sling.* London: Weidenfield and Nicolson, 1970.

————. *The New Middle East.* New York: Henry Holt, 1993.

Powell, Colin L. *My American Journey.* New York: Random House, 1996.

Qaddafi, Muammar al. *The Green Book.* Tripoli: World Center for Research and Study, 1973.

Rabin, Yitzhak. *The Rabin Memoirs.* Boston: Little, Brown, 1979.

Rafael, Gideon. *Destination Peace: Three Decades of Israeli Foreign Policy, a Personal Memoir.* New York: Stein and Day, 1981.

Reagan, Ronald. *An American Life.* New York: Simon and Schuster, 1990.

Rogers, William P. "A Lasting Peace in the Middle East: An American View." *Department of State Bulletin* 62 (5 January 1970): 7–11.

————. *United States Foreign Policy, 1969–1970: A Report by the Secretary of State.* Washington, D.C.: Government Printing Office, 1971.

Roosevelt, Elliot, ed. *F.D.R.: His Personal Letters, 1928–1945.* 2 vols. New York: Duell, Sloan and Pearce, 1947–50.

Rusk, Dean. *As I Saw It.* New York: Norton, 1990.

Safire, William. *Before the Fall: An Inside View of the Pre-Watergate White House.* Garden City, N.Y.: Doubleday, 1975.

Shuckburgh, Evelyn. *Descent to Suez: Foreign Office Diaries, 1951–1956.* New York: Norton, 1986.

Shultz, George P. *Turmoil and Triumph: My Year As Secretary of State*. New York: Scribner's, 1993.

Sick, Gary. *All Fall Down: America's Tragic Encounter with Iran*. New York: Random House, 1985.

Taylor, Maxwell D. *Swords and Ploughshares*. New York: Norton, 1972.

———. *The Uncertain Trumpet*. New York: Harper, 1960.

Truman, Harry S. *Years of Trial and Hope*. Vol. 2 of *Memoirs*. Garden City, N.Y.: Doubleday, 1956.

Vance, Cyrus. *Hard Choices: Critical Years in America's Foreign Policy*. New York: Simon and Schuster, 1983.

Weinberger, Caspar W. *Fighting for Peace: Seven Critical Years in the Pentagon*. New York: Warner Books, 1990.

Wise, Stephen Samuel. *Challenging Years: The Autobiography of Stephen Wise*. New York: Putnam, 1949.

Newspapers and Magazines

Atlantic Monthly
Business Week
Jerusalem Post
Middle East Policy
National Geographic Magazine
New York Times
North American Review
Washington Post

Secondary Sources

Books

Abzug, Robert H. *Inside the Vicious Heart: Americans and the Liberation of the Nazi Concentration Camps*. New York: Oxford University Press, 1985.

Ajami, Fouad. *The Dream Palace of the Arabs: A Generation's Odyssey*. New York: Random House, 1998.

Allen, Gardner W. *Our Navy and the Barbary Corsairs*. 1905. Reprint, Hamden, Conn.: Archon Books, 1965.

Allison, Robert J. *The Crescent Obscured: The United States and the Muslim World, 1776–1815*. New York: Oxford University Press, 1995.

Anderson, Irvine H. *Aramco, the United States, and Saudi Arabia: A Study of the Dynamics of Foreign Policy, 1933–1950*. Princeton: Princeton University Press, 1981.

Antonius, George. *The Arab Awakening: The Story of the Arab National Movement*. New York: Lippincott, 1939.

Arendt, Hannah. *Eichmann in Jerusalem: A Report on the Banality of Evil*. New York: Viking, 1963.

Arzt, Donna E. *Refugees into Citizens: Palestinians and the End of the Arab-Israeli Conflict*. New York: Council on Foreign Relations, 1997.

Baker, Raymond William. *Egypt's Uncertain Revolution under Nasser and Sadat*. Cambridge: Harvard University Press, 1978.

Bamford, James. *Body of Secrets: Anatomy of the Ultra-Secret National Security Agency from the Cold War through the Dawn of a New Century*. New York: Doubleday, 2001.

———. *The Puzzle Palace*. Boston: Houghton Mifflin, 1983.

Baram, Phillip J. *The Department of State in the Middle East, 1919–1945*. Philadelphia: University of Pennsylvania Press, 1978.

Barnhart, Michael A. *Japan Prepares for Total War: The Search for Economic Security, 1919–1941*. Ithaca, N.Y.: Cornell University Press, 1987.

Barrett, Laurence I. *Gambling with History: Ronald Reagan in the White House*. Garden City, N.Y.: Doubleday, 1983.

Bar-Zohar, Michael. *Ben-Gurion: A Biography*. New York: Delacorte Press, 1978.

Batatu, Hanna. *The Old Social Classes and the Revolutionary Movements of Iraq*. Princeton: Princeton University Press, 1978.

Bill, James A. *The Eagle and the Lion: The Tragedy of American-Iranian Relations*. New Haven: Yale University Press, 1988.

Bills, Scott L. *The Libyan Arena: The United States, Britain, and the Council of Foreign Ministers, 1945–1948*. Kent, Ohio: Kent State University Press, 1995.

Blair, John M. *The Control of Oil*. New York: Random House, 1976.

Blitzer, Wolf. *Territory of Lies*. New York: Harper and Row, 1989.

Blum, John Morton. *The Republican Roosevelt*. 1954. Reprint, Cambridge: Harvard University Press, 1977.

Blundy, David, and Andrew Lycett. *Qaddafi and the Libyan Revolution*. Boston: Little, Brown, 1987.

Bodansky, Yossef. *Bin Laden: The Man Who Declared War on America*. Roseville, Calif.: Prima Publishing, 1999.

Bowden, Mark. *Black Hawk Down: A Story of Modern War*. New York: Simon and Schuster, 1999.

Brands, H. W., Jr. *Into the Labyrinth: The United States and the Middle East, 1945–1993*. New York: McGraw Hill, 1994.

———. *T. R.: The Last Romantic*. New York: Basic Books, 1997.

Brenchley, Frank. *Britain and the Middle East: An Economic History, 1945–87*. London: Lester Cook, 1989.

Bryson, Thomas A. *Tars, Turks, and Tankers: The Role of the United States Navy in the Middle East, 1800–1979*. Metuchen, N.J.: Scarecrow Press, 1980.

Brzezinski, Zbigniew. *Between Two Ages: America's Role in the Technetronic Era*. 1970. Reprint, Westport, Conn.: Greenwood Press, 1982.

Buchheit, Lee C. *Secession: The Legitimacy of Self-Determination*. New Haven: Yale University Press, 1978.

Bundy, McGeorge. *Danger and Survival: Choices about the Bomb in the First Fifty Years*. New York: Random House, 1988.

Burgat, Francois, and William Dowell. *The Islamic Movement in North Africa*. Austin: Center for Middle East Studies, University of Texas at Austin, 1993.

Burleigh, Michael, and Wolfgang Wippermann. *The Racial State: Germany, 1933–1945*. New York: Cambridge University Press, 1991.

Burns, William J. *Economic Aid and American Policy toward Egypt, 1955–1981*. Albany: State University of New York Press, 1985.

Buzzanco, Robert. *Masters of War: Military Dissent and Politics in the Vietnam Era.* New York: Cambridge University Press, 1996.

Callahan, David. *Unwinnable Wars: American Power and Ethnic Conflict.* New York: Hill and Wang, 1998.

Cannon, Lou. *President Reagan: The Role of a Lifetime.* New York: Simon and Schuster, 1991.

Chafets, Ze'ev. *Double Vision: How the Press Distorts America's View of the Middle East.* New York: Morrow, 1985.

Christison, Kathleen. *Perceptions of Palestine: Their Influence on U.S. Middle East Policy.* Berkeley: University of California Press, 1999.

Cockburn, Andrew, and Leslie Cockburn. *Dangerous Liaisons: The Inside Story of the U.S.-Israeli Covert Relationship.* New York: Harper Collins, 1991.

Cohen, Michael J. *Palestine: Retreat from the Mandate — the Making of British Policy, 1936–45.* New York: Holmes and Meier, 1978.

———. *Palestine and the Great Powers, 1945–1948.* Princeton: Princeton University Press, 1982.

———. *Truman and Israel.* Berkeley: University of California Press, 1990.

Cooley, John K. *Libyan Sandstorm.* Boston: Holt, Rinehart and Winston, 1982.

Cooper, Chester L. *The Lion's Last Roar: Suez, 1956.* New York: Harper and Row, 1978.

Crabb, Cecil V., Jr. *The Doctrines of American Foreign Policy: Their Meaning, Role, and Future.* Baton Rouge: Louisiana State University Press, 1982.

Daniels, Jonathan. *The Man of Independence.* New York: Lippincott, 1950.

Dann, Uriel. *King Hussein and the Challenge of Arab Radicalism: Jordan, 1955–1967.* New York: Oxford University Press, 1989.

Davis, John. *The Landscape of Belief: Encountering the Holy Land in Nineteenth-Century American Art and Culture.* Princeton: Princeton University Press, 1995.

Dawn, C. Ernest. *From Ottomanism to Arabism: Essays on the Origins of Arab Nationalism.* Urbana: University of Illinois Press, 1973.

Day, Arthur R. *East Bank/West Bank: Jordan and the Prospects for Peace.* New York: Council on Foreign Relations, 1986.

Divine, Robert A. *Eisenhower and the Cold War.* New York: Oxford University Press, 1981.

Draper, Theodore. *A Very Thin Line: The Iran-Contra Affairs.* New York: Simon and Schuster, 1991.

Eddy, William A. *F. D. R. Meets Ibn Saud.* New York: American Friends of the Middle East, 1954.

Edwards, Holly, ed. *Noble Dreams, Wicked Pleasures: Orientalism in America, 1870–1930.* Princeton: Princeton University Press, 2000.

Engler, Robert. *The Politics of Oil: A Study of Private Power and Democratic Directions.* Chicago: University of Chicago Press, 1961.

Esposito, John L. *The Islamic Threat: Myth or Reality?* New York: Oxford University Press, 1992.

Farid, Abdel Magid. *Nasser: The Final Years.* Reading: Ithaca Press, 1994.

Farouk-Sluglett, Marion, and Peter Sluglett. *Iraq since 1958: From Revolution to Dictatorship.* New York: KPI, 1987.

Field, James A., Jr. *America and the Mediterranean World, 1776–1882*. Princeton: Princeton University Press, 1969.

First, Ruth. *Libya: The Elusive Revolution*. Middlesex: Penguin, 1974.

Fraser, T. G. *The USA and the Middle East since World War 2*. New York: St. Martin's Press, 1989.

Freedman, Lawrence, and Efraim Karsh. *The Gulf Conflict, 1990–1991: Diplomacy and War in the New World Order*. Princeton: Princeton University Press, 1993.

Friedman, Thomas L. *From Beirut to Jerusalem*. New York: Doubleday, 1990.

Fromkin, David. *A Peace to End All Peace: Creating the Modern Middle East, 1914–1922*. New York: Henry Holt, 1989.

Fulbright, J. William. *The Arrogance of Power*. New York: Vintage, 1966.

Ganin, Zvi. *Truman, American Jewry, and Israel, 1945–1948*. New York: Holmes and Meier, 1979.

Garthoff, Raymond L. *Détente and Confrontation: American Soviet Relations from Nixon to Reagan*. Rev. ed. Washington, D.C.: Brookings Institution, 1994.

Gendzier, Irene. *Notes From the Minefield: United States Intervention in Lebanon and the Middle East, 1945–1958*. New York: Columbia University Press, 1997.

Ghareeb, Edmund, ed. *Split Vision: The Portrayal of Arabs in the American Media*. Washington, D.C.: American Arab Affairs Council, 1983.

Gibb, George Sweet, and Evelyn H. Knowlton. *History of the Standard Oil Company (New Jersey)*. Vol. 2., *The Resurgent Years, 1911–1927*. New York: Harper and Row, 1956.

Gibson, James William. *The Perfect War: The War We Couldn't Lose and How We Did*. New York: Atlantic Monthly Press, 1986.

Golan, Galia. *Soviet Policies in the Middle East from World War II to Gorbachev*. Cambridge: Cambridge University Press, 1990.

Golden, Peter. *Quiet Diplomat: A Biography of Max M. Fisher*. New York: Cornwall Books, 1992.

Goode, James F. *The United States and Iran, 1946–51: The Diplomacy of Neglect*. New York: St. Martin's Press, 1989.

Goodrich, Frances, and Albert Hackett. *The Diary of Anne Frank*. New York: Random House, 1956.

Gordon, Joel. *Nasser's Blessed Movement: Egypt's Free Officers and the July Revolution*. New York: Oxford University Press, 1992.

Green, Stephen. *Taking Sides: America's Relations with a Militant Israel*. New York: Morrow, 1984.

Griswold, A. Whitney. *The Far Eastern Policy of the United States*. New York: Harcourt Brace, 1938.

Grose, Peter. *Israel in the Mind of America*. New York: Knopf, 1983.

Hackett, David A., ed. and trans. *The Buchenwald Report*. Boulder, Colo.: Westview, 1995.

Haddawy, Husain, trans. *The Arabian Nights*. New York: Norton, 1990.

Hahn, Peter L. *The United States, Great Britain, and Egypt, 1945–1956: Strategy and Diplomacy in the Early Cold War*. Chapel Hill: University of North Carolina Press, 1991.

Halberstam, David. *The Best and the Brightest*. New York: Random House, 1972.

———. *War in a Time of Peace: Bush, Clinton, and the Generals*. New York: Scribner, 2001.

Halpern, Manfred. *The Politics of Social Change in the Middle East and North Africa*. Princeton: Princeton University Press, 1963.

Hammond, Thomas. *Red Flag over Afghanistan: The Communist Coup, the Soviet Invasion, and the Consequences*. Boulder, Colo.: Westview, 1984.

Hart, Alan. *Arafat: A Political Biography*. Bloomington: Indiana University Press, 1989.

Hathaway, Robert M. *Great Britain and the United States: Special Relations since World War II*. Boston: Twayne, 1990.

Heater, Derek. *National Self-Determination: Woodrow Wilson and His Legacy*. New York: St. Martin's Press, 1994.

Heikal, Mohamed H. *The Cairo Documents: The Inside Story of Nasser and His Relationship with World Leaders, Rebels, and Statesmen*. Garden City, N.Y.: Doubleday, 1973.

———. *Cutting the Lion's Tail: Suez through Egyptian Eyes*. London: Andre Deutsch, 1986.

Heiss, Mary Ann. *Empire and Nationhood: The United States, Great Britain, and Iranian Oil, 1950–1954*. New York: Columbia University Press, 1997.

Hersh, Seymour M. *The Samson Option: Israel's Nuclear Arsenal and American Foreign Policy*. New York: Random House, 1991.

Hoopes, Townsend, and Douglas Brinkley. *Driven Patriot: The Life and Times of James Forrestal*. New York: Random House, 1992.

Hourani, Albert. *A History of the Arab Peoples*. Cambridge: Harvard University Press, 1991.

Howard, Harry N. *The King-Crane Commission: An American Inquiry in the Middle East*. Beirut: Khayats, 1963.

Howe, George F. *Northwest Africa: Seizing the Initiative in the West — United States Army in World War II: The Mediterranean Theater of Operations*. Washington, D.C.: Department of the Army, 1957.

Hunt, Michael H. *Crises in U.S. Foreign Policy: An International History Reader*. New Haven: Yale University Press, 1996.

———. *Ideology and U.S. Foreign Policy*. New Haven: Yale University Press, 1987.

Huntington, Samuel P. *The Clash of Civilizations and the Remaking of World Order*. New York: Simon and Schuster, 1996.

Irwin, Ray W. *The Diplomatic Relations of the United States with the Barbary Powers, 1776–1816*. 1931. Reprint, New York: Russell and Russell, 1970.

Jentleson, Bruce W. *With Friends Like These: Reagan, Bush, and Saddam, 1982–1990*. New York: Norton, 1994.

Kaplan, Robert. *The Arabists: The Romance of an American Elite*. New York: Free Press, 1993.

Karetzky, Stephen, ed. *The Media's War against Israel*. New York: Steimatzky Shapolsky, 1986.

Karsh, Efraim, and Inari Rautsi. *Saddam Hussein: A Political Biography*. New York: Free Press, 1991.

Kaufman, Burton I. *Trade and Aid: Eisenhower's Foreign Economic Policy, 1953–1961.* Baltimore: Johns Hopkins University Press, 1982.

Keddie, Nikki R. *Roots of Revolution: An Interpretive History of Modern Iran.* New Haven: Yale University Press, 1981.

Kenen, I. L. *Israel's Defense Line: Her Friends and Foes in Washington.* Buffalo, N.Y.: Prometheus Books, 1981.

Kerr, Malcolm H. *The Arab Cold War: Gamal 'Abd al-Nasir and His Rivals, 1958–1970.* 3rd ed. New York: Oxford University Press, 1971.

Khadduri, Majid. *Modern Libya: A Study in Political Development.* Baltimore: Johns Hopkins University Press, 1963.

———. *Republican Iraq: A Study of Iraqi Politics since the Revolution of 1958.* New York: Oxford University Press, 1969.

Kinnard, Douglas. *The Certain Trumpet: Maxwell Taylor and the American Experience in Vietnam.* New York: Brassey's, 1991.

Kunz, Diane B. *The Economic Diplomacy of the Suez Crisis.* Chapel Hill: University of North Carolina Press, 1991.

Kyle, Keith. *Suez.* New York: St. Martin's Press, 1991.

Laffin, John. *The Arab Mind Considered: A Need for Understanding.* New York: Cassell, 1975.

Lake, Anthony. *Third World Radical Regimes: U.S. Policy under Carter and Reagan.* New York: Foreign Policy Association, 1985.

Lawrence, T. E. *Revolt in the Desert.* London: G. H. Doran, 1927.

———. *The Seven Pillars of Wisdom.* 1926. Reprint, New York: Doubleday, 1935.

Leffler, Melvyn P. *A Preponderance of Power: National Security, the Truman Administration, and the Cold War.* Stanford, Calif.: Stanford University Press, 1991.

Lenczowski, George. *American Presidents and the Middle East.* Durham, N.C.: Duke University Press, 1990.

Lerner, Daniel. *The Passing of Traditional Society: Modernizing the Middle East.* Glencoe, Ill.: Free Press, 1958.

Lesch, David. *Syria and the United States: Eisenhower's Cold War in the Middle East.* Boulder, Colo.: Westview, 1992.

Liddell Hart, B. H. *T. E. Lawrence: In Arabia and After.* London: Jonathan Cape, 1934.

Litwak, Robert. *Detente and the Nixon Doctrine: American Foreign Policy and the Pursuit of Stability, 1969–1976.* New York: Cambridge University Press, 1984.

Louis, William Roger. *The British Empire in the Middle East, 1945–1951: Arab Nationalism, the United States, and Postwar Imperialism.* New York: Oxford University Press, 1984.

Love, Kennett. *Suez: The Twice-Fought War.* New York: McGraw Hill, 1969.

Lucas, W. Scott. *Divided We Stand: Britain, the U.S., and the Suez Crisis.* London: Hodder and Stoughton, 1991.

Lutz, Catherine A., and Jane L. Collins. *Reading National Geographic.* Chicago: University of Chicago Press, 1993.

Lytle, Mark Hamilton. *The Origins of the Iranian-American Alliance, 1941–1953.* New York: Holmes and Meier, 1987.

McCullough, David. *Truman.* New York: Simon and Schuster, 1992.

McFadden, David. *Alternative Paths: Soviets and Americans, 1917–1920*. New York: Oxford University Press, 1993.

Mackey, Sandra. *Passion and Politics: The Turbulent World of the Arabs*. New York: Dutton, 1992.

Marsden, Peter. *Taliban: War, Religion, and the New Order in Afghanistan*. New York: Zed Books, 1998.

Martin, David C., and John Walcott. *Best Laid Plans: The Inside Story of America's War against Terrorism*. New York: Harper and Row, 1988.

Matthews, Christopher. *Kennedy and Nixon: The Rivalry That Shaped Postwar America*. New York: Simon and Schuster, 1996.

Melman, Yossi, and Dan Raviv. *Friends in Deed: Inside the U.S.-Israel Alliance*. New York: Hyperion, 1994.

Melville, Herman. *The White Jacket, or the World in a Man-of-War*. 1849. Reprint, London: Constable, 1922.

Merrill, Dennis, and Thomas G. Paterson, eds. *Major Problems in American Foreign Relations*. 5th ed. Boston: Houghton Mifflin, 2000.

Michener, James. *The Source*. New York: Random House, 1965.

Miller, Judith, and Laurie Mylroie. *Saddam Hussein and the Crisis in the Gulf*. New York: Times Books, 1990.

Miller, Merle. *Lyndon: An Oral Biography*. New York: Putnam, 1980.

Morris, Benny. *The Birth of the Palestinian Refugee Problem, 1947–1949*. New York: Cambridge University Press, 1987.

———. *Righteous Victims: A History of the Zionist-Arab Conflict, 1881–1999*. New York: Knopf, 1999.

Mutawi, Samir. *Jordan in the 1967 War*. New York: Oxford University Press, 1987.

Neff, Donald. *Fallen Pillars: U.S. Policy towards Palestine and Israel since 1945*. Washington, D.C.: Institute for Palestine Studies, 1995.

———. *Warriors against Israel*. Brattleboro, Vt.: Amana Books, 1988.

———. *Warriors at Suez: Eisenhower Takes America into the Middle East*. New York: Simon and Schuster, 1981.

———. *Warriors for Jerusalem: The Six Days That Changed the Middle East*. New York: Simon and Schuster, 1984.

Noyes, James H. *The Clouded Lens: Persian Gulf Security and U.S. Policy*. 2nd ed. Stanford, Calif.: Hoover Institution Press, 1982.

Nutting, Anthony. *Nasser*. New York: E. P. Dutton, 1972.

Packenham, Robert A. *Liberal America and the Third World: Political Development Ideas in Foreign Aid and Social Science*. Princeton: Princeton University Press, 1973.

Painter, David. *Oil and the American Century: The Political Economy of U.S. Foreign Oil Policy, 1941–1954*. Baltimore: Johns Hopkins University Press, 1986.

Palmer, Michael A. *Guardians of the Gulf: A History of America's Expanding Role in the Persian Gulf, 1833–1992*. New York: Free Press, 1992.

Parker, Richard B. *Politics of Miscalculation in the Middle East*. Bloomington: Indiana University Press, 1993.

———, ed. *The Six Day War: A Retrospective*. Tallahassee: University of Florida Press, 1996.

Parmet, Herbert S. *Richard Nixon and His America*. Boston: Little, Brown, 1990.

Patai, Raphael. *The Arab Mind*. New York: Scribner, 1973.

———. *The Arab Mind*. Rev. ed. New York: Scribner, 1983.

Pieragostini, Karl. *Britain, Aden, and South Arabia: Abandoning Empire*. New York: St. Martin's Press, 1991.

Poole, Walter S. *The History of the Joint Chiefs of Staff: The JCS and National Policy*. Vol. 4, *1950–1952*. Washington, D.C.: Office of Joint History, Office of the Chairman of the Joint Chiefs of Staff, 1979.

Prados, John. *Keepers of the Keys: A History of the National Security Council from Truman to Bush*. New York: Morrow, 1991.

Pryce-Jones, David. *The Closed Circle: An Interpretation of the Arabs*. New York: Harper, 1989.

Quandt, William B. *Camp David: Peacemaking and Politics*. Washington, D.C.: Brookings Institution, 1986.

———. *Decade of Decisions: American Policy toward the Arab-Israeli Conflict, 1967–1976*. Berkeley: University of California Press, 1977.

———. *Peace Process: American Diplomacy and the Arab-Israeli Conflict since 1967*. Washington, D.C.: Brookings Institution, 1993.

Quandt, William B., Fuad Jabber, and Ann Mosely Lesch. *The Politics of Palestinian Nationalism*. Berkeley: University of California Press, 1973.

Rashid, Ahmed. *Taliban: Militant Islam, Oil, and Fundamentalism in Central Asia*. New Haven: Yale University Press, 2000.

Raviv, Dan, and Yossi Melman. *Every Spy a Prince: The Complete History of Israel's Intelligence Community*. Boston: Houghton Mifflin, 1990.

Rockefeller Brothers Fund. *Prospect for America: The Rockefeller Panel Reports*. Garden City, N.Y.: Doubleday, 1961.

Rostow, W. W. *The Diffusion of Power: An Essay in Recent History*. New York: Macmillan, 1972.

———. *The Stages of Economic Growth: A Non-Communist Manifesto*. Cambridge: Cambridge University Press, 1960.

Rubin, Barry. *Cauldron of Turmoil: America in the Middle East*. New York: Harcourt Brace Jovanovich, 1992.

———. *Paved with Good Intentions: The American Experience and Iran*. New York: Oxford University Press, 1980.

Sachar, Howard M. *A History of the Jews in America*. New York: Knopf, 1992.

Safran, Nadav. *Saudi Arabia: The Ceaseless Quest for Security*. Cambridge: Harvard University Press, 1985.

Said, Edward W. *Covering Islam: How the Media and Its Experts Determine How We See the Rest of the World*. New York: Pantheon, 1981.

———. *Culture and Imperialism*. New York: Knopf, 1993.

———. *Orientalism*. New York: Random House, 1978.

Saikal, Amin. *The Rise and Fall of the Shah*. Princeton: Princeton University Press, 1980.

Sampson, Anthony. *The Seven Sisters: The Great Oil Companies and the World They Shaped*. New York: Bantam, 1976.

Sanders, Ronald. *The High Walls of Jerusalem: A History of the Balfour Declaration and the Birth of the British Mandate in Palestine*. New York: Holt, Rinehart and Winston, 1983.

————. *Shores of Refuge: A Hundred Years of Jewish Emigration*. New York: Holt, Rinehart and Winston, 1988.

Saunders, Harold H. *The Other Walls: The Politics of the Arab-Israeli Peace Process*. Washington, D.C.: American Enterprise Institute, 1985.

Schiff, Ze'ev, and Ehud Ya'ari. *Israel's Lebanon War*. New York: Simon and Schuster, 1984.

Schoenbaum, David. *The United States and the State of Israel*. New York: Oxford University Press, 1993.

Schoenbaum, Thomas J. *Waging Peace and War: Dean Rusk in the Truman, Kennedy, and Johnson Years*. New York: Simon and Schuster, 1988.

Schulzinger, Robert D. *Henry Kissinger: Doctor of Diplomacy*. New York: Columbia University Press, 1989.

————. *The Wise Men of Foreign Affairs: The History of the Council on Foreign Relations*. New York: Columbia University Press, 1984.

Schwartzkopf, H. Norman, Jr. *It Doesn't Take a Hero*. New York: Bantam, 1992.

Sciolino, Elaine. *The Outlaw State: Saddam Hussein's Quest for Power and the Gulf Crisis*. New York: Wiley, 1991.

Seale, Patrick. *The Struggle for Syria: A Study of Post-War Arab Politics, 1945–1958*. New Haven: Yale University Press, 1965.

Seale, Patrick, and Maureen McConville. *The Hilton Assignment*. New York: Praeger, 1973.

Sha'ban, Fuad. *Islam and Arabs in Early American Thought: The Roots of Orientalism in America*. Durham, N.C.: Acorn Press, 1991.

Shaheen, Jack G. *The TV Arab*. Bowling Green, Ohio: Bowling Green University Popular Press, 1984.

Shapely, Deborah. *Promise and Power: The Life and Times of Robert McNamara*. Boston: Little, Brown, 1993.

Sheehan, Edward R. F. *The Arabs, Israelis, and Kissinger*. New York: Reader's Digest Press, 1976.

Shlaim, Avi. *The Iron Wall: Israel and the Arab World*. New York: Norton, 2000.

Shwadran, Benjamin. *The Middle East, Oil, and the Great Powers*. New York: Praeger, 1955.

Silver, Eric. *Begin: The Haunted Prophet*. New York: Random House, 1984.

Simon, Reeva S. *Iraq between the World Wars: The Creation and Implementation of a Nationalist Ideology*. New York: Columbia University Press, 1986.

Skeet, Ian. *Opec: Twenty-five Years of Prices and Politics*. London: Faber and Faber, 1988.

Smolansky, Oles. *The Soviet Union and the Arab East under Khrushchev*. Lewisburg, Pa.: Bucknell University Press, 1974.

Spector, Ronald H. *U.S. Marines in Grenada, 1983*. Washington, D.C.: Government Printing Office, 1987.

Spiegel, Steven L. *The Other Arab-Israeli Conflict: Making America's Middle East Policy, from Truman to Reagan*. Chicago: University of Chicago Press, 1985.

Stephens, Robert. *Nasser: A Political Biography*. New York: Simon and Schuster, 1971.

Stivers, William. *America's Confrontation with Revolutionary Change in the Middle East, 1948–83*. New York: St. Martin's Press, 1986.

————. *Supremacy and Oil: Iraq, Turkey, and the Anglo-American World Order, 1918–1930*. Ithaca, N.Y.: Cornell University Press, 1982.

Stoff, Michael B. *Oil, War, and American Security: The Search for a National Policy on Foreign Oil, 1941–47*. New Haven: Yale University Press, 1980.

Stork, Joe. *Middle East Oil and the Energy Crisis*. New York: Monthly Review Press, 1975.

Strober, Gerald S., and Deborah H. Strober. *Nixon: An Oral History*. New York: Harper Collins, 1994.

Suleiman, Michael W. *The Arabs in the Mind of America*. Brattleboro, Vt.: Amana Books, 1988.

Sulzberger, C. L. *The Last of the Giants*. New York: Macmillan, 1970.

————. *The World and Richard Nixon*. New York: Prentice Hall, 1987.

Summers, Harry G., Jr. *On Strategy: A Critical Analysis of the Vietnam War*. Novato, Calif.: Presidio Press, 1982.

————. *On Strategy II: A Critical Analysis of the Gulf War* New York: Dell Books, 1992.

Terzian, Pierre. *OPEC: The Inside Story*. Translated by Michael Pallis. London: Zed Books, 1985.

Tessler, Mark A. *A History of the Israeli-Palestinian Conflict*. Bloomington: Indiana University Press, 1994.

Tillman, Seth P. *The United States in the Middle East: Interests and Obstacles*. Bloomington: Indiana University Press, 1982.

Tivnan, Edward. *The Lobby: Jewish Political Power and American Foreign Policy*. New York: Simon and Schuster, 1987.

Tocqueville, Alexis de. *L'Ancien Regime*. 1856. Translated by M. W. Patterson. Oxford: Basil Blackwell, 1952.

————. *Democracy in America*. 2 vols. 1831. Reprint, New York: Knopf, 1945.

Twain, Mark. *The Innocents Abroad: Roughing It*. 1869. Reprint, New York: Viking, 1984.

Uris, Leon. *The Haj*. Garden City, N.Y.: Doubleday, 1984.

Victor, Barbara. *A Voice of Reason: Hanan Ashrawi and Peace in the Middle East*. New York: Harcourt Brace, 1994.

Westad, Odd Arne, ed. *The Fall of Détente: Soviet-American Relations during the Carter Years*. Oslo: Scandinavian University Press, 1997.

Wilson, Jeremy. *Lawrence of Arabia: The Authorized Biography of T. E. Lawrence*. New York: Atheneum, 1990.

Wilson, John A. *Signs and Wonders upon Pharaoh: A History of American Egyptology*. Chicago: University of Chicago Press, 1964.

Wittner, Lawrence S. *American Intervention in Greece, 1943–1949*. New York: Columbia University Press, 1982.

Woodward, Bob. *The Commanders*. New York: Simon and Schuster, 1991.

Wright, John. *Libya: A Modern History*. Baltimore: Johns Hopkins University Press, 1982.

Wyman, David S. *The Abandonment of the Jews: America and the Holocaust, 1941–1945*. New York: Pantheon, 1984.

Yergin, Daniel. *The Prize: The Epic Quest for Oil, Money, and Power*. New York: Simon and Schuster, 1991.

Yousaf, Mohammad, with Mark Adkin. *The Bear Trap: Afghanistan's Untold Story*. London: L. Cooper, 1992.

Zahniser, Marvin. *Uncertain Friendship: American-French Relations through the Cold War*. New York: Wiley, 1975.

Articles

Abercrombie, Thomas J. "Behind the Veil of Troubled Yemen." *National Geographic Magazine*, March 1964, 402–45.

Abu-Amr, Ziad. "Hamas: A Historical and Political Background." *Journal of Palestine Studies* 22 (summer 1993): 5–19.

Adams, Harnet Chalmers. "Cirenaica, Eastern Wing of Italian Libia." *National Geographic Magazine*, December 1930, 689–726.

Akins, James E. "The Oil Crisis: This Time the Wolf Is Here." *Foreign Affairs* 51 (April 1973): 462–90.

"Arab Lands beyond the Jordan." *National Geographic Magazine*, December 1947, 753–68.

Arden, Harvey. "Eternal Sinai." *National Geographic Magazine*, April 1982, 420–61.

Ashton, Nigel John. "The Hijacking of a Pact: The Formation of the Baghdad Pact and Anglo-American Tensions in the Middle East, 1955–1958." *Review of International Studies* 19 (1993): 123–27.

Badeau, John S. "The Middle East: Conflict in Priorities." *Foreign Affairs* 36 (January 1958): 232–40.

Bassett, Lawrence J., and Stephen E. Pelz. "The Failed Search for Victory: Vietnam and the Politics of War." In *Kennedy's Quest for Victory: American Foreign Policy, 1961–1963*, edited by Thomas G. Paterson, 223–52. New York: Oxford University Press, 1989.

Békés, Csaba. "New Findings on the 1956 Hungarian Revolution." *Cold War International History Project Bulletin* 2 (fall 1992): 1–3.

Buruma, Ian, and Avishai Margalit. "Occidentalism." *New York Review of Books*, 17 January 2002, 4–7.

Cassandra [pseud.]. "The Impending Crisis in Egypt." *Middle East Journal* 49 (winter 1995): 9–27.

Chalabi, Fadhil J. Al. "The World Oil Price Collapse of 1986: Causes and Implications for the Future of OPEC." In *After the Oil Price Collapse: OPEC, the United States, and the World Oil Market*, edited by Wilfrid L. Kohl, 1–27. Baltimore: Johns Hopkins University Press, 1991.

Chase, Francis, Jr. "Palestine Today." *National Geographic Magazine*, October 1946, 501–16.

Christison, Kathleen. "The Arab in Recent Popular Fiction." *Middle East Journal* 41 (summer 1987): 397–411.

Clark, Harlan B. "Yemen: Southern Arabia's Mountain Wonderland." *National Geographic Magazine*, October 1947, 631–72.

Cobbs Hoffman, Elizabeth. "Diplomatic History and the Meaning of Life: Toward a Global American History." *Diplomatic History* 21 (fall 1997): 503–18.

Cogan, Charles G. "Partners in Time: The CIA and Afghanistan since 1979." *World Policy Journal* 10, no. 2 (summer 1993): 73–82.

Cohen, Michael J., "The Zionist Perspective." In *The End of the Palestine Mandate*, edited by William Roger Louis and Robert Stookey, 79–103. Austin: University of Texas Press, 1986.

Danner, Mark. "America and the Bosnia Genocide." *New York Review of Books,* 4 December 1997, 55–65.

———. "Slouching toward Dayton." *New York Review of Books,* 23 April 1998, 59–65.

Doran, Michael Scott. "Somebody Else's Civil War." *Foreign Affairs* 81 (January/February 2002): 22–42.

Elon, Amos. "Israel and the End of Zionism." *New York Review of Books,* 19 December 1996, 22–27.

———. "Israel's Demons." *New York Review of Books,* 21 December 1995, 42–46.

Eran, Obed. "Negotiating the Anglo-Egyptian Relationship between the World Wars." In *Imperialism and Nationalism in the Middle East: The Anglo-Egyptian Experience, 1882–1982,* edited by Keith M. Wilson, 56–75. London: Mansell, 1983.

Gardner, Lloyd C. "Harry Hopkins with Hand Grenades? McGeorge Bundy in the Kennedy and Johnson Years." In *Behind the Throne: Servants of Power to Imperial Presidents, 1898–1968,* edited by Thomas J. McCormick and Walter LaFeber, 204–31. Madison: University of Wisconsin Press, 1993.

Gasiorowski, Mark. "The 1953 Coup d'Etat in Iran." *International Journal of Middle East Studies* 19 (August 1987): 261–86.

Gause, F. Gregory. "Saudi Arabia over a Barrel." *Foreign Affairs* 79 (May/June 2000): 80–94.

Gerner, Deborah J. "Missed Opportunities and Roads Not Taken: The Eisenhower Administration and the Palestinians." *Arab Studies Quarterly* 12 (winter/spring 1990): 67–100.

Glidden, Harold. "The Arab World." *American Journal of Psychiatry* 128 (February 1972): 99.

Glueck, Nelson. "An Archaeologist Looks at Palestine." *National Geographic Magazine,* November 1947, 739–52.

Goldberg, Jeffrey. "Letter from Cairo: Behind Mubarak." *New Yorker,* 8 October 2001, 48–55.

Goode, James F. "Reforming Iran during the Kennedy Years." *Diplomatic History* 15 (winter 1991): 13–29.

Grose, Peter. "The President versus the Diplomats." In *The End of the Palestine Mandate,* edited by William Roger Louis and Robert Stookey, 32–60. Austin: University of Texas Press, 1986.

Gwertzman, Bernard. "Reagan Turns to Israel." *New York Times Magazine,* 27 November 1983, 63–88.

Haddad, Mahmoud. "The Rise of Arab Nationalism Reconsidered." *International Journal of Middle East Studies* 26 (May 1994): 201–22.

Halperin, Samuel, and Irvin Oder. "The United States in Search of a Policy: Franklin D. Roosevelt and Palestine." *Review of Politics* 24 (July 1962): 320–41.

Harbutt, Charles. "Eyewitness to War in the Holy Land." *National Geographic Magazine,* December 1967, 782–97.

Hersh, Seymour. "Annals of National Security: King's Ransom." *New Yorker,* 22 October 2001, 35–39.

————. "Target Qaddafi." *New York Times Magazine,* 22 February 1987, 17–26, 48, 71–74, 84.

Hyman, Sidney. "When Bundy Says, 'The President Wants—,'" *New York Times Magazine,* 2 December 1962, 30, 131–33.

"An Interview with Nabil Shaath." *Journal of Palestine Studies* 23 (autumn 1993): 5–6.

Kagan, Robert. "The Benevolent Empire." *Foreign Policy* 111 (summer 1998): 36–47.

Kaplan, Robert D. "Looking the World in the Eye." *Atlantic Monthly,* December 2001, 68–82.

Kaufman, Burton I. "Mideast Multinational Oil, U.S. Foreign Policy, and Antitrust: The 1950s." *Journal of American History* 63 (March 1977): 937–59.

Keith-Roche, Edward. "Changing Palestine." *National Geographic Magazine,* April 1934, 493–527.

————. "The Pageant of Jerusalem." *National Geographic Magazine,* December 1927, 635–81.

Khouri, Fred J. "The Policy of Retaliation in Arab-Israeli Relations." *Middle East Journal* 20 (autumn 1966): 435–55.

Latham, Michael E. "Ideology, Social Science, and Destiny: Modernization and the Kennedy-Era Alliance for Progress." *Diplomatic History* 22 (spring 1998): 199–229.

Lebow, Richard Ned. "Woodrow Wilson and the Balfour Declaration." *Journal of Modern History* 40 (December 1968): 501–23.

Lendenmann, G. Neal. "Arab Stereotyping in Contemporary Political Cartoons." In *Split Vision: The Portrayal of Arabs in the American Media,* edited by Edmund Ghareeb, 345–53. Washington, D.C.: American-Arab Affairs Council, 1983.

Lewis, Bernard. "License to Kill: Usama bin Laden's Declaration of Jihad." *Foreign Affairs* 77 (November/December 1998): 14–19.

————. "The Roots of Muslim Rage." *Atlantic Monthly,* September 1990, 47–60.

Lewis, Samuel. "The United States and Israel: Constancy and Change." In *The Middle East: Ten Years after Camp David,* edited by William Quandt, 217–57. Washington, D.C.: Brookings Institution, 1988.

"The Libyan Revolution in the Words of Its Leaders." *Middle East Journal* 24 (spring 1970): 212–19.

Little, Douglas. "Choosing Sides: Lyndon Johnson and the Middle East." In *The Johnson Years,* edited by Robert A. Divine, vol. 3, *LBJ at Home and Abroad,* 150–97. Lawrence: University of Kansas Press, 1994.

————. "Cold War and Covert Action: The United States and Syria, 1945–1958." *Middle East Journal* 44 (winter 1990): 51–75.

————. "From Even-Handed to Empty-Handed: Seeking Order in the Middle East." In *Kennedy's Quest for Victory: American Foreign Policy, 1961–1963,* edited by Thomas G. Paterson, 156–77. New York: Oxford University Press, 1989.

————. "His Finest Hour? Eisenhower, Lebanon, and the 1958 Middle East Crisis." *Diplomatic History* 20 (winter 1996): 27–54.

————. "The Making of a Special Relationship: The United States and Israel, 1957–68." *International Journal of Middle East Studies* 25 (November 1993): 564–73.

————. "The New Frontier on the Nile: JFK, Nasser, and Arab Nationalism." *Journal of American History* 75 (September 1988): 501–27.

————. "Pipeline Politics: America, TAPLINE, and the Arabs." *Business History Review* 64 (summer 1990): 255–85.

————. "A Puppet in Search of a Puppeteer? The United States, King Hussein, and Jordan, 1953–1970." *International History Review* 17 (August 1995): 512–44.

Loftus, John A. "Oil in United States Foreign Policy." *Department of State Bulletin* 15 (11 August 1946): 276–81.

Louis, William Roger. "The British and the Origins of the Iraqi Revolution." In *The Iraqi Revolution of 1958: The Old Social Classes Revisited*, edited by Robert Fernea and William Roger Louis, 31–61. London: I. B. Tauris, 1991.

————. "Dulles, Suez, and the British." In *John Foster Dulles and the Diplomacy of the Cold War*, edited by Richard H. Immerman, 133–58. Princeton: Princeton University Press, 1990.

————. "The Tragedy of the Anglo-Egyptian Settlement of 1954." In *Suez 1956: The Crisis and Its Consequences*, edited by William Roger Louis and Roger Owen, 43–71. New York: Oxford University Press, 1989.

Mahan, Alfred Thayer. "The Persian Gulf and International Relations." In *Retrospect and Prospect: Studies in International Relations Naval and Political*, edited by Alfred Thayer Mahan, 209–51. Boston: Little, Brown, 1902.

Malley, Robert, and Hussein Agha. "Camp David: The Tragedy of Errors." *New York Review of Books*, 9 August 2001, 59–65.

Manela, Erez. "Friction from the Sidelines: Diplomacy, Religion, and Culture in American-Egyptian Relations, 1919–1939." In *The United States and the Middle East: Diplomatic and Economic Relations in Historical Perspective*, edited by Abbas Amanas, 39–68. New Haven: Yale Center for Area Studies, 2000.

Mart, Michelle. "Tough Guys and American Cold War Policy: Images of Israel, 1948–1960." *Diplomatic History* 20 (summer 1996): 357–80.

Michalek, Laurence. "The Arab in American Cinema: A Century of Otherness." *The Arab Image in American Film and Television*, special supplement to *Cineaste* 17, no. 1 (1989): 3–4.

Nagourney, Adam. "Sound Bites over Jerusalem." *New York Times Magazine*, 25 April 1999, 42–70.

Neff, Donald. "The Clinton Administration and UN Resolution 242." *Journal of Palestine Studies* 23 (winter 1994): 20–30.

Newhouse, John. "No Exit, No Entrance." *New Yorker*, 28 June 1993, 44–51.

Noble, George B. "The Voice of Egypt." *Nation*, 3 January 1920, 861–64.

Ovendale, Ritchie. "Great Britain and the Anglo-American Invasion of Jordan and Lebanon." *International History Review* 16 (May 1994): 284–303.

Pastor, Robert. "The United States and the Grenada Revolution: Who Pushed First and Why?" In *Revolution Aborted: The Lessons of Grenada*, edited by Jorge Heine, 181–214. Pittsburgh: University of Pittsburgh Press, 1990.

Peretz, Don, and Gideon Doron. "Israel's 1996 Elections: A Second Political Earthquake?" *Middle East Journal* 50 (autumn 1996): 529–46.

Power, Samantha. "Bystanders to Genocide: Why the United States Let the Rwandan Tragedy Happen." *Atlantic Monthly*, September 2001, 84–108.

Quandt, William B. "Lyndon Johnson and the June 1967 War: What Color Was the Light?" *Middle East Journal* 46 (spring 1992): 198–228.

Quester, George H. "Nuclear Weapons and Israel." *Middle East Journal* 37 (autumn 1983): 547–64.

Rahme, Joseph G. "Ethnocentric and Stereotypical Concepts in the Study of Islamic and World History." *History Teacher* 32, no. 4 (August 1999): 483–85.

Remnick, David. "Letter from Jerusalem: The Outsider." *New Yorker*, 25 May 1998, 80–95.

"Report of Earl G. Harrison." *Department of State Bulletin* 13 (30 September 1945): 455–63.

Rotter, Andrew J. "Saidism without Said: Orientalism and U.S. Diplomatic History." *American Historical Review* 105, no. 4. (October 2000): 1205–17.

Savir, Uri. "Why Oslo Still Matters." *New York Times Magazine*, 3 May 1998, 50–54.

Schiff, Zeev. "The Green Light." *Foreign Policy* 50 (spring 1983): 73–85.

Schmemann, Serge. "Outside In." *New York Times Magazine*, 23 November 1997, 55–59, 74–77.

Schrag, Robert L., and Manoocher N. Javidi. "Through a Glass Darkly: American Media Images of Middle Eastern Cultures and Their Potential Impact on Young Children." In *The U.S. Media and the Middle East: Image and Perception*, edited by Yahya R. Kamalipour, 212–21. Westport, Conn.: Praeger, 1995).

Scofield, John. "Israel: Land of Promise." *National Geographic Magazine*, March 1965, 395–434.

Shlaim, Avi. "Conflicting Approaches to Israel's Relations with the Arabs: Ben Gurion and Sharett, 1953–1956." *Middle East Journal* 37 (spring 1983): 180–201.

———. "Woman of the Year." *New York Review of Books*, 8 June 1995, 24–27.

Shor, Franc. "Crusader Road to Jerusalem," "Conquest of the Holy City," and "Holy Land Today." *National Geographic Magazine*, December 1963, 797–857.

Simpich, Frederick, Jr. "Americans Help Liberated Europe Live Again." *National Geographic Magazine*, June 1945, 747–68.

———. "Change Comes to Bible Lands." *National Geographic Magazine*, December 1938, 695–750.

Singer, Mark. "Home Is Here." *New Yorker*, 15 October 2001, 62–70.

Solarz, Stephen J. "The Stakes in the Gulf." *New Republic*, 7, 14 January 1991, 18–25.

Stanger, Cary David. "A Haunting Legacy: The Assassination of Count Bernadotte." *Middle East Journal* 42 (spring 1988): 260–72.

Stein, Janice Gross. "The Wrong Strategy in the Right Place: The United States in the Gulf." *International Security* 13 (winter 1988/1989): 142–67.

Stockton, Ronald. "Ethnic Archetypes and the Arab Image." In *The Development of Arab-American Identity*, edited by Ernest McCarus, 119–53. Ann Arbor: University of Michigan Press, 1995.

Szulc, Tad. "Who Are the Palestinians?" *National Geographic Magazine*, June 1992, 84–113.

Tal, Lawrence. "Britain and the Jordan Crisis of 1958." *Middle Eastern Studies* 31 (January 1995): 39–57.

Thacher, Nicholas G. "Reflections on US Foreign Policy towards Iraq in the 1950s." In *The Iraqi Revolution of 1958: The Old Social Classes Revisited*, edited by Robert Fernea and William Roger Louis, 62–76. London: I. B. Tauris, 1991.

Tucker, Robert. "Oil: The Issue of American Intervention." *Commentary,* January 1975, 21–31.

Van Der Meulen, D. "Into Burning Hadhramaut." *National Geographic Magazine,* October 1932, 387–429.

Villiers, Alan. "Sailing with Sindbad's Sons." *National Geographic Magazine,* November 1948, 675–88.

Weaver, Mary Anne. "Blowback." *Atlantic Monthly,* May 1996, 24–36.

———. "Children of the Jihad." *New Yorker,* 12 June 1995, 40–48.

Weiner, Tim. "Blowback from the Afghan Battlefield." *New York Times Magazine,* 13 March 1994, 52–55.

Whiting, John D. "Among the Bethlehem Shepherds." *National Geographic Magazine,* December 1926, 729–53.

———. "Bethlehem and the Christmas Story." *National Geographic Magazine,* October 1932, 699–735.

Williams, Maynard Owen. "East of Suez to the Mount of the Decalogue." *National Geographic Magazine,* December 1927, 709–43.

Wright, Claudia. "Behind Iraq's Bold Bid." *New York Times Magazine,* 26 October 1980, 43, 109–17.

Dissertations

Bick, Etta Zablocki. "Ethnic Linkages and Foreign Policy: A Study of the Linkage Role of American Jews in Relations between the United States and Israel, 1956–1968." City University of New York, 1983.

Thomas, Teresa Ann. "From Orientalism to Professionalism: U.S. Foreign Service Officers in the Middle East since 1946." Clark University, 1996.

INDEX

Abdel-Shafi, Haidar, 299
Abdullah I (emir and king of Jordan), 54
Abu Nidal, 292, 295
Acheson, Dean, 161–62; and Egypt, 164, 165, 166, 176–77; and Iran, 57, 215; and Truman Doctrine, 123
Adams, John Quincy, 12
Aden, 25, 118, 140, 184, 187, 308
Adonis (Ali Ahmed Said), 315
Afghanistan, 3, 119, 124, 227; and bin Laden, 153, 264; and 1978 revolution, 223; Soviet invasion of, 5, 117, 147, 149–52, 244, 311; U.S. covert intervention in, 152–54; U.S. war in, 75, 264–66, 315, 317
Agency for International Development, 205
Akins, James, 67, 68, 212
Aladdin, 11, 40–41, 314
Alam, Asadollah, 219

Al-Aqsa Intifada, 304–6
Albania, 264
Albright, Madeline, 303
Algeria, 3, 27, 175, 232; oil of, 59, 67
Allen, George, 171
Alliance for Progress, 5
Allon, Yigal, 269
Al-Qaeda, 1, 2, 42, 75, 308, 315, 317; in Afghanistan, 314; and attacks on U.S. embassies in Tanzania and Kenya, 191, 264, 314; and U.S. war against, 231, 265
American Israel Public Affairs Committee (AIPAC), 78, 88, 94, 102, 104, 107, 108, 109–10, 114, 286, 297, 298, 300
American Jewish Committee, 89
American University in Beirut, 2, 197
American University in Cairo, 183
American Zionist Council, 88, 92
American Zionist Emergency Council, 21

Amini, Ali, 219

Amir, Yigal, 302

Amitay, Morris, 108, 109

Amouzegar, Jamshid, 70

Anderson, Robert, 61, 203, 275–76

Anglo-American Committee of Inquiry, 81

Anglo-American Oil Agreement, 50–51

Anglo-Egyptian Treaty (1936), 160, 163

Anglo-Iranian Oil Company (AIOC), 56–57, 60, 215, 216

Anglo-Persian Oil Company, 46, 47, 52; and Kuwait, 48, 49. *See also* Anglo-Iranian Oil Company

Anne Frank: Diary of a Young Girl, 29

Anti-Semitism, 309; in America, 4, 11, 12, 19, 20, 41, 77, 79; in Arab world, 40, 191; in Europe, 15, 19, 20, 23; Nixon and, 33

Arab-American Anti-Discrimination Committee, 41

Arab Americans, 39, 40, 42

Arabia, 18, 141

Arabian American Oil Company (ARAMCO), 56, 60, 67; formative years of, 53–55; Saudi takeover of, 72; and Six Day War, 63–64

Arab League, 137, 273

Arab Liberation Army, 269

Arab nationalism, 5, 14, 31, 35, 62, 77, 155, 157, 162, 181, 188; and First World War, 159–60; and Nasser, 5, 27, 28, 136, 137, 167–68, 169, 172, 193; and 1958 Middle East crisis, 93–94, 136; and Suez crisis, 132, 179, 180–81

Arab Petroleum Congress, 60

Arabs: American stereotypes of, 10–11, 13, 17, 18, 24, 26–28, 30–31, 34–39

Arafat, Yasser, 7, 37–38, 114, 246, 279, 283, 289, 306; and Clinton, 301–4; and Israel, 287, 316; and George Bush, 298–99; and Oslo Accords, 113, 267–68; and Reagan, 292, 293–94, 295–96

Arens, Moshe, 39, 294, 297

Armacost, Michael, 251

Armenia, 14

Armenians, 12, 16

Armitage, Richard, 251

Ashman, Howard, 40

Ashrawi, Hanan, 298, 299, 300

Assad, Hafez al-, 39, 186, 242, 287, 311

Aswan Dam, 130, 168–71, 172, 188, 274

Atlantic Charter, 158, 161, 162

Atlantic Monthly, 36

Atta, Mohammed, 192

Austin, Warren, 85

Australia, 142, 174

Azerbaijan, 121, 316

Aziz, Tarik, 260

Ba'ath Party, 199; in Iraq, 203, 204, 205, 206, 227; in Syria, 182, 186

Back to the Future, 38

Badeau, John S., 32, 158, 183, 190, 198

Badr, Mohammed al-, 238

Baghdad Pact, 129–30, 131, 136, 168, 199

Bahrain, 51, 141, 263, 264

Baker, James, 253; and Gulf War, 255, 258, 260; and Israel, 112–13; and Palestinian-Israeli peace process, 297–99, 300

Bakoush, Abdul Hamid, 207–8

Bakr, Ahmed Hassan al-, 205, 206

Balfour, Arthur, 16

Balfour Declaration, 16, 19, 20, 22, 41, 272

Balkans, 6, 123, 158, 263

Ball, George, 225–26

Bandar bin Sultan (prince of Saudi Arabia), 153

Barak, Ehud, 7, 113–14, 303–4, 312

Barbary Wars, 12, 28, 41, 229, 230, 231, 249

Barger, Thomas, 63

Baruch, Bernard, 82

Begin, Menachem, 7, 38, 113, 268, 312; and Camp David Accords, 109–10, 290–92; and Irgun, 81, 82, 83, 269; and Lebanon, 111–12, 293–95, 297; and occupied territories, 289–90; and Reagan, 110–11

Ben Bella, Ahmed, 279

Ben Gurion, David, 89, 97, 106, 115, 275, 285; and creation of Israel, 85; and Eisenhower, 93–94, 103, 114; and Kennedy, 95, 96; and Nixon, 284; and Palestine, 20, 81; and Palestinians, 269–70, 271, 276, 278; and Suez crisis, 90–93, 176; and Truman, 78, 88

Ben Halim, Mustafa, 208

Berle, Adolf, 26

Bernadotte, Folke, 88, 269–70

Bevin, Ernest, 80, 82

Bible, 11, 12

Biden, Joseph, 265

Biltmore declaration, 21

Bingham, Caleb, 12

Bin Laden, Osama, 42, 155, 191–92; and Afghan mujahadeen, 153; and al-Qaeda, 264, 308; Islamic extremism of, 314, 317; and Saudi Arabia, 75, 316; and September 11 attacks, 1, 8, 154, 265, 305, 314–15, 316

Black Sunday, 38

B'nai B'rith, 89

Bosnia, 263

Bowles, Chester, 183

Bradley, Omar, 126

Brandeis, Louis, 16, 19, 20, 21

Brezhnev, Leonid, 145, 243

Bridgman, Frederick Arthur, 13

British Petroleum Company (BP), 60, 67, 72

Brookings Institution, 288

Brown, Charles R., 234

Brown, George, 141

Brown, William, 35

Bruce, David, 142

Brzezinski, Zbigniew, 147, 252; and Afghan mujahadeen, 154; and Carter Doctrine, 151, 152; and Iranian revolution, 224, 226; and modernization, 196–97

Bulganin, Nikolai, 180

Bundy, McGeorge, 95, 236, 237

Buruma, Ian, 315

Bush, George, 11, 35; and Gulf War, 6, 45, 73–74, 154–55, 230, 252, 255–62,

311; and Iraq, 253–55; and Israel, 112; and PLO, 296–97; and Somalia, 263; as vice president, 252, 297; and Vietnam syndrome, 262, 267

Bush, George W., 114; and Arab-Israeli peace process, 7, 264, 305–6, 312, 316; and "axis of evil," 318; and oil, 74; and September 11 attacks, 2, 264; and war in Afghanistan, 231, 264–65, 317; and Vietnam syndrome, 266

Byrnes, James F., 121

Byroade, Henry, 28, 127, 171

Caffery, Jefferson, 163, 164, 165, 171

California Arabian Standard Oil Company (CASOC), 47, 48, 49

Camp David Accords (1978), 34, 110, 289–93

Camp David Summit (2000), 7, 114, 304, 306

Canada, 65, 73

Caradon, Lord, 282

Carter, Jimmy, 119, 146, 196, 230, 312, 316; and Camp David Accords, 289–92; and Iran, 223–27, 244–45; and Israel, 78, 109–10; and Libya, 214; and Palestinians, 288–90; and Sadat, 34; and Soviet Union, 117

Carter Doctrine, 5, 119, 146–52, 154, 244

Carville, James, 113

Casey, William, 153, 252

Castro, Fidel, 190

Central Asia: oil of, 312, 316–17

Central Command (CENTCOM), 255, 256, 257

Central Intelligence Agency (CIA), 30, 94, 96, 106, 123, 134, 206, 242; and Afghanistan, 152–54, 223; and al-Qaeda, 308; and Arabs, 26, 32; and Egypt, 171, 172, 186; and Iran, 144, 146, 217, 218, 223–24; and Iraq, 200, 201, 202; and Libya, 210, 212, 249; and Middle East oil, 62, 71; and Palestinians, 281; and Syria, 182, 280

Central Treaty Organization (CENTO), 136, 138

Chad, 214

Chafets, Ze'ev, 39

Chamberlain, Neville, 114

Chamoun, Camille, 134–35, 183, 234–35, 273

Chase Manhattan Bank, 205

Cheney, Richard, 255, 257, 259, 260

Chiang Kai-shek, 215

China, 14, 32, 45, 88, 124, 127, 158, 159, 162, 216, 315; and Iran, 251; and Nasser, 170

Christopher, Warren, 226

Church, Frank, 71–72

Churchill, Winston, 79, 119, 131, 168, 215, 232, 307; as colonial secretary, 19; and Egypt, 128, 163, 167

Clapp, Gordon, 271–72, 278, 305

Clark, Harlan B., 25

Clifford, Clark: and Arabs, 26; and creation of Israel, 85, 86–87; and USS *Liberty*, 241

Clinton, Hillary, 303

Clinton, William ("Bill"): and Balkans, 6, 263, 264, 311; and Camp David Summit (2000), 7, 304–5; and Israel, 78, 113–14; and Oslo Accords, 268, 301, 302–3; and Persian Gulf, 264, 313

Clinton Doctrine, 155

CNN, 2, 257, 314

Cogan, Charles, 153

Colby, Bainbridge, 46

Cole, USS, 308

Collins, Jane, 10

Collins, Lawton, 126

Colman, Ronald, 17

Colonialism, 195

Columbian World Exposition (1893), 13

Commission on Integrated Long-Term Strategy, 252

Communism, 20, 55, 82, 126, 138, 195, 196, 313; and Afghanistan, 150; and Arabs, 68, 87, 110; in China, 124; in Egypt, 27, 161, 162, 165, 166, 183, 186, 187; in France, 163; in Greece, 122; in Iran, 27, 149, 216, 217, 224, 226, 227; in Iraq, 194, 199, 200, 202, 203–4,

205–6; in Lebanon, 135; in Libya, 209, 213, 214; in Middle East, 117, 132–33, 162, 182, 197; and Palestinians, 270, 272; in Syria, 182; in Vietnam, 237, 244

Compagnie Française des Petroles (CFP), 47, 52, 58, 67

Congo, 183, 185, 186, 236

Congress, U.S., 19, 71, 231, 247, 288; and arms sales to Saudi Arabia, 109, 111; and Eisenhower Doctrine, 131–33; and foreign aid, 185, 196; and Gulf War, 259–61; and Iran-Contra affair, 250; and Israel, 92, 94, 101, 104, 107, 108–9, 111–12, 113, 286, 300; and Middle East oil, 50, 51; and reflagging Kuwait tankers, 250–51; and Saddam Hussein, 254; and Suez crisis, 174; and Truman Doctrine, 123; and UNRWA, 275; and Vietnam War, 239

Continental Oil Company (Conoco), 59–60

Cooley, John, 37

Coolidge, Calvin, 19, 47

Coon, Carleton, 26

Council on Foreign Relations, 194, 197, 274, 346 (n. 2)

Crane, Charles, 160

Cromer, Lord, 15

Crowe, William, 250

Cuba, 118, 150, 158, 214, 236

Cyprus, 93, 177, 235

Czechoslovakia, 85, 114, 130, 134, 151, 274

Daoud Khan, Mohammed, 223

Dardanelles, 120, 121, 122, 230, 233

Darwish, Mahmoud, 299

Davies, Rodger, 184

Dayan, Moshe, 90, 91, 241, 242, 289, 354 (n. 41)

Dayton Accords, 263

Dean, Patrick, 141, 142

Decatur, Stephen, 231, 233

DEFCON 3 nuclear alert (1973), 243, 244

Defense Department, U.S., 53, 123, 125,

237; and CENTCOM, 257; and Middle
East oil, 56, 61
Defense Intelligence Agency, 255
De Gaulle, Charles, 139
DeGolyer, E. L., 50
Delta Force, 38
DeMille, Nelson, 41–42
Democratic Party, 22, 26, 82, 174, 250,
260
Development Loan Fund, U.S., 217
Dewey, Thomas, 85, 87
Diego Garcia, 139, 140, 143, 146
Diem, Ngo Dinh, 237
Dienbienphu, 203
Disney Studios, 40–41, 314
Dodge, Bayard, 197
Dubai, 72
Dulles, Allen, 200, 216, 217
Dulles, John Foster, 127, 137; and Eisen-
hower Doctrine, 131–34, 181; and Iran,
28; and Iraq, 201; and Israel, 89, 92–93,
94; and Kuwait, 235; and Lebanon,
135–36; and Middle East oil, 60; and
Nasser, 28, 166, 168, 169, 170–71; and
Operation Alpha, 274–75; and Pales-
tinians, 272–73; and Suez crisis, 172–
79, 181; and Syria, 182; and Wheelus
Field, 208
Dutch East Indies, 48
Dwight, Harrison Gray Otis, 12

Eagleburger, Lawrence, 112, 255, 263
Eban, Abba, 6, 94, 269, 292, 304; and Palestinians, 268; and Six Day War, 100,
101, 102, 281–82; and Suez crisis, 93
Economic Survey Mission (1949), 271
Eden, Anthony, 128, 163, 168, 169, 170;
and Operation Alpha, 273–74; and
Suez crisis, 172–77, 179–81
Egypt, 5, 13, 15, 28, 31, 88, 98, 108, 119,
128, 147, 158, 193, 198, 200, 203, 208,
226, 231, 257, 274, 277, 317; ancient,
17; British presence in, 160–61; and
Camp David Accords, 110, 291; and
JFK, 95; and MEC, 126; and MEDO,
127; during Mubarak era, 191–92; and

1952 revolution, 163–68; and October
War, 69, 106–7, 287; during Sadat era,
33–34; and Six Day War, 63, 64, 99–
101, 281–84; and Suez crisis, 58–59,
90, 93, 169–81; and Yemen, 238. *See
also* Soviet Union; United Arab
Republic
Eichmann, Adolf, 29
Eisenhower, Dwight D. ("Ike"), 7, 28, 94,
101, 166, 167, 195, 272, 312, 316; and
Arabs, 27; and Iran, 57–58, 68, 216–
18, 226; and Iraq, 194, 199–204; and
Israel, 78, 88–94, 102; and Lebanon, 6,
27, 93, 230, 234–36, 244; and Libya,
208–10, 214; and Middle East defense,
127–30; and Nasser, 5, 168, 169–71,
182–83, 191; and oil imports, 65; and
OPEC, 61–62; and Palestinians, 272–
76, 278; and Suez crisis, 58–59, 131,
172–81. *See also* Eisenhower Doctrine
Eisenhower Doctrine, 5, 119, 132–37,
154, 181–82, 313
Enron, 75
Epstein, Eliahu, 271
Eshkol, Levi, 99, 104, 106, 285; and JFK,
97; and LBJ, 98, 102–3, 109, 283; and
Six Day War, 100–101, 242
Esposito, John, 36
Ethiopia, 93
Ethridge, Mark, 123, 270
Evron, Ephraim, 100, 101
Executive Decision, 39
Exodus, 29, 30, 32, 38
Export-Import Bank, 206
Exxon, 4, 66, 68, 69, 71, 72, 73

Fahd (king of Saudi Arabia), 256, 257
Fairbanks, Douglas, 17
Faisal (crown prince and king of Saudi
Arabia), 187; and defense of Persian
Gulf, 140, 143, 144; and oil, 68–69;
and Yemen, 184, 238, 239
Farouk (king of Egypt), 160–61, 163–65,
172, 184, 191, 200
Fatah, 279–80, 283, 359 (n. 52)
Federal Trade Commission, 55, 56

Feinberg, Abraham, 100
Feis, Herbert, 50
Feisal (emir and king of Iraq), 159, 199
Fekini, Mohieddine, 210, 211
Feldman, Myer, 95, 96, 98, 277, 278
First World War, 15, 29, 74, 134, 158–59;
    oil and, 46
Flemming, Arthur, 177
Ford, Gerald, 147, 316; and Iran, 146,
    222–23, 224, 287–88; and Israel, 78,
    107–9; and Sadat, 34
Foreign Petroleum Supply Committee, 64
Forrestal, James: and Middle East oil, 52,
    53; and Palestine, 82, 84; and Sixth
    Fleet, 233, 234
Fortas, Abe, 101
Fourteen Points, 158, 159, 160
Fox, Michael J., 38
France, 21, 46, 67, 74, 125, 132, 246, 257,
    270; and Algeria, 27; and American
    Revolution, 79; and French Revolution
    (1789), 157, 158, 181, 183; and Israel,
    94, 95, 99; and mandates, 159–60; and
    Second World War, 232; and Suez cri-
    sis, 58, 91, 173–81
Frank, Anne, 29, 32, 40
Frankfurter, Felix, 21
Franks, Oliver, 126
Front for the Liberation of South Yemen,
    141
Fulbright, J. William, 135, 190–91

Gallman, Waldemar, 199–200, 201, 203
Garment, Leonard, 286
Gati, Toby, 315
Gaza, 7, 309; Palestinian homeland in,
    268; and Suez crisis, 90–93. See also
    Occupied territories
Gazit, Mordechai, 96, 97
Germany, 85, 120, 159, 259; and Israel,
    98; and Jews, 12, 80, 81; and Middle
    East oil, 46, 49; and Nazi regime, 19,
    20, 21, 23, 207, 215, 232, 315
Gérôme, Jean-Léon, 13
Ghana, 185
Ghareeb, Edmund, 37–38

Glaspie, April, 254–55
Glenn, John, 259
Glidden, Harold, 30, 34, 36
Glubb, John, 169
Golan Heights, 7, 32, 99, 106, 111, 242,
    268, 280, 287, 309
Goldberg, Arthur, 98, 282
Goldmann, Nahum, 82–83
Goldwater, Barry, 98
Goodwin, Richard, 183
Gorbachev, Mikhail, 253, 311
Gore, Albert, Jr. ("Al"), 260, 261
Grady, Henry F., 82
Grady-Morrison plan, 82
Great Britain, 45, 51, 74, 96, 118, 150,
    162, 231, 232, 257; and decolonization
    in Middle East, 5, 27, 119–20, 124–30,
    132–36, 139, 146, 154, 233, 309; and
    Egypt, 160–61, 163–65; and Iran, 56–
    57, 215; and Iraq, 63, 199–200; and
    Kuwait, 137–38, 204; and Libya, 207,
    208, 211–12, 213; and Middle East oil,
    46, 49–50; and Nasser, 168–71, 183;
    and 1958 Middle East crisis, 93, 234–
    35; and Operation Alpha, 273–74; and
    orientalism, 10–11, 27, 29; and Pales-
    tine mandate, 19, 20–21, 22, 49, 79–
    84, 159–60, 162; and Six Day War, 63,
    64, 282; and Suez Base agreement, 128,
    129, 166–67; and Suez crisis, 58, 91,
    130–31, 172–81. See also Persian
    Gulf
Greece, 125, 126, 132, 138; and Truman
    Doctrine, 119, 122–24, 127, 152; war
    for independence of, 12
Grenada, 246, 259, 262
Gromyko, Andrei, 101
Guevara, Ernesto "Che," 186
Gulbenkian, Calouste, 47, 48, 52
Gulf Oil Company, 60, 71; and Iran, 58;
    and Kuwait, 47–48, 49, 68, 72
Gulf War (1990–91), 3, 6, 73–74, 112,
    230, 236, 252–62, 266, 298, 311

Habib, Philip, 111
Haganah, 20

Haig, Alexander, 243; and Israel, 110, 111, 246, 292–93
Haiti, 263
Haj, The, 38
Halliburton, 74–75
Halpern, Manfred, 197–98
Hamas, 296, 301, 302, 314, 315
Hamilton, Lee, 255
Hammarskjöld, Dag, 91, 93, 276
Hammer, Armand, 66
Hanania, Ray, 39
Harbord, James, 17
Harding, Warren G., 19
Hare, Raymond, 182
Harman, Avraham, 101
Harper's Magazine, 13
Harr, Karl, 210
Harriman, Averell, 98, 142, 188, 211
Harris, Thomas, 38
Harrison, Earl G., 80
Hart, Parker, 137, 138
Hasan (crown prince of Libya), 210
Hay, John, 45
Hebrew University in Jerusalem, 2
Heikal, Mohamed, 31
Hejaz, 18
Helms, Richard, 100
Henderson, Loy, 87, 120
Herter, Christian, 60, 136
Herzl, Theodore, 15
Herzog, Yitzhak, 304
Hilali, Neguib, 164, 165
Hirohito, 315
Hitler, Adolf, 20, 23, 29, 32, 119, 134, 207, 315; compared to Nasser, 173, 174, 187; and oil, 49; compared to Saddam Hussein, 256, 259
Hizbollah, 250
Hoaglund, Jim, 37
Ho Chi Minh, 31
Holloway, James L., 244
Holman, Eugene, 60
Holocaust, 4, 21, 23, 29, 32, 33, 41, 77, 80, 87, 114; and Hollywood, 40; and Reagan, 282
Holst, Johann Jurgen, 301

Hong Kong, 141
Hoover, Herbert C., 19, 48
Hoover, Herbert C., Jr., 57, 129, 131, 172
Hopkins, Harry, 237
Hoskins, Harold B., 162–63
House of Representatives, U.S.; Committee on Foreign Affairs, 133, 288; Committee on International Relations, 191; Subcommittee on the Middle East, 255
Hull, Cordell, 21, 50, 51
Humphrey, George, 178
Humphrey, Hubert, 96, 98, 103, 132, 133
Hungary, 150, 177–78, 179–80, 311
Hunt, Michael, 10
Huntington, Samuel, 315
Hurley, Patrick, 119, 161
Hussein (king of Jordan), 96, 133, 169, 183, 198, 230, 234, 256, 268, 273, 296; and LBJ, 31; and 1958 crisis, 93, 134, 135, 201, 235; and 1970 crisis, 105–6, 287, 310; and Reagan Plan, 294; and Six Day War, 240, 281, 282
Hussein (sharif of Mecca), 159
Hussein, Ahmed, 170–71
Hussein, Saddam, 6, 11, 33, 192, 206, 308, 310; and Gulf War, 112, 230, 257–62, 311; invades Kuwait, 45, 73–74, 253–56; U.S. assistance for, 253; and war with Iran, 227, 249–50

Ibn Saud, Abdul Aziz (king of Saudi Arabia), 18, 26, 49, 54, 55, 138; and oil, 47, 48; and Palestine, 22, 23, 79, 82; and Roosevelt, 307–8, 310
Ickes, Harold, 49, 50
Idris (king of Libya), 6, 193, 207, 211; and Eisenhower, 208–9; and Libyan oil, 59–60, 209–10; overthrow of, 66, 212
India, 49, 83, 139, 147, 161
Indian Ocean, 48, 118, 119, 120, 129, 138, 139, 145, 149, 151, 235, 244
Indochina, 135, 203. *See also* Vietnam War
Indonesia, 63, 139, 142, 185; and Bandung Conference, 168

Innocents Abroad, The, 2, 13–14, 26, 40, 318

Interior Department, U.S., 56

Internal Revenue Service (IRS), 55, 58, 71

Inter-Services Intelligence Agency (ISI), 152–53, 316

Intifada (1987–88), 39, 295–97, 299, 300, 312

Iran, 6, 36, 47, 59, 83, 93, 110, 119, 126, 127, 132, 133, 135, 136, 139, 150, 155, 179, 192, 193–94, 317, 318; and Baghdad Pact, 129; and Britain, 56–57; and defense of Persian Gulf, 5, 119, 136–37, 138, 140–41, 143, 144–46, 147–49; modernization in, 218–20; Mossadegh regime, 27, 28, 56–58, 68, 216–17; and 1979 revolution, 3, 5, 72, 149, 154, 224–27, 244, 310; oil of, 43, 46, 60, 198, 211; and OPEC, 61; post-Khomeini era, 313; Qajar dynasty, 14, 215; and Soviet Union, 117, 120–21, 123, 124, 125; at war with Iraq, 249–52, 253, 254; and White Revolution, 194, 219–22, 223–25, 226

Iran-Contra Affair, 112, 249–50

Iran-Iraq war, 6, 72, 249–52, 253, 254

Iraq, 6, 18, 26, 27, 28, 59, 110, 132, 179, 182, 192, 193, 217, 221, 226, 269, 309, 314, 318; and Baghdad Pact, 129; and British empire, 159–60, 161, 199, 200; and Gulf War, 73–74, 112, 230; and Kuwait, 137, 253–56, 311; during 1990s, 155, 313; oil of, 43, 46–47, 48, 58, 60, 68, 72, 74, 198; and OPEC, 61, 62, 65; and Palestinians, 271; and revolution of 1958, 62–63, 134, 194, 198, 201–5, 209, 235; and revolution of 1963, 30–31, 96, 205–6; and Six Day War, 63; and terrorism, 247; and war with Iran, 227, 249–52, 253, 254. *See also* Soviet Union

Iraq National Oil Company (INOC), 62

Iraq Petroleum Company (IPC), 52; creation of, 46–47; nationalization of, 68, 72; and Qassim, 62–63, 204–5

Irgun Zvai Leumi, 81, 82, 83, 90, 109, 269

Irving, Washington, 13

Islam, 154, 160, 161, 220, 296; in Afghanistan, 150–51, 223, 311; American stereotypes of, 9–10, 15, 18, 22, 27, 28, 35; and "Clash of Civilizations," 36, 168, 310, 315; in Egypt, 161, 167; and fundamentalism, 36, 155, 194, 314; and George W. Bush, 42; in Iran, 151, 310; in Libya, 207, 214

Islamic Group, 34, 191, 192, 317

Islamic Jihad, 315; in Egypt, 191, 192; in Lebanon, 247

Ismail (khedive of Egypt), 231

Israel, 30, 33, 41, 74, 77, 117, 124, 125, 129, 203, 235, 308, 314; and Egypt, 166, 168, 169; and Intifada (1987–88), 39; and Lebanon, 39, 111–12, 246; and nuclear weapons, 4, 78, 94–99, 101–3, 104, 107, 114, 310; and October War, 69–70, 242–43; and Oslo Accords, 301–5; and Palestinians, 6–7, 35, 267–71; and PLO, 279–80; and Six Day War, 25, 31–32, 63, 64, 99–103, 187–88, 240–42; and Suez crisis, 91–93, 131, 176–79; and war of independence, 25, 29. *See also* Occupied territories
—and relations with United States, 3, 4, 28, 68, 75, 78–79, 115, 240, 311, 312; and Carter, 109–10, 288–92; and Clinton, 113–14, 301–5; and Eisenhower, 89–90, 93–94, 273–75; and Ford, 107–9, 287–88; and George Bush, 112, 297–300; and George W. Bush, 114, 305–6; and JFK, 94–98, 276–78; and LBJ, 97–103, 279–84; and Nixon, 103–7, 284–87; and Reagan, 110–12, 292–97; and Truman, 26, 86–87, 88

Italy, 159, 232, 246, 257; and Libya, 18, 72, 207, 213, 233

Jackson, Samuel L., 41

Jacobsen, Eddie, 84

Japan, 120, 142, 232, 315; oil needs of, 48, 58

Jarring, Gunnar, 283, 284, 285

Javits, Jacob, 96, 131

Jefferson, Thomas, 5, 157, 192, 229, 231
Jenkins, Roy, 141
Jennings, Peter, 37
Jernegan, John, 62, 203
Jerusalem, 83, 110, 114, 240, 268, 280, 281, 288, 297, 301, 302–3, 304
Jewish Agency, 82
Jews: in Holy Land, 9–10, 11, 12; and immigration to Palestine, 15, 20, 22, 23, 29, 80–81, 82; and immigration to United States, 12–13, 19, 41
Johnson, Joseph, 276–78
Johnson, Lyndon B. (LBJ), 5, 6, 30, 103, 196, 198, 245, 312; and Arab-Israeli peace process, 282–84; and Iran, 138, 219, 221; and Israel, 78, 92, 94, 97–103, 104, 109, 185; and Libya, 211; and Nasser, 31, 185–88, 191, 309; and Palestinians, 279; and Persian Gulf, 139–43, 154; and Six Day War, 32, 100–101, 240–42, 280–81; as vice president, 97; and Vietnam War, 144, 238, 239–40; and war in Yemen, 239
Johnson Plan, 277–78, 305
Johnston, Eric, 273, 275
Johnston Plan, 273, 275, 277, 278
Joint Chiefs of Staff (JCS), 216, 234, 243, 256
Jones, Lewis, 61, 204
Jordan, 31, 134, 147, 169, 179, 183, 185, 198, 206, 240, 274; and 1958 crisis, 93, 135–36, 201–2, 234–35; and 1970 crisis, 105–6, 310; and Six Day War, 280–81; and TAPLINE, 53–54. See also Palestinians
Jordan, Hamilton, 151
Justice Department, U.S., 53, 55–56, 57, 59, 61, 66

Kadar, Janos, 179
Kahan, Yitzhak, 294–95
Kaiser, Philip, 140
Kamel, Mustapha, 185
Karameh, Battle of (1968), 283
Karetzky, Stephen, 39
Karmal, Babrak, 152

Kellogg, Minor, 12
Kemp, Geoffrey, 227
Kenen, I. L., 92, 94, 104, 108
Kennan, George F., 26, 121
Kennedy, Edward M., 259
Kennedy, John F. (JFK), 5, 6, 7, 30, 31, 32, 157, 198, 284, 312; and Iran, 218–21; and Iraq, 204–5; and Israel, 79, 94–98; and Kuwait, 137; and Libya, 210–11, 214; and limited war, 236–37, 245; and modernization, 195–96, 218; and Nasser, 95, 96, 97, 183–85, 309; and Palestinians, 276–78, 279; and Persian Gulf, 138–39, 154; and Vietnam, 237–38; and Yemen, 238–39
Kerensky, Alexander, 5, 158, 166, 167, 191, 202
Khalid (king of Saudi Arabia), 143
Khartoum (1967 Arab Summit), 281
Khatami, Mohammed, 313
Khobar Towers bombing, 264
Khomeini, Ayatollah Ruhollah, 6, 149, 151, 192, 194, 313, 317; and 1979 revolution, 214, 224–27, 310; and war with Iraq, 249–50, 252; and White Revolution, 220–21
Khrushchev, Nikita, 130, 134, 177–78
King, Henry, 160
King-Crane Commission, 160
Kissinger, Henry, 284; and energy crisis, 70–71, 252; and Holocaust, 33; and Iran, 221–23; and modernization, 195, 196, 197; and Nasser, 189; and 1970 Jordan crisis, 105–6, 287, 309; and Nixon Doctrine, 145–46, 148; and October War, 106–7, 243–44; and Rogers Plan, 286, 287, 288
Knowland, William, 92, 174
Komer, Robert, 30, 139, 205, 206; and Israel, 96, 97, 98; and Yemen, 238
Koran, 11
Korean War, 88, 125, 126, 132, 216, 245, 262
Kosovo, 264, 311
Ku Klux Klan, 19
Kurds, 14, 16, 17, 199

Kuwait, 6, 47, 60, 64, 135, 206, 235, 279;
Iraqi invasion of, 45, 73–74, 227, 230,
253–62, 311; and 1961 crisis, 137, 204;
oil of, 48, 49, 50, 51, 68, 72; and OPEC,
61, 70, 243; and Six Day War, 63; and
"Tanker War," 250–51, 252

Labor Party (Israel), 109, 300, 303
Labour Party (Great Britain), 5, 80, 139,
140, 141–42
Laffin, John, 35, 36
Lake, Anthony, 214
Landis, James, 197
Lang, Patrick, 255
Lansing, Robert, 159–60
Latin America, 5, 195, 196; oil of, 45, 64,
70
Lavon, Pinhas, 90
Lawrence, T. E., 14, 17, 18, 29, 30
Lawrence of Arabia, 29–30
League of Nations, 19; and mandates, 159,
160
Lean, David, 29
Lebanon, 6, 36, 58, 114, 162, 183, 201,
226, 231, 249, 268, 287; civil war in,
37; and French mandate, 159, 160; and
Israeli invasion (1982), 39, 111–12,
293–95; and TAPLINE, 53–54; U.S.
intervention (1958) in, 27, 134–36,
202, 230, 234–36, 244; U.S. interven-
tion (1982) in, 246–48, 252
Lehrer, Jim, 37, 38
Leishman, John, 14
LeMay, Curtis, 239
Lend Lease Act, 49
Lenin, Vladimir Ilyich, 5, 167, 168, 194;
and Russian revolution, 158–59
Lerner, Daniel, 197
Lewis, Anthony, 37–38
Lewis, Bernard, 36, 38
Lewis, Samuel, 111
Liberia, 83
Liberty, USS, 240–42, 244, 354 (n. 41)
Libya, 6, 28, 119, 134, 185, 192, 193–94,
226, 232; Italian colonialism in, 18; oil
of, 44, 59–60, 66–67, 72, 198, 206–7;

and OPEC, 63; and petroleum boom,
208–10; Qaddafi's revolution in, 212–
14; and Six Day War, 211; and terror-
ism, 214, 252; U.S. air raid on, 248–49,
256, 259. See also Soviet Union
Lie, Trygve, 83
Likud Party, 109, 114, 300, 302, 304, 314
Limited war, 6; and 1958 Middle East cri-
sis, 235–36, 244; and Vietnam,
235–36, 245–46, 260
Lloyd, Christopher, 38
Lloyd, Selwyn, 136, 169, 173, 176, 183,
201
Lloyd George, David, 16
Lodge, Henry Cabot, 179
Loftus, John, 51, 52
Lovett, Robert, 86–87
Lutz, Catherine, 10

Macatee, Robert, 84
McClintock, Robert, 26, 235
McCloy, John J., 97; and Middle East oil,
66, 67, 69–70, 71, 72
McDonald, David, 241
McFarlane, Robert, 153, 245, 248, 252
McGhee, George, 55, 124, 162
McGranery, James P., 55
McKinley, William, 45
Macmillan, Harold, 133, 134, 168, 183,
184; and 1958 Middle East crisis, 135,
202, 234; and Suez crisis, 130, 175, 180
McNamara, Robert, 139, 236, 237, 240,
241, 283
Madison, James, 231
Madrid Peace Conference (1991), 112,
267, 299
Mahan, Alfred Thayer, 118
Mahir, Ali, 164
Mahmud (sultan of Turkey), 231
Makins, Roger, 171, 176
Malaysia, 139
Malik, Charles, 272
Malley, Robert, 304
Mao Zedong, 190, 215–16, 315
Margalit, Avishai, 315
Marines, U.S.: in Grenada, 246; in Leb-

anon (1958), 6, 93, 135–36, 234–35; in
Lebanon (1982), 246–48
Marshall, George C., 53, 123, 233, 270;
opposes recognition of Israel, 86
Marshall Plan (European Recovery Pro-
gram), 44, 53, 123
Marx, Karl, 164
Mayaguez, 245
Meir, Golda, 93, 96, 98, 288; and Nixon,
104, 106, 107, 109, 242; and Palestin-
ians, 278, 285–86, 287
Melbourne, Roy, 205
Mellon, Andrew, 48
Melville, Herman, 79
Menderes, Adnan, 133
Menken, Alan, 40
Menzies, Robert, 174, 175
Mexico, 73, 158
Meyer, Armin, 221, 278
Michener, James, 32
Middle East Command (MEC), 126, 128,
154
Middle East Committee, 170
Middle East Defense Organization
(MEDO), 127–28, 154
Middle East Emergency Committee, 59
Milosevic, Slobodan, 264, 311
Missionaries, 12, 14
Mitchell, George, 305–6, 317
Mobil Oil, 52, 53, 60, 71, 72; and Iran, 57;
and Iraq, 68
Modernization, 193, 194, 227, 229; in
Afghanistan, 223; and bin Laden, 316;
in Iran, 215, 219–22, 223, 224, 226; in
Iraq, 199, 205, 206; in Libya, 210–11;
and Middle East, 5–6, 11, 197–98; and
social science theory, 195–96, 218, 309
Mohammed (prophet), 12, 14, 194
Mohammedanism. *See* Islam
Mollet, Guy, 175–76, 177, 179
Monroe, James, 118, 120
Monroe Doctrine, 5, 118, 154
Morocco, 11, 135, 160, 294
Morrison, Herbert, 82
Mossad, 106
Mossadegh, Mohammed, 28, 69, 226,

317; and AIOC crisis, 56–57, 216–17
Mubarak, Hosni, 191, 192, 256, 317
Mufti of Jerusalem, 81, 83
Mujahadeen, 153–54, 223, 316
Mukhtar, Omar, 207, 213
Multinational corporations, 4; and U.S.
national security, 43–45, 52, 55–56,
69, 71–72
Multinational Force (Lebanon), 246, 247
Murphy, Robert, 28, 202, 208
Murray, Wallace, 20, 23, 51
Musharraf, Pervez, 316
Muslim Brotherhood, 161, 167, 296
Mussolini, Benito, 232; compared to Nas-
ser, 169, 179; and Libya, 18, 207
Mutual Security Program, 94, 126, 195

Naguib, Mohammed, 165, 166–67, 191
Nagy, Imre, 178, 179
Nahas, Mustafa, 163, 164
Najibullah, Mohammed, 152, 153, 311
Nasser, Gamal Abdel, 30, 32, 93, 105, 194,
199, 200, 203, 207, 225, 234, 317; and
Aswan Dam, 168–71; and British imperialism, 127–28; and JFK, 95, 97; and
LBJ, 31; legacy of, 191–92; and Libya,
209, 210, 211, 212; and 1952 revolution, 158, 163, 165–68, 189–90; and
Operation Alpha, 274–75; and Palestinians, 276, 279–80, 287; *Philosophy
of the Revolution*, 167, 173, 174, 189;
and Six Day War, 99–101, 104, 186–
88, 281; and Soviet Union, 130, 168,
169, 189, 214, 240; and Suez crisis,
58–59, 90–91, 172–81, 194, 309; and
UAR, 181–84, 201, 203; and Yemen,
184–85, 238–39. *See also* Arab nationalism
National Geographic, 4, 10–11, 41; and
Arab world, 17–19, 25, 30; and Holocaust, 23–24; and Palestinians, 300; and
Sadat's assassination, 34; and Six Day
War, 32
National Iranian Oil Company (NIOC),
57, 72
National Security Act (1947), 123

National Security Council (NSC), 71, 123

Navy, U.S., 244; and Barbary Wars, 230–31; and Fifth Fleet, 244, 263; and Iran-Iraq war, 250–51; and Lebanon, 247; and Libya, 248; and Second World War, 232; and Seventh Fleet, 235; USS *Liberty*, 240–42. *See also* Sixth Fleet, U.S.

Nelson, Wesley, 200

Netanyahu, Benjamin, 7, 113, 114, 268, 302–3, 304, 305–6, 312

Netherlands, 175

Newman, Paul, 29

Newsom, David, 211, 212

New York Times, 2, 19, 37, 39, 42, 237, 315

Nicaragua, 250

Niles, David, 84, 87

Nixon, Richard, 6, 33, 34, 103, 109, 136, 147, 181, 196, 198, 236, 287, 309, 316; and Iran, 221–22, 224; and Israel, 78, 103–7; and Libya, 212–13; and Middle East oil, 65, 68–69, 70; and Nasser, 188–89, 191; and October War, 242–43; and Palestinians, 284–85, 287; and Rogers Plan, 286. *See also* Nixon Doctrine

Nixon Doctrine, 5, 119, 143–46, 147, 148, 149, 154, 313

Nkrumah, Kwame, 185, 188

Nonproliferation treaty (NPT), 99–100, 103

Noriega, Manuel, 253, 256

Norris, Chuck, 38

North, Oliver, 250

North Africa, 5, 27, 28, 123, 130, 173, 208, 231; oil of, 58, 59, 65, 67, 71; and Second World War, 207, 229, 232

North American Review, 12

North Atlantic Treaty Organization (NATO), 125, 126, 127, 139, 178, 181, 208, 219, 230; and Gulf War, 260; and Kosovo, 311

Northern Alliance, 265, 316

Northern Tier, 129, 130, 135, 136, 230

North Korea, 214

Noyes, James, 144

NSC-68, 125

Nunn, Sam, 250–51, 259

Nutting, Anthony, 167

Occidentalism, 315

Occidental Petroleum, 44, 66

Occupied territories, 113, 281–84, 287; and Carter, 288, 289, 290–92; and George Bush, 300–301; and Olso Accords, 302–5; and Reagan, 292–94, 295–97. *See also* Gaza; West Bank

October War, 33, 106–7; and Arab oil embargo, 69–71, 242–43, 287

Office of Defense Mobilization, 177

Oil, 77, 83–84, 141, 169, 198, 310, 311, 318; and aftermath of September 11, 316–17; and early Cold War, 52–58; and energy crisis, 72–73; and Gulf War, 73–74; Middle Eastern discoveries of, 46–47; and October War, 69–71, 243; and rise of multinational oil companies, 3, 4, 43–45; and rise of OPEC, 61–62; and Second World War, 48–51; and Six Day War, 63–65; and Suez crisis, 58–59, 174–75, 177, 180; U.S. domestic reserves of, 14, 48, 53, 65. *See also individual oil companies and oil-producing countries*

Oil Consultative Commission, 60

Olympic games: in Moscow (1980), 151; in Munich (1972), 33, 34, 41, 287

Oman, 145, 147, 151, 152

Operation Alpha, 273–75, 278, 305

Operation Blue Bat, 235–36

Operation Desert Falcon, 263

Operation Desert Shield, 253, 257

Operation Desert Storm, 6, 230, 258, 261–62, 311

Operation Eagle Claw, 244

Operation Earnest Will, 251

Operation El Dorado Canyon, 249, 252

Operation Enduring Freedom, 265, 266

Operation Hard Surface, 239, 244

Operation Just Cause, 253

Operation Praying Mantis, 251, 252
Operation Restore Hope, 311
Operation Torch, 232
Organization for Economic Cooperation and Development (OECD), 64
Organization of Arab Petroleum Exporting Countries, 65
Organization of Petroleum Exporting Countries (OPEC), 4, 44, 74, 245, 312, 316; and energy crisis, 72; establishment of, 58, 61–62; and Gulf War, 73; and Libyan revolution, 66–67; during 1960s, 63, 65; and October War, 69–71, 243, 310
Orientalism, 3–4, 309; in cartoons, 37; defined, 10–11; in feature films, 17, 29–30, 38–39, 40–42; and news media, 37–38; persistence of, 314–18; in popular fiction, 29, 32, 38, 41–42; in popular nonfiction, 34–36; pre-1920 manifestations of, 11–17; in television, 36–37, 40. See also *National Geographic*
Oslo Accords, 7, 268, 301–2, 313
O'Toole, Peter, 29
Ottoman Empire, 12, 13, 14, 15, 52, 199, 207; and Arab nationalism, 159; and First World War, 16, 17; and oil, 46, 47, 74

Pahlavi, Mohammed Reza (shah of Iran), 6, 27, 193, 194, 198, 215; and Afghanistan, 223; and Carter, 147, 148–49; and modernization, 218; and Mossadegh, 56, 57, 216–17; and Nasser, 186, 188; and oil, 72; overthrow of, 224–26; and regional defense, 129, 137, 138, 140–41, 143, 144–46; and White Revolution, 219–22, 310, 318
Pahlavi, Reza Shah, 215
Pakistan, 127–28, 129, 135, 136, 139, 147, 151, 170; and Afghan mujahadeen, 152–53, 223, 316
Palestine, 13, 25, 26, 77, 90, 183, 189, 272; and Balfour Declaration, 15–16; British mandate in, 18–19, 49, 159, 160, 161; Jewish immigration to, 15, 19, 20, 22, 23, 79, 80–81; and 1939 White Paper, 20–21, 80; partition of, 80–86, 162, 300, 305
Palestine Conciliation Commission, 270, 271
Palestine Liberation Front, 298
Palestine Liberation Organization (PLO), 31, 106, 185, 273, 278, 287, 288, 290, 293, 294; and Camp David Accords, 291; establishment of, 279; and Karameh, 283; in Lebanon, 111–12, 246, 291–92; and Madrid Peace Conference, 267, 298–99; and Oslo Accords, 301–2, 306; and Shultz initiative, 295–97; and Six Day War, 280; and terrorism, 268
Palestine National Congress, 280
Palestinian Authority, 7, 301–2, 305
Palestinian-Israeli peace process, 6–7, 266; and Carter, 288–92; and Clinton, 301–5, 313–14; and George Bush, 296–301; and George W. Bush, 305–6, 317; and Nixon, 284–88; and Reagan, 292–97. *See also* Oslo Accords
Palestinians, 38, 92, 93, 96, 279; and Camp David Accords, 110; and creation of Israel, 83, 84; and Johnson Plan, 276–78; and Jordan, 105, 271, 283, 286, 293, 294, 296; in Lebanon, 39, 111–12, 246, 269, 287, 294–95; and Oslo peace process, 113–14; as refugees, 269–72, 274–75; and Six Day War, 99, 280–81; and terrorism, 33, 34, 35, 39, 106, 214
Panama, 253, 254, 256, 258, 259, 260, 262
Patai, Raphael, 34–35, 36
Patton, George S., 23
Pearson, Richmond, 14
Pentagon talks (1947), 123–24
People's Democratic Party of Afghanistan, 223
Peres, Shimon, 113, 301, 302, 303
Perez Alfonso, Juan Pablo, 54, 60
Persia, 159
Persian Gulf, 27, 68, 118, 119, 127, 136, 138–39, 170; and Britain, 135, 137,

140–43, 144, 145, 147, 151, 221, 222, 235; and Carter Doctrine, 149–52, 244; oil of, 44–46, 48, 50, 51–52, 59, 61, 65, 70, 72, 124, 204; and sheikdoms, 186; and Soviet Union, 120, 125, 146, 148. *See also* Gulf War; Iran

Petroleum Administration for War, 49

Petroleum Reserves Corporation (PRC), 49–50

Pew, Joseph, 51

Philippines, 83, 172, 214, 303

Piercy, George, 72

Pineau, Christian, 174, 176

Podhoretz, Norman, 39

Point Four Program, 195

Poland, 311

Pollard, Jonathan, 112

Popular Front for the Liberation of the Occupied Arab Gulf, 141

Portugal, 175

Powell, Colin: and Lebanon, 248; and Palestinians, 312; and Panama, 253, 256; and Vietnam, 253, 258, 259, 262; and Gulf War, 255, 256–59, 261–62; and Yugoslavia, 263

Powell Doctrine, 154–55

Pryce-Jones, David, 35–36

Public Law 480 (Food for Peace program), 183, 185, 186, 206

Public opinion, U.S.: and Israel, 32, 89, 92, 101, 104, 109, 113; and Jewish voters, 78, 82, 86

Puritans, 9, 79, 89

Qaddafi, Muammar al-, 6, 192, 194, 207, 225, 230; and foreign oil firms, 66, 67, 72; and radical Islam, 213–14; seizes power, 212; U.S. air raid against, 248–49, 256

Qassim, Abdel Karim, 214, 217, 227, 309; Ba'athists overthrow, 205–6; and IPC, 62–63; and 1958 revolution, 194, 198–204, 207

Qatar, 63, 72, 243

Qavam, Ahmad, 121

Quandt, William, 291

Qutb, Sayyid, 315

Quwatly, Shukri, 54

Rabat (1974 Arab Summit), 287

Rabin, Leah, 302

Rabin, Yitzhak, 283, 284, 304, 312; assassination of, 7, 302; and Carter, 289; and Ford, 109; and Israeli nuclear weapons, 102–3; and Nixon, 104, 106, 107; and Oslo Accords, 113, 267, 300–302

Rabinovitch, Itamar, 113

Rahim, Mohammed, 165

Rapid Deployment Force, 151, 152, 244

Rayburn, Sam, 174

Razmara, Ali, 216

Reagan, Ronald, 35, 45, 73, 157, 316; and Afghanistan, 152–53; and Iran-Iraq war, 227, 249–52; and Israel, 78, 110–12; and Lebanon, 6, 246–48; and Libya, 214, 248–49; and Palestinians, 292–94, 296; and Reagan Doctrine, 153, 154; and Vietnam Syndrome, 245–46, 253

Reagan Plan (1982), 293–94, 295, 297, 305

Red Line Agreement, 47, 52

Reid, Ogden, 94

Republican Party, 22, 174, 195, 260

Revolutionary Command Council (RCC), 165, 166, 167

Riad, Mahmoud, 240

Richards, James P., 133, 200, 208

Robert College, 14

Roche, John, 31, 100

Rockefeller, John D., 45, 46, 47

Rockefeller, Nelson, 195, 223

Rogers, William P., 104, 144, 213, 284–85, 287

Rogers Plan, 285–86, 287, 288

Romania, 49, 311

Roosevelt, Franklin D. (FDR), 50–51, 89, 142, 161, 162, 191, 197, 232; and Ibn Saud, 307–8, 310; and Middle East, 119; and Palestine, 20–21, 22, 23, 79–80; and Saudi oil, 48, 49. *See also* Atlantic Charter

Roosevelt, Theodore, 14–15

Ross, Archibald, 171
Rostow, Eugene D., 98, 212, 284
Rostow, Walt W., 98, 283, 284; and modernization, 195–96, 197; and Nasser, 186, 187–88; and Persian Gulf, 140, 141–42; and Six Day War, 64, 102, 212, 240, 281
Rothschild, Lionel Walter, 16
Rountree, William, 170
Rowson, Susanna, 12
Royal Dutch Shell, 44, 47, 52, 60; and TPC consortium, 46; and Venezuela, 54; and Iran, 58
Rusk, Dean, 98, 279; and Britain, 141–42; and Johnson Plan, 276–78; and Nasser, 31, 185; and shah, 138, 220; and Six Day War, 101, 102, 240, 241, 242, 280, 281
Russell, Francis, 275
Russell, Richard, 132, 133
Russia, 15, 45, 118; and Bolshevik revolution, 157, 158–59, 165, 167. *See also* Soviet Union
Rwanda, 263

Sabah, Jabir al-Ahmed al- (emir of Kuwait), 254
Sadat, Anwar, 165, 268; assassination of, 33–34, 191, 292, 317; and Camp David Accords, 110, 289–91; and October War, 242–43, 287
Safire, William, 221
Said, Edward, 10, 35
Said, Nuri, 193, 199–200, 201, 202, 205
Saif (prince of Yemen), 26
Sallal, Abdallah al-, 184
San Remo agreement, 46
Sarraj, Abdel Hamid al-, 182
Saud (king of Saudi Arabia), 138, 238
Saudi Arabia, 26, 134, 138, 139, 154, 179, 185, 187, 206, 226, 263, 264, 265; and ARAMCO, 53–55, 60, 72; and bin Laden, 153; and defense of Persian Gulf, 5, 119, 140–41, 143, 144, 146, 147; and Gulf War, 6, 73, 74, 255–59; and Kuwait, 137; oil of, 23, 43, 47, 48, 49, 50,

51, 58, 82, 211, 316; and OPEC, 61, 65–66, 67–69, 310; and September 11, 75; and Six Day War, 63–64; U.S. arms sales to, 109, 110–11; and Yemen, 184, 238–39
Saunders, Harold, 99–100, 102, 104, 187, 242, 280, 281, 288
Scheherazade, 11, 18, 36
Schindler, Oskar, 40
Schindler's List, 4, 40
Schlesinger, James, 107
Schwartzenegger, Arnold, 39
Schwartzkopf, Norman, 255, 257, 258, 261
Scowcroft, Brent, 255, 256
Scranton, William, 285, 288
Second World War, 4, 21–23, 28, 29, 74, 79, 152, 158, 237; and British Empire, 118, 119–20, 154; in Middle East, 161–62; and North Africa, 207, 232; and oil, 44
Senate, U.S., 133, 273; Armed Services Committee, 132, 250–51, 259; Foreign Relations Committee, 132, 137, 181, 190, 208, 212, 251, 285; and Israel, 96, 102, 108; Subcommittee on Multinational Corporations, 71–72
September 11 terrorist attacks, 1, 2, 8, 42, 75, 114, 154, 192, 264, 305, 314, 315, 318
Serbia, 264, 311
Seven Sisters, 44, 60, 62, 65, 69
Shah of Iran. *See* Pahlavi, Mohammed Reza
Shamir, Yitzhak, 7, 113, 268, 302, 312; and Reagan, 112, 295, 296–97; and George Bush, 298–300
Sharett, Moshe, 88, 90, 93, 270, 271
Sharon, Ariel, 7, 268, 316; and invasion of Lebanon, 111, 293, 294–95, 297; as prime minister, 114, 305, 306, 312
Shazar, Zalman, 99
Sheik, The, 17
Shepilov, Dmitri, 171
Short, Michael, 264
Shukairy, Ahmed, 273, 279

Shultz, George, 252; and Arafat, 295–97; and Israel, 293–95; and Lebanon, 246–47

Sick, Gary, 148, 149, 150, 224, 226, 227

Siege, The, 42

Silver, Abba Hillel, 21, 22

Singapore, 139, 141

Sirry, Hussein, 165

Sisco, Joseph, 189, 286–87

Six Day War, 3, 5, 7, 25, 31–32, 104, 141, 187–88, 240–42, 268, 280–81, 283, 305, 309, 312; and Israel, 99–103; and oil supplies, 44, 63–65

Sixth Fleet, U.S., 97, 230, 233–34, 235, 236, 238, 240–42, 246, 247, 248, 249

Slim, William J., 126

Slocombe, Walter, 152

Solarz, Stephen, 261

Somalia, 152; U.S. intervention in, 263, 311

Sophie's Choice, 40

Sorensen, Theodore, 237

Source, The, 32

South Korea, 244

South Yemen, 146

Soviet Union, 21, 26, 78, 85, 129, 139, 147, 184, 208, 230, 236, 308; and Afghanistan, 5, 117, 149–54, 223, 244, 311, 316; and Arabs, 92, 95, 98, 102, 119, 124, 140, 162, 186, 187; collapse of (1989–91), 36, 153–54, 267, 311; and Egypt, 90, 97, 105, 124, 130, 140, 165, 166, 169–71, 189, 190, 217, 240, 274; and Hungary, 177–78, 179–80; and Iran, 27, 51, 117, 120–21, 215, 216, 218; and Iraq, 62, 63, 140, 146, 183, 194, 202, 203–4, 205, 206, 240, 310; and Jordan, 106; and Kuwait, 250–51; and Libya, 208, 209, 213, 214, 249; Middle East policies of, 5, 56, 61, 87, 110, 115, 117–18, 119–20, 123–27, 132, 135–36, 142, 166, 187, 234, 313; and October War, 243; oil reserves of, 49; and Palestine, 82, 84, 86, 270; and Persian Gulf, 145–46, 148, 150–52; and Six Day War, 99–100, 101, 241–42, 280; and Suez crisis, 174, 180–81;

and Syria, 99, 133–34, 182, 187, 217, 240, 242, 247, 310; and Turkey, 121–22, 233

Special Coordinating Committee, 152

Spielberg, Steven, 40

Stalin, Josef, 120, 121, 122, 130, 215, 307

Standard Oil Company, 45

Standard Oil Company of California (Socal), 60, 71; and Iran, 58; and Saudi Arabia, 47, 48, 49, 53, 72

Standard Oil Company of New Jersey, 44, 45–47, 48, 52, 60, 66; and ARAMCO, 53; and Iran, 57; and Iraq, 62; and OPEC, 61; and Suez crisis, 59; and Venezuela, 54. *See also* Exxon

Standard Oil Company of New York (SOCONY), 46–47, 48, 52. *See also* Mobil Oil

Stark, USS, 250, 251

Stassen, Harold, 178–79

State Department, U.S., 124, 197; anti-Semitism of, 20, 26; and Middle East oil, 46–47, 48, 50, 52, 55–56, 57, 61, 63, 66, 67, 71; and "open door policy," 45; and Palestine, 80–81, 84–85; and Rogers Plan, 104

Stettinius, Edward R., 51, 80

Stevens, Roger, 204

Stevenson, Adlai, 91

Stone, Charles, 231

Streep, Meryl, 40

Strong, Robert, 205

Stufflebeem, John, 265

Sudan, 160, 163

Suez Canal, 118, 124, 126, 128, 131, 161, 163

Suez Canal Users Association (SCUA), 175

Suez crisis, 3, 5, 27, 64, 78, 91, 131–32, 170–81, 194, 275, 309, 311; and Iraq, 200; and Israel, 89–93; and oil supplies, 44, 58–59

Sukarno, Achmed, 185, 188

Suleiman, Abdullah, 26

Sullivan, William, 224, 225

Sulzberger, Arthur Hays, 19

Sulzberger, Cyrus L., 167, 177, 191
Summers, Harry, 245–46, 262
Sun Oil, 51
Supreme Court, U.S., 45, 46
Sykes-Picot Agreement, 159
Symmes, Harrison, 210
Syria, 14, 26, 39, 88, 89, 96, 147, 181,
    186, 190, 198, 199, 234, 235, 272; and
    French mandate, 159, 160; and Leb-
    anon, 247; and 1970 Jordanian crisis,
    106; and October 1973 War, 34, 69,
    106–7, 287; and Palestinians, 269,
    271, 277; and Six Day War, 31, 32, 64,
    242, 280; and Suez crisis, 58, 59; and
    TAPLINE, 53–54; and UAR, 182, 184,
    201. See also Communism; Soviet
    Union
Syrian Protestant College, 14

Taft, Robert, 22
Tal, Wasfi al-, 287
Talbot, Phillips, 62, 204–5, 219, 221
Taliban, 1, 154, 223, 264–65, 316, 317
Tanter, Raymond, 111
Tappin, John, 208
Tariki, Abdullah, 60, 66
Taylor, Maxwell D., 236–37, 239
Tennessee Valley Authority (TVA), 271,
    273
Terrorism, 110, 214, 252; and al-Qaeda,
    231, 265; as depicted in American pop-
    ular culture, 4, 37–39; and Palestini-
    ans, 33–34, 99, 196
Texaco, 4, 44, 48, 60, 68, 71; and Iran, 58;
    and Saudi Arabia, 47, 49, 53, 72
Thieu, Nguyen Van, 143
Thousand and One Arabian Nights, 11,
    12, 13, 25, 31
Tito, Jozef, 168
Tocqueville, Alexis de, 191, 192, 194
Trans-Arabian Pipeline (TAPLINE), 53–
    54, 58
Transjordan, 18
Treasury Department, U.S., 55
Tripartite Declaration, 125–26, 240
Troutbeck, John, 27

Troye, Edward, 13
True Lies, 4, 39
Truman, Harry S., 7, 11, 23, 25, 71, 151,
    162, 177, 195, 233, 278, 305, 309, 312,
    316; and Arabs, 25–26, 27; and Egypt,
    164, 166; and Iran, 57, 121, 216; and Is-
    rael, 33, 77, 86–87, 88, 89, 114, 268,
    270–71; and Middle East defense, 126–
    27; and Middle East oil, 53, 56; and Pal-
    estine, 80–86; and Soviet Union, 117,
    230. See also Truman Doctrine
Truman Doctrine, 5, 119, 122–24, 125,
    127, 152, 154, 157, 162
Tucker, Robert, 243
Tudeh Party, 216, 217
Tunisia, 232
Turkey, 11, 13, 15, 59, 83, 93, 125, 219,
    221, 231, 263, 270; and Arab revolt,
    159; and Middle East defense, 127–28,
    129, 132, 133, 135, 136, 138; Soviet
    Union and, 120, 121–22, 233; and Tru-
    man Doctrine, 119, 123–24, 127, 152;
    and Young Turks, 14
Turkish Petroleum Company (TPC), 46
Turkmenistan, 316
Turks, 16; American stereotypes of, 13,
    17
Turner, Stansfield, 153
Tutankhamen (king of Egypt), 17, 41
Twain, Mark, 2, 3, 7, 13–14, 317–18

United Arab Emirates (UAE), 144, 254,
    257
United Arab Republic (UAR), 182, 183,
    184, 185, 186; and Iraq, 201, 202, 203;
    and Yemen, 238
United Kingdom (UK). See Great Britain
United Nations, 88, 98, 104, 110, 121,
    123, 168, 184–85, 252, 315, 318; and
    Gulf War, 73, 255, 257; and Libya, 207;
    and Palestine, 81–85, 270; and Pales-
    tinians, 268, 269, 271, 276; and Suez
    crisis, 91–93, 131, 175, 176, 177, 178,
    179, 180
United Nations Emergency Force, 93, 100,
    187, 240

United Nations Relief and Works Agency (UNRWA), 271, 275, 277

United Nations Security Council Resolution 242 (1967), 281–82, 285, 286, 287, 288, 289–90, 292, 293, 295, 296, 297, 305

United Nations Special Committee on Palestine (UNSCOP), 83–84, 329 (n. 19)

United States Information Agency (USIA), 31, 185, 286

Uris, Leon, 29, 38

Uzbekistan, 265

Valentino, Rudolph, 17, 34

Vance, Cyrus, 289; and Afghanistan, 150, 151; and Camp David Accords, 291; and Iran, 147, 148

Veliotes, Nicholas, 294

Venezuela, 53, 65, 73, 118; and oil companies, 54, 55, 56; and OPEC, 60, 61

Versailles Peace Conference, 20, 159–60

Vessey, John, 246, 250

Viet Cong, 5, 31, 186, 239, 279

Vietnam War, 32, 78, 98, 139, 141, 145, 146, 152, 186–87, 203, 221, 231, 243, 309; and limited war, 235–38; and Nixon Doctrine, 143–44; and Six Day War, 99, 101, 102; and Tonkin Gulf incident, 239–40; and Vietnam syndrome, 6, 230, 244, 245, 246, 252, 256, 258–61, 262, 263, 265–66, 267, 311, 317

Villard, Henry, 28

Vincennes, USS, 251–52

Wadsworth, George, 162

Wafd Party, 160–61, 163, 164

Wagner, Robert, 22

Wallace, Henry, 82

Walters, Barbara, 34

War Department, U.S., 231

Warnke, Paul, 103

War of Attrition (1969–70), 189

Washington, Denzel, 42

Washington, George, 79

Watergate scandal, 68, 107, 147, 243, 245, 287, 289

Webster, William, 255

Weinberger, Caspar, 245–47, 248–49, 250

Weizmann, Chaim, 16, 79, 81, 82–83, 84; and Truman, 85, 270–71

West Bank, 7, 32, 240, 264, 268, 269, 271, 272; and Camp David Accords, 290–91; and Six Day War, 280–81, 282, 284, 309. *See also* Occupied territories

Western Europe, 58, 169, 175, 308; and Marshall Plan, 44, 53, 56; oil needs of, 59, 61, 64, 173, 177, 211, 310

Wheelus Field, 208, 209, 211, 213

Willis, Bruce, 42

Wilson, Charles, 178

Wilson, Harold, 140, 141–42

Wilson, Woodrow, 17, 19; and Arab nationalism, 159–60, 191; and Balfour Declaration, 15–16; and Middle East oil, 44, 45, 46; and revolutions, 158–59, 165

Wise, Stephen, 19, 20; and Balfour Declaration, 16; and FDR, 21, 22, 23

World Bank, 169, 171, 217, 237

World Trade Center, 1, 42, 75, 114, 154, 192, 305, 308, 316

World Zionist Organization, 15

Wright, Michael, 124

Wye Memorandum (1998), 303, 304

Yahya (imam of Yemen), 25–26

Yamani, Ahmed Zaki, 65–66, 68, 69–70, 72

Yemen, 25–26, 30, 41, 124, 133, 186, 190; and 1962 revolution, 184–85, 238–39; and USS *Cole*, 308

Yemen Arab Republic (YAR), 184

Yishuv, 20

Yugoslavia, 26, 168, 263, 264

Yusuf (pasha of Tripoli), 231

Zaghlul, Saad, 160, 163

Zahedi, Ardeshir, 148

Zahedi, Fazlollah, 217

Zahir (king of Afghanistan), 223
Zaim, Husni, 54
Zanzibar, 25
Zawahiri, Ayman al-, 191
Zayyat, Montasser al-, 192
Zhou En-lai, 168
Zia al-Haq, Mohammed, 152
Ziegler, Ronald, 285

Zimmermann, Warren, 263
Zionism, 11, 19, 29–30, 38, 69; in America, 19–20, 21, 23, 24, 79, 84–85; and creation of Israel, 81–83; and First World War, 15–16; origins of, 15
Zionist Organization of America, 19–20
Zorlu, Fatin, 135